Connecticut à la Carte

The Art of Fine Food

Connecticut à la Carte

West Hartford, Connecticut

1982 Edition

First Printing:	June 1982	10,000 copies
Second Printing:	October 1982	10,000 copies
Third Printing:	September 1983	20,000 copies
Fourth Printing:	March 1987	10,000 copies

To order additional copies of *Connecticut à la Carte,*
use the order blanks in the back of the book, or write directly to:

Connecticut à la Carte
P.O. Box 17-158
West Hartford, Connecticut 06117

Checks should be made payable to Connecticut à la Carte
for $21.95 plus $2.00 postage/handling plus $1.65 CT sales tax
(if applicable) per book.
For large quantity ordering or wholesale ordering,
address inquires to the above or telephone (203) 233-5981.
Mastercard and Visa accepted.

ISBN: 0-9607352-0-8
Library of Congress Number: 81-70304

Artist Copyright © 1982
by
Francie Bergquist

Printed in the United States of America by
S. C. Toof & Co.
Memphis, Tennessee
Graphic Design: Karin Deeks, Imprint

Connecticut à la Carte

Edited by Melinda M. Vance

Junior League of Hartford

The Junior League of Hartford is an organization of women, committed to promoting voluntarism and to improving the community through the effective action and leadership of trained volunteeers. The word "commitment" is the essence of the organization. Each year the membership demonstrates this commitment by giving over 60,000 hours of service to community organizations, funding a variety of service projects, and training its membership in skills development.

Since the founding of the Junior League of Hartford in 1921, the organization has acted as a catalyst for community problem solving, bringing about results no one organization could have accomplished on its own. Capable and well-trained, League members leverage small amounts of resources into meaingful results for the elderly, children and youth, and the handicapped. These are groups in the community whose rights and needs can easily be overlooked. Our resources include our members and the dollars needed to support our community projects. The sale of this cookbook, *Connecticut à la Carte,* is one of the ways in which the Hartford League raises funds. All monies raised by the sale of this book are returned to the community through projects, grants, scholarships and gifts.

Membership in the Junior League of Hartford is open to all women between the ages of 20 and 40 who demonstrate an interest in and commitment to voluntarism. The Hartford League is one of the 267 individual Leagues belonging to the Association of Junior Leagues with a total membership of over 165,00 women in the United States, Canada, Mexico and the United Kingdom.

In March 1985 the Junior League of Hartford purchased *Connecticut à la Carte* from the five Hartford arts organizations that produced it in 1982: Connecticut Opera, Hartford Ballet, Hartford Stage Company, Hartford Symphony Orchestra and Wadsworth Atheneum. In addition to the monies realized in the purchase, the League returns fifteen percent of gross sales to the Five Arts. The remaining proceeds from the sales of *Connecticut à la Carte* are returned to the Greater Hartford community through service projects of the Junior League of Hartford.

There were many reasons why this transfer of ownership was mutually beneficial to the non-profits involved but two are noteworthy. First, because several League members were instrumental in developing the book (including the chairman/editor and the artist), and because Junior Leagues across the country have experience in cookbook production, the Hartford Junior League was a natural group to assume ownership. Second, the Hartford League has actively supported arts activities during its history and this was an excellent way to reaffirm its commitment to the arts in Hartford.

This fourth printing in Spring 1987 is the first printing which displays the name of Junior League of Hartford as publishers. Excepting the name change in several locations, the content — menus, recipes, historical material, index — remains unchanged.

For more information about our organization or the contents of this book, call or write: The Junior League of Hartford, Inc., 139 N. Main St., West Hartford, CT 06107 (203) 523-4670.

Volunteer Acknowledgement

This cookbook is not only a compilation of recipes, but a philosophy or a way of thinking about creatively preparing and serving fine food, developed and tested by many individuals — individuals representing many variants in character, taste and ethnic background. *Connecticut à la Carte* could not have been published without the hundreds of volunteers from the 5 Arts organizations in the Greater Hartford area, who submitted, tested, retested, sampled and compiled all the data for the 495 recipes in this book. As editor of *Connecticut à la Carte*, I am deeply indebted to each of these volunteers as well as their families, for the thousands of hours devoted to this time-consuming task over a 3½ year period. Because space does not permit, I am unable to name each volunteer, but I wish to express my heartfelt thanks to each one of them. Their contribution has not only made my job easier, but more importantly, has made *Connecticut à la Carte* a most unique and outstanding cookbook.

Additional Acknowledgements

Nancy Bailey, Nancy Woodworth, Lynn Blau and *Ann Feenstra* for contributions in many areas; *Robert Siegel,* attorney for Day Berry and Howard for legal consultation; *Alexander C. McNally,* wine consultant; *Melanie R. Polk,* R.D., M.M.Sc., and Assistant Professor Program in Dietetics at University of Connecticut at Storrs for consultation on nutrition; *Adeline Greenberg,* M.Sc., formerly Associate in Nutrition Columbia University, New York City and instructor Pratt Institute and Sarah Lawrence College for consultation on nutrition; *Nancy Johnson,* Home Economist for the Plymouth Electric Company for microwave testing; *Joan Hopper,* Home Economist for Appliance Distributors of Connecticut, Inc. for microwave testing; *Christine Sweklo,* Home Economist and microwave consultant for microwave testing. Some recipes were adapted from Paula Wolfet.

And special thank you to *Thelma Pressman,* noted pioneer in the field of microwave cooking. In 1969 she started the first microwave cooking school, which initiated quality education for the consumer. From this effort her role as consultant for different microwave manufacturers developed, as well as her affiliation with *Bon Apetit* magazine as their microwave consultant and columnist. Mrs. Pressman reviewed the entire microwave conversion section of the manuscript. She retested recipes where necessary, suggested removal of certain microwave conversions when results were not superior, and provided conversions for additional recipes.

Original Cookbook Committee

Chairman and Editor
Melinda M. Vance
Assistant to Chairman
Lee M. Grimmeisen
Production Staff
Bernice Kuzma
Kathleen J. Schwartz
Sarah C. Seymour
Menu Text
Alice F. Evans
Recipe Testing Chairman
Sarah C. Seymour
Menu Co-ordinator
Gloria J. Holtsinger
Nutrition
Diane L. Burgess
Microwave Conversion Chairmen
Renee P. Dubin
Beaubette Kagey
Metric Conversions
Sybille Brewer
Restaurant Recipe Solicitation
Kathleen J. Schwartz
Proofreading Chairman
Sybille Brewer
Index
Bernice Kuzma
Maryann Reuben
Printing Production
Melinda M. Vance
Treasurer and Business Manager
Sharon P. Carlos
Chairman, Board of Directors
Gloria S. McDonagh
Cookbook Office Manager
Joan D. Larkins
Marketing Chairmen
Patricia M. Mitchell
Jacqueline A. Gfeller
5 Arts Liaison
Anne Healey
Public Relations Co-ordinators
Pauline Livingston
Betty Barrett

The Program

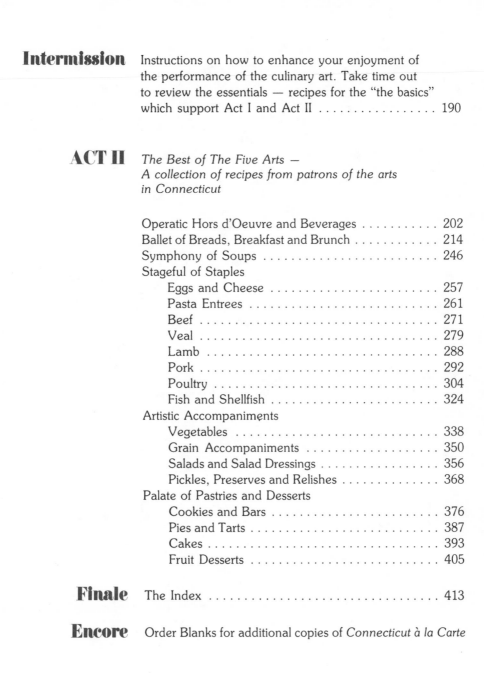

Program Notes

These introductory remarks are designed to facilitate and enhance the use of this book as well as document its special features.

There is **art** in *Connecticut à la Carte*. In fact, cooking has been described as one of the performing arts. That five major art organizations — Connecticut Opera, Hartford Ballet, Hartford Stage, Hartford Symphony and Wadsworth Atheneum art museum — should create and stage a cookbook is an appropriate and natural extension of their métier. *Connecticut à la Carte* presents a sixth art — the art of cooking and entertaining. Performance of this art calls for setting the stage, directing the cast of guests and presenting food that has visual excitement. There are drama and ritual, the decorative pattern of a well executed meal and the delicate blending of fine food and wine. Adding a special flair are recipes and menus which have been inspired by the unique art, history and setting of our state of Connecticut.

We are *à la carte* not only because we present the *art* of fine food and entertaining, but also because this term implies and emphasizes the creative aspect of cooking, as opposed to *prix fixe*, which denotes a preselected meal at a fixed price. *A la carte* refers to the listing of individual specialties offered by a kitchen. Ordering *à la carte*, one selects dishes to complement one another.

Nothing in this book is *prix fixe!* Everything is *à la carte!* You are invited to indulge your creativity. Make your own selections. The recipes are not formulas, but guidelines to let your imagination and senses gratify your fantasies.

Even the twenty menus in this book are *à la carte*. They are purposely very extensive culinary collages to allow freedom of choice. The menus are designed to let a particular setting in Connecticut inspire a special entertainment of your own. We urge you to challenge traditional rules. Try preparing a seafood celebration, serving fish in *every* course, not merely a fish course. Substitute fresh seasonal produce or herbs when a specified recipe ingredient is not available or does not suit your palate. Experiment with substituting whole grain flours or reduced calorie products. Make changes to suit your personal taste and lifestyle. That's truly creative cooking. That's *Connecticut à la Carte*.

Two questions were behind *every* decision made during the preparation of this cookbook: Is it of the finest quality? Is it really useful? There is an abundance of cookbooks on the market; new ones appear daily. There was no reason for *Connecticut à la Carte* to exist if it could not present exceptional recipes and a distinctively useful format. With that philosophy foremost in our minds we developed the following features:

● **Recipes:**
There are 495 recipes presented within these pages plus innumerable variations. Most are recipes for special entertaining. They were selected because they represent the finest, be it the most unusual pound cake, the best carrot cake, the finest beef stew, the best example of coq au vin or trifle, the decidedly unique recipe for cranberry bread or cheesecake. Each recipe was tested and rated before final selections were made. Then each recipe was *retested* using uniform guidelines. Further refinement was provided by six separate committees. Each received a copy of the recipe and added the "garnishes" which make this cookbook not only unique, but extremely useful.

● **Editing:**
Each recipe was edited according to (1) standardized language and format; (2) clear, precise and chronological enumeration of ingredients; (3) explicit and thorough description of preparation method; (4) advance preparation and serving suggestions to facilitate the ease of entertaining without help; (5) cooking definitions, recipe title translations and culinary folklore to enhance the recipe as well as entertain non-cooks.

● **Nutrition:**
Since practicality dictates that every day cannot be an extravagant culinary celebration, nutrition information is provided to assist in our endeavor to eat wisely. Nutritional Notes suggest ways in which we might modify our operatic extravaganzas, make them more suitable to the sensible diets we need to follow at least during weekday meals. Every ingredient in *every* recipe was carefully measured — the amount of oil absorbed during frying, the amount of crumbs *actually used* to bread a veal cutlet, or the amount of marinade consumed as opposed to drained off. The results were calculated according to useful serving sizes. That there are 5376 calories in 4 pints of jam is not especially useful information. That there are 42 calories per tablespoon is more meaningful.

Emphasis is on fresh ingredients. Very few recipes in this book use processed or canned ingredients. Not only are these ingredients more expensive, but their often high sodium content, chemical additives and reduced amounts of natural vitamins and minerals make them less healthful.

Because recipes are meant to be used creatively, symbols were designed to identify recipes that play multiple roles. The symbols are a quick and easy means of identifying these recipes.

FIRST COURSE DISHES

This symbol identifies any dish that is suitable for serving as a first course. In this book "first course" and "appetizer" are interchangeable. Adjustment in serving size or in manner of presentation is usually required when changing an entree or salad into a first course dish.

LUNCHEON DISHES

This symbol identifies entree recipes that are appropriate for lunch or brunch. Generally, they are the lighter entrees and one may easily reduce the serving size.

VEGETARIAN DISHES

This symbol identifies recipes considered suitable for the lacto-ovo-vegetarian. It is used to indicate a dish that could become an entree in the vegetarian diet. Each of these dishes contains a basic alternative source of protein.

FOOD PROCESSOR APPLICATION

This symbol identifies a recipe where the use of a food processor significantly alters the preparation time or where special food processor techniques are described.

QUICK GOURMET

This symbol identifies dishes in which total preparation plus cooking time is no more than 1 hour. It does, however, assume that a number of basic ingredients are on hand and that you are working continuously during the 60 minutes.

LOW CALORIE DISHES

This symbol identifies dishes that are *relatively* low in calories in relation to their serving size. Guidelines used were approximately 300 calories per serving for an entree, 160 calories per serving for a vegetable dish, and 200 calories per serving for a dessert.

● **Food Processor:**

While the food processor can be used in the preparation of a majority of the recipes in this book, the special food processor symbol and specific directions were given only when the technique suggested was significantly different from the conventional method. Chopping, mincing or grating of ingredients was not highlighted even though use of the food processor for these steps could reduce preparation time. The specialized food processor techniques have been delineated in the recipes either by being printed in italics or by a separate heading and paragraph. The food processor directions were written based upon the results obtained with a Cuisinart DLC-7. If using a smaller bowl or food processor of another manufacturer, it may be necessary to process the recipe in two batches. In this case the directions given should be a *guide* for how to use your own machine.

● **Microwave:**

Since many of the selected recipes are "gourmet" and therefore usually time consuming, and today we have many duties away from the home, microwave adaptations would allow us the best of both worlds — quality dishes with shorter preparation time. It is important to note than none of the 495 recipes originated as a recipe designed for microwave use. All recipes were first "conventional" recipes. Then microwave conversion instructions were written and the recipe was tested in the microwave oven. Some recipes were found unsuitable for microwave cooking, but those which were found successful consequently show both methods of preparation on the same page. Confirmed conventional cooks may break down and give the microwave a try!

● **Wine Suggestion:**

A consultant knowledgeable in both wine and fine food carefully studied a copy of each recipe, selected an appropriate wine, and offered serving suggestions.

● **Metric Conversions:**

Metric conversions for ingredients have been given immediately following the standard measurements. Conversions were not given for very small measurements or for spices and herbs. In the ingredient column of each recipe, the metric equivalents might appear as follows:

½ **cup** *(65g)* **finely chopped walnuts**
2 **cups** *(120g)* **soft fresh breadcrumbs**
½ **cup** *(120ml)* **dry white wine**

The reason for providing two methods of measurement has not so much to do with the anticipated conversion to the metric system in America, but rather with the advantage of weighing in cooking. When using the metric system solids are weighed and liquids are measured, as compared to the American system of measuring the volume of both solids and liquids. The standard form of measuring in cupfuls — i.e., 4 cups cubed eggplant, ½ cup chopped onion, 1 quart sliced apples, 1 cup flour or ½ cup ground almonds — leaves several important questions unanswered. How much eggplant should you purchase at the market to obtain 4 cups? Was the cup of flour sifted before measuring, was it firmly packed into the cup, or was it rounded or leveled off? How do you avoid grinding too many or too few almonds to accurately measure ½-cup ground almonds? Exactly how many almonds are needed to make ½ cup ground? That depends on whether you start with whole, slivered or coarsely chopped almonds. Measuring each in a ½-cup measure will give a different result once ground. In distinction, the metric measurement, 65 grams almonds, is exact, regardless of the shape.

By measuring in cupfuls we are limiting our cooking in two ways: (1) Creativity in substituting ingredients or altering a recipe to suit individual palates is restricted. We need to know the weight of the ingredient specified in the recipe in order to substitute another ingredient of a different shape or density. (2) The more exact science of baking and pastry-making is thrown off if accurate measurements are not followed. Consider the advantages of weighing ingredients either in metric system measurements or pounds and ounces, then buy a good kitchen scale so that you have the freedom to adjust ingredients as well as to be precise when making pastry.

To be consistent, conversion for temperatures is provided below as well as handy formulas for doing your own conversions:

TEMPERATURES

Fahrenheit	Celsius	Fahrenheit	Celsius
85°F	29°C	325°F	165°C
110	43	350	180
120	49	375	190
200	95	400	205
225	110	425	220
250	120	450	230
300	150	500	260

To convert to Celsius: subtract 32, multiply by 5, divide by 9

To convert to Fahrenheit: multiply by 9, divide by 5, add 32

LIQUID MEASURE

Ounces to milliliters: multiply ounces by 29.57
Quarts to liters: multiply quarts by 0.95
Milliliters to ounces: multiply milliliters by 0.034
Liters to quarts: multiply liters by 1.057

WEIGHING

Ounces to grams: multiply ounces by 28.35
Grams to ounces: multiply grams by 0.035

MEASUREMENT BY LENGTH

Inches to centimeters: multiply inches by 2.54
Centimeters to inches: multiply centimeters by 0.39

● **Index:**

Many good cooks judge a cookbook by its index. It should be thorough, easy to read as well as have a philosophy that supports the rest of the book. It is especially important that you make good use of our Index because approximately ⅓ of the recipes immediately follow one of the 20 menus. This means, for example, that not all soups are in the soup section of the book. Approximately 13 of the 28 soup recipes will be scattered throughout the menus. But the Index lists all the soups alphabetically in one easy-to-read column. The Index is also a useful tool to help you find alternative uses for various recipes — e.g., a poultry stuffing given in one recipe is also suitable as a crepe filling or as a ravioli filling. Using the Index will allow you to quickly find these variations.

Should the foregoing material have been more than you cared to digest, and you skipped to this last paragraph, the "Program Notes" serve mainly to document the rationale for each feature of the book. It is hoped that this particular presentation of menus and recipes will lead you to a more fulfilling experience of the fine art of cooking. If you think more creatively about food preparation and entertaining, apply newly learned techniques, acquire confidence in your own palate and ability to execute a dish, or convert a recipe for special dietary needs, or make use of the benefits of microwave cooking, then *Connecticut à la Carte* has attained its objectives.

Nutrition Foreword

Concern with good nutrition and diet has never been greater. Simultaneously, interest in foods and cooking has increased significantly over the last several years. Health-conscious Americans with a passion for gourmet cuisine are seeking a solution to this seeming paradox. Nutrition-minded individuals now are adapting many rich gourmet recipes and traditional family favorites to their lighter eating habits.

As we learn more about the essential role of good nutrition in preventive and therapeutic health care, we become increasingly aware of the importance of discretion in our eating patterns. Many of us are giving careful thought to reliable nutrition information based on scientific data rather than the muddle of nutrition misinformation that floods the media. Although the scientific community is not in total agreement over many questions, the results of many studies point to the need for dietary changes. As a result, we are attempting to modify our food intake by cutting down on excess and empty calories and salt. Total fat, saturated fat and cholesterol, as well as refined carbohydrates and alcohol are being reduced, and our consumption of complex carbohydrates and fiber is increasing. "Meat and potatoes" meals are being replaced by lighter food combinations. Vegetarian dishes, whole grain breads, cereals and pasta products, lowfat dairy products including skim milk, lowfat cheeses and yogurt, and the "nouvelle cuisine" are often preferred in this trend toward healthier eating.

This is not a diet cookbook. It is, rather, a collection of gourmet ideas to be used most often for entertaining and special occasions. Many of the recipes have been highlighted with "nutritional notes" relating to the above trends toward eating wisely. Such information will, hopefully, help to identify food items or ingredients that should be eaten with discretion and aid in building prudent daily eating patterns.

A number of the recipes in this cookbook can be modified easily to meet the specifications of many restricted diets. The occasional inclusion of foods high in calories, sodium, fat, and cholesterol is certainly not inadvisable for the general public. However, individuals with medical conditions that dictate the reduction of these food components will note the inappropriateness of certain recipes that cannot be easily adapted to a modified diet regimen.

In order to increase nutrition awareness, as well as to alert individuals who must comply with dietary restrictions, information on nutrition has been incorporated into this book in several ways:

1. Computerized nutritional analysis data were collected by students from the Department of Nutritional Sciences at the University of Connecticut. The resulting carbohydrate, protein, and fat values were used in order to calculate calories per serving and per yield. The data provided are based on *approximate* figures and should be used accordingly to serve only as a *guideline* to individuals interested in the modification of their dietary intake. Data do not include optional ingredients and garnishes, microwave options, or suggested variations, and were calculated on the basis of the smaller amount of an ingredient if a range is given, (e.g. ½-1 cup milk uses ½ cup milk in nutritional analysis) and the smaller serving size (e.g. information given for a recipe yielding 6-8 servings is based on 8 servings.) Also, where water, broth or stock, or wine is suggested, water was used in the nutritional analysis. Calories are given either by yield or serving size as are grams of carbohydrate, protein and fat.

2. Recipes were reviewed for ingredients that contribute a significant amount of cholesterol and sodium. Only recipes estimated as containing large amounts of cholesterol and sodium are highlighted. Thus, individuals adhering to strict diets may need to rely on more specific information not provided within the scope of this book, since such restrictions may preclude the consumption of even moderate amounts of these dietary components. Additional information regarding the cholesterol and sodium content of selected food items is given on pages 14 and 15.

3. "Nutritional Notes" written by the nutrition committee are included with many recipes to provide more detailed information to the reader concerning the nutritive value of certain ingredients as well as the possible alteration of ingredients to suit a modified diet regimen or the needs of an individual who is attempting to eat more wisely. Lack of commentary, however, does not necessarily endorse the consumption of the item by all individuals, but may indicate that the recipe cannot be altered easily or that ingredient modification could drastically change the quality of the product. We encourage experimentation

with ingredient modifications suggested or alteration of recipes in accordance with individualized diet restriction, as prescribed by a physician or registered dietitian.

The nutrition-conscious individual may wish to consider decreasing serving sizes and experimenting with other ingredients and cooking methods when selecting a healthy diet:

1. *Decreasing serving sizes:* Note that the calorie content per serving of certain recipes in this book is fairly high. Although not often realized, most food items do not necessarily need to be eliminated from the food intake of those interested in weight loss or weight maintenance. Instead, *moderation* is emphasized; the number of servings obtained from each recipe may be increased. Smaller serving sizes eliminate deprivation yet provide the experience of tasting a variety of foods. Traditionally forbidden foods often can become occasional treats in small quantities. Unless a strict diet is necessary, virtually any food can be incorporated into the diet when eaten in small quantities and only on special occasions.

2. *Experimenting with alternate ingredients and cooking methods:* In numerous cases ingredient alternatives are suggested in "Nutritional Notes" and "Microwave Conversion Instructions." Generally microwave cooking incorporates less fat or oil, less coating mediums and less liquid for substantial savings in calories. In addition, many other substitutions can be tested in your own kitchen. Experiment with adapting a recipe to your individual diet, budget or taste. Some examples of adaptations that may be tried include:

- Decreasing total fat in a recipe; using polyunsaturated margarine or oil to decrease satuurated fat and cholesterol where butter is indicated
- Decreasing amount of meat suggested
- Substituting whole wheat flour for a portion of the flour called for in order to increase fiber and trace nutrients
- Adding bran and/or wheat germ to breads and casseroles to increase fiber and nutritional content, respectively
- Substituting lowfat yogurt for a portion of the specified amount of sour cream or mayonnaise in order to decrease fat and calories, being careful not to allow mixture to reach a high temperature
- Using brown rice in place of white rice
- Substituting lowfat (1% fat) or skim milk for whole milk
- Steaming vegetables instead of sauteing in order to decrease calories and retain more nutrients

- Reducing sugar by as much as one half in some recipes, and adding more vanilla, cinnamon, nutmeg, grated orange peel, orange juice concentrate, raisins, or other naturally sweet ingredients
- Making use of lowfat, low sodium, or "light" food products. Some of the "light" foods available include:

    Imitation cheeses (butterfat is replaced by polyunsaturated oils to decrease cholesterol)
    Imitation mayonnaise (contains approximately 45 calories per tablespoon; regular mayonnaise contains about 100)
    "Fruit spreads" instead of preserves, decreasing sugar content by one third
    Fruits canned in their own juice or in light syrup, rather than heavy syrup
    Salt-free products: salt-free broth or stock (either homemade or commercial), unsalted butter or margarine, and salt-free bread or bread crumbs.

- Skimming off excess fat from cooked food prior to eating. If refrigerated, hardened fat can be removed from soups and gravies within several hours. If not refrigerated, a bristle type utensil or spouted cup especially designed for "degreasing" may be used for removal of the fat layer, and therefore, excess calories
- Broiling meats on a metal rack so that fat drips off and calories, fat and cholesterol are reduced. All visible fat should be removed from the meat prior to cooking.

In addition to the above suggestions for recipe modification, the following information may be helpful to those attempting to build prudent eating patterns.

Protein: Protein serves an essential function in the diet since it is responsible for providing the building blocks necessary for the maintenance and repair of body tissues, enzymes, and other life-supporting substances. According to the Recommended Dietary Allowances (1979), the "average" healthy male needs about 56 grams of protein each day, while the adult female needs about 44 grams. Americans, however, tend to eat approximately twice as much protein as is needed. In addition, a large amount of fat is sometimes combined with the protein. For example, a three-and-one-half ounce rib-eye steak contains about 20 grams of protein, 40 grams of fat, and about 440 calories. Thus, by decreasing consumption of protein, we often are decreasing our fat and calorie intake as well.

An alternative which generally is lower in calories, saturated fat, and cholesterol, as well as lower in cost, is the consumption of "complementary proteins." Vegetarians are well aware of the necessity of combining specific vegetable proteins in order to form a "high quality protein." Animal proteins — meat, fish, eggs, poultry, milk — are of high quality, while proteins from vegetable sources are incomplete. When vegetable proteins are combined in a complementary manner, however, high quality protein is formed.

High quality protein can be obtained by using combinations of non-animal products as follows:

- Cereal grains and legumes, e.g. rice with beans, whole grain bread with beans, tofu (soybean curd) with rice or split pea and barley soup
- Legumes and nuts/seeds, e.g. soybean/sunflower seed/peanut snack
- Rice and seeds, e.g. sesame seed and rice casserole
- The quality of vegetable protein can also be greatly improved by adding small amounts of animal protein, e.g. bean soup with small amounts of meat, bulgur salad with yogurt-based dressing, stir-fried vegetables with small amounts of meat. Included in this cookbook are a number of Oriental style dishes where small amounts of meat are used, or where meat can be eliminated in favor of combining non-meat proteins to form complete proteins.

Fats and Cholesterol: Essential components of the diet, fats carry fat-soluble vitamins (A, D, E, K), provide calories for energy and essential fatty acids, and add flavor to foods. In addition, they generally remain in the stomach longer than protein and carbohydrates, and, therefore, a meal containing fat will delay a hungry feeling for a longer period of time than one that is fat-free.

On the other hand, a diet containing a large quantity of fat is not recommended. Protein and carbohydrate both contribute four calories per gram, whereas fat provides nine calories per gram, thereby contributing a significant percentage of calories to the diet when consumed in large amounts. At present, scientific data are being collected regarding other effects of large amounts of fat in the diet.

Quality of fat is also important. Although, as of this writing, many controversies exist concerning the effect of saturated, monounsaturated, and polyunsaturated fat, many scientists believe that saturated fat (present in animal products such as whole milk products, egg yolk and meat) is associated with increased levels of blood cholesterol, which is considered to be one of the risk factors associated with heart disease. Polyunsaturated fats (found in plant foods and oils derived from corn, safflower, sesame, soy, sunflower and cottonseed) tend to decrease

cholesterol levels, while it appears that monounsaturated fats (found in olive and peanut oils and avocado) do not alter cholesterol levels.

Although the cholesterol question remains controversial, many dietitians and nutritionists are recommending the restriction of cholesterol to approximately 300 milligrams per day for individuals with elevated cholesterol levels. (The "average" American consumes about 500 milligrams per day.) It is also felt that the general public would not be harmed by decreasing the intake of high cholesterol foods.

Some substitutions are recommended in the cookbook in order to modify cholesterol intake. Give attention to recipes indicated as high in cholesterol by altering ingredients when possible and/or decreasing serving sizes.

Carbohydrates and Fiber: Carbohydrates are often considered to be the cause of overweight, and have been eliminated or drastically decreased by many individuals who "battle the bulge." Contrary to popular opinion, *calories,* rather than carbohydrates, are the culprit. It is important to remember, however, that carbohydrates are classified in two groups — the complex (starches) and the simple (sugars). It is the latter that is largely responsible for our intake of "empty calories," or foods which provide a large amount of calories with very little nutritional value. Carbohydrates contained in cookies, cakes, sugar, honey and other sweets are the "simple" form, and should be decreased in the diets of individuals attempting to achieve their ideal body weight. On the other hand, grain products and vegetables contain complex carbohydrates and provide the body with essential nutrients and relatively fewer calories. Enriched whole grain bread, pasta and potatoes, for example, contain complex carbohydrates and will not cause weight gain. Of course, any food can cause weight gain if eaten in large enough quantities. Again, concern is with *total number of calories, rather than the carbohydrate* content.

Within the past ten years scientific research has found much evidence of the value of complex carbohydrate and fiber in the diet. Fiber, the portion of plant material that is resistant to digestive enzymes, includes a group of carbohydrate substances including cellulose, hemicellulose, pectin, and gums and the noncarbohydrate lignin. These substances hold water in the intestinal tract and help to prevent constipation. Lack of fiber in the diet has been linked to diverticular disease and other health disorders, and the effects of dietary fiber are presently being studied.

Fiber can be obtained from whole grain breads and cereals, including bran, raw fruits and vegetables, legumes (dried beans and peas) and nuts and seeds, and should be included in the nutritionally adequate diet. Unprocessed bran can be added easily to many of the recipes in this cookbook, including breads, stuffings and casseroles. If bran or high fiber foods have not been consumed previously on a regular basis, add them to the diet gradually in order to avoid excessive flatulence and abdominal discomfort.

Sodium: A taste for salty foods is said to be established at an early age. Since the association between salt and high blood pressure has become recognized, many individuals are attempting to shake the salt habit. Although salt consumption varies, Americans are presented with a plethora of sodium-laden processed "convenience" foods, fast foods, salty snacks, cured meats, and canned items, which makes the "average" consumption of sodium approximately 5 to 10 grams per day.

Dietitians and nutritionists are recommending a decrease of sodium in the diet to approximately *2 to 4 grams*, depending on whether hypertension (high blood pressure) exists. For many individuals, this is a difficult challenge. However, most who have tried to cut down on salt have stated that one adapts within several weeks to the natural flavor of foods and to alternate seasonings. Suggested ways of cutting down on salt include:

- Seasoning foods with garlic, onions, oregano, curry powder, basil, marjoram, rosemary, pepper, orange juice, lemon juice, etc., etc., etc. Experiment with various spices and herbs to find the ones preferred!
- Using fresh foods instead of canned or convenience frozen
- Avoiding canned soups, canned vegetables, cured meats, pickles, olives, sauerkraut, ketchup, mustard, soy sauce, whenever possible. Read labels to note items containing salt or sodium (e.g. *monosodium* glutamate). Avoid salty snack foods

- Removing the salt shaker from the table. If salt is needed, it is used only in minimal amounts, and only *after tasting.*

Basics of a Healthy Diet: A variety of foods should be eaten daily in order to obtain essential nutrients, including the following:

- 4 to 5 oz. *(115 to 140g)* of high quality protein foods, such as lean meat, fish, poultry without skin, eggs, nuts, dried beans and peas. As already discussed, protein complementation, or the combining of specific vegetable sources to obtain higher quality protein can provide variety and a nutritious change to the diet.
- Lowfat milk and milk products, including yogurt and cheeses
- Fresh fruits and vegetables, including those that are dark green and orange/yellow for Vitamin A (e.g. carrots, squash, spinach, sweet potatoes); and Vitamin C (e.g. oranges, grapefruits, strawberries, cantaloupe, green pepper, broccoli, etc.)
- Whole grain breads and cereal products (bread, pasta, brown rice, wheat germ, dry and cooked cereals, dishes made from whole grains)

It is hoped that the information included in this book will help the nutrition conscious to adapt more healthful eating patterns, revise favorite recipes, and modify some of the recipes presented. The word "diet" is being erased from the vocabulary of many dietitians and nutritionists because it suggests a *temporary way of life* and has a negative connotation. *Good eating habits are a lifelong process.* Eating habits aren't changed overnight. Learning more about nutrition, skipping the fads, and making gradual changes in the way we eat are an excellent, nutritious beginning!

Melanie Rodin Polk, R.D., M.M.Sc.

SODIUM AND CHOLESTEROL CONTENT OF SELECTED FOODS

———— SODIUM CONTENT ————

FOOD	AMOUNT	MILLIGRAMS
Bacon	1 slice	71
Baking Powder	1 tsp.	219
Low Sodium Baking Powder	1 tsp.	Trace
Baking Soda	1 tsp.	821
Bread	1 slice	117
Unsalted Bread	1 slice	Trace
Broth — Canned and		
reconstituted	1 cup	737
Dry Broth	1 T.	2431
Homemade Unsalted Broth	1 cup	Trace
Butter or Margarine — Regular	1 tsp.	41
Sweet Butter or Margarine	1 tsp.	Trace
Cheese		
Cheddar	1 oz.	197
Creamed Cottage Cheese	½ cup	258
Uncreamed Cottage Cheese	½ cup	459
Grated Parmesan	1 T.	93
Cream Cheese	2 T.	84
Low Moisture Mozzarella	1 oz.	116
Part Skim Mozzarella	1 oz.	148
Ricotta	½ cup	104
Part Skim Ricotta	½ cup	155
Clams	4 large	36
Dry Cereal —		
Shredded Wheat	1 cup	5
Other (with Salt)	1 cup	150-300
Egg	1 medium	59
Fish, fresh	3½ oz.	50-100
Ham	3 oz.	837
Mayonnaise	1 T.	84
Meat (Beef, Veal, Pork,		
Lamb, Chicken)	1 oz.	25
Mussels	3½ oz.	289
Olives —		
Black	5 large	435
Green	3 large	280
Oysters	5-8 medium	73
Peanut Butter	1 T.	18
Unsalted Peanut Butter	1 T.	Trace
Pickle —		
Dill Pickle	1 large	1428
Prepared Mustard	1 tsp.	65
Prepared Salad Dressings	1 T.	290
Salt	1 tsp.	1955
Soups — Canned		
Cream of Celery	1 cup	980
Cream of Mushroom	1 cup	880
Tomato	1 cup	770
Shrimp	3½ oz.	140
Soy Sauce	1 T.	858
Sweet Relish	1 T.	107
Tomato Juice	2/5 cup	200
Unsalted Tomato Juice	2/5 cup	Trace
Worcestershire Sauce	1 tsp.	49

———— CHOLESTEROL CONTENT ————

FOOD	AMOUNT	MILLIGRAMS
Bacon	2 slices	13
Beef	3½ oz.	70
Butter	1 tsp.	11
Cheese —		
Cheddar	1 oz.	30
Creamed Cottage Cheese	½ cup	17
Uncreamed Cottage Cheese		
1% fat	½ cup	4
Mozzarella	1 oz.	25
Part Skim Mozzarella	1 oz.	15
Muenster	1 oz.	27
Ricotta	½ cup	63
Part Skim Ricotta	½ cup	40
Chicken	3½ oz.	60
Cream —		
Half & Half	1 T.	6
Heavy	1 T.	20
Light	1 T.	10
Sour	1 T.	5
Duck	3½ oz.	70
Egg	1	272
Egg White	1	0
Fish, fillets, steaks	3½ oz.	60
Goose	3½ oz.	75
Ice Cream (16% fat)	½ cup	42
Ice Milk	1/6 qt.	13
Kidney	3½ oz.	375
Lamb	3½ oz.	70
Liver (Calves)	3½ oz.	300
Margarine	1 tsp.	0
Mayonnaise —		
Regular	1 T.	10
Imitation	1 T.	5
Milk —		
Whole	1 cup	34
Lowfat	1 cup	10
Skim	1 cup	5
Buttermilk (From Skim)	1 cup	10
Evaporated Skim	1 oz.	1
Nuts	3½ oz.	0
Pork	3½ oz.	70
Salt Pork	1 oz.	31
Shellfish —		
Canned Crab	½ cup	62
Lobster	3½ oz.	200
Oysters	5-8 medium	200
Scallops	3½ oz.	35
Shrimp	3½ oz.	150
Sherbet	½ cup	7
Yogurt (Lowfat)	1 cup	10

* Information obtained from *Bowes and Church's Food Values of Portions Commonly Used*, 13th edition, by Pennington and Church

EAT A VARIETY OF FOODS WITHIN EACH OF THE BASIC 4 FOOD GROUPS

AVERAGE ADULT DAILY RECOMMENDATIONS*: I: 2 SERVINGS   II: 4 SERVINGS   III: 4 SERVINGS   IV: 2-2 oz. SERVINGS

GROUP I — MILK, MILK PRODUCTS

Food	Serving	Cal.
Cheese		
American	1½ oz.	160
Brie/Camembert	1½ oz.	126
Cheddar	1½ oz.	168
Cottage		
Creamed	½ Cup	120
Lowfat	½ Cup	88
Roquefort	1½ oz.	167
Swiss	1½ oz.	156
Milk		
Buttermilk	1 Cup	88
Whole, 3.5% fat	1 Cup	159
Skim/Nonfat	1 Cup	88
Ice Cream, 12% fat	⅔ Cup	186
Ice Milk	⅔ Cup	137
Yogurt		
from skim milk	1 Cup	122
from whole milk	1 Cup	151

GROUP II — GRAINS

Food	Serving	Cal.
Bread		
Enriched White	1 slice	62
Pumpernickel	1 slice	79
Rye	1 slice	60
Whole Wheat	1 slice	56
Cereal, Ready to Eat		
Bran Flakes (40%)	1 Cup	135
Cheerios	1 Cup	102
Corn Flakes	1 Cup	95
Rice Krispies	1 Cup	107
Shredded Wheat	1 Biscuit	84
Special K	1 Cup	60
Wheaties	1 Cup	104
Crackers		
Saltine	5	70
Shredded Wheat	3	63
Ritz	4	72
Cream of Wheat	½ Cup-c	67
Grits	½ Cup-c	75
Oatmeal	½ Cup-c	74
Pasta		
Enriched (al dente)	½ Cup-c	106
Egg Noodles	½ Cup-c	100
Rice		
Brown	½ Cup-c	89
Enriched White	½ Cup-c	82
Wild Rice	½ Cup-c	74

GROUP III — VEGETABLES AND FRUIT

VEGETABLES

Food	Serving	Cal.
Asparagus	6 spears-c	26
Bean Sprouts	½ Cup-r	10
Beets	½ Cup-c	27
Bell Pepper	large-r	22
Broccoli	⅔ Cup-c	26
Brussels Sprouts	7 sprouts-c	36
Cabbage	½ Cup-r	12
Carrot	large-r	42
Cauliflower	½ Cup-c	13
Celery	½ Cup-r	9
Corn	medium ear-c	100
Cucumber	½ medium	8
Eggplant	½ Cup-c	19
Green Beans	½ Cup-c	16
Green leafy (Spinach, Kale, Turnip, Mustard, etc.)	½ Cup-c	22
Green Peas	⅓ Cup	36
Lettuce	10 small-r	5
Mushrooms	medium-r	28
Onions	½ Cup-c	29
Parsnips	½ Cup-c	66
Potatoes		
Sweet	small-c	141
White	3¼" diameter-c	139
Pumpkin	½ Cup-c	38
Squash		
Yellow/Green	½ Cup-c	15
Winter	½ Cup-c	65
Tomato	medium-r	33

FRUIT

Food	Serving	Cal.
Apple	medium	87
Apricots	3	51
Avocado	½	167
Banana	small, 6"	85
Berries (Blue, Black, Rasp.)	½ Cup	47
Cantaloupe	¼	30
Cranberries	½ Cup	23
Dates	5	137
Grapefruit	½	41
Grapes, Seedless	½ Cup	51
Lemon, juice from	1 medium	12
Lime, juice from	1 medium	8
Orange	med. - 3" diameter	73
Peach	medium	38
Pear	medium	90
Pineapple	½ Cup	35
Plums	3 medium	75
Prunes	4	172
Raisins	¼ Cup	103
Strawberries	½ Cup	28

UNSWEETENED JUICES

Food	Serving	Cal.
Apple	¾ Cup/6 oz.	87
Grapefruit	¾ Cup/6 oz.	74
Orange	¾ Cup/6 oz.	84
Pineapple	¾ Cup/6 oz.	104
Prune	¾ Cup/6 oz.	138
Tomato	¾ Cup/6 oz.	34
V-8	¾ Cup/6 oz.	31

GROUP IV — MEAT / FISH / POULTRY, Etc.

Food	Serving	Cal.
Almonds	12-15	93
Bacon, 3 Strips	1 oz. - c	147
Beef		
Flank Steak	3½ oz.	196
Hamburger		
Lean	3½ oz. - c	219
Chuck	3½ oz. - c	286
Rump Roast - L	3½ oz. - c	347
Sirloin - L	3½ oz. - c	216
Tenderloin	3½ oz. - c	224
Bologna, 3 slices	3½ oz. - c	221
Calf Liver	3½ oz. - c	206
Clams	3½ oz. - r	80
Chicken		
Fried	3½ oz. - c	242
Roast	3½ oz. - c	183
Chicken Liver	3½ oz. - c	165
Cod	3½ oz. - c	171
Crab	3½ oz. - c	93
Dried Beans	½ Cup - c	120
Duck	3½ oz. - c	311
Egg	1 large	88
Frankfurters (2)	3½ oz. - c	248
Flounder/Sole	3½ oz. - c	202
Goose	3½ oz. - c	330
Halibut	3½ oz. - c	175
Ham		
Cured Butt	3½ oz. - c	348
Cured Shank	3½ oz. - c	371
Fresh	3½ oz. - c	306
Lamb		
Leg, Roast	3½ oz. - c	242
Loin Chop	3½ oz. - c	302
Rib Chop	3½ oz. - c	423
Lentils	½ Cup - c	80
Lobster	3½ oz. - c	95
Oysters	3½ oz. - r	66
Peanut Butter	2 T.	190
Pork		
Boston Butt	3½ oz. - c	283
Loin Chop	3½ oz. - c	357
Sirloin Roast	3½ oz. - c	297
Tenderloin	3½ oz. - c	239
Pork Sausage	link (3" × ½") - c	94
Salmon/Swordfish	3½ oz. - c	180
Scallops	3½ oz. - c	112
Shrimp	3½ oz. - r	91
Soyabean Curd/Tofu	4 oz.	140
Tunafish		
in oil, drained	3½ oz.	197
in water	3½ oz.	127
Turkey, Roast	3½ oz. - c	200

Miscellaneous

Food	Serving	Cal.
Alcohol (av.)	1½ oz.	125
Beer	8 oz.	100
Butter	1 T.	100
Catsup	1 T.	21
Cola	8 oz.	105
Cookies		
Choc. Sand.	1	50
Fig	1	55
Graham	1	27
Vanilla Wafers	1	15
Cream		
Half & Half	1 oz/2 T.	40
Heavy/Whipping	1 oz/2 T.	106
Light	1 oz/2 T.	64
Sour	1 oz/2 T.	57
Donut - yeast, plain	3¾" diameter	175
Gelatin Dessert	½ Cup	80
Jam/Jelly	1 T.	52
Margarine	1 T.	100
Mayonnaise	1 T.	65
Mustard	1 T.	11
Potato Chips	10	113
Salad Dressings		
French	1 T.	70
Italian	1 T.	82
Sweeteners		
Honey	1 T.	64
Maple Syrup	1 T.	50
Molasses	1 T.	50
Sugar, White	1 T.	46
Unsweetened Coffee, Tea, Soda Water		0
Vegetable Oil/Shortening	1 T.	124
Wine, dry (av.)	4 oz.	95
Wine, sweet (av.)	4 oz.	190

This group contains foods which are generally high in calories and low in nutritive value. Their use should be in *addition* to an already well balanced diet and the amounts determined by individual caloric needs.

— c = cooked (baked, broiled or steamed) — r = raw — L = lean meat

* Items are listed according to portions commonly used and do not always represent recommended serving size. Caloric information is based on Bowes and Church, *Food Values of Portions Commonly Used* and U.S. Department of Agriculture, *Composition Of Foods.*

Wine Selection Guide

Like a good marriage, the wedding of food and wine completes an equation: one without the other cannot be whole. Once complementary tastes are combined, there results a natural mesh of gastronomic delights that makes a harmonious treat infinitely more pleasing and natural than either could provide alone. A good dish, well prepared and served, is appealing to the eye and to the palate; with the appropriate wine, the taste and effect are enhanced, appreciated, digested, completed. The bouquet and taste of wine enormously enhance the flavors of food. Wine also aids digestion and induces a feeling of well-being. Wine has enhanced, since antiquity, the tradition of dinner table society with the exchange of ideas and stimulating conversation.

Unfortunately, the last hundred years of recessions, wars, depressions and social upheaval produced a dark age for food and wine, a period of underground gourmets and clandestine cocktails. Fortunately, the thread was not broken and the books not all burned; the bottles were not all emptied and the vineyards not all left fallow. The vines struggled to raise their fruit above the earth. By 1960, a good dozen years after Second World War hostilities ended and replanting began, wine started to find its way upon the table. After decades of neglect, wine has regained its dignified role on top of the dinner table.

The fact that wine and food go together so well was discovered by our earliest ancestors. The ancients, epitomized by Roman general Lucius Licinius Lucullus, consumed vast repasts washed down by jugs of new wine fresh from the wood. As a general and consul, Lucullus enjoyed considerable success in his military and political career. Tired of the active life of public service, he retreated (67 B.C.) to his villa in Rome which soon became famous for its gardens and banquets. To appreciate the progress of gastronomy in his day, the excellence and variety of food supplies at the gourmet's disposal for varied combinations, we must refer to the Thirteenth Book of Martial's *Epigrams*. In this passage appears a lengthy series of the many foods available to the wealthy citizen of ancient Rome. Not a few items have a distinctly "modern" flavor: smoked cheeses, goose livers, truffles, capons, sausages and no less than *nineteen* different varieties of wines are mentioned.

Fish were caught in the gulfs and bays adjacent to the city; the shell-fish, large and small, in the Mediterranean. Game abounded in the Laurentine and Ciminian forests. The open country near at hand supplied from its flocks and herds meat and milk in every form, the cheeses of Trebula and Vestini, and also vegetables of every sort: cabbages and lentils, beans and lettuce, radishes and turnips, gourds and pumpkins, melons and asparagus. Picenum and the Sabine country were renowned for the quality of their oils. The pickles with which eggs were seasoned came from Spain. Pork came from Gaul, spices from the East, wines and fruits from all sections of Italy and the world; apples, pears and figs from Chios, lemons and pomegranates from Africa, dates from the oases, and plums from Damascus.

To accompany these victuals one could include the most famous of all classical wines, Falernian, which came from the hills forming the boundary between Latium and Campania. The wine appears to have been like a red Rhone such as Chateauneuf-du-Pape, but with a much more powerful bouquet. Martial wrote that he "wanted not merely to drink the kisses left in the loved one's cup, but to kiss lips moist with old Falernian." Like so many Italian red wines of our own time, Falernian seems to have had a remarkable capacity for aging: Petronius, in Nero's time, makes the *nouveau-riche* Trimalchio serve his guests the most expensive wine obtainable in Rome — a hundred-year-old Falernian.

The appreciation of wine with food persisted through the centuries. Invention of the glass bottle was a landmark in the 1700s, allowing wine to mature in small containers in individual cellars, making possible more private parties and the immediate family gathering or gourmet group. By 1800 wine was no longer a refreshing beverage to gulp down in gluttony. The country gentleman still dined heartily and often drank three bottles a day. But the Renaissance led to the development and refinement of fine French cuisine, leading to the time of Careme and other great chefs. Meals began to be planned with care and attention to detail. Carefully selected bottled wines were appreciatively sniffed and sipped. Nevertheless, throughout the nineteenth century, dinners remained large and long with a redoubtable range of glasses with each course.

But now the match-making must be done anew — a new generation of foods and a new generation of wines must find each other. Let us establish some useful ground rules: good servants but bad masters.

Today, although we may eat and entertain more sparingly, it is again increasingly popular to arrange a special dinner where three or more wines are served, each course planned so that the accompanying bottle may build the taste experience on the one before. The meal might begin with a dry white wine (French Chablis or California Pinot Chardonnay) with fish, continue with red (Burgundy, Bordeaux or California Cabernet Sauvignon) for meat, and add a more mature red (aged French Burgundy, California Pinot Noir or Charbono) with cheese. Depending on the courses served, there could be three wines, starting with the youngest and ending with the oldest. Historically, cheese is served before a sweet dessert and the best red wine is furnished with this course. Then a luscious dessert wine complements the coda of the meal (French Sauternes, German or Austrian Trockenbeerenauslese or California Chateau Beaulieu Sauvignon Blanc) with cakes, pies, souffles, or sweet fruits and ices. After the last dish, Bristol Cream or Port will satisfy a lingering appetite for nuts and cookies.

Traditionally, certain wines go with certain foods (the wine snob's rule that is a bad master rather than a good servant), such as "Chablis and oysters go together like bread and butter." Many of the guidelines are good, however, the summary of centuries of experiment — of trial and error. Generations of triers have found that dry white wines taste best before red wines, finer or more complex wines taste better following younger or lesser ones of a similar type. White wines seem best with fish and seafood, although the acidity of some German and Austrian wines perfectly complements meats, roast goose, turkey and chicken (not to mention red wine with Bordelais lamprey). Sweet wines just don't fit with main course meats — they are sublime with desserts: sweet with sweet is the best match.

Thus, even though we should make up our own minds in pairing wines and foods, the rules can be useful shortcuts tested by our experience. In selecting a wine for a meal, it is our own perception and pleasure that must judge. Time and place are important factors: the Lancers Rose that goes perfectly with anything at lunch may be overcome by a complicated *piece de resistance* dish at dinner. That same cool rose enjoyed on a warm summer's day would not do with a hearty roast on a cold winter's night. The elegant Beaulieu Cabernet Sauvignon just clashes with that spring chef's salad and cold cuts while bringing to perfection the taste experience of Chateaubriand with Sauce Bearnaise.

Some foods fight with some wines. A spicy curry kills a Cabernet when an Inglenook Gewurztraminer (strong flavored) fights back and strikes a balance. Finally, briney things like anchovies or kippered herrings and vinaigrette salad dressing murder all wines and never should be served together.

Certain wines drink well all alone or with a cracker, particularly sparkling, semi-sweet or sweet types, such as Champagne, California Johannisberg Riesling, Gewurztraminer or sweet Sauvignon Blanc, French Sauternes or Barsac, German or Austrian Auslesen, Beerenauslesen and Trockenbeerenauslesen, or Oloroso Sherry, Port and Madeira. Still dry table wines, however, are incomplete without harmonious food accompaniment. And a great recipe requires an equivalent wine to make the taste equation work.

For the love of food and wine, therefore, still table wines are the beverage we drink with meals. They are simply the naturally fermented juice of fresh ripe grapes and normally attain 10% to 14% alcohol. They may be red, white or rose; dry, semi-sweet or sweet; light, medium or heavy bodied.

Dry white table wines have usually been paired with fish and seafood. California Pinot Chardonnay or Bouchard Pere & Fils White Burgundy go perfectly with shrimp or lobster (but also well with veal or chicken in a white wine sauce). California Chenin Blanc or Johannisberg Riesling mate marvelously with sole or poached fish. Generally, as dry white wines tend to be light, they best accompany light, delicately flavored dishes.

Sweet white table wines go best with dessert courses, cakes, pies and sweet fruits. The sugar content tends to sate the appetite and, therefore, such wines would spoil appreciation of a meal if served at the beginning, whereas at the end they serve to satisfy and engender contentment.

Dry red table wines are the worldwide staple dinner beverage. Everywhere but in the United States more red wine is consumed than white. White wine in this country is still drunk as a cocktail in addition to being a meal accompaniment. The salient characteristic of red wines is their diversity, ranging from light elegance to full-bodied robustness, all depending on grape type, microclimate and subsoil. Heavier meats demand fuller red wines with tannins to cut the taste sinews. Red meats and pasta with meat sauce want sturdy wines. The very best companion for red wine is cheese — not strong (Cheddar) or soft-ripened (Camembert or Brie), but mild (Swiss, Gruyere, Muenster or Port Salut). The cheese sets off the natural gastronomic gearwork that brings out the best of both. Neither should be too strong, rather complementary in their organic origins and our ability to perceive them.

Sparkling wines are shrined in the name "Champagne." That, of course, is the place of birth in France. The world has borrowed the name and production process; each has its individual taste. Versatility is Champagne's claim, good as aperitif or "passe partout" throughout the meal. For such general use, however, the effect is bubbly and unbalanced, although a festive underpinning to celebration. For launching ships, toasting the New Year or the new bridge, Champagne shows better than on the dinner table: *prima donna* not needing the service of food.

Aperitif and dessert wines (16%-20% alcohol) may be red, white, dry or sweet. Sherry, from mellow Bristol Cream to dry Tico Fino, is traditional as the before-a-wine-dinner aperitif. After dinner, a tawny Directors Bin Port is felt to deliver perfect bliss. There are others, although rarer in availability, such as Portuguese Moscatel de Setubal. Of course, none of these wines would be appropriate with meals, except Tico Sherry with turtle soup.

In summary, there are countless combinations of food and wine; we find new matches for the taste marriage every day of every generation. We need not, however, make needless mistakes and sacrifice good wine if we heed the advice of our "good servant" rules:

- Dry white table wines go best before reds, matched to fish or light meats.
- Red table wines should be poured youngest first and continue (according to quality) to the oldest and most complex. Red meat, game and cheese are the background fabric of the experience.
- Some strong flavor components (sour, bitter and salty) do not fit with wine. Vinegar and pungent ingredients like onions, garlic, curry, and hot mustard cancel the delightful balance of a wine and food match.

Otherwise, don't worry. Open bottles and experiment. For the love of food and wine, like love and marriage, wine makes food a most glorious carriage!

Microwave Introduction

To write a cookbook today and leave out microwave instruction would be to ignore the wonderful world of modern technology. With less time and many more commitments these busy days, more people are looking for shortcuts to make their lives easier.

The beginning of microwave cookery in 1948 started an evolution in the kitchen that makes it possible to produce the finest meals in a matter of minutes. The sophistication of the most recent ovens allows even the newest of cooks to serve elegant and delicious meals quickly, saving hours of time formerly spent in the kitchen. Cooking foods by microwave retains the bright natural colors of vegetables and keeps food moist and delicious. It saves energy because it is cooler and faster, and only uses the amount of energy needed to cook the foods. Microwave energy does not heat the cavity of the oven as does a conventional oven and is only attracted to the moisture in food, creating friction, and thus heat. Therefore, it is not suggested for the cooking of foods that need a hot, dry environment.

Microcookery fits into today's lifestyle and allows us the pleasure of a full day of work or play followed by a quick, nutritious and creative meal. With much of today's population watching calories and cholesterol, microwave cookery is ideal. Most fats and salt can be eliminated from recipes with little change in the finished dish and with better nutrition as a result. Use of the oven saves labor, money and time, and with a little planning, leftovers can be frozen easily and reheated for another meal.

In this cookbook "Microwave Conversion Instructions" have been given only for recipes that were extremely successful when converted. Many tested microwave conversions have been omitted because the end product, while acceptable, was not equal or superior to the conventional recipe. Many of the converted recipes utilize a combination of microwave and conventional cookery with good results. Unless the use of a microwave oven produces an equally good or better dish, or saves time, adapting is not recommended.

Remember, too, that *recipe cooking times vary with the cook, the oven and the conditions*. It is important to remember that foods are better undercooked than overcooked and that a minute can make the difference between success and failure. Food can easily be returned to the oven for additional cooking, but an overcooked dish can ruin an otherwise perfect meal. Variables, such as starting temperature of the food and the voltage regulating electricity at different times of the day, should be considered when determining cooking times.

In spite of the number of individual microwave ovens found in homes today, many cooks still use them exclusively for defrosting foods, heating snacks or "convenience" foods, and/or reheating leftovers. The frustration of such limitations is widespread. In this cookbook we are pleased to enlarge the scope of microwave knowledge. The converted recipes represent a significant concentration of truly "gourmet" microwave recipes that should satisfy the most adventurous of microwave cooks as well as stimulate an interest in microwave cooking in those who have previously criticized its performance.

Once the mechanical process detailed in the manufacturer's microwave oven manual for operating the oven is mastered, a whole world of epicurean delights awaits us. One must realize, however, that the manufacturer's use and care manual takes precedence over any suggestions or directions included in this book. Recipes should be read thoroughly and ingredients assembled before proceeding. Before the "Microwave Conversion Instructions" begin, the word "Note" indicates significant changes that must be made in the ingredients or equipment before proceeding. It is also necessary to read through the conventional recipe preparation method before reading the microwave conversion located beneath. We suggest reading through the following microwave glossary and the various microwave conversions at your leisure. Then when cooking, you will be familiar with the terms and processes used throughout this book.

The tips, suggestions, procedures and definitions are your guide to successful microwave cookery. We hope you find as much enjoyment in using the microwave recipes in this book as we did in testing them in our kitchens.

Microwave Glossary

Altitude: Use the same guidelines as for conventional cooking. It may be necessary to increase cooking time slightly.

All converted recipes in this book have been tested in ovens with wattage ranging from 600- to 700-watt microwave units. For a 400- to 500-watt oven, add 30 seconds to each minute of cooking time. For a 500- to 600-watt oven, add 15 seconds to each minute of cooking time. Read individual recipes carefully for special instructions.

Bread Rising: Conventionally, yeast dough should rise at a temperature of about 75° to 80°. Covering the dough with a dry, clean dish towel helps to maintain a warm environment. The dough is placed in a well-greased large bowl and turned over once so that the entire surface is lightly greased. Then the dough is allowed to double in bulk which can take anywhere from 45 minutes to 3 hours or sometimes overnight. In a microwave oven this rising time can be reduced significantly. Follow any one of the 3 methods given below:

1. Place dough in a well-greased bowl, large enough to hold the dough when it is doubled in bulk. Lightly grease all surfaces. Place a glass measuring cup of water in a corner of the oven. Heat 4 minutes on High. Leave heated water where placed and put bowl with dough in center of oven; cover loosely with cloth or waxed paper. Heat 3 minutes on Low (10%). If your oven does not have a 10% setting, use Medium (50%) 1 minute. Let stand. Repeat after 15 minutes.

2. Place bowl containing the dough inside a pan of warm water. Use same timing as in #1. In this method, the dough should be turned over every 15 minutes. Repeat process of heating, standing and rotating bowl until dough is doubled in bulk. Check manufacturer's cookbook for any other possible instructions.

3. If your oven has a touch-panel, set your micro-computer to 10% energy level and let bread rise at 10% for 10 minutes. Let rest 15 minutes; then repeat. Approximately half the waiting time for bread to rise can be saved by using the microwave oven.

Dough has risen sufficiently in these methods if fingerprints remain when the dough is touched. Then punch dough down and shape as your recipe directs. Place shaped product in a dish that will be used for baking. If bread is to be baked conventionally, be sure dish is safe for conventional oven. Use any of the above methods once again, repeating the microwave heating and standing, until dough has reached desired volume.

When baking breads or cakes, do not flour the greased pans. If using a bundt-shaped pan, lightly grease; then dust with sugar, graham cracker crumbs or chopped nuts.

Browning: High fat items, like bacon, will brown rapidly as the fat cooks. Meats that are cooked for longer periods of time will brown somewhat, but results will be more attractive if paprika, a commercial browning agent, or a topping mix that you prepare yourself, is used on roasts, poultry and smaller cuts of meat. See BROWNING DISHES for cooking small food items such as steaks, chops, hamburgers and fried eggs. Other possibilities to promote browning of meats and fish are: soy or teriyaki sauce, melted butter and paprika, taco seasoning mix, dry onion soup mix, Worcestershire or steak sauce.

TOPPING MIX

1 T. paprika	½ tsp. pepper
6 tsp. flour	6 T. salt (optional)

When using mix, eliminate salt and pepper from meat recipe. Sprinkle over meat or poultry evenly and rub lightly over surface to promote browning. Other seasonings, such as garlic powder, onion powder, etc., can be added according to individual taste.

Yeast breads and pastries will not brown, but ingredients can be included to make them appear as we would normally expect to see them. Food coloring and orange juice as well as cinnamon and wheat germ can give added color. Some ovens have a browning unit. For others, the microwave can be used to speed up the initial stages of cooking; then the broiler or conventional oven can be used.

Avoid overcooking milk. It has a tendency to boil over very quickly. Use a container large enough for the boiling action, usually twice as large as one normally used.

Browning Dishes: These dishes are designed for microwave use only. The underside is coated with tin oxide to absorb microwave energy when the dish is preheated. This provides a hot surface for "grilling" foods such as steaks, chops, fried eggs or hamburgers. (If both sides of the foods are to be grilled, it is necessary to preheat the dish again.) Temperature inside the dish can reach up to 500° when preheated to its maximum absorption. See the instruction manual for each model for proper preheating times. Times will vary with the size of the browning dish.

Clay Pot: This pot is excellent for braising meats and cooking less tender cuts of meat and poultry. Follow manufacturer's directions for presoaking top and bottom.

To soften cream cheese, remove foil wrap. Heat on Medium (50%) 30 to 45 seconds.

Grated cheese cooks more quickly and evenly than cheese cut into chunks.

Cleaning: Spills and splatters do not bake on since there is no heat in the cavity. It is simple to wipe these off with a soapy, soft cloth. Allowing food to accumulate in the oven may interfere with the cooking pattern.

Covering: Glass covers, plastic wraps, paper towels (not the recycled type), waxed paper and china plates have all been used successfully. Glass covers and plastic wrap are used to tenderize, steam or retain heat during standing time and are good for foods that require hot moisture to cook. Paper towels prevent splattering and help absorb moisture. Waxed paper is used to retain moisture where tenderizing or steaming is not needed. It is also used on foods that may have a high sugar or fat content which would melt plastic wrap. Never use a plastic wrap that melts during the heating. Be careful when removing plastic wrap from a dish since the steam inside could cause a burn. Pierce it or cut a little away to allow steam to escape, then remove.

OVEN WATTAGE

To determine output wattage, fill a 2-cup glass measure with water. Record the water temperature, then microwave on High, 1 minute. Take the new, heated water temperature and subtract the first figure from it. Multiply the difference by 18.5 to get the approximate output wattage. (To illustrate: 104 degrees microwave heated water temperature less 68 degrees tap water temperature equals 36 degrees. Multiplied by 18.5, that is approximately 666 output wattage.) The higher the wattage, the less cooking time foods will need.

Wooden food picks may be substituted for metal skewers and clamps to truss meat and poultry.

Defrosting: All frozen foods should be defrosted before cooking, unless the recipe specifies otherwise. It is best to remove defrosted section as food thaws to prevent overcooking. A 10-oz. *(285g)* package of frozen food may be defrosted right in its container on High about 3 to 4 minutes. Allow 5 minutes standing time. Always place box on end in a dish to catch possible drippings.

Density: Foods have different molecular structures. Dense foods, such as meats, take longer to cook or heat than porous foods because microwaves do not penetrate deeply. Light, porous items, such as breads, will absorb microwave energy faster. The timing should be adjusted to conform with the particular characteristics of the food being cooked.

Dish Shape: The amount of food should match the size of the dish, with some consideration given to bubbling over of food or liquids that might accumulate. If dish is too large, sauces will spread out and overcook. Since microwaves travel from the outside in, a round dish will give the most uniform cooking pattern. Ovals also work well, since, like the round dish, they do not have corners. Square or rectangular dishes tend to overcook the foods in the corners; so cooking speed must be slowed when using those dishes to assure that food in the center will get done before the corners overcook. Foil can be used on sharp corners to prevent this (See SHIELDING). A shallow casserole will cook more efficiently than a deeper casserole of the same volume. Straight sides on a container are better than sloping sides, since the latter allows the volume of food to thin out and to overcook. Dishes should be filled only half to two-thirds full.

Unshelled eggs, unshelled shellfish, popovers and angel food cakes do not cook well in the microwave.

Explosions: Foods that are protected by tight membranes, such as eggs, livers, hot dogs, snails, etc., will build up pressure and pop open when heated. The process is similar to dropping cold food into hot fat. To avoid this in shelled eggs, simply pierce the yolk several times with a toothpick. The yolk will not run. Liver can be cut into pieces. Using a Medium (50%) cooking level will also reduce the chances of popping, but only if the membranes are pierced or cut.

Food Shape and Arrangement: Minimize difference in density. Variations in food shapes, such as chicken legs and broccoli, can be used to good advantage since microwaves travel from the periphery of the food to the center with diminishing heating capacity. Therefore, place the denser, or thicker, food near the outside of the dish where the heating takes place first.

Reheating: When possible, use a probe and the suggested guide to internal temperature settings (See TEMPERATURE PROBE) to reheat foods. Place the probe at an angle toward center of the food. Use a reheat setting if one appears on the manufacturer's guide; or use Medium High, 70% or 80%, depending upon the manufacturer. If reheating a dinner with a combination of foods, place the denser food, such as meat, at the outer edges, and the more porous food, such as bread, toward the center. Food that cooks the quickest will also reheat the fastest and should be at the center where somewhat less microwave energy is received. Wrap breads and sandwiches in paper napkins to absorb moisture and prevent sogginess. Elevate them on a rack, preferably with holes for drainage, to prevent steaming. As a general guide to reheating a plate of food, start with 2 minutes for each cup of solid food and add time as needed. To retain moisture during reheating, cover food with a lid. If food has a crisp texture, cover with paper towel. Recommended reheating times can only be approximate, since starting temperatures, amount, shape and food characteristics will vary.

CHOCOLATE

Melt chocolate by heating 6 oz. (170g) on High, uncovered, 1½ minutes; then stir. Or place unwrapped 1-oz. (28g) squares in a shallow dish. Cook 1 square on High 2 minutes. Cook 2 squares on High 2½ to 3 minutes.

To toast nuts, spread about ¼ cup nuts on a paper plate or a glass pie plate. Cook on High, uncovered, about 3 minutes, or until toasted. Stir frequently.

To shell nuts easily, place pecan or Brazil nuts in 2-qt. (2L) bowl. Add 1 cup water. Heat 4 to 5 minutes on High.

Roasting Rack: Use microwave rack inside a large dish to catch moisture and drippings. Use whenever foods need to be kept out of moisture and liquid. A rack is also useful for reheating bread and rolls and for baking potatoes.

Rotating: Food should be turned if it appears to be cooking unevenly. This will vary with the food being cooked and with the oven. If necessary, turn dish ¼ or ½ turn as needed (See STIRRING). Do not rotate dish more than three times.

To dry croutons, use leftover bread, herbs and butter. Cut bread slices into ½-inch cubes; cook on High 6 to 7 minutes; stir once.

Safety: Never switch on an empty microwave oven. With no food to absorb them, the waves bounce back to the magnetron, the "heart" of the oven that converts electrical energy into microwave energy and produces invisible waves. This shortens the life of the oven.

There is much misunderstanding about radiation. If there is a concern about leakage, ovens can be checked. Types of radiation are differentiated by wave length and frequency. Light waves are in the middle between the very long and the very short waves. Infrared, microwaves and broadcast bands (TV and Radio) are all longer than light waves and are used safely in our daily lives. X-rays and gamma rays, which can be harmful, are not in the same spectrum as microwaves.

To warm pancake syrup, heat 1 cup at room temperature on High 1½ minutes.

Sensitive Ingredients: Some ingredients, such as cheese, cream, eggs, condensed milk, sour cream, mayonnaise, snails, oysters and kidney beans are sensitive, respond to microwaves quickly and can overcook in a very short time. Use lower power settings for these ingredients. They may also be cooked conventionally and then added to the other recipe ingredients. Check individual recipes for variations in the case of large volumes of these foods cooked at one time. High power may cause some of these foods to curdle or "pop."

Shielding — Use of Metal: Many cookbooks recommend shielding of square or rectangular corners to avoid overcooking. If round or oval dishes are used, this problem does not occur. If the manufacturer recommends limited use of aluminum foil, follow the suggestions in the manual. Portions of food that might appear to be overcooking, i.e. narrow ends of roasts, poultry wings and drumsticks, may be shielded from further cooking by blocking out microwave energy with small patches of foil. As long as there is enough food unshielded in the microwave cavity, there is no damage possible. Foil should never come in contact with the sides of the oven which is metal lined. Arcing (a "snap" and a "spark") occurs where two metals touch; therefore, be sure that foil patches are securely in place and at least 2 inches away from another metal surface. Cakes and quick breads, baked in pans with corners, can be shielded with foil for half the cooking time; remove foil for the remainder of the cooking time.

INTERNAL TEMPERATURE CHART
(Before Standing Time)

120° — Fully Cooked Ham, Rare Roast Beef
125° — Medium Rare Roast Beef, Rare Lamb
130° — Medium Roast Beef
135° — Medium Lamb
140° — Fish Steaks and Fillets, Well Done Beef
150° — Vegetables, Hot Drinks, Soups, Casseroles
155° — Veal
160° — Well Done Lamb
165° — Well Done Pork
170° — Poultry Parts, Whole Fish
180° — Well Done Whole Poultry

Starting Temperature: A most important influence on required cooking or heating time is the starting temperature. Refrigerated or cold foods require longer cooking periods than foods started from room temperature. Food that has been frozen and has not completely defrosted will need extra cooking time.

Stirring: This allows the food to cook more evenly by bringing the area of food that is cooking the most toward the center, just as stirring the foods on a conventional range top keeps the contents on the bottom from overcooking. Flour mixtures need more stirring than those made with cornstarch. Only those recipes where stirring does not disturb the end product would benefit from this technique. It is not advisable to stir more than three times.

SUGGESTIONS FOR PORK

Cook only after consulting manufacturer's time directions.

Rotate during cooking.

Wrap in foil for several minutes after cooking to increase effectiveness of equal heating.

Check with a meat thermometer to make sure ALL PARTS are cooked to 140° to 160° after standing time.

Standing Time: This technique is also called *Holding* or *Resting Time*. It is the removal of food from the oven before it is done, thus allowing it to finish cooking by internal heat. This prevents overcooking and saves energy. After a period of microwave cooking, the food develops enough internal heat to continue cooking by itself. How long the food continues to cook depends on its volume, density and amount of exposed surface. As it stands, the hot food loses some warmth to the cooler air around it. To get the full benefit of standing time, aluminum foil may be used to wrap the food to hold in the heat.

Toast coconut by spreading ½ cup flaked coconut in pie plate. Cook, uncovered, on High 3 to 4 minutes. Crumble if desired. Store in airtight container.

23

Temperature Probe: A sensor or microwave food thermometer can measure the internal temperature of the food during cooking. Only a thermometer designed for microwave use is advisable. Conventional thermometers use materials which are not compatible with microwave energy. A probe can be valuable in several ways. It can give you a "reading" as you cook. Also, it can be used in reheating foods, for proper water temperature for instant coffee, for regular coffee warm-ups, for casseroles and for soups. Once a desired temperature is decided, food can be reheated to that level. A conventional thermometer can be inserted only *after* food is removed from the oven.

To test whether dishes are suitable for the microwave oven, place a glass measuring cup of tap water inside the oven. Place the empty dish to be tested near the cup. Turn microwave on High for 45 seconds. The water will be warm and the dish should still be cool. If the dish gets hot, it has absorbed microwave energy and cannot be used. If the dish absorbs any energy, it is not transparent to microwaves and eventually will crack.

Utensils: Refer to manufacturer's instructions for individual ovens. Metal and paint-trimmed containers should be avoided as well as those with handles held by metal screws. Most metal containers should be avoided. Food in metal dishes will not cook since metal acts as a barrier to microwaves. Use only plastics made for the microwave oven. Plastics which melt or soften should never be used to heat foods. Unglazed pottery may absorb moisture and become hot. Paper, china and heavy glass are usually safe but should be checked. Delicate glasses may crack. Straw and wooden dishes should be used only for short-term cooking. Many utensils can be used both for cooking and for serving. *Active Microwave Cooking Products* are a variety of utensils designed to absorb microwave energy and to cook foods within the metal itself. Only the heated metal cooks the food. The food does not receive any microwave energy. Like a browning, dish, it is preheated. Unlike a browning dish, it completely encloses the food. For method of using, carefully follow the manufacturer's directions.

DRYING HERBS

To dry herbs, remove stems. Rinse and dry thoroughly such herbs as fresh parsley, chives, basil, sage and mint. Spread about 1 cupful on paper towel. Cook on High 2 to 3 minutes. Crumble as soon as dry to touch. Cool. Store in airtight container.

High (100%)
Medium High (70%)
Medium (50%)
Medium Low (30%)
Low (10%)

Variable Power: Varying the power in a microwave oven is similar to varying the heat on a conventional range, like turning a burner higher or lower. Because microwaves produce no heat, the amount of energy entering the food at any one time is varied. As an example, at 50% power, or Medium, microwave energy is being emitted 50% of the time, allowing the food to rest 50% of the time. This occurs within a specified time base, usually a 12-second interval, i.e. 6 seconds power on and 6 seconds resting. If an oven does not have a Medium-high (70%) setting, use Medium (50%) power. Add about 1 minute to each 5 minutes of cooking time as directed in recipe. More time will be required for recipes containing large amounts of liquid. Dense (solid) foods, such as meat loaf, will not require as much added time. To prevent overcooking, begin testing for doneness after the allotted time in the recipe. It is better to make changes in small increments.

Volume: When the volume of food put into the microwave oven is increased, the concentration of microwaves in a given food item decreases; therefore, the more food cooked at one time, the longer that food will take to cook. For example, two potatoes take longer to cook than one potato. It is better to cook in small batches and to repeat the cooking procedure than to cook a large quantity at once.

DRYING FLOWERS

Choose flowers that are in late bud but not full bloom. It is important that they are picked in early morning or late afternoon when any trace of dampness has totally dried. Trim stems to within 1 inch of head. Place flowers face down in a box that has 2 inches of silica gel in bottom. Do not allow flowers to touch each other. Gently sprinkle more gel over flowers so they are completely covered. Put box in microwave oven along with 1 cup (240ml) water. Cook on High as follows:

Daffodils and Pansies	*1 to 1½ minutes*
Carnations and Daisies	*2½ to 3 minutes*
Chrysanthemums	*3 minutes*

Standing time in gel is 12 hours. Great care must be taken in removing flowers from gel. Gently pour gel into a container for future use, collecting flowers as they appear. Form new stems with florist's tape and wire; very gently brush any clinging crystals from petals.

A Taste of
Our Heritage

Iced Pink Sumacade
(Indian "Lemonade")

Hot Goldenrod or **Bergamot Tea**

Sunseed Delight
(Sunseed Energy Mix)
p. 28

**Popcorn with Raw
Peanuts and Currants**
p. 28

Chilled Yellow Squash Soup
p. 29

**Crayfish and Mussels
on Platter of
Wild Rice, Nuts and Berries**
p. 30

Fried Squash or Pumpkin Blossoms
p. 29

Quinnetukut Succotash
p. 30

Milkweed Pods Vinaigrette
p. 366

Purslane Salad with Dressing
Garnish of Watercress, Fresh Coriander, Nasturtium Leaves
p. 359

Wild Strawberry Bread   **Beach Plum Jam**

Indian Pudding
p. 31

**Black Birch or Blackberry
Leaf Tea**

Beechnut Coffee

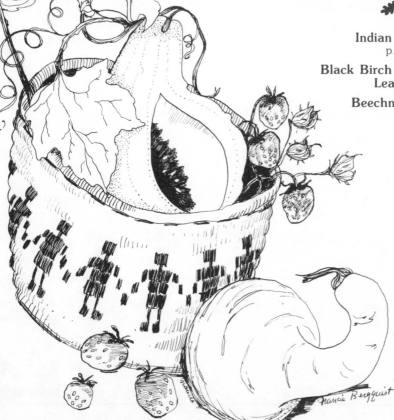

Algonquian Indian Mid-Summer Celebration

A menu based on the wild and cultivated harvests of Connecticut's Indian ancestors that is as comfortably modern as it is 400 years old.

The Native Americans who greeted the first European settlers to New England preceded them by more than 9,000 years. Over the centuries the Indians had learned the secrets of cultivating and living off the bounty of the countryside. The Algonquian Indians who inhabited New England in the 17th century not only gave the settlers the name "Quinnetukut" or Connecticut, meaning "the long tidal river" and the names of countless other rivers, hills and lakes, they also taught the settlers how to survive in a harsh new world.

Though dependent on the seasons for both quantity and variety of food, Algonquian women experimented with herbs and developed intricate methods of soaking, grinding, stewing and baking which maximized the flavors of the natural ingredients. From them the settlers learned to line a deep sand pit with hot stones, add shellfish and seaweed, then reap the harvest of a clambake. They also learned to make a V-shaped gash in the trunk of a maple tree, place a birch bark pail at the base and catch the sap in the early spring. The watery sap was slowly boiled over open fires until a heavier syrup formed. This was poured out into shallow pans to dry in the sun and harden into sugar.

The Indians taught the settlers how to prepare an earth oven and slowly simmer dried beans in maple syrup for many days — the predecessor of New England baked beans. Our Algonquian heritage also includes such American classics as succotash, hominy, popcorn and cranberries. Because of the high nutritional value of the squash, corn and beans farmed by the Indians and of the available fruits and wild game, the Indians were generally stronger and healthier than the 16th century European colonists.

Though today few live on the four remaining reservations, more than 5,000 Indians now live in Connecticut. One of these reservations, the smallest preserve in North America, is the ¼ acre Golden Hill Preserve of the Paugusett Tribe located near Trumbull. The Schaghticoke Reservation is in Kent near the Housatonic River, and the Mashantucket and Paucatuck Pequot Reservations are in southeastern Connecticut. Many Mohegan Indians live as private landowners in historic Uncasville, which was named after the famous Mohegan chief, Uncas. At one time these tribes were all linked by the common Algonquian language.

A unique educational and research center for Indian life in New England, is the American Indian Archaeological Institute in Washington, Connecticut. The Institute is dedicated to discovering, preserving and disseminating the pre-European history of Native Americans. One significant focus of the Institute is ethnobotany, the study of a society through the foods a people cultivated, cooked and ate. A visitor to the Institute can learn from archaeological exhibits of Indian homes, crafts, food products and utensils; on summertime field trips one learns how to search out squash blossoms, elderberries, and hazelnuts. An additional wealth of information can be gleaned from Barrie Kavasch's *Native Harvests: Recipes and Botanicals of The American Indian* (New York: Random House, 1979). This is the source of most of the recipes for the Mid-Summer Celebration.

As Connecticut's Native Americans once significantly enriched the lives of the early settlers, so can their history offer us today exciting new ways of relating to our environment. Based on a naturally abundant harvest of goldenrod, milkweed pods, crayfish and beechnut, the Algonquian Indian menu celebrates one aspect of this valuable heritage.

Sunseed Energy Mix

YIELD: 30 Servings
CALORIES PER SERVING: 229
CARBOHYDRATES: 10g
PROTEIN: 9g
FAT: 17g
PREPARING: 15 Minutes
COOKING: None

3 cups *(170g)* dried apples
2 cups *(240g)* raw sunflower seeds
2 cups *(130g)* raw pumpkin seeds
1 cup *(130g)* beechnuts
2 cups *(285g)* currants or wild raisins
1 cup *(60g)* sea dulse (a marine vegetable, available, dried, in health food stores)
1 cup *(170g)* bee pollen (available in health food stores)
1 cup *(120g)* walnuts
1 cup *(140g)* raw peanuts

A super energy snack.

Combine all ingredients and serve in a pottery or wooden bowl.

Barrie Kavasch, Bridgewater, CT

Nutritional Notes: This is truly a nutritious snack. Seeds and nuts supply a good amount of protein and carbohydrates for energy. Bee pollen used to be removed from the legs of bees; now it is removed directly from the flowers. Currants contain the same nutritional value as a corresponding weight of raisins. Sea dulse is very salty and may be omitted for sodium-restricted diets.

Popcorn, Peanuts and Currants

YIELD: 30 Servings
TOTAL CALORIES: 3720
CALORIES PER SERVING: 124
CARBOHYDRATES: 10g
PROTEIN: 3g
FAT: 8g
PREPARING: 20 Minutes
TOASTING: 10 Minutes

⅓ cup *(80ml)* sunflower seed oil
½ cup *(100g)* popping corn
¼ cup *(60g)* nut or seed butter
2 cups *(285g)* shelled raw peanuts
2 cups *(285g)* dried currants

This native classic is a fundamental, botanical grace of friendship among three distinctly different indigenous foods.

In large saucepan with lid, heat oil to 'popping point'. Test by dropping in one kernel of corn; then add the remainder. With lid held on securely, shake pan until corn stops popping. Pour immediately into large bowl.

Place nut butter and peanuts into warm pan; return to moderate heat to melt butter. Stir to coat nuts. Heat, stirring until nuts are toasted. Pour over popcorn. Pour currants into a "nest" in the center of popcorn.

Barrie Kavasch, Bridgewater, CT

Nutritional Notes: A nutritious snack that is a good source of fiber. The mixture may also be sprinkled with wheat germ for additional nutritional value. This snack may be appropriate for a sodium-restricted diet if *salt-free* nut butter is used and no salt is added.

Microwave Conversion Instructions: Note: Eliminate oil. Place popping corn in microwave popcorn popper. Follow manufacturer's directions or cook about 4½ to 5½ minutes on High. Place nut butter and peanuts in 1-qt. *(1L)* casserole. Heat on High 3 to 5 minutes, stirring twice, until nuts are toasted.

Yellow Squash Soup

This is a delicious mid-summer potage.

Squash was almost as important as corn to the Indians of the East because of its nourishment and versatility. In the winter, squash was frequently baked whole, particularly the rich, sweet-meated acorn and butternut varieties, using fat and honey or maple syrup for seasoning. The delicate summer squashes were sometimes boiled and blended into a smooth fragrant soup. And from the Indians the colonists learned to plant squash to counteract the debilitating effect on the soil of growing corn year after year.

YIELD: 8 Servings
TOTAL CALORIES: 432
CALORIES PER SERVING: 54
CARBOHYDRATES: 8g
PROTEIN: 1g
FAT: 2g
PREPARING: 10 Minutes
SIMMERING: 35 Minutes

Combine squash, scallions, honey, oil and water in large pot. Cover; simmer for 30 minutes or until squash is tender.

Cool slightly; mash to a puree; add dill.

Return to heat; simmer 5 minutes. If soup seems too thick, more water may be added.

Serve either hot or cold, garnished with seeds.

Barrie Kavasch, Bridgewater, CT

Microwave Conversion Instructions: Cook squash, scallions, honey, oil and water on High, covered, 15 to 20 minutes. Puree until smooth. Add dill. Return to casserole and reheat, uncovered, 2 to 3 minutes, or until hot.

2 lbs. *(900g)* medium yellow squash, cubed
2 scallions or wild onions, including tops, sliced
1 T. *(20g)* honey
1 T. *(15ml)* sunflower seed oil
1 qt. *(950ml)* water
1 T. chopped fresh dill
Shelled sunflower seeds or toasted squash seeds

Fried Squash Blossoms

There seem to be countless bright yellow blossoms from these prolific vines. What better way to appreciate them at day's end, after they have served their vital functions to the plants, than by collecting them to use further as a vegetable or to garnish a whole fish.

YIELD: 8 Servings
CALORIES PER SERVING: 105
CARBOHYDRATES: 3g
PROTEIN: 3g
FAT: 9g
PREPARING: 25 Minutes
FRYING: 25 Minutes

In bowl, blend milk, egg, flour, and seasoning with fork. Beat batter until smooth. Place mashed blossoms in batter, stir gently, and allow to soak for 10 minutes. Heat oil in cast-iron skillet until hot. Fry batter-coated blossoms, a few at a time, until golden, turning once. Drain on brown paper. Serve hot, garnished with chopped, fresh mint leaves or dill.

Barrie Kavasch, Bridgewater, CT with special credit to Edmind K. Swigart

Variations, Advance Preparation, and Serving Suggestions:
Day-lily buds can be substituted for squash blossoms. Additional ways to use squash blossoms are to add them to an omelette after they have been sauteed in butter. Also, try adding fresh alfalfa sprouts and sauteed green peppers, scallions, mushrooms and a dash of Tabasco.

1 cup *(240ml)* milk
1 egg
1 T. flour
1 tsp. dried ground sassafras leaves
3 dozen *male* blossoms (the male blossoms are the larger infertile blossoms without an ovary, the swelling at the base of the flower), picked just before they open, mashed
½ cup *(120ml)* oil
Fresh mint or dill

YIELD: 8-12 Servings
CALORIES PER SERVING: 247
CARBOHYDRATES: 37g
PROTEIN: 18g
FAT: 3g
PREPARING: 45 Minutes
COOKING: 1½ Hours
FREEZING: No

3 dozen fresh mussels, well-scrubbed
2 large stalks celery, cut in 1-inch
   (2.5cm) pieces
1 medium onion, coarsely diced
3 dozen fresh crayfish (or blanched,
   frozen; available at fish markets)
5 cups (1180ml) water
2 cups (340g) wild rice, washed in cold
   water
2 wild onions, diced
1 cup (125g) hazelnuts, chopped
1 cup (140g) dried blueberries (dried
   currants may be substituted)

Fresh watercress to garnish
Lemon to garnish

Crayfish and Mussels on Wild Rice with Hazelnuts and Blueberries

Place mussels in large enamel pot with celery and onion. Cover with boiling water to 1 inch (2.5cm) above contents. Simmer, covered, 5 minutes. Remove cover; add crayfish. Cover. Steam over low heat another 5 minutes. Remove from heat; cool several minutes. Drain water, reserving it to cook rice. Keep rest of ingredients covered and warm.

Combine reserved water with additional water, if necessary, to equal 5 cups. Pour into large kettle with rice and onions. Bring to boil; cover; simmer about 40 minutes, until most of liquid is absorbed. Add hazelnuts and blueberries; mix well. Steam, covered, 20 minutes more, stirring occasionally.

Arrange wild rice on large platter; top and surround with crayfish, mussels and vegetables. Garnish with watercress and lemon. Serve hot.

Barrie Kavasch, Bridgewater, CT with special appreciation to Ella Thomas/Sekatau of Kenyon, RI, who inspired this from her Narragansett heritage

Wine Suggestion: California Pinot Chardonnay, rich white; serve chilled.

Quinnetukut Succotash

M'sickquatash, the Indian word for corn boiled whole, became the succotash of the first settlers. This was one of the easiest Indian recipes adopted by the Pilgrims. The hearty mixture was usually sweetened with bear fat. As time went on, however, succotash developed into a more elaborate dish made of large white beans, hulled corn, corned beef, salt pork, onion, white turnip, and potato. A classic Algonquian dish, with many, many variations, we encourage you to try your own adjustments.

YIELD: 10 Servings
CALORIES PER SERVING: 100
CARBOHYDRATES: 16g
PROTEIN: 4.5g
FAT: 2g
PREPARING: 30 Minutes
COOKING: 20 Minutes

1 onion, chopped
1 green pepper, chopped
1 cup (240ml) water
2 cups (300g) shelled lima beans
2 cups yellow corn or 8 ears, scraped
2 T. (30g) nut butter

In large covered kettle, simmer all ingredients 20 minutes. Serve hot.

NUT BUTTER: In a food processor, grind enough shelled nuts of choice to paste to equal amount required.

Barrie Kavasch, Bridgewater, CT, with special appreciation to Courland Fowler of Uncasville, CT, who inspired this from his Mohegan heritage.

Microwave Conversion Instructions: Place all ingredients in 4-qt. (4L) casserole. Cover and cook 8 to 10 minutes on High until vegetables are done to desired taste.

New England Indian Pudding

Indian pudding was not a food of the Indians. It took its name from the main ingredient, cornmeal, which was called "Indian meal" by the settlers.

YIELD: 6 Servings
TOTAL CALORIES: 2856
CALORIES PER SERVING: 476
CARBOHYDRATES: 48g
PROTEIN: 8g
FAT: 28g
CHOLESTEROL: High
PREPARING: 30 Minutes
BAKING: 2-2½ Hours

Scald 3 cups *(710ml)* milk in top of double boiler. Mix 1 cup cold milk with cornmeal; pour cornmeal mixture slowly into hot milk. Place mixture over boiling water and cook 20 minutes, stirring occasionally.

Add sugar, butter and molasses and remove from heat. Add salt and spices; stir in beaten eggs and pour into well-buttered 1½-qt. *(1.5L)* shallow baking dish.

Bake in preheated 300° oven 2 to 2½ hours, stirring every 15 minutes during first hour. After first hour, pour cream over top of pudding and continue to bake without stirring in cream.

Serve *warm,* topped with whipped cream or vanilla ice cream.

Donna Howe, West Hartford, CT

4 cups *(950ml)* **milk**
½ cup *(75g)* **stone-ground yellow cornmeal**
⅔ cup *(140g)* **firmly packed brown sugar**
2 T. *(30g)* **butter**
½ cup *(120ml)* **molasses**
1 tsp. salt
½ tsp. freshly grated nutmeg
½ tsp. ginger
½ tsp. cinnamon
½ tsp. mace
2 eggs, beaten
1 cup *(240ml)* **heavy cream**

Nutritional Notes: The yellow stone-ground cornmeal and molasses are nutritional pluses in this recipe. Cornmeal is high in thiamine (vitamin B_1) and vitamin A. There are two types of molasses: Blackstrap molasses and unsulfured molasses. Blackstrap molasses is the product of refining sugarcane whereby a chemical process separates white sugar crystals from the "residue." This "residue," blackstrap molasses, has most of the original B vitamins, calcium, phosphorus and iron of the sugarcane. Unsulfured molasses, conversely, is not a by-product of sugarcane refining, but is manufactured for molasses itself. While unsulfured molasses has a milder flavor than the bitter blackstrap, it has the same nutritious content. Molasses is a sugar alternative which, even though the effects are similar to refined sugar and therefore is not recommended in large quantities, does have some nutritional merit.

Microwave Conversion Instructions: Note: Decrease milk to 3 cups and salt to ½ tsp. Place 2 cups milk in 2-qt. *(2L)* casserole; cook on High 3 to 4 minutes, or until scalded. Mix 1 cup cold milk with cornmeal. Pour cornmeal mixture slowly into hot milk. Cook on High 4 minutes or until mixture just comes to rolling boil. Complete recipe preparation for pudding except pour into a covered 2-qt. round casserole; cook on High 14 minutes, stirring well *every* 3 minutes, until smooth and thick. Uncover casserole and pour heavy cream over top of pudding without stirring in; cook uncovered 14 minutes on Medium (50%) rotating dish ¼ turn halfway through. Let stand on rack 10 minutes before serving. *To reheat in microwave oven:* 1 cup on Medium High (70%) 1 to 2 minutes, 2 cups on 70% 2 to 3 minutes, 3 cups on 70% 3 to 4 minutes, 4 cups on 70% 4 to 5 minutes.

Great River
Smoked Salmon
(Smoked Salmon Dipping Sauce)
p. 34

Oyster Cakes
(Oyster Croustades)
p. 204

Mussel Soup Sequin   or   **Corn Oyster Chowder**
p. 34

Spitted Venison

Roast Turkey
with
Warwick Maize Sausage
Stuffing
p. 98

Connecticut Roast Gosling
(Roast Goose with Cumberland Sauce)
p. 36

Chestnut Poultry Stuffing
p. 37

Wethersfield Onion   **Hartforde Towne Butternut Bake**   **Wyndsor Beans**
Shortcake   *(Autumn Apple Butternut)*
p. 38   p. 339

Cranberry Relish
p. 46

Pompion Pickles
(Pickled Pumpkin)
p. 37

Blueberry Johnnycake
p. 35

Mill Hollow Bread
p. 235

Raisin Tart
p. 133

Steamed Cranberry
Pudding
p. 39

Maple Nut Cream
(Maple Mousse)
p. 38

A River Plantations Thanksgiving

A Thanksgiving feast inspired by colonial plantation kitchens along the banks of the Great River (Connecticut River).

In 1631 a group of Podunk-Algonquian Indian braves, led by their chief Wanginnacut, traveled to Boston and Plymouth to urge the English settlers to move into the area now known as Connecticut. The Indians were seeking allies against the fierce invading Pequot Indians. Edward Winslow of Plymouth was one of the first Europeans to explore Connecticut for settlement. Soon after, in 1633, a trading post was built in Windsor and temporary settlement followed in Wethersfield, both on the banks of the Great River, later named the Connecticut.

A few months later the Puritan Thomas Hooker and a small band of colonists moved into the area. They purchased land at the juncture of the Great River and the Little River (Park) from the Saukiog-Algonquian Indians. This purchase contested the earlier claim to the land by the Dutch who had bought it from the invading Pequots. Though initially called Newtown, the new settlement was soon renamed Hartford, after the English town of Hertford, birthplace of the Rev. Samuel Stone, assistant to Thomas Hooker.

Within the next few years an increasing number of English Puritans moved inland from the coast along the fertile valley of the Great River to live in the settlements or "plantations" of Windsor, Wethersfield and Hartford. The settlers found the river provided transportation, a plentiful food supply of fish and shellfish, and fish fertilizer for their crops. It was largely through the aid of the friendly Algonquian Indians that these early settlers survived their first winters.

The Indians taught them how to search for edible nuts and berries, taught them methods of hunting deer, turkey, duck and geese, and how to grow crops of corn, squash and pumpkin. It was the pumpkin, which was grown easily and could be preserved through much of the winter, that often meant the difference between starvation and survival. To make this almost daily staple more palatable, the settlers learned to slice and roast it, add maple sugar to the softened pulp, bake it, and even knead the pulp with corn to make pancakes. One colonist wrote to a friend in England, "We have pompion at morning, pompion at noon. If t'were not for pompion we should be undone." The early settlers also learned the art of drying meat, fish and fruits. The slow smoking of salmon and other fish over a smudge fire not only discouraged flies, it produced a delicate flavor and enabled the preservation of the food for many weeks.

Ten years before the Connecticut settlers arrived, the Plymouth colony had been equally indebted to the Indians for survival. We learn from letters by Gov. William Bradford that after the colony's first harvest in October of 1621, the people celebrated with a feast to which both Indian and Pilgrim hunters brought deer, duck and geese. More than 200 years later, in 1863, Abraham Lincoln was to recognize this event by proclaiming an annual Thanksgiving to be celebrated on the last Thursday of November.

Originally, the thanksgiving feast was an annual autumn event in which the Indians recognized the bountiful harvest of vegetables, berries and wild game provided by the Great Spirit. As the early Connecticut settlers along the Great River adopted the Indian celebration, it became a time for families and communities to gather together. The women of each household would bring their favorite dishes to add to the feast — one can imagine the competition to excel in each offering. This may even have been the beginning of our "recipe swaps!"

In order to prepare hot meals our earliest housewives used such marvelous utensils as "flagons," "beere bowls," "beakers," "a caudle cup," "porrengers," "yron hooks," "andyrons," and an "old fire shovel." The open fire the Indians used had become more elaborate indoor hearths with a brick oven set in the back, and later to the side, of the fireplace. A special pit stored ashes to make soap and lye.

The River Plantations Thanksgiving menu represents the best of colonial cooking: a unique blending of Indian dishes; the cooking traditions which the settlers brought from their homeland; and the creativity inspired by the variety of tantalizing ingredients they found in the New World.

YIELD: 1½ Cups
TOTAL CALORIES: 1320
CALORIES PER TABLESPOON: 55
CARBOHYDRATES: 1g
PROTEIN: 1.5g
FAT: 5g
CHOLESTEROL: High
SODIUM: High
PREPARING: 10 Minutes
FREEZING: No

Smoked Salmon Dipping Sauce

8 oz. *(225g)* cream cheese, softened
⅓ cup *(75g)* sour cream
4 T. *(60ml)* fresh lemon juice
2 T. *(30ml)* drained horseradish
3 oz. *(84g)* smoked salmon, finely chopped
1 T. finely chopped fresh dill
Salt, freshly ground pepper
Cayenne pepper

Fresh dill sprigs to garnish

In a bowl, mix together the cream cheese, sour cream, lemon juice and horseradish. Fold in salmon and dill. *[FOOD PROCESSOR: Combine cream cheese, sour cream, lemon juice, and horseradish; blend with quick on/off turns. Add whole pieces of salmon and dill sprigs. Process until salmon is blended. Do not overprocess.]* Add salt, pepper and cayenne to taste.

Pour into serving bowl and garnish with fresh dill.

Maria M. Rossi, Brewster, MA

Variations, Advance Preparation, and Serving Suggestions:
May be prepared a day ahead and refrigerated, covered tightly.

Present this dipping sauce in a straw basket lined with a glass bowl. Set the basket on a straw tray and arrange crudites and/or homemade melba toast around the basket.

YIELD: 6 Servings
TOTAL CALORIES: 2016
CALORIES PER SERVING: 336
CARBOHYDRATES: 21g
PROTEIN: 9g
FAT: 24g
CHOLESTEROL: High
SODIUM: High
PREPARING: 20 Minutes
HEATING: 5 Minutes
STANDING: 5 Minutes
FREEZING: No

Corn Oyster Chowder

Jacques Pepin, renowned French chef, teacher and author, selects this simple New England chowder for us as a sample of the best in regional American cuisine.

2 T. *(30g)* unsalted sweet butter
½ cup *(100g)* grated sweet onion, (about 1 medium onion)
1 large clove garlic, peeled and grated or finely chopped
4 scallions, white and green part, finely minced
1½ cups *(355ml)* milk
1 cup *(240ml)* heavy cream
1½ tsp. coarse salt or ¾ tsp. regular salt
¼ tsp. freshly ground pepper
12 fairly large fresh oysters, halved (if fresh oysters are not available, canned oysters may be used)
1 cup *(240ml)* oyster liquor
2 cups fresh corn kernels, (about 4 ears corn)

1 T. chopped fresh chives

Melt butter in saucepan; add onions, garlic, scallions. Cook on medium heat one minute. Add milk and cream. Bring to boil. Add salt, pepper, fresh oysters, oyster liquor, corn. Return to boil. Remove from heat.

If using canned oysters, bring to boil with oyster liquor in a separate saucepan; skim off and discard any scum that may form on top of oysters. Add oysters and clear liquid to soup after it has been removed from heat.

Let stand five minutes. Serve with sprinkling of chives.

Jacques Pepin, Madison, CT

Microwave Conversion Instructions: Place onions, garlic, scallions in a 3-qt. *(3L)* bowl. Place butter on top of vegetables. Cook 3 minutes on High, uncovered, add milk and cream, continue to cook on High about 4 to 5 minutes, or until it boils. Add salt, pepper, oyster liquor, corn. Return to boil. Add oysters (see directions for using canned oysters.) Continue on Medium (50%) just until it returns to a boil, or oysters are heated through. Allowing it to stand 5 minutes will complete cooking.

Blueberry Johnny Cake

This recipe, which is still prepared by members of the Bushnell Macdonough family, has been in the family since 1716, when the Denison branch moved from Mystic to Old Saybrook. It is traditionally served by the family when the berries first ripen.

Ashcakes were called "Appones" by the Indians. They were made with cornmeal and water and shaped into flat cakes and "baked" in the ashes. Later, when these same cakes were baked inside in ovens, the name became corn pone. JONNY-CAKE is still another name for this cornmeal bread. Both Indians and colonists took it on trips and hunting, thus the actual name "Journey-cakes".

YIELD: 16 Medium Squares
TOTAL CALORIES: 3000
CALORIES PER SQUARE: 188
CARBOHYDRATES: 26g
PROTEIN: 3g
FAT: 8g
SODIUM: High
PREPARING: 15 Minutes
BAKING: 40 Minutes

Cream butter and sugar; add eggs; beat until light in color. Combine flour, cornmeal, baking powder and salt; add alternately with milk stirring until just mixed. *[FOOD PROCESSOR: Combine flour, cornmeal, baking powder and salt in work bowl and process 2 seconds. Remove mixture and set aside. Add sugar and eggs to work bowl and process 1 full minute. Add softened butter and process 1 full minute. With machine running pour milk through feed tube. Blend in reserved flour mixture by turning machine on/off 3 or 4 times or until flour just disappears. Do not overprocess. Transfer batter to a bowl.]* Fold in lightly floured blueberries. Pour into buttered and floured 9 × 13-inch *(22.5 × 32.5cm)* baking pan. Bake in preheated 350° oven for 40 minutes. Cool in pan on wire rack. When cool, cut into squares.

Gladys Macdonough, Wethersfield, CT

½ cup *(115g)* butter
1 cup *(200g)* sugar
2 eggs
1½ cups *(170g)* sifted flour
1½ cups *(225g)* stone-ground yellow cornmeal
4 tsp. *(12g)* baking powder
½ tsp. salt
1¼ cups *(300ml)* milk
2 cups *(300g)* fresh blueberries or wild blueberries (if frozen are used, must be *thoroughly* drained)

Variations, Advance Preparation, and Serving Suggestions: Accompany with scrambled eggs and country smoked bacon for a hearty breakfast or Sunday night supper.

Nutritional Notes: This recipe was successfully tested with the addition of ½ cup *(60g)* unprocessed bran and ½ cup *(60g)* wheat germ. Unsalted polyunsaturated margarine and skim or lowfat milk may be used.

Microwave Conversion Instructions: Note: Increase butter to ¾ cup, increase number of eggs to 3, reduce milk to 1 cup. Mix ingredients according to conventional recipe. Use 10-inch *(25cm)* square glass pan or 9 × 13-inch baking dish. Line with waxed paper. Pour batter into dish. Cook on Medium (50%) 6 minutes, rotating dish after 3 minutes. Increase power to High. Cook 2 to 5 minutes, or until center springs back when touched. Let stand directly on counter 5 minutes. Bottom should be checked to see that no unbaked batter appears in center of cake.

YIELD: 6 Servings Roast Goose
CALORIES PER SERVING: 422
PROTEIN: 38g
FAT: 30g
CHOLESTEROL: High

YIELD: 3 Cups Cumberland Sauce
CALORIES PER TABLESPOON: 22
CARBOHYDRATES: 5g
PREPARING: 10 Minutes
ROASTING: 2½-3 Hours
RESTING: 30 Minutes

Roast Goose with Cumberland Sauce

Cumberland Sauce, a traditional sweet and spicy port wine sauce from the Cumberland region of England, is often served with game as well as goose.

ROAST GOOSE:

1 domestic goose (9-11 lbs.) *(4-5kg)*
Lemon wedge
Salt
4 or 5 apples, cored and quartered

CUMBERLAND SAUCE:

½ cup *(120ml)* port wine
1 cup *(240ml)* freshly squeezed orange juice
½ cup *(120ml)* freshly squeezed lemon juice
1 cup *(285g)* red currant jelly
½ cup *(75g)* chopped onion
1 tsp. dry mustard
¼ tsp. ground ginger
Few drops Tabasco
1½ T. arrowroot
1 T. coarsely shredded orange rind
1 T. coarsely shredded lemon rind

ROAST GOOSE: Pull out all fat from body cavity of goose. Rinse inside and outside of goose with cold water. Cut out wishbone to make carving easier. Cut off wing tips. Rub cavity with lemon wedge; sprinkle with salt. Place apples inside cavity. Truss goose and secure neck opening and body opening with skewers or use a poultry needle and string. Then secure wings and legs to the body with either skewers or string. Prick skin at ½-inch *(1.25cm)* intervals around sides of breast, thighs and back. Place goose on a rack in a roasting pan.

In a preheated 400° oven, roast goose 60 minutes; lower heat to 325° and roast 1½ to 2 hours longer. For perfect results, use a meat thermometer inserted deep into the inside thigh muscle without touching the bone. It should register 180-185° degrees. *Do not overcook.* Allow the goose to rest about 30 minutes before carving.

CUMBERLAND SAUCE: In a saucepan, combine port, orange juice, lemon juice, jelly, onion, mustard, ginger and Tabasco. Bring mixture to a boil, stirring occasionally. Be careful as mixture may foam up and over the pan. Combine arrowroot with a little of the hot mixture in a cup; mix well, add to saucepan; cook over low heat, stirring constantly, until slightly thickened. Do not allow to boil. Add orange rind and lemon rind. Pass in a sauce boat. The sauce may be prepared a day in advance and gently reheated.

Gloria J. Holtsinger, West Hartford, CT

Nutritional Notes: Goose is higher in fat than chicken and turkey. Roasted properly, it compares to duck in fat and cholesterol content. The low-fat and low-sodium sauce is therefore an excellent accompaniment for this dish. The nutritional analysis uses 4 ⅔ oz. *(130g)* cooked goose meat per serving. For best flavor uncooked goose or duck should be kept no longer than 6 months in a freezer. Uncooked chicken and turkey should be kept no longer than 1 year in a freezer.

Wine Suggestion: Hungarian Egri Bikaver, zesty red; serve at room temperature.

Chestnut Poultry Stuffing

Before 1900, chestnut trees were plentiful along the eastern seaboard. Our forebearers learned to store this valuable fruit in sand to keep out mold. In 1900, the trees were attacked by a great blight. Fortunately, the European and Chinese varieties still survive. The distinctively delicious chestnut is used commonly as a nut or a vegetable or may be ground into flour. Chestnuts can be purchased fresh, canned, which saves the labor of peeling, or dried, which then need soaking and boiling.

YIELD: 6 Servings or Enough for 14-16 Lb. *(6-7kg)* Goose or Turkey
TOTAL CALORIES: 1476
CALORIES PER SERVING: 246
CARBOHYDRATES: 35g
PROTEIN: 4g
FAT: 10g
PREPARING: 40 Minutes
BAKING: 30 Minutes
FREEZING: No

TO PREPARE CHESTNUTS: With short-bladed oyster knife or sturdy paring knife, make 3 deep cross gashes on flat side of each chestnut. Place in heatproof baking pan, sprinkle with oil, place over medium heat. Stir to coat with oil. When chestnuts start to sizzle, place in preheated 350° oven on middle rack; bake 20 to 30 minutes or until chestnuts are soft. Shells will have puffed and inner skin will be crisp. Both can be flaked off as soon as chestnuts are cool. Chop into small pieces.

STUFFING: Put toasted bread through food chopper or food processor. Place in large bowl. Add seasonings, chestnuts, onion, cranberries, apples, celery; stir to mix well. Add water and butter, mix. Let cool.

Doris E. Farrington, Darien, CT

Microwave Conversion Instructions: To Prepare Fresh Chestnuts: With short-bladed oyster or paring knife, make 3 deep cross gashes on flat side of each chestnut. Place nuts in single layer in shallow pie plate. Cook, uncovered, on High 2 minutes, stirring once. Allow to cool before peeling.

12 fresh chestnuts
2-4 T. *(30-60ml)* olive oil
10 slices bread, toasted and cubed, to equal 4 cups
½ tsp. salt
¼ tsp. freshly ground pepper
¼ tsp. thyme
¼ tsp. sage
¼ tsp. parsley
1 medium onion, chopped
½ cup *(60g)* raw cranberries, chopped
2 tart apples, peeled, chopped
4 celery stalks, chopped
1 cup *(240ml)* boiling water
4 T. *(60g)* butter, melted

Pickled Pumpkin

Pumpkin, a member of the squash family, was called *pompion* by the Indians. They taught the colonists how to prepare it in a seemingly endless variety of ways. It became an almost daily staple in the New World and often was the difference between survival and starvation.

YIELD: 2½ Cups
TOTAL CALORIES: 1680
CALORIES PER TABLESPOON: 42
CARBOHYDRATES: 10g
PREPARING: 15 Minutes
CHILLING: 4 Hours Minimum
COOKING: 30 Minutes

In large saucepan combine sugar, vinegar, water, cinnamon, cloves, allspice, and lemon peel. Cook without stirring 5 minutes. Add pumpkin and simmer until tender, about 15 minutes. Pumpkin should be *just* tender, not too soft.

Transfer pumpkin to jar. Reduce syrup over high heat to 1 cup. Cool syrup and pour over pumpkin.

Chill at least 4 hours before serving. This will keep for 2 to 3 weeks in the refrigerator.

Grace E. Rubinow, Manchester, CT

1⅔ cups *(335g)* sugar
¾ cup *(175ml)* cider vinegar
½ cup *(120ml)* water
1 cinnamon stick, broken in half
6 cloves
6 whole allspice
6 2-inch *(5cm)* strips of lemon peel
2 cups *(475ml)* ripe pumpkin flesh cut into 1-inch *(2.5cm)* pieces (use a melon ball cutter to scoop out flesh)

Wethersfield Onion Shortcake

Connecticut was largely a farm state until the 1850s and was known as the "Provision State" during the Revolution. The land was rich and there was much traffic on the Connecticut River as sailing barges hauled loads of vegetables down the waterway on to New York for marketing. And many varieties of onions accounted for a large portion of those loads. One variety called Southport Globe is still available for planting today.

YIELD: 4 Entree Servings or
  6-8 Vegetable Servings
TOTAL CALORIES: 2584
CALORIES PER
  VEGETABLE SERVING: 323
CARBOHYDRATES: 23g
PROTEIN: 6g
FAT: 23g
CHOLESTEROL: High
SODIUM: High
PREPARING: 40 Minutes
BAKING: 55 Minutes

CRUST:

2 cups *(225g)* **flour**
4 tsp. baking powder
1 tsp. salt
6 T. *(85g)* **butter**
½-⅔ cup *(120-160ml)* **buttermilk**

FILLING:

8-10 medium baking onions,
  thinly sliced
6 T. *(85g)* **butter**
1 cup *(225g)* **sour cream or 1 cup**
  (240ml) **Creme Fraiche (page 200)**
2 eggs, slightly beaten
1 tsp. salt
Freshly ground white pepper

CRUST: Place flour, baking powder, and salt in bowl. Work in butter with finger tips until resembles coarse meal. Add buttermilk gradually, mixing until a somewhat sticky dough is formed. *[FOOD PROCESSOR: Place dry ingredients in work bowl; process 5 seconds. Add butter in pieces. Process until like coarse meal. With machine running, add buttermilk through feed tube. When dough starts to mass, stop machine.]* Turn onto floured board; knead briefly until smooth. Line 9-inch *(22.5cm)* spring-form pan. Chill until ready to use.

FILLING: Saute onions in butter until transparent; spread over dough. Mix sour cream and seasonings with beaten eggs; blend thoroughly. Pour mixture over onions. *[FOOD PROCESSOR: Cut onions to fit feed tube. Slice using medium slicing disc and medium pressure. Remove. Process eggs by turning machine on/off 3 times. Add sour cream, salt and pepper; blend.]* Bake in preheated 450° oven 10 minutes. Reduce temperature to 350°; bake 45 minutes longer. Slice in wedges and serve.

Melinda M. Vance, West Hartford, CT

Variations, Advance Preparation, and Serving Suggestions:
Serve with Fruited Pork Loin (page 296) or Roast Pork Loin Either/Or (page 294). For a lovely brunch dish, add 2 oz. *(60g)* slab bacon cut into fine julienne strips and browned, and ½ tsp. nutmeg.

Maple Nut Cream

A heavenly dessert that has been in Alyce Hild's family for years. Her father used to send her fresh maple syrup from his farm in Vermont.

YIELD: 4-6 Servings
TOTAL CALORIES: 1830
CALORIES PER SERVING: 305
CARBOHYDRATES: 32g
PROTEIN: 1.6g
FAT: 19g
CHOLESTEROL: High
PREPARING: 30 Minutes
CHILLING: 3 Hours

4 egg yolks
¾ cup *(175ml)* **maple syrup**
2 cups *(475ml)* **heavy cream, whipped**
Finely chopped walnuts or almonds

Beat yolks until light and they form a ribbon. Heat maple syrup in top of double boiler. When hot, add a little of hot syrup to eggs; mix well. Then add egg mixture to hot syrup, stirring constantly until thickened. Do not let mixture boil. Cool.

When cool, fold in whipped cream; pour into a wet 1-qt. *(1L)* mold or individual parfait glasses; chill or freeze. When ready to serve, sprinkle with finely ground walnuts. May be served directly from freezer in parfait glasses.

Alyce Hild, West Hartford, CT

Steamed Cranberry Pudding

Lighter, less dense than plum pudding, this dessert is perfect for Thanksgiving or Christmas. When the Pilgrims stepped ashore in Plymouth, Massachusetts, in 1620, they were greeted by a group of friendly Wampanog Indians bearing gifts of bright red berries. The Wampanog called the fruit "ibimi," or bitter berry, and they taught the newcomers to use its juice to preserve meat and dye clothing. But to the Pilgrims, the long pink blossoms of the berry's vine suggested the heads of cranes and they renamed this vitamin C rich food so essential to their survival, the *"crane berry"*.

YIELD: 6 Servings
TOTAL CALORIES: 2760
CALORIES PER SERVING: 460
CARBOHYDRATES: 64g
PROTEIN: 4g
FAT: 21g
CHOLESTEROL: High
PREPARING: 15 Minutes
COOKING: 1½-3 Hours
FREEZING: No

PUDDING: Sift 1 cup *(115g)* flour with salt and baking soda. Stir together molasses and water; add to flour. Combine ½ cup flour with cranberries; add to batter. Mix well. Pour into greased 1-qt. *(1L)* covered double boiler. Steam undisturbed over hot water on low heat 3 hours. Or pour pudding into greased 1-qt. pudding or other mold; cover tightly with mold cover or foil; tie foil with string. Place on a rack in deep kettle. Pour 1 to 2 inches *(2.5-5cm)* boiling water into kettle; cover; steam 1½ hours. Add more boiling water if necessary. Remove mold from kettle carefully; let cool 15 minutes. Unmold pudding.

SAUCE: Melt butter in small saucepan over low heat. Add brown sugar, stir until dissolved. Add cream, vanilla. Heat slowly. Serve hot over warm, unmolded pudding or over individual servings. Pass extra sauce separately.

M. Elsie Straube, Chester, CT

Variations, Advance Preparation, and Serving Suggestions:
Pudding can be made several hours to 1 day ahead; reheat gently to serve. Sauce can be made 2 to 3 days in advance and is also best when reheated gently. Recipe does not double well.

Wine Suggestion: California Lejon Champagne, semi-sweet sparkling white; serve chilled.

Microwave Conversion Instructions: Combine pudding ingredients as for conventional recipe. Pour mixture into well-greased 6-cup *(1½L)* ring mold. Place large shallow pan in oven with inverted saucer or meat rack in it. Add enough boiling water to cover saucer. Put ring mold on top of saucer; cover all with plastic wrap and cook on High 5 minutes. Continue to cook on Medium (50%) 12 minutes, or until pudding is set. Top will be moist, but firm. Allow 20 minutes resting time. Meanwhile, prepare sauce by melting butter in oven and adding remaining ingredients. Stir until well blended; cook on High 1½ to 2 minutes, stirring once.

PUDDING:
1½ cups *(175g)* flour, divided
½ tsp. salt
1 tsp. baking soda
½ cup *(120ml)* dark molasses
½ cup *(120ml)* very hot water
8 oz. *(225g)* whole fresh cranberries, about 2 cups (inspect and use only whole firm unblemished berries)

BROWN BUTTER SAUCE:
½ cup *(115g)* butter
½ cup *(100g)* dark brown sugar
½ cup *(120ml)* heavy cream
½ tsp. pure vanilla extract

Noah Webster Autumn Dinner by the Hearth

A special black kettle and brick oven menu from the great hearth of the Websters' 18th century farm house.

The man who was to become the "father of the American Language" was born in 1758 in the town now known as West Hartford. Young Noah Webster grew up on his father's 90 acre farm, was tutored by local Congregational ministers and attended Yale University in New Haven. During the revolutionary campaign of 1777, he served under his father who was a captain in the militia. He later married Rebecca Greenleaf, and they had seven children.

Noah Webster was involved in banking, he practiced law and was in the state legislature. He was a prolific writer and a deeply committed educator. After teaching in a number of schools and experiencing great inconsistency in English pronunciation and usage, he became convinced that the country should have its own national language with unified, simplified spelling and word definitions. He wrote and published widely used spelling and grammar books. He is best known for the first American dictionary which took twenty-five years to compile. He completed the revision of the appendix to his dictionary only a few days before his death in 1843.

Noah Webster also had a significant effect on the literary future of Hartford. In 1783 he urged Congress to pass the basis of our present copyright laws. An immediate result was that in 1796 the first American Cookbook, *American Cookery or The Art of Dressing Viands, Fish, Poultry and Vegetables,* was published in Hartford by Amelia Simmons. Under the protection offered by this federal law, the city of Hartford became by 1820 the publishing center of the country. This was an important factor in Samuel Clemens' (Mark Twain) and his literary friends' decision to make Hartford their home.

The birthplace of Noah Webster has been restored and is a National Historic Site open to the public as an excellent example of an 18th century farm house. Standing at 227 South Main Street, West Hartford, Connecticut, the house is operated under the auspices of the Noah Webster Foundation and Historical Society of West Hartford, Inc.

By the close of the 18th century the more monotonous menus of the early settlers were replaced by bountiful tables. Newly established travel routes brought Virginia hams, Carolina rice, and Pennsylvania sausage to New England. The importation of salt from Lisbon made meat storage easier. From the West Indies citrus fruits, sugar and rum added excitement to the normal daily fare. The introduction of apples provided another important supplement to dreary winter meals. Vast markets offering a wide variety of produce, meats and bread could now be found in the larger towns. Colonial housewives took pride in their herb gardens which were used not only to add delicate flavors to food, but for healing medicines as well.

Noah Webster's family often entertained local church officials and politicians, as well as neighbors and relatives. The main meal of the day was at noon. Special guest dinners were usually composed of home grown crops of corn, squash and beans, a chicken, pork or goose raised by Mrs. Webster, and small game such as rabbit. Several desserts testified to the variety of fruits available, the creative ingenuity of the colonial housewife, and the proverbial sweet tooth of the colonists. Noah Webster wrote home to his wife and mother on more than one occasion that he could hardly wait to get home to their pumpkin pies!

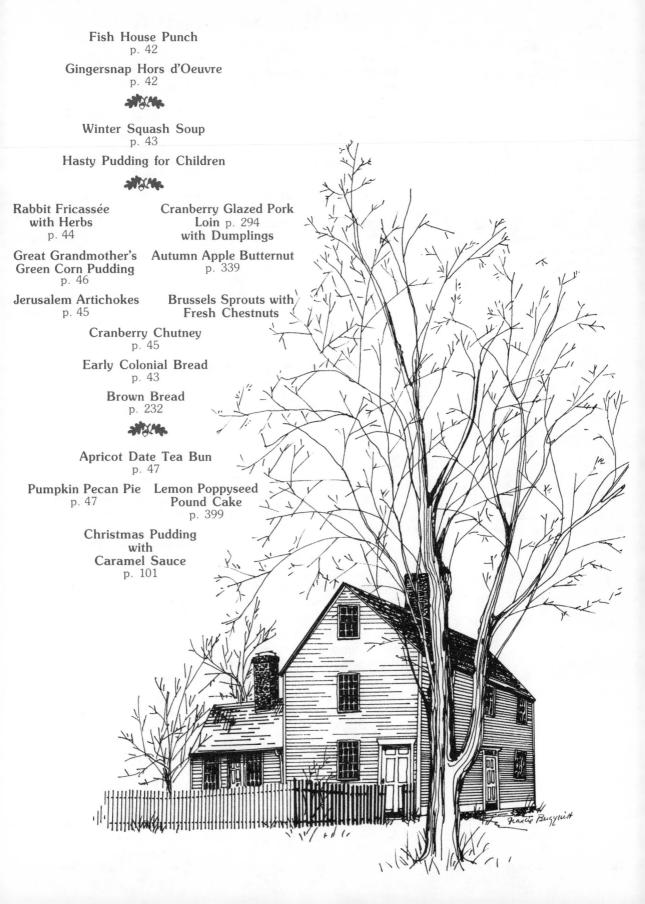

Francis Burghwist

Fish House Punch

A great traditional Colonial brew — but truly deadly! This potent punch originated with the men of The Fish House, Philadelphia's famed fishing and social club around 1732.

YIELD: 48 ½-Cup Servings
TOTAL CALORIES: 8200
CALORIES PER SERVING: 170
CARBOHYDRATES: 9g
PREPARING: 25 Minutes
STANDING: 2 Hours Minimum
FREEZING: Yes — Ice Ring

1½ cups *(300g)* superfine sugar
1 qt. *(950ml)* freshly squeezed lemon juice (about 24 medium lemons)
2 qts. *(1890ml)* dark Jamaican rum (Meyers's preferred)
2 qts. *(1890ml)* cold water (or substitute carbonated spring water like Perrier)
½ cup *(120ml)* peach brandy
1 qt. *(950ml)* cognac
1 block of ice or ice ring
1 cup *(200g)* peeled sliced peaches

Place sugar and lemon juice in punch bowl; stir to dissolve sugar completely. Add rum, water, peach brandy and cognac; stir. Let sit at room temperature for at least 2 hours, stirring occasionally. Just before serving, add ice; garnish with peaches.

Francie Bergquist, West Hartford, CT

Gingersnap Hors d'Oeuvre

A snappy addition to your hors d'oeuvre repertoire!

YIELD: 70 Cookies
TOTAL CALORIES: 2800
CALORIES PER COOKIE: 40
CARBOHYDRATES: 5g
PROTEIN: .75g
FAT: 2g
PREPARING: 1 Hour
BAKING: 10 Minutes
CHILLING: 2 Hours
FREEZING: Yes

GINGERSNAPS:

¼ cup *(50g)* dark brown sugar
⅓ cup *(80ml)* molasses
¼ cup *(60g)* unsalted sweet butter, room temperature
1 egg
1 tsp. baking soda
¼ tsp. salt
¼ tsp. each ground allspice, cinnamon, cloves, ginger
2¼ cups *(250g)* flour, divided

TOPPING:

1 pkg. (8 oz.) *(225g)* cream cheese
¼ cup *(60ml)* mango chutney, finely chopped

GINGERSNAPS: In a large bowl, cream sugar, molasses and butter; add egg, beat until fluffy. Into another bowl, sift baking soda, salt and spices, and ¾ cup of the flour. Add this mixture all at once to molasses mixture; beat just until ingredients are mixed. Stir in the remaining 1½ cups flour and beat to form a stiff dough. *[FOOD PROCESSOR: Put flour, soda, spices, and salt in work bowl; process 5 seconds and set aside. Process butter, molasses, and sugar 1 minute until creamed and fluffy. Add egg and process 30 seconds. Add flour mixture and turn machine on/off to combine, stopping as soon as flour has almost disappeared. Do not overprocess.]* Divide the dough in half, flatten the portions and wrap each in plastic wrap. Refrigerate at least 2 hours, preferably overnight.

On a lightly floured surface, roll out dough about ⅛ inch *(3mm)* thick. With a crimped pastry wheel, cut dough into 1 × 2-inch *(2.5 × 5cm)* rectangles. Place them on buttered cookie sheets. With a fork, prick each cookie in an even pattern.

Bake cookies in preheated 350° oven until crisp, about 10 minutes. Watch carefully to prevent burning. Transfer cookies to racks, cool completely.

TOPPING: Blend cream cheese with chutney. Transfer to serving bowl. Serve cookies with bowl of topping and let guests spread their own.

Carolyn Orsulak, Wethersfield, CT

Microwave Conversion Instructions: Place 15 to 20 cookies in a circular formation on shallow baking dish. Cook on High 2 to 3 minutes or until just dry. Timing will vary due to thickness of dough and amount placed on baking dish. Cookies will firm when cool.

Winter Squash Soup

Acorn, buttercup, butternut, hubbard and turban are all names for winter squash. You can take your pick of any of the five to make this soup.

YIELD: 2 Quarts or 8-10 Servings
TOTAL CALORIES: 2760
CALORIES PER SERVING: 276
CARBOHYDRATES: 13g
PROTEIN: 2g
FAT: 24g
CHOLESTEROL: High
SODIUM: High
PREPARING: 45 Minutes
COOKING: 15 Minutes
FREEZING: Yes

Saute onions, celery and garlic in 2 T. butter, until golden. Add chicken stock, cooked squash, rosemary, savory and parsley. Bring to a boil; reduce heat and simmer 10 minutes. Add remaining butter. Remove from heat; add cream. Season to taste with salt, pepper and nutmeg. Serve immediately.

Elizabeth Henstenberg, West Hartford, CT
via Noah Webster House

Nutritional Notes: Even boiled and mashed, winter squash is exceptionally high in vitamin A. Freshly harvested squash has somewhat less vitamin A than squash that has been stored for awhile as the carotenoid content increases during storage.

Microwave Conversion Instructions: Wash squash. Pierce rind several times in 4 to 6 places. Put squash on rack and cook on High 7 to 8 minutes per pound, or until squash begins to feel soft. Cool and cut squash in half. Scoop out centers and mash; set aside. Place onion, celery and garlic in large casserole. Put butter on top of vegetables. Cook, covered, on High 8 to 9 minutes. Add *heated* stock, reserved squash, rosemary, savory and parsley. Cook on High, uncovered, 9 minutes. Stir in cream. Season and serve immediately. If additional heating is necessary, cook on Medium (50%) 2 to 3 minutes.

3 large onions, chopped
1 cup *(110g)* chopped celery
1 clove garlic, minced
¼ cup *(60g)* butter
3 cups *(710ml)* chicken stock
2 cups *(275g)* winter squash, cooked and mashed
1 T. rosemary
1 T. savory
2 T. chopped fresh parsley
2 cups *(475ml)* heavy cream
Salt
Freshly ground pepper
Freshly grated nutmeg

Early Colonial Bread

YIELD: 2 Loaves
CALORIES PER LOAF: 1483
CARBOHYDRATES: 266g
PROTEIN: 35g
FAT: 31g
PREPARING: 45 Minutes
RISING: 1½ Hours
BAKING: 45 Minutes
FREEZING: Yes

Dissolve yeast in warm water. Add 1 tsp. sugar and set aside to proof.

Mix together boiling water, oil, molasses and salt.

Combine cornmeal and cold water; add to molasses mixture; cool.

Add yeast to cooled cornmeal mixture. Add whole wheat and rye flours; mix thoroughly. Gradually add about 3 cups white flour; turn out onto floured board and knead, adding white flour as needed, until dough is smooth and elastic. Place dough in greased bowl, turn to coat; cover and let rise until doubled in bulk, about 1 hour.

Punch down dough; divide into 2 pieces; let rest 10 minutes. Then shape into 2 loaves and place on a baking sheet sprinkled with cornmeal. Cover and let rise 30 minutes.

Bake in preheated 375° oven, 45 minutes. Cool on wire racks.

Elizabeth Henstenberg, West Hartford, CT
via Noah Webster House

2 pkgs. (¼ oz. each) *(14g)* active dry yeast
1 cup *(240ml)* warm water
1 tsp. sugar
1 cup *(240ml)* boiling water
¼ cup *(60ml)* vegetable oil
⅓ cup *(80ml)* molasses
2 tsp. salt
½ cup *(75g)* cornmeal
1 cup *(240ml)* cold water
1 cup *(120g)* whole wheat flour
1 cup *(100g)* rye flour
3½ cups *(400g)* white flour (approximately)

YIELD: 4-6 Servings
CALORIES PER SERVING: 614
CARBOHYDRATES: 10g
PROTEIN: 49g
FAT: 42g
CHOLESTEROL: High
PREPARING: 15 Minutes
COOKING: 1¼ Hours

Rabbit Fricassée with Herbs

6 T. *(85g)* butter
¼ lb. *(115g)* bacon, chopped
1 young domestic rabbit, cut in pieces
4 medium onions, chopped
1 bouquet garni — 4 whole cloves, 1
   sprig fresh parsley, thyme, marjoram,
   tied in muslin or cheesecloth bag
¼ tsp. freshly grated nutmeg
½ tsp. salt
¼ tsp. freshly ground black pepper
1 cup *(240ml)* white wine

SAUCE:
¼ cup *(30g)* flour
4 T. *(60g)* butter, softened
Reserved pan juices
2 egg yolks
¼ cup *(60ml)* white wine
Grated rind of ½ lemon

RABBIT: Melt butter and heat the bacon in a large frying or stew pan; add rabbit pieces and onions. Fry 3 minutes. Add bouquet garni, nutmeg, salt, pepper, wine. Bring to boil, cover, reduce heat. Simmer gently 50 minutes. Remove rabbit pieces to serving dish. Keep warm. Reserve pan juices.

SAUCE: Mix flour with butter in medium-sized, heatproof bowl. Add enough reserved pan juices to flour and butter to bring to consistency of thick gravy. Return mixture to frying pan. Stir well; simmer 5 minutes, stirring. Reduce heat to low.

In a bowl, beat the yolks, add wine, lemon rind. Pour into hot, not boiling mixture in frying pan. Stir well to heat through, do not let boil. Pour over meat.

Gloria Holtsinger, West Hartford, CT

Variations, Advance Preparation, and Serving Suggestions:
Chicken may be substituted for the rabbit in this recipe. In either case, rice is a good accompaniment. The dish may be prepared a day ahead and refrigerated. Reheat over a pan of hot water or on very low heat just until hot.

Wine Suggestion: California Ruby Cabernet, dry red; serve at room temperature.

Microwave Conversion Instructions: Place bacon in large casserole, cook on High 4 to 6 minutes, or until bacon is crisp. Drain and reserve 1 T. bacon fat; set aside. In a 2-qt. *(2L)* casserole combine butter and chopped onion, cover, cook on High 5 minutes. Combine indicated seasonings as directed with wine and onion mixture in large casserole with bacon chips; mix well. Add rabbit pieces, bone sides up, with thicker portions placed near outer edges. Baste with sauce and cover; cook on High 10 minutes, stir. Turn rabbit pieces, bone side down, again with thicker portions toward outer edges of dish, cover, cook on High 10 to 15 minutes until tender and no longer pink.

Remove rabbit pieces; keep warm. Reserve pan juices. In medium glass bowl, cook 4 T. butter until melted on Medium (50%) (about 90 seconds). Add flour, stir, cook 1 minute on High. Add enough reserved pan juices to flour and butter mixture to bring to consistency of thick gravy. Cook mixture 2 minutes on High, stirring once.

In glass bowl beat egg yolks; add wine and lemon rind. Carefully spoon some of hot gravy into mixture, stirring constantly. Add remaining gravy; cook 1 minute on Medium (50%) uncovered. Serve over rabbit.

Cranberry Chutney

Delicious with pork, ham, fowl, or cream cheese.

YIELD: 3 Cups
TOTAL CALORIES: 1392
CALORIES PER TABLESPOON: 29
CARBOHYDRATES: 5g
FAT: 1g
PREPARING: 30 Minutes
COOKING: 20 Minutes

Combine all ingredients in large saucepan. Bring to boil, stirring constantly and simmer uncovered 15 minutes, stirring occasionally. Chill, covered, in refrigerator before serving.

Cathy Power, Medfield, MA

Nutritional Notes: This recipe is low in sodium if onion powder is used instead of onion salt.

Microwave Conversion Instructions: Place all ingredients in 2-qt. *(2L)* bowl. Cook, uncovered, on High 10 minutes.

2 cups *(225g)* fresh cranberries
¾ cup *(150g)* packed brown sugar
½ cup *(85g)* raisins
½ cup *(55g)* chopped celery
½ cup *(125g)* peeled and chopped apple
¼ cup *(30g)* chopped walnuts
2 T. *(25g)* candied ginger, finely snipped
2 T. *(30ml)* fresh lemon juice
1 tsp. onion salt
¼ tsp. ground cloves
½ cup *(120ml)* water

Jerusalem Artichokes

The Jerusalem artichoke was so named by Samuel de Champlain in 1605 in the gardens of Indians at Cape Cod. But the Jerusalem artichoke is actually a tuber-bearing type of sunflower. It was cultivated extensively by the colonists because it stored well through long winters. The word "Jerusalem" is thought to be a corruption of *girasol,* meaning "turn to the sun."

YIELD: 6 Servings
CALORIES PER SERVING: 100
CARBOHYDRATES: 6g
PROTEIN: 1g
FAT: 8g
PREPARING: 25 Minutes
COOKING: 10 Minutes

Scrub artichokes well under running water. Cut away knobs and blemishes; scrape with vegetable peeler. Drop immediately into cold water.

Place artichokes in large saucepan with water and salt. Cover pan; simmer 8 to 10 minutes or until artichokes are tender and can easily be pierced with fork. Drain well. Mash or puree in food processor. Stir in butter, lemon juice, seasonings. Transfer to serving dish.

Cathryn Britton, West Hartford, CT

Variations, Advance Preparation, and Serving Suggestions: Can be made up to a day ahead. Reheat gently in buttered shallow 1-qt. casserole or individual ramekins. Substitute 2 to 3 tsp. hot mustard or ½ cup grated cheese for basil.

Nutritional Notes: Jerusalem artichokes are a good source of iron, are low in calories, and are low in fat and sodium (so they are an excellent food for dieters and diabetics). Caloric value of Jerusalem artichokes varies. According to *Bowes and Church Food Values of Portions Commonly Used (13th ed.)* values range from 7 calories per 3½ oz. *(100g)* for freshly harvested to 75 after long storage. The nutritional analysis uses freshly harvested. Stored Jerusalem artichokes would result in 188 calories and 25g carbohydrates per serving for the above recipe.

Microwave Conversion Instructions: Note: Reduce water to ½ cup. Place prepared artichokes in casserole and add salt and water. Cook, covered, on High 8 to 10 minutes or until fork tender. Drain well and proceed as directed above.

2 lbs. *(900g)* Jerusalem artichokes or sunchokes
1½ cups *(355ml)* water
1 tsp. salt
4 T. *(60g)* butter
1 T. fresh lemon juice
¼ tsp. dried basil, crumbled or 1 T. chopped, fresh basil
¼ tsp. dried oregano, crumbled
Salt
Freshly ground pepper
2 T. chopped parsley

Uncooked Fresh Cranberry Relish

YIELD: 10 ½-Cup Servings
TOTAL CALORIES: 1360
CALORIES PER SERVING: 136
CARBOHYDRATES: 23g
PROTEIN: 2g
FAT: 4g
PREPARING: 15 Minutes

1 lb. *(450g)* fresh raw cranberries, washed
1 apple, cored and quartered
1 orange, washed, quartered and seeded
1 fennel bulb, including 3 stalks, cut up
6 T. *(100g)* orange or tangerine marmalade
3 T. *(65g)* good quality honey
½ cup *(60g)* chopped walnuts

Sassamanesh is the native Indian word for cranberry. Indians taught the early pilgrims not only how to use it for food, but how to use its juices to preserve meat and dye clothing and for medicinal purposes. The colonists used this vitamin-C-rich berry to treat scurvy on long ocean voyages.

Grind cranberries, apple, orange and fennel with coarse blade of food grinder or in food processor. Add marmalade, honey and walnuts; stir until well mixed. Refrigerate until serving time.

Gloria J. Holtsinger, West Hartford, CT

Variations, Advance Preparation, and Serving Suggestions: Good for breakfast with sauteed chicken livers, sausage patties, and Cracked Wheat toast (page 53).

Nutritional Notes: A colorful and tangy accompaniment to many meals. It is relatively fat free and low in sodium, and can add variety to many restricted diets. Cranberries used raw rather than cooked require much less sweetener.

Great Grandmother's Green Corn Pudding

YIELD: 6-8 Servings
TOTAL CALORIES: 3216
CALORIES PER SERVING: 402
CARBOHYDRATES: 27g
PROTEIN: 6g
FAT: 30g
CHOLESTEROL: High
SODIUM: High
PREPARING: 30 Minutes
BAKING: 4 Hours
FREEZING: No

Colonists quickly came to depend on corn as a vital staple. When times were hard, it was not uncommon for them to eat some form of corn three times a day — fresh (green), dried, or ground into cornmeal. Lacking most fruits and vegetables during the winter months, the resourceful women brought variety to meals by using cornmeal to make a wide selection of porridges, breads, puddings, pancakes, and pies.

12 ears corn, grated *not* scraped (use a corn grater)
2 cups *(475ml)* heavy cream
1 T. sugar
1 tsp. freshly ground pepper
2 tsp. salt
Butter

Combine corn, heavy cream, sugar, pepper and salt. Mix together thoroughly. Pour mixture into a well-buttered 2-qt. *(2L)* casserole. Dot heavily with butter. Place in pan of hot water to reach halfway up the sides of casserole. Bake in preheated 300° oven, 3½ to 4 hours. Pudding should be nicely firm and brown. Use a knife to test if it is set. If not set, continue to bake a little longer. Serve hot.

Kathryn L. Britton, West Hartford, CT

Microwave Conversion Instructions: Note: Reduce heavy cream to 1½ cups *(360ml)*. Place thoroughly mixed ingredients in 2-qt. ring mold or 3-qt. *(3L)* casserole dish with inverted glass in center. Cover and cook on Medium High (70%) 25 to 30 minutes, rotating ½ turn 3 times. Check to determine if firm and set. Allow 5 minutes standing time before serving. If browned top is desired, place under conventional broiler, watching carefully.

Apricot Date Tea Bun

This is an unusually good compliment to a cup of coffee or tea.

YIELD: 2 Shortbreads or 12 Servings
CALORIES PER SERVING: 241
CARBOHYDRATES: 38g
PROTEIN: 2g
FAT: 9g
PREPARING: 25 Minutes
BAKING: 40 Minutes

Cut butter into flour; add baking powder, salt, and sugar; mix; add eggs, mixing well.

Divide dough into 4 equal parts. Use 2 pieces of dough to line 2 8-inch *(20cm)* cake pans. Dot each cake with dates and apricot jam. Divide remaining dough into 4 pieces and press flat, totally covering the filling. Press almonds on top in a pattern easy to cut around.

Bake in preheated 350° oven 40 minutes. Cut into wedges while warm; when cool, remove from tins.

Fiona Marlow, Bangor, Northern Ireland

1 cup *(225g)* butter, softened
2 cups *(225g)* flour
2 tsp. baking powder
Salt
1 cup plus 2 T. *(225g)* sugar
2 eggs
1½ cups *(225g)* dates, cut up
8-12 oz. *(225-340g)* apricot jam, depending on desired sweetness
¼ cup *(40g)* slivered almonds

Pumpkin Pecan Pie

In 1920, Yale students invented the new game of Frisbie when they discovered that the empty pie plates from Mrs. Frisbie's pies could be used to sail across the New Haven Green. With the cry "Frisbie", the plates were hurled aloft, and a national pastime was born from a national favorite, pumpkin pie.

YIELD: 6-8 Servings
TOTAL CALORIES: 4184
CALORIES PER SERVING: 523
CARBOHYDRATES: 56g
PROTEIN: 5g
FAT: 31g
CHOLESTEROL: High
PREPARING: 20 Minutes
BAKING: 1 Hour
CHILLING: 2 Hours
FREEZING: Yes

In medium bowl, combine eggs with pumpkin, corn syrup, sugar, cinnamon and salt. Pour into pie shell. Sprinkle with pecans.

Place on middle rack of preheated 350° oven. Bake 50 to 60 minutes, until knife inserted in center comes out clean. Remove from oven; let cool on rack to room temperature. Refrigerate several hours to chill.

TOPPING: Whip cream until soft peaks form. Gradually add sugar, whipping, until stiff peaks form. Spread over chilled pie.

Gloria Filhoff, Vernon, CT

Variations, Advance Preparation, and Serving Suggestions:
The cooled pie, without topping, may be frozen, well-wrapped, up to one month. Defrost, still wrapped; add topping while still cold. The pie can be served slightly warm from the oven (or gently reheated if made ahead) with topping served separately.

Nutritional Notes: Elimination of cream can significantly decrease cholesterol, calories and fat. One tablespoon sweetened whipped cream contains approximately 125 calories and 14 grams fat.

Wine Suggestion: California Sauvignon Blanc, sweet white; serve cold.

Microwave Conversion Instructions: Pour filling into *baked* pie shell. Cook on Medium (50%) 35 to 40 minutes, rotating ¼ turn every 8 to 9 minutes. Test for doneness by inserting knife midway between edge and center. Center should be set.

3 eggs, beaten until frothy
1½ cups *(425g)* pureed cooked or canned pumpkin
¾ cup *(175ml)* dark corn syrup
¾ cup *(150g)* sugar
½ tsp. cinnamon
¼ tsp. salt
1 9-inch *(22.5cm)* unbaked Pie Crust (page 198)
1 cup *(120g)* chopped pecans

TOPPING:
1 cup *(240ml)* heavy cream
2 T. *(25g)* sugar

Enfield Kitchen Sisters' Harvest Breakfast

Let the Shaker tradition of a hearty breakfast inspire great beginnings — nutritious weekday breakfasts, a grand weekend breakfast or a party brunch.

Two years before the signing of the Declaration of Independence, Ann Lee and her eight followers landed in New York after a difficult three month ocean voyage from England. Seeking freedom from religious persecution, the small band purchased a home in the wilderness at Niskeyvna, New York. Initially they experienced the same persecution as in England, but by the mid-1780s converts in growing numbers were attracted to the strict ideals of the community: a celibate life dedicated to hard work and the glory of God; common ownership of all property; and a communal life style removed from worldly politics and competition.

The group, officially called the United Society of Believers in the First and Second Appearance of Christ, was more commonly known as Shakers. This name, which members also applied to themselves, was derived from the free form of worship in which followers sang and danced. After the death of Mother Ann Lee, one of her original followers, James Whittaker, led the community. In 1787 the leadership passed to a devoted convert from Enfield, Connecticut, Joseph Meacham, who is credited with having shaped the doctrines and the orderly and practical way of life upon which future communities were designed. Prior to the Civil War, over 6,000 members lived in 18 colonies extending as far west as Ohio and south to Florida.

The Connecticut Shaker colony, founded in Enfield in 1792, existed there until 1917. At one point 200 members lived in a flourishing 3,000-acre model farm community. They lived communally in five "families," each with its own complex of buildings. The grist mill, cider mill and sawmill were powered by water generators; wind generators irrigated the fields and pumped running water into the homes. This same Shaker community developed the first packaging and shipping of vegetable and flower seeds.

Today most of the communal homes, barns, and mills have been razed. In their place stand factories and a state prison farm. The few buildings which remain, however, are eloquent reminders of Shaker design, with its harmony of line and space, and superior craftsmanship. The majestic, four-story brick dwelling of the Church family is the most striking of the remaining buildings.

The Shakers zealously followed Mother Lee's dictate to "Put your hands to work and give your hearts to God." They were committed to standards of thrift, cleanliness and excellence as they considered their communities "Heavens on earth." Hand-crafted items were no longer made for personal profit; time was of no consequence. The artisans let their imaginations flow; their gifts to us include the washing machine, the flat broom, packaged garden seeds and herbs, the screw propeller and the common clothespin.

Like the Shaker tools, furniture and architecture, their food was an expression of their simplicity, imagination and dedication to quality. The women, known as the Kitchen Sisters, were given the full responsibility for cooking and serving the meals, often to more than a hundred people. Long before the awareness of nutrition, the Shakers insisted on cooking fresh vegetables quickly in small amounts of water, stewing fruits unpeeled, and using natural whole wheat flour and home-grown ground cereals. Pies, limited in contemporary meals to dessert, were a customary part of any Shaker meal. One particular favorite was a lemon pie made with whole, thinly sliced lemons which maximized the nutritional value of the fruit.

The Shaker farm communities freely shared their prosperity with victims of natural disasters as well as with weary travelers. The fame of their bountiful meals spread. In the mid-19th century large numbers of city folk from "the World" would travel many miles to enjoy the Shaker hospitality. As is evident from the Sisters' menu for a Harvest Breakfast, the repasts were not only to satisfy bodily hunger. Their goal was also to "create enjoyment, joy and satisfaction to those partaking of them."

Today the only growing Shaker colony, one founded in 1794, is located in Sabbathday Lake, Maine. However, their heritage continues to live in the several communities preserved as museums or historic landmarks, in their imaginative handmade crafts, and in their delicious, wholesome recipes.

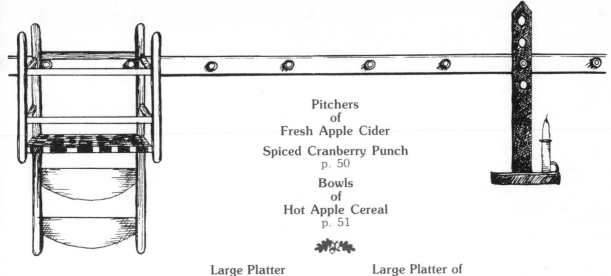

Pitchers
of
Fresh Apple Cider

Spiced Cranberry Punch
p. 50

Bowls
of
Hot Apple Cereal
p. 51

| Large Platter Corned Beef Hash with Baked Eggs p. 50 | Large Platter of Corn Fritters p. 52 and Pumpkin Griddle Cakes p. 51 |

Pitcher of Maple Syrup

Shaker Daily Loaf
(White Bread Deluxe)
p. 52

Graham Buttermilk Bread
(Cracked Wheat Bread)
p. 53

Raspberry Plum Butter
p. 54

Bing Cherry Jam
p. 54

Cider Apple Pie
p. 55

Sister Ann's Lemon Tart
(Lemon Chess Tart)
p. 55

YIELD: 12 Servings or
  22 ½-Cup Servings
TOTAL CALORIES: 2950
CALORIES PER ½ CUP: 134
CARBOHYDRATES: 16g
PREPARING: 15 Minutes
CHILLING: 3 Hours Minimum
COOKING: 5 Minutes
FREEZING: Yes — Ice Ring

Spiced Cranberry Punch

An especially festive punch for the Christmas holidays. And children love it if they are served just before the addition of the rum.

---

1 cup *(200g)* sugar
1 cup *(240ml)* water
1 tsp. whole cloves
4 cinnamon sticks, 3-4 inches *(7.5-10cm)* in length
2 cups *(475ml)* cranberry juice
½ cup *(120ml)* fresh lemon juice
1 cup *(240ml)* fresh orange juice
3 cups *(710ml)* ginger ale
3 cups *(710ml)* white rum

Combine sugar, water, cloves, and cinnamon; boil 5 minutes. Strain; cool.

Mix with fruit juices. Chill 3 hours or overnight.

Before serving pour into a punch bowl over a decorative ice ring mold. (Use green leaves and cranberries.)

Add ginger ale and rum.

Mary Fish, Cashiers, NC

YIELD: 4 Servings
CALORIES PER SERVING: 418
CARBOHYDRATES: 14g
PROTEIN: 32g
FAT: 26g
CHOLESTEROL: High
SODIUM: High
PREPARING: 10 Minutes
BAKING: 35 Minutes
FREEZING: Yes

Corned Beef Hash with Baked Eggs

This is an easy dish to make for a brunch party.

½ lb. *(225g)* new potatoes, cooked, finely diced
2 cups *(340g)* finely chopped cooked corned beef, about ¾ lb.
1 small onion, minced
¼ cup *(20g)* minced scallion, green and white parts
¼ cup minced parsley
¼ tsp. freshly grated nutmeg
½ tsp. cayenne pepper
Salt, freshly ground black pepper to taste
⅓ cup *(80ml)* heavy cream
2 T. *(30g)* unsalted sweet butter, melted
4 eggs
Minced parsley to garnish

In a large bowl, combine potatoes, beef, onion, scallion, parsley, seasonings and cream. Transfer mixture to a well-buttered 1-qt. *(1L)* baking dish. Make 4 depressions in the hash with the back of a large spoon. Brush the top of the hash with butter. Place the baking dish in the upper third of a preheated 375° oven. Bake 25 minutes. Remove from oven. Crack 1 egg carefully into each depression. Reduce oven to 350°. Return dish to oven. Bake 5 to 8 minutes, or until eggs are set. Sprinkle dish with parsley. Serve hot.

Kathleen J. Schwartz, Avon, CT

Variations, Advance Preparation, and Serving Suggestions: The hash may be prepared a day or two ahead. Reheat it in the oven at serving time, at 350°, then crack eggs into dish and finish baking. (The hash, without eggs, may be frozen for several months.) The hash may be doubled or tripled and served in a separate dish for those who don't fancy eggs.

Serve with Sourdough Fruit Bread (page 238) or Sourdough English Muffins (page 239) or a variety of Six Weeks Bran Muffins (page 225).

Wine Suggestion: California Navalle Zinfandel, dry red; serve at room temperature.

Nutritional Notes: Corned beef is processed by soaking or marinating beef in a salty, spicy water, under refrigeration, for up to 3 weeks. Salt peter (sodium nitrate) is used in the soaking medium to prevent botulism. It also reddens the meat.

Hot Apple Cereal

Originally breakfast cereals had to be cooked for hours before they were digestible. Women had to get up before dawn to begin cooking the cereal, if it was to be ready in time for breakfast.

YIELD: 6-8 Servings
CALORIES PER SERVING: 408
CARBOHYDRATES: 54g
PROTEIN: 11g
FAT: 16g
PREPARING: 15 Minutes
BAKING: 45 Minutes

In a saucepan, combine milk, brown sugar, butter, salt and cinnamon; scald. Set aside.

In a mixing bowl, combine oats, apples, walnuts and raisins. Add hot milk mixture to ingredients. Pour mixture into a buttered 2-qt. *(2L)* casserole; cover.

Bake in preheated 350° oven 45 minutes until most of liquid is absorbed.

Inger Hansen, Goshen, CT

4 cups *(950ml)* **milk**
½ cup *(100g)* **brown sugar, firmly packed**
2 tsp. butter
½ tsp. salt
½ tsp. cinnamon
2 cups *(170g)* **rolled oats**
2 cups *(500g)* **apples, peeled and coarsely chopped**
1 cup *(120g)* **chopped walnuts**
1 cup *(170g)* **raisins**

Nutritional Notes: Each serving can be reduced by forty calories if skim milk is used, or even less calories if made in microwave oven.

This recipe serves as a nutritious family breakfast; but, to increase the nutritional value add wheat germ and bran to the cereal. Rolled oats are formed by rolling groats (oat with hulls removed) and steaming them to a specific thickness. The thicker the flake, the more cooking time required. The thinner the flake, the less cooking time required, but also less vitamins and minerals remain as they are lost in the steaming process.

Microwave Conversion Instructions: Note: Reduce milk to 2 cups, use only 1 tsp. butter. Combine 2 cups milk, brown sugar, 1 tsp. butter, salt and cinnamon in a 2-qt. covered casserole; cook 2 to 2½ minutes on High or until mixture is hot. Add rolled oats, apples, walnuts and raisins; recover, cook on Medium (50%) 7 to 10 minutes. Allow 2 minutes standing time.

Pumpkin Griddle Cakes

When the autumn air turns crisp, serve these griddle cakes for a wonderful weekend breakfast.

YIELD: 4 Servings
CALORIES PER SERVING: 494
CARBOHYDRATES: 58g
PROTEIN: 16g
FAT: 22g
CHOLESTEROL: High
SODIUM: High
PREPARING: 20 Minutes
COOKING: 8-10 Minutes
FREEZING: No

Sift together dry ingredients. Combine milk, pumpkin, egg yolks, butter. Stir into dry ingredients until just blended.

Beat egg whites until stiff, not dry; fold into batter. Pour about ½ cup *(120ml)* of batter at a time onto a hot, lightly greased griddle or large skillet. When top of each cake is bubbly, turn. Cook until lightly browned.

Serve with additional butter. Pass a pitcher of warmed pure maple syrup.

Melinda M. Vance, West Hartford, CT

2 cups *(225g)* **flour**
2 T. *(25g)* **sugar**
4 tsp. *(12g)* **baking powder**
1 tsp. salt
1 tsp. cinnamon
1½ cups *(355ml)* **milk**
1½ cups *(425g)* **canned pumpkin**
4 eggs, separated
¼ cup *(60g)* **melted butter**

Additional butter
Pure maple syrup

Nutritional Notes: This recipe was tested with good results substituting whole wheat flour, and increasing the milk by ½ cup (total 2 cups milk). Lowfat or skim milk may be used if desired.

Corn Fritters

Also known as Corn Oysters or Mock Oysters, they owe their revival to Civil War cooking. Severe food shortages in the South forced Southerners to use their ingenuity in devising many new recipes as well as reviving old ones.

YIELD: 6-8 Servings
CALORIES PER SERVING: 220
CARBOHYDRATES: 23g
PROTEIN: 5g
FAT: 12g
PREPARING: 25 Minutes
COOKING: 20 Minutes

½ cup *(120ml)* **milk**
2 cups **corn**, about 8 ears, scraped, and as fresh and tender as possible for best results, cooked, or use canned corn
2 **eggs**, beaten
1 cup *(115g)* **flour**
½ tsp. **salt**
2 tsp. *(6g)* **baking powder**
Freshly ground **pepper**
Peanut or **vegetable oil** for frying
Real maple syrup

In mixing bowl, add milk to corn, then eggs. Stir in dry ingredients.

Heat 3 inches *(7.5cm)* oil in wok or electric skillet to 375°. Drop batter by heaping tablespoonfuls into hot fat. Fry on each side until light golden-brown. Drain on paper toweling. Keep in warm oven while frying remaining fritters and for up to 30 minutes before serving.

Serve with real maple syrup.

Joyce Anne Vitelli, Manchester, CT

Nutritional Notes: Nutritional analysis estimates that 5 T. of oil are absorbed during frying.

White Bread Deluxe

YIELD: 3 Loaves
CALORIES PER LOAF: 1640
CARBOHYDRATES: 287g
PROTEIN: 31g
FAT: 41g
PREPARING: 25 Minutes
RISING: 3½ Hours
BAKING: 30 Minutes
FREEZING: Yes

1 pkg. *(¼ oz.) (7g)* **active dry yeast**
½ cup *(100g)* plus 1 T. *(15g)* **sugar**
2½ cups *(600ml)* **warm water**
8-9 cups *(900-1000g)* **unbleached bread flour**
½ cup *(115g)* **shortening** (lard preferred), melted
1 **egg**
2 tsp. **salt**

Combine yeast, 1 T. sugar and ½ cup warm water. Let proof.

Place 5 cups flour in large bowl. Add 2 cups warm water, ½ cup sugar, the shortening, egg and salt; mix. Add yeast mixture; mix. Gradually add flour, ½ cup at a time, until dough is too stiff to stir. Put dough on floured board; knead, adding flour as needed, until dough is smooth and elastic, about 10 minutes. *[FOOD PROCESSOR: Divide ingredients in half and process dough in 2 batches. Put 3 cups flour, salt and yeast mixture into work bowl; process to mix. With machine running, pour warm water and shortening through feed tube; process until well mixed. Add remaining flour and process until dough is smooth and elastic.]* Put dough in large greased bowl, turning to coat. Cover with plastic wrap and a towel. Let sit in warm place until doubled in bulk, about 2 hours.

Punch dough down; let rise again until doubled in bulk.

Punch dough down again; turn out onto floured board. Divide into 3 equal parts. Shape each piece into an oval; turn ends under and put in greased 9 × 5 × 3-inch *(22.5 × 12.5 × 7.5cm)* loaf pan. Cover; let rise until doubled in bulk.

Place loaves in a cold oven. Turn oven to 400°. Bake 15 minutes. Then turn temperature down to 350°; bake 15 minutes longer or until bread is rich brown color. Cool on wire racks.

Peg Rice, Darien, CT

Nutritional Notes: Unbleached bread flour is an unbleached wheat flour with a higher portion of gluten (protein) than other all-purpose flours — both enriched and non-enriched. This extra gluten gives the dough more elasticity and allows for better yeast reaction. It is, however, a flour that has been highly processed, as most commercial flours — air-blasted, mechanically separated, washed, dried and steel rolled. The result of this processing is the separation of the germ and bran from the endosperm. The product, unbleached flour, is often then chemically bleached. While aging will also whiten flour, the commercial treatment is faster and also "sanitizes" the flour for a longer shelf life. Though most flours are now "enriched," they do not contain all of the nutrients available in the original whole wheat. Specifically, they are lacking in some minerals and fiber. As a rule, the most nutritious flours are in descending order: (1) stoneground or unbolted whole wheat and non-wheat flours; (2) enriched flours; (3) unbleached flours; (4) all-purpose flours; (5) self-rising flours (white flour to which sodium bicarbonate or leavens and salt is added); (6) cake flours; and (7) instantized flours.

Cracked Wheat Bread

Graham flour, developed by Dr. Sylvester Graham, is a ground whole-wheat grain that includes the bran of the grain kernels.

YIELD: 3 Medium Loaves or 2 Large Loaves
CALORIES PER MEDIUM LOAF: 1074
CARBOHYDRATES: 198g
PROTEIN: 30g
FAT: 18g
PREPARING: 30 Minutes
RISING: 2-3 Hours
LET STAND: 60 Minutes
BAKING: 45 Minutes
FREEZING: Yes

Place cracked wheat in bowl; pour boiling water over it and let stand 60 minutes or longer.

In saucepan heat buttermilk to simmer; add molasses, honey, butter and salt. Stir to mix; cool to lukewarm.

In large mixing bowl, dissolve yeast in warm water. Add ½ tsp. sugar or honey and set aside to proof.

To proofed yeast, add lukewarm buttermilk mixture and 2 cups white flour. With electric mixer beat 2 minutes or 200 strokes by hand. Stir in cracked wheat. Gradually add whole wheat flour and enough additional white flour to make dough that leaves sides of bowl. Turn out onto floured board and knead adding more flour if dough is too sticky to work with. Knead until dough is resilient but still tacky. [FOOD PROCESSOR: Put whole wheat flour, 2 cups white flour and yeast and buttermilk mixtures into work bowl; process a few seconds to combine. Add cracked wheat mixture and process until well mixed, about 20 seconds. Add remaining white flour and process until smooth and elastic, about 40 to 60 seconds.] Place dough in buttered bowl, turn to coat or brush top with melted butter. Cover and let rise until doubled in bulk.

Punch down dough; turn out onto lightly floured board, knead a few times. Cover and let rest 10 minutes.

Cut dough into 2 pieces and place in 2 9 × 5-inch (22.5 × 12.5cm) loaf pans. Brush tops with melted butter. Cover and let rise again until doubled in bulk.

Bake in preheated 350° oven, 45 minutes or until the bottoms of loaves sound hollow when tapped. If you like a glossy crust, about 10 minutes before loaves are done, brush tops with egg beaten with 2 T. milk or water. Remove from pans and cool on wire racks.

DOUGH:
¾ cup (125g) cracked wheat or bulgur
1½ cups (355ml) boiling water
1 cup (240ml) buttermilk
¼ cup (60ml) unsulphured molasses
2 T. (40g) honey
¼ cup (60g) unsalted sweet butter
2 tsp. salt
2 pkgs. (¼ oz. each) (14g) active dry yeast
¼ cup (60ml) warm water
½ tsp. sugar or honey
3 cups (340g) unbleached white flour (approximately)
2 cups (240g) stone-ground whole wheat or graham flour

GLAZE:
1 egg
2 T. (30g) milk or water

Dean Lindsay, Darien, CT

YIELD: 5½ Cups
TOTAL CALORIES: 3454
CALORIES PER TABLESPOON: 42
CARBOHYDRATES: 10g
PREPARING: 1 Hour
COOKING: 15 Minutes
PROCESSING: 10 Minutes
FREEZING: Yes

4 cups *(600g)* **bing cherries, pitted and chopped**
1 pkg. (1¾ oz.) *(50g)* **powdered pectin**
¼ cup *(60ml)* **freshly squeezed lemon juice**
¼ cup *(60ml)* **Amaretto liqueur**
¼ tsp. salt
¼ tsp. ground cinnamon
¼ tsp. ground cloves
4½ cups *(900g)* **sugar**

Bing Cherry Jam

Bing cherries are large red sweet cherries shaped like hearts. A sweet cherry tree must receive pollen from another variety of cherry tree before it can produce fruit.

Place all ingredients except sugar in 6-qt. *(6L)* kettle; bring mixture to boil that cannot be stirred down. Immediately add sugar. Bring mixture to boil again and continue boiling 2 minutes. Skim jam and immediately ladle into hot sterilized jars. Adjust caps; process 10 minutes in boiling water bath.

Melinda M. Vance, West Hartford, CT

Variations, Advance Preparation, and Serving Suggestions: The purchase of a small, inexpensive cherry pitter fitted to top of canning jar will save time, aggravation, and stained hands!

Microwave Conversion Instructions: Note: Reduce cherries to 3 cups, Amaretto liqueur to 2 T., cloves to ⅛ tsp. and sugar to 2 cups. Combine all ingredients except sugar in 8-cup *(2L)* bowl. Cook on High 5 to 6 minutes until it reaches a rolling boil. Stir in sugar. Bring mixture back to a boil and boil for exactly 2 minutes. Complete as directed above.

Raspberry Plum Butter

YIELD: 4 Pints
TOTAL CALORIES: 5000
CALORIES PER TABLESPOON: 40
CARBOHYDRATES: 10g
PREPARING: 25 Minutes
COOKING: 1½ Hours

In the depth of winter, to taste last summer's conserve on warm toast is reassurance enough that spring will come again.

4 lbs. *(1.8kg)* **plums, quartered and pitted**
2 pkgs. (10 oz. each) *(285g each)* **frozen raspberries or fresh when available**
2 cups *(475ml)* **water**
5 cups *(1kg)* **sugar**
¼ cup *(60ml)* **fresh lemon juice**

Combine plums, raspberries and their juice, and water in heavy 10-qt. *(10L)* kettle. Bring mixture to boil. Reduce heat and cook, stirring, until fruit is tender. Remove contents of kettle and puree in blender or food processor. Put puree back into kettle and add all remaining ingredients. Cook over low heat until all sugar is dissolved. Increase heat and cook, stirring constantly, until butter is thick and glossy, about 45 minutes to 1 hour. It is ready when it sheets from a spoon. Place butter in hot sterilized jars and seal.

Edith Bruce, Evanston, IL

Microwave Conversion Instructions: Note: Cut recipe in half. Cut plums into small pieces and combine with remaining ingredients in 4-qt. *(4L)* casserole. Cook on High, covered, 5 to 7 minutes or until mixture comes to a boil, stirring several times. Puree contents of casserole in blender or food processor. Return to oven and cook on High another 5 to 7 minutes. Stir and check for sheeting. Continue cooking on High until sheeting occurs. Mixture will thicken during standing time.

Lemon Chess Tart

This tasty lemon tart has been handed down through four generations.

YIELD: 6 Servings
CALORIES PER SERVING: 334
CARBOHYDRATES: 48g
PROTEIN: 4g
FAT: 14g
PREPARING: 30 Minutes
BAKING: 1 Hour
FREEZING: No

Thoroughly mix together egg yolks and sugar until light and pale in color. Add milk, butter, cornstarch, lemon juice and lemon rind.

Beat egg whites until stiff. Fold whites into lemon mixture. Place filling in unbaked tart shell.

Bake in preheated 300° oven 60 minutes. Cool. When completely cool, sprinkle top with confectioners' sugar.

Ann Houston Feenstra, Houston, TX

2 eggs, separated
1¼ cups *(250g)* sugar
¼ cup *(60ml)* whole milk
2 T. *(30g)* butter, melted and cooled to lukewarm
¼ tsp. cornstarch
1 large lemon, juice and grated rind
1 9-inch *(22.5cm)* tart or quiche pan with removable bottom lined with cream cheese pastry or Pie Crust dough (page 198) or Rich Tart Pastry (page 196)
Confectioners' sugar

Cider Apple Pie

This is a recipe that has been passed down through generations of the Hooker, Butler and Clark families. These families have been in Connecticut and Massachusetts since the elder William Brewster was the minister on the Mayflower and Thomas Hooker helped in the founding of Hartford.

YIELD: 8 Servings
TOTAL CALORIES: 2896
CALORIES PER SERVING: 362
CARBOHYDRATES: 57g
PROTEIN: 2g
FAT: 14g
PREPARING: 30-40 Minutes
BAKING: 25 Minutes

Roll out half of dough and line deep 8-inch *(20cm)* pie pan.

Simmer apples in cider until soft and plump, 20 to 25 minutes. Add sugar and spices; mix well and cook about 10 minutes longer. By then, apples will have absorbed most of liquid. Pour into pie shell. Dot with pieces of butter. Roll out remaining dough; cut into strips. Place strips over apples to form a woven lattice.

Bake in preheated 400° oven 25 to 30 minutes, until golden brown.

Janet Clark, West Hartford, CT

Nutritional Notes: Dried fruits are rich in natural sugar and provide all the vitamins and minerals of their fresh counterpart. The two methods of removing moisture from fresh fruit are sun-drying and heat evaporation. The heat evaporation process generally includes the use of sulfur dioxide, though some commercial "sun-dried" methods also include this chemical. This is particularly true of "Golden Raisins" and other bright or light colored fruits. Look for this information on the package label.

Microwave Conversion Instructions: Note: Reduce cider to 2 cups and use a prebaked (page 196) pie crust. Place apples and cider in casserole. Cook, covered, on High 10 to 12 minutes until soft and plump. Add sugar and spices; mix well. Cook 4 to 5 minutes or until apples have absorbed most of the juice. Pour into baked pie shell. Dot with butter. Cook on High 9 to 12 minutes. To form a lattice: Cut out lattice strips and place on sheet of waxed paper. Cook 4½ to 5 minutes on High. Cool. Remove from waxed paper and place on pie before baking.

Dough for 2 crust 9-inch Pie Crust (page 198)

½ lb. *(225g)* dried apples
3 cups *(720ml)* apple cider
½ cup *(100g)* sugar
½ tsp. cinnamon
¼ tsp. nutmeg
2 T. *(30g)* butter

**Terrine of Sole and Scallops
with Watercress and
Salmon**
p. 58

**Cold Cucumber, Tomato
and Avocado Soup**
p. 60

Stuffed Eggs à la Parisienne　　　**Chilled Marinated Steak**
p. 257　　　　　　　　　　　　　　　p. 60

Couscous Salad
p. 367

Cold Beets in Mustard Sauce　　　**Snow Pea Salad**
p. 61　　　　　　　　　　　　　　　p. 61

Tomato Bread　　　**Sweet Muenster Bread**
p. 62　　　　　　　　　　p. 240

Lime Pickles
p. 62

Individual Fresh Fruit Tartlets

Blueberry　　　**Cherry**
p. 391　　　　　p. 391

Strawberry
p. 390

Rhubarb　　　**Grape**
p. 391　　　　p. 391

or

Lindy's Cheesecake
p. 63

Charter Oak Summer Picnic

A tribute to summer's bounty, served on wicker trays and baskets under the spreading limbs of a great Connecticut oak.

As their new colony would be in the wilderness many miles west of the settlements of Boston and Plymouth, Thomas Hooker and his Puritan congregation had received from the New England agent of the Earl of Warwick authority to issue decrees and make their own laws. The first General Court of Connecticut was established in Hartford in 1638. Soon after this, Connecticut's first constitution, the Fundamental Orders, was adopted by the Court. However, the legal basis of the fledgling government was seriously threatened when Oliver Cromwell, the Puritan Protector of England, died and Charles II ascended the throne.

In contrast to Connecticut's unique self-government, most American colonies were ruled by an appointed Royal Governor. Fearing this outcome, the Connecticut colonists selected John Winthrop, Jr. to travel to England and procure a coveted Royal Charter to insure self-rule. Historians seem baffled by Winthrop's success, for the Puritans were in disfavor in royal circles. Yet the new charter not only contained a solid legal basis for self-government, it increased the geographical area of the colony. Connecticut would henceforth be bounded on the east by Narragansett Bay; its western boundary would be the Pacific Ocean!

In 1685 James II followed Charles to the throne. He commissioned Sir Edmund Andros to suspend all Royal Charters and consolidate the New England colonies under his rule as Royal Governor. Andros traveled to Hartford with a company of seventy-five men to seize the charter from Connecticut, the only colony which had not surrendered to his authority. The charter was kept in a wooden box in view of all who came before the Assembly. After many hours of heated debate with the colonists, Andros demanded the charter. At the last moment, however, the candles went out and the assembly room was plunged into darkness.

There are a number of theories to explain the sudden darkness. Some say a gust of wind rushed through an open window; others suggest a colonist feigning illness fell over the candles! Whatever the cause, it took only a moment to relight them, but in that moment the charter had disappeared. No amount of searching on the part of Andros or his soldiers could produce the valuable document. Many months later it was learned that the charter had been whisked away and hidden by Captain Joseph Wadsworth in an old oak tree on the nearby Wyllys' estate.

According to legend, the tree was once known as the Sachem's tree, a sacred oak where the Indians gathered to hold their councils. Each spring when the tree's budding leaves were "as large as a squirrel's ears", it was time for the planting of crops. The tree, which purportedly stood for 1,000 years, became known to the settlers as the Charter Oak.

Though the colonists still lost control of their colony to Andros, he was recalled to England within two years, and the new Connecticut government was reestablished according to the Royal Charter. The charter also became a model for many elements of the U.S. Constitution composed in Philadelphia. The Charter Oak, until it was destroyed by a storm in August of 1856, was a living symbol of the independence and resourcefulness of the Connecticut colony. Today wood from the Charter Oak frames the original Royal Charter which hangs in Memorial Hall between the Connecticut State Library and the Supreme Court in Hartford.

The setting for the Charter Oak, the Wyllys' estate located on the banks of the Little River, was considered one of the most beautiful estates in New England. For generations on warm summer afternoons, friends and relatives would gather on the spacious grounds and picnic under the spreading limbs of the proud oak. Though our own picnic menu is contemporary, it is inspired by the romantic story and setting of the Charter Oak.

Terrine of Sole and Scallops with Watercress and Salmon

YIELD: 8-10 Servings
CALORIES PER SERVING: 424
CARBOHYDRATES: 8g
PROTEIN: 17g
FAT: 36g
CHOLESTEROL: High
SODIUM: High
PREPARING: 40 Minutes
BAKING: 1½ Hours
COOLING: 3 Hours
FREEZING: Yes

A fish terrine, delightful to behold, layered with pink salmon and delicate green watercress. Serve it hot as a first course or luncheon dish, or take it cold, in its terrine, on a picnic.

1 large bunch fresh watercress, or ½ lb. (225g) spinach, leaves only, washed and minced
4-5 scallions, white and light green parts, minced
2 T. (30g) butter
1½ lbs. (675g) very fresh sole or flounder fillets cut in 2-inch (5cm) pieces
½ lb. (225g) very fresh sea or bay scallops, washed and drained
2 cups (240g) fresh breadcrumbs, lightly packed
2 eggs
2-3 cups (475-710ml) heavy cream
¼ cup (60ml) fresh lemon juice
⅛ tsp. freshly grated nutmeg
1 T. salt
⅛ tsp. freshly ground white pepper
¼ lb. (115g) good quality lightly smoked salmon or nova lox

SOUR CREAM SAUCE:

Reserved cooking liquid
1 cup (225g) sour cream or Creme Fraiche (page 200)
½ cup (120ml) heavy cream
1 tsp. prepared horseradish
¼ tsp. Dijon mustard
Few drops fresh lemon juice
1 T. fresh dill, minced, or 1 tsp. dried dill
Salt
Freshly ground white pepper

Saute watercress or spinach with scallions in butter until soft. Set aside in small bowl.

In food processor, puree sole pieces with scallops. Add breadcrumbs, eggs, 2 cups cream, lemon juice, seasonings; puree 30 to 45 seconds. Scrape sides of work bowl with rubber spatula, process until smooth. Puree should hold a soft shape; add more cream in small amounts until desired consistency is reached. (If work bowl is small, make puree in two batches, halving ingredients for each batch; beat together in large mixing bowl.)

Layer a 6-cup (1½L), 8½ × 4½ × 2½-inch (21.5 × 11.5 × 6.5cm) loaf pan or terrine with about 1 cup puree. Smooth top with back of spoon dipped in cold water.

Mix some of puree into the reserved watercress, using twice as much puree as watercress. Spread this mixture over puree in terrine, smooth top. Spread another layer of plain puree in terrine, again smoothing top. Remove about 1 cup puree from work bowl; set aside.

Add salmon to processor work bowl. Puree until smooth; spread evenly in terrine. Layer reserved plain puree over all. Cover terrine tightly with buttered waxed paper, then aluminum foil.

Place terrine in a larger baking pan. Pour hot water into baking pan to come half way up sides of terrine. Place in preheated 350° oven. Bake 1½ hours or to 160° on meat thermometer inserted in center of terrine. Top should be springy, sides should easily come away from pan.

To serve hot: Leave terrine in pan of water in turned-off oven with door ajar until serving time. Cut slices directly from terrine. Serve with melted butter, or with Beurre Blanc (page 155) or Hollandaise (page 191).

To serve cold: Remove terrine from oven and let cool. Drain off accumulated cooking liquid and reserve for sauce. When cool, cover with plastic wrap; refrigerate. Cut slices directly from terrine and serve with sauce.

SOUR CREAM SAUCE: If cooking liquid measures more than 4 T., reduce it to that amount by boiling over high heat in small saucepan. Transfer to small mixing bowl; add remaining ingredients, mix well. To serve, spoon sauce onto each serving dish. Place chilled slice of terrine gently on top.

Patricia K. Anathan, Simsbury, CT

Variations, Advance Preparation, and Serving Suggestions:
To serve unmolded, line terrine with buttered waxed paper before baking. Baked terrine keeps several days in refrigerator. Can be frozen, but texture will become slightly grainy. Sauce does not freeze well, but keeps several days in refrigerator. If using fresh dill, mix into sauce no more than 3 or 4 hours before serving.

Nutritional Notes: Sour cream contains 57 calories per 1 oz.; sour half & half, 43 calories; imitation sour cream, 35 calories; and plain lowfat yogurt, 20 calories. Any of the latter can be substituted in whole or in part for sour cream according to individual taste. The advantage of substituting lowfat yogurt is that it not only reduces calories and fat appreciably, but it brings more protein and calcium to the dish.

Wine Suggestion: California Pinot Chardonnay, full white; serve chilled.

Microwave Conversion Instructions: Note: Eliminate butter and reduce salt to 1½ tsp. Prepare a 9 × 5-inch *(22.5 × 12.5cm)* glass loaf dish by cutting waxed paper strips to run in both directions being careful to have enough waxed paper to fold over loaf when assembled. Place watercress or spinach with scallions in a covered glass casserole; cook on High 5 minutes. Drain thoroughly. Prepare remaining ingredients as indicated being careful to eliminate any unnecessary liquids. Cover terrine loosely with buttered waxed paper; cook on High 10 minutes, rotating dish ¼ turn 2 times. Cook on Medium (50%) 20 to 25 minutes rotating dish ¼ turn every 5 minutes. Check for doneness — top will be springy and sides will pull away. Cool as indicated; leave terrine in loaf dish overnight. *Sauce:* Prepare as indicated. If less than 4 T. of cooking liquid remain, onion broth may be substituted. Note: If corners appear to be overcooking, shield them with small pieces of aluminum foil if approved by your oven manufacturer.

YIELD: 8 Servings
TOTAL CALORIES: 2160
CALORIES PER SERVING: 270
CARBOHYDRATES: 11g
PROTEIN: 4g
FAT: 23g
CHOLESTEROL: High
SODIUM: High
PREPARING: 20 Minutes
COOKING: 25 Minutes
CHILLING: 2-3 Hours
FREEZING: Yes

¼ cup *(60g)* butter
1 cup *(150g)* chopped onion
¼ cup *(30g)* flour
4 cups *(400g)* garden fresh tomatoes,
　peeled and cubed
4 cups *(800g)* cucumbers, peeled and
　cubed
Salt
Freshly ground pepper
4 cups *(950ml)* chicken stock
1 ripe avocado
1 cup *(240ml)* heavy cream

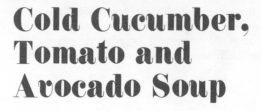

Cold Cucumber, Tomato and Avocado Soup

Do you know how to ripen an avocado? Store it in a brown paper bag at room temperature. It will ripen in 2 to 3 days.

In large skillet, melt butter; add onion. Cook, stirring until onion is soft. Sprinkle in flour; mix. Add tomatoes, stirring rapidly with whisk. Add cucumbers, salt, pepper and stock. Simmer 25 minutes.

In small batches, puree in food processor or blender; strain; chill. It may be made in advance up to this point and refrigerated or frozen.

Several hours before serving, peel and chop avocado; add to soup. Stir in cream; chill.

Kathryn K. Masius, West Hartford, CT

Nutritional Notes: Our tester felt soup was delicious even with cream omitted. In doing so, calories are decreased by 110 per serving and fat/cholesterol are also lowered.

Microwave Conversion Instructions: In a 4-qt. *(4L)* casserole, combine onion and butter. Cook, uncovered, on High 3 to 4 minutes, until onion is soft. Stir in flour until dissolved, then add tomatoes, stirring rapidly with whisk. Add cucumbers, salt, pepper and *heated* stock. Cook, covered, on High 20 minutes. Follow above directions for completion.

YIELD: Marinade for 3 Lb. Steak
CHOLESTEROL: High
SODIUM: High
PREPARING: 5 Minutes
BROILING: 15-20 Minutes
CHILLING: Overnight Minimum

Chilled Marinated Steak

Easy elegance for a hot summer day.

MARINADE:
1 large clove garlic, crushed
1 tsp. salt
½ tsp. freshly ground pepper
½ tsp. dry mustard
1½ T. blue cheese
2 tsp. instant coffee
2 T. *(30ml)* dry vermouth
½ cup *(120ml)* olive oil

Sirloin steak up to 3 lbs. *(1350g)*, cut
　2 inches *(5cm)* thick, trimmed

Combine marinade ingredients and blend with whisk until you have a smooth paste. Rub marinade on both sides of steak and marinate at room temperature several hours, turning occasionally. Broil steak or grill outside for best flavor on each side to rare. Use any remaining marinade to brush on meat while grilling. Let cool at room temperature for 30 minutes. Wrap in heavy foil and refrigerate overnight for more pronounced flavor. Slice thinly and serve.

Amy W. Hamilton, Avon, CT

Wine Suggestion: French Valbon Rouge, dry red; serve at room temperature.

Nutritional Notes: Nutritional analysis has been omitted because figures are dependent upon size of steak. It is estimated that a slice of broiled sirloin, 4½ oz. *(130g)*, is equal to 260 calories, 32g protein and 14g fat.

Cold Beets
in Mustard Sauce

YIELD: 6-8 Servings
CALORIES PER SERVING: 113
CARBOHYDRATES: 7g
PROTEIN: 1g
FAT: 9g
PREPARING: 45 Minutes
CHILLING: 4 Hours Minimum
COOKING: 30 Minutes

In a small bowl combine vinegar, lemon juice, and sugar; when sugar has dissolved, add mustard and olive oil; whisk until dressing is well blended and creamy; blend in parsley and dill.

Pour dressing over beets; season with salt and pepper. Cover and refrigerate at least 4 hours prior to serving.

Garnish with chopped egg and dill.

Sarah Seymour, West Hartford, CT

Nutritional Notes: For optimum red color, cook beets whole and unpeeled. If steaming, sliced beets should be steamed for a maximum of 6 to 8 minutes.

1 T. white cider vinegar
2 T. *(30ml)* fresh lemon juice
2 tsp. sugar
¼ cup *(60g)* Dijon mustard
⅓ cup *(80ml)* olive oil
1 T. finely chopped fresh parsley
3 T. finely chopped fresh dill
4 cups *(900g)* fresh beets, cooked, drained, and cut into fine julienne strips
Salt
Freshly ground pepper
2 hard-cooked eggs, finely chopped
Sprigs of fresh dill

Snow
Pea Salad

YIELD: 6 Servings
TOTAL CALORIES: 972
CALORIES PER SERVING: 162
CARBOHYDRATES: 6g
PROTEIN: 3g
FAT: 14g
PREPARING: 30 Minutes
CHILLING: Up to 24 Hours
COOKING: 2 Minutes

This colorful salad has no limits. Its versatility permits you to include it at a brunch, a buffet, or a gourmet picnic. Except when sweet red bell peppers leave the market for a short time, this salad is for all seasons.

Remove strings from peas. Blanch peas 1½ to 2 minutes, depending on desired crispness. Immediately place under cold running water to stop cooking. Drain well. Slice each snow pea in half on diagonal. Halve pepper lengthwise, cut in thin strips; cut each strip in half. Combine oil, vinegar, lemon juice, garlic, sugar and salt; mix well. Combine snow peas, mushrooms and pepper. Pour dressing over salad and gently toss to coat vegetables. Refrigerate up to 24 hours in glass serving bowl. Just before serving, mix lightly and sprinkle sesame seeds over salad.

Bernice Kuzma, West Hartford, CT

½ lb. *(225g)* fresh snow peas or sugar snap peas
1 large sweet red bell pepper
⅓ cup *(80ml)* salad oil
2 T. *(30ml)* white wine vinegar
1 T. *(15ml)* fresh lemon juice
1 clove garlic, minced finely or ⅛ tsp. garlic powder
1 T. sugar
½ tsp. salt
½ lb. *(225g)* fresh mushrooms, very thinly sliced
2 T. *(15g)* sesame seeds, toasted in skillet until lightly golden

YIELD: 7 Pints
TOTAL CALORIES: 3209
CALORIES PER CHUNK: 15
CARBOHYDRATES: 4g
PREPARING: 45 Minutes
STANDING: 2 Days
COOKING: 45 Minutes

Lime Pickles

Do not be surprised at the use of ordinary garden lime; these are delicious semi-sweet pickles.

2 cups *(850g)* **lime powder, ordinary garden variety**
2 gallons *(7.5L)* **water**
7 lbs. *(3.2kg)* **cucumbers,** *unpeeled* **and cut into 1-inch** *(2.5cm)* **chunks**

SYRUP:

2 qts. *(2L)* **cider vinegar**
5 lbs. *(2.25kg)* **sugar**
1 tsp. celery seed
1 T. pickling spice
1 T. salt

Combine lime powder and water, stirring until dissolved. Soak cucumbers in lime water 24 hours, stirring frequently. Drain well; place in crock. Cover with cold water for 4 hours; drain well.

SYRUP: In saucepan, combine ingredients for syrup; gently heat but *do not boil.* Pour syrup over cucumbers; let stand 12 hours, stirring often.

Place in kettle and heat thoroughly but *do not boil.* Place in jars. Seal and store in dry, cool place. Refrigerate after opening.

Marion Brennwald, Avon, CT

YIELD: 1 Loaf
TOTAL CALORIES: 2652
CARBOHYDRATES: 430g
PROTEIN: 62g
FAT: 76g
SODIUM: High
PREPARING: 20 Minutes
BAKING: 1-1¼ Hours

Tomato Bread

Excellent for buffets and picnics. Delightful served in the summer spread with cream cheese and watercress.

1⅓ cups *(320ml)* **milk, scalded**
⅔ cup *(75g)* **Grape Nuts**
¼ cup *(60g)* **butter, melted**
2 eggs, beaten
1 cup *(100g)* **chopped and peeled tomatoes**
2¼ cups *(250g)* **flour**
¾ cup *(150g)* **sugar**
1 T. baking powder
1½ tsp. salt

Pour scalded milk over Grape Nuts; cool.

Stir in melted butter and eggs; add tomatoes and stir carefully. Add dry ingredients; stir just until moist. Pour into buttered and floured 9 × 5 × 3-inch *(22.5 × 12.5 × 7.5cm)* loaf pan.

Bake in preheated 375° oven for 1 to 1¼ hours. Cool on wire rack. When completely cooled, wrap in plastic wrap and refrigerate or freeze.

Nancy McKinney, Glastonbury, CT

Nutritional Notes: Calories, sodium, and saturated fat can be decreased somewhat by using skim or lowfat milk, decreasing salt, and by using unsalted polyunsaturated margarine. The fortified cereal included adds a small amount of fiber, in addition to vitamins and minerals.

Microwave Conversion Instructions: Note: Decrease milk to ¾ cup, increase butter to ½ cup, decrease salt to ¾ tsp., and add ¼ cup fine graham cracker crumbs.

Scald milk by cooking 1½ to 2 minutes on High in 2 cup glass measuring cup. Do not boil. Pour over grape nuts and cool.

Melt butter in glass mixing bowl. To be sure unnecessary liquid will not be added to batter, use only tomato pulp. Combine ingredients as for conventional recipe. Pour batter into tube pan, which has been buttered and lightly dusted with graham cracker crumbs. (Crumbs will improve appearance of finished product.) Cook on Medium (50%) 10 minutes, turning pan ¼ turn every 2 to 3 minutes. Cook on High 2 minutes or until top springs back lightly when touched.

Lindy's Cheesecake

When Lindy's restaurant in Manhattan closed in 1969, it was the "assumed" end of a legend in many ways. The restaurant was fabled for many dishes, but especially for its cheesecakes. The owner, Leo Lindermann, would not part with the recipe. But Kay Pellizari's mother obtained this recipe from a chef at Lindy's 30 years ago!

YIELD: 12-15 Servings
TOTAL CALORIES: 7440
CALORIES PER SERVING: 496
CARBOHYDRATES: 33g
PROTEIN: 10g
FAT: 36g
CHOLESTEROL: High
PREPARING: 50 Minutes
BAKING: 1 Hour 20 Minutes
CHILLING: Overnight
FREEZING: Yes

SHORTBREAD CRUST: Combine all ingredients; mix with fingertips or in food processor. Shape approximately ⅔ of dough into a ball. Place ball on bottom of a buttered 10-inch (25cm) springform pan (sides removed). Cover ball with waxed paper; roll out to fit bottom of pan. Place pan on bottom rack of preheated 400° oven; bake 8 to 10 minutes, until light golden. Remove from oven; let cool on rack. Attach sides of springform pan to bottom.

Shape remaining ⅓ dough into another ball. Roll out, cut into 3 strips. Line sides of pan, overlapping dough. Make sure sides meet bottom all the way around.

FILLING: In bowl of electric mixer or in food processor blend cream cheese, sugar, flour, lemon and orange rinds and vanilla. Beat in eggs and yolks, one at a time, beating well after each addition. Add heavy cream, beat well. Pour into crust-lined springform pan. Place on middle rack of preheated 450° oven; bake 10 minutes. Lower heat to 250°; bake 60 minutes. Remove pan from oven; let cool on rack 2 hours. Then chill overnight in refrigerator.

OPTIONAL GLAZES:

PINEAPPLE: Combine all ingredients in medium saucepan. Simmer until glaze is thick and clear, stirring frequently. Let cool. Spread over cooled cake in springform pan. Chill in refrigerator 10 to 12 hours.

STRAWBERRY: Crush about 1 cup strawberries; place in saucepan with sugar, water, cornstarch and salt. Simmer 2 to 3 minutes, stirring constantly. Add butter, stir well. Let cool slightly. Decorate top of cheesecake with remaining strawberries; spoon glaze over them. Chill in refrigerator several hours.

LEMON: Combine sugar, cornstarch and salt in medium saucepan. Mix together water, lemon juice and egg yolk. Add to saucepan. Simmer several minutes, stirring constantly, until mixture is thick and clear. Add butter and lemon rind, stir well. Let cool slightly. Spread over cheesecake. Chill in refrigerator at least several hours or overnight.

Kay Pellizari, Glastonbury, CT

Variations, Advance Preparation, and Serving Suggestions:
Cheesecake, without glaze, can be made several days in advance and refrigerated. It will also freeze well, thoroughly wrapped, for up to a month.

Nutritional Notes: Glazes not included in nutritional analysis.

SHORTBREAD CRUST:

1 cup (115g) sifted flour
¼ cup (50g) sugar
1 tsp. freshly grated lemon rind
½ tsp. pure vanilla extract
1 egg yolk
¼ cup (60g) butter, softened

FILLING:

5 pkgs. (8 oz. each) (1135g) cream cheese, softened
1¾ cup (350g) sugar
3 T. (20g) flour
2 tsp. freshly grated lemon rind
2 tsp. freshly grated orange rind
½ tsp. pure vanilla extract
5 eggs plus 2 egg yolks
¼ cup (60ml) heavy cream

OPTIONAL GLAZES:

PINEAPPLE:

2 T. (25g) sugar
4 tsp. cornstarch
2 cans (8¼ oz. each) (465g) crushed pineapple, undrained
2 T. (30ml) lemon juice

STRAWBERRY:

1 qt. (600g) fresh stawberries, washed and hulled
¾ cup (150g) sugar
¼ cup (60ml) water
1½ T. cornstarch
⅛ tsp. salt
1 tsp. butter

LEMON:

½ cup (100g) sugar
1½ T. cornstarch
¼ tsp. salt
¾ cup (180ml) water
⅓ cup (80ml) freshly squeezed lemon juice
1 egg yolk
1 T. butter
1 tsp. freshly grated lemon rind

Clam Bloody Marys

Peach Blossom   or   **Sherman Sunrise**
p. 66   p. 67

Crudités and Dipping Sauce
p. 208

Pickled Shrimp   **Cocktail Mussels**
p. 66   *(Moules Ravigote)*
                                       p. 67

Corn Oyster Chowder   or   **Clam and Spinach Soup**
p. 34   p. 68

**Whole Poached Glazed
Salmon**

**Poached Scallops
with
Green Sauce**   **Shellfish Mold**
p. 69   p. 334

**Baked Rice with
Tomatoes and Cheese**   **Steamed Carrots**
p. 350

Snow Pea Salad   **Bibb Lettuce and Watercress
Lemon Dijon Dressing**
p. 61   p. 148

Hot Herb Bread

**Fresh Fruit Terrine
with
Raspberry Sauce
and
Crème Anglaise**
p. 70

or

Apricot Chocolate Torte
p. 71

Mystic Seaport Seafood Salute

A fabulous fish and shellfish festival celebrating the treasures of the sea.

Early settlers, who found coastal Connecticut rocky and difficult to farm, soon turned to the sea for sustenance. By the end of the 17th century, coastal shopkeepers and sea captains had established lucrative businesses by exchanging inland farm surplus for Eastern spices and myriad other items such as lace, tea and cord not produced in the colonies. There was an active trade with the West Indies which included exchanging agricultural products for salt, sugar and fruits.

During these years shipbuilding began to flourish. Substantial stands of New England spruce, oak and pine led to the emergence of this industry in the coastal towns of Branford, Guilford and New Haven. By the mid-1800s the village of Mystic had become the center of Connecticut's shipbuilding.

A significant number of Mystic ships were constructed for the thriving whaling industry. Whaling expeditions, some lasting as long as two or three years, could reap great profits for investors from the sale of whale oil, spermaceti and whale bone. The adventurous Yankee sailors endured often brutal seagoing conditions for the promise of a small percentage of the final profit.

Today in Mystic Seaport a visitor can reenter the 19th century shipyard and waterfront whaling community. Situated on a forty-acre site, the period buildings house contemporary artisans engaged in the early arts of mast carving, sailmaking, cooping and printing. One can even board the Charles W. Morgan, built in 1841, the last of the wooden whaling ships. On board this "floating time machine" the visitor has a special opportunity to appreciate the rigorous lifestyle of the captain, crew and particulary the cook. His awesome task was to prepare daily meals for over forty men on one tiny iron stove in a galley only a few feet square.

The style of cooking in coastal Connecticut was heavily influenced by the treasures brought home from the sea. These included not only fish and shellfish, but also fragrant ginger and cinnamon brought from the Orient, and tropical fruits from the southern islands. During the later colonization of New England, nearly every ship carried cows to supply milk for the children. The introduction of cow's milk to the coastal towns provided butter and cheese, unknown to the Indians, and also provided a significant ingredient for many New England recipes. Early housewives, cooking in a single pot over an open hearth fire, turned delicate English soups into whole, nourishing meals called "chowder" with the addition of milk, fish and vegetables.

As Mystic developed into a productive whaling and shipping community, there were also developments in the style of cooking. In the earliest indoor fireplaces pots and kettles hung over the fire on pot hooks attached to a heavy "lugstick" made of green wood. A housewife had to replace this thick stick frequently lest it dry out, break and spill her dinner into the fire. However, in the early 18th century the greatly improved "swinging crane" was introduced. This was composed of two metal bars which were hinged inside the fireplace and could swing the kettle off the fire. Now the housewife could season or serve her meal without scorching her apron or inhaling soot and smoke.

Some fifty years later, in the most "modern" kitchens, one might find the unique invention of American born Benjamin Thompson, later known as Count Rumford. He developed the first cookstoves on the principle that the most efficient cooking unit should contain heat in as small a space as possible. His small box-like stove, which could be moved, and a special saucepan, which fitted over the fire, were the beginnings of our contemporary stoves.

Strolling along the waterfront and entering the homes and businesses of Mystic Seaport, a visitor can step back in time and recognize the early stages of many facets of our lives today. Not the least important legacy from this part of our past are treasured recipes from the sea-faring community. These have inspired this contemporary Mystic Seaport Salute to Connecticut's abundant and varied supply of seafood.

YIELD: 5 Servings
CALORIES PER SERVING: 232
CARBOHYDRATES: 38g
PREPARING: 5 Minutes
CHILLING: 3 Hours

Peach Blo3som

A delightful brunch drink.

1 can (1 lb.) *(450g)* **peaches in heavy syrup**
1 can (6 oz.) *(180ml)* **frozen lemonade concentrate**
6 oz. *(180ml)* **Seven-Up**
6 oz. *(180ml)* **vodka**

Several hours before serving, remove peaches and juice from can and freeze in plastic container with cover from which they can be easily removed. Immediately before serving, place all ingredients in blender; mix until just slushy. Serve in stemmed glasses.

Judy Kunisch, West Hartford, CT

YIELD: 2 Quarts
TOTAL CALORIES: 3192
CARBOHYDRATES: 31g
PROTEIN: 227g
FAT: 240g
CHOLESTEROL: High
SODIUM: High
PREPARING: 30 Minutes
CHILLING: 24 Hours
FREEZING: No

Pickled Shrimp

An unusual hors d'oeuvre, easy and impressive to serve.

2 lbs. *(900g)* **medium-sized raw shrimp, (approx. 21-25 per lb.)**
1 large **onion,** ¼-inch *(½cm)* **slices, separated into rings**
2 **lemons,** ⅛-inch *(3mm)* **thick slices**
1 1-inch *(2.5cm)* **piece fresh ginger, peeled, julienned**
¼ cup **fresh parsley, minced**
4 small **bay leaves**
2 cups *(475ml)* **cider vinegar**
2 T. **mixed pickling spice**
½ tsp. **dry mustard**
¼ tsp. **ground mace**
2 tsp. **salt**
½ cup *(120ml)* **olive oil, combined with** ½ cup *(120ml)* **vegetable oil**

Shell and devein shrimp, leaving tails on. To lightly salted boiling water add shrimp and boil briskly. Cook 3 minutes, or until shrimp turn pink and firm. Drain. Pat dry with paper towels. Place shrimp in deep bowl. Add onion, lemon, ginger and parsley. Toss together lightly and thoroughly. Divide mixture evenly between 2 wide-mouthed quart jars. Tuck 2 bay leaves down sides of each jar. In 1- to 1½-qt. *(1-1.5L)* enamel or stainless steel saucepan, combine and bring to boil over high heat, vinegar, pickling spice, mustard, mace and salt. Stir until mustard and salt dissolve completely. At once pour by the tablespoon hot spiced liquid over shrimp mixture. Allow each spoonful to flow completely through to the bottom of the jars before adding more.

To make the jars airtight place a tablespoon upside down in the top of each jar and very slowly pour the oil over the back of the spoon, letting it trickle off onto the top of the shrimp. Cover the jars with their lids and chill for at least 24 hours before serving. When ready to serve, place partially drained shrimp in a crystal bowl; provide toothpicks.

Nancy Webster Woodworth, West Hartford, CT

Variations, Advance Preparation, and Serving Suggestions: Tightly covered and refrigerated, the shrimp can safely be kept for approximately 1 month.

Nutritional Notes: Actual calories consumed per serving will depend on amount of marinade absorbed by shrimp. 1 medium unmarinated raw shrimp contains 17 to 20 calories.

Wine Suggestion: California Gewurztraminer, spicy white; serve chilled.

Sherman Sunrise

A somewhat sweet drink that would be ideal for a hot summer's eve.

YIELD: 2 Servings
CALORIES PER SERVING: 107
CARBOHYDRATES: 7g
PREPARING: 4-5 Minutes

Mix together vodka, apricot brandy, grapefruit juice and lemon juice. Add grenadine syrup to add color and sweetness, the degree of sweetness depending upon the amount of syrup used.

Serve on the rocks.

Brenda Larsen, North Granby, CT

2 T. *(30ml)* vodka
1 T. *(15ml)* apricot brandy
½ cup *(120ml)* grapefruit juice
2 T. *(30ml)* freshly squeezed lemon juice
Grenadine syrup

Moules Ravigote

COLD MUSSEL SALAD IN CAPER SHALLOT MAYONNAISE

Ravigote sauce is one of the most important of the classical French sauces. The warm version begins with a veloute sauce whereas the cold is really a spicy mayonnaise.

YIELD: 6 First Course Servings
TOTAL CALORIES: 2100
CALORIES PER SERVING: 350
CARBOHYDRATES: 14g
PROTEIN: 15g
FAT: 26g
CHOLESTEROL: High
PREPARING: 30 Minutes
CHILLING: 3 Hours Minimum
COOKING: 3 Minutes

Place mussels in large, flat roasting pan with cover. *Do Not Add Any Liquid.* Cover pan; place over very high heat 3 minutes, tossing mussels once during cooking period. Remove mussels from pan immediately to stop further cooking; discard any unopened shells. Reserve accumulated liquid from pan. When cool enough to handle, gently remove mussels from shells. Save deeper halves of shells, if you plan to serve individual cocktail mussels.

Refrigerate mussels in their reserved cooking liquid for several hours or overnight. Drain mussels; pat completely dry with paper toweling.

SHALLOT MAYONNAISE: In small saucepan, combine shallots, vinegar, wine and tarragon. Cook until moisture has completely evaporated. Add shallot mixture, capers, parsley and chives to mayonnaise. Season with salt, pepper and Dijon mustard.

Add just enough shallot mayonnaise to mussels to lightly coat them. Toss *very gently* as mussels are fragile. Refrigerate until serving time. Serve in lettuce cups.

Jared I. Edwards, West Hartford, CT

Variations, Advance Preparation, and Serving Suggestions:
For cocktail mussels: Refrigerate mussels in cooking liquid; drain. Fill deeper halves of shells with shallot mayonnaise; half submerge a chilled mussel in each. Top with dill, tarragon or parsley leaf. Refrigerate until ready to serve. (1 cup shallot mayonnaise will fill approximately 3 dozen medium mussel shells.) The shallot mayonnaise can be made into Remoulade Sauce by adding ½ tsp. finely minced garlic and 1 hard-cooked egg, chopped.

6 lbs. *(2700g)* fresh mussels, thoroughly scrubbed under cold running water.

SHALLOT MAYONNAISE:
3 T. *(30g)* chopped shallots
¼ cup *(60ml)* tarragon wine vinegar
¼ cup *(60ml)* white wine
1 T. finely minced fresh tarragon or dill
1 T. small capers (if not small, chop them)
1 T. finely minced fresh parsley
1 T. fresh, chopped chives
1½ cups *(340g)* Homemade Mayonnaise (page 190), made with whole eggs
Salt
Freshly ground pepper
2 tsp. Dijon mustard

Lettuce cups

YIELD: 6-8 Servings
CALORIES PER SERVING: 349
CARBOHYDRATES: 8g
PROTEIN: 14g
FAT: 29g
CHOLESTEROL: High
SODIUM: High
PREPARING: 40 Minutes
COOKING: 20 Minutes

Clam and Spinach Soup

The spinach adds a touch of color to this nice variation of clam chowder.

3 dozen clams (cherrystone preferred)
¾-1 lb. (340-450g) fresh spinach, cleaned and stems removed
¼ lb. (115g) salt pork, cut into ½-inch cubes
1 cup (200g) onion, finely minced
1 clove garlic, finely minced
4 anchovy fillets, finely minced
½ cup (115g) unsalted sweet butter
2 T. (15g) flour
4 cups (950ml) chicken stock (2 cups of broth from cooking clams may be substituted for 2 cups of chicken stock)
1 cup (240ml) heavy cream
Salt
Freshly ground white pepper

Thoroughly wash clams. Put clams in a kettle and add cold water; cover and bring to a boil. Reduce heat to medium; cook until clams open, about 5 minutes. Cool until they can be handled.

Meanwhile, cook spinach until just wilted; drain and squeeze out moisture. Chop coarsely; set aside.

Heat salt pork in small skillet until it renders 1 T. fat, about 15 minutes. Discard pork solids. Saute onion and garlic in remaining fat, until soft; add anchovy; stir, set aside.

In large casserole, melt butter. Add flour; mix; cook 2 minutes, stirring. Add stock, whisking constantly. Add onion and anchovy mixture.

Coarsely chop clams. To the casserole, add clams, spinach, cream, salt and pepper to taste. Bring to a simmer and serve piping hot with a dot of butter on each serving. May cook a day ahead and gently reheat before serving.

Patricia K. Anathan, Simsbury, CT

Nutritional Notes: Unsalted broth can be used to decrease sodium. In addition, a portion or all the cream can be replaced by evaporated milk or evaporated skim milk. Squeezing spinach if not absolutely necessary, as in this recipe, is not recommended as valuable vitamins and minerals are also removed.

Microwave Conversion Instructions: Place 12 clams in pie plate. Cook on High, removing clams as soon as shells *begin* to open. Cooking beyond that point will make them tough and chewy. Repeat until all clams have been cooked, discarding any that do not open. Place cleaned spinach in casserole, adding 3 T. water. Cook, covered, on High 2 minutes or just until it begins to steam. Allow to cool; then chop coarsely. Place salt pork in 1-qt. *(1L)* glass measure. Cover with paper towel. Cook on High until it renders 1 T. fat. Discard pork solids. Add onion and garlic and cook on High 3 to 4 minutes or until soft; add anchovy. Stir and set aside. In large casserole, melt butter 1 minute on High. Stir in flour and cook on Medium (50%) 1 minute. Using a whisk, add *heated* stock, whisking until well blended. Add onion and anchovy mixture. Coarsely chop clams. Combine all ingredients in casserole. Cook on Medium (50%) until soup begins to simmer, about 2 to 3 minutes, stirring once.

Poached Scallops with Green Sauce

A most delicate and light dish.

YIELD: 4 Servings
TOTAL CALORIES: 1740
CALORIES PER SERVING: 435
CARBOHYDRATES: 10g
PROTEIN: 29g
FAT: 31g
CHOLESTEROL: High
SODIUM: High
PREPARING: 15 Minutes
COOKING: 20 Minutes
FREEZING: No

SCALLOPS: Place scallops, wine, mushrooms, salt in a large non-aluminum saucepan over medium heat. Bring almost to boil, stirring occasionally. Simmer gently until barely cooked. Drain scallops and mushrooms, reserving liquid. Cover scallops and mushrooms.

SAUCE: Return reserved liquid to saucepan; stir in watercress, spinach, herbs. Bring to full boil, stirring. Remove wilted greens with slotted spoon. Place in container of food processor or blender. Continue boiling liquid until it is reduced to about ¼ cup. Add to greens. Add egg yolks and cream. Blend until smooth. Add pepper. Slowly add oil, blending as for mayonnaise. The sauce should be the consistency of salad dressing.

Place some sauce (about ¼ cup (60ml)) on each individual serving plate. Divide scallops and mushrooms evenly among plates. Decorate with strips of tomato skin. Serve warm or at room temperature.

Patricia K. Anathan, Simsbury, CT

Variations, Advance Preparation, and Serving Suggestions:
Both scallops and sauce may be prepared early in the day and held at room temperature.

Nutritional Notes: When liquor or wine is brought to a boil in a recipe, the alcohol and calories are burned off, but the flavor remains.

Wine Suggestion: French Meursault, full white; serve chilled.

Microwave Conversion Instructions: *Scallops:* Place wine, mushrooms and salt in 3-qt. *(3L)* casserole. Cook on High 5 minutes. Stir in scallops. Cook, covered, on High 6 to 8 minutes, until just cooked. Do not overcook. Drain scallops and mushrooms, reserving liquid; set aside. *Sauce:* Return reserved liquid to casserole. Stir in watercress, spinach and herbs. Bring to a boil on High. Stir. Bring to a boil again. Remove wilted greens with slotted spoon; puree. Cook reserved liquid, uncovered, on High until reduced to ½ cup, about 5 to 7 minutes. Add to pureed greens. Complete as directed above.

SCALLOPS:
1½ lbs. *(675g)* fresh bay scallops
1 cup *(240ml)* dry white wine
1 tsp. salt
2 cups *(170g)* mushrooms, coarsely chopped, about 6 oz.

SAUCE: 2 Cups
Reserved poaching liquid
1 cup *(30g)* watercress leaves
2 cups *(65g)* spinach leaves
⅛ cup tarragon (or ½ tsp. dried) and/or mint leaves
2 egg yolks
2 T. *(30ml)* heavy cream
¼ tsp. freshly ground white pepper
1 cup *(240ml)* olive oil, preferably virgin
2-3 small strips tomato skin (optional)

YIELD: 10 Servings
TOTAL CALORIES: 7800
CALORIES PER SERVING: 780
CARBOHYDRATES: 76g
PROTEIN: 13g
FAT: 47g
CHOLESTEROL: High
PREPARING: 2 Hours
CHILLING: 6 Hours Minimum
FREEZING: No

Fresh Fruit Terrine with Two Sauces

The colorful drama and artistic presentation of this dessert make it perfect for any important dinner.

GENOISE:

5 eggs at room temperature
⅔ cup (135g) sugar
2 tsp. pure vanilla extract
Grated rind of 1 lemon or orange
1½ cups (170g) sifted cake flour
4 T. (60g) unsalted sweet butter, clarified

ALMOND CREAM: 3½ Cups

¾ cup (170g) unsalted sweet butter, at room temperature
1¼ cups (160g) confectioners' sugar
1½ cups (6 oz.) (170g) very finely ground blanched almonds
¼ tsp. almond extract
2 T. (30ml) Grand Marnier or Cointreau
1 cup (240ml) heavy cream

RASPBERRY SAUCE: 2 Cups

1½ cups (200g) fresh raspberries or 2 pkgs. (10 oz. each) (570g) frozen, thawed and drained
¼ cup (50g) superfine sugar
1 T. fresh lemon juice

CREME ANGLAISE: 2½ Cups
(page 200)

FRESH FRUITS:

24-30 small firm fresh strawberries
½ cup (75g) fresh blueberries
4 kiwi fruits, pared and sliced in half, vertically

GENOISE: Line with waxed paper, butter and flour 9 × 9 × 2-inch (22.5 × 22.5 × 5cm) or 9-inch (22.5cm) round cake pan. Set aside.

Place eggs, sugar, and flavoring in bowl. Set bowl over pan of almost simmering water and beat until mixture is foaming and doubled in volume, 5 minutes at least. Remove from heat and continue to beat until cool. Very quickly, fold in flour by hand, sifting ¼ flour over egg mixture at a time. When almost incorporated, fold in 1 T. butter and then flour. Repeat this process until all flour and butter have been incorporated. Immediately turn batter into prepared cake pan, tipping pan in all directions to run batter up sides, so cake will not puff in middle; bang pan lightly on table to settle batter. Set pan in middle of preheated 325° oven and bake 35 to 40 minutes. Remove from oven and cool 10 minutes, then turn out onto cake rack, peel off paper and allow to cool completely.

ALMOND CREAM: Cream butter with confectioners' sugar. Beat in ground almonds and flavorings. Separately beat cream until stiff. Fold into nut mixture until just blended. Do not overfold.

RASPBERRY SAUCE: Puree berries in blender or food processor, pass through food mill to remove seeds. Mix in sugar and lemon juice. Refrigerate, covered.

TO ASSEMBLE TERRINE: Lightly oil an 8½ × 4½ × 2⅝-inch (21.5 × 11.5 × 6.5 cm) loaf pan. Line with plastic wrap, leaving overhang on each side. Cut Genoise in half to make 2 pieces, each 8 × 4 inches (20 × 10cm). Shave off and discard brown crusts from all surfaces of cake with long sharp knife (optional). Carefully slice each piece horizontally into thirds. Place 1 layer in bottom of pan. It should fit snugly. Line sides of pan, reserving 1 piece for top. Discard excess cake. Cake should extend about 1 inch (2.5cm) above sides of pan.

Spread ¼ of Almond Cream over bottom of cake-lined pan. Arrange hulled strawberries on top of cream. Spread with another ¼ of cream. Arrange blueberries and kiwi over next layer. Spread with ¼ of cream. Arrange a final layer of strawberries. Spread remaining cream on top. Always pack gently, but be sure to fill all spaces. Cover with final layer of cake. Fold up overhanging layer of plastic wrap. Refrigerate at least 6 hours or overnight.

TO SERVE: 20 minutes before serving, unmold terrine. At same time, remove sauces from refrigerator. Cut terrine into ¾-inch (2cm) thick slices and place flat in center of large dessert plate. Ladle

Raspberry Sauce and Creme Anglaise around sides of terrine, not on top of it. Pass remaining sauce separately.

Maureen Moghtader, West Hartford, CT

Variations, Advance Preparation, and Serving Suggestions:
Part of the fun of this dessert is the freedom to create your own pattern of fruits. Just keep the emphasis on what is seasonal and what will create an attractive pattern when terrine is sliced. Terrine may be assembled day before serving. Genoise should be at least 1 day old or may be made ahead and frozen. Sauces can be made several days ahead. Substitute Apricot Sauce (page 408) for Raspberry Sauce.

Wine Suggestion: California Tejon Champagne, semi-sweet; serve chilled.

Apricot Chocolate Torte

YIELD: 10-12 Servings
TOTAL CALORIES: 5064
CALORIES PER SERVING: 422
CARBOHYDRATES: 50g
PROTEIN: 6g
FAT: 22g
PREPARING: 45 Minutes
BAKING: 40 Minutes
FREEZING: No

FILLING: Combine all ingredients in heavy saucepan. Over low heat, bring to boil; simmer 25 minutes until thick, resembling jam. Mash any large pieces remaining. Cool.

CRUST: Combine chocolate, nuts, flour, sugar, and salt; mix well. Add butter, water, and vanilla; mix until just crumbly. *[FOOD PROCESSOR: Add chocolate broken into four pieces and chop roughly. Then add nuts, chopping coarsely. Add flour, sugar, and salt to blend with pulse motion. Butter should be cut into small pieces, not melted. Add pieces of butter; blend. Add water and vanilla; mix until just crumbly.]*

Pat ⅔ dough on bottom and 1 inch *(2.5cm)* up sides of 9-inch *(22.5cm)* springform pan. Add filling. Sprinkle with remaining dough. Bake in preheated 350° oven 40 minutes. Cool in pan. Remove pan and garnish with shaved chocolate or chocolate curls.

Margaret J. Trainor, Storrs, CT

Wine Suggestion: California Muscat Blanc, semi-sweet white; serve chilled.

Microwave Conversion Instructions: Note: Reduce water to ½ cup and precook crust as directed below. *Filling:* Combine all ingredients in 8-cup *(2L)* glass measure. Cook on High 3 minutes, or until it comes to a boil. Simmer on Medium (50%) 10 to 14 minutes, until thick like a jam. Mash any large pieces. Cool. *Crust:* Combine crust ingredients. Place in 9-inch microwave-designed cake pan, reserving a little dough to crumble over filling. Cook crust on High 4 minutes. Pat dough in place where it has bubbled. Cook an additional 3 to 4 minutes on High, or until set. Allow to cool. Place cooled filling into crust. Sprinkle reserved crust mixture over filling. Cook on High 6 to 9 minutes, until it appears set.

FILLING:

1 box (11 oz.) *(310g)* **dried apricots, finely chopped**
1½ cups *(300g)* **sugar, can be decreased to ¾ cup** *(150g)*
¾ cup *(175ml)* **water**
3 T. *(20g)* **flour**
Juice of ½ lemon

CRUST:

3 oz. *(85g)* **unsweetened chocolate, finely chopped**
2 cups *(240g)* **whole walnuts, finely chopped**
1½ cups *(170g)* **flour**
¾ cup *(150g)* **light brown sugar, packed**
½ tsp. salt
½ cup *(115g)* **butter, melted and cooled**
2 T. *(30ml)* **cold water**
2 tsp. pure vanilla extract

GARNISH: (optional)
1 oz. *(30g)* **semisweet or milk chocolate, shaved**

Samuel Colt
Game Dinner at Armsmear

A menu befitting the grand, flamboyant style of Samuel Colt and the opulence of Armsmear.

"Rough!" "half-educated," "genius," "brash," "aggressive," "shrewd," "colorful," — all of these words have been used to describe Samuel Colt. Born in Hartford in 1814 to a genteel family, he soon displayed his independent spirit, his genius for invention and his fascination with firearms. In his early teens he was expelled from school for setting off "an underwater explosion" — the forerunner of underwater harbor mines. His father then sent him to sea as a midshipman. The primary result of the voyage seems to have been the wooden prototype of a six chamber revolver which Sam whittled from a ship's tackle block during his long hours at sea.

In the ensuing years, determined to have funds to finance the production of his revolver, Colt followed a variety of careers, the most fascinating and lucrative that of a showman. He learned the formula for nitrous oxide, named himself "Dr. Coult, Entertainer and Scientist," and traveled throughout the country demonstrating the effects of "laughing gas" on incredulous small town farmers and businessmen.

By 1830 he had applied for a patent for his revolver and set up a gun factory in New Jersey. This initial endeavor failed. However, widespread use of the firearm on the western frontier by Texas Rangers, U.S. troops and pioneers, who dubbed the revolver "Judge Colt" and "Peacemaker," insured the success of his second factory built in Hartford.

Colt turned his talent for showmanship to the promotion of his products and became a world traveler. He was received with grand ceremony in the courts of Europe and Russia. Colt returned to the U.S. with massive orders for firearms, a need for expansion and many new ideas. For a nominal sum he bought an enormous tract of marshy, unused land on the banks of the Connecticut River. Colt then drained the land, built a dike patterned after the ones he had seen in Holland and constructed the largest privately owned armory in the world.

With the acknowledged assistance of his superintendent, Elisha K. Root, Samuel Colt then applied his genius to new methods of mass production, used the revolutionary new steam power and invested only in the best of machinery. His attention to quality was also applied to his employees for whom he built one of the first industrial parks in the country. This included restaurants, a recreation center and homes. He introduced the shorter ten hour day and paid the highest wages in the industry. One indicator of the great success of Colt's policies, and of the friction his unorthodox policies created with local politicians, is the fact that Colt paid one tenth of the entire tax bill of the city of Hartford.

Many credit the Colt Armory with significantly influencing the subsequent development of Hartford as a manufacturing center and with making substantial contributions to the advancement of machine tools and American concepts of mass production.

Turning his thoughts to domesticity, in 1856 Colt married Elizabeth Hart Jarvis, the daughter of an Episcopal clergyman. Following a four month European honeymoon, they settled at Armsmear (meadow of arms), the palatial home Colt had built for his wife. Though rebuilt and redesigned, the main structure still stands on Wethersfield Avenue.

In the height of its glory Armsmear was described by Mrs. Colt as "of massive stone, spacious, towered, domed, with large halls for state occasions and crowds, as well as cozy cabinets and boudoirs for household comfort and genuine sociability . . ." The house was adorned with "onion domes" similar to the blue, star-studded onion-shaped dome atop the armory, assumed by many to have been inspired by Russian architecture.

The magnificent grounds contained a deer park, an artificial lake with swans and an enormous "grapery" from which the gardeners plucked a ton of grapes a year. The glass covered greenhouse, half a mile long, also contained more than 2,000 fruit trees.

One can imagine entertainment at Armsmear to have been as dramatic and flamboyant as Sam Colt himself. The wild quail and pheasant would surely have been hunted with a Colt gun, and the exotic fresh fruits gathered from the Armsmear greenhouses. The menu also reflects the cosmopolitan tastes of the world traveler who reveled in the extraordinary and gleaned the best from every new experience.

Caviar Mousse
p. 144

Duck Rillettes
p. 74

Clear Consomme

White House Soufflé Crackers
p. 136

Sole Walewska
p. 75

Cranberry Sorbet

Pheasant à la Normande
p. 76

Quail Véronique
(Quail with Grapes)
p. 322

Watercress and Endive Salad

Tarragon Sesame Salad Dressing
p. 76

Onions Monégasque
p. 77

Soufflé
Carrot Ring
filled with
Fresh Buttered Peas

Wild Rice
Casserole
p. 77

Brie, Roquefort, Gruyere Cheeses

Riz à l'Impératrice
with Apricot Sauce
p. 78

Pavlova with
Sliced Kiwi
and Mango
p. 79

Spanish
Coffee
p. 79

YIELD: 1½-Quart Terrine
TOTAL CALORIES: 10,160
APPROXIMATE CALORIES
  PER TABLESPOON: 101
PROTEIN: 5g
FAT: 9g
CHOLESTEROL: High
SODIUM: High
PREPARING: 30 Minutes
CHILLING: 3 Hours Minimum
COOKING: 4 Hours
FREEZING: Yes

2 ducks, halved, without breasts
2 T. *(30ml)* water
1 lb. *(450g)* pork shoulder, cubed
½ cup *(120ml)* dry vermouth
1 cup *(240ml)* rich chicken
  stock (page 198)
1 bay leaf
½ tsp. dried thyme
1 clove garlic, minced
1 shallot, minced
1 T. coarse salt
½ tsp. freshly ground black pepper
2 T. *(30ml)* Armagnac or cognac,
  flamed, cooled
½ cup *(115g)* goose or duck fat or lard

Duck Rillettes

Originally a French method of preserving meat, rillettes are shredded pieces of duck or pork cooked very slowly in fat and stock or water. They are very flavorful.

Skin duck pieces; place skin in saucepan with any pieces of fat from ducks, and the water. Cook on low heat until fat is rendered. Strain; reserve and refrigerate 1½ cups *(340g)* fat.

Place duck pieces, pork, chicken stock, vermouth, bay leaf, thyme, garlic, shallot, salt and pepper in a 3-qt. *(3L)* Dutch oven. Mix well. Simmer gently over low heat, uncovered, about 4 hours, or until meat falls from bones, stirring occasionally. Remove from heat. Pour contents into colander set over a large bowl. When cool enough to handle, remove meat pieces. Shred by hand or process in batches in food processor with Armagnac and chilled, reserved fat. Process in short on-off bursts just enough to shred meat coarsely, about 10 seconds. Pack meat in a 1½-qt. *(1.5L)* terrine or baking pan. Refrigerate until chilled.

Pour thin layer of melted fat or lard over terrine. Cover. Refrigerate at least 3 days before serving.

Kathleen J. Schwartz, Avon, CT

Variations, Advance Preparation, and Serving Suggestions:
The rillettes need a few days of chilling time to produce a mellowed flavor. Leftovers may be frozen, but will keep well in refrigerator for up to 10 days.

Serve from an earthenware crock or terrine surrounded by chunks of crusty French bread.

Wine Suggestion: French Cotes du Rhone, dry red; serve at room temperature.

Sole Walewska

Walewska was the name of a beautiful Polish countess, with whom Napoleon is said to have had an affair!

YIELD: 6 Servings
TOTAL CALORIES: 2070
CALORIES PER SERVING: 345
CARBOHYDRATES: 4g
PROTEIN: 36g
FAT: 21g
CHOLESTEROL: High
PREPARING: 60 Minutes
POACHING: 10-15 Minutes
FREEZING: No

LOBSTER BUTTER: Melt butter over hot water and add crushed lobster shells. Add a little water. Cook 10 minutes without boiling. Strain into a small bowl. Add a little boiling water to the shells and strain into the same bowl. Refrigerate. Skim off butter when cold.

COURT BOUILLON: Poach fish fillets in equal parts white wine and water seasoned with salt and pepper. When the fish are poached, about 10 minutes, remove from pan and keep warm. Reserve poaching liquid.

SAUCE: Make roux by melting butter in medium saucepan and adding flour. Cook 1 minute. Add 1½ cups reserved poaching liquid to roux and bring to a boil. Boil 1 minute. Meanwhile, reduce remaining stock by half. Blend egg yolks and cream. Add some hot sauce to the egg mixture, stirring constantly, then return to hot sauce. Add reduced stock. Warm cut-up lobster in sauce and add 3 T. lobster butter.

Pour sauce over fish fillets. Garnish with parsley.

Frances Bibow, Paris, France

Wine Suggestion: Hungarian Badacsonyi Szurkebarat, soft white; serve chilled.

Microwave Conversion Instructions: Place fillets in glass baking dish. Pour in ¾ cup *(180ml)* white wine and ¾ cup *(180ml)* water. Season with salt and pepper; cover with plastic wrap. Depending on thickness of fillets, cook on High 8 to 10 minutes. Keep fish warm and remove liquid to another container. *Sauce:* Melt 2 T. butter on Medium (50%); add flour, stir, cook on High 1 minute. Using a wire whip, beat 1½ cups poaching liquid into flour mixture; cook on High 3 minutes stirring occasionally. Beat egg yolks with fork. Add sauce as indicated. Add cream (and reduced stock if necessary). Put in cut up lobster; cook 5 to 8 minutes on Medium (50%), stirring occasionally. Add lobster butter and serve over warm sole.

2 boiled lobsters, meat removed, shells reserved

LOBSTER BUTTER:
¼ cup *(60g)* **butter**
Crushed lobster shells
Water

COURT BOUILLON:
Water
White wine
Salt
Pepper

2 lbs. *(900g)* **fillet of sole or flounder**

SAUCE:
2 T. *(30g)* **butter**
3 T. *(20g)* **flour**
Reserved poaching liquid
2 **egg yolks**
½ cup *(120ml)* **heavy cream**
3 T. *(45g)* **lobster butter**

Chopped parsley

Tarragon Sesame Salad Dressing

Because of its honey-sweet flavor, this dressing can be used with fresh fruit as well as with mixed greens.

YIELD: 1¼ Cups
CALORIES PER TABLESPOON: 70
CARBOHYDRATES: 4g
FAT: 6g
PREPARING: 15 Minutes

½ cup *(120ml)* **vegetable oil**
¼ cup *(60ml)* **tarragon vinegar**
1 tsp. **sea salt or regular salt**
¼ cup *(85g)* **honey**
¼ cup *(30g)* **sesame seeds, toasted in oven or non-stick skillet over low heat until golden**
½ tsp. **dried tarragon**

In food processor or blender, mix oil, vinegar, salt, honey. Pour into jar, add sesame seeds, tarragon; shake well. Can be served immediately or chilled for future use. Will keep several days refrigerated, but may need re-blending.

Carolyn Orsulak, Wethersfield, CT

Pheasant à la Normande

PHEASANT WITH APPLES

YIELD: 4 Servings
CALORIES PER SERVING: 592
CARBOHYDRATES: 23g
PROTEIN: 35g
FAT: 40g
CHOLESTEROL: High
PREPARING: 30 Minutes
BAKING: 1 Hour

2 **pheasants**
Salt and pepper
3 T. *(45ml)* **oil**
1 medium **onion, minced**
1 lb. *(450g)* **eating apples, sliced**
3 T. *(45g)* **butter**
½ cup *(120ml)* **brown stock**
1½ oz. *(45ml)* **brandy or Calvados**
½ cup *(120ml)* **whipping cream**

Rub cavities of birds with salt and pepper. Heat oil in large heavy casserole with lid; brown birds; remove to a side platter. Soften onions in same casserole; add apples. Place birds on top of apples; dot with butter; add stock and brandy.

Bake, covered, in preheated 350° oven until tender, approximately 1 hour. Transfer birds to a heated platter. Carve into individual portions.

Place apple-onion mixture in blender or food processor; puree. Add cream and blend. Correct seasoning; pour sauce over birds and serve.

Frances Bibow, Paris, France

Variations, Advance Preparation, and Serving Suggestions:
This recipe was successfully tested using 2 large Rock Cornish game hens.

Nutritional Notes: Nutritional analysis uses 4½ oz. *(125g)* cooked pheasant meat per serving.

Wine Suggestion: Portuguese Lancers Vinho Branco, semi-dry white; serve chilled.

Microwave Conversion Instructions: Note: Do not season cavities of birds. In small glass-covered casserole, place butter and minced onion; cook 4 to 5 minutes on High or until onions soften. In large glass casserole layer onions, then apples; place pheasants breast side down, on top. Dot with butter, add stock and brandy; cover; cook on High 10 minutes. Reduce to Medium (50%) and continue to cook 10 minutes. Turn pheasants breast side up and cover; cook 8 to 12 minutes on Medium (50%) until pheasant is tender and legs move freely. Complete sauce as indicated in conventional recipe.

Onions Monégasque

YIELD: 12 Servings
CALORIES PER SERVING: 159
CARBOHYDRATES: 21g
PROTEIN: 3g
FAT: 7g
PREPARING: 10 Minutes
COOKING: 30 Minutes
FREEZING: Yes-Very Well

This sweet and tangy dish is a cross between an hors d'oeuvre and a relish. It is typically served with pate, cold sliced meats or as part of an hors d'oeuvre platter.

Peel onions, being careful not to remove too much of the root end so that onions will remain in one piece during cooking. Put onions in saucepan with wine, oil, vinegar, thyme, bay leaf, garlic and salt. If necessary, add enough water to cover onions. Bring to boil, covered; reduce heat. Simmer gently until almost tender, about 20 minutes. Stir in tomato paste, saffron, sultanas. Continue simmering about 5 minutes, until *al dente*. Remove from heat. Serve warm as an entree accompaniment, or chill to serve as an appetizer or hors d'oeuvre. They keep well, refrigerated or freeze beautifully.

Nancy Bailey, Prospect, KY

Microwave Conversion Instructions: Put onions in casserole with wine, oil, vinegar, thyme, bay leaf, garlic and salt. Cook, covered, on High 10 to 15 minutes. Add remaining ingredients and continue cooking on High 5 minutes until *al dente*.

60-65 white pearl onions
1 cup *(240ml)* white wine
6 T. *(90ml)* olive oil
4 T. *(60ml)* wine vinegar
1 tsp. dried thyme
1 bay leaf, crumbled
2-3 cloves garlic
1 tsp. salt
3-4 T. *(25-35g)* tomato paste
¼ tsp. saffron
4 oz. *(115g)* sultanas or white raisins

Wild Rice Casserole

YIELD: 12 Servings
CALORIES PER SERVING: 189
CARBOHYDRATES: 13g
PROTEIN: 5g
FAT: 13g
SODIUM: High
PREPARING: 15 Minutes
BAKING: 1½ Hours

Wild rice is not a rice but actually an aquatic grass. The Chippewa Indians of the Great Lakes region call themselves *Menominee* which means "wild rice people." This delicious food is native to both Asia and North America. It is still harvested today in the Indian fashion using a canoe in northern Minnesota.

Soak rice in water overnight; drain.

Mix all ingredients except hot water and ¼ cup cheese; place in buttered 3-qt. *(3L)* casserole. (May be prepared in advance to this point and set aside.)

Before cooking, stir in hot water. Cover and bake in preheated 350° oven 1½ hours (1 hour if recipe is cut in half), checking several times to make sure it doesn't dry out. Add more water if necessary. Rice should be tender. Before serving, sprinkle with extra cheese.

Sarah C. Seymour, West Hartford, CT

Variations, Advance Preparation, and Serving Suggestions:
In spite of the strange ingredients which one might think would spoil good expensive wild rice, all turns out deliciously in the end! This is definitely an all purpose wild rice casserole that goes well with meats, game, and poultry, regardless of what sauce is used with the entree dishes.

Microwave Conversion Instructions: Precook wild rice separately before adding other ingredients. To cook rice: Place rice and 3 cups *(710ml)* water in a 3-qt. casserole. Cook, covered, on High 7 minutes. Cook on Medium (50%) 30 to 35 minutes, checking after 25 minutes to see if water has reduced. Cook until fork tender, adding more water only if necessary. Combine with remaining ingredients. Cook on High, covered, 8 to 10 minutes.

1 cup *(170g)* wild rice, washed
1 cup *(115g)* grated Cheddar cheese
1 cup *(115g)* sliced ripe olives
1 cup *(225g)* canned tomatoes and their juice
1 cup *(80g)* sliced fresh mushrooms
½ cup *(75g)* chopped onions
½ cup *(120ml)* vegetable oil
Salt
Freshly ground pepper
½ cup *(120ml)* hot water

YIELD: 8-10 Servings
TOTAL CALORIES: 5260
CALORIES PER SERVING: 526
CARBOHYDRATES: 86g
PROTEIN: 5g
FAT: 18g
CHOLESTEROL: High
PREPARING: 2 Hours
BAKING: 35-40 Minutes
CHILLING: 4 Hours Minimum
FREEZING: No

Riz à l'Impératrice

BAVARIAN CREAM WITH RICE AND FRUITS
This glorious mixture of rice, custard and glaceed fruits was
named for Napolean III's consort, the Empress Eugenie.

---

1 cup *(225g)* **finely diced glaceed fruits
such as pear, orange, peach and
quince purchased at a specialty food
store**
3 T. *(45ml)* **kirsch**
1⅓ T. *(10g)* **unflavored gelatin**
½ cup *(100g)* **long grain white rice**
4 qts. *(4L)* **boiling water**
1⅔ cups *(400ml)* **milk**
⅓ cup *(65g)* **sugar**
2 T. *(30g)* **butter**
1 T. **pure vanilla extract**

CREME ANGLAISE:

5 **egg yolks**
¾ cup *(150g)* **sugar**
1 tsp. **cornstarch**
1½ cups *(355ml)* **boiling milk**
1 T. **pure vanilla extract**
3 T. *(45g)* **strained apricot preserves**
1 cup *(240ml)* **heavy cream, whipped**

Apricot Sauce (page 408)

Additional *whole* glaceed fruits for final
decoration

Mix fruits in small bowl with kirsch. Sprinkle with gelatin; set aside.

Sprinkle rice into boiling water; boil 5 minutes. Drain thoroughly.
Bring milk, sugar and butter to a boil in fireproof casserole. Stir in
rice and vanilla. Bring to a simmer. Lay buttered round of waxed
paper over rice, cover casserole. Bake in preheated 300° oven 35 to
40 minutes, until milk has been absorbed and rice is very tender.

Meanwhile make CREME ANGLAISE: Put yolks in mixing bowl.
Gradually beat in sugar; continue beating until mixture is pale yellow
and forms a ribbon. Beat in cornstarch, then boiling milk by droplets.
Pour mixture into saucepan, stir over moderate heat until custard
lightly coats a spoon (170°). Do not bring near simmer. Remove
from heat; immediately stir in glaceed fruits and gelatin mixture, stirring until gelatin has thoroughly dissolved. Add vanilla and apricot
preserves. Stir rice into custard, a spoonful at a time if rice is hot.
Chill, stirring occasionally, until cold *but not set.* When rice custard
has cooled, carefully fold in whipped cream. Turn mixture into a
lightly oiled 6-cup *(1.4L)* mold, (turk's head mold preferred). Cover
with oiled waxed paper and refrigerate 4 hours or overnight.

When ready to serve, dip mold in hot water 1 second. Unmold onto
chilled serving platter. Surround with Apricot Sauce and whole
glaceed fruits. Pass remaining sauce separately.

Dr. Colin Atterbury, West Haven, CT

Wine Suggestion: French Sauternes, sweet white; serve cold.

Microwave Conversion Instructions: Note: Reduce milk used in
rice mixture to 1½ cups. Eliminate sugar. While 4 qts. water is boiling on conventional stove, cook milk and butter in glass bowl on
High 2 minutes, stirring once. Add rice to boiling water on stove;
cook 5 minutes. Meanwhile, cook 1½ cups milk for Creme Anglaise
2 to 3 minutes on High. Drain rice; continue with Creme Anglaise as
per conventional recipe. Add drained rice, vanilla, milk-butter mixture to 3-qt. *(3L)* casserole. Cover with waxed paper or plastic wrap
(small slit must be made in plastic wrap for steam to escape); cook
on High 12 to 14 minutes stirring several times. Do not allow milk to
boil over. Allow 2 to 3 minutes standing time. Gradually add custard
mixture. Refrigerate until cool enough to add whipped cream. Pour
into mold, chill until set.

Pavlova

Lovely to look at, delightful to eat. A delicious New Zealand and Australian classic named in honor of a visit to those countries by the celebrated Russian ballerina.

YIELD: 10-12 Servings
CALORIES PER SERVING: 216
CARBOHYDRATES: 34g
PROTEIN: 2g
FAT: 8g
PREPARING: 25 Minutes
BAKING: 1 Hour

With electric mixer, beat egg whites until they begin to hold their shape. Gradually add sugar and beat until smooth and sugar is dissolved. Fold in vinegar and vanilla. Prepare greased baking sheet with greased brown paper. Mound meringue in large circle on paper. Place in preheated 425° oven; immediately reduce to 200°. Bake 60 minutes. Allow to cool. Loosen carefully with spatula; place on silver serving platter. (At this point, may be stored with airtight covering several days). Whip cream with sugar until thick and fluffy. Fill center and spread over sides of Pavlova. Chill until serving time. (Will keep refrigerated several days). Decorate with sliced kiwi and drizzle with accumulated fruit juice. Serve immediately.

6 egg whites
2 cups *(400g)* superfine white sugar
1 T. *(15ml)* cider vinegar
1½ tsp. pure vanilla extract
10 oz. *(300ml)* whipping cream
1 T. *(15g)* sugar
4-5 kiwi fruit and juice

Janice Niehaus, West Hartford, CT

Variations, Advance Preparation, and Serving Suggestions:
The center of this cosmopolitan delight has a marshmallow consistency. Ice cream may replace the whipped cream. Substitute 1 qt. strawberries, fresh or frozen, with some added juice, or any other seasonal fruit.

Nutritional Notes: Kiwi fruit are a delightful and festive fruit and one should not be misled by the dark brown fuzzy covering. Its flesh is a bright lime-green dotted with tiny black seeds. Its flavor is somewhere between watermelon, grape and strawberry. It is rich in vitamin C and has only 30 calories per fruit. Chilling kiwi facilitates peeling.

Wine Suggestion: Sauternes, semi-sweet white; serve chilled.

Spanish Coffee

An elegant way to bid your guests good night.

YIELD: 1 Drink
CALORIES PER DRINK: 355
CARBOHYDRATES: 11g
PROTEIN: 1g
FAT: 17g
PREPARING: 5 Minutes

Place spoon in jumbo stemmed glass. Add cognac and Kahlua; pour in hot coffee. Stir. Remove spoon. Add 3 heaping T. whipped cream.

1 oz. *(30ml)* cognac
1 oz. *(30ml)* Kahlua
10 oz. *(300ml)* brewed coffee, hot
3 T. *(45ml)* heavy cream, sweetened
   and whipped

Carol Ann Smoragiewicz, West Hartford, CT

Microwave Conversion Instructions: To reheat brewed coffee: Must use a microwave safe stemmed glass, or mug. Heat on High 3 to 4 minutes, depending on size of container. Add cognac and Kahlua. Stir. Add whipped cream.

June Luncheon on a Nook Farm Veranda

A garden party invitation to dine with the late 19th century's most famous literary sisters, Harriet Beecher Stowe and Catherine Beecher.

During the mid-19th century, Hartford's famous Nook Farm Community became a center for the cultural and intellectual life of the day. It was particularly known to the literary world for the number of authors who built homes near one another. Though Harriet Beecher Stowe and Mark Twain were the two most distinguished authors, other nationally known residents included: Francis Gillette, U.S. Senator and abolitionist; Gillette's son William, an actor and playwright who popularized Sherlock Holmes; Charles Dudley Warner, author and editor of the *Hartford Courant;* and Isabella Beecher Hooker, the Connecticut leader of the woman suffrage movement. Several of the original houses were part of the "underground railway" and contained secret areas to hide escaped slaves prior to the Civil War.

Harriett Beecher Stowe is perhaps best known for her influential anti-slavery novel, *Uncle Tom's Cabin.* When she was first introduced to President Abraham Lincoln, he is reputed to have remarked, "So, you're the little lady who started the war." However, Harriett, in collaboration with her sister Catherine Beecher, published in 1869 an equally influential and immensely popular work, *The American Woman's Home.*

Harriett and Catherine lived in a world in which the woman's role was significantly changing. In the colonial years of America, when the primary economy of the nation was agriculture, a woman worked in the home and on the farm on an equal basis with her husband. However, with the advent of the Industrial Revolution, men flocked to the cities and became primary wage earners in industries outside the home. The home soon became the vocation and the "exclusive domain" of women.

Catherine Beecher urged women to apply the efficiency principles of industry to their home, particulary to the kitchen. Harriet Beecher Stowe's house at Nook Farm was designed around her sister's domestic theories. Catherine expressed disgust with the large, disorganized kitchens of her time and promoted instead continuous work surfaces and built-in cupboards and shelves. The kitchen was no longer to be considered a separate part of the house, but was to be the core around which other rooms were situated. A kitchen garden was another recommendation: "If flowers and shrubs be cultivated around the doors and windows . . . it will add very much to their agreeable appearance."

A significant factor which Catherine Beecher predicted and which influenced the development of American kitchens was the decreasing availability of domestic servants. The age of slavery and of the indentured servant was coming to an end. The new immigrants, many of whom had begun life in America as domestics, began to aim higher. Catherine and Harriett wrote, "Every young woman who expects to have a household of her own to manage should be able to do it well herself." Consequently the era of mechanical "workers" was introduced, and industries began to direct attention to the development of such ingenious devices as Stanley's Patent Cookstove with a revolving top and the Garland stove with flat burners and an elevated warming oven. The modern kitchen was on its way!

In the Nook Farm community entertaining neighbors and friends was a way of life. The Nook Farm luncheon on the veranda is planned for just such a gathering of good friends. To prepare the entire menu would surely require the efficiency and organization of Catherine Beecher. But the final product would be reminiscent of Mark Twain's delightful description in *The Portable Mark Twain:* In the summer the table was set in the middle of that shady and breezy floor, and the sumptuous meals — well, it makes me cry to think of them!

Ramos Fizz
p. 83

d Lemonade   Mint-Flavored Punch
                              p. 82

heese Straws   Rosemary Pecans
ennese Cigarettes)   p. 121
p. 164

Southern Peanut Spread
p. 82

hilled Sour Cream and Shrimp Soup
p. 83

Ham Braised in Wine with
Madeira Cream Sauce
p. 84

Mustard Custard
p. 85

Green Beans with Sunflower Seeds
p. 85

Variegated Salad
with Sweet and Sour Honey Dressing
p. 175

Corn Herb Batter Bread
p. 124

Sourdough English Muffins
p. 239

Pear Chip Preserve
p. 86

Peppermint Stick Ice Cream
p. 140

Strawberry Ice Cream Sodas
(Strawberry Ice Cream)
p. 140

Plate of Assorted Cookies:

Cracked Sugar Cookies
p. 87

Cracked Gingersnaps
p. 87

Almond Lace Wafers
p. 382

Chocolate Italian   Coconut Oatmeal
Cookies   Crisps
p. 86   p. 141

Rocky Ripple Fudge Bars
p. 379

Mint Flavored Punch

YIELD: 13 4-oz. Servings
TOTAL CALORIES: 1161
CALORIES PER SERVING: 89
CARBOHYDRATES: 22g
PREPARING: 15 Minutes
CHILLING: 4 Hours Minimum

In 1853 the first artificial ice-making machine was patented in Connecticut by Alexander Catling Twining.

⅔ cup *(130g)* sugar
½ cup lightly packed fresh mint leaves, snipped
2 cups *(475ml)* boiling water
2 cups *(475ml)* red grape juice, chilled
2 cups *(475ml)* fresh orange juice, chilled
¾ cup *(175ml)* fresh lime juice, chilled
Crushed ice
Fresh mint leaves

Combine sugar, mint, and boiling water; stir until sugar dissolves; chill.

Strain, reserving liquid; discard mint leaves. Stir together reserved liquid and fruit juices.

Pour over crushed ice; garnish with fresh mint leaves.

Nancy Webster Woodworth, West Hartford, CT

Southern Peanut Spread

YIELD: 2⅔ Cups
TOTAL CALORIES: 3180
CALORIES PER TABLESPOON: 76
CARBOHYDRATES: 6g
PROTEIN: 2.5g
FAT: 5g
PREPARING: 15 Minutes
CHILLING: 4 Hours Minimum
FREEZING: No

Peanuts, a vine of the pea family, also called Spanish nuts, are groundnuts native to South America. Cultivated by Incas and Mayans, peanuts were taken to Spain and Africa by Spanish explorers. They were brought back to the New World as food on slave ships.

1 cup *(200g)* sugar
1 egg, well beaten
1 T. prepared mustard
½ cup *(120ml)* vinegar
1¼ cups *(320g)* crunchy peanut butter

Combine sugar, egg, mustard, and vinegar in saucepan. Cook until mixture thickens. Add peanut butter and mix well with wire whisk. Chill at least 4 hours. Serve with raw vegetables or unsalted crackers.

Joy Tripp, West Hartford, CT

Variations, Advance Preparation, and Serving Suggestions: For a dramatic presentation, hollow a large Savoy cabbage and fill with peanut spread just before serving.

Nutritional Notes: Use unsalted peanut butter or homemade peanut butter made from freshly ground peanuts. This will help to reduce salt and fat content. Store unused portion of spread in refrigerator.

Microwave Conversion Instructions: Combine first four ingredients in 4-cup measure. Cook on High 2 minutes, stir. Cook on Medium (50%) 1 to 1½ minutes or until mixture is thickened. Stir in peanut butter.

Ramos Fizz

Another brunch, lunch, anytime drink.

YIELD: 3 Servings
TOTAL CALORIES: 310
CALORIES PER SERVING: 103
CARBOHYDRATES: 6g
PROTEIN: 2g
FAT: 3g
PREPARING: 5 Minutes

Place all ingredients in blender. Cover and blend one minute. Serve immediately in slender stemmed glasses.

Marion Kuzma, West Hartford, CT

Variations, Advance Preparation, and Serving Suggestions:
Make several batches of Ramos Fizz and fill a crystal pitcher for larger gatherings.

1 egg
1 T. sugar
2 oz. *(60ml)* **vodka or gin**
1 oz. *(30ml)* **lemon juice**
Generous splashes of:
   orange juice
   half and half
   orange flower water
Cracked ice

Chilled Sour Cream, Shrimp and Cucumber Soup

MEDITERRANEAN OKROCHKA

There are many versions of Okrochka. It can be made with different kinds of fish, fish and meat mixed, or simply with pieces of cold cooked chicken. The essential ingredients are cucumbers, fennel and dill which impart its characteristic flavor. Russians serve this soup with sliced radishes and omit the shrimp. Danes use only shrimp and add sauerkraut juice. This soup is especially appropriate during the hot summer months or preceding a rich entree at other times of the year.

YIELD: 6 Servings
CALORIES PER SERVING: 243
CARBOHYDRATES: 16g
PROTEIN: 20g
FAT: 11g
CHOLESTEROL: High
SODIUM: High
PREPARING: 30 Minutes
CHILLING: 4 Hours Minimum
COOKING: 5 Minutes
FREEZING: No

Combine all ingredients except bouquet garni and shrimp. Chill at least 4 hours, preferably overnight. Meanwhile, bring 4 cups water to boil in a saucepan with the bouquet garni. Add the shrimp. As soon as the water returns to a boil, take the saucepan off the heat and let shrimp cool in the water. When cool, shell and devein shrimp; dice. Add shrimp to soup just before serving. Garnish with dill sprigs.

Melinda M. Vance, West Hartford, CT

4 cups *(950ml)* **buttermilk**
2 cups *(450g)* **sour cream or Creme Fraiche (page 200)**
2 small **cucumbers, peeled, seeded and diced**
2 cloves **garlic, finely minced**
Salt
Freshly ground white pepper
3 T. finely minced fresh dill
½ cup finely minced fennel tops (optional if not available)
½ cup finely minced fresh chives
½ cup *(120ml)* sauerkraut juice
1 bouquet garni (dried thyme, bay leaf, fresh parsley, tied in cheesecloth bag)
¾ lb. *(340g)* fresh raw shrimp
Dill sprigs for garnish

YIELD: 16 Servings
CALORIES PER SERVING: 612
CARBOHYDRATES: 7g
PROTEIN: 29g
FAT: 52g
CHOLESTEROL: High
SODIUM: High
PREPARING: 1 Hour
BAKING: 2 Hours
FREEZING: No

Ham Braised in Wine with Madeira Cream Sauce

2 T. *(30g)* butter
1 T. oil
1 cup *(115g)* sliced carrots
1 cup *(135g)* sliced onions
1 8-10 lb. *(3.5-4.5kg)* cooked ham
6 parsley sprigs
1 bay leaf
6 peppercorns
½ tsp. thyme
3 whole cloves
4 cups *(950ml)* dry white wine
4-6 cups *(950-1325ml)* white or brown
   stock

SAUCE:
2 lbs. *(900g)* fresh mushrooms, sliced
3 T. *(45g)* butter
1 T. oil
3 T. *(30g)* minced shallots or green
   onions
Salt and pepper
½ cup *(120ml)* Madeira wine
4 T. *(30g)* flour mixed to a paste with
   4 T. *(60g)* butter
2-3 cups *(475-720ml)* whipping cream
Ham braising liquid

Saute vegetables in butter and oil until tender and lightly browned in a roaster or casserole just large enough to hold ham.

Place ham over vegetables with its fattiest side up; add rest of ingredients. Bring to a simmer on top of stove, cover and place in preheated 350° oven, regulating heat so ham is barely simmering for about 2 hours. Baste every 20 minutes.

SAUCE: Dry the mushrooms in a paper towel; saute in hot butter and oil until lightly browned; stir in shallots or green onions; saute for a minute more; season to taste and set aside.

Degrease braising liquid in roaster; set roaster over high heat, reduce liquid to about 3 cups; add wine; simmer for a minute or two.

Strain sauce into saucepan; beat in flour/butter paste; beat in 2 cups cream; stir in mushrooms; simmer 5 minutes. The sauce should be just thick enough to coat a spoon lightly. Stir in more cream if the sauce seems too thick.

Serve ham with sauce passed separately.

Sarah C. Seymour, West Hartford, CT

Nutritional Notes: Nutritional analysis uses 4 lbs. boned, skinned, cured, butt ham with lean meat and fat. It assumes that all the sauce is consumed.

Wine Suggestion: California Pinot Noir, dry red; serve at room temperature.

Microwave Conversion Instructions: Note: Cut recipe in half, using a 4-lb. *(1.8kg)* ham.

Combine carrots, onions, butter and oil. Cover with plastic wrap. Cook on High for 5 minutes. Stir and test for doneness. Add ham, fat side up, and rest of ingredients. Use only 1 cup *(240ml)* dry white wine and 1 cup *(240ml)* stock. Cover with plastic wrap. Cook 30 minutes on Medium (50%) basting twice.

Sauce: Make conventionally using 1½ cup *(355ml)* liquid from pan in which ham was cooked.

Mustard Custard

YIELD: 12 Servings
CALORIES PER SERVING: 141
CARBOHYDRATES: 13g
PROTEIN: 2g
FAT: 9g
CHOLESTEROL: High
SODIUM: High
PREPARING: 25 Minutes
CHILLING: 2-3 Hours

Not only is this a lovely accompaniment to ham or pork and cold meats, but it can be used in place of mayonnaise in some sandwiches.

Soften gelatin in ¼ cup water. Beat eggs in top of double boiler. Add ½ cup water, sugar, mustard, vinegar, salt and softened gelatin. Cook over boiling water, stirring constantly until thickened. Cool. Thoroughly fold in whipped cream. Pour into a 4-cup (1L) ring mold; chill until firm. Unmold onto a lettuce-lined plate.

Peggy Stanwood, Bloomfield, CT

Wine Suggestion: French Monbagillac, semi-sweet white; serve chilled.

1 T. unflavored gelatin
¾ cup (180ml) water
4 eggs
¾ cup (150g) sugar
1 T. dry mustard (Coleman's preferred)
½ cup (120ml) cider vinegar
1½ tsp. salt
1 cup (240ml) heavy cream, whipped

Green Beans with Sunflower Seeds

YIELD: 4-6 Servings
CALORIES PER SERVING: 122
CARBOHYDRATES: 6g
PROTEIN: 2g
FAT: 10g
PREPARING: 15 Minutes
COOKING: 15 Minutes

Did you realize that green beans are a very tender variety of a kidney bean?

HERB BUTTER: Combine butter, marjoram, basil, chervil, parsley, chives, savory and thyme; mix until smooth. Refrigerate.

In a large skillet, add barely enough water to cover bottom. Add salt. Bring to a boil; add onion and garlic. Then add green beans; cover and cook until crisp yet tender, 10 to 15 minutes. Pour off excess water; add herb butter and sunflower seed kernels; swirl to melt butter. Add salt and pepper to taste; toss over medium heat 1 minute. Serve immediately.

Terry Oakes Bourret, Cromwell, CT

Microwave Conversion Instructions: Melt butter in glass measure on High 45 seconds. Add seasonings and set aside. Place onions and garlic in bottom of round casserole. Add ¼ cup (60ml) water and beans. Cook, covered, on High 10 minutes, stirring halfway through. Drain. Add sunflower seeds and toss with herb butter. Heat, covered, 1 to 2 minutes on High.

HERB BUTTER:
¼ cup (60g) butter
½ tsp. marjoram
½ tsp. basil
½ tsp. chervil
1 tsp. parsley, chopped
1 tsp. chives, chopped
⅛ tsp. savory
⅛ tsp. thyme

Water
1 tsp. salt
1 small onion, chopped
1 clove garlic, mashed
1 lb. (450g) green beans, washed and ends removed
¼ cup (30g) sunflower seed kernels
Sea salt
Freshly ground pepper

Pear Chip Preserve

YIELD: 4 Pints
CALORIES PER PINT: 1550
CALORIES PER TABLESPOON: 48
CARBOHYDRATES: 14g
PREPARING: 15 Minutes
COOKING: 2½ Hours

This preserve recipe came to Connecticut from Virginia's Shenandoah Valley. It is equally delicious made with pumpkin.

3½ lbs. *(1585g)* sugar
4 cups *(950ml)* water
4 lbs. *(1800g)* firm Bartlett or Seckel pears, peeled, cored, thinly sliced in ½-inch *(1.2cm)* squares or
4 lbs. pumpkin flesh, thinly sliced in ½-inch *(1.2cm)* squares
2 lemons, thinly sliced
4 oz. *(115g)* crystallized ginger, finely chopped, about 3 T.

Combine sugar and water in large saucepan over medium heat and stir until sugar dissolves. Raise heat to high and bring to boil; boil until syrup is reduced to about two-thirds. Add pear (or pumpkin) chips, lemon and ginger; return to boil. Reduce heat and cook gently until pears are transparent, about 2 hours or longer.

Transfer to sterilized jars, filling to ½ inch *(1.2cm)* of top. Seal jars with paraffin.

Francie Bergquist, West Hartford, CT

Variations, Advance Preparation, and Serving Suggestions:
Serve this condiment in honey or jam pots with meat entrees, or use as a spread on English muffins. Wrap preserve jars in calico to give as holiday or hostess gifts.

Chocolate Italian Cookies

YIELD: 144 Cookies
TOTAL CALORIES: 9504
CALORIES PER COOKIE: 66
CARBOHYDRATES: 11g
PROTEIN: 1g
FAT: 2g
PREPARING: 3 Hours
BAKING: 10-12 Minutes Per Sheet
FREEZING: Yes-Unglazed

8 cups *(900g)* flour
2 cups *(170g)* cocoa
2½ cups *(300g)* sugar
3 tsp. baking powder
1 cup *(195g)* vegetable shortening, melted and cooled (Crisco preferred)
1 cup *(120g)* chopped nuts
1½ tsp. baking soda
1½ tsp. cloves
1½ tsp. cinnamon
2 cups *(340g)* raisins, ground
½ orange with peel, grated
½ cup *(125g)* applesauce
2½ cups *(600ml)* cold coffee
Confectioners' sugar combined with milk to make glaze

Combine all ingredients in large bowl adding coffee last, a little at a time. Using hands, mix dough thoroughly.

Rub hands with oil; roll a teaspoonful of dough into a ball. Roll until ball is shiny and has no cracks in it. This takes at least 1 minute per cookie.

Place cookies on a lightly greased baking sheet 1 inch *(2.5cm)* apart. Bake in preheated 375° oven for 10 to 12 minutes. Remove from sheet; when completely cool, dip each cookie into thin glaze.

Janet Russo, West Hartford, CT

Cracked Gingersnaps

These cookies, an old family favorite, crack on top. Do not overbake — they are better on the chewy side.

YIELD: 48-60 Cookies
TOTAL CALORIES: 3360
CALORIES PER COOKIE: 56
CARBOHYDRATES: 8g
PROTEIN: .5g
FAT: 2.5g
PREPARING: 10 Minutes
BAKING: 8-10 Minutes Per Sheet
CHILLING: 2 Hours Minimum

Cream shortening and sugar. Add molasses and egg, beating well. Sift dry ingredients together. Add to batter and mix until smooth. Refrigerate batter at least 2 hours.

Form chilled batter into 1-inch (2.5cm) balls; roll in granulated sugar. Place 2 inches (5cm) apart on greased baking sheet. Bake one sheet at a time in center rack of preheated 375° oven 8 to 10 minutes. Let cool briefly before removing from sheet to wire rack.

Carolyn P. Wardner, West Hartford, CT

Microwave Conversion Instructions: Place 12 balls 3 inches apart on a sheet of parchment paper in a ring formation. Cook on Medium (50%) 5 minutes. They will be slightly soft, but become firm as they cool.

¾ cup *(145g)* shortening
1 cup *(200g)* brown sugar
4 T. *(60ml)* molasses
1 egg
2 cups *(225g)* flour
2 tsp. baking soda
1 tsp. cinnamon
1 tsp. cloves
1 tsp. ginger
½ tsp. salt
Extra granulated sugar for coating

Cracked Sugar Cookies

A chewy sugar cookie that goes well with many desserts.

YIELD: 48 Cookies
TOTAL CALORIES: 4224
CALORIES PER COOKIE: 88
CARBOHYDRATES: 12g
PROTEIN: 1g
FAT: 4g
PREPARING: 15 Minutes
BAKING: 10 Minutes Per Sheet

Sift together flour, baking soda, cream of tartar and salt; set aside.

Cream butter and vanilla; add 2 cups sugar and continue to beat until fluffy. Add egg yolks, one at a time, beating after each until well-blended. Add dry ingredients, in fourths, beating until just blended. *[FOOD PROCESSOR: Combine first 4 ingredients in work bowl; mix briefly. Remove and set aside. Mix sugar, egg yolks, and vanilla in work bowl 1 full minute, stopping machine once to scrape down sides of bowl. Add butter and process 1 more minute. Return dry ingredients to work bowl and mix with on/off turns just until flour is incorporated; do not overprocess or dough will be tough.]* Form dough into 1-inch (2.5cm) balls; roll in additional sugar. Place 2 inches apart on ungreased baking sheet.

Bake in preheated 350° oven 10 minutes or until edges are golden in color. Do not let edges get dark. The outside of the cookie should be dry and crisp and the interior should be moist and slightly chewy.

Jan Granberry, Houston, TX

2½ cups *(285g)* sifted flour
1 tsp. baking soda
1 tsp. cream of tartar
¼ tsp. salt
1 cup *(225g)* unsalted sweet butter
1 tsp. pure vanilla extract
2 cups *(400g)* sugar
3 egg yolks
Extra sugar to coat (Use colored sugar crystals for holidays)

Mark Twain and Mrs. Clemens Entertain — May 11, 1887

An actual late 19th century banquet prepared and served for ten guests in Mark Twain's Hartford home. The menu is authentic but the recipes are contemporary.

"A man accustomed to American food and American domestic cookery would not starve to death in Europe; but I think he would gradually waste away and eventually die."

Mark Twain's delightful and not so subtle appreciation of American "cookery" in *A Tramp Abroad* reflects the growing distinctiveness of American meals in the 19th century. The great abundance and variety of field and garden crops as well as meats and fish now stood in contrast to the comparatively small quantity of food products available in much of Europe. Cooking for the average American housewife came to be based on the quantity and quality of the food rather than on the intricacy of sauces. In one of his comments on special favorites, Twain (Samuel Clemens) expressed particular fondness for strawberries "which are not to be doled out as if they were jewelry, but in a more liberal way."

The incredible variety of dishes represented on this menu actually served by the Clemens on May 11, 1887 — bears witness to 19th century America's bounty and gastronomic expectations! The guest list on this date included Mr. and Mrs. John Day, Mr. and Mrs. Watson, Mr. and Mrs. Taylor and Mr. and Mrs. Holcombe. Carefully preserved records also tell us that the table was a large round one set with a profusion of flowers. Bread was served in napkins. There were dinner cards and bowls of olives, almonds and candies on the table.

This sumptuous feast was served in the Clemens' Hartford home located in Nook Farm. Designated as a National Historic Landmark, meticulously restored to its original elegance, and now open to the public for guided tours, this remarkable Victorian residence was home to the Clemens and their children for seventeen years. Built in 1874 at the height of Clemens' financial prosperity, the house was designed by Edward Tuckerman Potter. Its sweeping roof lines, geometrically patterned red and white bricks, and intricate gables attest to Clemens' extravagance and unique exuberance.

There always seemed to be a steady stream of visitors to the Clemens' home where an "open house" policy prevailed. Excellent food was a ready accompaniment to their generous hospitality. The magnificent dining room, decorated by Louis Comfort Tiffany was the perfect setting for the famous and very lively dinner parties. Art objects and elegant table settings collected on the Clemens' many trips abroad added to the effect of "cluttered splendor."

In an article in *Eruption*, Twain wrote: "A banquet is probably the most fatiguing thing in the world except ditchdigging. It is the insanest of all recreations. The inventor of it overlooked no detail that could furnish weariness, distress, harassment, and acute and long-sustained misery of mind and body."

However, inspite of his caustic comments, Clemens has been described as an engaging host, regaling his guests with often hilarious anecdotes and occasionally striding across the dining room waving his dinner napkin to emphasize a point. The charming Olivia ("Livy") Clemens would serenely and competently preside as the perfect hostess while she gave her obstreperous husband secret coded signals to mind his manners!

Another side of the flamboyant author, lecturer, riverboat pilot and publisher can be glimpsed in the adjoining library where he often sat in the evening with his three daughters. To either side of the ornately carved mantlepiece were bookshelves lined with family treasures. In *The Autobiography of Mark Twain* we learn that "At one end of the procession was a framed oil-painting of a cat's head; at the other end was a head of a beautiful young girl . . . an impressionist watercolor."

Between the two pictures was an assortment of bric-a-brac. The children would clamor for a story involving all of the objects. "I had to start always with the cat . . ." Clemens concludes this vignette by saying that in the course of time "the bric-a-brac and pictures showed wear. It was because they had so many and such tumultuous adventures in their romantic careers."

There seems to be striking contrast between these glimpses of Samuel Clemens. One portrays a cosmopolitan world traveler hosting a feast fit for kings and the other a loving father telling wonderful, imaginative stories to his children. Perhaps together they convey the diversity and depth of the frontier boy who attained world reknown but always retained his gentleness, humor, and love of a good tale.

Romaine Punch
p. 90

Champagne   **Claret Wine**

Clear Soup with Sherry

Clams on Half-Shell   **Dressed Cucumbers**   **Soft Shell Crabs**
(Cucumber Salata)
p. 91

**Shad Roe Balls with
Creamed Shad Sauce**

Creamed Sweetbreads   **Broiled Squab on Toast**   **Roast Lamb with**
(Sweetbreads with Port Wine Sauce)   **Parisian Potatoes**   **Curry Cream Sauce**
p. 92   *(New Potatoes in Savory Sauce)*
Peas   p. 91   **Creamed Asparagus**

Molded Tomato Jelly with Mayonnaise
(Tomato Aspic with Sour Cream Dressing)
p. 90

Fresh Strawberries in Cream   **Molded Ice Cream Flowers**
(Grand Marnier Sauce)   *(Homemade Ice Cream)*
p. 188   p. 140

Bonbons   **Candies**   **Bonbons**
(Orange Sugarplums)   *(Toffe Bars)*   *(Yum Balls)*
p. 93   p. 381   p. 93

Coffee in the Drawing Room

Romaine Punch

This is the punch served at Mark Twain's Hartford home on May 11, 1887. It was also served by President and Mrs. Grant at an elaborate breakfast in the State Dining Room after the marriage of their daughter Nellie.

YIELD: 4 Servings
CALORIES PER 5 oz. SERVING: 179
CARBOHYDRATES: 18g
PREPARING: 15 Minutes
FREEZING: 3 Hours Minimum

1⅔ cups *(400ml)* cold water
⅓ cup *(65g)* sugar
⅓ cup *(80ml)* fresh lemon juice
2 jiggers (3 oz.) *(90ml)* brandy
2 jiggers (3 oz.) *(90ml)* light rum

Combine water and sugar; stir until sugar dissolves. Stir in lemon juice.

Freeze at least 3 hours.

Remove from freezer about 1 hour before serving; thaw mixture to slush. Divide mixture evenly among 4 glasses. Combine brandy and rum; pour 1 jigger of the mixture into each glass. Stir well to mix.

Freeze until served.

Tomato Aspic and Dressing

YIELD: 4 Cups Aspic
CALORIES PER SERVING
 ASPIC: 164
CARBOHYDRATES: 37g
PROTEIN: 4g
SODIUM: High
CALORIES PER TABLESPOON
 DRESSING: 45
PREPARING: 15 Minutes
CHILLING: 24 Hours

3½ cups *(830ml)* tomato juice
½ tsp. celery salt
1 T. grated onion
6 whole cloves
2 pkgs. (3 oz. each) *(170g)* lemon gelatin
2 T. vinegar (1 T. white, 1 T. wine)
1 pkg. *(7g)* unflavored gelatin

SOUR CREAM HORSERADISH DRESSING:

½ cup *(115g)* sour cream or Creme Fraiche (page 200)
½ cup *(115g)* mayonnaise (preferably Hellmann's) or Homemade (page 190)
Horseradish to taste
¼ cup *(20g)* scallions, thinly sliced; white and green parts

Simmer first 4 ingredients 10 minutes; strain and pour mixture over gelatin. Add vinegar and additional gelatin. Pour into well-greased 1-qt. *(1L)* mold and chill until set.

Combine dressing ingredients to taste and chill overnight. Unmold aspic on decorative platter accompanied by dressing in small bowl.

Eloise W. Martin, Kenilworth, IL

Variations, Advance Preparation, and Serving Suggestions: Recipe doubles or triples easily. Mold may be made several days ahead. If using a ring mold, fill center with fresh shrimp and surround with sliced avocado.

Nutritional Notes: A reduced sodium version utilizes low-sodium tomato juice, low-sodium mayonnaise and eliminates celery salt.

Wine Suggestion: California Chenin Blanc, soft white; serve chilled. This suggestion applies if aspic is being served with shrimp and used as entree.

Cucumber Salata

This is a Hungarian recipe for cucumber salad.

YIELD: 6 Servings
CALORIES PER SERVING: 50
CARBOHYDRATES: 1g
FAT: 5g
SODIUM: High
PREPARING: 10 Minutes
STANDING: 3 Hours

Slice cucumbers and onion paper thin. Put in bowl with salt; let sit under weight 3 hours.

Mix together vinegar and oil.

Squeeze out water from cucumbers; add vinegar and oil mixture, season with white pepper and dill. Add sugar, place in oblong bowl or dish; sprinkle paprika over one-half of salad and freshly grated black pepper over other half. Can be prepared in the morning.

Peg Beakey, Wethersfield, CT

Nutritional Notes: Salting removes or leaches water soluble vitamins and minerals from cucumbers.

3 cucumbers
1 onion
Salt
¼ cup *(60ml)* **white wine vinegar**
2 T. *(30ml)* **vegetable oil**
Freshly ground white pepper
Chopped fresh dill
⅛ tsp. sugar
Paprika
Freshly ground black pepper

New Potatoes in Savory Sauce

Always a favorite — especially tasty with grilled fish, particularly swordfish, or a butterflied leg of lamb. This one is simple!

YIELD: 4-6 Servings
CALORIES PER SERVING: 210
CARBOHYDRATES: 27g
PROTEIN: 3g
FAT: 10g
PREPARING: 30 Minutes
COOKING: 20 Minutes
FREEZING: No

In 4-qt. *(4L)* saucepan, place unpeeled potatoes in salted water to cover. Bring to boil over medium heat, cook gently 15 to 20 minutes until fork tender. Drain. Peel potatoes or leave skins intact to preserve more nutritional value. Keep warm.

SAUCE: Heat butter and oil. Stir in rind, parsley, chives, nutmeg, flour, salt and pepper. Heat slowly while stirring. Do not boil. Sauce will thicken slightly. (Up to this point, may be made earlier in day; keep at room temperature until serving). At serving time, stir lemon juice into warmed sauce. Pour mixture over potatoes. Toss to coat.

Bernice Kuzma, West Hartford, CT

Nutritional Notes: Potatoes are rich in vitamin C. This vitamin ranges from about 26mg per 100 grams (average serving size) in newly dug potatoes to half this amount after 3 months of storage and even less after longer storage. Cooking potatoes in their skins preserves vitamin C and other vitamins and minerals which are found in the layer directly under the skin. Today "new" potatoes are sometimes dyed red. It is best to avoid the dyed potatoes as they generally spoil quickly.

Microwave Conversion Instructions: Peel band around center of potatoes and place in 2-qt. *(2L)* casserole with ¼ cup water. Cover, cook on High 15 to 18 minutes, stirring once. Drain and keep warm. In 2-cup *(475ml)* measure melt butter and heat oil by cooking on High 1 minute. Add grated lemon peel, parsley, chives, nutmeg, flour, salt and pepper. Cook on High 45 to 60 seconds, or until slightly thickened. Just before serving, stir in lemon juice and pour over potatoes; toss gently to coat.

2 lbs. *(900g)* **small new potatoes**

SAUCE:
¼ cup *(60g)* **butter**
1 T. olive oil
Grated rind of 1 lemon
¼ cup chopped fresh parsley or dill
2 T. snipped chives
⅛ tsp. freshly grated nutmeg
¼ tsp. flour
¼ tsp. salt
¼ tsp. freshly ground pepper
3 T. *(45ml)* **fresh lemon juice**

Sweetbreads in Port Wine Sauce

Sweetbreads were known to be among Mark Twain's favorite delicacies. It is possible that his recipe was from *The House-keeper and Healthkeeper*, written by Catherine E. Beecher in 1873, a sister of Harriet Beecher Stowe, Mark Twain's friend and nearest neighbor. The recipe reads: The best way to cook sweetbreads is to broil them thus: Parboil them, and then put them on a clean gridiron for broiling. When delicately browned, take them off and roll in melted butter on a plate, to prevent their being dry and hard. Some cook them on a griddle well buttered, turning frequently; and some put narrow strips of salt pork on them while cooking.

YIELD: 4 Servings
CALORIES PER SERVING: 427
CARBOHYDRATES: 14g
PROTEIN: 23g
FAT: 31g
CHOLESTEROL: High
SODIUM: High
PREPARING: 30 Minutes
SOAKING: 1½ Hours
COOKING: 20 Minutes
SIMMERING: Stock-5 Hours
FREEZING: Sauce Base

SWEETBREADS:

2 pairs large sweetbreads
1 T. fresh lemon juice
Salt
Freshly ground pepper
2 T. *(15g)* flour
2 T. *(30g)* butter

PORT WINE SAUCE:

1 cup *(240ml)* ruby port
Juice of 1 orange
1⅓ cups *(315ml)* Poultry Stock Sauce Base (page 198)
⅓ cup *(80ml)* heavy cream
Salt
Freshly ground pepper

SWEETBREADS: Soak sweetbreads for 1 hour in cold water. Drain. Put into saucepan with cold water and lemon juice; bring slowly to boil and simmer 5 minutes. Drain, put into a bowl of ice water for 15 minutes or until ready to use. Remove skin and sinews and dry. Season with salt and pepper; dust with flour. Brown sweetbreads on both sides in butter over moderate heat. Remove and keep warm while preparing sauce.

PORT WINE SAUCE: In 2-qt. *(2L)* saucepan, reduce port wine and orange juice to syrupy glaze. Add Poultry Stock Sauce Base and boil until reduced by half. While sauce is still boiling hard, add the cream; do not stir. Boil vigorously 5 minutes or until surface is full of small tight bubbles. Then stir gently until sauce is thick enough to coat spoon. Remove from heat. Season to taste with salt and pepper. Set over very low heat to keep warm while sauteing sweetbreads.

For each serving, arrange half a sweetbread on a hot plate and nap with ¼ cup *(60ml)* sauce.

Melinda M. Vance, West Hartford, CT

Variations, Advance Preparation, and Serving Suggestions: 1¼ lbs. *(570g)* calves liver, cut into 4 slices ⅓-inch (8mm) thick or an equal amount chicken livers may be used instead of sweetbreads.

Wine Suggestion: California Navalle Burgundy, soft red; serve at room temperature.

Orange Sugarplums

Visions of these goodies will dance in your head!

YIELD: 84-96 Sugarplums
TOTAL CALORIES: 7100
CALORIES PER SUGARPLUM: 74
CARBOHYDRATES: 9g
PROTEIN: .5g
FAT: 4g
CHOLESTEROL: High
PREPARING: 1 Hour
BAKING: None
FREEZING: Yes-Very Well

Mix all ingredients (use only 8 oz. thawed orange juice concentrate) except coconut together. Mixture should be slightly sticky. If too dry, add more orange juice concentrate.

Roll dough into small balls and then *finely* flaked coconut. Store in cookie tin between layers of waxed paper.

Ann Houston Feenstra, Houston, TX

1 lb. *(450g)* vanilla wafers, crushed
1 cup *(225g)* melted butter
1 lb. *(450g)* confectioners' sugar
1 cup *(170g)* finely chopped pecans
1 can (12 oz.) *(360ml)* frozen orange juice concentrate, thawed
Finely flaked coconut

Yum Balls

A wonderful healthy treat to have around. They don't become dry when left out.

YIELD: 36 Balls
TOTAL CALORIES: 3924
CALORIES PER BALL: 109
CARBOHYDRATES: 13g
PROTEIN: 3g
FAT: 5g
PREPARING: 10 Minutes
COOKING: None

Combine all ingredients except coconut; shape into 1-inch *(2.5cm)* balls and roll in coconut.

The Happy Cookers, Anita MacDonald and
Mary Cagenello, Bloomfield, CT

Nutritional Notes: This is a nutritious snack for children. If preferred, salt-free peanut butter or "natural" peanut butter may be used. Natural peanut butter can be made at home by simply grinding roasted peanuts in a food processor or nut-butter machine. Since the oil will rise to the top in time, stirring to blend will be necessary. Keeps best in the refrigerator. Generally, commercial peanut butter contains quite a bit of salt, sugar, dextrose and additional oil which acts as an emulsifier. Consequently, peanut butter, which is a very rich source of protein, can be as high as 55% fat or approximately 70% of its total calories.

1 cup *(250g)* peanut butter
½ cup *(170g)* honey
1 cup *(85g)* regular oats
1 cup *(170g)* raisins or chopped dried fruit
½ cup *(60g)* wheat germ
1 cup *(75g)* coconut

Insidious Rum Punch
p. 96

Ginger-Snap Hors d'Oeuvre
p. 42

Oyster Croustades
p. 204

Popcorn, Peanuts and Currants
p. 28

Mock Turtle Soup

Chestnut Soup
p. 96

**Mushroom Stuffed Beef Tenderloin
with Madeira Sauce**
p. 271

Smoked Scallops New Zealand
p. 97

Roast Turkey
p. 98

Pheasant Cumberland
p. 321

**Baked Apples with
Spiced Sweet Potatoes**
p. 346

Pomfret Parsnips
p. 100

Succotash
p. 30

Flamed Mushrooms
p. 97

**Soused Gourmet
Onions**
p. 343

Pickled Oranges
p. 100

Cranberry Relish
p. 46

Pickled Watermelon Rind
p. 375

**Aunt Lily's Mincemeat
Pies**
p. 375

Pumpkin Pecan Pie
p. 47

**Christmas Pudding
with Caramel Sauce**
p. 101

Christmas on Main Street

A Holiday Celebration at the Butler-McCook Homestead with noted guest, Horace Bushnell.

No picture of life in historic Connecticut is complete without recalling the special celebration which surrounds a New England Christmas dinner. Some of the most delightful records we have are from the diaries of the Reverend John James McCook, who writes in detail of Christmas days with his family from 1873 through 1926, and from an essay, "Christmas in the Old Days," written by his daughter Frances.

One of the earliest entries in the diary records the tantalizing sights and smells of that special day when John McCook, his wife and their five young children lived together in Hartford. The wonderful scent of "roasted turkey, fresh greens, gingerbread and popcorn" pervaded the home. The mouthwatering "aromas of Christmas cooking" mingled with the crisp fragrance of evergreen and holly that Aunt Mary had brought in to decorate the pictures and windows.

The site of these festivities was a marvelous ten room home surrounded by extensive gardens. Today, on the National Register of Historic Places and open to the public, the home is a delightful "oasis of yesteryear" located in the center of downtown Hartford. Original parts of the house date back to 1740. The area which is now the kitchen was purchased in 1882 by Daniel Butler and remodeled with several additions. The Butler family married into the McCook family who then lived in the home continuously for 186 years. The antique furniture, children's toys, musical instruments, and especially the box of Christmas ornaments which was found carefully preserved in the "7th heaven" (loft) of the garret — just as the diary indicated — gives the modern visitor to the home a special glimpse into the personal life of this lively family.

Friends were often included in the Christmas festivities. One of John McCook's most distinguished friends was a fellow clergyman, the Reverend Horace Bushnell who is said to have dined with the McCook family on Christmas day, 1875. Bushnell was the minister of Hartford's North Congregational Church and was known for his powerful sermons as well as numerous articles, essays and books, including the well known *Christian Nurture*. His basic philosophy stressed the call for society to be "interdependent and mutually helpful." This was in strong contrast to the spirit of the times which stressed individualistic achievement. Horace Bushnell's concern for society led him to invest his energies in the development of better public schools, better roads and Hartford's first public water system. Through his efforts, land which was occupied by an unsightly slum area was purchased by the city of Hartford. The handsome new park which replaced the slum became "the first public park in the world to be voted and paid for by a city." After Bushnell's death in 1876, a memorial was built in his honor by his daughter, Dotha Bushnell Hillyer. The auditorium, which she had designed and constructed with the assistance of her daughter and son-in-law, Mr. and Mrs. Charles Seavernes, and a small group of equally dedicated citizens, became a significant addition to the life of the community. Connecticut theatergoers now come to the Bushnell Memorial Hall, fully modernized in 1973, to enjoy performances of the Hartford Symphony Orchestra, Connecticut Opera Association, the Hartford Ballet, as well as to enjoy the talents of leading artists and speakers from around the world. A building which serves the city so well was a fitting memorial to Bushnell and his passionate concern for his fellow citizens.

Curators of the Butler-McCook Homestead indicate that a Christmas meal shared with the McCook family would have included "thick mock turtle soup with a piece of lemon and hard boiled egg in it, roast turkey, potatoes, onions, mushrooms, succotash, olives, celery, cranberries, mince and pumpkin pies, frozen pudding, nuts and fruits, with a toast in cider." This special dinner was truly a filling and festive occasion!

Insidious Rum Punch

YIELD: 48 ½-Cup Servings
CALORIES PER SERVING: 173
CARBOHYDRATES: 11g
MARINATING: 24 Hours — Tea
FREEZING: Yes — Ice Ring

Well made plans enable the party giver to relax and graciously accept compliments for this beverage. Remember to serve coffee before your guests bid adieu!

2 qts. *(1.9L)* green tea, hot and *very* strong
1 lb. *(450g)* brown sugar
1 qt. *(950ml)* fresh lemon juice, (approx. 8 large lemons)
2 qts. *(1.9L)* dark Jamaican rum
1 qt. *(950ml)* cognac
2 lemons, thinly sliced
Decorative ice ring

Strain tea over brown sugar; add lemon juice, let sit overnight. Next day add rum, cognac and lemon slices. Pour into bowl over ice ring.

Emilie de Brigard, Higganum, CT

Chestnut Soup

Today the world's leading chestnut is *Castanea sativa*, the European chestnut. It is known as the Spanish chestnut in England, and as the *marron* in France. This large brown nut has been popular as a nutritious and versatile food since the time of ancient Greece. The kernel when peeled and cooked is sweet and slightly floury and may be prepared in a great variety of ways. It is used in stuffings, soups and sauces and is widely popular as a sweet when pureed or glazed with sugar.

YIELD: 8-10 Servings
TOTAL CALORIES: 1240
CALORIES PER SERVING: 124
CARBOHYDRATES: 11g
PROTEIN: 2g
FAT: 8g
SODIUM: High
PREPARING: 15 Minutes
SIMMERING: 18 Minutes

¼ cup *(30g)* chopped celery
¼ cup *(30g)* chopped carrots
¼ cup *(40g)* chopped onion
2 T. *(30g)* butter
4 cups *(950ml)* chicken stock
2 sprigs parsley
1 bay leaf
1 clove
1 cup *(450g)* fresh cooked chestnuts or 1 can (1 lb.) chestnuts, drained
¼-½ cup *(60-120ml)* Madeira wine or sherry
½ cup *(120ml)* cream
Salt
Freshly ground pepper

In a large saucepan, saute celery, carrot and onion in butter until tender. Add chicken stock, parsley, bay leaf and clove; bring to boil; simmer 15 minutes.

Puree chestnuts, add to stock; add Madeira, simmer 3 minutes. Remove parsley, bay leaf and clove; put contents of pan in blender or food processor; puree. Return to pan, add cream; stir over moderate heat until hot, but do not let boil. Add salt and pepper to taste. Add more Madeira, if desired, and serve.

Diane Burgess, Hartford, CT

Microwave Conversion Instructions: Note: Decrease chicken stock to 3 cups and Madeira to ¼ cup. In covered casserole, cook celery, carrots and onion in 2 T. butter 5 minutes on High. Stir in chicken stock and parsley, bay leaf and clove. Cook on High 5 minutes. Stir often. Remove parsley, bay leaf and clove. Puree chestnuts in blender or food processor. Add to stock mixture with scant ¼ cup Madeira. Simmer 1½ minutes on Medium (50%). Blend all ingredients in food processor or blender. Return to casserole. Add cream. Heat on Medium (50%) 1 minute. Season and serve.

Champignons Flambés

FLAMED MUSHROOMS

In ancient Egypt, mushrooms were grown for food, but only for the Pharaohs; mushrooms were thought to be much too good for the common people of Egypt. This is a fun dish to prepare at the table.

YIELD: 6 Servings
TOTAL CALORIES: 660
CALORIES PER SERVING: 110
CARBOHYDRATES: 3g
PROTEIN: 2g
FAT: 10g
PREPARING: 10 Minutes
COOKING: 15 Minutes

Remove stems from mushrooms and save for soup. Melt butter in saute pan; saute mushrooms. Season with salt, pepper and tarragon.

Heat cognac in small pan. As soon as mushrooms begin to brown, pour cognac over them and flame. When flame has died down, spoon liquid over mushrooms; cook 2 minutes more; serve.

Joyce Anne Vitelli, Manchester, CT

1½ lbs. *(680g)* mushrooms
5 T. *(75g)* butter
½ tsp. salt
Freshly ground pepper
1 tsp. crushed tarragon
½ cup *(120ml)* cognac

Smoked Scallops New Zealand

This recipe comes to us courtesy of Jonathan Walker, former Executive Chef of the BROWNSTONE Restaurant, from a chef who served the dish at the Mansion House Hotel on Kawua Island, New Zealand.

YIELD: 4 Servings
CALORIES PER SERVING: 276
CARBOHYDRATES: 3g
PROTEIN: 30g
FAT: 16g
SODIUM: High
PREPARING: 15 Minutes
COOKING: 10 Minutes
FREEZING: No

Heat saute pan over medium heat. Add clarified butter. Cook scallops in butter 2 to 3 minutes, or until halfway done. Add mushrooms and wine. Simmer about 2 more minutes. Add cream and dill. Simmer until sauce is reduced and thickened, about 3 minutes. Add salt and pepper.

Variations, Advance Preparation, and Serving Suggestions: Garnished with watercress, this dish makes an unusual buffet presentation. The recipe may be doubled or tripled.

Wine Suggestion: French Chablis, crisp white; serve chilled.

1 T. *(15g)* clarified butter
1 lb. *(450g)* smoked sea scallops, halved (available at smokehouses and specialty food markets)
½ cup *(40g)* sliced fresh mushrooms
¼ cup *(60ml)* white wine
½ cup *(120ml)* heavy cream
½ tsp. snipped fresh dill
Salt
Freshly ground white pepper to taste

Roast Turkey in Paper Bag with Warwick Maize Sausage Stuffing

This method for roasting turkey is foolproof! The bird emerges extremely moist, a beautiful rich golden brown with absolutely no watching, basting or worrying.

In fall of 1492, two Spaniards returned from America and reported to Christopher Columbus that they had come upon "a sort of grain they called maize, which was well-tasted, bak'd, dry'd and made into flour." It was thus that Europe became aware of the existence in America of its only native cereal. Maize is the world's second most plentiful cereal, behind rice but ahead of wheat. And it is certainly the only cereal, probably the only food plant, and possibly the only living producer of food, animal or vegetable, which cannot reproduce itself without the aid of man which is why the original habitat of maize is unknown. But actually Indian folklore knows exactly how maize originated! It grew out of the feathery headdress of a buried Indian warrior. A warrior descended from heaven and struggled with a brave. The brave conquered the warrior, and out of the head of the warrior's grave sprouted the maize for which the starving Indians had been praying.

YIELD: 1 15-Lb. Stuffed Turkey
  or 15 Servings
TOTAL CALORIES: 10,185
CALORIES PER SERVING
  INCLUDING STUFFING: 679
CARBOHYDRATES: 15g
PROTEIN: 49g
FAT: 47g
CHOLESTEROL: High
SODIUM: High

TURKEY STOCK:

Turkey neck and giblets
Celery, coarsely chopped
Onion, coarsely chopped
Water
Carrot, coarsely chopped
Salt
Freshly ground pepper

WARWICK MAIZE STUFFING:

2 cups *(110g)* **toasted bread cubes**
6 cups *(725g)* **day-old cornbread or**
  buttermilk cornbread
¼ cup minced parsley
3 T. sage
1 tsp. marjoram
1 tsp. thyme
1 T. salt
1 tsp. freshly ground pepper
½ lb. *(225g)* **hot bulk sausage, crumbled**
4 T. *(60g)* **butter**
1½ cups *(225g)* **finely chopped onion**
Turkey liver
1 cup *(115g)* **finely chopped celery**
1 pint *(475ml)* **fresh oysters**

TURKEY STOCK: Cook neck and giblets with celery, onion, water, carrot, salt and pepper. (Turkey stock may be made a day in advance).

STUFFING: For a 12- to 15-lb. turkey. Crumble bread and cornbread in large bowl; combine with parsley, sage, marjoram, thyme, salt and pepper. Set aside.

Saute crumbled sausage in a large heavy skillet. Drain on paper towels; add to cornbread mixture. Add butter to sausage drippings and saute onion and liver for 10 minutes. Add celery, cook 5 minutes more. Transfer to cornbread mixture, add oysters to skillet and cook until the edges curl. Remove and add to dressing. Combine dressing with enough turkey stock to moisten.

ROAST TURKEY: Stuff and truss turkey. Place ½ lb. butter, broken into small pieces in the bottom of brown paper bag. (Be certain the seam side of bag is on the top — not on the bottom where you are placing butter). Rub outside of turkey thoroughly with remaining butter. Put turkey in bag and seal by stapling open end together, so that no air can get in. If sealed well, turkey will be very moist. Place bag on as high a rack as possible in oven over roasting pan filled with 1½ inches *(4cm)* water. Roast turkey in preheated 325° oven according to chart. When time is up, slit open bottom of bag while still in oven, so that all juices will drain into remaining liquid in roasting pan; check for doneness with meat thermometer. If not done, finish roasting turkey in conventional manner. When done, remove from oven and let rest 20 to 30 minutes. Make gravy while turkey rests.

TURKEY GRAVY: Pour fat and meat juices from roasting pan into bowl, leaving all brown bits in pan. Let fat rise to top; skim it off, but reserve in another bowl. For each cup of gravy desired, measure

1 T. fat and put back in roasting pan. Set over low heat. Measure 1 T. flour for each cup gravy. Blend flour into fat in pan. Cook until bubbly, stirring constantly. Brown flour to obtain more color for gravy. You will need 1 cup liquid for each cup of finished gravy. Use reserved pan juices and turkey stock. If extra liquid is needed, use canned chicken stock. Add lukewarm stock to flour mixture all at once. Cook, stirring constantly, until thickened, scraping up all brown bits. Add chopped cooked giblets, if desired. Season to taste.

Gloria J. Holtsinger, West Hartford, CT
Melinda M. Vance, West Hartford, CT

Nutritional Notes: Nutritional analysis uses 4⅔ oz. *(130g)* cooked turkey meat per serving and does not include gravy. Gravy generally contains approximately 30 calories per tablespoon, although calories and fat can be decreased when prepared from scratch.

Wine Suggestion: California Charbono, robust red; serve at room temperature or California Beaumont Pinot Noir, dry red; serve at room temperature.

Microwave Conversion Instructions: *Turkey Stock:* Coarsely chop celery, onion and carrot. Cut giblets into slices. Cut neck into 3 sections. Place in casserole and add 2 cups *(475ml)* water. Cook, covered, on High 20 minutes or until tender.

Warwick Stuffing: Prepare bread and cornbread with seasonings as directed above. Place crumbled sausage and chopped onion in large glass measure. Cook, uncovered, on High 3 to 4 minutes, stirring once or twice to keep sausage crumbly. Cook until sausage is no longer pink. Drain on paper towels and add to cornbread mixture. Add chopped celery to sausage drippings; cook, uncovered, 2 minutes. Add coarsely chopped turkey liver; cook on Medium (50%), covered, 2 minutes or until liver is no longer pink. Transfer to cornbread mixture. Add oysters to drippings; cook on High 3 minutes, just until oysters curl around edges. Remove and add to dressing. Combine dressing with just enough turkey stock to moisten. Save remaining stock for gravy.

For *Turkey up to 14 lbs.:* Stuff turkey. Close opening with heel of bread or toothpicks. Blend 1 T. commercial browning sauce with 1 T. oil and brush over turkey. *Leave bag open.* (Place in oven at an angle if necessary.) Cook on High 20 minutes. Turn turkey rack or pan around to reverse position. Cook on Medium High (70%) 30 minutes. Remove turkey from bag and baste with drippings. Turn turkey over. Brush again with browning sauce if necessary. Return turkey to bag. Continue to cook on Medium High (70%) until it reaches an internal temperature of 170°. If not using probe, time should be 7 minutes per pound *total cooking time.* Allow turkey to rest 20 to 30 minutes before carving. Cover with foil during this standing period.

Turkey Gravy: Pour fat and meat juices into large bowl along with all brown bits to add flavor and color. Let fat rise to top; skim and reserve in a second bowl. For each cup gravy, measure 1 T. fat and put back in roasting dish. Cook on High until melted. Measure 1 T. flour for each cup gravy. Blend flour into fat in dish; stir until flour is completely dissolved. Cook, uncovered, on High until bubbly, stirring once. Cook until flour is slightly brown. Add 1 cup pan juices for each cup gravy. If more gravy is needed, use turkey broth made by cooking giblets. Add lukewarm broth to flour mixture all at once. Cook on High, uncovered, stirring frequently until sauce is thickened. Correct seasonings.

ROAST TURKEY:

1 6-30-lb. *(2700-13500g)* **turkey, stuffed**
1 lb. *(450g)* **butter**
1 or 2 large brown paper bags

ROASTING TIMES IN 325° OVEN:

WEIGHT	HOURS
6-8 lbs.	2-2½
8-12 lbs.	2½-3
12-16 lbs.	3-3¾
16-20 lbs.	3¾-4½
20-24 lbs.	4½-5½
24-30 lbs.	5½-6½

TURKEY GRAVY:

Fat
Flour
Pan juices
Turkey stock

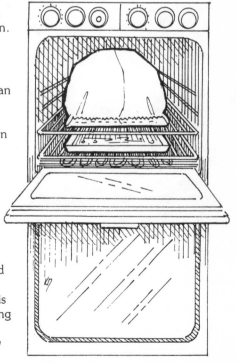

Pomfret Parsnips

YIELD: 6 Servings
CALORIES PER SERVING: 186
CARBOHYDRATES: 13g
PROTEIN: 2g
FAT: 14g
CHOLESTEROL: High
SODIUM: High
PREPARING: 15 Minutes
COOKING: 20 Minutes

From the GOLDEN LAMB BUTTERY in Brooklyn, Connecticut, a very charming and personal restaurant ensconced in an authentic, storybook red barn on a 1,500 acre working farm, Hillandale.

8-10 medium parsnips, peeled and cut into rounds or chopped into small pieces
Chicken stock (about 1 cup)
1 tsp. seasoned salt
5 T. *(75g)* **butter, divided**
1 cup *(240ml)* **cream**
Paprika

Cover parsnips with chicken stock; add seasoned salt. Cook slowly until tender and almost all liquid has evaporated.

Using either food processor or potato masher, mash parsnips; add 4 T. butter and enough cream to make parsnips consistency of very soft mashed potatoes.

Put in 1½-qt. *(1.5L)* casserole. In center of the mixture, add 1 T. butter, sprinkle with paprika and put in preheated 200° oven to keep warm for up to 30 minutes.

Nutritional Notes: Small to medium-sized parsnips usually have a less thick woody center which can be bitter and tough when cooked. Steaming and removing peel after cooking preserves vitamins and minerals as well as flavor and texture. Parsnips are available October through April. They contain a moderate amount of vitamin C, as well as B vitamins and potassium. For optimum vitamin C content use them during the winter months as the vitamin C supply can diminish by half during long storage.

Pickled Oranges

YIELD: 6-8 Servings
TOTAL CALORIES: 1888
CALORIES PER ORANGE: 236
CARBOHYDRATES: 58g
PROTEIN: 1g
SODIUM: High
COOKING: 1 Hour
BAKING: 1½ Hours

Particularly delicious with chicken or roast turkey.

6-8 juice oranges
1 tsp. salt
2½ cups *(500g)* **sugar**
½ cup *(120ml)* **water**
¼ cup *(60ml)* **light corn syrup**
½ cup *(120ml)* **cider vinegar**
24 whole cloves
6 whole cinnamon sticks

Prick orange skins. Place oranges in saucepan with salt and water to cover. Boil 20 minutes; drain. Add fresh boiling water; boil 20 minutes. Drain and let cool.

Cut oranges into quarters and discard seeds. Place oranges in shallow baking dish.

Combine sugar, ½ cup water, corn syrup and vinegar in saucepan. Boil until sugar dissolves. Add cloves and cinnamon sticks. Boil 10 minutes more. Pour syrup over oranges. Bake, covered, in a preheated 275° oven 1½ hours. Let cool to room temperature. Refrigerate until chilled. Serve cold. Oranges keep indefinitely, refrigerated.

Paula Smith, West Hartford, CT
from *Not Chopped Liver*

Nutritional Notes: Nutritional analysis uses 8 oranges and assumes that ⅔ of the syrup is consumed.

Microwave Conversion Instructions: Prick orange skins. Place oranges in a circular formation on floor of oven. Heat on High 5 to 6 minutes. Cool. Cut into quarters and place in shallow baking dish. In a 4-cup *(1L)* glass measure combine sugar, water, corn syrup and vinegar. Boil until sugar dissolves, about 4 minutes, stirring once. Pour syrup over orange quarters. Cover and cook on High 12 to 15 minutes. Let cool to room temperature. Refrigerate.

Christmas Pudding with Caramel Sauce

No single dish is more synonymous with Christmas feasting than the English plum pudding, fragrant with spices, darkly rich with fruit and handsome with its sprig of holly and wreath of blue-burning brandy flames. Its origin dates back to Druid times when legend has it that Daga, the god of plenty, mixed a pudding of the best meats, fruits and spices in celebration of the winter solstice. The word "plum" usually used in the title of a pudding that contains none refers back to the time when the main ingredient was prunes, later replaced by raisins. But the pudding recipe presented here is neither English nor plum! It comes from the donor's German grandmother and uses carrots and potatoes.

YIELD: 10 Servings
CALORIES PER SERVING
   INCLUDING SAUCE: 545
CARBOHYDRATES: 69g
PROTEIN: 2g
FAT: 29g
CHOLESTEROL: High
CALORIES PER TABLESPOON
   CARAMEL SAUCE: 64
PREPARING: 30 Minutes
BAKING: 1 Hour
COOKING: 5 Minutes
FREEZING: Yes

PUDDING: Mix baking soda with carrots and potatoes. Set aside. Cream butter and sugar together; sift flour and spices over mixture; add raisins, carrot and potato mixture. Blend well. Place in buttered, 5-cup (1¼L) oven-proof mold. Place mold in larger baking pan. Pour enough hot water into pan to come halfway up sides of mold. Place pan on middle rack of preheated 350° oven. Bake 60 minutes, or until pudding is set but still moist and begins to leave sides of mold. Remove pan from oven. Set mold on rack to cool to room temperature. Unmold onto serving plate. (If plate is oven-proof, pudding may be re-warmed briefly in 300° oven, if desired.)

CARAMEL SAUCE: Melt sugar and butter in top of double boiler set in hot water over low heat. Add cream slowly, stirring well. Remove pan from heat. Stir in vanilla.

Pass warm sauce separately or pour over pudding.

Gloria McDonagh, West Hartford, CT

Variations, Advance Preparation, and Serving Suggestions: Pudding and sauce can be prepared a day ahead. Re-warm sauce gently over low heat. Unmolded pudding can be frozen for 1 month, wrapped in foil. Defrost still wrapped. Bring to room temperature. Re-warm in 300° oven. Sprinkle pudding with whisky or brandy if dry. Pudding and sauce can be doubled successfully.

Wine Suggestion: French Chateau Voigny Sauternes, sweet white; serve cold.

Microwave Conversion Instructions: Note: Do not soak or rinse raisins in hot water. Place pudding mixture in 2-qt. (2L) casserole. Cook, covered, on High 6 minutes. Rotate ½ turn. Continue to cook on High 3 to 5 minutes.

PUDDING:

1 tsp. baking soda
1 cup (120g) raw, finely grated carrots
1 cup (250g) raw, finely grated potatoes
½ cup (115g) butter, softened
1 cup (200g) sugar
1 cup (115g) flour
1 tsp. cinnamon
1 tsp. freshly grated nutmeg
1 tsp. ground cloves
1 cup (170g) raisins, rinsed in hot water, drained

CARAMEL SAUCE:

1 cup (200g) brown sugar
½ cup (115g) butter
1 cup (240ml) heavy cream
1 tsp. pure vanilla extract

Connecticut Hunt
Breakfast Buffet

Join the hunters after the chase in front of a roaring fire for lively conversation and a satisfying meal.

The crisp autumn air rushes past the brightly clad riders as they gallop their mounts across broad fields. The fever pitch, as the hounds "give tongue," urges the riders to hurdle yet another stream and stone wall in pursuit of their quarry. . . . A scene from 19th century England? Hardly. This could well describe a bright November morning for many members of the Fairfield County Hounds who would affirm that fox hunting is alive and well in Connecticut.

Though the origin of fox hunting is generally traced to England, it actually had strong supporters in the colonies as early as 1650. One hundred years later both George Washington and Thomas Jefferson were known as avid fox hunters.

There have been interesting differences, however, between the English and American versions of the hunt. In England the hunt was a sport reserved for the landed aristocracy. The dress and hunt codes were rigidly enforced. In unsettled rural America the attitude was much more casual and individual. Though many American hunt clubs today adhere to English hunt terminology and tradition, the rules are primarily enforced to ensure the safety of the hunters and their animals. A typical "field" might include a pre-teen on a shaggy pony as well as the elegantly garbed master of the hounds mounted on a handsome thoroughbred hunter.

According to Peter Beckford (1740-1811), an early hunt enthusiast, there is also a distinct difference in the North American climate and terrain, making it "much easier for the hounds to follow the line of the fox by scent" in England than in America. For this reason "it is impossible to use only one type of foxhound," and distinct American fox hounds have been bred.

The American Master of Fox Hounds Association indicates that there are currently three active hunt clubs in Connecticut: Fairfield County Hounds; Mr. Haight's Litchfield County Hounds; and the Connecticut Fox Hunters Association. This third club is located in Broad Brook and holds an annual field trial with between sixty and seventy hounds. In the past Connecticut fox hunters were able to boast of at least ten recognized hunts and dozens of clubs. As late as 1945, the Hartford Fox Club organized hunts on both Talcott and Cedar Mountains. But population growth, highways and building developments have all contributed to the demise of most of the hunting grounds as well as most of the foxes.

On a typical Connecticut hunt the dogs begin to search for the scent of a fox. When one is "raised" the mounted hunters chase the baying hounds who chase the fox. If the dogs lose the scent, they stop baying. This actually happens often, for in Connecticut the fox frequently escapes. The New England terrain offers so many hiding places and thick underbrush that both hounds and hunters are hindered or halted in their pursuit. Some of the biggest concerns for the hunter are that the hounds will chase a deer instead of the fox or that the hounds will come upon a porcupine. Rather than chase the live fox, several Connecticut hunts are organized as "drag hunts." A huntsman has dragged a line of scent some twelve miles across the countryside, skillfully simulating the path a cunning live fox might take. This might be along fence rails or across a brook, yet the huntsman carefully avoids areas which might be dangerous for a large field of riders.

Following the ancient custom of feasting after a successful hunt, fox hunters usually observe the rite of a hunt breakfast. In the United States one of the most elaborate breakfast feasts of the year is traditionally on Thanksgiving morning. Our first Thanksgiving celebration could even be labeled a hunt breakfast, for the main course of the Plymouth Colony's midmorning feast was the fresh venison provided by the Indians.

After an exhilarating chase through the Connecticut countryside, the hounds are kenneled, the horses carefully rubbed down and stabled, and the riders served a sumptuous feast before a blazing fire.

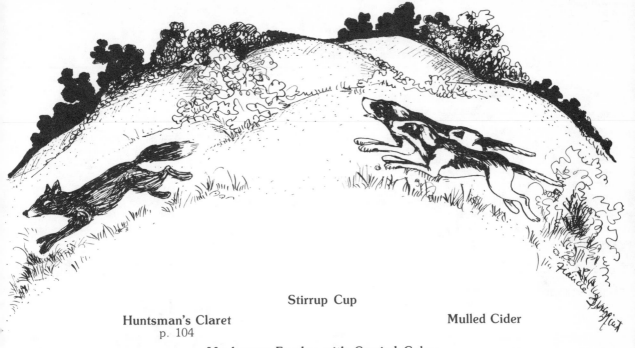

Stirrup Cup

Huntsman's Claret
p. 104

Mulled Cider

Mushroom Fondue with Curried Cubes
p. 104

Shellfish Mold
p. 334

Spinach Roulade with Smoked Salmon
Brunch Filling
p. 106

Keshy Yena
p. 105

Creole Eggs Casserole
p. 107

Nectarine Chutney
p. 107

Whole Wheat Irish
Soda Bread
p. 108

Individual Brioche
p. 226

Sourdough English
Muffins
p. 239

Bibb Lettuce, Endive and Watercress
with Sesame Salad Dressing
p. 108

English Fruit Trifle
p. 109

Huntsman's Claret

15 whole cloves
8 cinnamon sticks
1 T. freshly grated nutmeg
1 qt. *(950ml)* water
Rind of 4 lemons, grated
Rind of 2 oranges, grated
8 liters red wine
1 liter Ruby port

In a large kettle, combine spices, water, and grated fruit rinds; simmer 15 minutes.

Strain; add wine and port; heat until almost boiling.

Remove from heat; garnish with strips of lemon rind; serve immediately.

Deitra Bardon, Groton Long Point, CT

YIELD: 12 Hors d'Oeuvre Servings or
  6 Entree Servings
TOTAL CALORIES: 4122
CALORIES PER ENTREE SERVING: 687
CARBOHYDRATES: 51g
PROTEIN: 15g
FAT: 47g
CHOLESTEROL: High
TOTAL CALORIES FONDUE
  WITHOUT CUBES: 1512
PREPARING: 50 Minutes
FREEZING: Yes

MUSHROOM FONDUE:

4 T. *(60g)* butter
¾ lb. *(340g)* fresh mushrooms, chopped
1 medium onion, chopped
3 oz. *(85g)* Cheddar cheese, chopped
3 T. *(20g)* flour
1 cup *(240ml)* milk
½ cup *(120ml)* heavy cream
Salt and freshly ground pepper
2 T. fresh Italian parsley, chopped

CURRIED BREAD CUBES:

1 loaf *(425g)* French bread
½ cup *(115g)* butter
4 T. *(60ml)* oil
4 tsp. curry powder

Mushroom Fondue with Curried Cubes

An unusual and wonderful variation on a classic theme.

MUSHROOM FONDUE: In large skillet, melt butter and saute mushrooms and onion until soft, approximately 10 minutes. In blender or food processor, puree mixture. Return to skillet; add cheese, cooking slowly until melted. Sprinkle with flour and add milk. Bring to boil; cook gently until thickened, 2 minutes. Add cream, season to taste. Sprinkle with parsley. (Up to this point may be prepared ahead, reheat in fondue pot).

Pour into fondue pot for serving. Keep hot over low heat on fondue stand. Let each person spear chunks of curried bread cubes on long-handled fondue fork and dip in mixture.

BREAD CUBES: Remove crust from bread and cut in cubes. In large skillet, melt butter, add oil and curry powder, stir.

Saute bread cubes until butter is absorbed and cubes are golden brown. Cool.

Janice Niehaus, West Hartford, CT

Wine Suggestion: Swiss Neuchatel or Valais, light white; serve chilled.

Microwave Conversion Instructions: In a 2-qt. *(2L)* glass measure or bowl place chopped onion, with 4 T. butter on top of onion. Cook on High uncovered 3 minutes; stir in chopped mushrooms; continue to cook 2 minutes, or until soft. In blender or food processor, puree mixture. Return to bowl, stir in flour and milk. Cook on High until thick and bubbly, about 5 to 6 minutes, stirring twice. Add cheese (grated is easier to melt), stir until melted. Add cream, cook on High one minute. Season to taste. Sprinkle with parsley. Follow above directions for completion.

Keshy Yena

A Curacaon recipe, the name derives from Spanish "queso" for cheese, and "llena", meaning filled. In Curacao, it is served in a hollowed-out Edam cheese. The top of the cheese is used as a cover and when the "lid" is lifted, a tantalizing aroma fills the air.

YIELD: 8-10 Servings
CALORIES PER SERVING: 506
CARBOHYDRATES: 16g
PROTEIN: 43g
FAT: 30g
CHOLESTEROL: High
SODIUM: High
PREPARING: 45 Minutes
BAKING: 30 Minutes
FREEZING: Yes

Coat beef strips with ¼ cup flour mixed with salt and pepper. Melt ½ cup butter in heavy skillet. Add beef, stir and cook until browned. Add 2 T. flour; cook, stirring, 1 minute. Add wine. Cook 2 minutes more. Remove from heat.

Melt ¼ cup butter in heavy frying pan. Add peppers, onions, mushrooms. Saute until soft. Add tomatoes, cayenne, salt. Cook, stirring, until most of liquid has evaporated. Remove from heat. Stir in pickle, raisins, olives. Combine with beef and wine mixture. Add water. Correct seasoning.

Line a 3-qt. *(3L)* casserole with sliced cheese. Fill casserole with meat and vegetable mixture. Grate any remaining cheese and sprinkle over top. Bake, uncovered, on bottom rack of preheated 350° oven for 30 minutes, or until cheese is melted and bubbly. Garnish with parsley.

Marjorie Chapin, Manchester, CT

Variations, Advance Preparation, and Serving Suggestions:
Can be made with 2 lbs. *(900g)* chicken meat, or 2 lbs. red snapper cut in strips or cubed. Tastes even better a day or so after baking. Refrigerate. To serve, bring to room temperature, rewarm in 300° oven. Leftovers may be frozen.

If you wish to serve it in a cheese, peel the wax off and hollow a 6 lb. Edam cheese to about ½-inch *(1.25cm)* thickness. (Small, individual cheeses are more readily available). Wrap in foil to prevent melting.

Serve with Variegated Salad (page 175) and a dark bread. Apple Mousse with Apricot Sauce (page 408) provides a refreshing finale.

Wine Suggestion: California Petite Sirah, peppery red; serve at room temperature.

2 lbs. *(900g)* round steak, cut in thin strips (partially freeze meat to facilitate slicing)
¼ cup *(30g)* plus 2 T. *(15g)* flour
½ tsp. salt
¼ tsp. freshly ground pepper
¾ cup *(170g)* butter
½ cup *(120ml)* red wine
2 medium green or red peppers, coarsely chopped
½ cup *(70g)* finely sliced onions
½ lb. *(225g)* mushrooms, sliced
2 medium tomatoes, coarsely chopped
¼ tsp. cayenne pepper
Salt to taste
1 T. finely chopped sweet pickle
¼ cup *(40g)* seedless raisins
6 small stuffed green olives, finely chopped
1 cup *(240ml)* water
1 2-lb. *(900g)* Edam cheese, rind removed and cut into ¼-inch *(6mm)* slices
Chopped fresh parsley

YIELD: 8 Servings
TOTAL CALORIES WITH
  MUSHROOM FILLING: 2480
CALORIES PER SERVING: 310
CARBOHYDRATES: 12g
PROTEIN: 14g
FAT: 23g
CHOLESTEROL: High
PREPARING: 30 Minutes
BAKING: 15 Minutes
FREEZING: No

ROULADE:

3 lbs. *(1350g)* well-washed fresh spinach
  or 3 pkgs. **(10 oz. each)** *(855g)* frozen
  spinach, thawed, squeezed dry,
  chopped but not cooked
Salt
Freshly ground pepper
Freshly grated nutmeg
6 T. *(85g)* butter
4 eggs, separated
Breadcrumbs
¼ cup *(30g)* grated Parmesan cheese

MUSHROOM FILLING:

½ lb. *(225g)* mushrooms, finely minced
3 T. *(15g)* finely minced scallions
2 T. *(30g)* butter
8 oz. *(225g)* cream cheese
2-3 T. *(30-45g)* sour cream
Salt
Freshly ground pepper
1 T. chopped fresh dill

BRUNCH FILLING:

3 T. *(45g)* butter
4 eggs, beaten
¼ lb. *(115g)* smoked salmon, minced
1 T. finely minced chives
Salt
Freshly ground pepper
Creme Fraiche (page 200)

Spinach Roulade

A *roulade* is a flat souffle baked in a rectangular shape, then rolled up with a filling. The variety of both the roll and filling is limited only by your imagination. It may be served as a first course for a luncheon or supper, or as the vegetable accompaniment for a main course.

ROULADE: If using fresh spinach, cook until just wilted. Thoroughly drain spinach, squeezing out as much moisture as possible. Put spinach in large bowl; add seasonings to taste. If spinach is cold, put bowl in hot water to help absorption of butter. Beat in butter and egg yolks, mixing well.

In another bowl, beat egg whites until they form soft peaks. Fold into spinach mixture.

Spread souffle mixture into a 15½ × 10½-inch *(40 × 26.5cm)* jelly roll pan that has been buttered, lined with waxed paper leaving an extra 1 inch at each end and then buttered again and sprinkled with breadcrumbs. Sprinkle Parmesan cheese over top.

Bake in preheated 350° oven 12 to 16 minutes. Unmold onto foil or a dish towel. If not planning to fill it immediately, roll up in foil or towel, keep a few hours at room temperature or a day in refrigerator. When ready to fill, unroll roulade and spread evenly with filling; roll up lengthwise. Serve at room temperature or warm. It may be made ahead, filled, stored at room temperature covered with foil and then reheated in a preheated 200° oven, 15 to 20 minutes.

MUSHROOM FILLING: Saute mushrooms and scallions in butter. In bowl blend together cream cheese and sour cream. Add mushrooms and scallions and mash well. Season to taste and add dill. If not firm, chill a few minutes in refrigerator until *slightly* firm.

BRUNCH FILLING: Melt butter in skillet; begin to scramble eggs. While eggs are still soft, add remaining ingredients; blend well. Spread mixture over roulade and roll. Serve with a side dish of Creme Fraiche. Garnish with watercress and sauteed cherry tomatoes.

Melinda M. Vance, West Hartford, CT

Wine Suggestion: Hungarian Keknyelu, soft white; serve chilled.

Microwave Conversion Instructions: If using frozen spinach, defrost in package 15 minutes on High. Melt butter 45 seconds on High. Finish spinach souffle according to conventional directions. *Mushroom Filling:* Melt butter 45 seconds on High. Add mushrooms and scallions. Cook 4 minutes on Medium (50%). Soften cream cheese 4 minutes on Low (10%). Blend with sour cream. Combine mushrooms and cheese mixtures with seasonings. *Brunch Filling:* Melt butter 20 seconds on High. Add eggs. Cook 1½ minutes on High. Stir to break up outside edges. Push eggs to center. Add salmon, chives and seasonings. Cook 1 to 1½ minutes more on High. When spinach roulade is assembled, reheat 3 to 5 minutes on Medium (50%).

Nectarine Chutney

A delight for chutney lovers, and a great accompaniment to lamb curry.

YIELD: 2 Pints
TOTAL CALORIES: 2112
CALORIES PER TABLESPOON: 33
CARBOHYDRATES: 6g
FAT: 1g
PREPARING: 20 Minutes
COOKING: 1 Hour

In a large, heavy saucepan, combine all ingredients. Bring to a boil, stirring constantly. Simmer uncovered for 1 hour or until dark brown in color.

May be preserved in canning jars by processing 15 minutes.

Meredith Robbins, Avon, CT

Microwave Conversion Instructions: Note: Decrease cider vinegar from 1½ cups to 1 cup. Combine all ingredients in large casserole. Cook on High 20 to 25 minutes or until dark brown in color and softened. Stir 2 to 3 times during cooking.

6 nectarines, pitted and cut into small pieces
¾ cup *(130g)* raisins
1 tsp. ground ginger or **2 T.** *(30g)* fresh ginger, finely chopped
1 cup *(200g)* dark brown sugar
½ cup *(60g)* chopped walnuts
1½ cups *(355ml)* cider vinegar
¼ cup *(40g)* finely chopped onion
¼ tsp. cayenne pepper
½ tsp. salt

YIELD: 6 Servings
CALORIES PER SERVING: 390
CARBOHYDRATES: 18g
PROTEIN: 16g
FAT: 28g
CHOLESTEROL: High
SODIUM: High
PREPARING: 20 Minutes Plus Boiling Eggs
BAKING: 15 Minutes
SIMMERING: 25 Minutes
FREEZING: Yes

Creole Egg Casserole

Melt butter; add chili powder (browning removes the bitter taste). Saute celery, onion, and bell pepper until lightly browned.

Add tomato soup; simmer 20 minutes; add mushroom soup, mushrooms, salt, pepper, Worcestershire and tabasco sauces; simmer 5 more minutes.

Place eggs in buttered 9 × 13-inch *(22.5 × 33cm)* casserole; cover with sauce, cracker crumbs, finish with grated cheese.

Bake uncovered in preheated 450° oven 15 minutes.

Joyce Anne Vitelli, Manchester, CT

Variations, Advance Preparation, and Serving Suggestions: May be made a day in advance and reheated before serving, or it may be frozen until ready to bake.

Wine Suggestion: California Chenin Blanc, semi-dry, white; serve chilled.

Microwave Conversion Instructions: In large glass casserole, add celery, onion and bell pepper; place cut up butter on top along with chili powder. Cover, cook on High 10 minutes. Add tomato soup, stir and cover; cook on High 5 minutes. Add mushrooms, mushroom soup, salt, pepper, Worcestershire and tabasco sauces; cook uncovered, 5 to 7 minutes on Medium (50%) until heated through. Place eggs in buttered 9 × 13-inch casserole; cover with sauce, cracker crumbs and grated cheese. Cook, uncovered, 15 minutes on Medium, or until cheese is melted and eggs are heated through. Rotate dish halfway through cooking.

4 T. *(60g)* butter
1 tsp. chili powder
5 stalks celery, chopped
1 medium onion, chopped
1 small bell pepper, chopped
1 can (10¾ oz.) *(305g)* tomato soup
½ lb. *(225g)* fresh mushrooms, sliced
1 can (10¾ oz.) *(305g)* cream of mushroom soup
Salt and pepper to taste
Dash Worcestershire sauce
Dash tabasco sauce
8 eggs, hard-boiled, sliced
½ cup *(60g)* cracker crumbs
1 cup *(115g)* grated sharp Cheddar cheese

Fresh Greens with Sesame Salad Dressing

YIELD: 10 Servings
TOTAL CALORIES: 1600
CALORIES PER SERVING: 160
CARBOHYDRATES: 5g
PROTEIN: 1.5g
FAT: 15g
CHOLESTEROL: High
SODIUM: High
PREPARING: 10 Minutes

This recipe came from Phyllis' sister, Lois Schobert, a cooking instructor in Milwaukee.

¼ cup *(30g)* sesame seeds
¼ cup *(60g)* butter
¼ cup *(30g)* freshly grated Parmesan cheese

DRESSING:
1 cup *(225g)* sour cream or Creme Fraiche (page 200)
½ cup *(115g)* mayonnaise (page 190)
1 T. tarragon vinegar
1 T. sugar
½ tsp. salt
¼ tsp. freshly grated pepper
Salad greens of your choice
Cucumber (optional)
Green pepper (optional)

Toast sesame seeds in hot skillet, watching carefully that they do not burn. When toasted, add butter and stir until melted. Add Parmesan cheese and remove from burner; set aside to cool.

DRESSING: Combine sour cream, mayonnaise, vinegar, sugar, salt and pepper. Set aside until ready to use.

Just before serving, toss greens and other salad ingredients of your choice with dressing and crumble cheese mixture over it.

Phyllis Janiszewski, West Hartford, CT

Irish Whole Wheat Soda Bread

YIELD: 1 Pound Loaf
CALORIES PER LOAF: 1990
CARBOHYDRATES: 372g
PROTEIN: 69g
FAT: 25g
SODIUM: High
PREPARING: 15 Minutes
BAKING: 35 Minutes
FREEZING: Yes

Soda bread was traditionally baked over a peat fire in an iron pot with three legs that could be raised or lowered over the fire to regulate the heat.

¼ cup *(30g)* wheat germ
2 cups *(240g)* whole wheat flour
2 cups *(225g)* unbleached white flour
1 T. baking soda
2 tsp. sugar
1 tsp. salt
2 cups *(450g)* plain yogurt

Mix together dry ingredients; add 1 cup yogurt. Add more yogurt in ¼ cup increments until mixture is consistency of soft dough, like biscuit dough, but firm enough to hold its shape. Knead on lightly floured board until smooth and velvety, about 2 minutes. Shape into oval; put on well-buttered baking sheet. With very sharp floured knife, cut a ¼ inch *(6mm)* deep X in center of loaf to within 1 inch *(2.5cm)* of edge. Bake in preheated 375° oven 35 minutes or until loaf is browned and sounds hollow when tapped with your knuckles. Cool, then thinly slice and serve with butter. Soda bread should never be cut into thick slices.

Deitra Bardon, Groton Long Point, CT

Variations, Advance Preparation, and Serving Suggestions:
For white soda bread, use 4 cups *(450g)* unbleached white flour, but decrease baking soda to 2 tsp. Otherwise ingredients and methods remain the same.

Nutritional Notes: This bread is appropriate for the fat-restricted diet if lowfat yogurt is used. Whole grain ingredients add additional nutrients and fiber to bread.

English Fruit Trifle

Trifle is a traditional English dessert sometimes called "tipsy cake" because it was originally made with stale cake restored to its full flavor with liberal sprinklings of rum. One became a little "tipsy" after a generous serving. Its excellence depends in large measure on the quality of the custard and the liquors used. Our version is unquestionably the finest that can be found — no mere trifle!

YIELD: 12-14 Servings
TOTAL CALORIES: 6818
CALORIES PER SERVING: 487
CARBOHYDRATES: 56g
PROTEIN: 5g
FAT: 27g
CHOLESTEROL: High
PREPARING: 1 Hour
MARINATING: 1½ Hours
CHILLING: 1-2 Hours

CUSTARD SAUCE: Dissolve cornstarch in ¼ cup *(60ml)* cream. Beat egg yolks until light; combine with cornstarch. In saucepan, heat remaining cream, do not boil. Add sugar, stirring to dissolve. Pour about 1 cup *(240ml)* of this mixture over yolks, stirring constantly. Return all to mixture in saucepan. Continue cooking over low heat, stirring. Add gelatin, if desired, to thicken. Cook 5 minutes or until sauce is slightly thickened. Remove from heat, blend in vanilla. Let cool to room temperature, covered with plastic wrap.

Place half the ladyfingers and jam in bottom of crystal or decorative serving bowl about 8 inches *(20cm)* in diameter and 4 inches *(10cm)* deep. Sprinkle with half of lemon rind, then half of sherry and brandy. Cover with layer of half of macaroons and fruit. Let stand about 1 hour. Pour half of custard sauce over top.

Repeat layers of remaining ladyfingers, jam, lemon rind, sherry, brandy, macaroons, fruit. Let stand about 30 minutes. Cover with custard sauce. Refrigerate until thoroughly chilled, about 1 to 2 hours. Just before serving, top with whipped cream and almonds. Garnish with additional fruit.

Diane Burgess, Hartford, CT

Variations, Advance Preparation, and Serving Suggestions:
Trifle is at its best served the day made, but if fruits are well-drained, it will spend a night in the refrigerator. Flavors will be combined, less distinct, but perhaps *improved*, to the taste of some. Moist chocolate almond macaroons can be substituted for coconut macaroons.

CUSTARD SAUCE:
1½ T. *(15g)* cornstarch
2 cups *(475ml)* light cream, divided
4 egg yolks
½ cup *(100g)* sugar
1 tsp. unflavored gelatin (optional)
1 tsp. pure vanilla extract

24 ladyfingers, spread with: 1 cup *(285g)* good quality strawberry or raspberry jam
Grated rind of 1 lemon
½-1 cup *(120-240ml)* good dry sherry (can use cream sherry if desired)
3 T. *(45ml)* good brandy
12 coconut macaroons, coarsely crushed, about 2 cups
2 cups diced, sliced, halved seasonal fresh fruit:
    Winter — bananas, pineapple, kiwi
    Summer — peaches, nectarines, berries
2 cups *(475ml)* heavy cream, whipped
½ cup *(60g)* toasted slivered almonds

Pitcher of Bullfrogs

Spinach Water Chestnut Dip
p. 112

Southern Peanut Spread
p. 82

Italian Clam Soup
p. 112

or

Ceviche de Acapulco
p. 113

**Poached Scallops
with Green Sauce**
p. 69

or

**Steamed Fish in Lettuce
with Ginger Lemon Sauce**
p. 114

Baked Rice with Tomatoes and Cheese
p. 350

Snow Pea Salad
p. 61

Cauliflower Slaw
p. 362

Portuguese Sweet Bread
p. 115

Fresh Strawberries and Brie

Amaretti Chocolate Almond Cheesecake
p. 116

or

Blueberry Cheese Charlotte
p. 117

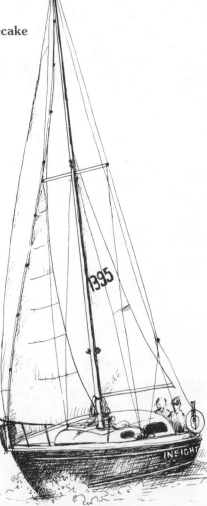

Off Soundings Supper

A galley slave's reprieve, this menu is a perfect combination of make-at-home dishes and simple preparation of the fresh catch of the day.

For centuries the waterways of Connecticut have been a sailor's boulevard. They have enticed the adventurous from the early Indians, to explorers, colonists, whalers, traders, and today even the land-locked suburbanite.

Historically, both the inland waterways and the coastline, bounded by Long Island Sound, were central to the development of the state. By 1662 when the Connecticut Charter was issued by Charles II of England, there were seventeen towns located along the Sound and the Connecticut River. In the 1800s a vibrant steamboat trade plied Connecticut's inland waterways. This era is recalled in the impressively restored Steamboat Dock Museum in Essex. The thriving whaling and shipbuilding industries of early Connecticut are relived in the reconstructed village of Mystic Seaport.

Today Groton, dubbed the "Submarine Capital of the World," is home to the largest United States naval submarine base as well as to the Electric Boat Division of General Dynamics. New London was originally settled because of its excellent deep-water harbor, considered by many to be the best on the Atlantic Coast. At one time it was the busiest whaling port in the world. Today its coastline is the home of the U.S. Coast Guard Academy.

As these and other towns have developed, there have been dramatic changes along the coast over the past 300 years, with houses and commercial buildings now dominating much of the skyline. However, as much of the Connecticut coast is rocky, there has been little erosion. For centuries the physical shoreline has remained remarkably intact. Crabs still scamper through sandy pools, gulls dive for fish, and water laps beside protected salt water marshes. Hardshell clams are still harvested in significant numbers, and juicy scallops can still be found in Niantic Bay. Both residents and visitors to the coast can reap the bounty of the sea, taking not only shellfish but flounder, striped bass, black fish (tautaug) and bluefish. Still thousands of other non-fisherfolk take to the sea in ships — from rubber rafts and rowboats to powerboats, sailboats and yachts for the sheer delight of being on the water.

Throughout the summer months the coastal waters sparkle with brightly colored sails of all shapes and sizes. Sailing in the Sound provides a special treat for today's adventurer, whether one is seeking a relaxed escape from the nine-to-five job or a vigorous competition with nature. Of particular interest to both sailors and landlubbers are the sailboat races sponsored by the Off Soundings Club, founded in 1933. On an Off Soundings weekend over one hundred sailboats, belonging to members from all over the country, gather in New London harbor to compete in eight different cruising classes. The races are held on Friday and Saturday mornings, usually in early June and late September.

Whether it's the sea breeze or the salt air, a sailor's appetite is always hearty. The galley — a kitchen in motion — becomes a most important asset to any vessel. Essentially work space is limited in all but the most elaborate yachts. Just as modern navigation tools and charts have eased the task of the sailor, modern technology has provided vast improvements in refrigeration, stove units and storage for today's galley gourmet. The experienced sailor knows that appliances should be well anchored in case of rough weather. Modern technology has not been able to remedy the problems of stormy seas! Non-breakable utensils and dishes are highly recommended.

No matter how skilled a cook one is, shipboard meals should be simple and well planned. Entrees and one dish casseroles which can be prepared ahead of time and reheated are a boon. A few useful tips suggested by seasoned sailors: when cooking breakfast, boil extra water and store in a Thermos for "instant" soups, coffee or tea; always keep on board emergency stores of dried and canned foods; and always carry saltine crackers for the fair weather sailors! It is also a good idea to have between meal snacks readily available. Wax-coated cheeses such as Edam or Gouda, nuts and dried fruits all keep well.

The successful galley gourmet places emphasis on creating casual, imaginative menus which can be prepared in a small space with a minimum of effort. A challenge, but definitely possible! When the sun has set, celebrate the victory of a glorious day of sailing with this tempting Off Soundings Supper.

111

YIELD: 4 Cups
TOTAL CALORIES: 1600
CALORIES PER TABLESPOON: 25
CARBOHYDRATES: 1g
PROTEIN: 1g
FAT: 2g
SODIUM: High
CHOLESTEROL: High
PREPARING: 5 Minutes
CHILLING: 4 Hours
FREEZING: No

1 pkg. (10 oz.) *(285g)* chopped spinach, thawed, well-drained
2 cups *(450g)* sour cream
1 pkg. (1⅝ oz.) *(40g)* Knorr Swiss vegetable soup mix
½ cup *(115g)* mayonnaise
1 can (8 oz.) *(225g)* water chestnuts, drained, chopped

Spinach Water Chestnut Dip

This will become one of your favorites.

Combine all ingredients. Mix well. Refrigerate at least 4 hours or overnight. Serve with water biscuits or favorite crudites arrangement.

Lois F. Sykes, Niantic, CT

Nutritional Notes: Imitation sour cream and low-sodium imitation mayonnaise may be used in place of *a portion* of above ingredients. Low-sodium soup powders are now available, and will significantly decrease sodium content of this recipe.

YIELD: 4-6 Servings
TOTAL CALORIES: 1284
CALORIES PER SERVING: 214
CARBOHYDRATES: 11g
PROTEIN: 11g
FAT: 14g
PREPARING: 30 Minutes
COOKING: 20 Minutes
FREEZING: No

⅓ cup *(80ml)* olive oil
½ cup *(75g)* chopped onion
4 cloves garlic, finely minced
1 tsp. dried basil or 6 fresh leaves, finely chopped
1 tsp. oregano
1 tsp. saffron, powdered (optional)
1 can (6 oz.) *(170g)* tomato paste
1 cup *(240ml)* dry white wine
2 cups *(475ml)* water
40 littleneck clams, rinsed under cold water
Salt
Freshly ground black pepper

Zuppa di Vongole

ITALIAN CLAM SOUP

Very successful as a main course for a family supper.

Heat olive oil in a large kettle. Add onions and garlic and saute until transparent. Add spices and cook 5 minutes. Add tomato paste, wine, and water; stir. Simmer 5 minutes.

Add clams; cover and steam, stirring with a wooden spoon and shaking the kettle occasionally until the clams open, 5 to 10 minutes. Add salt and pepper to taste. Serve in warmed soup plates with an extra bowl for discarded shells or, as in Italy, bring the pot to the table and serve the clams a few at a time so they do not get cold.

Judith Jordan, West Hartford, CT

Variations, Advance Preparation, and Serving Suggestions: As part of an authentic Italian dinner, this soup is an all-purpose first course that can be followed by any fish course, giving preference, however, to robust rather than delicate flavors. It goes well with Stuffed Squid (page 329).

Clams almost always contain sand. In terms of flavor when clams are to be served in their shells, as in this soup, the most satisfactory method is to allow them to release their juices directly into sauce. There may be a little sand, but it quickly settles to bottom of pot, and with a little care in lifting out clams and spooning sauce into soup plates it will be left behind.

A slice of toasted whole wheat Italian bread can be added to each soup plate before ladling on clams and sauce.

Microwave Conversion Instructions: Place oil, onion and garlic in deep casserole. Cook on High, uncovered, 3 minutes. Add spices and cook 2 minutes. Stir in tomato paste, wine and water. Cook on High 7 minutes. Add clams and cook, covered, on High, stirring frequently, until clams open, about 5 to 10 minutes. Once open, do not cook further as clams become tough. Add salt and pepper to taste.

Ceviche de Acapulco

The word "cebiche" is thought to come from the word "cebar", using its meaning "to saturate". This refers to the fact that the raw fish is saturated or marinated in fresh lime juice. The "cooking" is done by the lime juice rather than by any form of heat, although the fish looks and tastes as though it has been poached. It is white and has lost any raw or translucent look.

YIELD: 6 Entree Servings or
  12 Appetizer Servings
TOTAL CALORIES: 3192
CALORIES PER
  APPETIZER SERVING: 266
CARBOHYDRATES: 7g
PROTEIN: 19g
FAT: 18g
SODIUM: High
PREPARING: 20 Minutes
MARINATING: 6-24 Hours
CHILLING: 4-24 Hours
FREEZING: No

Cut fish and scallops into small cubes, no larger than ½-inch (1.25cm). Marinate fish in lime juice a minimum 6 hours or overnight.

Combine all remaining ingredients except lettuce and avocado; mix lightly but thoroughly.

Drain fish well; add to the sauce and toss well. Chill at least 4 hours before serving. Serve on top of shredded lettuce with avocado slices arranged attractively on top.

Dean Lindsay, Darien, CT

Variations, Advance Preparation, and Serving Suggestions:
Makes a delicious light luncheon dish (especially nice in the center of an avocado mousse ring mold), a cool summer dinner dish, an elegant fish course. After preparation, keeps 1 week refrigerated.

Nutritional Notes: Sodium can be modified by eliminating olives and salt, and decreasing chili sauce. Lime juice contributes vitamin C to the recipe which already has a good distribution of vitamins and minerals.

For an especially low-calorie version yielding 5 cups at 150 calories each, use the following proportions: 1½ lbs. bay scallops or other firm white fish, 1 cup fresh lime juice, 1½ cups chopped fresh tomato, ½ cup chopped green onion, 2 T. chopped green chilies, 10 small pitted green olives, sliced, 1 T. chili sauce, 2 T. tarragon vinegar, 1½ tsp. crushed oregano, 1½ tsp. crushed basil, salt and pepper.

Wine Suggestion: Hungarian Leanyka, dry white; serve chilled.

1½ lbs. *(675g)* haddock (or other firm white fish such as halibut, pompano, red snapper)
1 lb. *(450g)* bay or sea scallops
2 cups *(475ml)* fresh lime juice (about 10 limes)
2 cups *(200g)* peeled, chopped tomato
1 cup *(85g)* sliced green onion (white and green parts)
⅓ cup *(115g)* chopped green chilies
16 pitted green olives, sliced
½ cup *(120ml)* olive oil
¼ cup *(60ml)* dry white wine or dry vermouth
2 T. *(30ml)* white vinegar
2 T. *(30ml)* chili sauce
1 tsp. crumbled oregano
3 T. minced parsley
Salt to taste
Freshly ground pepper to taste
Shredded lettuce
2 avocados, thinly sliced

Steamed Fish in Lettuce Packages with Ginger Lemon Sauce

YIELD: 4 Servings
CALORIES PER SERVING: 442
CARBOHYDRATES: 19g
PROTEIN: 33g
FAT: 26g
SODIUM: High
PREPARING: 40 Minutes
COOKING: 20 Minutes

Light, interesting and elegant dish, with a wonderful texture.

4 serving-size pieces of a firm white fish
   fillet (sole, flounder, cod, or halibut),
   about 6 oz. *(170g)* each
1 head of Boston, red leafed or other
   soft leafed lettuce
4 thin slices onion
12 slices cucumber, peeled and seeded
Salt
Freshly ground pepper

COURT BOUILLON:

4 cups *(950ml)* water
1 T. salt
1 tsp. ground cloves
1 clove garlic, minced
6 peppercorns
6 whole allspice

GINGER LEMON SAUCE:

1 cup *(240ml)* frozen reconstituted
   lemonade
2 T. *(30ml)* fresh lemon juice
2 cups *(475ml)* double-strength chicken
   stock
2 T. *(30g)* finely chopped fresh ginger
¼ lb. *(115g)* butter
½ cup *(120ml)* fish steaming liquid
2 tsp. potato starch mixed with 1 T. cold
   water

One at a time, place pieces of fish on top of several thicknesses lettuce; top each piece with a slice of onion and 3 slices cucumber; salt and pepper to taste.

With additional lettuce leaves, wrap the fish pieces to form a package.

COURT BOUILLON: Combine all ingredients in bottom of steamer. Simmer 15 minutes before using.

Place packages in a steamer and steam over court bouillon 20 minutes. Do not overcook.

GINGER LEMON SAUCE: Simmer all ingredients except potato starch and water 15 minutes; strain if desired and add potato starch-water mixture to thicken. Nap over lettuce and fish.

Adair Burlingham, Cambridge, MA

Variations, Advance Preparation, and Serving Suggestions:
Truly elegant when served in a Chinese steamer or on platter garnished with parsley and steamed mussels in their shells. For large crowds, the fish may be poached in the court bouillon in a preheated 350° oven for approximately 30 minutes. This dish may also be served cold with the Ginger Lemon Sauce or a soy sauce vinaigrette dressing, and then is appropriate for picnics.

Wine Suggestion: California Muscot Blanc, perfumed white; serve chilled.

Microwave Conversion Instructions: Note: Increase potato starch to 3 T. Combine sauce ingredients, except potato starch, in 1½-qt. *(1½L)* casserole. Cook on High 10 minutes or until mixture comes to a boil. Reduce power to Medium (50%) and continue cooking 3 minutes. Stir in dissolved potato starch. Cook on High 3 to 4 minutes. Place 3 cups *(710ml)* court bouillon in 8-inch *(20cm)* round baking dish. Cover with plastic wrap. Cook 8 to 10 minutes on High until it starts to boil. Continue cooking 3 to 4 minutes. Remove plastic wrap. Place fish packages on roasting rack with holes, set over court bouillon. Cook, covered, on High 8 to 10 minutes or just until fish turns opaque. (Timing is for 1½ lbs. *(680g)* fish.)

Portuguese Sweet Bread

This rich yeast loaf with a close, fine texture will remind you of the round loaves of sweet Portuguese bread originally found on Nantucket or Cape Cod.

YIELD: 3 Loaves
CALORIES PER LOAF: 1890
CARBOHYDRATES: 350g
PROTEIN: 49g
FAT: 33g
PREPARING: 40 Minutes
RISING: 3½ Hours
BAKING: 40 Minutes
FREEZING: Yes

Pour milk into large mixing bowl. Add sugar and salt; cool to lukewarm. When cool, beat in eggs; add butter.

Dissolve yeast in warm water with 1 tsp. sugar and set aside to proof. Add to milk with 4 cups flour. Beat well; add remaining flour gradually until dough is stiff.

On floured board, knead dough until smooth and elastic, about 10 minutes. *[FOOD PROCESSOR: Divide ingredients in half. Process in 2 batches. Put flour, unmelted butter, sugar and salt into work bowl; blend by turning machine on/off about 6 times. Add yeast mixture, eggs and warm milk; process 30 to 40 seconds or until dough is thoroughly mixed.]* Form dough into a ball; place in an oiled bowl; turn dough to coat; cover bowl. Put in warm place to double in bulk, about 2 hours.

Punch dough down and let rise again until doubled in bulk, about 50 minutes.

Divide dough into 3 parts; shape into flattened 8-inch *(20cm)* round loaves. Place in well-buttered 9-inch *(22.5cm)* round cake pans. Cover; let rise until doubled in bulk, about 45 minutes.

Bake in preheated 400° oven 40 minutes or until a wooden toothpick inserted in loaf comes out clean and dry. Cool on racks. Serve with sweet butter and jam.

Nancy Bailey, Prospect, KY

2 cups *(475ml)* milk, scalded
1½ cups *(300g)* sugar
2 T. salt
4 eggs
¼ cup *(60g)* butter, melted and cooled
2 pkgs. *(¼ oz. each) (14g)* active dry yeast
¼ cup *(60ml)* lukewarm water
8-9 cups *(900-1000g)* unbleached flour

Variations, Advance Preparation, and Serving Suggestions:
This bread may also be shaped into loaves called "carocois". Roll ⅓ of dough into a 30-inch *(75cm)* long rope. Coil it in a 9-inch *(22.5cm)* pan; brush it with beaten egg and decorate it with a dozen raisins.

Plain rolls can be made with dough by fashioning smooth balls of dough, about 1 inch *(2.5cm)* in diameter, and putting them about ¼ inch *(6mm)* apart in a lightly greased 9-inch *(22.5cm)* square pan.

YIELD: 12-16 Servings
TOTAL CALORIES: 8400
CALORIES PER SERVING: 525
CARBOHYDRATES: 34g
PROTEIN: 8g
FAT: 40g
CHOLESTEROL: High
SODIUM: High
PREPARING: 1 Hour
BAKING: 45 Minutes
CHILLING: 4-6 Hours Minimum
FREEZING: Yes

Amaretti Chocolate Almond Cheesecake

While the Italian macaroons and Italian liqueur used to flavor this cake are almond-flavored, they are both made with apricot kernels, not almonds.

CRUST:

7 oz. *(200g)* **amaretti macaroons (use Amaretti di Saronno, Lazzaroni & Co. brand)**

2 T. *(25g)* **sugar**

1 oz. *(30g)* **unsweetened chocolate**

5 T. *(70g)* **unsalted sweet butter**

FILLING:

8 oz. *(225g)* **extra bittersweet chocolate (Lindt preferred)**

7 oz. *(200g)* **amaretti macaroons**

3½ oz. *(100g)* **almond paste**

⅓ cup *(80ml)* **Amaretto di Saronno liqueur**

3 pkgs. (8 oz. or *225g* **each) cream cheese, at room temperature**

½ cup *(100g)* **sugar**

3 eggs

½ cup *(120ml)* **heavy cream**

Chocolate shavings (optional)

CRUST: Butter sides only of 9-inch *(22.5cm)* springform pan. Crush the macaroons very fine in blender or food processor. You should have about 1½ cups. Place crumbs in bowl; add sugar. Melt chocolate and butter together in double boiler; add to macaroon crumbs and blend thoroughly. Turn mixture into prepared springform pan. Spread crumbs evenly over bottom (not sides); press to make firm, compact layer on bottom. Refrigerate until ready to use.

FILLING: Melt chocolate in top of double boiler over hot water. Remove and set aside to partially cool. Crush macaroons and set aside. Break up almond paste into small pieces and place in mixing bowl. Very slowly beat in liqueur. Beat until thoroughly blended; set aside.

In large bowl of electric mixer or in food processor beat cream cheese until smooth. Add sugar and beat again until smooth. Add almond paste mixture; beat again until thoroughly mixed. Add melted chocolate; beat well again. Slowly beat in 1 egg at a time. Beat only until each is incorporated. Add heavy cream and beat only until smooth.

Gently fold in crushed macaroons. Pour mixture into prepared crust. Rotate pan to level batter. Place cake on shelf ⅓ up from bottom in preheated 350° oven. Bake 45 minutes. Remove from oven; set aside at room temperature until completely cool. Then carefully remove sides of pan.

Refrigerate cake minimum 4 to 6 hours, but best made 3 to 5 days ahead. Serve as is or top with chocolate shavings.

Arlene J. Parmelee, West Hartford, CT

Wine Suggestion: Italian Reciotto Amarone, sweet red sparkling; serve chilled.

Microwave Conversion Instructions: Note: Construct a microwave-safe springform pan as follows. Bottom: Cut a 9-inch circle from heavy cardboard; place on bottom of a 9-inch cake or pie plate. Side: Cut a strip of cardboard 2½ inches wide and long enough to ring a 9-inch circle. Tape edges with masking tape, so that sides can be cut away after cheesecake has set. *Crust:* Cook chocolate and butter together in small glass bowl on High 90 seconds, or until melted. Continue with crust as in conventional recipe. *Filling:* Cook chocolate and butter together in small glass bowl on High 90 seconds, until melted. Set aside to cool slightly. Note: If cream cheese is refrigerator cold, unwrap each block, place on paper plate to soften in oven on Low (10%) 4 minutes per 8 oz. block. Prepare filling as in conventional recipe. Once crushed macaroons are folded in, pour mixture into large glass bowl; cook on Medium (50%) 12 to 14 minutes, or until mixture is very warm, stirring every 2 minutes. Pour warm mixture onto crust bottom. Cook 15 minutes (or until set) on Medium (50%), rotating every 3 to 5 minutes. Remove from oven, cool, refrigerate overnight before serving.

Blueberry Cheese Charlotte

YIELD: 8 Servings
TOTAL CALORIES: 2960
CALORIES PER SERVING: 370
CARBOHYDRATES: 37g
PROTEIN: 6g
FAT: 22g
CHOLESTEROL: High
PREPARING: 40 Minutes
CHILLING: 2 Hours Minimum

"A plum of a job," "the apple of my eye," "peachy-keen!" and "top banana" use fruit as a metaphor for excellence. Exception: "What a lemon." This charlotte recipe "is the berries."

Sprinkle gelatin over water; set aside to soften, about 5 minutes. Add softened gelatin to hot pineapple juice; stir until dissolved. Add lemon juice. Chill until syrupy.

Beat egg whites until foamy; continue beating and gradually add sugar. Beat until stiff peaks form. In another bowl, beat cream cheese and liquor until fluffy. Whip gelatin mixture until it becomes foamy; fold into egg whites. Then fold in cream cheese mixture and then half the blueberries.

Line 1½-qt. *(1.5L)* mold with ladyfingers or strips of sponge cake. Put gelatin mixture into lined mold. Chill several hours or overnight. Unmold on serving plate; garnish with whipped cream and remaining blueberries.

Pauline Livingston, Avon, CT

1 env. *(7g)* **unflavored gelatin**
2 T. *(30ml)* **cold water**
1 cup *(240ml)* **pineapple juice or other fruit juice, heated**
1 T. *(15ml)* **fresh lemon juice**
3 **egg whites**
½ cup *(100g)* **sugar**
2 pkgs. (3 oz. each) *(170g)* **cream cheese**
2-4 T. *(30-60ml)* **rum, brandy or kirsch**
1 pt. *(300g)* **blueberries**
12 whole **ladyfingers or sponge cake strips**
1 cup *(240ml)* **heavy cream, whipped**

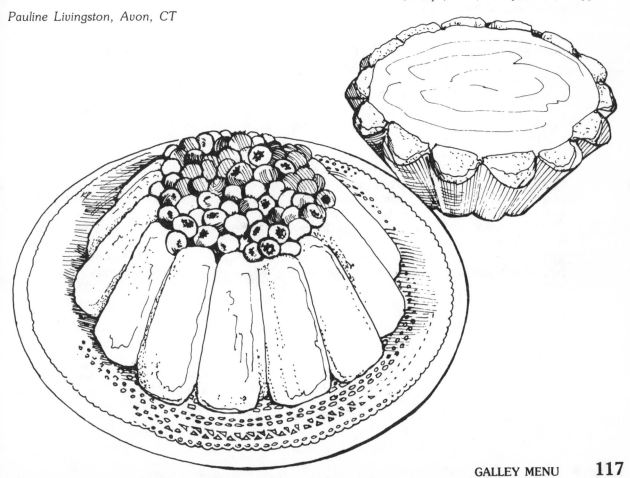

Spring Herb Luncheon

Let your own garden or a friend's tempt you to use nature's gifts to create this special lunch — a lunch to linger over and to savor.

The gently rolling hills of the Connecticut countryside are scored by miles of picturesque stone walls, reminiscent of days gone by. As the early colonial farmer laboriously dug up fieldstones to clear his land for crops, he judiciously and skillfully used these same stones to partition his fields. Today tucked into the crevices of these stone walls are fragrant sprays of wild mint, chive, and thyme. Also evoking images from the past, these are probably escapees from the "Yarb Gardens" which were planted outside the kitchen door of every early colonial home.

Herbs have been a very important part of New England culture. The colonial housewife made use of these indispensible plants not only for culinary but also for cosmetic and medicinal purposes. In the still-room she concocted the many items which made life more comfortable and enjoyable for her family.

Herbs and spices have had a significant role in cooking for more than 5,000 years. No doubt herbs were eaten for their flavor long before it was recognized that they possessed various other beneficial properties. In about 950 B.C. King Solomon was visited by the Queen of Sheba who brought gifts of Arabian spices and herb seeds.

Biblical references to herbs and spices, and oils obtained from them, abound in both the Old and New Testaments. In Proverbs (XV:17) we find "Better is a dinner of herbs where love is than a stalled ox and hatred therewith."

The 15th century term "peppercorn rent" arose from the occasional practice of paying rent to landlords in specified weights of peppercorns. Rent paid in peppercorns was often preferred because it held its value better than unstable coinage — suggesting problems with inflationary currency even in those days. Herbs are often associated with specific dates, often religious festivals. The earliest Shrove Tuesday pancakes were tansy-flavored; bitter herbs still symbolize the Jewish Passover; on Good Friday (traditionally free of devilish influence) cuttings of bay, lavender, sage, rosemary and thyme are planted to insure their healthy growth; on May 1st the German Mai-Bowle, a white wine cup flavored with woodruff and early strawberries, is prepared.

In 1933 a small group of herb growers who spent their summers on or near Cape Ann first met in Gloucester, Massachusetts to form what they proudly and ambitiously named the Herb Society of America. The society has since grown by leaps and bounds. The Connecticut unit of the Herb Society of America celebrated its twenty-fifth anniversary in 1980. The National Herb Garden, located in the arboretum in Washington D.C., was also dedicated in 1980. This marked the culmination of many years of fund raising and hard work on the part of all units of the Herb Society.

The Connecticut unit is one of the most active in the Society, and its members some of the most well-known herbalists of the present time. Adelma G. Simmons and Gertrude B. Foster have written books on herbs which are widely read. Mrs. Foster, who is editor of *Herb Grower Magazine* collaborated with her husband and daughter, Rosemary Louden, to write *Success with Herbs,* which has been published by the Park Seed Company. Mrs. Foster's garden in Falls Village and the century-old Logee's Greenhouse in Danielson, which is owned by Mrs. Joy Martin, are nationally known to herb growers. Another well-known Connecticut site is Caprilands Herb Farm located between Manchester and Willimantic. These gardens contain over 300 varieties of herbs. The visitor can take in the pungent aroma of herbs in the well-stocked shop or enjoy a tempting variety of herbal luncheon dishes.

In addition to the use of herbs in cooking, there is much interest in the legend and folklore which is connected with herbs. "Eat Thou of Sage and Thou wilt live for aye." "If Thou wise would be, drink a cup of Mint tea." One is also urged to eat calendula or pot marigold petals for "they warmeth the heart, cooleth the brain and lifteth the spirit." In turning to the delicate flavors of the Spring Herb Luncheon, recall the delightful insight of Millicent Jones: "Tis said that those who delve into the magic of herbs possess a joy unknown to others."

Capriland's May Wine
p. 120

Rosemary Pecans   Spring Green Spread
p. 121   p. 121

Spring Vegetable Soup
p. 122

Marigold Buns
p. 122

Paupiettes of Sole Pesto
p. 123

Deep Fried Parsley
p. 123

White Bean Salad with
Fresh Herbs
p. 364

Corn Herb Batter Bread
p. 124

Purslane Salad
with Wild Herb Dressing
p. 359

Anne's Dilly Bread
p. 124

Rose Geranium Peach Crisp
p. 125

or

Connecticut Wild Black Raspberry
Chiffon Pie
p. 125

Iced Mint Tea

Rosemary

Black Fennel

Bay

Purple-leaved Sage

Lavender

Bergamot

Thyme

Cotton Lavender

Borage

Chives

Curry

Parsley

Francie Berquist

Capriland's May Wine

A horticultural treat!

Woodruff *(Asperula odorata)* is a dwarf perennial with green leaves on 6-inch stems, and clusters of tiny white flowers in early summer. It is available fresh in spring and summer. The scent only develops as leaves begin to dry out. While used to flavor beverages, it is not used in cooking. Woodruff makes a charming ground cover plant preferring moist soil and some shade.

YIELD: 48 ½-Cup Servings
CALORIES PER SERVING: 82
CARBOHYDRATES: 8g
PREPARING: 3-7 Days

---

12 or more sprigs of sweet Woodruff
1 gal. *(3.75L)* **Rhine wine**
2 cups *(475ml)* **brandy (optional)**
1 pkg. (10 oz.) *(285g)* **sliced frozen strawberries**
1 cup *(200g)* **sugar**
1 qt. *(600g)* **fresh strawberries or 1 bag (20 oz.)** *(570g)* **frozen whole strawberries**

GARNISH:
Fresh Woodruff
Violets
Johnny-jump-ups
Woodruff blossoms

Heat freshly picked Woodruff in preheated 250° oven to bring out the coumarin. Let stand in wine 3 to 7 days to bring out flavor.

To prepare punch bowl put in block of ice; ladle wine over it to chill; add optional brandy. Mash sliced strawberries with sugar; add to wine; remove Woodruff if desired.

Garnish with flowers; float a few whole strawberries in bowl; place a whole strawberry and a floating flower in each cup as it is served.

Adelma Simmons, Coventry, CT

Variations, Advance Preparation, and Serving Suggestions:
Champagne is traditional for May wine punch. Half a bottle of champagne may be added just before serving. Serve immediately to avoid diluting the wine too much.

Spring Green Spread

The green is burnet, a wonderful salad herb which often stays green throughout the winter and is ready for early spring cutting. It has a true cucumber flavor, which is especially evident if combined with cream cheese or butter and left overnight.

YIELD: ½ Cup
TOTAL CALORIES: 350
CALORIES PER TABLESPOON: 44
CARBOHYDRATES: 1g
PROTEIN: 1g
FAT: 4g
PREPARING: 10 Minutes
CHILLING: 4-24 Hours
FREEZING: No

Combine all ingredients and blend well. Cover and refrigerate several hours or overnight.

Adelma Grenier Simmons
Caprilands Herb Farm, Coventry, CT

3 oz. *(85g)* cream cheese, softened
4 T. burnet, finely chopped
2 T. chives or garlic chives, chopped
¼ cup lettuce, chopped
¼ cup parsley, chopped
2 T. *(30ml)* dry white wine
Salt
Freshly ground pepper

Rosemary Pecans

Why not make your own seasoned nuts? Properly stored, they will keep for weeks. They're handy to have for the cocktail hour.

YIELD: 2 Cups
TOTAL CALORIES: 1656
CARBOHYDRATES: 26g
PROTEIN: 19g
FAT: 164g
PREPARING: 5 Minutes
BAKING: 10 Minutes
FREEZING: No

In preheated 350° oven, melt butter in jelly roll pan. Combine remaining ingredients with butter and bake until nicely browned, about 10 minutes. Stir and shake pan occasionally. Spread on brown paper and let drain 3 minutes. Place on clean piece of brown paper, let cool. Store in airtight, sealed containers. Can be served warm or cold.

Nashville Herb Society

2 T. *(30g)* butter
1½ tsp. rosemary, crumbled
1 tsp. salt
¼-½ tsp. cayenne pepper
2 cups *(240g)* pecan halves

Nutritional Notes: Pecans provide protein and calcium. By roasting pecans yourself, the amount and quality of oil can be controlled and a lot of the "extras" (salt, sugar, starch, MSG, vegetable gum and chemical preservatives) can be eliminated.

Microwave Conversion Instructions: Place pecans in 1½ qt. *(1½L)* casserole. Sprinkle with rosemary, salt, and pepper. Cut butter into 4 pieces and space evenly on top of pecans. Cook uncovered on High 3 to 4 minutes, stirring once or twice during cooking to distribute butter. Follow above directions for completion.

YIELD: 8 Servings
TOTAL CALORIES: 2592
CALORIES PER SERVING: 324
CARBOHYDRATES: 20g
PROTEIN: 7g
FAT: 24g
CHOLESTEROL: High
SODIUM: High
PREPARING: 30 Minutes
COOKING: 30 Minutes
FREEZING: No

4 T. *(60g)* butter
4 T. *(30g)* flour
6 cups *(1425ml)* well-degreased and warmed chicken stock or vegetable stock
3 small new potatoes, peeled and cubed
3 carrots, peeled and cubed
2 leeks, *well cleaned* and sliced
1½ cups *(300g)* shelled fresh peas
1½ cups *(170g)* fresh asparagus cut into 1-inch *(2.5cm)* pieces
2 cups *(65g)* fresh spinach, thoroughly washed
1 small head Boston lettuce, leaves separated and washed
1 cup *(240ml)* heavy cream
2 T. chopped fresh chives
Salt
Freshly ground white pepper

Spring Vegetable Soup

In a large heavy casserole heat butter, add flour and whisk for 1 or 2 minutes. Remove casserole from heat, add *warm* stock. Whisk until mixture is smooth. Return casserole to a low simmer, add potatoes and carrots. Cook 2 minutes and then add leeks. Simmer soup until vegetables are almost tender. In the meantime cook the peas separately in a little water, with a pinch of salt and 1 tsp. sugar until barely tender; drain. Add peas and asparagus to soup and cook 5 more minutes. Add spinach, lettuce and cream. Season with salt and pepper. Sprinkle with chopped chives and serve hot immediately or spinach and lettuce leaves will wilt.

Melinda M. Vance, West Hartford, CT

Variations, Advance Preparation, and Serving Suggestions: Serve with Anne's Dilly Bread (page 124) or Mill Hollow Bread (page 235.)

Nutritional Notes: This soup is rich in vitamins and minerals, using fresh vegetables at the peak of their nutritional potency.

Microwave Conversion Instructions: Melt butter in large casserole 1 minute on High. Add flour, using whisk to blend. Add *heated* stock; continue whisking until flour and butter are completely dissolved and mixture is smooth. Add potatoes, carrots and leeks. Cook, covered, on High 20 minutes. Add asparagus and peas; cook on High, covered, 5 minutes. Check that all vegetables are fork tender. Add cream and cook, uncovered, on High until heated. Add spinach and lettuce. Garnish and serve immediately.

YIELD: 18-20 Buns
TOTAL CALORIES: 2360
CALORIES PER BUN: 118
CARBOHYDRATES: 14g
PROTEIN: 2g
FAT: 6g
PREPARING: 10 Minutes
BAKING: 10 Minutes

Marigold Buns

The flowers of Pot Marigolds have been used since the fifteenth century in England and France to flavor and color foods. It is sometimes used in place of saffron.

½ cup *(100g)* sugar
½ cup *(115g)* butter
2 eggs, beaten
2 cups *(225g)* flour
2½ tsp. baking powder
¼ tsp. salt
Petals from 2 or 3 fresh calendula (Pot Marigold) blossoms

Cream sugar and butter. Add eggs; mix well. Then add flour, baking powder, salt and marigold petals. Stir well to distribute petals throughout dough. Drop by tablespoonfuls onto buttered baking sheet.

Bake in preheated 350° oven 10 minutes until lightly browned, but not hard.

Rosemary Louden, New Hartford, CT

Nutritional Notes: Unsalted polyunsaturated margarine can be used. Substitution of whole wheat flour is not recommended since it overpowers marigold flavor. A small amount, ¼ to ½ cup *(30-60g)* wheat germ may be added.

Paupiettes
of Sole Pesto

Pesto was first made by the Genoese. They claim that it is not authentic pesto unless made with the small-leaved basil found in Genoa and ground in a marble mortar!

YIELD: 6 Servings
CALORIES PER SERVING: 462
CARBOHYDRATES: 8g
PROTEIN: 31g
FAT: 34g
PREPARING: 20 Minutes
BAKING: 20 Minutes

PESTO: Mix garlic, basil and pine nuts in blender or food processor until well mixed, or grind together in a mortar with a pestle until well-mixed. Add cheese, then slowly add olive oil mixing well until mixture becomes a fine paste.

Spread each fillet with pesto; roll up. In a buttered 8 × 8-inch *(20 × 20cm)* pan, cover bottom with half the tomato slices. Place rolled fillets on top. Cover with remaining tomato slices; season with salt and pepper; dot with butter.

Bake in preheated 350° oven 20 minutes, uncovered. Garnish with Fried Parsley when serving.

Louise Gens, New Canaan, CT

Microwave Conversion Instructions: Sole has a fine line of bone running through middle of fillet; carefully cut fillet into two pieces, thus removing bone and making pieces more appropriately shaped for microwave preparation. Follow conventional recipe except for baking. In a 13 × 9 × 2-inch *(33 × 23 × 5cm)* glass dish place fillet rolls alongside each other at dish edges. (Season with salt and pepper after baking rather than before.) Cover casserole with plastic wrap; cook on High 12 to 15 minutes.

PESTO:
2 cloves garlic
1 cup fresh basil leaves
⅓ cup *(50g)* **pine nuts or** *(40g)* **walnuts**
½ cup *(65g)* **freshly grated Parmesan cheese**
½ cup *(120ml)* **olive oil**

2-2½ lbs. *(900-1125g)* **sole or haddock fillets**
5 or 6 sliced tomatoes
Salt
Freshly ground pepper
4 T. *(60g)* **butter**
Fried Parsley (page 123)

Deep Fried Parsley

Fried parsley is crisp in texture, bright in color, and especially attractive when served with grilled fish, a roast or a sweet and sour entree. In *haute cuisine,* it is a must with all breaded dishes.

Choose curly parsley sprigs without thick stalks. Wash and pat dry. In deep skillet or small deep fryer, heat oil. Toss parsley into deep fat and cook about 1 minute. Drain and serve hot. Sprinkle with salt and pepper if desired.

Ann Pinto, Bloomfield, CT

Variations, Advance Preparation, and Serving Suggestions:
Can deep fry a few hours ahead of serving and reheat in 350° oven. Another colorful garnish is mustard greens which can be prepared in the same manner.

Nutritional Notes: Parsley is very high in Vitamin A, which is available in significant amounts even in small sprigs used for garnish.

Fresh parsley
Oil for deep-fat frying
Salt
Freshly ground pepper

YIELD: 2 Loaves
CALORIES PER LOAF: 1379
CARBOHYDRATES: 209g
PROTEIN: 39g
FAT: 43g
PREPARING: 10 Minutes
RISING: 45-60 Minutes
BAKING: 45 Minutes
FREEZING: Yes

This bread has an interesting mushroom shape when baked and is especially good toasted.

1 pkg. (¼ oz.) *(7g)* **active dry yeast**
½ cup *(120ml)* **warm water**
⅛ tsp. **ground ginger**
3 T. *(35g)* **sugar**
2 tsp. **celery seed**
1½ tsp. **ground sage**
⅛ tsp. **marjoram**
1 can (13 oz.) *(385ml)* **undiluted evaporated milk**
1 tsp. **salt**
2 T. *(30ml)* **vegetable oil**
½ cup *(75g)* **yellow stone-ground cornmeal**
3½-4 cups *(390-450g)* **unbleached flour**

Dissolve yeast in warm water in large mixing bowl; blend in ginger and 1 T. sugar. Let proof.

Stir in 2 T. sugar, celery seed, herbs, milk, salt and vegetable oil. Using low speed on electric mixer, beat in cornmeal; add flour, 1 cup at a time, beating well after each addition. Beat in last cup of flour with wooden spoon; add only enough flour to make a heavy stiff dough that is too sticky to knead. *[FOOD PROCESSOR: Combine 3½ cups flour, cornmeal, celery seed, salt and herbs in work bowl. With machine running add yeast mixture, milk and oil; process until well blended. Add additional flour, a tablespoon at a time, if necessary to make a stiff dough.]*

Place into 2 well-greased one-pound coffee cans. Cover with well-greased plastic lids. Put in warm place until dough pops off lids, 45 to 60 minutes. Discard lids. Bake in preheated 350° oven 45 minutes, or until golden brown.

Let cool on wire racks 10 minutes; then loosen crust around edge of can; slide bread from cans. Cool upright on rack. If cooled completely, then wrapped tightly, this bread can be frozen.

Anne Pinto, Bloomfield, CT

Anne's Dilly Bread

YIELD: 1 Loaf
TOTAL CALORIES: 1495
CARBOHYDRATES: 240g
PROTEIN: 66g
FAT: 30g
PREPARING: 15 Minutes
RISING: 1 Hour
BAKING: 40-45 Minutes

Unlike other herbs, dill is most tasty when flowering.

1 pkg. (¼ oz.) *(7g)* **active dry yeast**
¼ cup *(60ml)* **warm water**
2 T. *(25g)* **sugar**
1 cup *(225g)* **cottage cheese, warmed**
1 T. *(15g)* **butter**
1 T. **dill seed**
1 tsp. **salt**
¼ tsp. **baking soda**
1 **egg**
2½ cups *(285g)* **sifted flour**

Dissolve yeast in warm water. Add 1 T. sugar; set aside to proof.

To warm cottage cheese, add proofed yeast; mix. Then add 1 T. sugar, butter, dill seed, salt, baking soda and egg. Mix together, add enough flour to make a stiff dough; set aside to rise until doubled in bulk, about 60 minutes.

Beat dough down with a spoon, place in well-buttered 8½ × 4½ × 3-inch *(21.5 × 11.5 × 7.5cm)* loaf pan. Put softened butter on top of dough; set aside to rise until almost doubled in bulk.

Bake in preheated 325° oven 25 minutes, then increase heat to 350° and continue baking 15 to 20 minutes more until bread is golden and sounds hollow when tapped on bottom. Remove to wire rack and cool.

Anne P. Pinto, Bloomfield, CT

Variations, Advance Preparation, and Serving Suggestions:
This bread is delicious with many soups, with salads, and especially nice for roast beef sandwiches or other cold meat sandwiches in the summer. 1 tsp. dill weed can be added to give the bread green flecks. It can also be baked in an 8-inch *(20cm)* round casserole.

Connecticut Wild Black Raspberry Chiffon Pie

The lucky author of this recipe has wild black raspberries in her own back yard! Her pie took second place in a Fourth of July contest on the Wethersfield green.

YIELD: 6-8 Servings
TOTAL CALORIES: 2174
CALORIES PER SERVING: 272
CARBOHYDRATES: 28g
PROTEIN: 4g
FAT: 16g
CHOLESTEROL: High
PREPARING: 35 Minutes
CHILLING: 4 Hours Minimum

Soften gelatin in water 10 minutes. Heat raspberries without bringing to boil; add egg yolks beaten with ½ cup sugar. When slightly thickened, add gelatin.

Remove from heat and add salt. Cool thoroughly until mixture begins to congeal, *not set.*

Beat egg whites until stiff while gradually adding remaining ¼ cup sugar.

Fold egg whites and half of whipped cream into berry mixture. Pour into crust; spread remaining whipped cream around rim of plate leaving center exposed. Refrigerate at least 4 hours before serving.

Helen Kowalczyk, Wethersfield, CT

1 T. unflavored gelatin
½ cup *(120ml)* cold water
1 pt. *(275g)* fresh black or red raspberries, crushed
3 eggs, separated
¾ cup *(150g)* sugar
¼ tsp. salt
½ cup *(120ml)* heavy cream, whipped
1 graham cracker crust or baked Pie Crust (page 198)

Rose Geranium Peach Crisp

Rose geranium leaves can be chopped and frozen in small quantities to use all year long in this fruit crisp. The use of rose geraniums as a flavoring agent is a result of Southern ingenuity during the Civil War. The fragrant and delicately flavored leaves provided a tasty substitute for more common, but unavailable flavorings. Today, this geranium variety known as *Pelargonium Graveolens,* is available either in seed or plant form from local or mail order greenhouses in the spring.

YIELD: 6 Servings
TOTAL CALORIES: 1968
CALORIES PER SERVING: 328
CARBOHYDRATES: 51g
PROTEIN: 4g
FAT: 12g
PREPARING: 20 Minutes
BAKING: 40 Minutes
FREEZING: No

Butter 6 × 10-inch *(15 × 25cm)* or 8-inch *(20cm)* square baking dish. Gently toss peaches with mixture of 2 T. flour, ¼ cup sugar and mace. Place in baking dish.

Combine with fork until crumbly the remaining flour and sugar, baking powder, salt, geranium leaves and egg. Spread over peaches. Pour butter over dough. Sprinkle with nutmeg.

Bake on next-to-lowest rack of preheated 350° oven 40 minutes. Remove from oven. Serve warm with small pitcher of heavy cream.

Betty Stevens, Cobalt, CT

Variations, Advance Preparation, and Serving Suggestions:
The crisp may be made a day ahead (do not need to refrigerate). Cover with foil and re-warm in slow oven to serve. Substitute apples, fresh or frozen rhubarb for peaches.

5-6 cups *(1000-1200g whole fruit)* peeled, sliced peaches (may use frozen if fresh not available)
1 cup *(115g)* flour, divided
¾ cup *(150g)* sugar, divided
½ tsp. mace
1 tsp. *(3g)* baking powder
½ tsp. salt
1 T. finely chopped rose geranium leaves
1 egg
⅓ cup *(75g)* melted, cooled butter
Freshly grated nutmeg to taste
Heavy cream

Yale Tailgate Picnic

Even if your team loses, this picnic is bound to be a winner. It is equally suitable for an outdoor concert, for a box at the baseball game, or for a tranquil site on a country hillside.

If by chance, when you hear the word "tailgating" an image forms of The Holland Tunnel during rush hour traffic — read on. Tailgating actually refers to pre-game picnics in football stadium parking lots. *The Official Preppy Handbook* offers this description: "Picnics with Bloodies are arranged on the open tailgates . . . the men develop bone-crushing handshakes . . . there is much backslapping and the talk is very, very hearty." To truly understand tailgating one must go back to the beginning of football (mid 1800s), the beginning of the station wagon (early 1920s), and finally, the beginning of the college scene.

Yale University was founded in the early 1700s and it has since grown to encompass over 150 acres in the center of New Haven. In 1914 the Yale Bowl (seating over 70,000) was built on a 720-acre athletic area less than two miles west of the campus. Yale finally had a home for the sport it had started to play officially in 1872. Her color was blue, her mascot the bulldog; two of the more famous and still surviving football songs were written by Cole Porter (B.A. 1913). During his undergraduate years Porter entered various football songwriting competitions. His first success was "Bingo! Bingo!" and in 1911 the famous "Bull Dog! Bull Dog! Bow Wow Wow!".

Whether it was Porter's cheering songs, or the college's enthusiastic fans, or simply the teams themselves, Yale was the biggest Ivy League football winner for the first one hundred years of the game. In 1976 Yale held 701 wins, Princeton 621, and Harvard 620.

To understand tailgating one must remember that college stadiums were usually built in rural settings which had the space to accommodate the size of the facility. When one then considers the swarm of spectators descending on the area for a football game, it becomes obvious why the few restaurants available were unable to satisfy the demands. Tailgating therefore evolved as a fashionable solution to the dilemma of the starving spectator.

Originally high society arrived in buggies and picnics were prepared near the playing field. The word "tailgating" was probably first used when the station wagon (hence the tailgate) became popular immediately after World War II. The tradition begins around noon when hundreds of station wagons and other vehicles line up or form a circle or surround various tents designated for certain alumni or supporters. As John McCallum would explain, it all becomes a "convention of John O'Hara characters."

The tailgate picnic may consist of fried chicken with beer or caviar with champagne. Bloody Marys are a familiar sight, although ginger ale will do just as well as long as one maintains the spirit of the occasion. And for some the spirit means the whimsical competition of tailgating: who can outdo whom. Various status accoutrements have included: lace tablecloths with sterling placesettings, Lenox china, Waterford crystal. Candelabra have been placed near slow revolving rotisseries and finally, one group has arrived with a flatbed truck to hold a baby grand piano for music to tailgate by. It is all in the spirit and comradeship of the game. Whether Yale's team wins or loses, the tailgate picnic should keep up one's spirits right through the bumper-to-bumper traffic during the ride home.

126

Bullshots

Gravlax and/or **Cold Poached Artichokes**
p. 128

with Mustard Dill Sauce
p. 128

Thermos of Herbed Carrot Soup
p. 129

or

European Cream of Barley Soup
p. 130

Dill Bread with Sweet Butter Curls
p. 124

**Ballotine de Boeuf
with Light Tomato Sauce**
p. 131

Cold Curried Rice Salad
p. 130

**Mixed Green Salad
with Dressing Fromage**
p. 129

Apple Rings Spread with Blue Cheese

Raisin Tart
p. 133

Petit Gâteau au Chocolat
p. 132

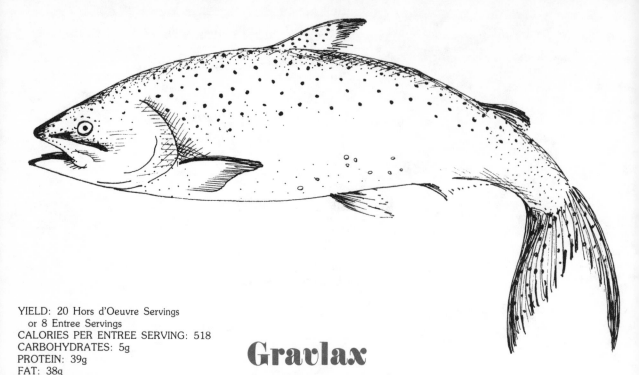

YIELD: 20 Hors d'Oeuvre Servings
 or 8 Entree Servings
CALORIES PER ENTREE SERVING: 518
CARBOHYDRATES: 5g
PROTEIN: 39g
FAT: 38g
SODIUM: High
PREPARING: 35 Minutes
MARINATING: 2 Days
FREEZING: No

Gravlax

SWEDISH MARINATED SALMON

A Swedish tradition to serve on New Year's Eve, Midsummer Night and the first day of spring.

GRAVLAX:

3-4 lbs. *(1350-1800g)* **middle cut fresh salmon, sliced in half lengthwise, boned**
1 large bunch fresh dill
½ cup *(150g)* **salt**
½ cup *(100g)* **sugar**
20 white peppercorns, coarsely crushed
Lemon slices to garnish
Fresh dill to garnish

MUSTARD SAUCE:

2 T. hot prepared mustard
1 T. sugar
1 egg yolk
2 T. *(30ml)* **white vinegar**
½ cup *(120ml)* **olive oil**
2 T. chopped fresh dill
Salt
Freshly ground pepper

GRAVLAX: Wipe fish with damp cloth dipped in salt (do not wash fish.) Arrange half of dill in bottom of non-metal dish just large enough to fit salmon. Place one piece of salmon, cut surface up, on top of dill. Place remaining dill over fish. Mix salt, sugar, peppercorns; sprinkle over dill. Place remaining piece of salmon on top, cut surface down. Place a heavy board or plate on fish; top with a 4-lb. *(1800g)* weight. (May use foil-wrapped bricks). Refrigerate 48 hours, turning every 12 hours and basting with salmon juices.

Drain fish, discard seasoning and dill. Set salmon on carving board, skin side down. Cut flesh in very thin slices with sharp knife. Arrange on platter with lemon slices and fresh dill. Serve sauce separately.

MUSTARD SAUCE: Mix mustard, sugar, egg yolk and vinegar together in a small bowl. Beat in oil, a little at a time, until mixture thickens, as for mayonnaise. Beat in rest of oil in a steady stream. Add dill, salt and pepper to taste.

Elizabeth af Jochnik, West Hartford, CT

Variations, Advance Preparation, and Serving Suggestions:
Serve this salmon as a main course with poached eggs, creamed spinach and new boiled potatoes for a taste of Scandinavian heritage.

Nutritional Notes: Some salt-soluble proteins are lost during the marinating process. Salmon is high in potassium.

Carrot Soup with Herbs

YIELD: 8 Servings
TOTAL CALORIES: 1648
CALORIES PER SERVING: 206
CARBOHYDRATES: 21g
PROTEIN: 8g
FAT: 10g
SODIUM: High
PREPARING: 1 Hour
COOKING: 40 Minutes
FREEZING: Yes-Very Well

In large soup pot saute bacon until limp. Add butter, carrots, onions, celery, and turnips; saute until onions are transparent, about 5 minutes. Add flour gradually and continue cooking 2 minutes, stirring constantly. (Mixture will be quite dry). Add chicken stock and bring to a boil. Reduce heat; add herbs and simmer covered 15 minutes.

Cool slightly and puree in batches in blender or food processor.

Return mixture to pot; add milk, salt and pepper; bring to boil; reduce heat and simmer uncovered 5 minutes.

Winnie White, North Conway, NH

Nutritional Notes: Water soluble vitamins and protein are preserved in soups, which from a nutritional standpoint are generally "good quality" foods. Carrots are particularly high in vitamin A which is good for eyesight, skin and normal growth in the young.

Microwave Conversion Instructions: Note: Divide recipe by half for microwave preparation. Cut bacon into pieces. Place in a 3-qt. *(3L)* casserole. Cook covered with paper towel on High 2 minutes. Add butter, carrots, onion, celery, and turnips, cook covered 10 minutes. Add flour, stirring to dissolve. Stir in *heated* broth, cook on High, covered, 10 minutes, stirring twice. If vegetables are not completely soft, cook an additional few minutes. Cool slightly and puree in batches. Return mixture to casserole. Add *heated* milk, salt and pepper, bring to a boil on High uncovered. Cover and allow to sit 5 minutes.

4 slices *(100g)* uncooked bacon, chopped
¼ cup *(60g)* butter
2 lbs. *(900g)* carrots, peeled and chopped
1 medium onion, peeled and thinly sliced
1 cup *(100g)* chopped celery
½ cup *(50g)* peeled and chopped turnips
½ cup *(60g)* flour
2 qts. *(2L)* chicken stock
2 tsp. chopped fresh parsley
1 bay leaf
1 tsp. thyme
1½ cups *(355ml)* milk
Salt and pepper to taste

Dressing Fromage

YIELD: 3½ Cups
CALORIES PER TABLESPOON: 74
CARBOHYDRATES: 1g
PROTEIN: .5g
FAT: 8g
CHOLESTEROL: High
SODIUM: High
PREPARING: 5 Minutes
FREEZING: Not Necessary

A more unusual dressing to bind traditional salad greens.

In mixing bowl combine eggs, sugar, salt, mustard and Worcestershire sauce. Using wire whisk beat 2 to 3 minutes. Blend in horseradish. Very slowly pour in ½ cup *(120ml)* oil, beating constantly with whisk. Mix in vinegar and lemon juice alternately with remaining oil; beating 2 to 3 minutes longer. Transfer mixture to blender or food processor and mix until creamy. Do not allow to become the consistency of mayonnaise. Add cheese and scallions; blend briefly. Refrigerate. Dressing will keep several weeks refrigerated.

Cathy Power, Medfield, MA

2 eggs
2 tsp. brown sugar
1½ tsp. salt
1 tsp. Worcestershire sauce
1 tsp. dry mustard
1 tsp. prepared horseradish
2 cups *(475ml)* salad oil
¼ cup *(60ml)* vinegar
¼ cup *(60ml)* lemon juice
¼ cup *(30g)* Cheddar cheese, grated
3 scallions, finely chopped

YIELD: 4-6 Servings
TOTAL CALORIES: 1200
CALORIES PER SERVING: 200
CARBOHYDRATES: 21g
PROTEIN: 6g
FAT: 10g
CHOLESTEROL: High
SODIUM: High
PREPARING: 10 Minutes
COOKING: 1¼ Hours

1 T. butter
1 carrot, finely chopped
1 medium onion, finely chopped
1 whole leek, finely chopped
2 stalks celery, finely chopped
5 cups *(1.2L)* chicken stock
½ cup *(100g)* pearl barley
Salt
Freshly ground pepper
3 egg yolks
½ cup *(120ml)* heavy or light cream
2 T. finely chopped chives

European Cream of Barley Soup

In a large saucepan, melt butter and saute chopped carrot, onion, leek and celery for 5 minutes. Add chicken stock, barley, salt and pepper to taste; simmer, uncovered 1 hour. Remove from heat.

Beat together egg yolks and cream. To the cream mixture, add about ½ cup of soup and stir quickly to prevent curdling. Stir cream mixture into the soup; reheat but do not let soup boil.

Sprinkle each serving with chopped chives.

Lee M. Grimmeisen, West Hartford, CT

Nutritional Notes: Barley provides carbohydrates and some protein. It has about half the protein of rolled oats. Barley eaten along with legumes such as lentils or peas forms complete vegetable protein.

Microwave Conversion Instructions: Note: Heat stock before using and increase butter to 3 T. Saute carrot, onion, leek and celery with butter 7 minutes on High, covered. Stir once. Add heated stock, barley, salt and pepper. Cook on High, covered, 30 minutes. Uncover and cook an additional 3 minutes. Follow above directions for addition of cream and egg yolks. Reheat soup on Medium (50%), uncovered, until heated through. Do not let soup boil.

YIELD: 8 Servings
CALORIES PER SERVING: 335
CARBOHYDRATES: 40g
PROTEIN: 10g
FAT: 15g
PREPARING: 15 Minutes
COOKING: 30 Minutes
CHILLING: 8 Hours

4 cups *(265g raw)* cooked white rice, cooled
¾ cup *(75g)* celery, thinly sliced
1 cup *(200g)* cooked peas, cooled
¾ cup *(115g)* slivered almonds, toasted

CREAMY CHUTNEY CURRY DRESSING:

½ cup *(115g)* sour cream
½ cup *(115g)* mayonnaise (page 190)
⅓ cup *(150g)* mango chutney, chopped
2 tsp. curry powder or to taste
Salt
Freshly ground pepper

Cold Curried Rice Salad

Combine rice, celery, peas, and almonds.

Mix dressing ingredients.

Gently toss dressing with rice mixture; chill at least 8 hours before serving.

Sarah C. Seymour, West Hartford, CT

Nutritional Notes: Imitation sour cream or mayonnaise may be utilized to decrease calories and fat.

Ballotine de Boeuf

COLD STUFFED FLANK STEAK

Ballotine, an early name for galantine, is a French term describing meat, fowl, game or fish that is boned, stuffed and rolled into the shape of a bundle.

YIELD: 6 Servings or 10 ¾-Inch Slices
TOTAL CALORIES: 4340
CALORIES PER SLICE: 434
CARBOHYDRATES: 12g
PROTEIN: 39g
FAT: 25.5g
CHOLESTEROL: High
SODIUM: High
PREPARING: 45 Minutes
BRAISING: 1¼ Hours
CHILLING: 2 Hours Minimum
FREEZING: No

Cut a pocket into flank steak, leaving a ¾-inch *(2cm)* border on all 3 sides.

STUFFING: Soak bread in milk 15 minutes. Blanch carrots in boiling salted water 2 minutes. Squeeze bread dry. In a large bowl combine bread, carrots, prosciutto, veal, pork, cheese, spinach, parsley, eggs, herbs, and salt and pepper to taste. In a small skillet, saute shallots and garlic in butter for 2 minutes. Add to stuffing mixture and mix well. Stuff pocket of flank steak and sew opening closed. Tie meat at 1-inch *(2.5cm)* intervals.

In a large flameproof casserole, brown the stuffed flank steak in 2 T. butter and 1 T. oil over moderately high heat; remove meat. Add the remaining 2 T. butter and cook chopped carrot, celery, and onion 5 minutes. Add beef stock, red wine, tomatoes and bay leaf. Return meat to casserole; bring liquid to boil. Transfer casserole to preheated 350° oven and braise the meat, *covered,* for 1¼ hours. Transfer steak to a platter and allow it to cool. When cool, refrigerate. Strain liquid remaining in pan into a saucepan. Bring to a boil and reduce to ½ cup, or until it is a thick glaze. When steak is chilled, brush it with glaze and chill until ready to slice.

Arrange slices overlapping on a platter. Spoon a band of Light Tomato Sauce around the rim and place remaining sauce in a sauce boat. Decorate with a few sprigs of watercress.

LIGHT TOMATO SAUCE: Place shallots, vinegar, tarragon, tomato paste and water in a saucepan and reduce over high heat to ⅓ cup. Cool slightly, then place in blender or food processor. Add tomato and puree until smooth. Add oil; blend. Add tomato juice and blend, then season with salt and pepper.

Melinda M. Vance, West Hartford, CT

Wine Suggestion: French Beaujolais Villages, light red; serve slightly chilled.

---

1 2¼-lb. *(1000g)* flank steak

STUFFING:
1 cup *(30g)* crustless white bread, torn into cubes
½ cup *(120ml)* milk
¾ cup *(100g)* carrots, cut into ½-inch *(1cm)* cubes
6 oz. *(170g)* prosciutto, cut into ½-inch *(1cm)* cubes
6 oz. *(170g)* ground veal
6 oz. *(170g)* ground lean pork
½ cup *(65g)* freshly grated Parmesan
½ cup *(35g)* firmly packed shredded spinach
½ cup minced fresh parsley
2 eggs, lightly beaten
1 T. minced rosemary (or 1 tsp. dried)
1 T. minced fresh thyme (or 1 tsp. dried)
1 tsp. minced fresh sage (or ¼ tsp. dried)
½ tsp. salt
Freshly ground pepper to taste
½ cup *(50g)* chopped shallots
2 cloves garlic, minced
Butter

4 T. *(60g)* butter
1 T. oil
1 carrot, chopped
1 stalk celery, chopped
1 onion, chopped
1 cup *(240ml)* beef stock
½ cup *(120ml)* dry red wine
2 tomatoes, chopped
1 bay leaf

LIGHT TOMATO SAUCE:
1 T. chopped shallots
½ cup *(120ml)* wine vinegar
1 tsp. dried tarragon
1 T. tomato paste
⅓ cup *(80ml)* water
⅔ cup *(100g)* fresh tomato, peeled, seeded and diced (about 1 large)
1 cup *(240ml)* oil, ½ safflower and ½ olive oil
2 cups *(475ml)* tomato juice
1 tsp. salt
½ tsp. freshly ground pepper

YIELD: 8 Servings
TOTAL CALORIES: 5480
CALORIES PER SERVING: 685
CARBOHYDRATES: 82g
PROTEIN: 6g
FAT: 37g
CHOLESTEROL: High
PREPARING: 1 Hour
BAKING: 30 Minutes
FREEZING: Yes-Without Icing
RESTING: 6½ Hours

Petit Gâteau au Chocolat

FRENCH CHOCOLATE CAKE

A very special cake and incredibly delicious! It is a single layer cake, compact, dense, dark, moist, rich and bittersweet with a shiny chocolate glaze — a sophisticated and elegant dessert.

CAKE:

¼ cup *(35g)* **currants**
¼ cup *(60ml)* **Scotch**
8 oz. *(225g)* **sweet chocolate (Maillard's preferred)**
5 T. *(75ml)* **strong coffee**
½ cup *(115g)* **unsalted sweet butter, room temperature**
3 **eggs, separated, room temperature**
⅛ tsp. **salt**
⅔ cup *(135g)* plus 1 T. **sugar**
4½ T. *(30g)* **cake flour**
⅔ cup *(125g)* **finely ground almonds**

ICING:

3 oz. *(85g)* **semisweet chocolate, (Lindt Extra-Bittersweet preferred)**
3 T. *(25g)* **confectioners' sugar**
3 T. *(45g)* **unsalted sweet butter**

CAKE: Butter an 8- or 9-inch *(20 or 22.5cm)* cake pan. Line pan with buttered waxed paper.

Place currants in a small bowl with Scotch. Melt chocolate with coffee in top of double boiler. Stir to smooth. Remove from heat, let cool to room temperature. Whisk in butter in pieces.

In mixing bowl, beat egg yolks with salt and ⅔ cup sugar until well combined. Stir in chocolate mixture. Add flour and almonds. Mix just until thoroughly combined. Stir in currants and Scotch.

In another bowl, beat egg whites until soft peaks form. Sprinkle 1 T. sugar over whites. Beat until stiff. Gently fold whites into chocolate mixture, just until no whites show. Pour batter into pan. Place on next-to-lowest rack of preheated 375° oven. Bake 25 to 30 minutes. Remove pan from oven. Let cool on rack 10 minutes. Unmold cake onto serving plate. Let cake remain at room temperature at least 6 hours or overnight.

ICING: Melt chocolate in top of double boiler. Add sugar, stir until melted. Add butter, stir until melted. Cover cake with icing. Let remain at room temperature 30 minutes before serving.

Patricia M. Mitchell, Avon, CT

Variations, Advance Preparation, and Serving Suggestions: Dark rum (Myers's preferred) may be substituted for Scotch. Raspberry sauce (page 70), passed separately, accompanies this cake nicely.

Wine Suggestion: French Vouvray or Sancerre, semi-sweet white; serve chilled.

Microwave Conversion Instructions: Note: Decrease coffee from 5 T. to 3 T. Combine currants and Scotch in covered small glass casserole; cook 1 minute on High to plump. Butter a 9-inch round glass cake dish and line with a circle of waxed paper. Melt chocolate with coffee by placing in glass bowl; cook on High 4 to 5 minutes, or until chocolate is almost melted, stir to complete melting. Prepare cake batter as for conventional recipe, pour into glass dish; cook on Medium (50%) 14 minutes rotating dish every 2 to 3 minutes. Cook on High 1 minute — cake should be pulling away from side of dish and appear basically set. Cool in dish and cover overnight. Place chocolate in glass bowl; cook 2 minutes on High or until melted. Stir in sugar and butter until smooth. Unmold cake and peel off waxed paper. Ice. Let stand at room temperature 30 minutes.

Raisin Tart

Absolutely superb!

Raisins have been known and used since ancient times. Up to the latter part of the 19th century, raisins were almost exclusively from grapes grown in the vineyards of Malaga and Greece and districts bordering the eastern Mediterranean. Then in 1873 in California's San Joaquin Valley, the summer was so hot and dry that grapes dried on the vines. One enterprising grower, refusing to see a year's work wasted, shipped the dried grapes to a grocer friend in San Francisco. The grocer, just as enterprising, marketed them as "Peruvian delicacies" because a ship from Peru happened to be in port. The promotion was such a success that it inspired the beginnings of the raisin industry in California.

YIELD: 8-10 Servings
TOTAL CALORIES: 3240
CALORIES PER SERVING: 559
CARBOHYDRATES: 72g
PROTEIN: 7g
FAT: 27g
PREPARING: 30 Minutes
BAKING: 1 Hour

Line 10-inch *(22.5cm)* tart pan with removable bottom with tart pastry.

Combine all filling ingredients in large bowl; mix well. Pour into unbaked tart shell. Bake in preheated 350° oven 50 to 60 minutes. Cool. When ready to serve, garnish with whipped cream on the side.

Phillip Johnston, Pittsburgh, PA

Wine Suggestion: German Rhine Beerenauslese, sweet white; serve chilled.

Microwave Conversion Instructions: Note: Prebake (page 196) Tart Pastry and set aside. Combine ingredients for tart in large bowl and mix well. Pour into prebaked pastry shell. Cook on Medium (50%) 18 to 20 minutes, until it appears set. Cool.

1 recipe Walnut Tart Pastry (page 197)
  or Rich Tart Pastry (page 196)

FILLING:
½ cup *(115g)* butter, melted
1½ cups *(300g)* sugar
3 eggs, beaten
1 cup *(170g)* raisins, plumped in ⅓ cup
  (80ml) warm dark Jamaican rum
1 T. white vinegar
1 tsp. pure vanilla extract
½ tsp. salt
1 T. flour

TOPPING: (optional)
Whipped cream sweetened with sugar
  and vanilla

Orange Kir Royale
p. 154

Salted Cashews

Black Olive Canapés   White House Soufflé Crackers
p. 206   p. 136

Mushroom Cheese
p. 136

Garden Fresh Tomato Soup
p. 137

Coulibiac of Salmon
in Brioche
p. 138

Mustard Carrots   Tiny Fresh Green Beans
p. 139   with Lemon Butter

Fresh Fruit Salad
Honey Dressing
p. 137

Anastasia's Rice Pudding
(Old Fashioned Rice Pudding)
p. 406

or

Homemade Ice Cream   Coconut Oatmeal Crisps
p. 140   p. 141

Hill-Stead Dinner Invitation

A distinctive meal to complement the ambience of this truly remarkable Connecticut home.

Hill-Stead, the Farmington home of Theodate Pope and John Wallace Riddle, is now a museum open to the public. However, the term "museum" is perhaps a misnomer, for Hill-Stead, situated on a hilltop overlooking the Farmington Valley and surrounded by 150 acres of fields and woods, is more properly a period country estate. It is also an immaculately preserved example of distinguished turn-of-the-century living.

With inspiration from plans drawn by Theodate Pope later to become an architect in her own right — Stanford White completed the design for the house which was built in 1901. Hill-Stead's principal contribution to our times, however, is to be found throughout its interior. The rooms and halls are furnished and adorned to be lived in and enjoyed by a family of wealth, culture and taste. The magnificent Neo-Impressionist collection of paintings, which includes works by Degas, Monet, Manet, and Cassatt, are today precisely as they were when first acquired by the Popes. The paintings are displayed family-style, to be lived with comfortably as parts of the total decor. And this is true of everything in the house — furniture, books, prints, fine porcelain and clocks, even down to the contents of the linen closets — all frozen in time and carefully tended.

It is small wonder that Hill-Stead's unique qualities are well-known in this country and abroad. To quote a contemporary poem about Hill-Stead by Alan Hunter, ". . . to walk on the porch and gaze over the valley one can feel life here. It is not a dead museum, but a home for all time."

After John Riddle's retirement from foreign service, having been both Ambassador to Russia and our first Ambassador to Argentina, he and Mrs. Riddle moved permanently to Hill-Stead. However, friends from across the country continued to enjoy their company. The famed novelist Henry James visited at Hill-Stead. He was a close friend of Theodate Pope. Theodore Roosevelt was also a friend and guest. His sister, Anna Roosevelt Cowles, and her husband, Rear Admiral William S. Cowles, were good friends and frequent guests. It was Anna Cowles who first introduced Theodate Pope to John Riddle.

Visitors to Hill-Stead might best have experienced the warmth and beauty of this lovely home through a coveted invitation to dinner. One must add that dinner was a formal occasion — every night. It was remarked that none were invited to stay for dinner who did not have the proper attire. Mrs. Riddle was as strict about dress in her home as she was about the boys' clothing at Avon Old Farms School, which she designed and founded.

A handsome flower arrangement from the Hill-Stead gardens graced the center of the massive mahogany dining table. An elaborate silver service, crystal goblets, and beautiful china completed the magnificent table. In the family collection one finds Meissen, Limoge, Wedgwood, Crown Derby, Coalport, Queensware, Flow Blue and Canton.

A well equipped bar, even in Prohibition, contained the makings of all variety of drinks. Ernest, the devoted family butler for 62 years, served with great style. Salted nuts, cheese crackers and canapes accompanied drinks in the library or the drawing room. Paul Martin and Donald Carson, foster sons of the Riddles, lived at Hill-Stead, and their friends were often entertained there, as were boys from Avon Old Farms School. Mrs. Riddle allowed the collegiate group to help themselves at the bar, but any who over-indulged were not invited back.

The food at Hill-Stead was described by one frequent guest as "perfection." Mrs. Riddle had her cooks trained at the famous Boston Cooking School. The Hill-Stead kitchen was equipped with a coal stove, which many considered superior to the wood stove. One of the mandatory components of the Cooking School's program of instruction was the correct use and care of the stove. The many steps included blackening it with stove polish while cold, sifting ashes for half-burned coal, and skillfully regulating the dampers for uniform heat.

It has been said that all food served at Hill-Stead was tastefully prepared and beautifully served. Menus often featured roast meat, vegetables from the garden when they were available, and locally grown fruits. Like the best home-cooking of its time, the food was noted for being wholesome and delicious. For dessert one of Mrs. Riddle's personal treats was rice pudding rich with cream, generously given by Anastasia, the Hill-Stead cow. Homemade ice cream was also a favorite. Though actual recipes and menus of the family could not be located, our Dinner at Hill-Stead is one which those now associated with the museum feel would have been typical.

135

White House Soufflé Crackers

YIELD: 12 Crackers
CALORIES PER CRACKER: 67
CARBOHYDRATES: 5g
PROTEIN: .5g
FAT: 5g
PREPARING: 10 Minutes
BAKING: 45 Minutes
FREEZING: No

An unusual but simple conversation piece, these crackers go well with soup. They have been served at the White House mess for many years, but their origin is unknown.

Crackers are sheets of lightly leavened biscuits. Their inventor found that if he scored a pan of crisp biscuits, they "cracked" into regular squares.

---

12 Saltine crackers
Ice water
¼ cup *(60g)* butter (do not substitute)

Optional:
Dill seeds
Caraway seeds

Float crackers in pan of ice water until well soaked but not falling apart. This will take 1½ to 2 minutes and crackers should be turned once with spatula.

With a spatula, carefully place crackers on well-buttered baking sheet. Leave about ½ inch *(1.5cm)* between each cracker. Tilt baking sheet to drain excess water. Brush top of each cracker with melted butter. A light touch with a feather or soft brush is essential. (Crackers can be sprinkled with dill or caraway seeds or other herbs before baking.)

Place in preheated 400° oven for 15 minutes. Reduce heat to 300° and bake until a deep golden brown, about 20 to 30 minutes. Watch carefully as they can go quickly from a perfect brown to overdone. The crackers will puff up about ½ inch *(1.5cm)* but will not puff evenly.

When cool, store in airtight container to maintain crispness.

Phyllis R. Lappen, West Hartford, CT
James McE. Brown, Stonington, CT

Mushroom Cheese

YIELD: 2 Quarts Pate
TOTAL CALORIES: 7560
CALORIES PER TABLESPOON: 63
CARBOHYDRATES: .5g
PROTEIN: 1g
FAT: 6.3g
PREPARING: 1 Hour 15 Minutes
COOKING: 25 Minutes
CHILLING: 4 Hours Minimum
FREEZING: Yes-Very Well

The title of this recipe is purposely deceptive. There is no cheese in the pate! Over the years the donor had many requests for the recipe. Not willing to part with it, nor reveal its ingredients, she simply replied that it was "Mushroom Cheese."

2½ lbs. *(1125g)* fresh mushrooms, sliced
2 lbs. *(900g)* unsalted sweet butter
1 lb. *(450g)* chicken or calves' liver
1½ T. salt
1½ T. pepper
1½ T. imported curry powder

GARNISH:
Cherry tomatoes
Plain crackers
Imported pumpernickel bread, cut into triangles
Watercress

In a skillet saute mushrooms in ½ lb. *(225g)* butter. In another skillet saute livers in ½ lb. butter. Cream remaining butter and set aside. Divide seasonings between mushrooms and liver while they are cooking.

Combine sauteed mushrooms and liver; chop coarsely. Cool mixture 20 to 30 minutes.

Put some of creamed butter in blender or food processor. Add some of chopped mixture and blend or process until smooth but not runny. Check seasonings. Repeat process until all ingredients have been combined. Place in 2 large or 4 small molds. Refrigerate up to 1 week ahead of serving or freeze. Unmold and leave at room temperature 30 minutes before serving. Garnish and serve.

Garden Fresh Tomato Soup

An excellent solution to an abundance of ripe tomatoes.

YIELD: 9 Servings
TOTAL CALORIES: 1044
CALORIES PER SERVING: 116
CARBOHYDRATES: 16g
PROTEIN: 4g
FAT: 4g
PREPARING: 15 Minutes
COOKING: 45 Minutes
FREEZING: Yes

Combine all ingredients except butter and flour in large soup pot. Bring to boil, reduce heat, cover and simmer until vegetables are soft, about 20 to 30 minutes. Puree in batches in blender or food processor. (May be frozen at this point.)

Force mixture through a sieve or food mill to remove seeds and skins while retaining as much pulp as possible. Melt butter, add flour and cook for a few minutes, stirring constantly. Add soup mixture; stir to combine. Season with salt and pepper.

Dr. Sybille Brewer, West Hartford, CT

Variations, Advance Preparation, and Serving Suggestions:
Vegetables may be cooked in pressure cooker for 5 minutes after pressurization is reached.

Microwave Conversion Instructions: All ingredients should be reduced by half for microwave preparation. Combine all ingredients except butter and flour in a 4-qt. *(4L)* covered casserole. Cook on High 18 to 20 minutes, stirring twice. Puree mixture and then strain through food mill. Place flour and butter in measuring cup and cook 45 seconds on High; stir into soup mixture. Salt and pepper to taste. Return all ingredients to covered casserole; cook on Medium (50%) 5 to 7 minutes. Do not allow soup to boil.

4 lb. *(1800g)* **garden fresh tomatoes**
4 stalks **celery with leaves, sliced**
2 **carrots, sliced**
1 large **onion, quartered**
1 **parsnip, sliced**
4-5 **scallions including greens, sliced**
2 large **bay leaves**
16 whole **allspice**
32 whole **peppercorns**
4 sprigs **parsley**
¾ cup *(175ml)* **water**
3 T. *(45g)* **butter**
3 T. *(20g)* **flour**
Salt and pepper to taste

Honey Salad Dressing

Superb for fresh fruit salads!

YIELD: 2½ Cups
CALORIES PER TABLESPOON: 76
CARBOHYDRATES: 6.5g
FAT: 5.5g
PREPARING: 15 Minutes
FREEZING: Not Necessary

In 3-qt. *(3L)* saucepan, combine all dry ingredients. Add onion, honey, vinegar and lemon juice; blend well. Over moderate heat begin to add oil very slowly, beating constantly. If possible use electric hand mixer to obtain nice thick dressing.

When cool, pour into jar and refrigerate until ready to use. Dressing doubles or triples easily and keeps several months tightly covered in refrigerator. Stir well each time before using.

Eloise W. Martin, Kenilworth, IL

⅔ cup *(135g)* **sugar**
1 tsp. **dry mustard**
1 tsp. **imported paprika**
1 tsp. **celery seed**
1 T. **grated onion**
¼ tsp. **salt**
½ cup *(170g)* **good quality honey**
5 T. *(75ml)* **white vinegar**
1 T. **fresh lemon juice**
1 cup *(240ml)* **salad oil**

YIELD: 12 First Course Servings
  or 6 Entree Servings
TOTAL CALORIES: 5106
CALORIES PER ENTREE SERVING: 851
CARBOHYDRATES: 33g
PROTEIN: 29g
FAT: 67g
CHOLESTEROL: High
SODIUM: High
PREPARING: Brioche Day Ahead
  then 45 Minutes
BAKING: 30 Minutes
RISING: 25 Minutes
FREEZING: Very Well

Coulibiac

When asked to name a single favorite recipe, this Coulibiac has been the editor's choice for over 14 years!

Kulebyaka is a traditional Russian hot fish pie, usually made with pike-perch or sterlet, but when these are not available, salmon or turbot are used. The filling can also be made with meats. It became well-known in France and England as Coulibiac, when the French chef Escoffier prepared it in Monte Carlo for the Ballet Russe.

1 recipe Large Quantity (20 oz.) *(570g)*
  Brioche Dough (page 226)

FILLING:
3 T. *(45g)* **butter, melted**
2 T. *(15g)* **breadcrumbs**
3 hard-cooked eggs, finely chopped
1 cup *(225g)* **sour cream**
½ lb. *(225g)* *smoked* **salmon**
1½ cups *(340g)* **cooked shrimp (about**
  ¾ lb.), sliced in half lengthwise
½ lb. *(225g)* **fresh mushrooms, sliced**
  and sauteed in 2 T. *(30g)* **butter**
½ cup snipped fresh dill

GLAZE:
1 egg yolk beaten with 2 tsp. water

SAUCE:
½ lb. *(225g)* **melted butter**

On a very heavily floured board, roll out dough to ¼-inch *(0.6cm)* thickness making a 15 × 15-inch *(38 × 38cm)* square. If using this method, a standard bread pan 9 × 5-inch *(22.5 × 12.5cm)* will be needed. (An alternate method which looks especially impressive is to line one of the various French pate molds with removable sides with the brioche dough and then layer in the filling. If using this method, roll out ¾ of the dough for the lining of the mold and the other ¼ for the top piece and decorations.) Reserve small amount of dough for decorations.

Brush dough with melted butter; sprinkle with breadcrumbs. In center of dough and within an area of 9 × 5 inches *(22.5 × 12.5cm)*, put a layer of chopped egg on top of dough and dot with sour cream. On top of this, put thin slices of smoked salmon, some shrimp, some mushrooms; sprinkle with dill. Repeat this process until all filling is used. Fold each side of dough over on top of the filling. Lift entire loaf-shaped coulibiac up, turn over and place in a well-greased bread tin. All seams should be on the bottom, and top should look like a loaf of unbaked bread. Cut out a few pastry decorations such as a branch with leaves. Secure decorations on top of dough with a little water. Cover bread pan with cloth and put in a warm place to rise for 25 minutes. Brush top with glaze; bake in pre-heated 425° oven 30 minutes. Remove from oven. Turn out of tin; let rest 10 to 15 minutes. At this point, coulibiac may be sliced and served, or it may be frozen. If you plan to freeze the coulibiac, omit the egg whites when layering the other ingredients in the filling. If serving immediately, slice coulibiac as you would a loaf bread, only into slightly thicker slices. (End slices of brioche will not be consumed.) Heat melted butter and pass in a sauceboat. It is absolutely imperative to dribble the melted butter over each serving! It is an important part of the finished product, not merely a garnish.

Melinda M. Vance, West Hartford, CT

Variations, Advance Preparation, and Serving Suggestions:
Well-wrapped, cooled Coulibiac freezes 2 to 3 months. Thaw and bring to room temperature before reheating in 325° oven 30 minutes. Cover top if it browns too much.

Serve with seasonal green vegetable and fresh fruit salad with Honey Dressing (page 137) or Variegated Salad (page 175). Serve Fresh Apple Mousse (page 408) or Blueberries In Lemon Mousse (page 405) for dessert.

Wine Suggestion: Hungarian Nemes Kadar, semi-sweet rose; serve chilled.

Mustard Carrots

Sometimes, the easiest recipes are the best; this one fits in that category.

YIELD: 4 Servings
CALORIES PER SERVING: 140
CARBOHYDRATES: 16g
PROTEIN: 1g
FAT: 9g
PREPARING: 10 Minutes
COOKING: 15 Minutes

Combine butter, mustard, and sugar in skillet; stir over low heat until sugar is dissolved.

Add carrots; cook stirring occasionally until carrots are tender and glazed but still slightly crunchy, about 15 minutes.

Doris Hornblow, Farmington, CT

3 T. *(45g)* butter
2 tsp. prepared Dijon mustard
1 T. brown sugar
3 cups *(400g)* thinly sliced carrots

Nutritional Notes: Carrots are very rich in vitamin A (carotene). The richest vegetable sources of this vitamin, however, are chard, kale, spinach and other "greens". The skin and the flesh just beneath the skin of the carrot are especially rich in vitamins and minerals. Peeling carrots removes many of these valuable nutrients. Unless the skin is discolored or thick, a good, brisk washing is preferable to peeling. Generally carrots with fresh green tops are fresher than the more common bagged variety which can be stored for several weeks before reaching the consumer.

Microwave Conversion Instructions: Melt butter on High in 1-qt. *(1L)* casserole. Stir in mustard and brown sugar. Add carrots. Stir to coat. Cook, covered, on High 10 minutes or until carrots are tender, stirring once.

Homemade Ice Cream

TOTAL CALORIES
VANILLA: 3580
CALORIES PER ½ CUP: 358
CARBOHYDRATES: 16g
PROTEIN: 1.6g
FAT: 32g
CHOLESTEROL: High

TOTAL CALORIES
CHOCOLATE FUDGE: 5810
CALORIES PER ½ CUP: 415
CARBOHYDRATES: 27g
PROTEIN: 2.5g
FAT: 33g
CHOLESTEROL: High
PREPARING: 20 Minutes
CHILLING: 6 Hours Minimum
FREEZING: 15-60 Minutes

No commercial ice cream can compare with the lightness and honest flavor of homemade ice cream. You use no artificial flavorings, nor do you adulterate it with stabilizers or emulsifiers. And beyond the consideration of taste goes the creative pleasure of mixing and freezing flavors limited only by your imagination.

While using a hand cranked ice cream freezer may provide a fun family activity, on a regular basis it is too tedious. An electric ice cream freezer with its own built-in refrigeration unit and thus the elimination of the need for crushed ice and salt, is ideal although very expensive. The alternative is a small electric ice cream freezer that is placed inside the freezer compartment of a refrigerator.

VANILLA: YIELD 1¼ Quarts
1 qt. (950ml) heavy cream
1 very fresh vanilla bean
¾ cup (150g) sugar
Few grains salt
1 T. pure vanilla extract

CHOCOLATE FUDGE: YIELD 1¾ Quarts
1½ cups (300g) sugar
Few grains salt
½ cup (120ml) water
6 oz. (170g) Lindt Extra Bittersweet Chocolate
1 qt. (950ml) heavy cream
1 T. pure vanilla extract

COFFEE KAHLUA: YIELD 1¼ Quarts
¾ cup (180ml) very strong freshly brewed coffee with 1 tsp. instant coffee crystals added
1 qt. (950ml) heavy cream
¾ cup (150g) sugar
Few grains salt
1 T. pure vanilla extract
¼ cup (60ml) Kahlua

MAPLE WALNUT: YIELD 2 Quarts
1 qt. (950ml) heavy cream
Few grains salt
2½ cups (590ml) pure maple syrup
1 cup (115g) coarsely chopped walnuts

PUMPKIN: Yield 1¼ Quarts
1 qt. (950ml) heavy cream
½ cup (100g) brown sugar
1 cup (280g) canned pumpkin
1 T. pure vanilla extract
¾ tsp. cinnamon
½ tsp. each allspice, ginger, nutmeg, cloves
¼ tsp. salt

VANILLA: Scald heavy cream, adding seeds scraped from vanilla bean and the bean itself. Add sugar and salt and allow to dissolve completely. When mixture has cooled, add vanilla extract. Chill in refrigerator a minimum of 6 hours or up to 3 days. Transfer mixture to an ice cream machine and freeze as directed by manufacturer. Remove ice cream to storage containers and harden in freezer.

CHOCOLATE FUDGE: Dissolve sugar and salt in water in saucepan. Break chocolate into small pieces. Gradually add chocolate to dissolved sugar mixture; continue cooking until chocolate is completely melted, stirring frequently. Gradually stir in cream, cooking just until mixture comes to a boil before adding more cream. Stir well after each addition. Allow mixture to boil for 30 seconds after all cream has been incorporated. Cool and add vanilla. Chill in refrigerator a minimum 6 hours or up to 3 days. Transfer mixture to ice cream machine and freeze as directed. (This flavor always remains softer than others.) For regular CHOCOLATE, reduce amount of chocolate by half.

COFFEE KAHLUA: Combine coffee and scalded cream. Add sugar and salt and allow to dissolve completely. When cool, add vanilla and Kahlua. Chill in refrigerator and freeze as directed.

MAPLE WALNUT: Scald cream. Add salt and maple syrup. Blend well and cool. Chill in refrigerator and freeze as directed. As ice cream begins to thicken, add walnut pieces.

PUMPKIN: Scald cream. Remove from heat and add sugar and pumpkin. Stir until dissolved and well blended. When cool blend in remaining ingredients. Chill in refrigerator and freeze as directed.

BUTTERSCOTCH: Slowly melt butter and sugar together in saucepan, stir well and gently cook until sugar melts into brown syrup. Scald cream and gradually stir into cooled brown sugar syrup. Cool and then add salt and vanilla. Chill in refrigerator and freeze as directed.

STRAWBERRY: Combine mashed (do not puree) berries with sugar. Let mixture stand about 2 hours. Mix with remaining ingredients. Chill in refrigerator and freeze as directed.

BLUEBERRY: Mash berries and combine with sugar. Let mixture stand about 2 hours. Puree this mixture in blender or food processor and then simmer about 20 minutes, stirring often. Cool, then stir in remaining ingredients. Chill in refrigerator and freeze as directed.

RASPBERRY: Crush berries and add sugar. Let stand 2 hours. Mix in remaining ingredients. Taste for sweetness and adjust if necessary. Chill in refrigerator and freeze as directed.

PEPPERMINT STICK: Scald cream. Add sugar, salt and extract and allow to dissolve completely. Chill and freeze as directed. As ice cream begins to thicken, add crushed candy.

Melinda M. Vance, West Hartford, CT

Nutritional Notes: Because you are using superior flavorings, you do not have to rely on richness for good taste. Therefore, try using half-and-half, milk or skim milk and decide which type you find most suitable to your taste.

BUTTERSCOTCH: YIELD 1 Quart

2 T. *(30g)* butter
1 cup *(100g)* dark brown sugar
1 qt. *(950ml)* heavy cream
Few grains salt
1 T. pure vanilla extract

STRAWBERRY: YIELD 1½ Quarts

2 cups *(340g)* well *mashed* fresh
　strawberries
1¼ cups *(250g)* sugar
2 cups *(475ml)* heavy cream
1 T. pure vanilla extract
1 tsp. fresh lemon juice
Few grains salt

BLUEBERRY: YIELD 1 Quart

1½ cups *(225g)* fresh blueberries
1 cup *(200g)* sugar
2 cups *(475ml)* heavy cream
1 tsp. fresh lemon juice
1 T. pure vanilla extract

RASPBERRY: YIELD 1 Quart

2 cups *(275g)* fresh raspberries
1½ cups *(300g)* sugar
2 cups *(475ml)* heavy cream
1 tsp. fresh lemon juice

PEPPERMINT STICK: YIELD 1 Quart

1 qt. *(950ml)* heavy cream
½ cup *(100g)* sugar
Few grains salt
2 tsp. peppermint extract
1 cup *(255g)* crushed peppermint candy

Coconut Oatmeal Crisps

YIELD: 40-50 Cookies
TOTAL CALORIES: 4850
CALORIES PER COOKIE: 97
CARBOHYDRATES: 12g
PROTEIN: 1g
FAT: 5g
PREPARING: 15 Minutes
BAKING: 5-8 Minutes Per Sheet
FREEZING: Yes

Cream butter; add sugars and beat until light and creamy. Add beaten eggs and mix thoroughly. Add vanilla.

Sift together flour, baking powder, baking soda, and salt; add to batter. Gently mix in oats, coconut and Rice Krispies.

Drop by well-rounded teaspoonfuls onto greased baking sheet. Bake in preheated 350° oven 5 to 8 minutes.

Bobbi Evans, Duxbury, MA

½ lb. *(225g)* butter
1 cup *(200g)* granulated sugar
1 cup *(200g)* brown sugar
2 beaten eggs
1 tsp. pure vanilla extract
1¾ cups *(200g)* sifted flour
1 tsp. baking soda
¼ tsp. baking powder
½ tsp. salt
½ cup *(45g)* quick oats
1 cup *(75g)* flaked coconut
2 cups *(60g)* Rice Krispies

Society of Daniel Wadsworth Dinner at the Atheneum

Join us in Morgan Great Hall in Connecticut's leading art museum for a superb French banquet in honor of the museum's first patron.

Daniel Wadsworth, founder of America's first civic art museum, the Wadsworth Atheneum, was the son of Jeremiah Wadsworth, Commissary General to the Colonies during the Revolution. Daniel inherited a considerable fortune from his father, much of which he used to support and promote the arts in his native Hartford.

As a patron of the arts, Daniel Wadsworth took a material interest in the careers of the painters Thomas Cole, Frederic Church and Thomas Sully, to name just a few. As an amateur architect, he had a hand in determining the Neo-Gothic style of the Atheneum, which, when it opened in 1844, was devoted to art, science and literature. The museum was constructed on the site of the Wadsworth family homestead. At that time the one-building structure contained eighty-two works of art. Among these was John Trumbull's painting which is reproduced on the two dollar bill.

Today the museum comprises five distinct, interconnected buildings which form a square complex around an outdoor sculpture court. The buildings house a world-famous collection of art, consisting of over 40,000 objects ranging from early Greek, Roman and Egyptian artifacts to the work of living artists. Of particular note are: the collection of Baroque paintings; French 19th century paintings; 18th and 19th century American art; the Wallace Nutting collection of early American furniture and decorative arts; and Meissen porcelain given to the museum by one of its greatest benefactors, J.P. Morgan.

The museum also contains such attractions as Toulouse-Lautrec's portrait of Jane Avril, one of only four Caravaggio paintings in the United States, and a remarkably lifelike sunbather by Duane Hanson. Two particularly unique features of the Atheneum are the MATRIX Gallery, which highlights the latest developments in contemporary art, and the Lions Gallery of the Senses, which presents exhibitions exploring the use of all the senses, including taste and smell. The museum contains a shop and restaurant, as well as the celebrated Auerbach Art Library and a 300-seat theatre. The theatre opened in 1934 with the world premiere of Gertrude Stein and Virgil Thomson's "Four Saints in Three Acts."

The society of Daniel Wadsworth was founded in 1973, approximately 200 years after the birth of the museum's founder, to foster the tradition of support for the arts in Hartford. Members of the Society are honored each year by a dinner held at the museum. They are highlighted not only by the presence of distinguished speakers but by superb food. The following Society of Daniel Wadsworth Dinner is indicative of the strong influence of French cooking on the development of American cuisine. This elegant menu is clear evidence that American tastes and culinary skills have changed dramatically from those of our Puritan ancestors who served "Pompkins" — baked, boiled and stewed.

The first real introduction of French cooking to America came through Thomas Jefferson who followed Benjamin Franklin as the U.S. envoy to Paris. Jefferson became so enamored of French foods that he brought the first French chef to the White House and assigned two servants as apprentices to learn his skills. Invariably, the congressmen and constituents who dined at Jefferson's lavish table went home with a new appreciation for "the French style." A dish such as Chicken Marengo might well have been served by Jefferson and then zealously copied by an admiring American cook. This particular dish was created on June 14, 1800 by Napoleon's chef following the general's victory at Marengo. Legend suggests that the chef gathered garlic, olives, tomatoes, eggs, bread and a chicken — all that he could find in the countryside — and created this now famous dish on the battlefield.

Thomas Jefferson's impact on the introduction of French cooking was extended in 1803 when he negotiated the Louisiana Purchase. The French-dominated capital of New Orleans soon became famous for its delectable cuisine. The French influence could be detected in fresh Gulf seafood recipes such as *pompano en papillote* and *bouillabaisse* as well as in luscious desserts such as Pecan Roulade, which combines French culinary magic with plump Louisiana pecans. After purchase of the Territory, the following influx of settling Americans soon came to appreciate and adopt the distinctive French style of food preparation. In the same way, those who participate in this superb Wadsworth Society Menu will come to appreciate anew the French accent on our cooking heritage.

Champagne Punch
p. 144

Gougère
p. 145

Caviar Mousse
p. 144

Mouclade Maraichine
p. 146

Poulet Sauté à la Marengo
(Chicken Marengo with Croustades)
p. 146

Zucchini Julienne
p. 148

Garden Greens,
Lemon Dijon Dressing
p. 148

Pecan Roulade
p. 149

Charlotte Royale
à la Framboise
p. 150

YIELD: 30 5-oz. Servings
CALORIES PER SERVING: 140
CARBOHYDRATES: 10g
PREPARING: 20 Minutes
CHILLING: 4 Hours
FREEZING: Yes — Ice Ring

Champagne Punch

Lemon, orange slices for ice ring
2 qts. *(1.9L)* **club soda**
1 can (6-8 oz.) *(180-240ml)* **frozen
  lemonade concentrate**
2 cups *(475ml) very* **strong dark tea**
1½ cups *(355ml)* **Curacao**
1½ cups *(355ml)* **peach brandy**
1 cup *(240ml)* **maraschino cordial**
2 fifths *(1½L)* **champagne**

Make a decorative ice ring; use lemon and orange slices, if desired, or other seasonal fruits, berries, or leaves.

Chill all ingredients. Place ice ring in punch bowl large enough to hold approximately 5 quarts *(5L)* punch. Pour ingredients into bowl, adding champagne immediately before serving.

Gail Standish, West Hartford, CT

Variations, Advance Preparation, and Serving Suggestions:
Can be made a day in advance, but add club soda and champagne just before serving.

YIELD: 2 Cups
TOTAL CALORIES: 1858
CALORIES PER
   TABLESPOON: 58
PROTEIN: 2g
FAT: 5.5g
SODIUM: High
CHILLING: 4 Hours
FREEZING: No

Caviar Mousse

2 T. *(30ml)* **fresh lemon juice**
1½ T. dry vermouth
1 pkg. *(7g)* **unflavored gelatin**
2 tsp. anchovy paste
5 eggs, hard-boiled and sieved
¾ cup *(170g)* **mayonnaise**
1 tsp. Worcestershire sauce
1 T. grated onion
1 jar (3½ oz.) *(100g)* **black lumpfish
  caviar, rinsed lightly, drained**

Combine lemon juice and vermouth in cup, add gelatin and soften mixture over warm water. Stir in anchovy paste until dissolved. Add eggs, mayonnaise, Worcestershire sauce, onion, and gently fold in caviar. Pour into oiled 2-cup *(480ml)* mold. Cover. Chill minimum of 4 hours before serving. Unmold and garnish with watercress or parsley. Serve with pumpernickel rounds or crackers.

Clare Edwards, West Hartford, CT

Beverage Suggestion: Iced vodka.

Gougère with Optional Cheese Soufflé Filling

In its simplest form, a gougere is a rustic Burgundian cheese-enriched chou pastry, baked in the form of a ring. It is an ideal accompaniment to the wine of the region. The traditional manner for making a gougere is without the filling.

YIELD: 6-8 Hors d'Oeuvre Servings or
  2 Large Rings or 24-30 Individual Puffs
CALORIES PER ⅛ DOUGH: 260
CARBOHYDRATES: 12g
PROTEIN: 9g
FAT: 20g
CALORIES PER ⅛ DOUGH
  WITH CHEESE FILLING: 370
PREPARING: 1 Hour
BAKING: 45 Minutes
FREEZING: Yes

After last egg has been beaten into the pate a choux, beat in grated cheese. Grease and flour a baking sheet; draw a 6-inch *(15cm)* circle in center.

Fit a pastry bag with a #9 plain tube. Fill the bag with dough and pipe a ring around the outside of the circle. The ring should be about 1 inch *(2.5cm)* thick and as high as it is wide. Or shape dough with 2 large soup spoons and drop it by spoonfuls onto baking sheet, using circle as a guide. The rounds should touch.

Brush ring with egg wash; sprinkle ring with grated cheese.

Bake ring in the center of preheated 475° oven for 5 minutes; lower heat to 400° and bake 25 to 30 minutes longer, or until ring is golden brown and dry. Remove from oven and cool slightly on a wire rack. While ring is still warm, slice off top ⅓ with a serrated knife and lay it on the rack. (If you are planning to serve the ring plain without any type of filling, then do not remove this top piece.)

SOUFFLE FILLING: While pastry is baking, prepare the filling. Melt butter, add flour; cook stirring until roux is white and foamy, about 2 minutes. Whisk in hot milk and continue whisking over heat until mixture is smooth. Add salt, pepper, nutmeg and mustard. Remove from heat; whisk in grated cheese and then yolks. Return to heat and bring mixture just to a boil. Set aside and keep warm until needed. When ready to fill and bake gougere, beat egg whites until stiff, then fold them gently into souffle base.

Preheat oven to 450° Spoon or pipe most of mixture into bottom of the gougere. Place top piece (lid) on top of filling. Bake ring in the center of oven for 5 to 10 minutes or until lid starts to rise. Cover top with foil if it browns too quickly. Serve immediately, cut into wedges. The center should be soft and creamy.

Melinda M. Vance, West Hartford, CT

Variations, Advance Preparation, and Serving Suggestions:
The filled or unfilled Gougere can be served either hot or at room temperature.

If Gougere is to be used as a "bread" as part of a buffet, line center of ring with Boston lettuce leaves to form a cup and fill cup with Cold Beets In Mustard (page 61) or other salad of your choice.

Wine Suggestion: French Macon Villages Blanc, fresh white; serve chilled.

GOUGERE:
1 recipe Pate a Choux (page 195)
¾ cup *(90g)* freshly grated cheese
  (Swiss, Parmesan, or Gruyere)

GOUGERE TOPPING:
1 egg beaten with pinch salt
2 T. grated Gruyere cheese

OPTIONAL SOUFFLE FILLING:
2½ T. *(35g)* unsalted sweet butter
3 T. *(20g)* flour
1 cup *(240ml)* milk, gently heated
1 tsp. salt
Pinch freshly ground white pepper
Pinch freshly grated nutmeg
1 tsp. Dijon mustard
½ cup *(60g)* Gruyere cheese
3 eggs, separated

YIELD: 2 Servings
CALORIES PER SERVING: 576
CARBOHYDRATES: 13g
PROTEIN: 23g
FAT: 48g
CHOLESTEROL: High
SODIUM: High
PREPARING: 45 Minutes
COOKING: 10 Minutes
FREEZING: No

Mouclade Maraichine

MUSSELS COOKED IN CREAM WITH CURRY

This recipe comes from Poitou in southwestern France where the mussels are found along the wide sandy marshes. It is featured on the menu of RESTAURANT DU VILLAGE, Chester, Connecticut.

30 large fresh mussels
¼ cup *(60ml)* **dry white wine**
1 T. chopped shallots
1 T. chopped parsley
1 cup *(240ml)* **heavy cream**
1½ T. curry powder (Madras preferred)
1 tsp. coarse sea salt (sea salt is important for the flavor in the recipe)
Chopped parsley
Toasted French bread rounds

Carefully scrub mussels, remove "beards" and any barnacles. Place mussels, wine, shallots, parsley, cream, curry and salt in heavy saucepan; cover. Bring just to a boil, lower heat and simmer until mussels open. Remove mussels from cooking liquid; discard any that have not opened. Set aside.

Continue to rapidly cook cream and curry mixture until reduced to half and thick and light yellow in color.

Remove one shell from each mussel; arrange 15 mussels in their shells on each plate in an attractive circular pattern. Briefly place plates in a hot oven to make certain the mussels are hot before serving. Pour sauce into shells and over hot mussels. Garnish with chopped parsley and toasted French bread rounds.

Variations, Advance Preparation, and Serving Suggestions: Recipe can be adjusted to serve 8; additional quantities require two pots.

Wine Suggestion: French Chateau Olivier Blanc Graves, dry white; serve chilled.

YIELD: 6 Servings
TOTAL CALORIES: 3600
CALORIES PER SERVING
  INCLUDING GARNISHES: 621
CARBOHYDRATES: 15g
PROTEIN: 48g
FAT: 41g
CHOLESTEROL: High
SODIUM: High
PREPARING: 1¼ Hours
COOKING: 1½ Hours
FREEZING: No

Poulet Sauté à la Marengo

SAUTEED CHICKEN WITH SHRIMP AND FRIED EGGS

Named after the Napoleonic Battle of Marengo in 1800, this dish was said to have originated at the hand of Napoleon's cook, making use of the foods to be found at the farmhouses closest to the battle scene.

CHICKEN:
2 whole large chicken breasts, split (4 pieces)
4 chicken leg/thigh pieces, not split
Olive oil to saute
¼ cup *(60ml)* **cognac**
½ cup *(100g)* **fresh onion, minced**
¾ tsp. Italian seasoning
Salt
Freshly ground pepper

CHICKEN: Dry chicken with paper towels. Film a large skillet with olive oil. Heat to hot, not smoking. Saute chicken 4 to 5 minutes each side until golden. Pour cognac over chicken and carefully ignite. Let flame 1 minute, extinguish with skillet cover. Add onion, Italian seasoning, salt and pepper. Bring to simmer, cover. Simmer 10 to 12 minutes. Turn chicken and simmer another 10 to 12 minutes. Set aside, covered.

GARNISHES: *Mushrooms —* Place fluted caps in small stainless saucepan with 3 to 4 T. wine, ¼ tsp. salt, and butter. Bring to simmer, cover. Simmer slowly 5 minutes. Set pan aside.

Croutons — Heat a second large skillet with ⅛-inch olive oil over moderately high heat until hot, not smoking. Saute bread triangles 1 to 2 minutes on each side until lightly browned. Drain on paper towels.

Shrimp — In same skillet, saute shrimp in a bit more oil, swirling pan, until shrimp begin to stiffen. Season with salt, pepper. Pour in 2 to 3 tsp. wine. Swirl a minute more. With slotted spoon, transfer shrimp to bowl.

Sauce — Add another T. oil to skillet. Stir in mushroom stems, tomatoes, tomato paste, garlic, ¼ tsp. Italian seasoning, salt, pepper. Add liquid from mushrooms. (Reserve caps in bowl with shrimp.) Simmer, covered, 5 minutes. Remove cover. Simmer over medium heat until most of liquid has evaporated.

Eggs — In small stainless saucepan, heat 1 inch *(2.5cm)* oil until hot, not smoking. One at a time, break an egg into a ladle and tip into oil, being careful not to break yolk. Immediately roll egg against side of pan with a spoon to form oval shape. Let cook 2 minutes. Remove, drain on paper towels.

Remove chicken pieces from skillet. Spoon out excess fat. Pour in tomato sauce, return chicken to skillet. Baste and simmer 1 to 2 minutes to reheat chicken. Reheat shrimp and mushroom caps briefly in second skillet. Reheat croutons and eggs briefly in preheated 450° oven.

ASSEMBLY: Arrange chicken and sauce on a hot serving platter. Place croutons around edge. Top them alternately with an egg and 3 shrimp. Arrange mushroom caps and olives over chicken. Sprinkle parsley over eggs. Serve at once.

Sheila D'Agostino, West Hartford, CT

Variations, Advance Preparation, and Serving Suggestions:
Chicken and garnishes may be prepared several hours ahead of serving. Reheat and assemble just before serving. Easily doubled or tripled for a dramatic dinner party entree.

Wine Suggestion: Puligny-Montrachet or Corton-Charlemagne, full white; serve chilled.

Microwave Conversion Instructions: Note: This recipe uses a combination of conventional cooktop cooking and microwave oven. In a large microwave-safe skillet saute chicken on conventional cooktop. After chicken has been flamed, add onion, Italian seasoning, and salt and pepper to skillet. Cook on High, covered, 15 minutes, or until chicken is just done. Set aside, covered.

GARNISHES: *Croutons* — To absorb flavor of oil, best done on conventional cooktop.

Mushroom caps — Place mushroom caps, wine, salt, butter in small glass-covered casserole; cook 5 minutes on Medium (50%). Set aside.

Shrimp — Place 2 T. oil in shallow pie plate; arrange shrimp in ring with tails facing inside of plate. Cover with waxed paper; cook on High 1 to 3 minutes, just until they turn pink. Remove each shrimp as it turns color so that none get tough. When all are cooked, return them to plate; season with salt and pepper and stir in 2 T. wine. Swirl shrimp in liquid; transfer with slotted spoon to bowl.

Sauce — Add another 1 T. oil to same pie plate. Stir in mushroom stems, tomatoes, tomato paste, garlic, Italian seasoning, salt and pepper. Add liquid from mushroom caps. Cook, uncovered, on High until liquid has been reduced.

Eggs — Prepare on conventional cooktop.

Remove chicken from skillet. Spoon out excess fat. Pour in tomato sauce. Return chicken to skillet. Baste with sauce. Cook, uncovered, on High 3 to 4 minutes to reheat. Assemble as directed above.

GARNISHES:
12 large mushrooms, stems minced, caps fluted
5 T. *(75ml)* **dry vermouth or white wine, divided**
¼ tsp. salt
1 T. butter

Olive oil for frying

4 slices firm, white bread, crusts removed, cut in 8 triangles

12 large raw shrimp, peeled
Salt
Freshly ground pepper to taste

3-4 large tomatoes, peeled, seeded, chopped
2 T. tomato paste
2 large cloves garlic, minced
¼ tsp. Italian seasoning

6 eggs

10 small black olives
2 T. chopped fresh parsley

YIELD: 6-8 Servings
CALORIES PER SERVING: 143
CARBOHYDRATES: 7g
PROTEIN: 4g
FAT: 11g
PREPARING: 15 Minutes
COOKING: 8 Minutes

Zucchini Julienne

3 lbs. *(1350g)* **very firm zucchini**
4 cups *(950ml)* **chicken broth**
½ cup *(115g)* **butter**
1½ tsp. **salt**
1½ tsp. **freshly ground pepper**
¾-1 tsp. **tarragon, crumbled**

Slice zucchini into strips, 2 inches *(5cm)* long and ⅛ inch *(0.3cm)* thick with vegetable peeler. Do not use center containing seeds. Bring broth to boil in large saucepan. Add zucchini and cook 3 to 4 minutes. Remove and drain. (Save broth in which zucchini has been cooked to use as a soup base, liquid for rice, or to combine in cooking another vegetable.) Cool in single layer on large platter in refrigerator 1 to 2 hours. In large skillet, melt butter, add seasonings. Over high heat, quickly saute zucchini, about 3 minutes. Remove to serving dish. Serve immediately.

Deborah A. Cornwell, Farmington, CT

Nutritional Notes: Although the seeds are removed from the zucchini, the vitamin A content found mainly in the skin is preserved. The flesh contains no appreciable amounts of this vitamin.

Microwave Conversion Instructions: In covered 3 qt. *(3L)* casserole bring 1 cup stock to boil on High 2 to 3 minutes. Add zucchini. Cover and cook on High 1½ minutes. Drain and dry zucchini. Continue to saute conventionally or heat browning pan 5 minutes on High. Add butter, seasonings and zucchini. Stir well and cook on High 2 minutes.

YIELD: ¾ Cup
CALORIES PER TABLESPOON: 76
CARBOHYDRATES: 1g
FAT: 8g
SODIUM: High
PREPARING: 10 Minutes
CHILLING: 2 Hours Minimum
FREEZING: Not Necessary

Lemon Dijon Dressing

This is a very versatile salad dressing.

1 **egg**
2 tsp. **freshly grated Parmesan cheese**
½ tsp. **salt**
¼ tsp. **freshly ground pepper**
2 T. **Dijon mustard**
3 T. *(45ml)* **fresh lemon juice**
1 tsp. **Worcestershire sauce**
1 tsp. **sugar**
½ cup *(120ml)* **oil**

In small bowl, place all ingredients and beat until completely blended, using wire whisk (or blend briefly in food processor with plastic blade). Put ingredients in covered jar and refrigerate at least 2 hours. Shake thoroughly before serving.

Lee Grimmeisen, West Hartford, CT

Variations, Advance Preparation, and Serving Suggestions: Refrigerated, this dressing keeps well for at least 1 month. Recipe may be made in much larger quantities. For extra bite and added flavor, add 1 T. Italian balsamico vinegar to above recipe.

Pecan Roulade

YIELD: 8 Servings
TOTAL CALORIES: 3900
CALORIES PER SERVING: 488
CARBOHYDRATES: 25g
PROTEIN: 7g
FAT: 40g
CHOLESTEROL: High
PREPARING: 30 Minutes
BAKING: 20 Minutes

ROULADE: Beat egg yolks and sugar with electric mixer until thick and light. In separate bowl, beat egg whites and cream of tartar until stiff peaks form. Add pecans and baking powder to egg yolk mixture and blend; gently fold egg yolk mixture into egg whites. Spread mixture into a 10½ × 15½-inch (26.5 × 40cm) jelly roll pan that has been oiled and covered with oiled piece of waxed paper extending over edges of pan.

Bake in preheated 350° oven 20 minutes. The roulade will be puffy and light; it is done when it springs back and toothpick comes out clean. Cool to room temperature, then cover with slightly damp, not wet, towel. It may now be refrigerated for several days.

To fill, sprinkle sheet of waxed paper with confectioners' sugar. Turn roulade onto paper; peel off waxed paper.

FILLING: Whip cream with choice of flavoring and confectioners' sugar; spread on flat roulade. Top with sliced fruit and roll as you would a jelly roll. Sift additional confectioners' sugar over roulade and decorate with extra whipped cream and fruit.

Sharon Mann, Bloomfield, CT

Variations, Advance Preparation, and Serving Suggestions:
Walnuts may be substituted for pecans. In summer, decorate with fresh flowers and mint leaves.

Wine Suggestion: French Sauternes, sweet white; serve chilled.

ROULADE:

6 eggs, separated
¾ cup (150g) sugar
¼ tsp. cream of tartar
1½ cups (150g) pecans, coarsely ground or finely chopped
1 T. baking powder

FILLING:

2 cups (475ml) heavy cream
¼ cup (35g) confectioners' sugar
1 tsp. rum, brandy, almond or pure vanilla extract
1 cup fresh sliced peaches, (200g whole) bananas (200g) or strawberries (150g) or a combination

YIELD: 12 Servings
CALORIES PER SERVING: 475
CARBOHYDRATES: 68g
PROTEIN: 9g
FAT: 18.5g
CHOLESTEROL: High
PREPARING: 3 Hours
BAKING: 15 Minutes
CHILLING: Overnight
COOKING: 25 Minutes
FREEZING: Yes

Charlotte Royale
à la Framboise

A molded jelly roll filled with either a raspberry Bavarian cream or a creamy chocolate mousse, a dramatic finale to a fine meal. Absolutely habit forming!

RASPBERRY JELLY ROLL:

5 eggs, separated, room temperature
1 tsp. pure vanilla extract
½ cup (100g) sugar
½ tsp. baking powder
¾ cup (85g) sifted cake flour
1 cup (285g) good quality raspberry jelly

RASPBERRY BAVARIAN FILLING:

6 egg yolks, room temperature
¾ cup (150g) sugar
3 cups (710ml) milk, scalded
6 T. (90ml) framboise liqueur
2 env. (15g) unflavored gelatin
½ cup (140g) good quality raspberry jelly
Few drops red food coloring, (optional)
1½ cups (355ml) heavy cream

CHOCOLATE MOUSSE FILLING:

4 egg yolks
½ cup (65g) confectioners' sugar
2 T. (30ml) dark rum (Myers's preferred)
8 oz. (225g) semisweet chocolate (Lindt Extra-Bittersweet preferred), melted
½ lb. (225g) unsalted sweet butter, softened
8 egg whites

GLAZE:

½ cup (140g) good quality apricot jam
2 T. (30ml) framboise liqueur

RASPBERRY SAUCE:

2 pkg. (10 oz. each) (570g) frozen raspberries, thawed
4-6 T. (50-80g) sugar
2 T. (20g) cornstarch
¼ cup (60ml) framboise liqueur

RASPBERRY JELLY ROLL: Butter 10½ × 15½-inch *(26.5 × 40cm)* baking pan. Line pan with waxed paper or parchment, letting ends extend slightly. Butter and flour paper.

With electric mixer, beat egg yolks and vanilla until smooth. Gradually add sugar, beating until very thick and pale yellow, about 8 minutes. Combine baking powder and flour; sift over yolks, folding in lightly with a large rubber spatula. Beat egg whites until stiff, not dry. Gently stir ¼ of whites into yolk mixture. Gently fold in remaining whites until barely mixed.

Transfer batter to baking pan using large rubber spatula. Smooth top. Place pan on next-to-lowest rack of preheated 350° oven. Bake 13 to 15 minutes. Remove from oven; invert cake onto waxed paper on flat surface. Remove waxed paper or parchment lining. Invert cake so that it is right side up. While still warm, spread jelly evenly over cake. Starting with long end, gently roll cake up as tightly and compactly as possible. Wrap in plastic wrap or aluminum foil. Chill until ready to assemble Charlotte, or freeze up to one week.

Prepare either Raspberry Bavarian Filling or Chocolate Mousse Filling.

RASPBERRY BAVARIAN FILLING: Beat egg yolks and sugar with electric mixer until very pale yellow. Add milk while stirring vigorously. Transfer mixture to saucepan and cook over low heat, stirring constantly, until mixture thickens and coats back of spoon, about 20 minutes. Do not let custard boil. Place framboise in small bowl; stir in gelatin. Mix until gelatin is softened. Add gelatin mixture to hot custard; stir well until gelatin is dissolved. Add raspberry jelly, stir until well blended. If custard is lumpy, it may be passed through a fine sieve. If desired, add a few drops red coloring. Let cool completely. Whip cream until almost stiff; fold into custard. Let mixture remain at room temperature while lining a 2½-qt. *(2.5L)* round-bottomed bowl with plastic wrap. Starting with bottom center, line bowl with ½-inch *(1.25cm)* slices of raspberry jelly roll. Pour filling into center of bowl. Chill until top is firm. Cover with plastic wrap; refrigerate overnight.

CHOCOLATE MOUSSE FILLING: Combine yolks, sugar and rum in bowl. Beat until light and fluffy and pale yellow. Combine melted chocolate and softened butter; beat 1 minute; add to yolk mixture. Keep mixture lukewarm.

Beat egg whites until stiff, but not dry. Gently stir ¼ of egg whites into mixture. Gently fold in remaining whites. The mixture will lose some of its volume. Work quickly to prevent whites from becoming grainy. Pour filling into cake-lined bowl. Chill until top is firm. Cover with plastic wrap. Refrigerate overnight.

Invert bowl onto serving dish; unmold. Remove plastic wrap lining. Return to refrigerator.

GLAZE: Melt apricot jam in saucepan over low heat, stirring. Strain into small bowl; stir in framboise. Brush glaze over chilled Charlotte. Refrigerate until ready to serve.

RASPBERRY SAUCE: Puree raspberries. Pass puree through strainer to remove seeds. Combine puree with sugar and cornstarch in saucepan. Cook, stirring constantly, until thickened. Cool. Add framboise to taste. Chill until ready to serve.

To serve, place slices of Charlotte on individual plates; ladle sauce around each.

Kathleen J. Schwartz, Avon CT

Variations, Advance Preparation, and Serving Suggestions:
The well-wrapped jelly roll may be frozen. In a pinch, you may also freeze the assembled Charlotte. Defrost in refrigerator. Apply glaze just before serving. Creme Anglaise (page 200) may be served as a sauce. If using this sauce, sprinkle a few fresh raspberries or fraises de bois on top of the sauce surrounding each slice.

Wine Suggestion: California Chateau Beaulieu Sauvignon Blanc, semi-sweet; serve chilled.

Hartford Ballet
"Romeo and Juliet" Dîner à Deux

A perfect menu to celebrate an engagement, and anniversary or most any very special, romantic occasion.

That the Hartford Ballet menu should focus on "Romeo and Juliet" is a fitting tribute to the art of ballet which originated in Italy in 1450. Initially, ballet was a series of sophisticated social dances accompanied by sung or spoken words. The first "silent" ballet, called pantomime ballet, with only a musical accompaniment was introduced in 1734 in France. The romantic ballet as we know it today attained wide European acceptance by the mid-1800s. It was at this time that ballet began to appear in theatres in the United States, often through touring European companies. However, it was not until the early 1900s, when Diaghilev's Ballet Russe and the Ballet Russe de Monte Carlo toured the U.S. and received the public's enthusiastic acceptance, that the art of ballet began to flourish in American cities.

The Hartford Ballet was founded in 1972; within three years it became the most actively touring ballet company in the nation. Under the direction of nationally recognized dancer and choreographer Michael Uthoff, the Hartford Ballet has appeared in almost every state of the union, reaching an audience of over 120,000 annually. Uthoff uses both his own eclectic talent and that of other major choreographers (including: Balanchine, Tudor, Limon and Lubovitch) to formulate an extensive and diverse repertory of works that appeal to seasoned dance fans, new audiences and the most respected dance critics. Clive Barnes hailed the company as "a major cultural resource for America".

An important part of the organization is the School of the Hartford Ballet which serves as the official school for the company. It was founded in 1960 as Connecticut's first non-profit organization dedicated to dance. Under the direction of Enid Lynn the school has expanded to meet the growing demand for professional dance training and now operates branch schools in Bristol, Connecticut and Worcester, Massachusetts. In 1979 it was selected as one of the nation's first five private dance schools to be accredited by the Joint Commission on Dance and Theatre.

Our special "Diner a Deux" menu which honors this highly acclaimed production of "Romeo and Juliet" draws on a style of food preparation which is particularly suitable for a memorable, intimate meal for two. *Nouvelle Cuisine* is a controversial "new cooking" style developed in France. It highlights the individual texture and taste of fresh ingredients and focuses on the visual appearance of the food on the serving plate. Cooking techniques such as steaming and grilling the freshest, most tender cuts guarantee the original flavor of meats. Because starchy sauces and strong marinades are believed to camouflage delicate flavors, the new sauces are based on reduction and thus on the concentration of natural juices. Each imaginative dish is carefully arranged, ideally on oversized plates with shallow wells and wide rims. Julienne strips of colorful, contrasting vegetables or fruits complete the picture of a meal which can both satisfy the appetite and delight the eye.

Now lest we become too serious in our preparation of a romantic meal for two, recall that in the past there have been other associations between ballet and food. According to dance legend, the term "balletomane" originated in Russia during the 19th century when romantic ballet was at its height. Choreographers lavished their talents on the role of the ballerina, and an avid dance public known as "balletomanes" followed the career and exploits of their favorite ballerina. Marie Taglioni, the epitome of the ethereal 19th century ballerina, was vastly admired in Russia. In St. Petersburg balletomanes vied for her dance slippers, prepared them with a sauce and consumed them! It is our hope that those who prepare the luscious Diner a Deux will enjoy this repast much more than the unfortunate balletomanes who succeeded in winning the dance slipper!

Orange Kir Royale
p. 154

Camembert en Brioche
p. 154

Shrimp Beurre Blanc
p. 155

French Bread
p. 229

Juliet's Blush
(Pink Grapefruit Sorbet)
p. 155

Canard aux Poires
p. 158

or

Breast of Duckling Montague
(Broiled Duck Breast
with Raspberry Vinegar Sauce)
p. 156

Spinach Timbales   **Purée of Celeriac with**
p. 159   **Apples**
p. 157

Romaine, Endive and Walnut Salad
p. 160

Coeurs de Chocolat
(Individual Heart-Shaped Dacquoise)
p. 160

Orange Kir Royale

YIELD: 16 Servings or 62 oz.
TOTAL CALORIES: 2400
CALORIES PER SERVING: 150
CARBOHYDRATES: 10g
PREPARING: 5 Minutes

You'll lose some bubble but gain a few minutes if you prepare this champagne punch by the pitcher.

½ cup *(120ml)* **chilled fresh orange juice**
1 cup *(240ml)* **chilled Creme de Cassis**
2 bottles *(750ml each)* **dry chilled champagne**

Mix all together in a crystal pitcher.

James Mitchell, Avon, CT

Variations, Advance Preparation, and Serving Suggestions:
Substitute Campari for Cassis. Use following proportions for a variation: 4 cups *(950ml)* fresh orange juice, ¼ cup *(60ml)* Triple Sec, ¼ cup *(60ml)* Creme de Cassis, and 1 bottle *(750ml)* champagne. Float lime and orange slices on top.

Camembert en Brioche

YIELD: 2 Servings
CALORIES PER SERVING: 635
CARBOHYDRATES: 32g
PROTEIN: 21g
FAT: 47g
CHOLESTEROL: High
PREPARING: 15 Minutes
BAKING: 20 Minutes

Although brioche is wonderful on its own, it's especially good when used to wrap fish, meats, eggs and a variety of other foods. Here it is equally delicious as a casing for soft creamy melted cheese.

½ recipe **Small Quantity Brioche Dough** (page 226), about 6 oz. *(170g)*
4 oz. *(115g)* **imported Camembert cheese, crusts removed**

EGG GLAZE:
1 egg, mixed with 1 tsp. water

Make brioche dough; let rest overnight in refrigerator. On well-floured surface, roll out dough to a 6-inch *(15.2cm)* square, rolling the edges slightly thinner than the center. Place the Camembert in the center and bring the edges of dough up to overlap, wrapping cheese securely. Pinch dough together to seal. (Egg glaze may be brushed on edges before pinching to insure a good seal.)

Invert package onto lightly buttered shallow 5-inch *(13cm)* baking/serving dish. Cover loosely with buttered foil; set in warm (80°-85°) humid place 1½ to 2 hours, until dough is light and springy. Brush package with Egg Glaze. Set dish on preheated baking sheet on lower middle shelf of preheated 425° oven. Bake 10 minutes. Lower heat to 350°. Bake 10 minutes more. Cover lightly with foil if necessary during last minutes of baking to prevent over-browning. Serve warm.

Kathleen J. Schwartz, Avon, CT

Variations, Advance Preparation, and Serving Suggestions:
Can be baked until light brown early in day; reheat in oven just before serving to brown fully. Double or triple the recipe to serve the number you wish.

Wine Suggestion: French Lancillon Bordeaux Rouge, dry red; serve at room temperature.

Shrimp Beurre Blanc

A simple method to prepare shrimp with a sauce that appears frequently in discussions of nouvelle cuisine, although its French origin dates back many generations. It owes its renewed popularity to its delicate flavor and the ease with which it may be substituted for the heavier, more traditional hollandaise.

YIELD: 2 Servings
CALORIES PER SERVING: 410
CARBOHYDRATES: 10g
PROTEIN: 25g
FAT: 30g
PREPARING: 20 Minutes
COOKING: 20 Minutes
FREEZING: No

SHRIMP: Place ingredients in saucepan. Bring to boil over high heat, uncovered. Reduce heat to simmer; cook 2 minutes, stirring occasionally. Remove shrimp from heat; drain. Arrange shrimp in their shells on heated serving plates. Garnish center of each plate with a twisted lemon slice.

BEURRE BLANC: Place shallots and wine in small saucepan; bring to full boil over high heat. Continue boiling until wine is reduced to about ¼ cup. Begin adding butter in pieces, about a tablespoon at a time, while whisking briskly. When butter is incorporated, remove from heat; add salt and pepper to taste. Pass Beurre Blanc in small pitcher with the shrimp.

Kathleen J. Schwartz, Avon, CT

Variations, Advance Preparation, and Serving Suggestions:
Recipe easily doubles, triples, etc. Beurre Blanc can be made several hours ahead; let remain at room temperature. Reheat in top of double boiler. If sauce separates, it can be restored in food processor or blender. Beurre Blanc accompanies simply prepared fish and veal dishes nicely.

Wine Suggestion: French Graves Blanc, dry white; serve chilled.

SHRIMP:
¾ lb. *(340g)* **fresh, raw shrimp, unpeeled**
1 cup *(240ml)* **beer**
1 **bay leaf, crumbled**
6 **whole cloves**
6 **whole allspice**
1 **small clove garlic, peeled**
Salt
Freshly ground pepper
Lemon slices to garnish

BEURRE BLANC:
3 T. *(30g)* **peeled minced shallots**
¾ cup *(175ml)* **dry white wine**
6 T. *(75g)* **butter, at room temperature**
Salt
Freshly ground pepper

Pink Grapefruit Sorbet

A palate-cleansing sorbet rather than a dessert sherbet. Serve as an *intermezzo* between courses, or a cooling snack on a hot day.

YIELD: 1 Quart or 16 Servings
CALORIES PER SERVING: 78
CARBOHYDRATES: 19.5g
PREPARING: 45 Minutes
CHILLING: 2 Hours
FREEZING: Mandatory

Combine water and sugar in saucepan. Bring to boil over medium low heat, stirring just until sugar is dissolved. Wash down any sugar clinging to sides of pan with a brush dipped in cold water. Let syrup simmer 3 minutes. Cool to room temperature. Stir in grapefruit juice. Refrigerate 2 hours. Freeze in electric ice cream maker according to manufacturer's instructions.

Carolyn Orsulak, Wethersfield, CT

Variations, Advance Preparation, and Serving Suggestions:
Consistency is best the day it is made. If it becomes too icy after a few days in the freezer, let soften slightly, process in food processor or blender.

2¼ cups *(535ml)* **water**
1½ cups *(300g)* **sugar**
2 cups *(475ml)* **fresh pink grapefruit juice**

YIELD: 4 Servings
CALORIES PER DUCK BREASTS
  WITH SAUCE: 445
    CARBOHYDRATES: 13g
    PROTEIN: 24g
    FAT: 33g

CALORIES PER SERVING WHOLE
  ROASTED DUCK WITH SAUCE: 519
    CARBOHYDRATES: 13g
    PROTEIN: 29g
    FAT: 39g

CHOLESTEROL: High
SODIUM: High
BROILING: 5-8 Minutes
ROASTING: 1 Hour 10 Minutes
FREEZING: No

Broiled or Roasted Duck with Raspberry Vinegar Sauce

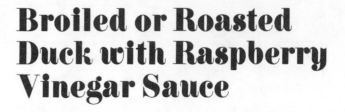

Two methods are given for preparing duck, one for roasting whole duck, the other broiling only the duck breasts. The latter is a relatively quick and simple process. A rich glaze of sauce complements either preparation.

RARE BROILED DUCK BREAST:

2 tsp. coarse (Kosher) salt
2 tsp. finely minced shallots
1 tsp. finely minced fresh parsley
½ tsp. crumbled dry bay leaf
¼ tsp. dried thyme
6 black peppercorns, crushed
2 small cloves garlic, minced
2 whole boneless duck breasts cut into 4 pieces, with skin, from 2 fresh or frozen 4-5 lb. (1800-2250g) ducks

WHOLE ROASTED DUCK:

1 4½-5 lb. (2000-2250g) duck
½ tsp. salt
½ tsp. freshly ground black pepper
1 T. (15ml) olive oil
1 T. (15g) butter
1-2 cups (240-475ml) chicken stock

RASPBERRY VINEGAR SAUCE:

¼ cup (50g) sugar
½ cup (120ml) Raspberry Vinegar (page 372)
½ cup (120ml) duck stock (made from cooking neck with a bouquet garni, onions and carrots)
¼ cup (60ml) heavy cream

RARE BROILED DUCK BREAST: Mix seasonings together well. Rub duck breasts with mixture; cover with plastic wrap. Refrigerate at least 6 hours, up to 24 hours.

Wipe breasts to remove excess seasonings. Score the skin. Arrange breasts on broiler rack, breast side down. Broil about 4 inches (10cm) from heat, for 2 minutes. Turn and broil 3 minutes for rare breasts. (Broil 2 to 3 minutes longer for less rare or for crisper skin.) Let breasts rest on carving board several minutes. Slice each on bias, crosswise.

Spoon Raspberry Vinegar Sauce in small pools on each of 4 warmed serving plates. Fan breast slices out on top of sauce.

WHOLE ROASTED DUCK: Remove as much fat as possible from the duck neck and cavity. Pat the cavity dry with paper towels. Season the cavity with salt and pepper. Truss the tail end of the duck so that it will brown more easily. Cut off excess neck skin and remove wishbone to facilitate carving. Prick skin with a fork.

Heat olive oil and butter in a large cast iron skillet. (Do not use enamelware as it will not brown well.) Brown duck on all sides, starting with breast side down, approximately 10 to 15 minutes in all. Place skillet on middle shelf of a preheated 400° oven 30 minutes. Lower temperature to 350°; continue roasting another 40 minutes. Baste duck with ¼ cup stock every 15 minutes. When duck is done, transfer to carving board. To carve, first remove backbone with poultry shears and discard it. With sharp knife or cleaver, cut down through the exact center of breastbone. Separate leg with thigh from breast with knife. Keep duck warm in a 300° oven if serving immediately or let remain at room temperature until serving time. Reheat by placing under broiler 1 to 2 minutes.

RASPBERRY VINEGAR SAUCE: Heat sugar and vinegar in a caramel pot or 2-qt. (2L) stainless steel saucepan over medium heat. Do not stir. Let mixture boil, shaking pan to blend sugar and vinegar. Cook until sugar caramelizes and mixture is consistency of corn syrup, about 5 to 8 minutes. Add duck stock and cream. Continue boiling, stirring occasionally, until sauce is reduced to a thick, syrupy consistency.

Kathleen J. Schwartz, Avon, CT

Variations, Advance Preparation, and Serving Suggestions:
For Rare Broiled Duck Breast, reserve the rest of the ducks for preparing Duck Rillettes (page 74).

Nutritional Notes: Nutritional analysis uses 3½ oz. *(100g)* cooked duck meat per serving for duck breast method and 4½ oz. *(125g)* cooked duck meat per serving for whole roasted duck method.

Wine Suggestion: California Gewurztraminer, semi-dry white; served chilled.

Microwave Conversion Instructions: *Whole Roasted Duck:* Prepare duck as directed above. Cut up excess neck skin; place skin, bouquet garni, 1 onion quartered, and 2 carrots cut in chunks in baking dish. Put a rack inside dish and place duck on rack, breast side up. Cook, covered with waxed paper, on High 15 minutes, basting with chicken stock once. Pour off drippings and set aside. Turn duck breast side down; continue to cook on High 10 minutes. Transfer duck to conventional roasting pan. Baste with chicken stock. Place in 400° oven until duck is crisp and brown, basting several times. Turn duck over if necessary for even browning. When duck is done, transfer to cutting board. Combine drippings from oven roasting pan with original drippings. After duck has rested 15 minutes to allow juices to redistribute, follow above directions for carving, catching juices and adding them to drippings.

Raspberry Vinegar Sauce: Prepare sauce while duck is crisping in oven. Place sugar and vinegar in a 4-cup *(1L)* glass measure. Bring to a boil on High. Allow to boil until sugar caramelizes about 5 to 8 minutes. Watch carefully to avoid burning. When syrup has caramelized, add ½ cup skimmed, strained duck stock to caramel. Add cream. Cook, uncovered, on High until it boils and cooks into a syrup. Stir once or twice.

Celeriac Purée with Apples

Celeriac, also known as knob celery or celery root is a variety of celery cultivated for its thick, turnip-like root. It came to England from Europe in the 18th century, from there a short sail to the tables of present-day Connecticut.

YIELD: 6 Servings
TOTAL CALORIES: 1200
CALORIES PER SERVING: 200
CARBOHYDRATES: 20g
PROTEIN: 7g
FAT: 10g
CHOLESTEROL: High
PREPARING: 15 Minutes
COOKING: 30 Minutes
FREEZING: No

Place celeriac chunks in saucepan, add enough milk to cover. Bring to boil. Reduce heat; simmer uncovered 10 minutes. Add apples, simmer 15 to 20 minutes more, or until celeriac is tender. Drain off liquid. Puree celeriac and apples in food processor or blender until smooth, adding enough cream to make a medium-thick puree. Add salt, pepper to taste. Puree may be passed through a fine sieve, if desired, for smoother consistency. Serve at room temperature or reheat over hot water.

Kathleen J. Schwartz, Avon, CT

1 lb. *(450g)* celeriac, peeled, coarsely chopped
4 cups *(950ml)* milk
2 large Golden Delicious apples, peeled, cored, quartered
¼ cup *(60ml)* heavy cream
Salt
Freshly ground white pepper

Variations, Advance Preparation, and Serving Suggestions:
Can be made a day ahead and reheated. Serve with Spinach Timbales (page 159): spoon or pipe puree around base of each timbale on heated serving plates. Garnish puree with julienne of lemon peel.

Canard aux Poires

DUCK WITH FRESH PEARS

LA FINE BOUCHE restaurant, Centerbrook, Connecticut, offers this fine roasted duck recipe as evidence of its extraordinary culinary talent. Chef Steven Wilkinson's emphasis on food, exquisitely prepared and presented, makes dining a most gratifying experience.

YIELD: 6 Servings
CALORIES PER SERVING: 543
CARBOHYDRATES: 4g
PROTEIN: 35g
FAT: 43g
PREPARING: 20 Minutes
BROILING: 5-10 Minutes
COOKING: Stock 2½ Hours
ROASTING: 30 Minutes
FREEZING: No

3 Long Island ducklings, defrosted if frozen
Coarse (Kosher) salt
¼ cup *(60ml)* brown veal stock
1 ripe Bartlett pear, cored, sliced
¼ cup *(60ml)* Pear William liqueur
4 T. *(60g)* unsalted butter, at room temperature

Cut wings off ducks. Arrange wings with necks and giblets in shallow roasting pan. Prick skin of duck breasts (do not pierce flesh) with fork. Sprinkle salt all over ducks. Place ducks on top of parts in roasting pan. Roast uncovered, in preheated 500° oven about 30 minutes, until lightly browned, but medium rare. Remove from oven. Set ducks aside until cool enough to handle. Remove breasts and legs. Reserve drumsticks for other use. Bone thighs. Place breasts and thighs on baking sheet, skin side up. Cover lightly.

Break up carcass; place in stock pot or large heavy pot with water just to cover. Bring to boil; reduce to simmer. Cook 2 hours, covered. Remove bones. Boil liquid over high heat until reduced to 1 cup *(240ml)*. Let cool; skim all fat.

Combine duck and veal stock in small pan. Boil over high heat until reduced to half. Add pear slices. Cook over medium heat until *al dente,* about 5 minutes. Stir in Pear William liqueur. Remove slices with slotted spoon to paper towel. Remove sauce from heat; whisk in butter by tablespoons. Return slices to sauce.

When ready to serve, remove covering from duck. Place under preheated broiler to reheat. Arrange pieces, in fan shape, on individual heated serving plates. Pour sauce and pears over each plate. Garnish with watercress.

Variations, Advance Preparation, and Serving Suggestions: Roast duck, make and reduce stock several hours ahead. Add pear slices and butter to sauce; broil duck just before serving.

Nutritional Notes: Nutritional analysis uses 5¼ oz. *(150g)* cooked duck meat per serving.

Wine Suggestion: California Cabernet Sauvignon, full red; serve at room temperature.

Spinach Timbales

The word timbale derives from the Arab-Persian *atabal,* meaning kettledrum. There are French dishes made of copper, tin or china, round in shape with straight or sloping sides, also called timbales. Egg souffles or custards cooked in such molds take their name from them. Individual dome-shaped tin gelatin molds are perfect for this spinach custard.

YIELD: 6 Servings
CALORIES PER SERVING: 145
CARBOHYDRATES: 7g
PROTEIN: 9g
FAT: 9g
CHOLESTEROL: High
PREPARING: 20 Minutes
BAKING: 45-55 Minutes
FREEZING: No

Melt 2 T. butter over low heat; add flour. Cook and stir until completely blended; do not let brown. Gradually add milk, stirring constantly with whisk. Cook sauce 3 to 5 minutes until thick and smooth.

Squeeze all water from spinach. In small skillet, saute onion and garlic in 1 T. butter 2 to 3 minutes until soft. Add spinach and sauce; stir well. When mixture is heated through, remove from heat, stir in egg yolks, nutmeg, salt and pepper to taste. Divide mixture evenly among six buttered ½-cup *(120ml)* timbale or other molds. Place molds in baking pan. Pour enough water into pan to come one third up sides of molds. Cover tops of molds with a single sheet of foil. Bake in preheated 375° oven about 45 to 55 minutes, until a knife inserted in center of timbale comes out clean. Remove molds carefully from baking pan. Let molds rest on rack 5 minutes. Run knife around inside edge of each mold, invert onto heated serving plate.

Melinda M. Vance, West Hartford, CT

Variations, Advance Preparation, and Serving Suggestions:
Timbales may be prepared a day ahead of serving. Reheat in molds in hot water bath. Invert each timbale onto broiled tomato slice for an attractive presentation.

Nutritional Notes: Spinach is an excellent source of vitamin A as well as potassium and calcium.

Microwave Conversion Instructions: Melt 2 T. butter by cooking 90 seconds on Medium (50%). Add flour and continue to cook 90 seconds on High. Stir and gradually add milk, stirring constantly with wire whisk; cook on High 2 minutes, stirring twice; set aside. Squeeze all water from spinach. In 2-qt. *(2L)* casserole add 1 T. butter, onion and garlic; cook on High 3 minutes, covered. Add spinach, stir well. Stir in egg yolks, nutmeg, salt and pepper to taste. Cover and cook 3 minutes on High, stirring occasionally. Divide mixture evenly into 6 buttered custard cups. Place in circular pattern in oven and cover with sheet of waxed paper. Cook on Medium (50%) 10 minutes or until set. Allow 5 minutes standing time before unmolding and serving.

3 T. *(45g)* butter, divided
2 T. *(15g)* flour
1 cup *(240ml)* milk
3 pkgs. (10 oz. each) *(855g)* frozen chopped spinach, thawed
1 small onion, finely chopped
1 clove garlic, minced
2 egg yolks
⅛ tsp. freshly grated nutmeg
Salt
Freshly ground pepper

Romaine, Endive and Walnut Salad

YIELD: 2-4 Servings
CALORIES PER SERVING: 324
CARBOHYDRATES: 6g
PROTEIN: 3g
FAT: 32g
PREPARING: 25 Minutes
CHILLING: 1 Hour Minimum

This salad is special enough to serve as a separate course, yet simple enough to serve with a rich or complicated entree.

WALNUT DRESSING:

¼ cup *(30g)* coarsely chopped walnuts
3 T. *(45ml)* sherry vinegar
½ cup *(120ml)* walnut oil
1 small clove garlic, peeled
Salt
Freshly ground pepper to taste

SALAD:

½ large head romaine lettuce
1 large head Belgian endive
½ cup *(70g)* sliced water chestnuts

WALNUT DRESSING: Spread walnuts in shallow baking dish. Bake 10 minutes in preheated 350° oven, stirring once. Transfer nuts to medium sized glass jar, let cool. Add vinegar, oil, garlic, salt, pepper; shake well. Chill at least 1 hour, preferably several hours.

SALAD: Crisp greens in ice water 15 minutes before serving. Dry gently in paper towels. Tear into bite-sized pieces.

Remove garlic from dressing, shake again. In bowl, toss greens with dressing. Divide among chilled salad plates. Garnish with water chestnuts.

Kathleen J. Schwartz, Avon, CT

Nutritional Notes: Walnut oil, as most oils — peanut, corn, olive and even lard, contains 124 calories per 1 T. or 14 grams fat. Walnut oil is a cold pressed oil that is low in saturated fats and contains no cholesterol.

Chocolate Dacquoise

YIELD: 12 Servings
CALORIES PER SERVING: 610
CARBOHYDRATES: 68g
PROTEIN: 6g
FAT: 35g
CHOLESTEROL: High
PREPARING: 2½ Hours
BAKING: 1 Hour
FREEZING: Not Preferred

A "dacquoise" is a layered meringue or Swiss broyage dessert made with nuts. The layers are filled with a rich butter cream. The word "dacquoise," however, is elusive. It is not in any French dictionary nor can it be found in current food encyclopedias.

MERINGUE CAKE:

6 egg whites, at room temperature
1 cup *(200g)* superfine sugar
4 oz. *(115g)* powdered almonds or a
    mixture of almonds and another nut

CHOCOLATE MOUSSE:

3 eggs, separated
⅓ cup *(65g)* superfine sugar
5 T. *(75g)* unsalted sweet butter,
    creamed
3 oz. *(85g)* semisweet chocolate, melted
    (Lindt Extra-Bittersweet preferred)

MERINGUE CAKE: Beat egg whites, adding 3 T. sugar, until mixture is thick. Dump almond powder and remaining sugar on whites; fold together quickly and *gently* with a spatula. Butter and flour 2 or 3 baking sheets; draw 3 9-inch *(22.5cm)* circles on baking sheets (or draw individual round, heart-shaped or other shapes as desired.) Spoon ⅓ of mixture into large pastry bag fitted with ½-inch *(1.25cm)* plain tube. Beginning at center of one of the circles, squeeze out meringue and form a continuous coil until you reach the end of the circle. Form remaining 2 circles in the same manner. Bake coils 60 minutes in preheated 200° oven. (After about 30 minutes, loosen each meringue with a spatula so it won't stick.) Remove baking sheets from oven. Let cool on racks. Carefully remove coils from baking sheets. If they stick, loosen over a low burner flame.

CHOCOLATE MOUSSE: Beat egg yolks and sugar until smooth and light in color. Beat in butter, then chocolate. Beat egg whites until stiff; fold into chocolate mixture. Refrigerate until ready to assemble.

CHOCOLATE BUTTER CREAM: Whisk yolks in mixer or food processor. Meanwhile, bring sugar and water to softball stage (238°). Dribble syrup into yolks with beater running or through feed tube with food processor running. Mix thoroughly. Let cool completely. Beat butter into yolk mixture; add chocolate and then praline paste. Refrigerate until of spreading consistency or freeze until needed.

TO ASSEMBLE DACQUOISE: Place one coil of the meringue on a serving plate. With a fluted pastry tube and bag filled with butter cream, pipe rosettes all around outer edge of coil. Fill center with half the chocolate mousse. Place second coil on top and repeat process. Add 3rd coil. Decorate entire top with butter cream rosettes. Refrigerate dacquoise, covered, until ready to serve. Dacquoise *must* stand at room temperature 20 minutes before serving.

Melinda M. Vance, West Hartford, CT

Variations, Advance Preparation, and Serving Suggestions:
The dacquoise may be made 3 to 4 days ahead of time, but is at its finest assembled the day it is to be served. It may also be frozen, but there is considerable loss of crispness to the meringue.

CHOCOLATE BUTTER CREAM:

4 egg yolks
¾ cup *(150g)* **sugar**
5½ T. *(80ml)* **water**
¾ lb. *(340g)* **unsalted sweet butter, creamed**
4 oz. *(115g)* **semisweet chocolate, melted (Lindt Extra-Bittersweet preferred)**
5 T. *(80g)* **praline paste (available commercially)**

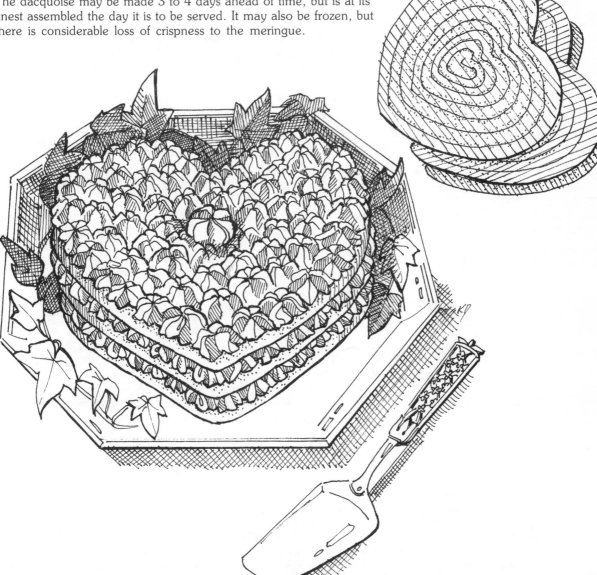

Hartford Symphony's Springtime in Vienna

This rich and varied menu harmoniously combines some of the best features of our Austrian-Hungarian culinary heritage.

Though he contributed to many musical forms, perhaps Austrian Joseph Haydn's greatest contribution to music was his development of the string quartet and the classical symphony as we now know them. Other composers whose works flourished in the appreciative Austrian environment were Mozart, Schubert, Strauss, Mahler, Bruckner, Berg and Schonberg.

Music was such an important part of Austrian society in old Vienna that families who considered themselves among the intelligentsia of music and literature had to have their own quartet of musicians to play for all special dinners. Weeks in advance the hostess would begin by inviting the first violin player and his wife to an informal dinner, during which the chamber music repertoire and possible dinner menu choices could be balanced and arranged to suit seasonal interests and foods. Naturally the specialties of the kitchen staff were inserted as key dishes in the menu. An imaginative Frau could visualize the harmonious combination of Kalb Metternich or the inevitable Salzburger Nockerln with Mozart or Cauliflower Polonaise with Chopin.

In the 18th century, when thousands of German-speaking Austrian-Hungarian immigrants flocked to the United States, they brought with them their deep love of music and their delight in good food. Though a live quartet and a fine meal may not be so readily combined in most homes today, consider the enticing combination of the Austrian Symphony Dinner followed by an evening with the Hartford Symphony.

The Austrian menu highlights distinctive aspects of Austrian-Hungarian cooking: the use of sour cream, a liberal sprinkling of paprika and the creation of marvelous desserts. The combination of paprika (the powdered form of the capsicum plant) and sour cream with meat is the basis of Austrian goulash. This particular dish made such an impact on American cooking that a 1969 Gallup poll found goulash to be one of the five most favored American meat dishes!

Austrian pastries have made an equally indelible impression on American cooking. Those who visit Vienna and find themselves gawking before the incredible display of confections arranged in the pastry shop windows celebrate with renewed fervor the Austrian love of sweets. Even the poorest of the Austrian-Hungarian immigrants to America are said to have always added a sweet to every meal. As the immigrants blended their culinary skills into the mainstream of American cooking, the baking achieved distinctive refinements. In 1850 the introduction of cream of tartar and later baking powder made possible even lighter pastries and cakes. And the competition created by women's "cake sales" to benefit schools and churches, as well as by agricultural fairs, particularly in the Midwest where the majority of Austrian-Hungarians settled, led to the development of luscious indigenous cakes and confections. Sample the spectacular Viennese Torte as a delicious reminder of one of Austria's culinary gifts to America.

To complete the perfect evening — on to the symphony! Already in its thirty-ninth year of operation, the Hartford Symphony Orchestra occupies a unique place as the largest part-time professional orchestra in New England. It has grown from a government subsidized organization to a thriving private, non-profit corporation. Its members are Greater Hartford residents, many of whom teach in local music schools and conservatories. Under the brilliant leadership of Music Director Arthur Winograd, the Orchestra has come a long way from a partially "imported" group of performers to a finely-honed ensemble of resident musicians, serving a metropolitan area of over 500,000 people. The Orchestra also plays a significant role each year in introducing over 50,000 area students to classical music through the Discovery Concert series and the Music-To-Go program, which includes school demonstrations.

In 1980 when the late Governor Ella Grasso designated "Hartford Symphony Week," she described "the symphony's incalculable contribution to our state's cultural heritage." Her statement continued: "From colonial days, music has been a great source of enjoyment and enrichment for the American people . . . The Hartford Symphony makes available to the people of our state and region the creativity of the world's music, past and present. Music has been called the universal language, and through the Orchestra's versatile and accomplished programming, it is ours to hear."

Tracing the earliest roots of the Hartford Symphony, we are indeed indebted to Austria for the development of this musical form. We celebrate as well a wonderful cuisine. The two make a heavenly combination.

Champagnerbowle
(Champagne Punch)
p. 144

Mai Bowle
(May Wine)
p. 120

Wiener Zigaretten
(Viennese Cigarettes)
p. 164

Karfiolpureesuppe Liane
(Cauliflower and Fennel Soup)
p. 165

Kalte Forelle
(Mushroom Stuffed Brook Trout)
p. 165

Kalbsrücken Metternich
(Veal with Paprika Sauce)
p. 166

Gemüsepudding Lukullus
(Molded Vegetable Pudding)
p. 167

Nudeln
(Homemade Noodles)
p. 192

Fruchtsalat Lenore
(Fresh Fruit Salad with Mint Vinaigrette)
p. 365

Wiener Torte
(Viennese Torte)
p. 169

or

Linzertorte
p. 168

YIELD: 20 Large Cigarettes
TOTAL CALORIES: 2560
CALORIES PER CIGARETTE: 128
CARBOHYDRATES: 10g
PROTEIN: 4g
FAT: 8g
CHOLESTEROL: High
PREPARING: 1 Hour
BAKING: 20 Minutes
CHILLING: 45 Minutes

Viennese Cigarettes

Patience is called for, but the end result is most impressive and worth the effort.

PASTRY:

1½ cups *(170g)* sifted flour
1 tsp. salt
¼ tsp. paprika
1 cup *(115g)* finely grated Swiss cheese
½ cup *(115g)* butter
3 T. *(45ml)* cream
½ cup *(60g)* flour mixed with ½ cup *(65g)* freshly grated Parmesan cheese
1 egg yolk beaten with 1 tsp. water
Additional grated Parmesan cheese

SPECIAL EQUIPMENT:

20 individual dowels *(¼ inch (0.6cm)* thick and approximately 4½ inches *(11.5cm)* long each)

Sift together flour, salt and paprika. Toss mixture with Swiss cheese; cut in butter. Add cream to make smooth dough. *[FOOD PROCESSOR: Grate Parmesan with steel blade; add ½ cup flour, process 5 seconds. Remove and set aside. Grate Swiss cheese with shredding disc. Remove disc and insert steel blade. Add 1½ cups flour, salt, and paprika; process 10 seconds. Add butter cut into several chunks. Turn machine on/off until mixture resembles coarse meal. With machine running pour cream through feed tube. As soon as pastry starts to mass, stop machine. Do not wait for ball to form.]* Chill about 30 minutes or until dough is easy to work with.

Lightly sprinkle work surface with some of flour/Parmesan mixture. Roll dough out into a rectangle; sprinkle with additional flour/Parmesan mixture. Using pastry spatula, fold dough in thirds like a business letter. Roll dough out again and sprinkle with more flour/Parmesan mixture; fold in thirds again but in the opposite direction. Roll out again using all remaining flour/Parmesan mixture. Fold in thirds a final time. Chill 15 minutes.

On lightly floured surface, roll out ⅛ inch *(0.3cm)* thick. Cut into strips ¾ inch *(2cm)* wide and 10 inches *(25cm)* long. Wrap each strip of dough around a well-buttered dowel. Hand warmth helps dough adhere to stick. Leave a little bit of dowel showing at one end to facilitate removal after baking. Brush each dowel with beaten egg yolk and water. Immediately roll each dowel in Parmesan cheese. Place cigarettes well apart on lightly greased baking sheets. Bake in preheated 375° oven for 20 minutes. Carefully draw out dowel while cigarettes are still hot. Serve immediately or cool on racks. Store in airtight containers until ready to serve.

Shirley Taylor, West Hartford, CT

Variations, Advance Preparation, and Serving Suggestions:
These are good chilled as well as warm. If made a day ahead, re-crisp on baking sheet in 300° oven just before serving. The large cigarettes are excellent as a "bread" accompaniment to soups, salads and light luncheon dishes. Make the cigarettes smaller if using as hors d'oeuvre.

Nutritional Notes: Cholesterol content can be reduced somewhat by using Swiss cheese made from skim milk, and polyunsaturated margarine instead of butter.

Cauliflower and Fennel Soup

An unusual combination of strong flavors.

YIELD: 8 Servings
TOTAL CALORIES: 752
CALORIES PER SERVING: 94
CARBOHYDRATES: 6g
PROTEIN: 4g
FAT: 6g
PREPARING: 15 Minutes
COOKING: 30 Minutes
FREEZING: Yes

Steam cauliflower and fennel until fork tender.

Puree vegetables in blender or food processor with small amount of cooking liquid.

Saute onion, celery, and bay leaf in butter until vegetables are soft. Add flour; stir in hot stock; add milk, salt, pepper, and curry powder. Bring to a simmer; combine with pureed vegetables and serve immediately.

Gloria J. Holtsinger, West Hartford, CT

Microwave Conversion Instructions: Place cauliflower, fennel, bay leaf and 3 cups liquid in a 4-qt. *(4L)* bowl. Cook covered, on High 5 to 7 minutes until fork tender (timing will depend on age of cauliflower). Place onion and celery in a 4-cup glass measure, place butter on top. Cook covered 3 to 4 minutes, until soft. Stir in flour, hot stock, *heated* milk, and seasonings. Continue to cook on High, uncovered, until it reaches a simmer. Add pureed vegetables and serve.

1 head cauliflower, broken into flowerets and sliced
1 knob fennel with green parts removed, sliced
½ medium onion, peeled and sliced
¼ cup *(55g)* celery, chopped
½ bay leaf
2 T. *(30g)* butter
2 T. *(15g)* whole wheat flour (or white flour)
2 T. *(15g)* soy flour (or white flour)
3 cups *(710ml)* hot veal or chicken stock or water
2 cups *(475ml)* milk
Salt and pepper
1-2 T. curry powder

Mushroom Stuffed Brook Trout

Perfect for a trout season opening day breakfast, cooked over an open fire or outdoor grill.

YIELD: 3 Servings
CALORIES PER SERVING: 434
CARBOHYDRATES: 17g
PROTEIN: 33g
FAT: 26g
PREPARING: 25 Minutes
COOKING: 10 Minutes
FREEZING: No

Saute onion in melted butter until soft; add mushrooms. Cook and stir over high heat until liquid evaporates. Stir in wine, cook rapidly until most moisture has evaporated. Remove from heat; add breadcrumbs, cheese, parsley and only enough milk to keep mixture firm. Season. (Up to this point, may be prepared ahead and set aside; stuff and cook just before serving). Stuff trout. Roll in flour, patting off excess. Heat oil in skillet large enough to accommodate 3 trout. Saute about 5 minutes per side. *Do not overcook.* (Alternate cooking method: Poach unstuffed fish 6 minutes, stuff with heated dressing, bake in preheated 375° oven 10 minutes.)

Bernice Kuzma, West Hartford, CT

Wine Suggestion: Pouilly-Fume Ladaucette, crisp white; serve chilled.

3 T. *(45g)* butter
½ cup *(100g)* minced onion
1 cup *(120g)* minced mushrooms
3 T. *(45ml)* sherry or Madeira wine
¼ cup *(15g)* fresh breadcrumbs
1½ T. *(12g)* freshly grated Parmesan cheese
3 T. minced fresh parsley
3 T. *(45ml)* or more milk
Salt
Freshly ground pepper
3 whole brook trout, about ½ lb. *(225g)* per fish, cleaned
Flour for dredging
¼ cup *(60ml)* oil for frying

YIELD: 8-10 Servings
CALORIES PER SERVING: 451
CARBOHYDRATES: 11g
PROTEIN: 32g
FAT: 31g
CHOLESTEROL: High
SODIUM: High
PREPARING: 45 Minutes
BAKING: 15 Minutes
COOKING: 30 Minutes
ROASTING: 1½-2 Hours
FREEZING: Yes

Kalb Metternich

VEAL WITH PAPRIKA SAUCE

VEAL:
1 boned 4½-5-lb. *(2-2.3kg)* veal roast, rolled and tied
½ cup *(115g)* melted butter

PAPRIKA SAUCE:
½ cup *(115g)* butter
¼ cup *(30g)* flour
1½ T. imported paprika (Kingred preferred)
1½ cups *(355ml)* milk
1 small onion, chopped
1 cup *(240ml)* hot beef stock
Salt
½ lb. *(225g)* fresh mushrooms, sliced and sauteed in 2 T. butter (optional)

TOPPING:
¾ cup *(95g)* freshly grated Parmesan cheese
½ cup *(115g)* melted butter
¾ cup *(90g)* dry breadcrumbs (herbed may be used)

VEAL: Place veal in roasting pan in preheated 300° oven. Roast for 25 minutes per pound, basting frequently with butter. Time will depend upon the quality of the meat. When roast is fully cooked, remove from oven and allow to cool, as it will be easier to slice. (Roast may be cooked a day ahead, refrigerated and brought to room temperature before proceeding with recipe.)

PAPRIKA SAUCE: Melt butter in saucepan; add flour, making a roux and cook 1 minute. Add paprika. Combine milk and onion in a separate saucepan; heat until onion is soft. Gradually add hot milk to flour mixture, whisking constantly. Add hot beef stock. Allow sauce to simmer over low heat 20 minutes, stirring. Add salt to taste.

Slice roast into ½-inch-thick *(1.25cm)* slices. Lightly brush an oval au gratin dish with melted butter and sprinkle with 1 T. of the bread crumbs. Arrange slices all in one layer, slightly overlapping in dish. Sprinkle each slice with sauteed mushrooms and spread with thin layer of sauce before adding next slice. Cover veal (evenly) with remaining sauce.

TOPPING: Sprinkle veal with Parmesan cheese. Carefully pour butter over cheese and sprinkle with breadcrumbs. It is important that cheese, butter and crumbs form a thick coating on meat.

Return meat to preheated 325° oven and bake 15 minutes or until cheese and crumbs form a crust.

Shirley Taylor, West Hartford, CT

Variations, Advance Preparation, and Serving Suggestions:
Before sprinkling each veal slice with mushrooms, top with *thin* slice of baked ham. To freeze, omit final 15 minutes baking. Wrap well and freeze until ready to use. Thaw casserole and bring to room temperature. Reheat in 325° oven until cheese and crumbs form a crust. Eight large well-trimmed veal chops can be substituted for veal roast. Season chops and saute over medium to high heat approximately 4½ to 5 minutes on each side. Complete recipe as above. Serve with Molded Vegetable Pudding (page 167) and Homemade Noodles (page 192).

Wine Suggestion: Austrian Blauburgunder, light red; serve at room temperature.

Microwave Conversion Instructions: This recipe has been modified considerably for microwave. Note: 8 veal chops or round steak cutlets ¼ inch *(0.6cm)* thick, 5 T. butter, 1 cup breadcrumbs,

1¼ cups Parmesan cheese, 1 chopped onion, ⅔ cup melted butter, ¼ cup flour, 1½ cups milk, 1 cup beef stock, 1½ T. paprika, sauteed mushrooms. *Veal:* Melt butter in glass dish. Coat veal chops with bread crumbs mixed with ½ cup of the Parmesan cheese. Preheat browning dish per manufacturer's directions. Place 4 chops at a time on dish; cook on High 2 minutes. Turn chops; cook on High 2 minutes more. *Sauce:* Put onion in glass dish; cook on High 2 minutes. Add butter, flour, milk and broth and blend until smooth; cook on Medium (50%) until thick, about 3 to 4 minutes. Add remaining Parmesan cheese and paprika. Whisk until smooth. Place veal in low casserole; cover with sliced mushrooms and pour sauce over veal. Cook on Medium (50%) 10 minutes or until sauce is bubbling.

Gemüsepudding Lukullus

MOLDED VEGETABLE PUDDING

YIELD: 6-8 Servings
CALORIES PER SERVING: 285
CARBOHYDRATES: 16g
PROTEIN: 9g
FAT: 20.5g
CHOLESTEROL: High
PREPARING: 1 Hour
COOKING: 1¼ Hours

PUDDING: Soak bread slices in enough cream to moisten all the bread.

Cream butter; add egg yolks and beat mixture until light and creamy. Add spinach, asparagus and mushrooms and mix. Then squeeze out excess cream from bread. Add bread, dry breadcrumbs, parsley and Parmesan cheese to vegetable mixture. Add salt and pepper to taste; mix well.

In another bowl, beat egg whites with salt until stiff. Fold into vegetable mixture.

Put mixture in generously buttered 2 qt. *(2L)* charlotte mold or other pudding mold and cover tightly. Set mold in pan that is taller and wider than the mold. Add enough boiling water to reach halfway up sides of mold; cover pan tightly and steam for 1 to 1¼ hours, adding more water if necessary. Watch carefully.

GARNISH: Unmold pudding onto serving dish and surround with large mushroom caps sauteed in butter and filled with *thick* mousseline sauce. Pipe rosettes of mousseline sauce onto top of pudding.

Shirley Taylor, West Hartford, CT

PUDDING:
6 slices white bread
Cream
½ cup *(115g)* butter
6 eggs, separated
¾ cup *(140g)* chopped spinach, parboiled and squeezed dry before measuring
½ cup *(80g)* finely chopped green asparagus, parboiled and squeezed dry before measuring
¼ cup *(20g)* minced raw mushrooms
½ cup *(60g)* dry breadcrumbs
2 T. finely chopped parsley
2 T. *(20g)* freshly grated Parmesan cheese
Salt
Freshly ground pepper

GARNISH:
Large mushroom caps
Mousseline Sauce (page 191)

Linzertorte

Linzertorte, an Austrian specialty named for the city of Linz on the Danube River, is really a tart rather than a torte. It is usually made with raspberry jam.

YIELD: 8-10 Servings
CALORIES PER SERVING: 500
CARBOHYDRATES: 56g
PROTEIN: 6g
FAT: 28g
PREPARING: 30 Minutes
BAKING: 50 Minutes

1 cup *(225g)* butter
1 cup *(200g)* sugar
1 T. grated orange peel or lemon peel
2 egg yolks
1½ cups *(170g)* sifted flour
1 tsp. baking powder
2 tsp. cinnamon
½ tsp. cloves
¼ tsp. salt
1 cup *(100g)* ground filberts, almonds, or walnuts
1 cup *(285g)* currant or plum preserves
1 cup *(150g)* blueberries
Sweetened whipped cream (optional)

Cream butter. Gradually add sugar and continue creaming. Add grated peel, then egg yolks, one at a time, beating well after each.

Sift together flour, baking powder, spices and salt. Slowly add to creamed mixture, stirring to mix. Stir in nuts. Mix with hands until all ingredients are thoroughly combined. *[FOOD PROCESSOR: Process nuts with flour, baking powder, salt and spices until nuts are finely chopped. Remove and set aside. Add butter, sugar, orange rind and egg yolks to work bowl; process on/off 4 times. Then process 10 seconds. Add nut/flour mixture and process until dough begins to mass. Do not overprocess. Do not allow dough to form a ball. Put dough into a plastic bag. Work bag to form dough into ball, then flatten it into a disc.]* Chill.

Pat ⅔ dough into 9-inch *(22.5cm)* tart pan with removable bottom. Spread preserves over dough, then sprinkle blueberries evenly on top of preserves. Roll remaining dough. Cut into strips and place over blueberries to form woven lattice.

Bake in preheated 350° oven 50 minutes or until edges of strips pull away from sides. If edges begin to brown too quickly, cover with foil.

Serve garnished with whipped cream if desired.

Phillip Johnston, Pittsburgh, PA

Wine Suggestion: Austrian Gumpoldskircher Spaetlese, semi-sweet; serve chilled.

Microwave Conversion Instructions: The dry heat of the microwave oven is perfect to keep Linzertorte's nut pastry crisp. Pat ⅔ dough evenly over bottom of 10-inch *(25cm)* pie plate. Fill and place lattice strips on torte as directed above. Put pie plate in oven over inverted saucer. Cook on High 10 minutes, rotating dish every minute, or until dough is set and no longer moist. Cool completely.

Viennese Torte

YIELD: 8-10 Servings
TOTAL CALORIES: 3680
CALORIES PER SERVING: 368
CARBOHYDRATES: 41g
PROTEIN: 6g
FAT: 20g
PREPARING: 1½ Hours
BAKING: 30 Minutes

Sift sugar, flour and 1 T. cocoa together into a large bowl; add hazelnuts. Set aside.

Beat egg whites until stiff. Fold into sugar mixture. Put mixture into pastry bag fitted with large star tip. Pipe or spread mixture onto 3 buttered and floured baking sheets to form 3 9-inch *(22.5cm)* meringue layers; smooth with spatula. Bake in a preheated 300° oven 30 minutes or until layers are barely golden. After removing from oven, run a metal spatula under each layer to prevent sticking. If layers stick, loosen from sheet over low flame. Cool completely.

Reserving scant ¼ cup of whipped cream, combine remaining whipped cream and rum. Spread this mixture between meringue layers, leaving enough to thinly cover top of the torte. Arrange marrons in a circle on top, putting a candied violet or other decoration between marrons.

Combine ¼ tsp. cocoa with reserved whipped cream and put in pastry bag fitted with decorative tip; pipe border around top of torte.

Nancy Bailey, Prospect, KY

Wine Suggestion: Austrian Tangenloiser Auslese, sweet white; serve chilled.

Microwave Conversion Instructions: Note: Tester indicates there is a lot of "watching" in microwave for this torte; however, finished product is easier to handle. Prepare all ingredients as for conventional recipe. Pipe 3 9-inch layers from pastry bag onto waxed paper-covered cardboard. Cook each layer on Medium (50%) 4 to 6 minutes, checking for doneness frequently. Continue with assembly as for conventional recipe.

1½ cups *(300g)* superfine sugar
⅔ cup *(75g)* flour, sifted
1 T. plus ¼ tsp. cocoa (Droste's or Van Houten preferred)
1 cup *(100g)* hazelnuts, skins removed and finely ground
9 egg whites
1 cup *(240ml)* heavy cream, whipped and sweetened to taste
1 T. rum

GARNISH:
12 marrons glaces (whole sugar-glazed chestnuts)
Candied violets

Connecticut Opera's Feast with Verdi

This dramatic dinner pays tribute to Italy's gifts of grand opera and an incomparable cuisine.

It is difficult to think of opera and not think of Italy. In turn, it is equally difficult to think of Italy and not be reminded of pasta, pizza, ices and generally scrumptuous foods. Our Evening at the Opera pays tribute to this closeknit trio as well as to the significant Italian influence on American arts and cuisine.

In the early part of the 19th century there were few Italian immigrants to the United States. In 1829 U.S. statistics record only three! However, by the end of the century the number increased dramatically. In rural areas many of these Italian immigrants entered farming and the wine industry. Those who remained in cities often became grocers or food importers. Their substantial clientele was composed of the thousands of laboring class Italian immigrants who insisted on pastas, olive oil, special cheeses and herbs for their food preparation. Italians who farmed introduced bell peppers, eggplant, broccoli and artichokes on a large scale basis. Those farmers closest to the cities soon began to sell their produce to non-immigrant neighbors. This was in an era when the Italian push cart vendors would take the time to teach their new customers the art of preparing these very different vegetables. Along the same line, the many Italians who became widely acclaimed as butchers passed along favorite recipes with their special cuts of meat.

In the cities working class people from many nationalities soon discovered the inexpensive, filling and especially flavorful food in the small restaurants which initially catered to Italians. These restaurants often had begun as boarding houses established by Italian wives for the many Italian men who immigrated alone to pave the way for their families. Then Prohibition gave Americans a new impetus to discover the gastronomic delights of Italian antipasto and minestrone. The "red ink joints" were flourishing speakeasies which served "red ink" (chianti) in coffee cups and soda bottles along with the usual array of Italian specialties. This distinctive cuisine made a clear impression on American palates; by 1970 pasta was being made in the United States in over 150 sizes and shapes, and more than two billion pizzas were being consumed annually!

Just as Italians have significantly affected the character of American cooking, so has their influence made an indelible impression on the arts, particulary on the world of opera. This most complex of art forms incorporates drama, orchestrated and vocal music, scenery, costumes and often ballet. Opera — a drama which usually tells a highly emotional story — had its beginnings in 16th century Italy. "Dafne," the first opera, was produced in 1597 with words by the poet Rinuccini and music by composer Jacopo Peri. The first opera house, called the Teatro San Cassiano, opened in Venice in 1637. With the introduction of additional refinements — music and dialogue in harmony, dramatic planning, ballet, poetry and scenery — opera flourished in Europe in the 17th and 18th centuries, but the Italian style dominated. Puccini and Verdi, two of the most prominent 19th century Italian composers, gave the world such renowned favorites as *Madama Butterfly*, *La Boheme* and *Aida*.

Opera in Connecticut had its inception in 1941 when Frank Pandolfi gathered several local students and dressed them in costumes sewn by themselves and his wife, Carmela. The troupe's performance of operatic excerpts was enthusiastically received by the public. The following year Pandolfi's two productions of *Carmen* and *Rigoletto*, performed in Bushnell Hall, were sellouts. Seven years and numerous successful performances later the Connecticut Opera Association was formed with Pandolfi as associate director. In the early 1950s the Connecticut Opera Guild was created to support the Opera Association financially and to encourage appreciation and understanding of opera in the community. The Guild sponsors auditions for six annual scholarship awards and offers a program of in-school opera presentations for area children.

On a wider scope the Opera Express, the touring arm of Connecticut Opera, brings opera to audiences throughout New England. Under the current ambitious leadership of General Director George Osborne, Connecticut Opera has tripled its subscription base, performs to 97 percent capacity audiences and continues its forty-year history of superb productions starring world renowned artists. Connecticut Opera's recent grand-scale production of Verdi's *Aida* achieved national acclaim and introduced thousands of new patrons to the exciting world of opera.

Fresh Figs with Prosciutto

Gnocchi Parisienne
p. 172

or

Spinach Linguini ai Quattro Formaggi
p. 173

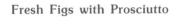

Veal Galliano
with Galliano Butter Sauce
p. 174

Bulgur Pignoli
Casserole
p. 350

Mario's Carrots
p. 174

Avocado, Orange and
Jerusalem Artichoke Salad
(Variegated Salad)
p. 175

Zuccotto
p. 176

or

White Chocolate Mousse in
Almond Wafer Cups with Fresh Berries
p. 177

Espresso

YIELD: 6-8 Servings
TOTAL CALORIES: 2910
CALORIES PER SERVING: 364
CARBOHYDRATES: 19g
PROTEIN: 9g
FAT: 28g
CHOLESTEROL: High
SODIUM: High
PREPARING: 15 Minutes
BAKING: 20 Minutes
COOKING: 30 Minutes
FREEZING: No

Gnocchi Parisienne

ITALIAN DUMPLINGS BAKED IN A CREAM SAUCE

This version of the classic first course — or light supper dish — is as easy to prepare as it is spectacular to serve.

Gnocchi (nyoh-KEE), the traditional dumpling-like pasta actually means "lumps." Pieces of flour and water plopped into boiling water could be mundane if they were served without the delicate sauce.

DUMPLINGS:

1 cup *(240ml)* **water**
½ cup *(115g)* **butter, cut into pieces**
1 cup *(115g)* **flour**
¼ tsp. **salt**
4 **eggs**
6 T. *(85g)* **freshly grated Parmesan cheese**

BECHAMEL SAUCE:

6 T. *(85g)* **butter**
4 T. *(50g)* **flour**
2½ cups *(600ml)* **milk, warmed**
1 tsp. **salt**
Freshly ground white pepper
Freshly grated nutmeg

DUMPLINGS: Combine water and butter in heavy saucepan. Cook over medium heat until butter is melted and water comes to boil. Reduce heat to low, add flour and salt all at once and stir vigorously with wooden spoon until mixture is smooth and leaves sides of pan forming a ball, (about 1 minute). Transfer mixture to bowl of electric mixer, or use hand mixer or food processor; add eggs one at a time, beating well after each addition, until smooth and well incorporated. Add cheese; beat vigorously.

In shallow 3-qt. *(3L)* pan, drop gnocchi mixture by teaspoon into salted simmering water. Cook until they puff and rise to surface, about 3 minutes. Drain on paper towel.

BECHAMEL SAUCE: In top of double boiler, melt butter; add flour, stirring with wire whisk. Cook for 2 minutes without letting mixture brown. Add milk; cook for about 15 minutes, stirring constantly until sauce is thickened and smooth. Season with salt, pepper and nutmeg to taste.

Arrange gnocchi in 1 layer in buttered decorative baking dish and spoon sauce over. Bake in preheated 400° oven, approximately 20 minutes. Gnocchi should have souffle appearance. Serve hot with freshly grated Parmesan cheese.

Florence Carriuolo, Farmington, CT

Variations, Advance Preparation, and Serving Suggestions:
Gnocchi may be placed in individual ramekins to bake and serve.

Wine Suggestion: Italian Salento Apulia, dry red, serve at room temperature.

Spinach Linguini ai Quattro Formaggi

SPINACH LINGUINI WITH FOUR CHEESES

This unique linguini recipe is from CAVEY's of Manchester, a restaurant Connecticut may take pride in. Here "quiet expertise and a high level of competence make dining out a total pleasure", according to Patricia Brooks in a New York Times review. Cavey's offers both Italian and French cuisine which reflect the high standard of excellence in food, service and decor.

YIELD: 6 Entree Servings
CALORIES PER SERVING: 1160
CARBOHYDRATES: 49g
PROTEIN: 32g
FAT: 93g
CHOLESTEROL: High
SODIUM: High
PREPARING: 10 Minutes
COOKING: 10 Minutes

In a 2-qt. *(2L)* heavy pan, melt butter on low flame. Add ginger, nutmeg and white pepper. Add Asiago, Fontina and Gorgonzola cheeses, stirring well, until they have all melted. Add ½ cup grated cheeses and all of the cream. Using a wire whisk, blend together, bring to a boil and stir until smooth. Set aside and keep warm.

In a large pot, bring one gallon salted water to a boil. Cook spinach linguini until *al dente*, 1½ to 3 minutes. Drain well and put back in pot. Pour sauce over pasta and stir over low heat until blended. Garnish with chopped parsley, remaining grated cheeses and a few twists of the pepper mill.

Chef Russell H. Pryzbek

Variations, Advance Preparation, and Serving Suggestions: If Asiago is hard to find, substitute a *very* aged Provolone.

Wine Suggestion: Italian Barbaresco, dry red; serve at room temperature.

Microwave Conversion Instructions: Put butter in 2-qt. *(2L)* glass or ceramic casserole. Cook on Medium (50%) 2-3 minutes or until melted. Add first three cheeses. Cook on Medium (50%) for 2 minutes. Stir. Continue cooking 2 minutes at a time, stirring after each 2-minute interval until cheeses are melted. Blend ½ cup grated cheese and all of heavy cream, using a wire whisk. Add to first cheese mixture. Continue cooking for 2 minutes at a time, stirring after each 2 minute interval until mixture boils. Set aside to keep warm and continue with recipe conventionally.

¾ lb. *(340g)* butter
Pinch each freshly grated nutmeg and ginger
¼ tsp. white pepper
¼ lb. *(115g)* **Asiago cheese**, grated
¼ lb. *(115g)* **Fontina cheese**, cubed
¼ lb. *(115g)* **Gorgonzola cheese**, crumbled
1 cup *(225g)* combined mixture of **Romano and Parmesan cheese**, grated
1½ cups *(355ml)* **heavy cream**
1 lb. 10 oz. *(835g)* fresh **Spinach Pasta** (page 192) linguini
3 T. Italian parsley, finely chopped

YIELD: 10 Servings
CALORIES PER SERVING: 778
CARBOHYDRATES: 9g
PROTEIN: 37g
FAT: 66g
CHOLESTEROL: High
SODIUM: High
PREPARING: 1 Hour
ROASTING: 2 Hours

Veal Galliano

A gala dish for a holiday buffet or an after-the-opera supper.

SPINACH STUFFING:

1 cup *(200g)* chopped cooked spinach
⅔ cup minced parsley
2 T. minced shallots
1 clove garlic, pressed
3 T. *(25g)* fresh breadcrumbs
½ cup *(200g)* diced prosciutto ham
½ cup *(120g)* ground veal
½ cup *(80g)* pine nuts
3 well beaten eggs

1 5-lb. *(2250g)* veal leg, boned but *not rolled or tied*

MIREPOIX:

2 carrots, finely chopped
2 onions, finely chopped
2 stalks celery, finely chopped
Parsley sprigs
1 cup *(240ml)* veal or chicken stock

GALLIANO BUTTER SAUCE:

1 lb. *(450g)* unsalted sweet butter
1½ tsp. salt
½ tsp. freshly ground pepper
½ tsp. oregano
1 cup *(240ml)* Galliano Liquore

SPINACH STUFFING: Combine all ingredients and spread stuffing mixture on inside of flattened piece of veal leg. (Depending on exact piece of meat, it may be necessary to make 3 long vertical ½-inch *(1.25cm)* slits down meat on underside to hold all the stuffing.) Form veal into a roll; tie at 2-inch *(5cm)* intervals.

MIREPOIX: Scatter chopped vegetables and parsley on bottom of shallow roasting pan. Place tied veal roast atop. Pour stock into pan around vegetables.

GALLIANO BUTTER SAUCE: Combine all ingredients in a saucepan and heat.

Baste roast with some of the Galliano Butter. Roast veal in preheated 325° oven for 2 hours, or until meat thermometer registers 170° (about 25-30 minutes per lb.) Baste frequently with Galliano Butter Sauce.

When roast is done, remove twine; place on bed of rice surrounded by snipped parsley. Slice meat and pass any remaining Galliano Butter in separate sauceboat.

Florence Carriuolo, Farmington, CT

Nutritional Notes: Nutritional analysis uses all the Galliano Butter Sauce, resulting in a relatively high calorie/fat content. If less sauce is consumed the calories and fat content can be significantly decreased.

Wine Suggestion: California Beau Velours Pinot Noir, dry red; serve at room temperature.

YIELD: 6-8 Servings
CALORIES PER SERVING: 76
CARBOHYDRATES: 9g
PROTEIN: 1g
FAT: 4g
PREPARING: 20 Minutes
COOKING: 25 Minutes

Mario's Carrots

3 T. *(45ml)* good quality olive oil
2 T. *(30g)* butter
2 lbs. *(900g)* carrots, peeled and cut into strips about 2½ × ¾-inch *(6.5 × 1.5cm)*
1½ cloves garlic, minced
Parsley or chives, chopped

Melt olive oil and butter in large skillet. Add carrots and garlic. Cover; cook over low heat, mixing occasionally 15 minutes or until carrots are tender but still crisp.

Just before serving, turn heat to high to brown carrots, mixing occasionally, about 5 minutes. Sprinkle with parsley or chives and serve.

Sarah Seymour, West Hartford, CT

Microwave Conversion Instructions: Cook olive oil, butter and garlic in a covered casserole just large enough to hold all ingredients, on High, just until garlic is softened, 1 to 2 minutes. Stir in carrots. Cook, covered, on High, stirring several times, 10 to 12 minutes or until carrots are fork tender. Sprinkle with parsley or chives.

Variegated Salad with Sweet and Sour Honey Dressing

ORANGE, AVOCADO AND JERUSALEM ARTICHOKE SALAD

A definite recommendation for a winter buffet table. The beautiful colors and sculpture of this salad create a striking presentation both for eye and palate.

YIELD: 10 Servings
CALORIES PER SERVING: 230
CARBOHYDRATES: 23g
PROTEIN: 3g
FAT: 14g
PREPARING: 1½ Hours

SALAD: Line 5-qt. (5L) salad bowl with large spinach leaves; tear remaining leaves into bite-size pieces and set aside. (Onion, cabbage and Jerusalem artichokes can be individually prepared with the aid of a food processor. Use slicing disc for onion and cabbage; julienne disc for Jerusalem artichokes.) Combine vegetables with reserved spinach. Place in spinach-lined salad bowl. Arrange orange slices, overlapping slices in circle on spinach leaves, allowing 1 inch (2.5cm) of green to show at edge of bowl. Slice avocado, toss lightly with lemon juice; arrange in center of salad bowl making an attractive design. Serve Honey Dressing separately.

DRESSING: In blender or food processor with metal blade in place, add parsley and onion. Process with off-on motion 6 times. Add remaining ingredients and process 10 seconds. Remove to serving bowl or pitcher.

Hipolit Narwid, West Hartford, CT

Variations, Advance Preparation, and Serving Suggestions: The Sweet and Sour Dressing lends itself to many other possibilities. Prepare salad greens the day before, construct the salad in serving bowl early in the day.

Nutritional Notes: Caloric value of Jerusalem artichokes varies depending upon length of time from harvesting to consumption. The values range from 7 calories per 3½ oz. (100g) for freshly harvested artichokes to 75 calories after long storage.

SALAD:

1 lb. (450g) flat spinach leaves, stems removed
1 bunch watercress, stems removed
1 small red onion (2 oz.) (55g), peeled, sliced
1 wedge red cabbage (2 oz.) (55g), thinly sliced
5 large Jerusalem artichokes (15 oz.) (425g), peeled and well scrubbed, julienned
5 small seedless eating oranges, peeled and sliced horizontally
2 large avocados, firm but ripe, split vertically, pitted
2 tsp. fresh lemon juice

SWEET AND SOUR HONEY DRESSING:
Yield: 1½ Cups (350ml)
4 T. chopped parsley
2 small onions (1 oz. each) (30g each), minced
1 tsp. dry mustard
1 tsp. Hungarian paprika
1 tsp. salt
1 tsp. celery seed
6 T. (130g) honey
6 T. (90ml) cider vinegar
2 T. (30ml) fresh lemon juice
⅔ cup (160ml) light oil

YIELD: 8 Servings
TOTAL CALORIES: 5020
CALORIES PER SERVING: 627
CARBOHYDRATES: 54g
PROTEIN: 6g
FAT: 43g
CHOLESTEROL: High
PREPARING: 45 Minutes
CHILLING: 6 Hours Minimum
FREEZING: Yes

Italian Zuccotto

Zuccotto is a dome-shaped Florentine specialty inspired by the cupola of Florence's Duomo. The Italian word *zucco* means pumpkin, and this dessert, before it is cut, looks like a pumpkin.

1 store-bought, rectangular pound cake (10-12 oz.) *(285-340g)*
¼ cup *(60ml)* Cointreau
2 T. *(30ml)* cognac
2 T. *(30ml)* maraschino liqueur (can substitute other favorite liqueur)
6 oz. *(170g)* semisweet chocolate chips
2 cups *(475ml)* heavy cream
¾ cup *(100g)* confectioners' sugar
4 oz. *(115g)* shelled, blanched almonds, chopped

Line 1½-qt. *(1.5L)* round-bottomed bowl with plastic wrap, allowing wrap to extend over edges of bowl. Cut 2-inch *(5cm)* piece off end of pound cake and set aside. Cut remaining cake lengthwise into ¼-inch *(0.6cm)* slices. Then cut each slice diagonally in half, making 2 elongated triangles of each slice. There will be a dark crust on one edge of each triangle. Combine liqueurs in shallow dish. Carefully, so as not to break cake, moisten each triangle, one at a time, then place against inside of lined bowl, pointed end at bottom center, until inside of bowl is completely lined with cake. Where one side of a triangle has crust on it, have it meet crustless side of section next to it. (When the dessert is unmolded, the lines of the crust should form indented ribs of a pumpkin.) Coarsely chop half the chocolate chips. Whip cream with confectioners' sugar until stiff; fold in almonds and chopped chocolate. Divide mixture in half; set aside one half; spoon other half into lined bowl, spreading it evenly over entire surface of cake. This should leave a still unfilled cavity in center. Melt remaining chocolate; fold into remaining whipped cream. Spoon into empty cavity; smooth off top. Cover with remaining end-piece of cake, sliced and moistened. Cover with plastic wrap; refrigerate overnight, or up to 2 to 3 days before serving.

When ready to serve, unmold onto serving plate; remove plastic wrap. Serve immediately or return to refrigerator for several hours before serving.

Maureen Rotenberg, West Hartford, CT

Wine Suggestion: Italian Moscato, sweet white; serve chilled.

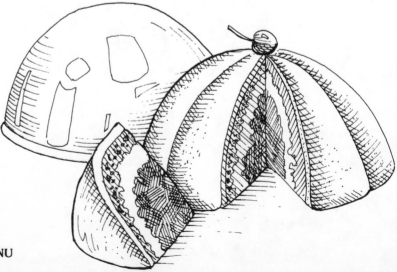

White Chocolate Mousse in Almond Lace Wafer Cups

White chocolate is a candy made from ivory-colored cocoa butter, highly condensed milk, sugar and vanillin. It tastes like a sweet, mild milk chocolate. It is not classified as a true chocolate because it does not contain chocolate "liquor," the chocolate essence that is extracted from cocoa beans.

YIELD: 10 Servings
CALORIES PER SERVING: 540
CARBOHYDRATES: 72g
PROTEIN: 4g
FAT: 26g
CHOLESTEROL: High
PREPARING: 1½ Hours
CHILLING: 4 Hours Minimum
COOKING: 15 Minutes

WHITE CHOCOLATE MOUSSE: Whip cream until very stiff; refrigerate until needed.

In small heavy saucepan, heat sugar and water until mixture reaches 250° on candy thermometer. While mixture is heating, beat egg whites until they form soft peaks. With mixer still running on low speed, add hot sugar syrup in slow, steady stream; continue to blend 3 minutes. Add white chocolate, continue beating until *most but not all* of it has melted and all is well blended.

Fold whipped cream into chocolate mixture. Chill several hours or up to 2 days before serving.

When ready to serve, place a scoop of mousse into center of Almond Lace Wafer Cup. Garnish with strawberries, blueberries or raspberries.

ALMOND LACE WAFER CUPS: To make cups follow recipe for Almond Lace Wafers except drop a tablespoonful of batter onto baking sheet rather than a teaspoonful. This will result in a much larger cookie. As soon as cookie can be lifted off baking sheet with a spatula, drape it over the outside of a 1 to 2 cup (¼-½L) size bowl or dish. With your fingers, quickly press cookie to conform to shape of bowl. As soon as cookie has hardened, gently remove it; store *very carefully* airtight until needed.

Melinda M. Vance, West Hartford, CT

WHITE CHOCOLATE MOUSSE:
2 cups *(475ml)* heavy cream, whipped
1 cup *(200g)* sugar
½ cup *(120ml)* water
3 egg whites at room temperature
1 lb. *(450g)* white chocolate, *coarsely* chopped

10 ALMOND LACE WAFER CUPS (page 382)

Strawberries, blueberries and/or raspberries (do not omit as they are essential to balance sweetness of mousse)

Variations, Advance Preparation, and Serving Suggestions:
Fill Almond Wafer Cups with Frozen Pumpkin Mousse: Combine 1½ cups *(300g)* sugar and 1½ cups *(355ml)* water in heavy saucepan and cook until it reaches 238°. Meanwhile, beat 6 egg whites with ¼ tsp. each salt and cream of tartar until soft peaks form. With machine running, add hot sugar syrup in slow steady stream; continue beating 10 minutes. Blend in 1 cup *(285g)* canned pumpkin and ¼ tsp. each cinnamon, ginger and nutmeg. Fold in 2 cups *(475ml)* heavy cream whipped with 3 T. *(45ml)* dark rum until soft peaks form (if too stiff mousse will be grainy). Freeze 3 to 4 hours. If freezing longer, soften in refrigerator 1 to 2 hours before serving.

Microwave Conversion Instructions: Place water and sugar in heat-resistant bowl and cook, uncovered, on High until mixture reaches 250°. If using a microwave candy thermometer it may be left in the bowl. If using regular candy thermometer, take mixture out of oven to test.

FRESH CRUDITÉS PLATTER WITH DIPPING SAUCES

Spinach Water Chestnut Dip
p. 112

Smoked Salmon Dipping Sauce
p. 34

Ham and Chutney Dipping Sauce
p. 206

Curried Yogurt Dip
p. 184

HOT HORS d'OEUVRE

Spinach Balls
p. 181

Sausage Mushroom Triangles
p. 302

Coconut Shrimp Dijon
p. 181

Chinese Pearl Balls with Dipping Sauces
p. 182

Happy Hour Mushrooms
p. 183

Oyster Croustades
p. 204

Graphic Cauliflower
p. 180

Caraway Fondue
p. 180

COLD HORS d'OEUVRE

Marinated Broccoli
p. 185

Cocktail Mussels
(Moules Ravigote)
p. 67

Duck or Pork Rillettes
p. 74 or 184

Curried Shellfish Mold with Wafers
p. 334

Caponata alla Siciliana Black Bread Rounds
p. 185

Fresh Fruit Kebabs with Sauce Grand Marnier
p. 188

Florentines
p. 386

Chocolate Truffles in Disguise
p. 188

Miniature Eclairs and Cream Puffs
p. 186

Hartford Stage Presents "The Cocktail Party"

A sumptuous and very elegant cocktail buffet for that once-in-a-lifetime party.

Come to the Hartford Stage Cocktail Party!

This invitation could have been for one of two significant Hartford Stage productions. First came an elegant 1980 revival of T.S. Eliot's play, "The Cocktail Party." This was followed a few months later by a special cocktail party given in honor of the Stage Company's producing director, Paul Weidner, as he prepared to move into a new profession after providing the city of Hartford with twelve seasons of vibrant theatre.

Eliot's "Cocktail Party" was only one of many successful productions which the Stage Company has brought to Hartford since its inception in 1964. Initially, the small local repertory company, under the direction of Jacques Cartier, was housed in a converted warehouse. During the next few years, however, the theatre blossomed into a nationally respected regional organization. Today the Stage Company attracts international stage and screen stars to perform in the new John W. Huntington Theatre, located in downtown Hartford. Much of this growth was under the guidance of Paul Weidner who had been an actor in the repertory company and who served as the theatre's director from 1968 to 1979. The present artistic director, Mark Lamos, has received national acclaim for his debut season and the list of regular subscribers who want to be assured a ticket to every production continues to grow.

In addition to six annual productions, the Stage Company sponsors a unique training program for inner-city teenagers which culminates in their production of a musical. Regular student matinee programs include prepared study guides and discussion of each play with the cast. The Company also sponsors theatre classes for adults and high school students. For several years the Touring Theatre has performed short dramas throughout Connecticut and New England. The dedicated auxiliary, called "Stagehands," has assisted the theatre with a variety of volunteer activities since 1969.

In contrast to the history of the Hartford Stage Company — and certainly to that of the theatre, which traces its origin to open air performances in ancient Greece — the cocktail party must look to a more uncertain and surely less auspicious beginning. We have several versions from which to choose. According to one tradition, the first "cocktails" served were literally just that. In 1796 a bar in Elmsford, New York offered customers the long feathers of a cock's tail to decorate a special drink mixture. This in turn may have come from the French word *coquetel* which described a mixed brandy drink originating in Bordeaux. A completely different tale(!) comes from New Orleans where Monsieur A.A. Peychard opened an apothecary shop in 1793. There he dispensed a tonic he called "bitters," made by a secret family formula. Peychard would sell customers suffering from various maladies a mixture of cognac and bitters. He served this in an egg cup, or *coquetier*, as it is called in French. It is said that Americans, who soon insisted on having bitters with other combinations of liquors, slurred *coquetier* into "cocktail." One of the earliest references to such a mixed drink is in a periodical called *The Balance*, dated May 13, 1806. The article describes the cocktail as "a stimulating liquor composed of spirits of any kind, sugar, water and bitters. It is vulgarly called bitter sling, and is supposed to be an excellent electioneering potion."

The combination of drinks and appetizers which can be held in one hand, "finger foods," is a much more recent phenomenon. Originally appetizers came from China via Russia (zakuska), Scandinavia (smorgasbord), Italy (antipasto), France ((hors d'oeuvre) and Greece (oretika). The first widespread use of appetizers in the U.S. was probably during the California gold rush when a "free lunch" was offered with a beer at bars competing for the miners' business. By the mid-20th century the serving of hot or cold savory tidbits with a drink became a popular way of entertaining.

The main ingredients for a successful cocktail party should be good friendship, warm hospitality, fine liquors and appetizers that are delectable both in taste and appearance. As in Eliot's "Cocktail Party" and the special farewell party for Paul Weidner, we would hope that your use of the cocktail recipes will lead to a delightful occasion filled with special meaning.

179

YIELD: 6-8 Servings
TOTAL CALORIES: 2080
CALORIES PER SERVING: 260
CARBOHYDRATES: 11g
PROTEIN: 3g
FAT: 23g
PREPARING: 5 Minutes
MARINATING: 15 Minutes
COOKING: 20 Minutes
FREEZING: No

Graphic Cauliflower

Milk is the secret ingredient that gives this finger food a fantastic crunch.

---

1 cauliflower, broken into flowerettes
1½ cups *(355ml)* milk
1 cup *(240ml)* olive oil
1 cup *(115g)* flour or breadcrumbs
Coarse salt (optional)

Dip cauliflower buds into milk and soak 10 to 15 minutes. Heat small amount of oil in skillet, preferably with non-stick surface. Roll cauliflower in flour or breadcrumbs or shake in paper bag and quickly fry. Add oil as needed. Vegetable must be crunchy.

Sprinkle with coarse salt. Serve immediately.

Ann Klein, West Hartford, CT

Variations, Advance Preparation, and Serving Suggestions:
Substitute green beans or zucchini for cauliflower.

Nutritional Notes: This recipe is low in sodium and cholesterol. It can be prepared using polyunsaturated oil (e.g. corn, safflower, soybean) and skim milk. Nutritional analysis is based on the absorption of 13 T. oil during frying.

YIELD: 6 Servings
CALORIES PER SERVING: 416
CARBOHYDRATES: 27g
PROTEIN: 23g
FAT: 24g
CHOLESTEROL: High
SODIUM: High
PREPARING: 30 Minutes
COOKING: 10 Minutes
FREEZING: No

Caraway Fondue

A nice change from conventional fondue, and great for after any 5 Arts performance.

---

1 loaf *(425g)* French or Italian bread
12-14 oz. *(350-400g)* Danbo cheese
4-6 oz. *(120-175g)* Gruyere cheese
¾ cup *(175ml)* dry white wine
3 T. *(45ml)* brandy
1½ T. *(15g)* cornstarch

Cube bread and let sit uncovered approximately 1 hour to slightly dry.

Grate or cube cheese (can be prepared day before or in morning; cover and refrigerate). Place in saucepan or fondue pot with glazed interior. Add wine. Gently simmer, stirring often until smooth. Mix brandy and cornstarch to make a smooth paste. Add to cheese. Stir constantly until thickened. (Up to this point, may be prepared ahead; rewarm by adding just a little more wine). If not prepared in fondue pot, transfer. Each bread cube should be speared with a fork and dipped into the warm fondue for serving.

Janice Niehaus, West Hartford, CT

Variations, Advance Preparation, and Serving Suggestions:
Use leftover bread cubes for croutons.

Microwave Conversion Instructions: Place wine in a 2-qt. *(2L)* glass measure. Heat on High 3 minutes. Stir in cheese (best if grated). Cook on Medium High (70%) uncovered for 2 to 3 minutes, just until cheese is melted, stirring once. Mix brandy and corn starch to make a smooth paste. Add to cheese, stirring constantly. Cook on High 1 minute, or just until mixture thickens. Pour into fondue pot.

Spinach Balls

An easy, hot hors d'oeuvre to freeze ahead for impromptu gatherings.

YIELD: 60-70 Balls
TOTAL CALORIES: 2450
CALORIES PER BALL: 35
CARBOHYDRATES: 1g
PROTEIN: 1g
FAT: 3g
CHOLESTEROL: High
SODIUM: High
PREPARING: 20 Minutes
BAKING: 15 Minutes
FREEZING: Mandatory

Combine all ingredients, mixing well. Roll into walnut-sized balls. Freeze, well-wrapped. When ready to serve, unwrap and place on baking sheet, still frozen.

Bake in preheated 350° oven 10 to 15 minutes, until heated through.

Phyllis R. Lappen, West Hartford, CT

Variations, Advance Preparation, and Serving Suggestions: Serve with hot Mustard Dip (page 373).

Nutritional Notes: As a general rule, frozen vegetables and fruits are preferable to canned as they contain most of the nutrients available in the fresh (sometimes even more, depending on how soon after harvest they are frozen vs. how long the "fresh" have been stored) whereas canned fruits and vegetables loose some nutrients through heat in the canning process and soaking in the canning liquids (which often contain acids, salt, sugar and chemicals).

Microwave Conversion Instructions: Place prepared balls in a circular pattern on a serving plate. Heat on Medium (50%) 4 to 5 minutes or until heated through.

2 pkgs. (10 oz. each) *(570g)* frozen chopped spinach, cooked, squeezed extremely dry
2 cups *(150g)* packaged stuffing mix
1 cup *(130g)* freshly grated Parmesan cheese
6 eggs, beaten
¾ cup *(170g)* butter, softened
Salt
Freshly ground pepper to taste

Coconut Shrimp Dijon

YIELD: 40 Pieces
TOTAL CALORIES: 2400
CALORIES PER PIECE: 60
CARBOHYDRATES: 5g
PROTEIN: 3.5g
FAT: 3g
CHOLESTEROL: High
PREPARING: 1½ Hours
COOKING: 45 Minutes
FREEZING: Yes

Cut each shrimp in half lengthwise; set aside. In small bowl combine egg, milk and sugar. Beat until well-blended. Gradually add flour, beating until smooth. Pour oil to 1 inch *(2.5cm)* depth in 10-inch *(25cm)* skillet; heat to 375°. Place ¼ of coconut in a shallow pan, adding more as needed. Grasp shrimp half from center back, dip into batter, coat with coconut. Fry 5 at one time in hot oil, maintaining 375° temperature, 4 to 5 minutes until golden, turning once. Drain on paper towels. Remove to decorative platter. Serve with mustard for dipping sauce.

Sheila D'Agostino, West Hartford, CT

Variations, Advance Preparation, and Serving Suggestions: After frying, shrimp may be refrigerated one day or frozen. Defrost before heating on baking sheet in 350° oven 5 to 7 minutes.

Nutritional Notes: Nutritional analysis is based on oil absorption of ¼ cup and consumption of 1 cup freshly grated, unsweetened coconut.

1 lb. *(450g)* medium, uncooked shrimp, 20 count; peeled and deveined
1 egg
¾ cup *(175ml)* milk
¼ cup *(50g)* light brown sugar, packed
1¼ cups *(140g)* flour
Vegetable oil for frying
2 pkgs. (7 oz. each) *(400g)* shredded coconut
1 jar (8 oz.) *(225g)* Dijon mustard

YIELD: 8 First Course Servings
   or 40-48 Balls
CALORIES PER BALL: 48
CARBOHYDRATES: 3g
PROTEIN: 2.5g
FAT: 3g
SODIUM: High
CALORIES PER TABLESPOON
   HOT SAUCE: 99
CALORIES PER TABLESPOON
   MILD SAUCE: 22
PREPARING: 1½ Hours
SOAKING: 2 Hours
STEAMING: 25 Minutes

Chinese Pearl Balls with Dipping Sauces

Glutinous rice, also known as sweet rice or sticky rice, is a significant part of this recipe since, when steamed, it has an opalescent quality which gives the dish its name.

PEARL BALLS:

⅔ cup *(130g)* glutinous or sweet rice
1 lb. *(450g)* lean pork, finely ground
6 water chestnuts, finely minced
6 dried Chinese mushrooms (soak in hot water 30 to 60 minutes), stems discarded, finely chopped
1 egg, lightly beaten
1 tsp. finely chopped fresh ginger
1 T. soy sauce
1 tsp. sesame oil
1 tsp. salt
½ tsp. sugar
2 scallions, finely chopped
2 tsp. cornstarch mixed with 1 T. water

Lettuce to line steamers

HOT DIPPING SAUCE:

1 cup *(240ml)* oil
½ cup *(45g)* crushed red pepper (can be purchased in powdered form)

MILD DIPPING SAUCE:

¼ cup *(60ml)* soy sauce
¼ cup *(60ml)* unseasoned rice vinegar
1 T. finely minced garlic
2 T. finely chopped scallions
2 T. finely minced fresh ginger
1 T. sesame oil
½ tsp. sugar

Rinse glutinous rice until water runs clear. (This may take eight washings.) Cover rice with cold water; let stand a minimum 2 hours.

In mixing bowl, combine remaining Pearl Ball ingredients. Using one hand, mix clockwise until meat holds together. Wet both hands and form mixture into balls approximately 1 inch *(2.5cm)* in diameter. Refrigerate.

Drain rice; allow to dry completely by spreading it out on a tea towel. Roll balls one at a time in the rice, thoroughly covering each ball.

Bring water to boil in bottom of wok or steamer. Place Pearl Balls on steamer rack lined with lettuce leaves, leaving ½ inch *(1.25cm)* between each ball. (The number of racks you need will depend upon the size of your steamer.) Cover and steam 25 minutes. Balls are done when the rice becomes transparent or pearly in appearance. Serve hot with Dipping Sauces.

HOT DIPPING SAUCE: Heat oil to hot but not steaming; add pepper powder and stir. Cool. Store covered in jar.

MILD DIPPING SAUCE: Combine all ingredients in covered glass jar. Refrigerate for several months and use as needed.

Bernice Kuzma, West Hartford, CT

Variations, Advance Preparation, and Serving Suggestions:
If you have an attractive Chinese bamboo steamer, serve directly from it with 2 small bowls of Dipping Sauces. Otherwise, arrange Pearl Balls on a platter surrounded by fresh coriander or Chinese parsley.

Can be prepared 1 day ahead. Steam 15 minutes first day, then steam another 10 minutes before serving.

Ground shoulder of veal can be substituted for pork.

Leftover Pearl Balls can be steamed again the next day for 5 minutes, or deep-fried in preheated 375° oil until brown.

Nutritional Notes: Soy sauce contains 850 milligrams sodium per tablespoon. If desired decrease soy sauce to taste.

Happy Hour Mushrooms

YIELD: 36 Stuffed Mushrooms
CALORIES PER MUSHROOM: 45
CARBOHYDRATES: 1g
PROTEIN: 1g
FAT: 4g
CHOLESTEROL: High
SODIUM: High
PREPARING: 30 Minutes
COOKING: 3-5 Minutes

Brush mushroom caps with melted butter or brush mushrooms with lemon juice or white wine before stuffing so they will retain their light color during cooking.

Combine softened butter, garlic and grated cheese; mix well. Add wine, soy sauce, onion dip mix and corn chips to make a paste.

Fill mushroom caps with mixture. Place on baking sheet; broil for 3 minutes or until bubbly and lightly browned.

Pauline Livingston, Avon, CT

Microwave Conversion Instructions: Wipe mushrooms with a damp towel. Remove stems. No need to brush with melted butter. Combine softened butter, garlic and grated cheese; mix well. Add wine, soy sauce, dip mix and crushed corn chips to make paste.

Fill mushroom caps with mixture. Place 18 in a circle on a microwave-safe serving dish. Cook on High about 3 minutes, just until filling is hot and mushrooms slightly cooked. Repeat with remaining mushrooms.

36 medium-sized fresh mushrooms, wiped and stems removed
3 T. *(45g)* butter, melted
¼ lb. *(115g)* butter, softened
1 clove garlic, minced
⅔ cup *(75g)* grated Monterey Jack cheese
2 tsp. *(10ml)* red wine
2 tsp. *(10ml)* soy sauce
1 envelope (1½ oz.) *(45g)* onion dip mix
⅓ cup *(30g)* finely crushed corn chips

Curried Yogurt Dip

YIELD: 2 Cups
CALORIES PER TABLESPOON: 48
FAT: 5g
PREPARING: 5 Minutes
FREEZING: No

This is particularly good with cold broccoli or kohlrabi.

1 cup *(225g)* mayonnaise (Hellmann's
  preferred) or Homemade Mayonnaise,
  (page 190)
1 cup *(225g)* plain yogurt
1 tsp. vinegar
⅛ tsp. thyme
1 tsp. chili powder
1 T. ketchup
1 tsp. honey or pure maple syrup
½ tsp. curry powder
1 T. chives, minced
1 T. onion, diced
2 T. dehydrated onion

Combine all ingredients and mix well. Chill. Serve with favorite raw vegetables.

Nancy Slonim Aronie, West Hartford, CT

Nutritional Notes: Using low fat yogurt will help to limit total calories and fat. Imitation mayonnaise will lower fat/calorie content even further. 1 cup yogurt made from skim milk contains 122 calories and 3g fat. 1 cup yogurt made from whole milk contains 155 calories and 7g fat.

Pork Rillettes

YIELD: 2 1-Quart Terrines
TOTAL CALORIES: 10,460
APPROXIMATE CALORIES
  PER TABLESPOON: 84
PROTEIN: 3g
FAT: 8g
CHOLESTEROL: High
SODIUM: High
PREPARING: 30 Minutes
BAKING: 4 Hours
MARINATING: Overnight
CHILLING: 3 Days Minimum
FREEZING: Yes

2 cloves garlic, finely minced
1 tsp. dried thyme
1½ T. coarse salt
¼ tsp. freshly ground black pepper
4 lbs. *(1.8kg)* pork shoulder, cubed
4 cups *(900g)* goose or duck fat, melted
1 cup *(240ml)* water

Pork rillettes are good for picnics with cornichons and plenty of French bread. In France, they are eaten on chunks of bread spread with the fat from atop the terrine.

Mix garlic with spices. Rub into cubed pork and place in non-metal bowl. Cover with plastic wrap; refrigerate overnight or up to 2 days.

Place meat in 9-qt. *(8.4L)* Dutch oven with goose fat and water. Cover and place on middle rack of preheated 250° oven. Bake 4 hours. Remove pot from oven. Pour contents into colander set over a large bowl. When cool enough to handle, process meat in food processor in batches with short, on-off bursts, just enough to shred meat coarsely, about 10 seconds.

Pack meat in 2 1-qt. *(1L each)* terrines or baking pans. Strain cooking liquid and pour over meat. Cover and refrigerate at least 3 days before serving.

Kathleen J. Schwartz, Avon, CT

Variations, Advance Preparation, and Serving Suggestions:
The rillettes need a few days of chilling time to produce a mellowed flavor. Leftovers can be frozen, but will keep well in the refrigerator for up to 10 days.

Wine Suggestion: French Valbon Rouge, dry red; serve at room temperature.

Marinated Broccoli

This disappears fast!

YIELD: 15-20 Hors d'Oeuvre Servings
PREPARING: 30 Minutes
MARINATING: 24 Hours

Separate broccoli into flowerettes, leaving an inch or so of stem on each.

3 bunches fresh broccoli

Combine marinade ingredients in a covered container large enough to hold all the broccoli. Add broccoli; cover and shake or turn container to baste. Refrigerate 24 hours, basting broccoli occasionally. Drain and serve in a crystal bowl. Have toothpicks handy.

MARINADE:
1 cup *(240ml)* cider vinegar
1 T. sugar
1 T. dill weed
1 T. Spike (available at health food stores)
1 tsp. salt
1 tsp. freshly ground black pepper
1 tsp. garlic salt
1½ cups *(360ml)* vegetable oil

Deborah Greenspan, West Hartford, CT
Lois Sykes, Bronxville, NY
Barbara Washburn, West Hartford, CT

Variations, Advance Preparation, and Serving Suggestions:
Leftover marinade may be refrigerated and reused. Fresh lemon juice and freshly minced garlic can be added.

Nutritional Notes: Nutritional analysis has been omitted since it is difficult to estimate how much marinade is absorbed. This is a relatively low-calorie hors d'oeuvre. For low-sodium version, omit salt and substitute garlic powder for garlic salt.

Caponata alla Siciliana

SWEET AND SOUR EGGPLANT SICILIAN STYLE

Caponata is a thick piquant mixture based on cooked eggplant. As a first course or as part of an antipasto presentation, spoon onto crisp lettuce and accompany with sliced crusty bread, or spread onto crisp crackers. Serve with meats like barbecued beef or lamb as a vegetable.

YIELD: 16 Appetizer Servings or
   8 Vegetable Servings
TOTAL CALORIES: 1264
CALORIES PER
   VEGETABLE SERVING: 158
CARBOHYDRATES: 14g
PROTEIN: 3g
FAT: 10g
SODIUM: High
PREPARING: 40 Minutes
COOKING: 20 Minutes
FREEZING: Yes

In heavy skillet heat 2 T. olive oil, add celery, cook over medium heat 10 minutes, stirring; add onions, saute until soft and lightly colored. With slotted spoon transfer vegetables to a bowl.

Add 2 T. oil to skillet; over *high heat* quickly saute eggplant stirring constantly until lightly browned. Add more oil only if necessary. Return celery and onion to skillet; stir in vinegar and sugar, tomatoes, olives, capers, salt and pepper. Bring to boil; reduce heat, simmer uncovered for 15 to 20 minutes. Stir in pine nuts; check seasonings; add extra vinegar if necessary. Chill. Keeps well 2 weeks refrigerated.

Mary Fish, Cashiers, NC

Wine Suggestion: Italian Azura, soft white; serve chilled.

¼ cup *(60ml)* good quality olive oil
2 cups *(225g)* celery, finely chopped
¾ cup *(115g)* onion, finely chopped
2 lbs. *(900g)* eggplant, peeled and cut into ½-inch *(1.2cm)* cubes
¼ cup *(60ml)* good quality red wine vinegar mixed with 2 tsp. sugar
2 cups drained *(425g)* Italian plum tomatoes
6 large green olives, pitted, slivered
2 T. capers
Salt
Freshly ground pepper
2 T. *(20g)* pine nuts (more can be added if desired)

Éclairs, Cream Puffs and Profiteroles

YIELD:
16 Eclairs or
16 Cream Puffs or
48 Profiteroles
PREPARING: 1½ Hours
BAKING: 20-35 Minutes
FREEZING: Yes-Unfilled

1 recipe Pate a Choux (page 195)
   YIELD: 2½ Cups Dough
   CALORIES: 1775

EGG WASH:
1 egg well beaten with pinch salt

FORMING ECLAIRS: Use baking sheet with non-stick coating or grease and flour a baking sheet. Fit pastry bag with #9 tube (¾ inch) (2cm) with plain tip and fill bag with pate a choux. Forming neat rows across sheet, pipe tube shapes about 1 inch (2.5cm) wide and 5 inches (12.5cm) long, spacing them about 1½ inches (4cm) apart. When you have reached desired length, keep tip in place and release pressure on bag. Flick tip down to sheet and then up, cutting off pastry as you lift up. Brush eclairs with egg wash, and then run back of tines of fork along length of each eclair; this increases inflation during baking.

BAKING ECLAIRS: Place baking sheet in center of preheated 475° oven and immediately turn temperature down to 400°. Bake eclairs until puffed and golden, about 20 minutes, then lower heat to 300° and bake until dry, another 10 to 15 minutes.

Remove eclairs from oven, poke small hole in each end, and cool completely on rack. When cool they are ready to be filled with pastry cream of your choice and frosted or stored for future use. If stored, whether frozen or just tinned, they are better if slightly reheated. Heat in 200° oven until crisp and firm, about 8 minutes.

FORMING CREAM PUFFS: Fit pastry bag with #6 (½-inch) (1.25cm) plain tube, and pipe dough onto prepared baking sheet into round puff about 1½ to 2 inches (4-5cm) in diameter and as high as they are wide. If you are using a teaspoon, form rough heaps of this size. Brush the shapes lightly with egg wash.

BAKING CREAM PUFFS: Preheat oven to 475°. Place sheet of puffs in center of oven and immediately lower heat to 400°. Bake until puffed, colored, and firm to touch, about 20 to 25 minutes; then lower heat to 300° and bake another 10 to 15 minutes. Remove pan from oven and poke hole in side of each puff. Cool thoroughly on a rack. Fill with pastry cream of your choice and frost.

FORMING PROFITEROLES: Fit pastry bag with #6 (½-inch) plain tube, and fill bag with pate a choux. Or use a teaspoon to spoon out pate a choux. Form ¾-inch (2cm) puffs, as high as they are wide, spacing them about ¾ inch (2cm) apart. Brush puffs lightly with egg wash.

BAKING PROFITEROLES: Place baking sheet in center of preheated 475° oven. After 5 minutes lower heat to 425° and bake 15 minutes. Then lower heat to 300° and continue to bake until puffs have dried, about 10 minutes. Remove from oven and poke small hole in each side. Cool on rack. Fill pastry bag with filling of your choice and pipe filling through small hole on side. Frost.

Éclair, Cream Puff and Profiterole Fillings and Frostings

BASIC PASTRY CREAM: Combine flour with ¼ cup cream or milk; stir until smooth. Gradually add remaining cream. Stir in salt and sugar. Cook mixture over medium heat, stirring until mixture becomes as thick as medium white sauce. Stir a little hot sauce into egg yolks. Then pour yolks into pan, stirring briskly. Return pan to low heat a few more minutes to thicken a little more, continuing to stir. Do not let sauce boil. Remove from heat and stir in additional flavorings. Beat in butter. Cool in refrigerator until ready to use, covered.

PRALINE PASTRY CREAM: Place confectioners' sugar and almonds in heavy saucepan. Place on medium heat and cook, stirring constantly until sugar starts to melt. Since there is no liquid this will take a few minutes. However, once it starts to melt, it will turn rapidly to caramel. This method produces a very hard and tight caramel. As soon as it turns to caramel, pour the mixture onto an oiled marble slab or an oiled tray. When cold, break into pieces and blend into a powder in food processor or blender. Fold into the basic pastry cream mixture.

CHOCOLATE FROSTING: Combine butter and chocolate in small saucepan. Heat, stirring until chocolate melts. Remove pan from heat and gradually blend in milk. Add sugar (sifted if lumpy) and stir briskly to blend.

MOCHA FROSTING: Melt butter in small saucepan and stir in coffee and confectioners' sugar. Stir briskly with wire whisk. Add cream and beat to blend. Let cool slightly to thicken before using.

Carol Renshaw, West Hartford, CT

BASIC PASTRY CREAM:
  YIELD: 1½ Cups
  CALORIES: 931
2 T. *(15g)* flour
1 cup *(240ml)* light cream or milk
⅛ tsp. salt
⅜ cup *(75g)* sugar
4 egg yolks, slightly beaten
1 T. pure vanilla or dark rum (Myers's preferred)
2 T. *(30g)* sweet unsalted butter

CHOCOLATE PASTRY CREAM:
  YIELD: 2 Cups
  CALORIES: 1440
Add 3 oz. *(85g)* melted semisweet chocolate to above Basic Pastry Cream

MOCHA PASTRY CREAM:
  YIELD: 1½ Cups
  CALORIES: 931
Add 1 T. instant coffee powder to above Basic Pastry Cream

PRALINE PASTRY CREAM:
  YIELD: 2½ Cups
  CALORIES: 1992
1 cup *(130g)* confectioners' sugar
½ cup *(70g)* almonds

CHOCOLATE FROSTING:
  YIELD: ⅓ Cup
  CALORIES: 772
2 T. *(30g)* butter
1½ oz. *(42g)* semisweet chocolate
2 T. *(30ml)* milk
½ cup *(65g)* confectioners' sugar

MOCHA FROSTING:
  YIELD: ½ Cup
  CALORIES: 1182
¼ cup *(60g)* butter
2 tsp. instant coffee crystals
1 cup *(130g)* confectioners' sugar
2 T. *(30ml)* heavy cream

YIELD: 10 Servings
CALORIES PER SERVING: 168
CARBOHYDRATES: 14g
PROTEIN: 1g
FAT: 12g
CHOLESTEROL: High
PREPARING: 20 Minutes
CHILLING: 30 Minutes
COOKING: 10 Minutes

Sauce Grand Marnier

A light sauce to serve with fresh fruits or berries, over fruit tarts or plain cake.

5 egg yolks
½ cup (100g) plus 2 T. (25g) superfine sugar
4 T. (60ml) Grand Marnier, divided
1 cup (240ml) heavy cream

Select 1½ or 2-qt. (1.5-2L) mixing bowl that will fit snugly on top of slightly bigger saucepan. Add about 2 inches (5cm) water to pan; bring to boil. Meanwhile, place yolks and ½ cup sugar in bowl. Beat thoroughly with whisk or portable mixer. Place bowl on saucepan. (Bottom of bowl should not touch water.) Continue beating 10 minutes, until yolks are pale yellow and very thick. Remove bowl from pan. Stir in 3 T. Grand Marnier. Let sauce cool to room temperature; cover, refrigerate until chilled.

Beat cream with 2 T. sugar until almost stiff. Fold cream lightly into sauce. Stir in remaining 1 T. Grand Marnier.

Jeanne L. Rossi, Rocky Hill, CT

YIELD: 40 Cookies
TOTAL CALORIES: 5320
CALORIES PER COOKIE: 133
CARBOHYDRATES: 11g
PROTEIN: 2g
FAT: 9g
PREPARING: 1 Hour
BAKING: 18-20 Minutes Per Sheet
FREEZING: Yes-Very Well

Chocolate Truffles in Disguise

PASTRY:
1 cup (8 oz.) (225g) butter
½ tsp. pure vanilla extract
½ cup (65g) confectioners' sugar
2 cups (225g) sifted flour

TRUFFLES:
8 oz. (225g) sweet chocolate very finely ground (cut coarsely; then add to food processor)
8 oz. (1⅔ cups) (225g) almonds, blanched or not; very finely ground
2 egg whites, jumbo or extra large
Confectioners' sugar

PASTRY: In large bowl of electric mixer cream butter; add vanilla and sugar and mix until smooth. On low speed, add flour, scraping bowl with rubber spatula and beating until mixture holds together. Transfer dough to piece of waxed paper. Flatten slightly and shape into an oblong. Wrap airtight; refrigerate briefly while preparing truffles.

TRUFFLES: Combine chocolate and almonds in food processor or bowl. Mix in unbeaten egg whites; knead until mixture holds together. Divide into 40 pieces, using 1 T. for each, placing on waxed paper.

Remove pastry from refrigerator; it should not be chilled hard. Cut into 40 pieces. Flatten a piece in palm of hand and wrap around truffle completely. Roll into ball between palms. (Dust hands with confectioners' sugar if dough sticks.) Place on ungreased baking sheets 1 inch (2.5cm) apart.

Bake on rack ⅓ down from top of preheated 375° oven 18 to 20 minutes until lightly colored. Reverse position of baking sheet if necessary during baking to insure even browning. Cool on baking sheets a minute or two; then with wide metal spatula transfer to rack to cool. Optional: Top cooled cookies with a bit of confectioners' sugar sifted over them.

Nancy Bailey, Prospect, KY

Intermission

Homemade Mayonnaise

YIELD: 1½ Cups
TOTAL CALORIES: 2208
CALORIES PER TABLESPOON: 92
PROTEIN: .5g
FAT: 10g
PREPARING: 15 Minutes

Anyone with serious interest in food should make homemade mayonnaise. Keeping in mind several guidelines, it is one of the easiest and quickest sauces to make. This mayonnaise will keep at least one week in a covered container in the refrigerator. Let it return to room temperature before using.

MAYONNAISE:

2 egg yolks (U.S. graded large or larger) or 2 whole eggs if lighter, less stiff mayonnaise is desired
½ tsp. salt
1 T. fresh lemon juice
1 tsp. prepared Dijon mustard
1-1¼ cups (240-300ml) olive oil, salad oil or a mixture of each
Freshly ground white pepper
⅛ tsp. sugar

COGNAC MAYONNAISE SAUCE:

1 T. tomato paste
2 T. (30ml) cognac

MUSTARD MAYONNAISE:

1 T. imported mustard

TARTAR SAUCE:

1 T. capers, well-drained
1 T. chopped sour pickles
1 T. finely chopped parsley
2 tsp. finely chopped shallot, onion or chives (optional)
1 tsp. chopped tarragon (optional)

REMOULADE SAUCE:

1 T. chopped anchovy fillets

GRIBICHE SAUCE: (page 367)

SAUCE VERT (GREEN MAYONNAISE):

1 cup coarsely chopped, loosely packed fresh spinach
½ cup coarsely chopped, loosely packed watercress
2 T. coarsely chopped parsley

CUCUMBER MAYONNAISE:

1 cup (110g) finely diced, peeled and seeded cucumbers
2 T. finely chopped parsley

ANCHOVY MAYONNAISE:

1 T. finely chopped anchovy fillets or 1 T. anchovy paste

WATERCRESS MAYONNAISE:

½ cup finely chopped watercress

GUIDELINES BEFORE STARTING: (1) All ingredients must be at room temperature. (2) Egg yolks must be beaten until pale yellow and creamy before adding oil. (3) Oil must be added drop by drop until oil thickens. Do not exceed ⅔ cup (160ml) oil per yolk. If you are not experienced making mayonnaise, do not use more than ½ cup (120ml) oil per egg yolk the first few times.

MIXER METHOD: In round-bottomed bowl, and using electric mixer set at medium speed, beat yolks together with salt until yolks are very pale yellow and the consistency of thick cream. Add mustard and lemon juice and beat again. Add oil, drop by drop, beating constantly. Stop pouring oil every few seconds while continuing to beat until you see that all the oil added has been absorbed by yolks and there is none floating free. Continue dribbling in oil and beating until sauce has become quite thick. When you have finished adding all the oil, (amount added will depend on variables such as yolk size) mayonnaise is done. Season to taste with salt, lemon juice, white pepper and sugar. (If sauce is to be used for fish, it should be a bit on the tart side.)

FOOD PROCESSOR METHOD: Place metal blade in food processor. Put in yolks, salt, lemon juice and mustard. Process 60 seconds. Slowly dribble in ¼ cup oil through feed tube, while machine is running. The remaining oil can be added gradually. When all oil has been added, immediately stop machine. Taste and adjust seasonings. Cover and refrigerate.

COGNAC MAYONNAISE: Add tomato paste and cognac to above mayonnaise and mix.

MUSTARD MAYONNAISE: Add mustard to above mayonnaise. Add more to taste if desired.

TARTAR SAUCE: Add capers, sour pickles and parsley to above mayonnaise. Shallots and tarragon can also be added.

REMOULADE SAUCE: Add chopped anchovies to above tartar sauce and mix.

SAUCE VERT (GREEN MAYONNAISE): Put spinach, watercress and parsley in a saucepan with boiling water to cover. When water returns to boil, simmer 1 minute. Drain in sieve, press gently to extract liquid. Put greens in square of cheesecloth and form a bag. Squeeze out as much vegetable juice as possible, reserving juice. Add reserved juice to above mayonnaise. Discard greens.

CUCUMBER MAYONNAISE: Add cucumbers and parsley to above mayonnaise and mix.

ANCHOVY MAYONNAISE: Add anchovy fillets or paste to above mayonnaise and mix.

WATERCRESS MAYONNAISE: Add watercress to above mayonnaise and mix.

Hollandaise Sauce

The difference in the preparation of a hollandaise and a mayonnaise is that hollandaise is made with egg yolks and butter, cooked over low heat and served with hot foods, while mayonnaise is made with egg yolks or whole eggs and oil, is not cooked and is served with cold foods.

YIELD: 1 Cup
CALORIES PER TABLESPOON: 76
PROTEIN: 1g
FAT: 8g
CHOLESTEROL: High
SIMMERING: 20 Minutes
FREEZING: No

MIXER METHOD: Place skillet on stove and add about ½ inch (1cm) water. Bring water to simmer.

Put egg yolks in small ovenproof glass bowl. Whisk in vinegar, salt, cayenne and heavy cream. Put bowl in simmering water and continue to whisk, keeping heat very low and water just simmering. If it boils, sauce may curdle. When mixture thickens enough to coat a spoon, continue to whisk, adding a piece of butter and whisking until it dissolves before adding another piece. Continue beating until all butter has been incorporated; then beat in lemon juice.

Cover bowl with plastic wrap to make it airtight, turn off heat under skillet and let hollandaise sit in pan of warm water up to 3 hours. If you want to reheat it, be sure to keep flame low under pan of water; do not let water boil or sauce may curdle. Stir sauce constantly when reheating.

FOOD PROCESSOR METHOD: Melt butter in saucepan over low heat.

Put metal blade in food processor and add egg yolks, vinegar, salt, cayenne and heavy cream. Process 10 seconds. Heat butter until bubbling. With processor running, gradually dribble in butter. Butter must be bubbling or sauce will not thicken. Add lemon juice and adjust seasonings.

MOUSSELINE SAUCE: Fold whipped cream into Hollandaise Sauce.

MALTAISE SAUCE: Add orange juice, grated orange rind and liqueur to Hollandaise Sauce.

BEARNAISE SAUCE: Before making Hollandaise Sauce, combine wine vinegar, shallots, tarragon and black pepper in a 1½-qt. (1.5L) saucepan. Bring to boil over direct heat and simmer until all vinegar evaporates. Remove from heat and cool slightly; then prepare hollandaise, omitting lemon juice and adding cooled shallot/tarragon mixture.

HOLLANDAISE SAUCE:

4 egg yolks
2 T. *(30ml)* **tarragon vinegar**
½ tsp. salt (scant)
Few grains cayenne pepper
¼ cup *(60ml)* **heavy cream**
¼ lb. *(115g)* **frozen, unsalted sweet butter, cut into very small pieces**
½ tsp. freshly squeezed lemon juice

MOUSSELINE SAUCE:

½ cup *(120ml)* **heavy cream, whipped**

MALTAISE SAUCE:

Juice of ½ medium orange
½ tsp. grated orange rind
2 tsp. Grand Marnier or Curacao liqueur

BEARNAISE SAUCE:

3 T. *(45ml)* **red wine vinegar**
1 T. finely chopped shallots
1 T. fresh tarragon or 1 tsp. dried
1 tsp. freshly grated black pepper

Fresh Homemade Pasta or Noodles

The words "fresh" and "homemade" are synonymous to an Italian since until comparatively recently, the only pasta consumed was made at home fresh daily. Today fresh still means homemade, not merely limp pasta made within the hour. Even if it is dry and brittle because it was made last week or last month, it is still fresh homemade pasta! And while making pasta at home requires some patience and practice, once the technique is mastered, you will discover that it is *vastly* superior to any store-bought or restaurant variety.

Directions for machine-made fresh pasta have been omitted on purpose. It simply is not as fine as hand-rolled. Machine pasta is slippery and rubbery and will not absorb as much sauce. Hand-rolled pasta is very light and delicate and absorbs sauce well. The steel rollers of the pasta machine compress the dough, while hand-rolling stretches the dough, resulting in its lighter texture.

YIELD: 3 Servings From
  1-Egg Pasta
TOTAL CALORIES: 618
CALORIES PER SERVING: 206
CARBOHYDRATES: 28g
PROTEIN: 5.5g
FAT: 8g
TOTAL CALORIES
  WHOLE WHEAT PASTA: 660
CALORIES PER SERVING: 220
CARBOHYDRATES: 29g
PROTEIN: 8g
FAT: 8g
PREPARING: 10 Minutes
RESTING: 30 Minutes
DRYING: 15-60 Minutes
COOKING: 1-9 Minutes
FREEZING: Not Necessary

BASIC EGG PASTA:

1 egg
3 T. *(45ml)* **heavy cream**
⅔ cup *(75g)* **cake flour (non-rising kind)**
⅓ cup *(35g)* **unbleached flour**
½ tsp. **salt**

SPINACH PASTA:

1 egg
3 T. *(45ml)* **heavy cream**
⅔ cup *(75g)* **cake flour**
⅓ cup *(35g)* **unbleached flour**
½ tsp. **salt**
2½ oz. *(70g)* **fresh or frozen spinach, dried or drained, chopped**

WHOLE WHEAT PASTA:

1 egg
3 T. *(45ml)* **heavy cream**
1 cup *(140g)* **whole wheat pastry flour (available at a health food store)**
½ tsp. **salt**

PIMIENTO PASTA:

1 egg
3 T. *(45ml)* **heavy cream**
⅔ cup *(75g)* **cake flour**
⅓ cup *(35g)* **unbleached flour**
½ tsp. **salt**
2 oz. *(60g)* **drained pimientos**

WORK TABLE METHOD: Mix together egg and cream; beat until foamy. Sift together flours onto pastry board or work table and add salt. Make a well in center of flour 10 inches *(25cm)* in diameter. Pour egg-cream mixture into well. Add chopped spinach now if making spinach pasta. Using a fork, start to mix in 2 T. flour at a time from inside rim of well. When it becomes difficult to use fork, continue with tips of your fingers. Form ball of dough as quickly as possible and knead with heel of your hand until dough is smooth. Cover dough with waxed paper; set aside for 30 minutes to relax.

Sprinkle flour on pastry board and rolling pin. Cut dough into 2 pieces. (This step is not necessary if you are an expert pasta maker. In Italy, a professional pasta roller can easily make 8-egg pasta in one roll. A novice must start with ½-egg pasta in order to get desired results before dough dries out and becomes tough and impossible to roll.) Roll out each piece of dough into a circle. Roll dough *as thin as possible*, until you can see grain of wood in your pastry board through dough. Flour table and rolling pin as much as needed.

Lay sheets of dough on top of towel and drape towel over back of chair, allowing dough to dry out just enough, so that it will not stick together when cut. It can take 15 to 60 minutes, depending on how dry and hot the kitchen is. *Do not*, however, let it dry out completely so that it is brittle.

Cut dough into size and shape noodle called for in the recipe you are preparing. If making long thin noodles, roll dough up jelly-roll fashion and with a sharp cleaver or large chef's knife, slice into appropriate widths. Uncoil strands and let dry until ready to cook, or indefinitely. If planning to store indefinitely, let noodles dry out several days to prevent mold from forming when wrapped airtight.

When ready to cook, drop into large amount of rapidly boiling water and cook *al dente*. Start testing after 1 minute. Drain thoroughly.

FOOD PROCESSOR METHOD: Beat together eggs and cream and herbs, spinach, or pimiento if applicable. All at once, dump in sifted flours and salt. Turn on machine and let run until ball is formed. Immediately stop machine and wrap dough in plastic wrap. Let rest, then follow above directions for completion of rolling dough.

ELECTRIC MIXER METHOD: Place eggs and cream in bowl; beat until well-blended. All at once, dump in sifted flours and salt. Beat until ball forms. Remove from bowl and knead with heel of hand until smooth. Wrap in plastic wrap, let rest, then follow above directions for completion of rolling dough.

Variations, Advance Preparation, and Serving Suggestions: When using delicately flavored foods like scallops choose egg pasta, as whole wheat pasta would overwhelm the delicate flavor.

Nutritional Notes: Pasta is readily combined with a variety of sauces, fresh, sauteed or steamed vegetables, and small quantities of meat, poultry or seafood. Pasta salads are gaining popularity as well. A large variety pasta — whole wheat, spinach, soy, etc. has made this food a versatile addition to most diets. Pasta is not necessarily fattening. Caloric value is dependent on (1) with what it is served (cream sauce vs. lower-calorie fresh tomato sauce) and (2) quantity eaten.

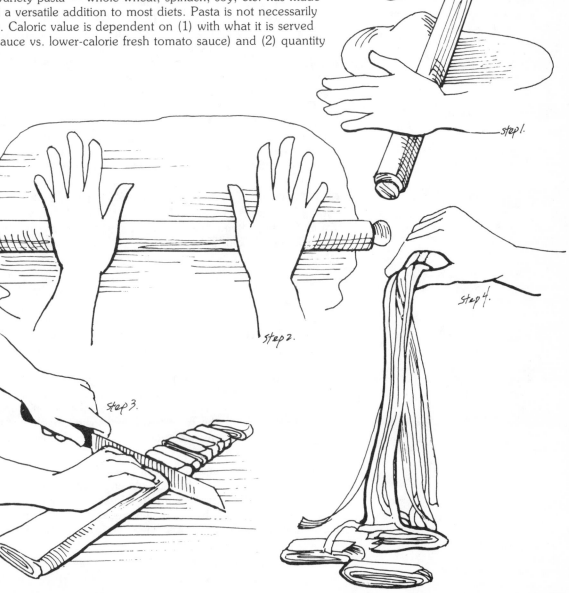

step 1.

step 2.

step 3.

step 4.

Feuilletage Classique

CLASSIC PUFF PASTRY

Homemade puff pastry is far superior to any commercial product on the market. Once the technique is mastered, large quantities can be made and frozen for later use.

YIELD: 1 lb. Pastry
CALORIES: 2403
CARBOHYDRATES: 167g
PROTEIN: 22g
FAT: 183g
CHOLESTEROL: High
PREPARING: 30 Minutes
CHILLING: 7-48 Hours
FREEZING: Yes-Very Well

PASTRY:

1 cup plus 6 T. *(155g)* all-purpose flour
6 T. *(40g)* non-rising cake flour
1 tsp. salt
3 T. *(45g)* unsalted sweet cold butter
½ cup *(120ml)* ice water

BUTTER PATTLE:

13 T. or 6½ oz. *(185g)* unsalted sweet cold butter

Extra flour for work table

Sift flours and salt together onto work table. Set aside for later use ¼ cup *(45g)* of this flour mixture. Make a well exactly 10 inches *(25cm)* in diameter in center of flour so that work surface is almost exposed. Quickly cut the 3 T. butter into small pieces; spread over bottom of well, but not on flour. Immediately pour ice water over butter in well. Now as fast as possible mix flour, butter and water together with fingertips, starting from inside rim of well until water will not escape, then swirl in all flour. Gather pastry with pastry scraper into a ball. At first, it will be very loose, but it will take shape. Work quickly. *[FOOD PROCESSOR: Place flours and salt in work bowl; process 2 seconds. Remove ¼ cup flour and reserve. Cut 3 T. butter into small pieces and place it over flour; process 2 seconds. With machine running, pour ice water through feed tube in a fast steady stream. As soon as a ball of dough forms, process 2 minutes.]* Wrap pastry in waxed paper and freeze ½ hour or refrigerate 1½ hours.

BUTTER PATTLE: Pound on 13 T. cold butter to make it workable. After 20 seconds or so, sprinkle reserved ¼ cup flour over butter. Then with heel of your hand, knead together so butter will be very smooth, yet still cold. Place butter on piece of waxed paper; shape into 6-inch *(15cm)* pattle. Wrap and refrigerate.

Lightly flour work table and rolling pin. Roll chilled pastry into 12-inch *(30cm)* circle. Place butter pattle in center. Wrap butter with pastry; place seam-side down on table. Roll pastry into rectangle 8 × 18 inches *(20 × 45cm)*. Start rolling with short strokes. You will have ridges on surface of pastry. Smooth them with rolling pin coming back toward you. Always roll from nearest to you to farthest and then come back toward yourself. Check under pastry to see that butter is not oozing out. Dust under pastry if necessary. Fold rectangle in thirds like business letter. The first fold is nearest you and the last fold farthest from you. You have now accomplished *one turn*. Then turn pastry counterclockwise so that it looks like a book with binding on left. On the right, pastry can be opened like a book. You are ready for *second turn*.

Roll out another rectangle of previous size. It will be harder to roll because butter is getting softer and gluten in pastry more elastic. Work quickly. Fold pastry again into thirds. With fingers, mark two indentations to indicate two turns have been made. Wrap pastry in waxed paper and then in plastic bag. Refrigerate a minimum 2 hours.

Roll pastry two more turns. Again mark with fingers to indicate *four turns* have been completed. Refrigerate overnight.

The next day roll pastry a final two turns and it is finished. Six turns have been completed. Let stand in refrigerator overnight. Next day, roll out and cut into any desired shape.

Variations, Advance Preparation, and Serving Suggestions:
Do not keep pastry more than 5 days in refrigerator. After pastry has been cut and shaped, it may be frozen until solid and then wrapped well. When ready to use, put directly into hot oven without thawing. Unshaped pastry can be frozen, but expect some loss of lightness since you will be reworking pastry. Best not to make on hot humid days. Cream can be used instead of water for extremely light, tender, delicate pastry. Once you have mastered the basic technique, you can easily double this recipe.

Pâte à Choux

CREAM PUFF DOUGH

This dough is used for eclairs, cream puffs, cocktail puffs, and classic French recipes like pommes dauphine, quenelles, and gougere. It is always made with a *panade* — a combination of butter, flour, and water — to which eggs are added.

YIELD: 2½ Cups Dough or
  2 Gougere Rings or
  16 Eclairs or
  16 Cream Puffs or
  48 Profiteroles
TOTAL CALORIES: 1775
CALORIES PER 1/16 DOUGH: 112
CARBOHYDRATES: 7g
PROTEIN: 3g
FAT: 8g
PREPARING: 10 Minutes
FREEZING: Yes

Into a saucepan measure water, butter and salt. Bring to a boil over moderate heat — butter should be just melted by that point. (If water boils before butter has melted, too much moisture may evaporate, altering consistency of paste. If lumps of butter remain when boiling begins, remove pan from heat and wait until butter has melted.)

Remove pan from heat; add flour all at once. Stir mixture quickly with a wooden spoon or spatula (it will resemble mashed potatoes) and return pan to medium heat. Stir vigorously to dry out pastry slightly, which should take about 30 seconds; when it has dried enough, it will be a shiny mass. Remove pan from the heat and allow the paste to cool for a moment or two.

You may now wish to transfer the mixture to a bowl before incorporating eggs, although it is not necessary; or you may complete the paste in an electric mixer (work on medium low speed) or food processor, which is especially helpful when making large batches. Add 2 of the eggs and beat to blend thoroughly. (Note, that when eggs are added, the pate a choux first separates into strands, which cohere with more beating.) Add remaining 2 eggs and again blend thoroughly. The pastry should now be soft enough to cling to sides of pan or bowl. If after incorporating all the eggs, the pastry is not soft enough to cling to spoon or spatula, you may need to add a little more egg so that pastry will puff when baked.

If paste is not to be used immediately, cover surface closely with plastic wrap to prevent skin forming. The paste will keep about 4 hours at room temperature; 3 or 4 days in the refrigerator; or 4 months, well wrapped and frozen.

1 cup *(240ml)* **cold water**
½ cup *(115g)* **unsalted sweet butter, cut into small pieces**
½ tsp. **salt**
1 cup *(115g)* **flour, dipped and levelled**
4 **large eggs**

2 T. *(25g)* **sugar and 1 tsp. pure vanilla extract should be added if making a sweet dough**

YIELD: 1 9-Inch Tart or
   30 Tartlet Shells
TOTAL CALORIES: 2460
CALORIES PER TARTLET: 82
CARBOHYDRATES: 7g
PROTEIN: 1g
FAT: 5.5g
CHOLESTEROL: High
PREPARING: 15 Minutes
CHILLING: 2 Hours Minimum
FREEZING: Yes-Very Well

Rich Tart Pastry

Tart pastry is easy to make, even for a beginner, because there is little danger in overhandling. Its consistency after being baked is not flaky; it is short, crisp, and delicate — comparable to a rich cookie dough. This crust may even outlast the edibility of its filling! Even after being kept for several days, crust will remain crisp and delicious.

2 cups *(225g)* **sifted flour**
3 T. *(40g)* **sugar**
¾ cup *(170g)* **butter (softened for mixer, but firm and broken into several pieces for processor)**
½ tsp. salt
1 T. grated lemon rind
3 hard-cooked egg yolks, mashed
2 raw egg yolks (or to make pastry less fragile and crisper in texture, substitute 2 egg whites)

HAND METHOD: Place flour in bowl. Make a well in the center; add remaining ingredients. Butter should not be ice cold, nor should it be so soft it is oily. With fingertips, make a paste of center ingredients, gradually incorporating flour to form a smooth firm ball of dough. Work quickly so butter does not become oily. When sides of bowl are left clean, pastry is finished. Wrap it in waxed paper; chill until firm enough to roll.

Roll pastry between sheets of waxed paper.

ELECTRIC MIXER METHOD: Place flour in largest bowl of electric mixer. Make a well in center; to it add remaining ingredients. With mixer on low speed, beat ingredients until well combined, pushing flour from sides to center of bowl with spatula. When flour is completely incorporated, stop machine. Form pastry into a ball, wrap in plastic wrap and chill until firm enough to roll.

FOOD PROCESSOR METHOD: Place flour, sugar, butter, salt, lemon rind and hard-cooked yolks in work bowl. Turn machine on/off until mixture resembles coarse meal. With machine running, add raw egg yolks or egg whites through feed tube. Once dough forms a ball, remove and press flat, wrap in plastic and chill.

Variations, Advance Preparation, and Serving Suggestions:
Unbaked tart pastry can be frozen for months and will taste even better because of the extra chilling. Freeze the dough as is or roll it out and cut it to fit a variety of tart pans or flan rings. The latter method allows you to have a complete tart ready on a moment's notice.

BAKING INSTRUCTION FOR VARIOUS TARTS: Always bake *a filled tart shell* on the lowest rack so maximum heat will be directed to the bottom of the pastry. *Unfilled tart shells* should be baked on the center rack of the oven. Tarts large and small are baked in 350° oven.

TO BAKE UNFILLED TARTLET SHELLS: Place tartlets on baking sheet. Bake on second rack from bottom, about 15 minutes or until shells are light brown. Prick each shell 2 or 3 times with a fork during first 5 minutes of baking when air bubbles appear. Cool baked pastry slightly before removing from tins.

TO BAKE FILLED TARTLET SHELLS: Fill tart ¾ full. Place on baking sheet and bake on lowest oven rack about 20 minutes, or until pastry is golden and filling is set.

TO BAKE UNFILLED TART SHELL: Prick bottom all over with a fork (if frozen, do not thaw) and place on second rack from bottom in oven. Prick 3 or 4 times during first 10 minutes of baking to prevent bottom from puffing up. Bake a total of 25 minutes, or until shell is golden brown.

Walnut Tart Pastry

A superb short pastry or sweet pie dough.

YIELD: 1 10- or 12-Inch Tart
TOTAL CALORIES: 2800
CALORIES PER 1/8 DOUGH: 350
CARBOHYDRATES: 38g
PROTEIN: 5g
FAT: 20g
PREPARING: 15 Minutes
FREEZING: Yes-Very Well

Combine flour, salt and cinnamon; mix with fork and add walnuts. Make a well in center of mixture. Put butter, sugar, egg, vanilla and water in well. Mix with fork until dough can be formed into a ball. *[FOOD PROCESSOR: Process unchopped nuts with flour, salt and cinnamon until nuts are finely chopped. Remove and set aside. Add remaining ingredients to work bowl and combine by turning machine on/off 4 times. Then process 10 seconds. Add nut/flour mixture and process just until mixture forms a mass of dough. Do not over-process. Do not allow dough to form a ball. Gather dough and place in plastic bag. Shape first into a ball and then flatten into a disc.]* Wrap in plastic wrap and chill 60 minutes. Roll between sheets of waxed paper.

Ann Howard Cookery, Farmington, CT
via Lee Grimmeisen, West Hartford, CT

2 cups *(225g)* **flour**
1/8 tsp. **salt**
2 tsp. **cinnamon**
1/2 cup *(65g)* **finely chopped walnuts**
10 T. *(140g)* **cold butter, cut into small pieces**
1/2 cup *(100g)* **sugar**
1 **egg**
1/2 tsp. **pure vanilla extract**
1 1/2 T. *(22.5ml)* **water (may not need if mixing in a food processor)**

Almond Short Pastry

This sweet pie dough is quite different from Basic Pie Crust. The texture is not flaky or tender, but rather is close to that of cookie dough. It is not at all elastic or springy. It makes an excellent shell for a sweet runny filling because it does not get soggy as easily as regular pie dough.

YIELD: 1 9-inch Tart or
      24 Tartlet Shells
TOTAL CALORIES: 3288
CALORIES PER
   TARTLET SHELL: 137
CARBOHYDRATES: 11g
PROTEIN: 3g
FAT: 9g
CHOLESTEROL: High
PREPARING: 15 Minutes
CHILLING: 2 Hours Minimum
FREEZING: Yes-Very Well

ELECTRIC MIXER METHOD: Cream together raw egg yolks and almond paste; set aside.

Place flour in largest bowl of electric mixer. Make a well in center; to it add creamed almond paste mixture and all remaining ingredients. Beating on low speed, mix until all ingredients are well combined, pushing flour from sides to center of bowl with a spatula. As soon as flour is completely incorporated, stop machine. Form pastry into a ball, wrap in plastic wrap and chill until firm enough to roll.

Roll between sheets of waxed paper.

FOOD PROCESSOR METHOD: Grind almonds with sugar in processor; set aside. Cream raw egg yolks and almond paste in processor; set aside. Wipe bowl clean and add flour, salt, lemon rind, butter, spices and cooked egg yolks. Turn machine on/off until mixture resembles coarse meal. With machine running, add almond paste mixture through feed tube. Once dough forms a ball, remove, press flat, wrap in plastic and chill.

3 raw **egg yolks**
1/2 cup *(115g)* **almond paste**
1 1/4 cups *(140g)* **sifted flour**
2/3 cup *(100g)* **unblanched ground almonds**
1/3 cup *(65g)* **sugar**
1/2 tsp. **salt**
1 tsp. **grated lemon rind**
1/2 cup *(115g)* **butter (softened for mixer but firm and broken into several pieces for processor)**
Pinch **ground cloves**
1/4 tsp. **cinnamon**
2 **hard-cooked egg yolks, mashed**

YIELD: Dough for 4 9-Inch Crusts
TOTAL CALORIES PER CRUST: 1272
CALORIES PER ⅛ OF 1 CRUST: 159
CARBOHYDRATES: 13g
PROTEIN: 2g
FAT: 11g
SODIUM: High
PREPARING: 15 Minutes
CHILLING: 15 Minutes Minimum
FREEZING: Yes-Very Well

4 cups *(450g)* flour
1¾ cups *(340g)* vegetable shortening
   (Crisco preferred)
¼ cup *(50g)* sugar (omit if filling is not
   sweet)
2 tsp. salt
1 T. white vinegar
1 egg
¼ cup *(60ml)* ice water

Basic Pie Crust

With pastry blender or fork, mix flour, shortening, sugar and salt together until mixture resembles coarse meal. In separate bowl beat together vinegar, egg and ice water. Add to flour mixture. Mix until moistened and form into ball. *[FOOD PROCESSOR: Put shortening, sugar, salt, egg, vinegar and water in work bowl. Combine them by turning machine on/off 5 or 6 times, then process 5 seconds. There may be small lumps of shortening. Add flour and process just until mixture forms a mass of dough. Do not overprocess. Do not allow dough to form a ball. Put dough and any scraps into plastic bag. Work through bag to press dough into a ball. Divide dough into 4 separate balls at this time and flatten each into a disc.]* Divide dough into 4 balls. Wrap dough in plastic wrap and chill a minimum 15 minutes, or overnight, or freeze.

Sandra P. Robinson, Farmington, CT

YIELD: 2 Quarts
TOTAL CALORIES: 1475
CALORIES PER 1 CUP: 184
CARBOHYDRATES: 6g
PROTEIN: 4g
FAT: 16g
SODIUM: High
PREPARING: 45 Minutes
COOKING: 5 Hours

2 T. *(30ml)* vegetable oil
1 carrot, diced
1 onion, diced
2 lbs. *(900g)* chicken or turkey bones or
   wings
2 lbs. *(900g)* veal bones, cut in pieces
1 cup *(240ml)* Madeira or ruby port wine
1½ cups *(355ml)* dry white wine
3 cups *(710ml)* red wine
1 qt. *(950ml)* commercial chicken stock
1 bouquet garni
4 cloves garlic
½ lb. *(225g)* salt pork, cubed and
   blanched
1 oz. *(30g)* dried imported mushrooms

Poultry Stock Sauce Base

An excellent *concentrated stock* that can be used any time a hearty recipe calls for a cup or two of good homemade stock as part of a sauce.

In large ovenproof casserole, heat oil. Add carrot and onion. Cover tightly and cook over moderate heat until vegetables wilt.

Add poultry pieces and veal bones and cook until meat turns golden. Immediately add Madeira and boil until reduced by half. Add white wine and again reduce by half. Add red wine, stock, bouquet garni, garlic, salt pork, and mushrooms. Bring to a boil; cover tightly and cook in 300° oven 5 hours. If necessary, add more chicken stock so that you end up with 2 qts. *(2L)* liquid.

Pour liquid through fine sieve into tall container. Cool completely and leave solid fat on top. Cover and refrigerate. Freeze in convenient portions for future use.

Variations, Advance Preparation, and Serving Suggestions: This stock base is not suitable for fish sauces or light colored sauces.

Microwave Conversion Instructions: In small covered glass container, cook onion and carrot 5 minutes on High. Set aside. Brown poultry pieces and veal bones in 2 T. oil in dutch oven on conventional range; add Madeira and boil until reduced by half. Add white wine and again reduce by half. Transfer mixture to very large glass casserole. Add red wine, stock, bouquet garni, garlic, salt pork (blanched by cooking in 1½ cups water 10 minutes on High) and mushrooms. Cover, cook 2 hours on Medium (50%) stirring occasionally. If necessary, add more chicken stock so that you have 2 qts. liquid.

Toast Boxes

An unusual and delicious way to serve any type of creamed dish or stew, boxes take the place of more traditional rice or noodle accompaniment.

YIELD: 12 Boxes
CALORIES PER BOX: 412
CARBOHYDRATES: 26g
PROTEIN: 5g
FAT: 32g
PREPARING: 35 Minutes
BAKING: 10-15 Minutes
FREEZING: Yes

Slice off all crusts from loaves. (Dry out all excess bread and crusts for homemade bread crumbs). Slice each loaf crosswise into 3 equal cubes. Each cube will be approximately 3 inches (7.5cm) square. To shape each box, place a single cube flat on a cutting surface. Cut around inside of cube a generous ¼ inch (0.6cm) from the sides and no deeper than ¼ inch (0.6cm) up from bottom. Then slip knife through only 1 side of box ¼ inch (0.6cm) up from bottom and cut across that one side to release center piece of bread. Lift the center cube out and discard or add to bread crumb reserves. Quickly dip bread boxes into melted butter on all sides and place on cookie sheet. Cover with plastic wrap and leave at room temperature or refrigerate overnight.

When ready to serve, bake in preheated 350° oven 10 to 15 minutes or until golden brown.

Variations, Advance Preparation, and Serving Suggestions:
Boxes can be prepared several days ahead and refrigerated until ready to bake. The recipe can be doubled, tripled, etc. to serve a large crowd. Toast Boxes can be used for scrambled eggs or other egg dishes such as Creole Egg Casserole (page 107). Other stews and casseroles suitable for serving with Toast Boxes include: Mushroom or Oyster Croustades (page 204), Chicken Armando (page 310), Blanquette of Lamb (page 290), Veal Marengo (page 282), Veal a l'Orange (page 283), Beef Curry (page 276) and Stifado (page 273).

4 loaves (1 lb. each) *(450g each)* unsliced, firm-textured white bread
1 lb. *(450g)* butter, melted (do not substitute margarine)

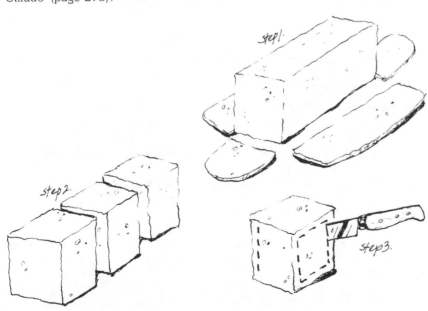

YIELD: 2½ Cups
TOTAL CALORIES: 1000
CALORIES PER ¼ CUP: 100
CARBOHYDRATES: 12g
PROTEIN: 4g
FAT: 4g
CHOLESTEROL: High
PREPARING: 30 Minutes

2 cups *(475ml)* **milk**
½ vanilla bean, split lengthwise and scraped
5 egg yolks, at room temperature
½ cup *(100g)* **sugar**

Crème Anglaise

ENGLISH CUSTARD SAUCE

Scald milk with vanilla bean in heavy saucepan. Meanwhile, beat yolks and sugar together on high speed until thick, pale yellow, and ribbony, about 5 minutes. Remove and discard vanilla bean. Very slowly pour hot milk into yolk mixture, whisking constantly. Transfer to heavy saucepan. Cook, stirring constantly with wooden spoon, over very low heat, until mixture thickens enough to coat spoon, 20 to 25 minutes. (Do not allow to boil or mixture will curdle.) Strain custard all at once into another bowl. Stir frequently until cool. Cover and refrigerate until cold. Stir again before serving.

Variations, Advance Preparation, and Serving Suggestions:
An excellent sauce for fresh fruits, Fresh Fruit Terrine (page 70), Lemon-Poppy Seed Pound Cake (page 399), and various hot or cold souffles.

Crème Fraîche

Creme fraiche is actually soured cream. However, it is far superior to commercial cream (although it has about twice the calories) and is widely used in French cooking. While sour cream may curdle in a hot sauce, creme fraiche will not and is therefore very practical to have. Unlike commercial sour cream, it can be whipped. Be careful not to overwhip because it can suddenly turn to butter. It can be kept in the refrigerator a month, and will get thicker and better. Sugared creme fraiche, whipped or plain, is a delicious accompaniment to baked apples, poached pears and all berries. It is lovely with fruit tarts and many chocolate desserts, and can also be used in many salad dressings or as a garnish with cold poached vegetables.

YIELD: 2 Cups
CALORIES PER ½ CUP: 400
CALORIES PER TABLESPOON: 50
CARBOHYDRATES: .5g
PROTEIN: .5g
FAT: 5g
CHOLESTEROL: High
PREPARING: 2 Minutes
STANDING: 24-48 Hours

2 cups *(475ml)* **heavy cream**
5 tsp. *(25ml)* **buttermilk**

Combine cream and buttermilk in screwtop jar. Shake jar for 60 seconds, then let stand at room temperature 24 hours. If room is especially cool, let it stand an extra 12 to 24 hours. When cream thickens refrigerate at least 24 hours, preferably longer, before using. Keeps well 2 to 4 weeks.

Variations, Advance Preparation, and Serving Suggestions:
For an even thicker consistency, more nearly duplicating that which is commercially available in France, use following ingredients and method: 1 cup *(240ml)* sour cream and 2 cups *(475ml)* heavy cream. Put sour cream in large mixing bowl. Slowly whisk in heavy cream until thoroughly mixed. Cover with plastic wrap and put in warm place 8 to 24 hours or longer, until mixture has thickened. Place a plastic coffee filter holder or a strainer in mixing bowl and insert coffee filter or double layer of cheesecloth. Pour thickened cream into filter or cheesecloth. Cover with plastic wrap, refrigerate and leave to drain 24 to 36 hours. Remove cream and place in a covered container until ready to use. Reserve the whey in mixing bowl for use in place of ice water in pie crusts or add to soup or soup stock.

The Best of
The Five Arts

Yellow Bird Punch

YIELD: 32 ½-Cup Servings
CALORIES PER SERVING: 155
CARBOHYDRATES: 14g
PREPARING: 10 Minutes
FREEZING: Yes — Ice Ring

You'll fly away after a sample of this brew!

1 can (46 oz.) *(1.36L)* pineapple juice
1 can (12 oz.) *(340g)* frozen orange juice
   concentrate mixed with 2 cans water
1 qt. *(950ml)* light rum
½ pt. *(240ml)* apricot brandy
½ pt. *(240ml)* Galiano

In a large punch bowl, combine all ingredients in order given. Add ice cubes or an attractive ice ring or mold.

"The Happy Cookers", Bloomfield, CT
Anita MacDonald
Mary Cagenello

Raspberry Punch

YIELD: 28 ½-Cup Servings
TOTAL CALORIES: 4816
CALORIES PER SERVING: 172
CARBOHYDRATES: 43g

This is an excellent punch for everyone; non-carbonated, non-alcoholic and not too sweet.

2 cups *(400g)* sugar
2 cups *(475ml)* water
2 cans (12 oz. each) *(710ml)* frozen pink
   lemonade concentrate
2½ pts. *(1425g)* frozen raspberries,
   thawed
½ gal. *(1.9L)* raspberry sherbet
1 sprig fresh mint (optional)

Mix together sugar and water; boil 5 minutes; set aside.

Dilute concentrated lemonade according to directions on lemonade containers.

In large pitcher, combine lemonade and sugar-water mixture. Crush 1 cup of raspberries, reserving the rest for a garnish; add to container.

When ready to serve, put sherbet in punch bowl; add ingredients from container, and remaining raspberries as garnish. Add a sprig of mint if desired.

Alyce S. Kohlmann, Granby, CT

Coffee Punch

YIELD: 20-30 Servings
CALORIES PER SERVING: 150
CARBOHYDRATES: 11g
PROTEIN: 2g
FAT: 11g
CHOLESTEROL: High
PREPARING: 30 Minutes
CHILLING: Overnight

A particularly good non-alcoholic punch! Especially appropriate for a late morning or early afternoon tea or holiday cookie exchange.

1 gal. *(3.75L)* very strong coffee, cooled
½ gal. *(1.9L)* good coffee ice cream
   (page 140)
1 pt. *(475ml)* good French vanilla ice
   cream (page 140)
1 pt. *(475ml)* heavy cream, whipped
Cinnamon

Chill coffee overnight. With a hand mixer, blend coffee and half of coffee ice cream to fairly thick consistency. Transfer to punch bowl, refrigerate. Make ice cream balls of vanilla ice cream and remaining coffee ice cream. Add to coffee mixture. Top with dollops of whipped cream. Sprinkle with cinnamon.

Judy Webb, Darien, CT

Variations, Advance Preparation, and Serving Suggestions:
You might like to add Kahlua to taste after you have blended the coffee and coffee ice cream.

Boursin Cheese

Commercial spiced French cheese with garlic and herbs is costly. Here is a duplicate you can create with your food processor in 5 minutes. Freeze portions for do-ahead holiday gifts.

YIELD: 5½ Cups
CALORIES PER TABLESPOON: 58
CARBOHYDRATES: Trace
PROTEIN: 1g
FAT: 6g
CHOLESTEROL: High
SODIUM: High
PREPARING: 5 Minutes
CHILLING: 2 Hours
FREEZING: Yes

In electric mixer or food processor, put garlic, cream cheese and butter; blend until smooth. Add dressing and optional seasonings; mix well. Place in individual containers, covered. Chill several hours before serving. Will keep in refrigerator two weeks. Serve with water crackers and crudites.

Mary D. Cianciolo, Simsbury, CT

Variations, Advance Preparation, and Serving Suggestions:
Freeze portions not being used. Thaw individual containers as needed at room temperature 2 hours before serving.

Wine Suggestion: California Navalle Chablis, dry white; serve chilled.

4 cloves garlic, finely minced
3 pkg. (8 oz. each) *(680g)* cream cheese, softened
¾ cup *(170g)* butter, softened
1 bottle (8 oz.) *(240ml)* Green Goddess dressing, chilled (Seven Seas preferred)
Dash freshly ground pepper (optional)
Pinch chives (optional)
Pinch parsley (optional)

Cheese Delights

An easy-to-make and savory addition to a cocktail party.

YIELD: 3 Cups Spread
TOTAL CALORIES EXCLUDING
   BREAD: 2050
CALORIES PER TABLESPOON: 43
CARBOHYDRATES: .5g
PROTEIN: 3g
FAT: 3g
CHOLESTEROL: High
SODIUM: High
PREPARING: 45 Minutes
COOKING: 3 Minutes
FREEZING: Yes

Put all ingredients except bread through food chopper or processor. Blend until smooth. Spread on party rye rounds. Broil 2 inches from direct heat until brown and bubbly.

"The Happy Cookers", Bloomfield, CT
Anita MacDonald and Mary Cagenello

Variations, Advance Preparation, and Serving Suggestions:
Spread rounds may be placed on baking sheet and frozen; remove to plastic bags. When ready to serve, place on baking sheet and broil.

Nutritional Notes: A reduced-sodium and saturated-fat version is possible with the use of cheese *made from skim milk* and the elimination of the bacon and salt. The green pepper and onion alone will lend a zesty flavor. The result also saves approximately 40 calories per serving. 1 slice party rye has 40 calories and 8g carbohydrates.

1 lb. *(450g)* sharp Cheddar cheese
½ green pepper
1 medium onion
3 strips *(75g)* raw bacon
Salt and freshly ground pepper
Dash Worcestershire sauce
1 egg
2 loaves party rye rounds

YIELD: 48 Pieces
TOTAL CALORIES WITH
 MUSHROOM FILLING: 5136
 CALORIES PER PIECE: 107
 CARBOHYDRATES: 9g
 PROTEIN: 2g
 FAT: 7g
TOTAL CALORIES WITH
 OYSTER FILLING: 4896
 CALORIES PER PIECE: 102
 CARBOHYDRATES: 9g
 PROTEIN: 3g
 FAT: 6g
PREPARING: 1 Hour
BAKING: 20 Minutes
FREEZING: Yes

Mushroom or Oyster Croustades

CROUSTADES:

48 slices thin white bread
½ lb. (225g) butter, melted

MUSHROOM DUXELLES FILLING:

1 lb. (450g) fresh mushrooms
¼ lb. (115g) unsalted sweet butter
6 shallots, chopped
Salt
Freshly ground black pepper
¼-½ cup (60-120ml) Madeira wine
½ cup (120ml) cream
1 tsp. lemon juice
1 T. chopped fresh parsley
½ cup (65g) freshly grated Parmesan cheese

CREAMED OYSTER FILLING:

1 medium onion, finely chopped
¼ lb. (115g) butter, melted
4-6 green onions, finely chopped
½ cup (50g) flour
48 small fresh oysters (approx. 2 pints) and their liquor, strained but reserved
⅓ cup chopped parsley
¼ cup (30g) finely chopped celery
½ tsp. thyme
1 scant tsp. salt
Dash cayenne pepper
2 bay leaves

CROUSTADES: Cut each slice of bread into a 3-inch *(7.5cm)* round. Brush each round with melted butter. Brush tiny muffin tins with melted butter. Carefully fit bread rounds into muffin tins. Bake in 400° oven 10 minutes. Remove to a baking sheet.

MUSHROOM FILLING: Wipe mushrooms with damp towel. Mince as finely as possible. A handful at a time, wring mushrooms out in a tea towel, extracting as much juice as possible.

Melt butter in skillet; add shallots and cook over high heat for a few minutes, stirring with wooden spoon until transparent. Do not let them brown. Add mushrooms, stirring constantly until all liquid is evaporated. (This may take 15 minutes.) Season with salt and pepper. Stir in Madeira; cook 2-3 minutes. Stir in cream, lemon juice, and parsley. Raise heat and cook until thickened. (Duxelles mixture may be frozen at this point.)

Fill croustades with duxelles mixture; sprinkle each with Parmesan. Bake about 10 minutes in 350° oven. Serve immediately.

CREAMED OYSTER FILLING: Saute onion in butter until light brown. Add green onion and flour, stirring until well blended. Add oysters and their liquor and all remaining ingredients. Simmer over low heat until oysters just curl. (May be done ahead to this point and gently reheated.) Fill croustades and reheat 10 minutes in 350° oven. Serve immediately.

Joan Larkins, West Hartford, CT

Variations, Advance Preparation, and Serving Suggestions:
Oyster Croustades make a lovely luncheon entree serving 6; make 6 Toast Boxes (page 199) instead of croustades.

Microwave Conversion Instructions: Prepare croustades as directed in recipe. Fillings may be prepared in the microwave, then baked in conventional oven as directed.

MUSHROOM DUXELLES FILLING: Prepare mushrooms as directed. Place shallots and butter in 2-qt. *(2L)* bowl. Cook High uncovered 2 minutes. Stir in mushrooms, continue cooking about 10 to 12 minutes, until all liquid is evaporated. Season with salt and pepper, stir in ¼ cup Madeira, cook 3 minutes. Stir in cream, lemon juice and parsley. Finish recipe conventionally.

CREAMED OYSTER FILLING: Place onion with butter on top in a 3-qt. (3L) bowl. Cook High uncovered 4 to 5 minutes, until light brown. Add green onion and flour, stir until well blended. Strain in the oyster liquor, add parsley, celery, and seasonings. Bring to a boil. Timing will depend upon the amount of liquid in oysters. When heated, stir in oysters. Cook uncovered, on Medium (50%) 2 to 3 minutes, stirring once or twice, until oysters just curl. Avoid over-cooking by removing oysters as they curl and allowing the remaining ones to finish.

Chinese Rumaki

The Chinese cook creates a harmony between salty foods and sweet ones. The rumaki are typical of the eastern region of China.

YIELD: 24 Bite-Size Pieces
TOTAL CALORIES: 600
CALORIES PER PIECE: 25
CARBOHYDRATES: 1g
PROTEIN: 1g
FAT: 2g
SODIUM: High
PREPARING: 25 Minutes
BAKING: 20 Minutes
MARINATING: 45 Minutes
FREEZING: Yes

Cut each water chestnut in half. Marinate in soy sauce to cover, 45 minutes. Drain. Roll in sugar. Wrap bacon around water chestnut and secure with a toothpick. (Up to this point may be made in morning). Place on rack on foil-lined pan. Bake in 400° oven, 20 minutes or until bacon is crisp. (Up to this point, prepare day before, cool, refrigerate, place on foil and reheat at 350° for 7 minutes). Serve immediately on decorative platter around a bowl of Indian chutney for optional dipping.

Marshall B. Beirne, Wethersfield, CT

1 can (8 oz.) (225g) water chestnuts, drained
Soy sauce
Granulated sugar
½ lb. (225g) bacon, cut in thirds

SAUCE:
Indian chutney

Variations, Advance Preparation, and Serving Suggestions: The recipe can be doubled or tripled successfully and the rumaki frozen; thaw briefly to reheat.

Nutritional Notes: Indian chutney generally has 14 calories per 1 teaspoon. Chinese water chestnuts, a product of the water plant which bears this fruit, have a very different nutritional make up than most common nuts. They are actually a vegetable and have about ⅛ the calories of an equal weight of common nuts.

Microwave Conversion Instructions: Follow directions for preparation. Place 12 at a time in a circle on paper towel-lined plate, or rack, cover with paper towel to absorb splatter. Cook on High 4 minutes, or just until bacon becomes crisp. Turn over, cover and cook an additional 1 to 2 minutes, or until bacon is cooked. Timing will depend on fat content and thickness of bacon used.

Reheating directions: Place on rack, or paper-lined plate in a circle, cover with paper towel. Reheat on Medium High (70%) for 2 to 3 minutes.

YIELD: 40 Canapes
CALORIES PER CANAPE: 100
CARBOHYDRATES: 4g
PROTEIN: 1g
FAT: 9g
SODIUM: High
PREPARING: 20 Minutes
BROILING: 3-4 Minutes
FREEZING: Yes

Black Olive Canapés

A tasty and easy-to-assemble hors d'oeuvre.

1½ cups *(225g)* minced black olives, about a 6-8 oz. can
½ cup *(115g)* mayonnaise (Hellmann's preferred) or use Homemade Mayonnaise (page 190)
2 T. *(25g)* minced fresh onion
¼ tsp. curry powder
1 cup *(115g)* grated sharp Cheddar cheese
5 whole English muffins

Combine all ingredients except muffins. Split muffins, cut into halves, then quarter each half. Spread mixture on pieces. Place under broiler 3 to 4 minutes until bubbly. Serve hot.

Levette C. Perkins, West Hartford, CT

Variations, Advance Preparation, and Serving Suggestions:
Spread may be prepared several days ahead and refrigerated. It will freeze well for a short period. Whole wheat English muffins may be used.

Wine Suggestion: California Navalle Rose, semi-dry rose; serve chilled.

YIELD: 1½ Cups
TOTAL CALORIES: 1650
CALORIES PER TABLESPOON: 69
CARBOHYDRATES: 4g
PROTEIN: 2g
FAT: 5g
CHOLESTEROL: High
SODIUM: High
PREPARING: 10 Minutes
FREEZING: Yes

Ham and Chutney Dipping Sauce

Hollow out a deep red cabbage as a serving vessel for this sauce.

½ lb. *(225g)* cooked ham, coarsely chopped
½ cup *(115g)* Homemade Mayonnaise (page 190) or mayonnaise (Hellmann's preferred)
½ cup *(115g)* sour cream
⅓ cup *(50g)* chopped water chestnuts
3 T. *(45ml)* minced sweet or hot mango or peach chutney
1½ tsp. curry powder, or to taste
1 tsp. fresh lemon juice
Pinch cayenne pepper
Salt to taste

Fresh dill or parsley sprigs to garnish

Blend ham and mayonnaise in food processor or blender until ham is minced. Transfer to mixing bowl, add remaining ingredients and mix well.

Place in serving dish. Garnish with fresh dill or parsley sprigs.

Maria M. Rossi, Brewster, MA

Variations, Advance Preparation, and Serving Suggestions:
Serve with crudites or chips. Prepare one or two days in advance. Also freezes well up to one month.

Nutritional Notes: You may substitute imitation mayonnaise or imitation sour cream to decrease fat and calorie content.

Dilly
Brussels Sprouts

YIELD: 10-12 Servings
CALORIES PER SERVING: 79
CARBOHYDRATES: 3g
PROTEIN: 1g
FAT: 7g
SODIUM: High
PREPARING: 15 Minutes
MARINATING: 24 Hours
FREEZING: No

Cook Brussels sprouts until barely tender. Rinse under cold water to stop cooking. Drain. Add remaining ingredients. Stir. Cover and chill overnight. Serve with wooden toothpicks.

Inger Brinckerhoff, Goshen, CT

2 pkgs. (10 oz. each) *(570g)* frozen Brussels sprouts (Seabrook baby sprouts preferred)
1 cup *(240ml)* Italian dressing
1 tsp. dried dill weed
2 T. *(10g)* minced scallions

Variations, Advance Preparation, and Serving Suggestions: Sprouts may be used as a salad. Serve on greens-lined plates and garnish with tomato slices.

Nutritional Notes: Nutritional analysis assumes consumption of ⅔ of dressing. For low-sodium version use salt-free dressing (available in the dietetic section of the supermarket, or may be prepared at home).

Microwave Conversion Instructions: Place sprouts in casserole just large enough to contain them. Add ¼ cup Italian dressing. Cook, covered, on High 6 to 7 minutes or until heated through. Add remaining dressing and seasonings.

YIELD: 40 Nuggets
CALORIES PER NUGGET: 49
CARBOHYDRATES: 1.5g
PROTEIN: 4g
FAT: 3g
PREPARING: 1¼ Hours
COOKING: 20 Minutes
FREEZING: No

Chicken Nuggets

Cut chicken in 1½-inch *(4cm)* cubes. Combine breadcrumbs, onion powder, cheese, salt and pepper. Dip chicken cubes in butter, then into crumb mixture. Arrange in ungreased roasting pan in 1 layer (Up to this point, may be made ahead in morning or day before, covered and refrigerated). Bake in preheated 375° oven 15 to 20 minutes, turning once. Bake until nicely browned.

Sandy Antonelli, West Simsbury, CT

4 large whole chicken breasts, skinned, boned
1 cup *(120g)* seasoned breadcrumbs
½ tsp. onion powder
¼ cup *(35g)* freshly grated Parmesan cheese
¾ tsp. salt
Freshly ground pepper
½ lb. *(225g)* butter, melted

Nutritional Notes: Adaptation for a moderately sodium-restricted diet is possible by eliminating the salt and using unseasoned breadcrumbs. Low-sodium breadcrumbs may be prepared at home with salt-free bread and unsalted seasonings (e.g. onion *powder*, garlic *powder*, oregano, basil, etc.)

Microwave Conversion Instructions: Prepare recipe as for conventional recipe. Add 1 tsp. paprika for color. Divide recipe into 4 portions; cook each portion 3 minutes 30 seconds on High, uncovered.

YIELD: 1 Cup
CALORIES PER TABLESPOON: 53
CARBOHYDRATES: 1g
PROTEIN: 1g
FAT: 5g
CHOLESTEROL: High
SODIUM: High
PREPARING: 15 Minutes
CHILLING: 4 Hours
COOKING: 15 Minutes
FREEZING: No

Crudités and Dipping Sauce

DIPPING SAUCE:

2 anchovy fillets, chopped
2 hard-boiled eggs, chopped
2 tsp. parsley, chopped
3 T. onion, chopped
¼ cup *(60ml)* olive oil
1 tsp. capers
1 tsp. lime juice
1 tsp. dill, chopped
½ cup *(115g)* sour cream
½ tsp. mixed-up salt (preferably Jane's Krazy) or coarse salt

CRUDITES:

Do Not Require Blanching:

Cucumbers
Radishes
Celery
Endive
Mushrooms
Cherry Tomatoes
Zucchini and yellow crookneck squash
Kohlrabi
Peppers
Jicama
Fennel

Require Blanching:
Cauliflower
Asparagus
String Beans
Snow Peas
Broccoli
Carrots

DIPPING SAUCE: Mix all ingredients in blender or food processor until smooth.

CRUDITES: Prepare vegetables in desired shapes, remembering to keep size appropriate for finger handling. Prepare vegetables early in the day, store wrapped and refrigerated or keep vegetables in a bowl of iced water. Drain at serving time.

TO BLANCH: In large pot bring salted water to boil. Drop prepared vegetable into boiling water for 1 to 3 minutes. Quickly remove with large skimmer and immerse in large tub of iced water to stop cooking. Do each vegetable separately.

Patricia K. Anathan, Simsbury, CT

Variations, Advance Preparation, and Serving Suggestions:
Place Dipping Sauce in hollowed green or red cabbage; surround with assorted crudites. For individual servings slice top, remove seeds and membrane from green bell peppers. Fill each with crudites assortment. Place in large shallow basket. Place Dipping Sauce around basket.

Wine Suggestion: California Navalle Chablis, dry white; serve chilled.

Pâté Quiche

Rich — although not sinfully so when served with a cold glass of champagne. A freeze-ease item for all seasons.

YIELD: 32 Servings or 2 Pies
TOTAL CALORIES: 8200
CALORIES PER SERVING: 256
CARBOHYDRATES: 8g
PROTEIN: 6g
FAT: 22g
CHOLESTEROL: High
SODIUM: High
PREPARING: 45 Minutes
BAKING: 50 Minutes
FREEZING: Yes

Separate 1 egg; combine yolk with remaining whole eggs, set aside. Beat 1 egg white and brush over bottom and sides of pie shells. Combine pate, ½ cup chopped onion, garlic, breadcrumbs and nutmeg. Mix well. Divide equally between pie shells, spreading evenly. Saute ¼ cup chopped onion in butter for 2 minutes or until lightly golden. Set aside. Beat together eggs and cream. Add salt, cayenne and nutmeg. Combine with sauteed onion mixture, cheese and sherry. Stir to mix. Pour half of this mixture over each pie shell. Freeze or refrigerate. When ready to serve, return to room temperature. Bake in preheated 375° oven, 40 to 50 minutes or until knife inserted 1 inch (2.5cm) from edge comes out clean. Cool on rack approximately 1 hour. Serve warm, not hot. Slice in very small wedges.

Emily M-S. MacKenzie, Manchester, CT

- 5 eggs
- 2 9-inch *(22.5cm)* pie shells, unbaked, (page 198)
- 1¾ lbs. *(750g)* canned liver pate
- ¾ cup *(115g)* onion, chopped
- 4 cloves garlic, crushed
- ½ cup *(60g)* dry breadcrumbs
- ½ tsp. nutmeg
- 2 T. *(30g)* butter
- 2 cups *(475ml)* heavy cream
- ½ tsp. salt
- ⅛ tsp. cayenne pepper
- ⅛ tsp. nutmeg
- ⅔ cup *(90g)* freshly grated Parmesan cheese
- ¼ cup *(60ml)* dry sherry

Nutritional Notes: To save calories and reduce fat content substitute 2 cups evaporated milk or evaporated skim milk for heavy cream. 2 cups heavy cream have 1688 calories and 180g fat. 2 cups evaporated milk have 704 calories and 40g fat. Evaporated skim milk has even less.

Wine Suggestion: California Jacques Bonet Champagne, sparkling white; serve chilled.

Microwave Conversion Instructions: Note: For better Microwave product, prepare only one quiche. Cut all ingredients in half. Recipe works better if prepared in porcelain quiche pan to eliminate slanted sides.

Brush pie shell with egg white. Cook on Medium (50%) 5 to 6 minutes or until slightly browned. Do not overcook. Prepare pate mixture as for conventional recipe. Cook chopped onion and butter, covered, 2 minutes on High. Prepare quiche topping as indicated in a glass bowl; cook on Medium (50%) 4 minutes, stirring frequently until mixture is warm. Pour over pate; cook uncovered 20 to 25 minutes on Medium (50%) or until center of quiche is just set. Rotate dish ¼ turn frequently during baking.

Note: If golden brown top is desired, place quiche under preheated broiler. Cool and serve as for conventional recipe.

YIELD: 3 lbs. Meat or 4 Salami Rolls
TOTAL CALORIES: 5200
CALORIES PER ⅛-INCH THICK SLICE: 26
CARBOHYDRATES: Trace
PROTEIN: 2g
FAT: 2g
SODIUM: High
PREPARING: 30 Minutes
BAKING: 4 Hours
CHILLING: 24 Hours
FREEZING: Yes

Picnic Salami

It's not like the dry Italian salami most people are familiar with, but more like the cured luncheon meat you can buy. For summer picnics or as an hors d'oeuvre it is tasty alone or with crackers. It also makes an exceptionally good year-round sandwich meat.

SMOKY BEEF SALAMI:

4 lbs. *(1800g)* **ground beef (maximum fat content 25%)**

¼ cup *(50g)* **meat curing salt (available in herb and spice shops, butcher's supply company, or directly from Morton Salt Co.)**

2 T. *(30ml)* **liquid smoke**

1½ tsp. **garlic powder**

1½ tsp. **freshly ground black pepper (or 2 tsp. whole black pepper)**

SPECIAL EQUIPMENT:

¼ yard *(25cm)* **nylon net (sold at most fabric stores)**

In a large bowl, mix all the ingredients very thoroughly. Cover and chill 24 hours.

Divide mixture into fourths. Shape each into compact 8-inch *(20cm)* log and place each on a 12 × 18-inch *(30 × 45cm)* piece of nylon netting. Roll up tightly; tie ends with string.

Place logs on broiler pan with rack and bake in preheated 225° oven for 4 hours.

Remove from oven and take off net. Pat rolls with paper towel to absorb excess fat. Cool slightly, then wrap in foil and refrigerate or freeze. The salami keeps up to 3 weeks refrigerated or 2 months frozen.

Slice to serve.

Judith Repp, West Hartford, CT

Variations, Advance Preparation, and Serving Suggestions:
For Herb Beef Salami: Prepare as directed above with these changes: Omit liquid smoke and add 3 T. *(45ml)* dry red wine. Reduce garlic powder to 1 tsp. and omit pepper. Instead, add 2 T. mustard seed, 1 T. *each* dry basil and oregano, 1 tsp. onion powder, and ⅔ cup *(150g)* grated Parmesan cheese.

For Spicy Beef Salami: Prepare as above with these changes: Omit liquid smoke and add 3 T. *(45ml)* dry white wine. Reduce garlic powder to 1 tsp. and omit pepper. Instead, add 2 T. chili powder, 2 tsp. crushed red pepper, and 1 tsp. ground cumin.

Nutritional Notes: Making your own salami permits you to control the fat content. Commercially made salami is usually 33% fat. You are able to eliminate use of nitrates and other chemicals as well.

Wine Suggestion: California Zinfandel, dry red; serve at room temperature.

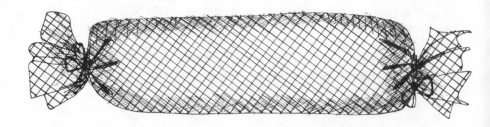

Sikil P'ak

MEXICAN PUMPKIN SEED DIP

A great way to start off a Mexican dinner.

YIELD: 1½ Cups
CALORIES PER TABLESPOON: 43
CARBOHYDRATES: 2g
PROTEIN: 2g
FAT: 3g
PREPARING: 25 Minutes
FREEZING: No

Heat a heavy frying pan and toast the seeds, stirring constantly, until hulls are well-browned and crisp. (Some types of seeds will start to pop open.) Set aside to cool. Meanwhile, toast the chili on a foil-covered baking sheet in a preheated 400° oven or toaster oven until the skin is blistered and black-brown in spots, turning occasionally.

In a saucepan, simmer the tomatoes in boiling water to cover, about 15 minutes. Drain, peel and set aside to cool.

Using an electric spice/coffee grinder, grind the toasted seeds, together with the salt, to a coarse powder. Transfer to a small serving bowl. Stir the tomatoes, coriander and chives into the seeds. Stir in the whole chili. (For a hotter dip, blend the chili with the tomato before mixing with the seeds.) The mixture should be the consistency of mayonnaise. Add a little water to thin it, if necessary. (Can be made several hours ahead, but keep at room temperature.)

Serve at room temperature with crisp, fried tortilla chips.

1¼ cups (90g) raw, unhulled pumpkin seeds, or any other squash seeds
1 chile habanero or any fresh, hot green chili
2 medium tomatoes, about 12 oz. (340g)
1½ tsp. salt, or to taste
2 heaping T. chopped coriander leaves
2 heaping T. chopped chives
Tortilla chips

Picadillo

Picadillo is Spanish for minced meat and usually refers to a meat and vegetable hash.

YIELD: 10 Hors d'Oeuvre Servings
TOTAL CALORIES: 1690
CALORIES PER SERVING: 169
CARBOHYDRATES: 10g
PROTEIN: 12g
FAT: 9g
CHOLESTEROL: High
SODIUM: High
PREPARING: 25 Minutes
COOKING: 25 Minutes
FREEZING: Yes

In a large skillet, cook onion in oil over medium heat until soft. Add pepper and garlic; cook and stir 3 minutes. Add beef and pork; cook, stirring, until meat is no longer pink. Add tomatoes, olives, raisins, brown sugar, vinegar, spices, salt and pepper.

Cook the mixture, stirring occasionally, until excess liquid is evaporated but mixture is still moist, about 20 minutes.

Serve hot, garnished with almonds or pine nuts, in a chafing dish as an appetizer with tortilla chips.

Kathleen J. Schwartz, Avon,CT

Variations, Advance Preparation, and Serving Suggestions:
Can be made a day or two in advance and refrigerated. Freezes well for a month or two. Serve over rice as a buffet entree.

Microwave Conversion Instructions: In a 3-qt. (3L) casserole, cook onion and oil on High, uncovered 3 minutes. Add pepper and garlic; cook an additional 3 minutes. Stir in beef and pork, cook 5 to 7 minutes on High, until meat is no longer pink, stirring once or twice to keep meat crumbly. Add tomatoes, olives, raisins, brown sugar, vinegar, spices, salt and pepper.

Continue cooking, stirring occasionally, until excess liquid is evaporated, about 10 to 13 minutes.

1 medium onion, chopped
2 T. (30ml) olive oil
½ cup (85g) chopped green pepper, about 1 small
3 large cloves garlic, minced
1 lb. (450g) ground lean beef
¼ lb. (115g) ground pork shoulder
1 can (16 oz.) (450g) plum tomatoes, chopped
⅔ cup (115g) chopped green olives with pimientos
⅓ cup (55g) raisins
2 T. (30g) brown sugar
1½ T. (22.5ml) white vinegar
1 tsp. chili powder
¼ tsp. dry mustard
⅛ tsp. cumin
⅛ tsp. cinnamon
⅛ tsp. ground cloves
Salt, freshly ground black pepper to taste
½ cup (70g) slivered almonds or ¼ cup (40g) pine nuts

Shanghai Spring Rolls

In China, Shanghai Spring Rolls are given as presents on New Year. In the lunar calendar, this usually comes at the end of January or February, which is the beginning of spring. When fried, Shanghai Spring Rolls resemble golden bars, which symbolize wealth for the New Year. Once you have made your own Shanghai Spring Rolls, you will be spoiled. Nothing in a restaurant will ever again taste the same. The wrappers are light and crunchy and greaseless, the filling distinguished, not merely cabbage. Egg rolls are an American variation, made with thicker skins.

YIELD: 10-12 Rolls
CALORIES PER ROLL: 138
CARBOHYDRATES: 5g
PROTEIN: 7g
FAT: 10g
SODIUM: High
PREPARING: 45 Minutes
SOAKING: 30-60 Minutes
COOKING: 10 Minutes
FREEZING: No

FILLING:

½ lb. *(225g)* **raw pork shreds (Boston butt is best cut to use)**
1 oz. *(30g)* **dried Chinese mushrooms**
1 T. **dry sherry**
2 T. *(30ml)* **dark soy sauce**
1 T. **oyster sauce**
½ tsp. **sugar**
2 T. *(30ml)* **peanut oil**
½ cup *(70g)* **shredded bamboo shoots**
½ cup *(30g)* **snipped fresh Chinese chives (not American chives)**
½ cup *(50g)* **shredded leeks (white part only)**
1 cup *(100g)* **shredded bok choy (white part only)**
1 cup *(80g)* **bean sprouts**

12 **spring roll sheets (do not use egg roll sheets as they are heavier)**
1 **egg, beaten**
Peanut oil for shallow frying

PREPARATION: Partially freeze pork to facilitate shredding. Then shred into matchstick-sized pieces. Rinse mushrooms, cover with warm water; soak 30 to 60 minutes or until soft. Discard stems. Finely shred mushrooms. Mix together in a bowl sherry, soy sauce, oyster sauce and sugar.

COOKING PROCEDURE: Place wok over high flame for 30 seconds. Add 2 T. oil and heat 30 seconds or until oil is very hot but not smoking. Add pork shreds; stir-fry 3 minutes, or until pork turns white.

Add mushrooms, bamboo shoots and leeks; mix well. Add sherry, soy sauce and sugar; mix well. Continue stir-frying over high flame for 3 minutes. Add bok choy and chives; toss for 30 seconds. Add bean sprouts and mix.

Dish into a strainer and set over a bowl to catch the drippings. (It is best to strain the mixture over a bowl in the refrigerator overnight.) The most important consideration in making the rolls is to have a *dry filling* and roll the wrapper *very tightly* around this filling to avoid breaking the wrapper and excessive absorption of oil.

Place a Shanghai spring roll wrapper with a corner facing you. Put 2 T. filling in lower center of diamond. Fold corner nearest you tightly over filling and roll away from you once.

With beaten egg on your fingertips, generously moisten the remaining 3 points of the diamond. Take the 2 side points and fold them in toward the bottom center. Make sure there is an overlap of at least 1 inch *(2.5cm)*. Roll this bulging envelope up, pressing the filling in tightly. Seal with the egg-moistened final point. Rolls may be made 3 to 4 hours ahead and refrigerated on a cookie sheet *very tightly covered.* Using a 12-inch *(30cm)* wok or skillet, fry 3 to 4 minutes, turning once after 2 minutes in 1½ inches *(4cm)* of 350° oil. *Drain well* on paper towels. Serve immediately with Plum Dip (page 373) and/or Mustard Dip (page 373).

Sarah Seymour, West Hartford, CT

Variations, Advance Preparation, and Serving Suggestions:
Chicken or shrimp can be substituted for pork, or use any combination of meats you like. When serving as hors d'oeuvre, make smaller spring rolls, or cut these in half after frying. While it is possible to freeze spring rolls, they are *definitely inferior* to fresh.

Nutritional Notes: Fat analysis assumes absorption of 3 tablespoons oil during frying.

Shrimp Toast

Now you can prepare shrimp toast, a favorite Chinese restaurant hors d'oeuvre, in your own kitchen. The processor makes it easy.

Water chestnut powder is a thickening agent like cornstarch, except that it is lower in carbohydrates and calories. It gives crunchiness to deep fried dishes. It has several drawbacks: it breaks down if you try to keep the dish warm for an extended amount of time and it is expensive.

YIELD: 24 Pieces
CALORIES PER PIECE: 82
CARBOHYDRATES: 4g
PROTEIN: 3g
FAT: 6g
CHOLESTEROL: High
SODIUM: High
PREPARING: 45 Minutes
CHILLING: 1 Hour Minimum
COOKING: 10 Minutes
FREEZING: Yes

Combine all but bread and oil. Mix until a paste is formed. (Can be done in food processor but add chopped water chestnuts by hand so that they do not become too finely minced. They should still have crunch.)

Refrigerate for at least 1 hour or up to 36 hours. Mixture becomes thicker and easier to spread after refrigeration. Cut each slice of bread into 4 triangles. Spread about 1 T. shrimp mixture over each triangle; smooth with butter knife. This may be done several hours ahead and placed on baking sheet in refrigerator.

Heat oil in a wok or electric skillet to 375°. Holding triangle in your fingers, gently lower into the oil with shrimp side down. After 1 minute, turn over and fry another minute or until it has turned a golden brown. Lift Shrimp Toast out of oil and let drain on paper towels. Blot the tops to remove excess oil. Serve immediately with Plum Dip (page 373) and/or Mustard Dip (page 373).

Patricia Mitchell, Avon, CT

½ lb. *(225g)* raw shrimp, finely minced
4 fresh water chestnuts, peeled and coarsely chopped
2 scallions, minced
1 tsp. minced fresh ginger root
1 tsp. salt
½ tsp. sugar
1 egg
1 T. water chestnut powder dissolved in ½ T. dark soy sauce and 1 tsp. dry sherry
6 slices thin-sliced stale white bread
2-3 cups *(475-710ml)* peanut oil for deep frying

Variations, Advance Preparation, and Serving Suggestions:
Freeze uncooked Shrimp Toast on baking sheet. When frozen solid remove to plastic storage bag. Just before serving, deep fry still frozen. Substitute fresh, peeled, coarsely chopped Jerusalem artichokes if fresh water chestnuts are not available.

Nutritional Notes: Absorption of ½ cup oil is estimated in calorie/fat analysis.

YIELD: 8 Cups
CALORIES PER ¼ CUP: 162
CARBOHYDRATES: 22g
PROTEIN: 5g
FAT: 6g
PREPARING: 20 Minutes
BAKING: 2 Hours
FREEZING: No

Peanut Granola

1 cup *(170g)* raisins, plumped in warm
  water then drained
¾ cup *(200g)* peanut butter
⅔ cup *(225g)* good quality honey
1 T. cinnamon
Dash cloves
1 T. pure vanilla
4 cups *(340g)* rolled oats
½ cup *(60g)* wheat germ
½ cup *(75g)* dates or figs, cut into
  small pieces
1 cup *(120g)* sunflower seeds or
  unsalted nuts

Set raisins aside until needed.

In saucepan, combine peanut butter, honey, cinnamon, and cloves. Heat through. Cool slightly; stir in vanilla.

Place oats in a large shallow roasting pan. Pour warm peanut butter mixture over oats. Gently stir with wooden spoon until oats are well-coated. Spread evenly in pan. Bake in preheated 300° oven 35 minutes, stirring several times. Turn oven off. Stir in raisins, wheat germ, dates or figs, sunflower seeds or nuts. Let granola dry in oven 1½ hours, stirring every 30 minutes. Store covered.

Bernice Kuzma, West Hartford, CT

Nutritional Notes: You can serve this as an additive and preservative-free breakfast, a party nibble or delicious after school snack that is high in nutritional value. If storing for a period of time, store in an airtight container in refrigerator. Remove portions needed and bring to room temperature.

YIELD: 32 ½-Cup Servings
CALORIES PER SERVING: 315
CARBOHYDRATES: 36g
PROTEIN: 8g
FAT: 16g
PREPARING: 30 Minutes
COOKING: 40 Minutes
FREEZING: No

Granola

4 cups *(340g)* rolled oats
1½ cups *(170g)* fresh, raw wheat germ
2 cups *(150g)* unprocessed bran
⅔ cup *(160ml)* oil
½ cup *(170g)* honey
½ cup *(100g)* brown sugar
1 cup *(140g)* almonds
1 cup *(120g)* pecans
1 cup *(120g)* walnuts
1 cup *(120g)* sunflower seeds
4 cups of any or a combination of: dried
  apples, dried apricots, dried raisins,
  dried figs and dried dates (cut or
  chopped as desired)

Place oats, wheat germ, and bran in large roasting pan; mix well. Drizzle ⅓ cup *(80ml)* oil and the honey over mixture; sprinkle with brown sugar.

Toast in preheated 350° oven 15 minutes; turn mixture; toast 15 minutes longer. Cool.

Spread nuts and seeds on separate baking sheet; drizzle with remaining ⅓ cup *(80ml)* oil; toast to a crisp crunch. Cool.

Combine toasted ingredients with dried fruits. Store in covered container in refrigerator.

Gloria J. Holtsinger, West Hartford, CT

Nutritional Notes: This granola recipe provides good nutrition as a breakfast cereal or high energy snack. It is a good source of vitamins, minerals and fiber. Oats, wheat germ, bran, nuts and seeds add protein and provide 2 to 4 times the amount of protein found in commercial cereals, even without the addition of milk! Since the wheat germ is highly perishable (it contains all the fat or oil from the wheat kernel), it, as well as the granola, should be stored in an airtight container in the refrigerator. Remove portions needed and bring to room temperature.

Puffed German Apple Pancake

A delicious way to start the day!

Mix together eggs, milk, flour and salt. Toss apple slices with 2 T. lemon juice.

Melt butter in a 13 × 9-inch *(33 × 22.5cm)* baking dish or a 12-inch *(30cm)* fluted porcelain quiche dish, in a preheated 425° oven. Remove dish from oven, lay apple slices evenly over bottom; return to oven until butter sizzles. Do not let it brown. Remove from oven; immediately pour batter over apples. Mix together brown sugar and cinnamon; sprinkle mixture over batter. Put back in oven; bake 20 minutes or until puffed and browned. Remove from oven; drizzle 2 T. lemon juice over top. Cut into pieces; serve immediately with warmed maple syrup.

Cathy Power, Medfield, MA

YIELD: 6 Servings
CALORIES PER SERVING: 304
CARBOHYDRATES: 31g
PROTEIN: 9g
FAT: 16g
CHOLESTEROL: High
PREPARING: 20 Minutes
BAKING: 25 Minutes
FREEZING: No

6 eggs
1 cup *(240ml)* milk
⅔ cup *(75g)* flour
½ tsp. salt
3 medium to large apples, peeled, cored and sliced
¼ cup *(60ml)* freshly squeezed lemon juice
4 T. *(60g)* butter
¼ cup *(50g)* firmly packed dark brown sugar
½ tsp. cinnamon
Pure maple syrup, warmed

Peanut Butter French Toast

Peanut butter aficionados — Arise to a good morning!

Make two sandwiches with bread and desired amount of peanut butter. Beat egg slightly, add salt, milk and cinnamon. Mix well. Dip sandwiches in custard mixture, coating until entire mixture is absorbed. Melt 1 or 2 T. butter in large skillet. Saute sandwiches until golden brown on both sides, adding more butter as needed. Serve hot with desired topping.

Thelma P. Glasband, West Hartford, CT

Variations, Advance Preparation, and Serving Suggestions: Change type of bread to raisin.

Nutritional Notes: Many modifications can be made in this recipe in order to make it acceptable for the restricted diet. (1) Egg substitute (low cholesterol) and skim milk can be used. (2) Salt-free peanut butter and salt-free bread would make this appropriate for the sodium-restricted diet. (3) Whole-grain bread substitution adds texture, fiber and trace minerals.

YIELD: 2 Servings
CALORIES PER SERVING: 443
CARBOHYDRATES: 34g
PROTEIN: 16g
FAT: 27g
PREPARING: 10 Minutes
COOKING: 10 Minutes
FREEZING: No

4 slices white bread
Chunky peanut butter
1 egg
¼ tsp. salt
⅓ cup *(80ml)* milk
Dash cinnamon
Butter

TOPPING:
Maple syrup or confectioners' sugar or cinnamon sugar

Orange Buttermilk Waffles

Light, easy, moist waffles with a tasty touch of orange and pecans.

YIELD: 4-6 Servings
CALORIES PER SERVING: 338
CARBOHYDRATES: 27g
PROTEIN: 8g
FAT: 22g
SODIUM: High
PREPARING: 15 Minutes
BAKING: 15 Minutes
FREEZING: Yes

1¾ cup *(200g)* flour
2 tsp. double-acting baking powder
1 tsp. baking soda
½ tsp. salt
3 eggs, lightly beaten
1½ cups *(355ml)* buttermilk
½ cup *(120ml)* oil
1 T. grated orange or tangerine rind
⅓ cup *(40g)* chopped pecans (optional)

Sift together dry ingredients. Combine eggs, buttermilk, and oil; add orange rind. Stir into dry ingredients just until batter is smooth. Pour about ¾ to 1 cup of batter at a time onto a preheated waffle iron, quickly sprinkle pecans over batter, close iron. Bake until steaming stops and waffle is golden.

Gloria J. Holtsinger, West Hartford, CT

Variations, Advance Preparation, and Serving Suggestions: To serve frozen waffles, unwrap and place directly on rack of preheated 300° oven. Bake until crisp.

Nutritional Notes: Buttermilk from skim milk contains half the calories of whole milk and was used in the nutritional analysis. Buttermilk from whole milk is also available.

Aunt Amie's Apple Muffins

Delectably moist, sweet muffins.

YIELD: 12-14 Muffins
TOTAL CALORIES: 2632
CALORIES PER MUFFIN: 188
CARBOHYDRATES: 27g
PROTEIN: 2g
FAT: 8g
PREPARING: 15 Minutes
BAKING: 25 Minutes

1 cup *(200g)* sugar
½ cup *(115g)* butter, softened
1 egg
1½ cups *(170g)* flour
1 tsp. baking soda
½ tsp. baking powder
½ tsp. salt
1 tsp. vanilla
2 cups *(250g)* cored, peeled, chopped
   apples (about 2 medium)

TOPPING:

1½ T. *(20g)* sugar, mixed with
   ¼ tsp. cinnamon
Confectioners' sugar

Cream together sugar and butter. Beat in egg. Sift together flour, baking soda, baking powder and salt. Add to egg mixture. Stir in vanilla and apples. *[FOOD PROCESSOR: Put flour, baking soda, baking powder and salt in work bowl; process 2 seconds. Remove and set aside. Coarsely chop cored, peeled and quartered apples by turning machine on/off several times. Remove and set aside. Add egg and sugar to work bowl and process 1 full minute. Add butter and vanilla and process 1 full minute. Blend in flour mixture by turning machine on/off just until flour disappears. Do not overprocess. Stir in apples by hand.]*

Fill 12 to 14 buttered 2½-inch *(6.5cm)* muffin tins or cups with batter to the top. Sprinkle with topping. Place muffin tins on next-to-lowest rack in preheated 375° oven. Bake 20 to 25 minutes. Remove from oven. Turn muffins out of tins. While still warm, sprinkle with confectioners' sugar.

Ann Howard Cookery, Farmington, CT

Microwave Conversion Instructions: Prepare batter as directed. Sprinkle muffins with topping *before baking.* Place 2 paper liners in each cup of microwave muffin pan. Fill cups ⅔ full with batter. Bake on High about 3 to 4 minutes for each pan, turning once if necessary.

Danish Pastry Dough

YIELD: 2 Large Rings or Braids or
    3 Medium Rings or Braids
    or 36 Individual Danish
TOTAL CALORIES DOUGH: 6406
CARBOHYDRATES: 575g
PROTEIN: 86g
FAT: 418g
CHOLESTEROL: High
PREPARING: 1¼ Hours
CHILLING: 4 Hours Minimum
FREEZING: Yes

In a small bowl mix yeast and 1 tsp. sugar, add water. Stir to dissolve yeast. Place bowl in a warm spot (over pilot light works well) for 8 to 10 minutes, or until yeast bubbles and doubles in bulk.

Place 4 cups of flour in large mixing bowl. Make a well in the center and add yeast mixture. Add all remaining ingredients. Mix together with your fingers until a soft dough is formed. *[FOOD PROCESSOR: Measure yeast, 1 tsp. sugar and warm water into work bowl fitted with metal blade. Stir by turning blade by hand until yeast is softened. Let proof. Then add milk, cardamom, eggs, salt and sugar; process on/off twice. Add flour all at once. Process until dough leaves sides of bowl. If processor overloads, scrape down both sides of bowl and blade. Process again until dough is smooth and elastic.]* Shape into ball and place on a floured pastry cloth or board. To knead dough, pull it into an oblong shape, fold it end to end, then press down and push forward several times with the heel of your hand. Continue kneading until dough is smooth and elastic. This will take at least 10 minutes. Sprinkle dough with flour, wrap in foil or plastic bag and refrigerate for 30 minutes.

BUTTER RECTANGLE: Meanwhile, remove butter from refrigerator and let it soften to the point where it is neither too soft nor too hard. If butter is in quarter-pound sticks, cut each stick into ¼-inch thick *(0.6cm)* slices lengthwise. Place each of these slivers on 2 separate sheets of waxed paper in the approximate shape of a 6 × 8-inch *(15 × 20cm)* rectangle. With your fingers, work butter until blended and you have 2 rectangles, each 6 × 8-inch. Wrap both halves in more wax paper and place in refrigerator.

Liberally sprinkle pastry board with flour. Roll chilled dough out on floured surface into a 9 × 18-inch *(23 × 46cm)* rectangle, ⅛ inch *(0.3cm)* thick. Place one sheet of butter across center of dough and bring end of dough farther from you over butter, sealing it along the sides with your fingers. Place other sheet of butter on top and bring other half of dough over that, again sealing the edges. Turn dough around so that the narrow side faces you. Roll out dough to an 8 × 18-inch *(20 × 46cm)* strip. Fold both narrow ends in to meet at the center, then fold in half, making 4 layers. Wrap again in foil and chill for 20 minutes. Repeat this procedure with the narrow side toward you and chill another 20 minutes. Remove from refrigerator, roll again into an 8 × 18-inch *(20 × 46cm)* rectangle. Finally, fold dough in half. Wrap again and chill for 2 to 3 hours or overnight before using. Use dough combined with fillings and toppings of your choice to make any of the Danish in the recipes that follow on pages 218 and 219.

Variations, Advance Preparation, and Serving Suggestions:
Dough may be frozen for short periods. Dough may also be kept in refrigerator 4 to 5 days, using varying amounts as needed to make fresh pastry each day.

2 pkgs. (¼ oz. each) *(14g)* active dry yeast
½ cup *(100g)* sugar
½ cup *(120ml)* warm (110°) water
5 cups *(570g)* unsifted flour (reserve 1 cup flour for pastry board)
½ cup *(120ml)* cold milk
1 T. unsalted sweet butter
2 whole eggs
1 tsp. salt
½ tsp. freshly ground cardamom (buy pods, remove skin and grind seeds in mortar.)
Grated rind 1 orange
2 tsp. pure vanilla

BUTTER RECTANGLE:
1 lb. *(450g)* unsalted sweet butter, chilled

Danish Pastry Shapes

LARGE DANISH RING:
½ recipe Danish Pastry Dough
Filling of your choice
Apricot Glaze
Almond Icing
Toasted Almonds

LARGE DANISH TWIST:
½ recipe Danish Pastry Dough
Filling of your choice
Apricot Glaze
Almond Icing or Coffee Glaze
Toasted Almonds

DANISH CLUSTER CAKE:
½ recipe Danish Pastry Dough
Filling of your choice
Apricot Glaze
Almond Icing
Toasted Almonds

INDIVIDUAL DANISH RINGS:
½ recipe Danish Pastry Dough
Nut Filling of your choice
Apricot Glaze
Icing
Toasted Almonds
Pearl Sugar

SMALL DANISH TWISTS:
½ recipe Danish Pastry Dough
Vanilla Butter Cream
Any filling of your choice, but this shape
   is very good for jams and more runny
   fillings that need to be contained
Apricot Glaze
Icing
Toasted Almonds
Pearl Sugar

COCKSCOMB:
½ recipe Danish Pastry Dough
Vanilla Butter Cream
Frangipane Filling
½ cup (75g) pearl sugar mixed with
   ½ cup (45g) sliced almonds
Almond Glaze or Coffee Glaze

LARGE DANISH RING: Roll out dough into a rectangle 6 × 25 × ¼ inch (15 × 60 × .6cm). Spread dough with thin layer of preferred filling. Fold lengthwise into thirds, making a strip 25 × 2 inch (60 × 5cm). Roll this strip gently with a rolling pin to flatten and lengthen slightly. With a knife, make 3 incisions lengthwise, spaced equally, almost full length of strip, leaving an inch (2.5cm) or so uncut at ends. Take one end in each hand. Turn and roll ends in opposite directions to form a long twist, stretching the dough slightly. Continue to hold ends so that they will not unwind. Shape into a ring, crossing ends and pressing them down firmly to join them. Holding joined ends down with one hand, flip ring over toward you with the other hand so that ends are concealed underneath. Place on a baking sheet. Press down top of ring to flatten it slightly. Bake at 400° for 15 to 20 minutes. Remove from oven and brush with Apricot Glaze. When cool drizzle with Almond Icing and sprinkle with Toasted Almonds.

LARGE DANISH TWIST: Roll out dough to make a square ⅛ inch (.3cm) thick. Spread dough thinly with preferred filling. Roll up tightly jelly-roll style. Press down with a rolling pin to flatten the filled roll slightly. Cut filled roll in half lengthwise, exposing the layers of filling. Entwine the strips together, keeping filling turned face up. Pinch ends to seal. Place on baking sheet. Bake at 400° for 15 to 20 minutes. Remove from oven and brush with Apricot Glaze. Drizzle with icing and sprinkle with Toasted Almonds.

DANISH CLUSTER CAKE: Roll and fill dough as in preceding recipe for Large Danish Twist. Cut roll into slices 2 inches (5cm) thick. Lay slices down in a 10-inch (25cm) tube pan. Lay them in an alternating pattern, one laying down flat and the next slice upright. Bake in a 350° oven for 40 to 45 minutes. Remove from oven and brush on Apricot Glaze. When cool drizzle on icing and sprinkle with Toasted Almonds.

INDIVIDUAL RINGS: Roll dough out to make a long strip ⅛ inch (.3cm) thick and twelve inches (30cm) wide. Spread filling over dough. Fold dough in half lengthwise to make a strip 6 inches (15cm) wide. Roll lightly over folded dough. Cut crosswise into ¾-inch (2cm) strips. Make an incision down the center of each strip almost to each end. Now follow twisting and shaping instructions for Large Danish Ring. Bake in a 400° oven for 12 to 15 minutes. Remove from oven and brush with Apricot Glaze. When cool drizzle with icing. Sprinkle with Toasted Almonds and Pearl Sugar.

SMALL DANISH TWISTS: Roll out dough to a strip ⅛ inch (.3cm) thick and 18 inches (45cm) long. (If you want larger pieces of Danish then roll dough out to 22 to 24 inches long (55-60cm). Cut into strips 18 × ¾ inches (45 × 2cm). Twist each strip by turning ends in opposite directions. Wind twisted strip around and around on a baking sheet to make a flat coil. Tuck ends underneath and in toward center to form a base in center of coil. Place a tsp. of Vanilla Butter Cream in the center of each twist. Place approximately 1 T. filling of your choice on top. Bake in a 400° oven for 12 to 15 minutes. Remove from oven and brush with Apricot Glaze. When cool, fill centers with a variety of fillings. Drizzle on an icing. Sprinkle on Toasted Almonds and Pearl Sugar.

COCKSCOMB: Divide the pastry in half. Roll each half, one at a time, into a 12-inch (30cm) square. Spread ½ the Vanilla Butter Cream down the center of the pastry and top with ½ the Frangipane Filling. Fold the top third over the filling; then fold the bottom third over to make a strip about 4 inches (10cm) wide. Press the pastry to seal it together. Roll slightly to widen the strip and even it out. Cut the dough crosswise into 2-inch (5cm) pieces. Then make parallel cuts (4 of them) along the long side of each piece, cutting to within ½ inch (1.25cm) of the edge. When all the pieces have been cut, have ready 2 bowls — one with water and one with the sugar-almond mixture. Dip the top of each piece first into the water and then into the almond mixture. As you lay the pieces on the baking sheet, bend slightly to form the combs or claws. Bake in a 400° oven 13 to 15 minutes.

Danish Pastry
Fillings, Glazes, Toppings

VANILLA BUTTER CREAM FILLING:
½ cup *(225g)* unsalted sweet butter
1 cup *(130g)* confectioners' sugar
1 tsp. pure vanilla

HAZELNUT FILLING:
1 cup *(125g)* hazelnuts (filberts) with
  brown skins on
1 cup *(200g)* sugar
2 T. *(30g)* butter
1 egg

GROUND NUT FILLING:
1½ cups *(200g)* almonds or nuts
  of your choice
3 eggs
½ cup *(100g)* sugar
½ cup *(115g)* melted butter
Grated rind 1 orange
½ cup *(85g)* white raisins
2 tsp. pure vanilla

ORANGE FILLING:
½ cup *(115g)* soft butter
½ cup *(150g)* orange marmalade
½ cup *(60g)* crushed walnuts or pecans

CREAM CHEESE FILLING:
¼ cup *(40g)* white raisins
1 T. dark rum
1 pkg. (8 oz.) *(225g)* cream cheese at
  room temperature
¼ cup *(50g)* sugar
1 T. flour
1 egg yolk
1 tsp. melted butter
1 T. sour cream
½ tsp. grated lemon rind
1 tsp. pure vanilla

FRANGIPANE FILLING:
½ cup *(115g)* soft butter
1 cup *(225g)* almond paste
2 eggs, beaten
1 tsp. grated lemon rind
2 tsp. flour

APPLE CUSTARD FILLING:
3 large apples, peeled
1 lemon, juice and rind
1 cup *(200g)* sugar
1 T. flour
2 egg yolks
2 T. *(30g)* butter
1 tsp. pure vanilla

RASPBERRY JAM FILLING
APRICOT JAM FILLING
BLUEBERRY JAM FILLING
CHERRY PIE FILLING

APRICOT GLAZE:
1 cup *(285g)* apricot jam
¼ cup *(50g)* sugar
2-4 T. *(30-60ml)* liqueur (dark rum or
  Grand Marnier)
1 T. fresh lemon juice

ALMOND ICING:
1 cup *(130g)* confectioners' sugar
2 T. *(30ml)* water
1 tsp. cooking oil
½ tsp. almond extract

COFFEE GLAZE:
1 cup *(130g)* confectioners' sugar
1 tsp. instant coffee dissolved in
  2 T. *(30ml)* water
2 T. *(30g)* butter

SLICED ALMONDS
PEARL SUGAR TOPPING

VANILLA BUTTER CREAM FILLING: Cream butter and sugar together until well blended; add vanilla. Will keep 2 to 3 weeks refrigerated.

HAZELNUT FILLING: Preheat oven to 300°. Toast nuts on baking sheet 10 minutes, or until crisp and nuts begin to darken. Grind nuts very fine. Add butter, sugar, and egg; process until a smooth paste is formed. Use at room temperature. Keeps 2 to 3 weeks refrigerated.

GROUND NUT FILLING: Finely chop nuts. Beat eggs and sugar for 5 minutes. Stir in nuts, butter, orange rind, raisins, and vanilla. Refrigerate. Keeps 2 to 3 weeks refrigerated.

ORANGE FILLING: Cream all ingredients together.

CREAM CHEESE FILLING: Mix raisins in rum. Cream together cheese, sugar, and flour. Stir in egg yolk, then melted butter, sour cream, lemon rind, and vanilla. Add soaked raisins. Keeps 2 to 3 weeks refrigerated.

FRAGIPANE FILLING: Cream butter. Stir in almond paste, a little at a time, adding beaten eggs alternately. Beat until smooth. Stir in remaining ingredients.

APPLE CUSTARD FILLING: Shred apples on coarse grater. Combine apples, lemon juice and rind, and sugar in saucepan. Cook over medium heat, uncovered, until almost boiling. Stir in flour. Stir until mixture is thickened. Stir 2 T. of hot filling into yolks. Pour egg-yolk mixture into pan containing filling, continuing to stir briskly. Return to low heat 3 to 4 minutes longer, stirring until filling is a little thicker. Remove from heat and stir in butter and vanilla.

JAM FILLINGS: Use only the finest commercial jams or preserves as fillings or your own homemade jams.

APRICOT GLAZE: Heat apricot jam and sugar in saucepan until boiling. Strain. Cool slightly and then add flavorings. Brush warm glaze on pastry. Extra glaze keeps indefinitely in refrigerator. Gently warm each time before using.

ALMOND ICING: Blend all ingredients together. Add more water if necessary to make an icing that can be drizzled.

COFFEE GLAZE: Blend all ingredients together.

SLICED ALMONDS: Place sliced (not slivered) almonds on a baking sheet and toast for 10 minutes in a 300° oven.

Croissants

Although identified with France, the croissant originated in Budapest. In 1668 the Turks, besieging the city, began to construct tunnels to make their passage through the walls. Bakers, working as they did in those quiet hours between dusk and dawn, heard the sound of tunneling, gave warning and saved the city. They were rewarded with permission to make pastry shaped in the form of a crescent, the emblem of the Turkish flag. Only later was it imported to Paris to be the accompaniment of the morning *cafe au lait*.

These golden rolls are best served warm, which intensifies the flavor of the buttery dough. The outer layers are flaky, the inner layers soft and light.

YIELD: 16 Croissants
TOTAL CALORIES: 3080
CALORIES PER CROISSANT: 193
CARBOHYDRATES: 16g
PROTEIN: 3g
FAT: 13g
CHOLESTEROL: High
PREPARING: 1½ Hours
BAKING: 15-20 Minutes
RISINGS: 4 Hours
CHILLING: 6 Hours
FREEZING: Yes

1 pkg. (¼ oz.) *(7g)* **active dry yeast**
3 T. *(40g)* **sugar**
1 cup *(240ml)* **milk, just barely warm**
2⅓ cups *(300g)* **flour**
1 heaping tsp. **salt**
8 oz. *(225g)* **unsalted sweet butter**
3 T. *(30g)* **flour**

SWEET GLAZE:

3 T. *(40g)* **sugar and** 3 T. *(45ml)* **milk**
  boiled until syrupy

EGG GLAZE:

1 egg beaten with 1 T. *(15ml)* **milk**

Combine the yeast, 1 tsp. of the sugar, and milk in a small bowl. Stir and allow to dissolve. Proof by making sure that a few bubbles are forming. Sift flour, sugar, and salt into bowl of a heavy-duty mixer. Make well in center of flour and pour in yeast mixture. Mix on medium speed for 3 minutes. *[FOOD PROCESSOR: Put flour, sugar, and salt into work bowl; turn machine on. With machine running, add yeast mixture through feed tube. Process 40 seconds.]* Croissant dough is much stickier than bread dough, so don't be alarmed if it seems rather moist. Put dough in covered bowl and allow to triple in volume. This may be done for minimum of 6 hours, or overnight, in refrigerator, or left out at room temperature for 2 to 3 hours.

With heel of hand or again with mixer, work or cream 3 T. flour and butter together. Make smooth paste consistency of soft butter. Reserve at room temperature.

1st ROLL: Roll out dough on *generously* floured work surface into rectangle 6 × 15 inches *(15 × 38cm)*. Lift dough gently once or twice to make sure it is not sticking. Evenly spread upper ⅔ of dough with butter, leaving ½-inch *(1.2cm)* border around top and sides. Smooth out butter with metal spatula dipped in warm water. The butter and dough should have about the same consistency. Fold dough like business letter. Fold bottom ⅓ up and with soft pastry brush clean off excess flour. Fold down the top ⅓ and clean off dough. Square up edges of dough. Turn dough counter-clockwise so it resembles a book with open flap on the right.

2nd ROLL: Again flour work surface generously and roll dough out as before. Fold as before, brushing off excess flour. Wrap dough well and refrigerate at least 4 hours or overnight if you like, up to 24 hours.

3rd ROLL: Roll out dough and fold as before, brushing off excess flour.

4th ROLL: Roll out dough again for 4th time. Refrigerate again for about 2 hours, just until dough becomes stiff enough to roll out again for cutting into triangles. Again, you may keep dough overnight.

Remove dough from refrigerator and cut in half lengthwise. Return one piece to refrigerator. You can keep half the dough overnight and have fresh croissants the second day as well.

Roll out the dough to a rectangle 5 × 20 inches *(12.5 × 50cm)*. Cut off one square and cut on diagonal to make 2 triangles. With rolling pin roll out each triangle so that it is more pointed, so that the sides are somewhat longer than the base.

With your finger, roll up this triangle of dough from the bottom ends. Place on lightly greased baking sheet. Bend ends of croissants inward slightly to make the crescent shape.

Brush all croissants with milk and let rise for about 1 hour at room temperature (70°) or until they increase 50% in volume. *Be careful here:* too much rising will cause them to fall during baking.

Preheat oven to 400°. (375° if oven is small)

Brush with Sweet Glaze or Egg Glaze. Bake at 400° until nicely browned, about 15 to 20 minutes. Serve before they are an hour old.

Melinda M. Vance, West Hartford, CT

Variations, Advance Preparation, and Serving Suggestions:

There is no question that croissants are superior when eaten within 1 hour of being baked. However, if this is an impossibility, underbake them by 5 minutes. When completely cool, freeze well wrapped. When ready to serve, take directly from the freezer, place on baking sheet in 400° oven for another 5 to 8 minutes.

For PETITS PAINS AU CHOCOLATE, roll out each piece of croissant dough into strips 21 × 6 inches *(52.5 × 15cm)*. Cut each strip into 7 pieces 3 × 6 inches. You will have 14 pieces of dough. Place a ½ oz. *(15g)* piece of chocolate across the short end and roll the dough up. Place dough on baking sheet; brush with milk and allow to rise until double. Brush with Sweet Glaze and bake in 400° oven for 12 to 15 minutes.

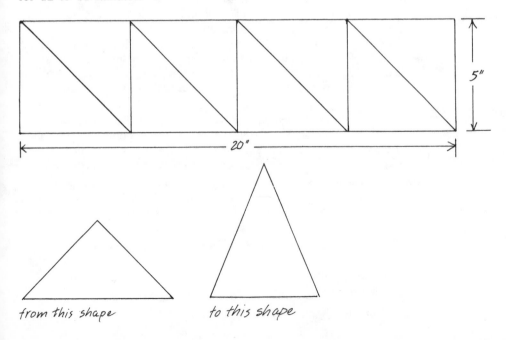

from this shape   to this shape

YIELD: 2 Large Coffeecakes
CALORIES PER CAKE: 4196
CARBOHYDRATES: 433g
PROTEIN: 112g
FAT: 224g
PREPARING: 2 Hours
RISING: 4 Hours Minimum
BAKING: 30-35 Minutes
COOLING: 30 Minutes
FREEZING: Yes

Garmish Nut Stollen

A stollen is a rich yeast dough. When times were hard in Europe, stollen was made using bread flour, water and a few raisins, but when times improved, butter, spices and sugar were added to make a much more elaborate yeast bread.

DOUGH:

1½ pkgs. (¼ oz. each) *(10g)* **active dry yeast**
⅓ cup *(80ml)* **warm water**
2 tsp. plus 2 T. *(25g)* **sugar**
1 cup *(240ml)* **milk**
½ cup *(115g)* **unsalted sweet butter**
1 tsp. **salt**
2 **eggs**
2 **egg yolks**
4½ cups *(510g)* **flour**
2 T. *(30g)* **unsalted sweet butter, melted**
2 tsp. **grated fresh lemon peel**
¼ tsp. **ground cardamom**
¼ tsp. **ginger**
¼ tsp. **freshly grated nutmeg**
1 cup *(170g)* **golden raisins**

NUT FILLING:

4 **egg whites, at room temperature**
2 cups *(200g)* **finely ground walnuts, almost a powder**
1½ cups *(180g)* **coarsely ground walnuts**
1 cup *(200g)* **sugar**
4 tsp. **water**
½ tsp. **cinnamon**

EGG GLAZE:

1 **egg**
1 T. **heavy cream**

CONFECTIONERS' SUGAR ICING:

1 cup *(130g)* **confectioners' sugar**
Water to moisten sugar
½ cup *(60g)* **chopped walnuts**

DOUGH: Dissolve yeast in warm water; add 2 tsp. sugar and set aside to proof, about 5 minutes.

Heat milk in small saucepan until hot; remove from heat. Stir ½ cup butter and salt into milk.

Put eggs and yolks into large mixer bowl; beat to mix. Gradually beat in 2 T. sugar until thick and lemon colored. Beat in milk mixture and 2 cups flour until smooth. Beat in yeast mixture. Stir in melted butter, lemon peel, cardamom, ginger, nutmeg and remaining flour to form a soft dough. Turn dough out onto lightly floured board and knead 5 minutes. Knead in raisins. Put in large greased bowl, cover and let rise in refrigerator until doubled in bulk, 4 to 5 hours or overnight.

NUT FILLING: Combine all filling ingredients in medium sized saucepan. Cook, stirring over low heat until warm and sugar dissolved, about 10 minutes; remove from heat. Cool to room temperature. Filling can be made up to 24 hours ahead and refrigerated covered. Bring back to room temperature before using.

Remove dough from refrigerator; let stand, covered 30 minutes. Place a 24 × 12-inch *(60 × 30cm)* piece of foil on dampened surface; lightly flour foil. Roll dough out on foil to form 22 × 12-inch *(55 × 30cm)* rectangle. Spread nut filling over dough, leaving 1-inch border on all sides. Mix ingredients for Egg Glaze in small bowl; brush border with some of glaze. Loosely roll up dough beginning at long edge, using foil to help turn dough. Pinch seam and ends to seal. Using long sharp knife, cut roll crosswise in half. Transfer pieces to floured well-greased baking sheet. Put first piece in refrigerator, covered.

Cut second piece lengthwise in half. Working quickly, twist halves together with sliced edges upward. Pinch ends together. Repeat with first piece. Let rise until doubled in bulk, about 45 minutes.

Bake in preheated 375° oven 15 minutes; brush with part of Egg Glaze. Reduce to 350°; bake 10 more minutes; brush with remaining glaze and sprinkle with 2 to 4 T. sugar. Continue to bake 5 to 10 minutes until golden and nut mixture is set. (Cover with foil if it browns too quickly.) Cool on wire rack 30 minutes.

Drizzle icing over stollen in decorative pattern; sprinkle with walnuts. Cool completely. Refrigerate tightly wrapped up to 4 days. Serve at room temperature.

Freezes well without icing.

Melinda M. Vance, West Hartford, CT

Swiss Pear Ring

This is an unusual sweet bread, using dried pears.

YIELD: 15-20 Servings or 1 Large Ring
TOTAL CALORIES: 4290
CARBOHYDRATES: 763g
PROTEIN: 80g
FAT: 102g
PREPARING: 30 Minutes
RISING: 2 Hours
BAKING: 35 Minutes
FREEZING: Yes

DOUGH: In large mixing bowl, soften yeast in warm water. Add salt, sugar, vanilla and warm milk. Mix in 2 cups flour; beat at medium speed until dough is smooth, elastic and pulls away from sides of bowl, 3 to 5 minutes. Mix in yolks and melted butter; stir in 1 cup more flour to make soft dough. On floured board, knead until smooth and satiny. *[FOOD PROCESSOR: Put 4 cups flour in work bowl. Add yeast mixture, egg yolks, and butter; process 20 to 30 seconds, or until dough is thoroughly mixed, smooth and satiny.]* Place dough in greased bowl; turn to grease. Cover; let rise in warm place until doubled in bulk, about 1 hour.

FILLING: While dough is rising prepare filling: in 2 qt. *(2L)* pan, combine 1½ cups water, coarsely chopped pears and lemon juice. Simmer uncovered, stirring often until pears are tender and liquid is absorbed, 10 to 15 minutes. Remove from heat and stir in all remaining ingredients. Set filling aside.

Punch down dough, then knead lightly on floured board until smooth. Roll out dough into 20-inch *(50cm)* square. Spread pear filling on top to within 1 inch *(2.5cm)* of dough edges. Tightly roll up, jelly-roll fashion; pinch to seal. Place roll, seam side down, on greased baking sheet; shape into ring. Moisten ends with water; pinch to seal. With sharp knife, make crosswise cuts about 2 inches *(5cm)* apart in top of ring, slashing just to filling. (Alternate method: cut slits through ring at 2 inch *(5cm)* intervals; turn each section on its side.) Beat egg white with ½ tsp. water; brush over ring; sprinkle with 2 T. granulated sugar. Let rise, uncovered, in warm place until almost doubled, about 50 minutes.

Bake in preheated 350° oven 30 to 35 minutes, until well browned. Loosen ring from sheet; let cool on sheet 10 minutes. Slide onto wire rack to cool to warm or cool completely, wrap and freeze. To reheat: wrap thawed loaf in foil; place in preheated 350° oven 20 minutes.

Lee Grimmeisen, West Hartford, CT

Microwave Conversion Instructions: Filling: Combine pears, 2 T. lemon juice and 1 cup water. Cook on High 10 minutes. Stir in remaining filling ingredients. Set aside.

First yeast rising: Place dough in greased bowl. Put bowl in glass pan containing 3 cups warm water. Grease top of dough. Cover bowl with plastic wrap. Cook on Warm (10%) for 40 minutes or until doubled.

Second rising: Conventional method so that dough is not disturbed after rising.

Bake in regular oven for best results.

DOUGH:

1 pkg. (¼ oz.) *(7g)* **active dry yeast**
¼ cup *(60ml)* **warm water**
½ tsp. salt
2 T. *(25g)* **sugar**
1 tsp. vanilla
¾ cup *(180ml)* **warm milk**
3-4 cups *(340-450g)* **flour**
3 egg yolks
¼ cup *(60g)* **butter, melted**

FILLING:

1½ cups *(355ml)* **water**
2 cups *(340g)* **coarsely chopped dried pears (about ¾ lb.)**
2 T. *(30ml)* **fresh lemon juice**
½ cup *(85g)* **golden raisins**
½ cup *(100g)* **brown sugar, firmly packed**
½ cup *(60g)* **chopped walnuts**
2 T. *(30ml)* **Kirsch**
1 tsp. grated lemon peel
1 tsp. cinnamon
½ tsp. crushed anise seed
½ tsp. ground cloves
¼ tsp. ground ginger
¼ tsp. coriander

GLAZE:

1 egg white
½ tsp. water
2 T. *(25g)* **sugar**

YIELD: 16-20 Servings or
  1 9-inch Tube Pan
TOTAL CALORIES: 5080
CALORIES PER SERVING: 254
CARBOHYDRATES: 30g
PROTEIN: 2g
FAT: 14g
CHOLESTEROL: High
PREPARING: 25 Minutes
BAKING: 55 Minutes
FREEZING: Yes

Prune Sour Cream Coffee Cake

A delicious variation of a sour cream coffee cake!

Boiling water
1½ cups (approximately 1 12 oz.
  (340g) box) pitted prunes
2 cups (225g) flour
1 tsp. baking powder
1 tsp. baking soda
½ tsp. salt
1 cup (225g) softened butter
1 cup (200g) sugar
1 T. grated lemon rind
2 eggs
1 cup (225g) sour cream
1 T. pure vanilla extract
½ cup (100g) dark brown sugar,
  firmly packed
1 T. cinnamon
⅔ cup (80g) chopped walnuts

Pour boiling water over prunes; let stand 15 minutes. Drain; cut into sixths; set aside.

Sift together flour, baking powder, baking soda and salt. Remove ¼ cup of flour mixture; toss with prunes.

Cream butter and sugar until fluffy; beat in lemon rind. Beat in eggs, one at a time. Slowly beat in flour mixture alternately with sour cream and vanilla, beginning and ending with flour. [FOOD PROCESSOR: Combine brown sugar, cinnamon and unchopped nuts in work bowl; process until nuts are coarsely chopped. Remove and set aside. Combine flour, baking powder, soda and salt in work bowl; process 2 seconds. Remove and set aside. Place eggs and sugar in work bowl; process 1 full minute. Add butter and lemon rind and process 1 full minute. Add sour cream and vanilla and combine. Blend in reserved flour mixture by turning machine on/off 3 or 4 times or until flour just disappears. Do not overprocess. Transfer mixture to a bowl.] Fold in prunes gently, using a spatula.

Combine brown sugar, cinnamon and nuts.

Spread ⅓ of batter carefully into a greased and floured 9-inch (22.5cm) tube pan. Sprinkle with ⅓ of brown sugar mixture; repeat layering 2 more times, ending with brown sugar mixture.

Bake in a preheated 350° oven 55 minutes, or until done; cake should be very moist. Cool in pan, on wire rack 10 minutes. Remove from pan; finish cooling on serving plate. If freezing, cool completely on wire rack, wrap tightly and freeze.

Edith Bruce, Evanston, IL

Nutritional Notes: This recipe was tested successfully with 2 cups (240g) whole wheat flour and butter or margarine decreased to ½ cup (115g).

Microwave Conversion Instructions: Treatment of prunes can be improved by using a microwave, leaving important nutrients intact. Place pitted prunes and ¼ cup (60ml) water (or wine) in 4 cup (1L) glass measure. Cover and cook on High 2 to 3 minutes, until softened.

Note: Add ¼ cup (30g) very fine graham cracker crumbs to coat greased tube pan rather than flour. Layer cake batter as directed above. Elevate tube pan or bundt mold on rack or inverted saucer. Cook on Medium (50%) 17 minutes, turning ¼ turn every 3 minutes. Cook on High 2 minutes or until top springs back and cake starts to shrink from sides of pan. Cool 20 minutes in pan on rack. Complete as directed above.

Six Weeks Bran Muffins

Here is a muffin batter you can stash away in your refrigerator and bring out at strategic moments in various guises. The batter will keep in the refrigerator up to 6 weeks. You can bake as many or as few at a time as suits you.

YIELD: 22 2½-Inch Muffins
TOTAL CALORIES: 4004
CALORIES PER MUFFIN: 182
CARBOHYDRATES: 28g
PROTEIN: 4g
FAT: 6g
PREPARING: 20 Minutes
BAKING: 15 Minutes
FREEZING: Yes

Put 100% bran cereal in a bowl and pour boiling water over it. Let cool.

Beat together shortening and sugar until light and fluffy. Add eggs, mix thoroughly.

Add flour, baking soda, Kelloggs All Bran, 100% bran cereal and buttermilk; mix well. Cover mixture and store in refrigerator until ready to bake muffins.

Fill buttered 2-inch (5cm) muffin cups two-thirds full. Bake in a preheated 400° oven, 12 to 15 minutes. Serve hot.

Lois Baker, West Hartford, CT

1 cup *(60g)* **100% bran cereal**
  (Nabisco preferred)
1 cup *(240ml)* **boiling water**
½ cup *(100g)* **vegetable shortening**
  (Crisco preferred)
1¼ cups *(250g)* **sugar**
2 **eggs**
2½ cups *(285g)* **flour**
2½ tsp. **baking soda**
2 cups *(170g)* **Kelloggs All Bran**
2 cups *(475ml)* **buttermilk**

Variations, Advance Preparation, and Serving Suggestions:
These muffins may be baked; cooled completely then frozen.

For variety you may add one or more of the optional ingredients.

Nutritional Notes: Buttermilk made from skim milk contains only a trace of fat and less cholesterol than if made from whole milk. Bran, provided in the cereals, is an excellent source of dietary fiber. Undigestible fiber does not supply calories and is an important component of a healthy diet. These muffins also have the advantage of the additional vitamin fortification of the cereal manufacturer.

Microwave Conversion Instructions: Note: This recipe is "use as needed", which is excellent for Microwave. Prepare batter as for conventional recipe. Place 2 paper cups in each cup of either a microwave muffin pan, or custard cups. Fill cups ½ full. Arrange in a ring when cooking 3 or more at a time. If using microwave muffin pan and only baking 2 or 3, alternate cups for more even baking. Cooking time on High is as follows: 1 muffin — 20 to 30 seconds, 2 muffins — 45 seconds to 1½ minutes, 4 muffins — 1½ to 2 minutes, 6 muffins — 2½ to 3½ minutes. Timing depends on quantity placed in cup and temperature of the batter before cooking.

Turn pan if it appears to be cooking unevenly.

OPTIONAL INGREDIENTS:
Select from following.

Nuts, raisins, currants, sunflower seeds, dried apricots, grated lemon or orange rind, grated fresh apple, dried figs, dates, prunes, well-drained crushed pineapple, minced citron

Pâte à Brioche

BASIC BRIOCHE DOUGH

Absolutely the finest recipe for brioche! No more the dry tasteless muffin so often found in bakeries or bread baskets. Brioche is a French yeast dough, very light and fluffy with an even crumb and hairline crust, perfectly balancing the taste of butter and egg. The finished article has as many different shapes as uses — from mere breakfast roll to sandwich bread, to hors d'oeuvre wrappings, to casings for meat and fish, to crusts for pies.

YIELD: 12 oz. (340g) Dough
TOTAL CALORIES: 1548
CARBOHYDRATES: 120g
PROTEIN: 33g
FAT: 104g
CALORIES PER 1 OZ.: 129
PREPARING: 25 Minutes
RISING: 7 Hours
BAKING: 17-45 Minutes
CHILLING: 8½ Hours
FREEZING: Yes

SMALL QUANTITY (12 oz.) (340g)

BRIOCHE DOUGH:

1 tsp. active dry yeast
2 T. (25g) sugar
2 T. (30ml) scalded milk, cooled to warm
1¼ cups (150g) flour
2 eggs, at room temperature
½ tsp. salt
7 T. (100g) unsalted sweet butter, softened

LARGE QUANTITY (20 oz.) (570g)

BRIOCHE DOUGH:

1½ tsps. active dry yeast or 2 tsps. fresh cake yeast
3 T. (40g) sugar
3 T. (45ml) scalded milk, cooled to warm
2 cups (225g) flour
3 eggs, at room temperature
¾ tsp. salt
10 T. (140g) unsalted sweet butter, softened

EGG GLAZE:

1 egg beaten with 1 T. cream

ELECTRIC MIXER METHOD: In a small bowl, dissolve yeast and a pinch of sugar in warm milk. Transfer mixture to bowl of electric mixer; add ¼ cup flour and 1 egg and beat until well combined. Sprinkle remaining flour over this mixture, but do not incorporate yet. Cover bowl; let stand at room temperature 1½ to 2 hours.

Add sugar, salt, and remaining egg(s) to bowl. Beat until dough is light. Beat in softened butter. Continue to beat until all butter is well incorporated. Scrape mixture from sides of bowl into a single mass at bottom of bowl. Dust top lightly with flour to prevent crust from forming. Cover bowl airtight. Let stand in warm (80°-90°) location 5 to 6 hours, until light and spongy and tripled in bulk.

Deflate dough by stirring down; refrigerate, covered, 1 hour, until slightly firm. Turn out onto lightly floured board. With floured hands, gently press out into a rectangle; fold in thirds like business letter. Turn dough 90°; press it out again and fold in thirds. Wrap well and refrigerate at least 8 hours or overnight. Dough will keep 3 days in refrigerator well-wrapped and weighted down, or it can be frozen for 1 week. To defrost, thaw overnight in refrigerator.

FOOD PROCESSOR METHOD: In a small bowl, dissolve yeast and a pinch sugar in warm milk. Transfer to food processor. Add ¼ cup flour and 1 egg. Process on and off to combine. Sprinkle remaining flour over mixture but do not mix. Cover and let stand 1½ to 2 hours.

Add sugar, salt and egg(s) to work bowl. Process 20 seconds. With machine on, quickly add butter a few pieces at a time through feed tube. When all butter has been added, process 30 to 45 seconds longer. Scrape mixture into a larger bowl. Dust top lightly with flour. Cover bowl airtight. Proceed with recipe as described above.

TO FORM AND BAKE BRIOCHE: (Directions that follow are for individual traditional brioche in shape of ball with small head known as *brioche a tete*.) Butter molds and divide dough into amounts appropriate for size mold you are using. Roll each piece of dough into a ball; pinch off a small piece of dough the size of a walnut. Form this piece into a teardrop shape. Place the original ball into bottom of each mold. With a sharp knife or small pair scissors, cut an "X" in top of each ball. Push two of your fingers into this "X" and enlarge the hole; insert narrow end of teardrop.

Cover molds with buttered sheet of waxed paper. Let rise in warm humid location 1½ to 3 hours or until dough has doubled in bulk. Place baking sheet on lower middle shelf of oven. Preheat to 425°. Lightly brush tops of brioche with Egg Glaze. Place molds on sheet.

Bake 5 minutes and then lower oven to 350° and bake 9 to 12 minutes longer. Check to see if browning too quickly after 5 minutes. Cover with foil if necessary. Unmold onto racks. Cool slightly before serving. Best served warm.

Maryann Reuben, West Hartford, CT

Variations, Advance Preparation, and Serving Suggestions:
Given below are the various molds and shapes for Brioche Dough and the appropriate amount of dough to use for each and corresponding baking time.

¼-cup *(60ml)* capacity molds	= 1 oz. *(30g)* Dough	Bake in preheated 425° oven 5 minutes and then lower to 350° 9 to 15 minutes
½-cup *(120ml)* capacity molds	= 1½ oz. *(45g)* Dough	Bake in preheated 425° oven 5 minutes and then lower to 350° 9 to 15 minutes
⅔-¾-cup *(160-180ml)* capacity molds	= 2 oz. *(60g)* Dough	Bake in preheated 425° oven 5 minutes and then lower to 350° 9 to 15 minutes.
1 10-inch *(25cm)* tart pan	= 12 oz. *(340g)* Dough	Fill and bake in preheated 400° oven 15 minutes and then lower to 300° for 30 minutes.
Brioche en Couronne 1½-qt. *(1.5L)* fluted brioche mold or charlotte mold	= 20 oz. *(570g)* Dough	Bake in preheated 425° oven 5 minutes and then lower to 350° 25 to 35 minutes.
Brioche Mousseline 5-cup *(1.2L)* mold or 1-lb. *(450g)* coffee can	= 12 oz. *(340g)* Dough	Bake in preheated 375° oven 35 minutes.
Brioche Mousseline 10-cup *(2.5L)* mold or 2-lb. *(900g)* coffee can	= 20 oz. *(570g)* Dough	Bake in preheated 425° oven 5 minutes and then lower to 375° 25 to 35 minutes.
Wrapped dishes such as Coulibiac, Beef Wellington	= 20 oz. *(570g)* Dough	Bake in preheated 425° oven 30 to 40 minutes.

YIELD: 20-24 Servings or 1 Large Loaf
TOTAL CALORIES: 6000
CALORIES PER SERVING: 250
CARBOHYDRATES: 35g
PROTEIN: 5g
FAT: 10g
PREPARING: 40 Minutes
RISING: 3 Hours
BAKING: 45 Minutes
FREEZING: Yes

Christopsoma

GREEK CHRISTMAS BREAD

The given decoration is the early form of a Christian cross. It can be fashioned into initials, names or dates to celebrate other occasions.

DOUGH:

2 pkgs. (¼ oz. each) *(14g)* **active dry yeast**
½ cup *(120ml)* **warm water**
½ cup *(120ml)* **milk, scalded and cooled**
1 cup *(225g)* **butter, melted and cooled to lukewarm**
4 eggs, slightly beaten
¾ cup *(150g)* **sugar**
1 tsp. salt
7 cups *(800g)* **unsifted flour**
9 candied cherries

EGG GLAZE:

1 egg white, slightly beaten

Combine yeast and warm water (110°-115°); let stand until softened, about 5 minutes. In large bowl combine yeast mixture, milk, butter, eggs, sugar and salt; blend thoroughly; gradually beat in flour. Turn dough out onto lightly floured board and knead until smooth and elastic, about 10 minutes. Place in large oiled bowl, turning to coat with oil; cover and let rise until almost doubled in bulk, about 2 hours.

Punch down dough; pinch off 2 pieces, each 3 inches *(7.5cm)* in diameter and set aside. On an unfloured board, knead remaining dough to form a smooth ball. Place on greased baking sheet; flatten to a 9 to 10-inch *(22.5 to 25cm)* round.

Shape each of 3-inch balls into a 15-inch *(38cm)* rope by rolling on unfloured board, using the palm of your hand. Cut a 5-inch *(12.5cm)* long slash into each end of the two ropes. Cross ropes on center of the round loaf *(do not press down)*. Curl slashed sections away from center of each rope. Place a candied cherry in each curl and one in the center of the cross. Brush loaf with beaten egg white. Lightly cover loaf; set in warm place to rise until almost doubled in bulk, (about 1 hour). The rope edges may slide during the rising process; if so, secure and bake with wooden toothpicks holding rope in place. Bake in preheated 350° oven 45 minutes or until wooden skewer inserted in center comes out clean. Serve warm or let cool on wire rack. Cut into wedges or slices. Serve with jam, or toast and serve with honey.

Maryann Reuben, West Hartford, CT

French Bread

Though French bread pans are best, it is possible to make this bread on greased baking sheets.

YIELD: 3-4 Loaves
TOTAL CALORIES: 2872
CALORIES PER LOAF: 718
CARBOHYDRATES: 150g
PROTEIN: 25g
FAT: 2g
PREPARING: 30 Minutes
RISING: 1½ Hours
BAKING: 42 Minutes
FREEZING: Yes

Combine yeast, sugar, and warm water in warm bowl; stir to dissolve. Put in warm place to proof, (about 10 min.)

Add salt and 4 cups of flour to yeast mixture; stir to blend well. Add more flour, stirring in ½ cup at a time, until dough leaves the sides of bowl almost clean. Add only enough flour to make a somewhat lumpy, sticky dough. Put dough onto well-floured board. Knead about 10 minutes, adding more flour if dough is too sticky. *[FOOD PROCESSOR: Divide ingredients in half and make dough in 2 batches. Put flour and salt in work bowl and turn on machine. With machine running, add yeast mixture through feed tube. Process for 40 seconds, or until dough is uniformly moist and elastic. If it is too wet add additional flour a teaspoon at a time until dough is proper consistency.]*

Cover sides and bottom of bowl with vegetable shortening. Put dough in bowl; turn to coat with oil. Cover with plastic wrap and towel; let rise in warm place until double in bulk, about 45 minutes.

Grease bread pans with vegetable shortening; set aside. Punch down risen dough and turn out onto bread board. Divide dough into 3 or 4 sections. Each section is then individually shaped as follows: pat dough into oval, and turn upper half over bottom half like a half-moon. With side of your hand pound across dough with 6 karate chops. Repeat process 8 to 10 times by folding over alternate sides, pounding each time. Then, with firm motion, roll out dough between your extended hands and table to form 12-inch *(30cm)* cylinder; place in greased bread pan. Set loaves aside to double in bulk.

Make diagonal slashes along length of breads with razor held at 45-degree angle. Paint dough with Egg Glaze. Place in preheated 450° oven for 12 minutes; lower temperature to 350°. Bake 30 minutes longer. During baking, check loaves to see if they are browning too quickly. If so, cover with foil for remainder of baking. Cool baked loaves on wire racks.

Ann Howard Cookery, Farmington, CT
via Maryann Reuben, West Hartford, CT

Variations, Advance Preparation, and Serving Suggestions:
To freeze: Place individual cooled loaves in foil; wrap tightly. To bake frozen, put in preheated 350° oven for 30 minutes. Open foil last 10 minutes if a crusty loaf is desired.

Nutritional Notes: Individuals with lactose intolerance, milk allergy, or fat intolerance can utilize French bread as a milk-free product that is almost fat-free as well.

DOUGH:
1 pkg. (¼ oz.) *(7g)* **active dry yeast**
1 T. **sugar**
2½ cups *(600ml)* **warm water**
   (105°-115°)
1 T. **salt**
7 cups *(800g)* **unbleached flour**
   (approximately)
Vegetable shortening

EGG WHITE GLAZE:
1 **egg white**
2 tsp. **water**

Challah

Challah (pronounced hal-la) is a beautiful egg-rich and light textured white bread steeped in Jewish history. The preparation of the dough for baking in the Jewish kitchen is itself the "act of Challah" in which the woman takes a small part of the dough to burn in the oven as an offering. She thereby reenacts her origin at the Creation when she sprang from man's rib. The remaining dough may then be baked as she chooses, most often in this braided form. The reason for the quantity of dough is based on the Hebrew law of Challah which requires that the flour to be kneaded be no less than the weight of 43 and 1/5 eggs (3½ lbs.) The portion to be removed as the Challah offering no less than the size of an olive.

YIELD: 2 Large Loaves
CALORIES PER LOAF: 2640
CARBOHYDRATES: 430g
PROTEIN: 62g
FAT: 75g
PREPARING: 30 Minutes
RISING: 8½ Hours
BAKING: 40-45 Minutes
FREEZING: Yes

DOUGH:

2 pkgs. (¼ oz. each) *(14g)* **active dry yeast**
2 tsp. *(9g)* **plus ½ cup** *(100g)* **sugar**
7¾ cups *(880g)* **flour (approximately)**
2¼ cups *(525ml)* **warm water**
½ cup *(120ml)* **plus 1 T.** *(15ml)* **oil**
2 T. kosher salt
2 eggs

EGG GLAZE:

1 egg
2 T. *(27g)* **sugar**
Poppy seeds

Place yeast, 2 tsp. sugar and 2 T. flour in tall tumbler; add ¾ cup warm (110°-115°) water; mix and set in warm place to proof.

In large bowl, place 4 cups flour; add 1½ cups water, ½ cup oil, ½ cup sugar, salt and eggs. Mix well. When yeast mixture reaches top of tumbler, add it to mixture in bowl. Mix well; gradually add 3 or more cups flour. On a floured board knead mixture until smooth and elastic. *[FOOD PROCESSOR: Divide ingredients in half and process dough in 2 batches. Pour warm water into a small bowl and stir in yeast and 1 tsp. sugar. Let proof 10 minutes. Put flour, salt, sugar, and oil in work bowl and combine by turning on/off about 6 times. Add yeast mixture and eggs; process until dough is smooth and elastic.]* Transfer dough to bowl, cover it and set in warm place until doubled in bulk, about 5 hours.

Punch down dough and add about ⅔ cup flour. Knead to form soft but not sticky dough. Cover top of dough with 1 T. oil. Cover, let rise until doubled in bulk, about 2½ hours.

Knead again; divide dough into 2 parts and shape into 2 loaves. Divide each loaf into fourths; braid 3 of these; divide remaining part into thirds, braiding these and attaching to top of first larger braid. Repeat process with other loaf of dough. Put loaves on greased baking sheet. Cover and let rise until doubled in bulk, about 1 hour.

Combine 1 egg and 2 T. sugar. Brush over tops of loaves; sprinkle with poppy seeds. Bake in preheated 350° oven, 40 to 45 minutes or until bread sounds hollow when tapped on bottom with knuckles. (Cover with foil during last 10 minutes if breads are browning too rapidly). Cool on wire racks.

Maryann Reuben, West Hartford, CT

Nutritional Notes: ½ cup *(60g)* wheat germ may be added with flour to increase nutritional value; it is particulary high in B vitamins and protein.

Greek Easter Bread

YIELD: 1 Large Loaf
TOTAL CALORIES: 3084
CARBOHYDRATES: 452g
PROTEIN: 85g
FAT: 104g
PREPARING: 1¼ Hours
RISING: 2¼ Hours
BAKING: 35 Minutes
COOKING: 20 Minutes
FREEZING: Yes

Red Easter eggs embedded in a braided bread ring.

In the traditional version, the dough is not braided. Instead, a triad of small loaves, together on a baking sheet, forms a cloverleaf. Representing the Trinity, the three joined loaves are sliced individually and a slice of each is served to each guest.

DOUGH: Combine milk and butter in a saucepan. Stir over low heat until butter is melted. Let cool to lukewarm. In large bowl, stir the yeast into ½ cup (120ml) of the milk mixture with 1 tsp. sugar: let proof 15 minutes in warm place until foamy. Add the remaining milk mixture, eggs, orange juice, ¼ cup sugar, orange rind and salt. Combine well. Stir in flour, using more if necessary to form a soft, sticky dough.

Transfer dough to floured surface and knead incorporating more flour if dough sticks, 8-10 minutes, until smooth. Form dough into ball, place in buttered bowl, turn to coat. Let dough rise in warm (80°-85°) humid place, loosely covered, 1½ hours, until double in bulk.

Punch down dough. Divide into thirds. Form each piece into 20-inch (50cm) long rope. Braid ropes together and form the braid into a round, pinching ends together and tucking them underneath. Transfer round to buttered baking sheet; nestle Red Easter Eggs among the braids. Let loaf rise, loosely covered, 45 minutes, until double in bulk. Brush with Egg Glaze made by beating egg and milk together. Place bread on lower middle shelf of preheated 375° oven; (check after 20 minutes to see if browning too rapidly; cover with foil if necessary.) bake 25 minutes. Remove from oven. Brush with Egg Glaze again, sprinkle with sesame seeds if desired. Bake 10 minutes more until bread sounds hollow when bottom is tapped. Watch carefully to prevent burning. Remove from oven, place on rack to cool.

RED EASTER EGGS: Mix the water, vinegar and food colorings in a large stainless steel saucepan. Add eggs, well rinsed, in one layer in the pan. Add more water, if necessary, to cover eggs. Bring to simmer over moderate heat. Simmer 12 minutes. Transfer with slotted spoon to rack to cool.

Kathleen J. Schwartz, Avon, CT

Variations, Advance Preparation, and Serving Suggestions:
On Easter morning, serve the braid with sweet butter and jam, scrambled eggs, baked ham and slices of fresh horseradish root.

The bread itself is delicious; bake it throughout the year.

Braid, minus eggs, may be frozen, well-wrapped, 3 to 4 weeks without loss of flavor.

DOUGH:
1 cup (240ml) milk
6 T. (85g) unsalted butter, cut into bits
1½ T. (10g) active dry yeast
¼ cup (50g) plus 1 tsp. (5g) sugar
2 large eggs, lightly beaten
¼ cup (60ml) fresh orange juice
1 T. grated orange rind
½ tsp. salt
4 cups (450g) flour (approximately)

GLAZE:
1 large egg
1 T. (15ml) milk

1 T. (7.5g) sesame seeds (optional)

RED EASTER EGGS:
2 cups (475ml) water
½ cup (120ml) white vinegar
3 T. (45ml) red food coloring
1 drop blue food coloring
6 white eggs

Maple Oatmeal Bread

YIELD: 2 Loaves
CALORIES PER LOAF: 2358
CARBOHYDRATES: 455g
PROTEIN: 58g
FAT: 34g
PREPARING: 20 Minutes
RISING: 3 Hours
BAKING: 45 Minutes
FREEZING: Yes

This is a loosely textured bread with an unusual light-brown color and a rich full flavor. It is especially good toasted and buttered.

1 tsp. sugar
2 pkgs. (¼ oz. each) *(14g)* active dry yeast
¼ cup *(60ml)* warm water
2 cups *(170g)* regular rolled oats
1 cup *(240ml)* real maple syrup
1 cup *(240ml)* hot strong decaffeinated coffee
⅓ cup *(75g)* butter
2 tsp. salt
6 cups *(675g)* flour (approximately)
2 eggs, lightly beaten

Place sugar and yeast in bowl; add warm water (110°-115°) and mix gently. Set in warm place to proof.

Combine and mix oats, maple syrup, hot coffee, butter, salt and 1 cup flour. Cool to lukewarm; add yeast. Beat in eggs until mixture is smooth. Mix in remaining flour; beat until dough is smooth and elastic. *[FOOD PROCESSOR: Divide ingredients in half and process dough in 2 batches. Put 2½ cups flour and salt into work bowl; combine by turning machine on/off a few times. Add yeast/oat mixture and eggs; process until dough is thoroughly mixed. Add additional flour, a few tablespoons at a time and process after each addition until dough is smooth and elastic.]* Form into ball; transfer to buttered bowl; turn dough in bowl to coat. Cover with towel; let rise 1½ to 2 hours until doubled in bulk.

Punch down dough; divide in half; form into 2 loaves and place in buttered 9 × 5 × 3-inch *(22.5 × 12.5 × 7.5cm)* loaf pans. Let rise until doubled in bulk, about 1 hour.

Bake in preheated 350° oven for 45 minutes or until bread sounds hollow when tapped on bottom with knuckles. Cool on rack in pan. If freezing, cool completely first.

Lee Grimmeisen, West Hartford, CT

Nutritional Notes: Oatmeal adds nutritional value to bread, especially protein, B vitamins and iron. When oats are processed, the bran and the germ remain in the oatmeal product. "Old Fashioned" or "steel-cut" oatmeals are preferable to "minute" or "quick" oats as the latter are highly processed and have lost some nutritional value.

Brown Bread

YIELD: 2 Loaves
CALORIES PER LOAF: 1209
CARBOHYDRATES: 229g
PROTEIN: 44g
FAT: 13g
PREPARING: 20 Minutes
RISING: 2 Hours
BAKING: 45 Minutes
FREEZING: Yes

This recipe won a $50 prize in a G. Fox and Co. department store cooking contest many years ago and has since been known in the Webster family as "Dale Webster's $50 G. Fox bread."

2 pkgs. (¼ oz. each) *(14g)* active dry yeast
¼ cup *(60ml)* lukewarm water
Pinch of sugar
2 cups *(475ml)* milk, scalded
½ cup *(120ml)* molasses
2 tsp. salt
2½ cups *(285g)* unbleached flour
2½ cups *(300g)* whole wheat flour
¼ cup *(30g)* wheat germ

In a small bowl, proof yeast in water with sugar. In another small bowl, mix together milk, molasses and salt. Let cool to lukewarm.

Place flours in large bowl. Add yeast and milk mixtures. Beat well with wooden spoon. Add wheat germ, mix well. *[FOOD PROCESSOR: Put flours, salt and wheat germ into work bowl. With the machine running, add yeast mixture and milk mixture through feed tube. Process until dough is uniformly moist and elastic, about 40 seconds.]* Let rise, covered, in a warm place until double in bulk, about 45 minutes or longer.

Punch dough down, beat again with wooden spoon. Divide dough in

half. Place each piece in buttered 9 × 5 × 3-inch
(22.5 × 12.5 × 7.5cm) loaf pans. Let rise, covered, in warm place until double in bulk, about 40 minutes or longer.

Place pans, uncovered, on lowest rack of preheated 375° oven. Bake 40 to 45 minutes. Cover with foil during last 20 minutes of baking if necessary to prevent over-browning. Remove pans from oven. Turn loaves out of pans. Cool on racks to room temperature.

Nancy Webster Woodworth, West Hartford, CT

Nutritional Notes: Wheat germ adds additional trace minerals and vitamins as well as fiber. Unbleached flour, creamy in color, has not been chemically bleached or sterilized as in the processing of white flour; therefore, it has more of the natural B and E vitamins which are eliminated in white flour milling process. Though many white flours are "enriched" (vitamins B and D, calcium, and iron added) they are still lacking some of the nutrients available in the original whole wheat flour, particularly trace minerals and fiber.

Welsh Buttermilk Wheat Bread

A fabulous recipe from one of Connecticut's finest breadbakers. Uncompromising quality is the keynote of Judith Saleeby's JUDIE'S EUROPEAN BAKED GOODS, Short Beach, CT, and this buttermilk and whole wheat bread is no exception. Whole wheat flour has a high gluten content, but the edges of the bran particles in the wheat are thought to cut the gluten strands, thus reducing the size of the loaf when compared to a loaf of white bread made using the same volume of flour.

YIELD: 2 Loaves
CALORIES PER LOAF: 2529
CARBOHYDRATES: 350g
PROTEIN: 82g
FAT: 89g
CHOLESTEROL: High
PREPARING: 35 Minutes
RISING: 1 Hour
BAKING: 35 Minutes
FREEZING: Yes

Dissolve yeast in warm water. Add ⅛ tsp. sugar; set aside to proof.

In large bowl, put milk, ricotta cheese, butter, salt, molasses, grated orange rind, 1 cup whole wheat flour and 2¼ cups white flour, stirring well. Add yeast and remaining 1 cup whole wheat flour and 2¼ cups white flour. Turn out onto floured board and knead about 10 minutes, until dough is no longer sticky. Place in a greased bowl; turn to coat. Cover and let rise about 1 hour.

Punch down dough; divide in half and shape into loaves. Place in 2 well-buttered 8 × 4½-inch *(20 × 11.5cm)* loaf pans; cover, let rise until doubled in size.

Slash tops of each loaf; then bake in a preheated 400° oven, 35 minutes or until bread sounds hollow when tapped gently on bottom of pans. Remove from pans; cool 60 minutes.

2 pkgs. (¼ oz. each) *(14g)* **active dry yeast**
⅓ cup *(80ml)* **warm water**
⅛ tsp. **sugar**
1 cup *(240ml)* **milk, boiled and cooled to lukewarm**
2 cups *(520g)* **ricotta cheese**
½ cup *(115g)* **butter**
2 tsp. **salt**
½ cup *(120ml)* **molasses**
1 T. **grated orange rind**
2 cups *(240g)* **stone ground whole wheat flour**
4½ cups *(500g)* **unbleached flour (approximately)**

Nutritional Notes: This is a nutritious bread. The milk and ricotta add protein and calcium. (Some ricotta contains sweeteners, carrageenan, citric acid, etc. and others have none of these additives. Check the label.) Stone grinding, an older and slower method of milling flours, distributes the grain's germ oil (contains most of the vitamins and minerals) evenly and keeps the grain cooler (thus preventing rancidity) than today's high speed milling process which necessitates removing the germ. Skim or lowfat milk, ricotta cheese made from skim milk, and unsalted polyunsaturated margarine may be substituted to decrease saturated fat/cholesterol. Salt may be eliminated.

Anadama Bread

YIELD: 2 Loaves
CALORIES PER LOAF: 2076
CARBOHYDRATES: 430g
PROTEIN: 53g
FAT: 16g
PREPARING: 30 Minutes
RISING: 2½ Hours
BAKING: 60 Minutes
FREEZING: Yes

A story circulated in the last century was that of the Massachusetts fisherman who became enraged with his wife, Anna. All she gave him for dinner was cornmeal and molasses — day after day. One night, when he could no longer control his anger, he tossed flour and yeast into cornmeal and molasses, put it all into the oven, and sat down later to eat a loaf of bread that had no name, mumbling, "Anna, damn her!" Polite society modified the name to "Anadama."

2 cups *(475ml)* **water**
½ cup *(75g)* **yellow stone-ground cornmeal**
2 T. *(30g)* **butter**
½ cup *(120ml)* **molasses**
2 tsp. **salt**
½ cup *(120ml)* **lukewarm water**
2 pkgs. (¼ oz. each) *(14g)* **active dry yeast**
7½ cups *(850g)* **unbleached flour (approximately)**

GLAZE:
2 T. *(30g)* **melted butter**

Bring 2 cups water to boil; gradually add cornmeal, stirring constantly to avoid lumps. Add butter, molasses and salt; cool to lukewarm. To the ½ cup lukewarm water, add yeast. When dissolved, add to cooled cornmeal mixture. Stir in enough flour to make stiff dough. On lightly floured board, knead until smooth and elastic. Put dough in buttered bowl and turn to coat with butter; cover. Let rise in warm place (80°-85°) until doubled in bulk, about 50 minutes.

Punch down dough; cover and let rise again until light, about 45 minutes.

Put on floured board and knead well, adding more flour if necessary. Shape into 2 loaves and place in greased 8½ × 4½ × 2½-inch *(21.5 × 11.5 × 6.5cm)* loaf pans. Cover and let rise in warm place until doubled in bulk.

Bake in preheated 400° oven 15 minutes, then reduce heat to 350° and bake 45 minutes longer or until bottom of bread sounds hollow when gently tapped. Brush with melted butter; remove from pans and cool on wire racks before slicing.

Jacqueline H. Moores, Bloomfield, CT

Norwegian Holiday Loaf

YIELD: 2 Loaves
CALORIES PER LOAF: 4218
CARBOHYDRATES: 645g
PROTEIN: 72g
FAT: 150g
LET STAND: 2 Hours
PREPARING: 2 Hours
BAKING: 50 Minutes
FREEZING: Yes

7 cups *(800g)* **flour (approximately)**
2 cups *(475ml)* **warm milk**
2 pkgs. (¼ oz. each) *(14g)* **active dry yeast**
1 **egg, at room temperature**
½ cup *(100g)* **sugar**
1 tsp. **salt**
1 cup *(225g)* **butter, at room temperature**
1 cup *(225g)* **glaceed cherries, halved**
1 cup *(225g)* **mixed candied fruit, finely diced**
1 cup *(150g)* **dates, chopped**
1 cup *(120g)* **pecans, coarsely broken**

In a large bowl, combine 2 cups flour, milk and yeast; mix. Cover bowl with plastic wrap. Let stand 2 hours.

Lightly beat egg and add to flour mixture. Add sugar, salt and butter; beat well. Continue beating while adding remaining flour, 1 cup at a time, until dough is soft and no longer sticky. (Up to this point, dough may be made in food processor). Turn out onto floured board and knead until dough is smooth and elastic, adding small amounts of flour if dough is still sticky.

Mix together glaceed cherries, candied fruit, dates and nuts.

Press dough flat and sprinkle half the fruit-nut mix on dough; work mixture into dough and repeat with remainder of fruit-nut mix. Knead until mixture is well-distributed throughout dough. Place dough in large bowl. Cover with plastic wrap; set aside to double in bulk.

Punch down dough; knead 30 seconds, pressing out air bubbles. Cut into 2 pieces. Shape each into a ball; let rest 4 minutes, covered with a towel.

Press each ball into flat oval to fit lengthwise into two greased 9 × 5-inch *(22.5 × 12.5cm)* loaf pans. Fold oval in half lengthwise and pinch seams tightly to seal. Tuck ends under; place in pan, seam down. Repeat with second ball. Cover pans with waxed paper and set aside to double in bulk.

Bake in preheated 350° oven, 50 minutes or until golden brown and bottoms sound hollow when tapped. If they begin to brown too quickly near the end of baking, cover with foil. Cool on racks.

Maryann Reuben, West Hartford, CT

Nutritional Notes: Glaceed fruits are generally commercially processed with corn syrup and other sugars, citric acid, artificial colors and flavors, and preservatives. They provide little nutritionally but calories. They do add flavor and eye appeal.

Microwave Conversion Instructions: Prepare dough as directed. Place dough in 2 lightly greased 9 × 5-inch glass or ceramic loaf pans. Set aside as directed until doubled in bulk. Brush each loaf with glaze made from 1 egg yolk beaten with 1 tsp. water. *Bake each loaf separately.* Bake 7 minutes on Medium (50%). Turn pan and bake 3 minutes on High. For attractive browning, bake in preheated 350° conventional oven 15 minutes.

Mill Hollow Bread

From Judith E. Saleeby of JUDIE'S EUROPEAN BAKED GOODS, Short Beach, CT, comes this relatively dense, yet light loaf with a crunchiness and taste that defy description. A must to make!

In the editor's opinion, this was the finest bread recipe to emerge from all those tested. It toasts well, makes interesting sandwiches, goes well with soups and stews, and is perfect as is!

YIELD: 3 Loaves
CALORIES PER LOAF: 2569
CARBOHYDRATES: 385g
PROTEIN: 66g
FAT: 85g
PREPARING: 35 Minutes
RISING: 2 Hours
BAKING: 35 Minutes
FREEZING: Yes

Dissolve yeast in warm water; add pinch of sugar and set aside to proof.

In large bowl, put boiled milk, butter, oil, salt, molasses, honey, maple syrup, wheat germ, bran flakes, wheat kernels and rye flour; mix well.

Add proofed yeast to milk mixture and mix thoroughly. Add whole wheat flour and enough white flour to still be able to stir mixture. Knead, in the bowl, 5 minutes. Add sunflower kernels. Turn out on to floured board and knead, incorporating enough remaining white flour to make an elastic dough, about 5 minutes. Cover and let rise 60 minutes.

Punch down dough; knead 5 minutes. Divide into 3 pieces and shape each piece to fit in 8½ × 4½-inch *(20 × 11cm)* loaf pan. Coat top of each loaf with safflower oil. Let rise 40 minutes or until bread forms peak above sides of each pan.

Bake in preheated 400° oven, 35 minutes. Remove from pans and cool on wire racks.

Nutritional Notes: This bread provides an interesting mixture of nutritious whole grains and is a good source of fiber.

2 pkgs. (¼ oz. each) *(14g)* **active dry yeast**
⅓ cup *(80ml)* **warm water**
Pinch of sugar
2½ cups *(600ml)* **boiled milk**
½ cup *(115g)* **unsalted sweet butter**
⅓ cup *(80ml)* **safflower oil**
2 tsp. **salt**
⅓ cup *(80ml)* **molasses**
⅓ cup *(115g)* **honey**
⅓ cup *(80ml)* **pure maple syrup**
½ cup *(60g)* **wheat germ**
½ cup *(40g)* **bran flakes**
½ cup *(100g)* **wheat kernels, coarsely ground**
½ cup *(50g)* **rye flour**
2 cups *(240g)* **stone-ground whole wheat flour**
6 cups *(675g)* **unbleached white flour**
⅔ cup *(80g)* **sunflower kernels, toasted**

Sourdough Rye Bread

Rye is not derived from wheat. It is a cereal grass that is closely related to wheat. Rye flour does not contain gluten; therefore, it is usually combined with other types of flours when making bread.

A starter in bread baking is defined by Bernard Clayton as "a mixture of flour and a liquid into which bacteria wild or otherwise, is introduced". The starter was used before yeast was available to the average person. Today it is used more for the flavor and aroma it imparts rather than for its rising abilities. Because starters tend to be unreliable, they generally are used in conjunction with packaged yeast.

YIELD: 2 Round Loaves
CALORIES PER LOAF: 1570
CARBOHYDRATES: 330g
PROTEIN: 51g
FAT: 5g
PREPARING: 4 Days including Making Starter
BAKING: 40-45 Minutes
FREEZING: Yes

SOURDOUGH RYE STARTER:

1 pkg. (¼ oz.) *(7g)* **active dry yeast**
2 cups *(475ml)* **warm water**
2 cups *(190g)* **medium rye flour**
1 small onion, peeled and speared
    several times with a fork

PHASE ONE — THE NIGHT BEFORE:

1 cup *(240ml)* **rye sourdough starter**
1½ cups *(355ml)* **warm water**
3 cups *(285g)* **medium rye flour**

PHASE TWO — THE NEXT MORNING:

1 pkg. (¼ oz.) *(7g)* **active dry yeast**
½ cup *(120ml)* **warm water**
¼ tsp. **sugar**
1 T. **salt (kosher preferred)**
1 T. **caraway seeds**
1½ tsp. **poppy seeds**
3½ cups *(400g)* **bread flour or all-**
    purpose flour

GLAZE:

1 **egg**
1 tsp. **water**

SOURDOUGH RYE STARTER: Dissolve yeast in warm water; add flour and stir. Add onion; place mixture in large glass or crockery container with lid; cover loosely. Let sit at room temperature overnight. In morning (starter will have risen and fallen back), remove onion, let mixture sit for one or two days at room temperature until mixture smells fermented. If it separates, stir to blend. Store in refrigerator, covered. After use, add equal amounts of flour and water and let mixture sit at room temperature a day before refrigerating again. If starter is not used in 3-4 weeks, discard half of it and add to starter all over again.

PHASE ONE: In large bowl, stir together all ingredients; cover with plastic wrap; let sit overnight at room temperature.

PHASE TWO: Dissolve yeast in warm water; add sugar and set aside to proof.

Add salt, caraway seeds, and poppy seeds to last night's mixture. Add proofed yeast and flour; stir to mix. Turn dough out onto floured board and knead until smooth. Place in ungreased bowl; cover and let rise until doubled in size.

Punch down dough; divide into 2 pieces. Form each piece into a round loaf. Place loaf on floured board. Flatten and fold into thirds, first from one direction and then from the other. Pinch dough to seal; pat into a round shape. Place loaves on greased baking sheet that has been sprinkled with cornmeal; cover; let rise until almost doubled in size.

Just before baking, brush with beaten egg mixed with 1 tsp. water. Bake in preheated 425° oven, 40 to 45 minutes, or until loaves sound hollow when tapped on bottom.

Leah W. Later, Wethersfield, CT

Herbed Croutons

YIELD: 15-20 Servings or 2 Cups
or 10-14 Croutons Per Serving
TOTAL CALORIES: 920
CALORIES PER SERVING: 46
CARBOHYDRATES: 4g
FAT: 3g
PREPARING: 5 Minutes
COOKING: 12-15 Minutes

Croutons generally are small bread cubes that are toasted in the oven or sauteed in butter in a pan. For variety, and an interesting taste and texture, try this recipe which uses shredded wheat in place of bread.

Melt butter in pan in preheated 400° oven. Add herbs and shredded wheat. Stir well to mix. Return to oven and cook 12 to 15 minutes, stirring twice, until golden brown. Cool and use in soups or salads

Winnie White, North Conway, NH

Nutritional Notes: Garlic powder may be substituted for garlic salt and unsalted polyunsaturated margarine used in order to obtain a low-sodium crouton. Shredded wheat is one of just a few ready-to-eat cereals low in sodium and it provides more vitamins, minerals and fiber, as a fortified cereal, than croutons made from white bread.

⅓ cup *(75g)* butter
½ tsp. crushed rosemary
½ tsp. garlic salt
¼ tsp. thyme
¼ tsp. mace
2 cups *(85g)* spoon size shredded wheat, halved

Raisin Rye Bread

YIELD: 3 Loaves
CALORIES PER LOAF: 2500
CARBOHYDRATES: 539g
PROTEIN: 43g
FAT: 19g
PREPARING: 30 Minutes
RISING: 1¾ Hours
BAKING: 40 Minutes
FREEZING: Yes

A richly flavored sweet brown bread, studded with raisins.

In a large bowl, proof yeast with water and sugar. Add all remaining ingredients except white flour. Stir with wooden spoon until well mixed. Stir in enough white flour to make a smooth, soft dough stiff enough to be handled. Turn out onto floured surface. Knead 10 minutes until smooth and elastic. Place dough in buttered bowl. Let rise, covered in a warm place (80°-85°) until double in bulk, about 1 hour. Punch dough down, turn out of bowl; divide in thirds.

Shape each piece into a smooth round ball. Flatten slightly into a circle about 7 inches *(17.5cm)* in diameter. Place in 3 buttered round pans or on buttered baking sheets. Cover; let rise in warm place (80°-85°) until double in bulk, about 45 minutes.

Prick tops of loaves in several places with a toothpick. Place pans on next-to-lowest rack of preheated 350° oven. Bake 25 minutes. Remove pans from oven. Quickly brush loaves lightly with Glaze. Return pans to oven, bake 10 to 15 minutes longer or until loaves sound hollow when tapped on bottom. Turn out of pans. Place on racks. Brush again lightly with Glaze. Let cool to room temperature.

Clare Edwards, West Hartford, CT

Variations, Advance Preparation, and Serving Suggestions:
As most breads, this tastes best the day it is made, but will keep a day or two, tightly wrapped. It toasts well. Fresh or toasted, it is good served with ham.

Nutritional Notes: The dark molasses provides varying amounts of vitamins and minerals that are not present in white sugar. Also, the raisins serve to sweeten bread, as well as provide a nutritional advantage of added vitamins and minerals, particularly iron.

DOUGH:
3 pkgs. (¼ oz. each) *(21g)* active dry yeast
¾ cup *(175ml)* lukewarm water (110°-115°)
Pinch of sugar
3 cups (2 12 oz. cans) *(710ml)* beer
1 cup *(240ml)* dark molasses
¼ cup *(60g)* butter, melted
Freshly grated rind of 1 large navel orange
1 cup *(170g)* raisins
2 tsp. anise seeds
1 T. salt
6 cups *(570g)* rye flour
5¾ cup *(650g)* white flour

GLAZE:
3 T. *(45ml)* dark molasses, mixed with 3 T. *(45ml)* water

YIELD: 2 Loaves
CALORIES PER LOAF: 2935
CARBOHYDRATES: 442g
PROTEIN: 69g
FAT: 99g
SODIUM: High
PREPARING: 30 Minutes
RISING: 10 Hours
BAKING: 1 Hour
FREEZING: Yes

Sourdough Fruitbread

This recipe comes from a cook who has kept her starter going for 20 years!

½ cup *(120ml)* **sourdough starter**
3 cups *(340g)* **flour**
2 cups *(475ml)* **homemade yogurt, sour milk, or milk**
¼ lb. *(115g)* **margarine**
1 cup *(200g)* **brown sugar**
4 **eggs**
1 cup *(85g)* **rolled oats**
1 tsp. **salt**
1 tsp. **baking soda**
1 T. **baking powder**

4 cups **your choice dried fruit and nuts:**
   1 cup *(170g)* **raisins**
   1 cup *(140g)* **peanuts, chopped**
   1 cup *(180g)* **apricots, chopped**
   1 cup *(60g)* **apples, chopped**
   1 cup *(120g)* **cashews, chopped**

Combine starter, flour, and yogurt. Cover bowl with towel, let batter rise at room temperature, away from draft, 6 to 8 hours or overnight. Cream margarine and sugar. Add eggs, beating well. Stir in oats. Add remaining ingredients and combine by hand with starter mixture. Place batter in two well-greased 9 × 5-inch *(22.5 × 12.5cm)* pans or 4 small loaf pans. Cover with towels and let rise in warm place until dough nearly reaches top of pans, 1 to 2 hours. Bake in preheated 375° oven, 1 hour. If using smaller pans, check after 45 minutes. Remove from pans and cool on racks.

Molly R.M. Fowler, West Hartford, CT

Variations, Advance Preparation, and Serving Suggestions:
Substitute 1 cup commercial yogurt and 1 cup lowfat milk or 1 cup cottage cheese and 1 cup lowfat milk for the homemade yogurt.

Compatible spices such as ginger, cinnamon, nutmeg can be additional ingredients. Leftover bacon, sausage or cheese can replace the fruit and nuts.

A delightful brunch or luncheon sweetbread. Toast it for a breakfast treat.

YIELD: 48 Rolls
TOTAL CALORIES: 3312
CALORIES PER ROLL: 69
CARBOHYDRATES: 13g
PROTEIN: 2g
FAT: 1g
PREPARING: 15 Minutes
BAKING: 12-15 Minutes
FREEZING: Yes

No Knead Refrigerator Rolls

This recipe is excellent for people who have difficulty with yeast dough.

2 pkgs. *(¼ oz. each)* *(14g)* **active dry yeast**
2 cups *(475ml)* **warm water**
½ cup *(100g)* **sugar**
2 tsp. **salt**
6½-7 cups *(750-800g)* **sifted flour**
1 **egg**
¼ cup *(50g)* **shortening (Crisco preferred)**

In mixing bowl, dissolve yeast in water. Add sugar, salt and about half the flour. Beat thoroughly, 2 minutes. Add egg and shortening. Gradually beat in remaining flour, until smooth.
[FOOD PROCESSOR: Mix yeast, 1 tsp. sugar, and warm water in a small bowl; let proof about 10 minutes. Put flour, sugar, salt, and shortening in work bowl and blend by turning machine on/off about 4 times. Add egg and yeast mixture, and blend until dough is smooth.] Cover with damp cloth; place in refrigerator. Occasionally punch down dough as it rises in the refrigerator.

About two hours before baking, cut off amount needed; return remaining dough to refrigerator. Form dough into desired shapes; place on greased baking sheet; cover and let rise until light, 1½ to 2 hours.

Bake in preheated 400° oven 12 to 15 minutes, until golden.

VARIOUS SHAPES:

OLD FASHIONED BISCUITS: Form dough into balls ⅓ desired size. Place close together in greased round pan.

PARKERHOUSE ROLLS: Roll dough ¼ inch *(6mm)* thick. Cut with biscuit cutter. Brush with melted butter. Make crease across center. Fold so top half slightly overlaps. Press edges together at crease. Place close together on baking sheet.

CLOVERLEAF ROLLS: Form bits of dough into balls about 1 inch *(2.5cm)* in diameter. Place 3 balls in each greased muffin cup. Brush with butter.

CRESCENTS: Roll dough scarcely ¼ inch *(6mm)* thick into 12-inch *(30cm)* circle. Spread with soft butter. Cut into 16 pie-shaped wedges. Beginning at base, roll up to point, place on baking sheet, point underneath, then bend into crescent.

PICNIC BUNS: Use ½ of dough. Divide into 2 parts. Roll each into a 7½-inch *(18.5cm)* square, ½ inch *(12mm)* thick. Cut into 2½-inch *(6.25cm)* squares. Yield: 18 buns.

Elizabeth Daggerhart, Granby, CT

Variations, Advance Preparation, and Serving Suggestions:
Dough will keep in refrigerator for 7 days, if kept covered with a damp cloth. To freeze: Bake rolls until set and beginning to brown slightly. Cool and freeze. Cook later as directed in recipe.

Microwave Conversion Instructions: Totally cook rolls as directed. Freeze. Place rolls on paper in oven. Cook 1½ minutes on Medium High (70%).

Sourdough English Muffins

Sourdough has been around for thousands of years. It has mystified cooks as to its self-replenishing substance. Today, we know that harmless bacteria found in milk cause fermentation.

Pioneers in every part of the country carried a sourdough starter in a crock or pot with them. They took great care in guarding their starters, which gave them a never-ending source of hotcakes every morning, biscuits and bread. Some starters became famous for their exceptionally good flavor and were passed down from generation to generation.

YIELD: 12 Muffins
TOTAL CALORIES: 1400
CALORIES PER MUFFIN: 116
CARBOHYDRATES: 23g
PROTEIN: 4g
FAT: 1g
PREPARING: 30 Minutes
RISING: 9 Hours
COOKING: 20 Minutes
FREEZING: Yes

Combine starter, milk, 2 cups flour, sugar, salt and baking soda; cover with a towel and let rise in a warm place 8 hours or ovenight. Turn out onto lightly floured surface. Knead until smooth and elastic, adding more flour if necessary. Dough will be sticky. Roll dough to ¾-inch *(2cm)* thickness. With a floured 3-inch *(7.5cm)* cutter, cut dough into rounds. Sprinkle sheet of waxed paper with some of the cornmeal, place muffins atop and sprinkle with remaining cornmeal. Cover muffins lightly and let rise in a warm place until puffy (about 45 minutes). Bake muffins on a lightly greased electric griddle preheated to 250-275° or in a lightly greased large skillet over low heat until muffins are golden brown (about 10 minutes on each side). Cool on wire racks. Split muffins in half with a fork, toast and serve with butter and/or preserves.

½ cup *(120ml)* **sourdough starter**
1 cup *(240ml)* **milk**
2¾ cups *(310g)* **flour**
1 T. **sugar**
¾ tsp. **salt**
½ tsp. **baking soda**
3 T. *(30g)* **cornmeal**

Molly R.M. Fowler, West Hartford, CT

Sweet Muenster Bread

YIELD: 1 Large Loaf
TOTAL CALORIES: 5726
CARBOHYDRATES: 329g
PROTEIN: 270g
FAT: 370g
CHOLESTEROL: High
PREPARING: 30 Minutes
RISING: 1½ Hours
BAKING: 60 Minutes

There are 2 Muenster or Munster cheeses. The French cheese originated in the Vosges Mountains of Alsace-Lorraine beginning in the seventh century. It is a soft cheese with a distinctively pungent flavor and odor. The American muenster was first made by German immigrants from the town of Munster in the Vosges region of Lorraine. Today, it is a semi-soft, mild-flavored cheese.

DOUGH:

2 pkgs. (¼ oz. each) (14g) active dry yeast
¼ cup (60ml) warm water
1½ T. (20g) sugar
1 cup (240ml) warm milk
1½ tsp. salt
½ cup (115g) butter, melted
3-4 cups (350-450g) flour

FILLING:

2 lbs. (900g) Muenster cheese, grated
1 egg, beaten
2 T. (30g) butter, melted

Dissolve yeast in ¼ cup warm water. Add 1½ tsp. sugar and let proof.

In mixing bowl, combine milk, 1 T. sugar, salt and melted butter. Blend well; add yeast mixture. Beat in 2 cups flour until mixture is smooth. Add enough flour to make soft, workable dough. Turn out onto floured surface; knead until smooth and satiny, about 8 minutes. *[FOOD PROCESSOR: Put 3 cups flour, sugar, salt, and unmelted butter cut into several pieces into work bowl and combine by turning machine on/off about 6 times. Add yeast mixture and warm milk; process 30 to 40 seconds or until dough is thoroughly mixed. Add enough additional flour, a tablespoon at a time, to make a soft dough, processing after each addition.]* Place in warm, greased bowl; turn to coat; cover with plastic wrap and let double in bulk, about 1 hour.

Punch down dough; cover and let rise again for 30 minutes.

Meanwhile prepare filling by mixing together Muenster cheese, egg and melted butter.

Again, punch down dough, turn out onto a lightly floured board; let rest 10 to 15 minutes.

Roll out into a circle 24 to 26 inches *(60-65cm)* in diameter; if dough resists, cover and let rest again. Fold dough in half; lay across half of a 10-inch *(25cm)* cake pan or a 9-inch *(22.5cm)* springform that has

been brushed with melted butter and put on a baking sheet; unfold and carefully lift and press dough to fit in pan, leaving a skirt of dough draped over pan rim. Mound the cheese mixture in the pan, forming it highest in the center. Pick up the skirt of dough and begin to pleat in loose folds around cheese, lifting and rotating pan as you progress. Gather ends of dough together on top and twist into a knob, giving it a firm twist. Encircling the bottom of knob with both hands, firmly twist it again. If any dough is torn, pinch it together. Set loaf aside for 15 minutes.

Then, again give it a twist. Bake in preheated 375° oven 60 minutes until golden. Check after 45 minutes; if browning too rapidly, cover top with foil for last 15 minutes. Let cool in pan on wire rack. Do not attempt to slice until bread has cooled enough so that the cheese has congealed. It can be reheated if you wish to serve it warm.

Ann Howard Cookery, Farmington, CT
via Clare Edwards, West Hartford, CT

Hartford Election Cake

During the 18th century this recipe was devised by thrifty colonial housewives who combined leftover fruits, bread dough and spices. The cake became one of the first foods to be associated with politics. In Hartford, Connecticut, it was named "Lection Cake" for it was often eaten while awaiting election returns or for celebrating an election victory. This particular version of Election Cake is based on a recipe used by Mary Todd Lincoln and is best served as a tea cake or at a brunch or breakfast.

YIELD: 12 Servings or
   1 10-Inch Cake
TOTAL CALORIES: 4658
CALORIES PER SERVING: 388
CARBOHYDRATES: 69g
PROTEIN: 5.6g
FAT: 10g
PREPARING: 30 Minutes
RISING: 4 Hours
SOAKING: Overnight
BAKING: 1 Hour 10 Minutes

DOUGH: Soak currants or raisins in brandy overnight, in a closed jar.

Dissolve yeast in warm water; add 1 T. sugar and set aside to proof. When milk is lukewarm, add yeast mixture. Add 1 cup flour; beat until blended. Cover; let rise until double in bulk, about 1 hour.

While dough is rising, drain currants or raisins, reserving the brandy. Cream butter and sugar until light and fluffy. Add eggs; beat well. Stir in lemon juice and grated rind; add yeast mixture and beat to mix. Add drained currants or raisins and reserved brandy. Combine 2½ cups sifted flour with salt, nutmeg or mace, and cinnamon. Gradually sift flour mixture into batter, beating well. Pour batter into well-buttered 10-inch *(25cm)* tube pan. Cover and let rise about 3 hours until doubled in bulk.

Place in cold oven. Turn oven to 300° and bake 35 to 40 minutes, than raise temperature to 350° and bake 30 minutes. Cool 10 minutes in pan, turn out onto serving plate.

GLAZE: Combine confectioners' sugar and lemon or orange juice. Mix until smooth. Brush over top of *warm* cake and let drizzle down sides. Do not try to ice sides of cake.

Ruth Hennessey, Morristown, NJ

DOUGH:

1 cup *(140g)* **currants or raisins** *(170g)*
½ cup *(120ml)* **brandy**
1 pkg. (¼ oz.) *(7g)* **active dry yeast**
¼ cup *(60ml)* **warm water**
1 cup *(200g)* **plus 1 T. sugar**
¾ cup *(175ml)* **milk, scalded**
3½ cups *(400g)* **flour, sifted**
½ cup *(115g)* **butter, softened**
2 **eggs**
2 tsp. **fresh lemon juice**
1 tsp. **grated lemon rind**
½ tsp. **salt**
¾ tsp. **freshly grated nutmeg or mace**
1 tsp. **cinnamon**

GLAZE:

1 cup *(130g)* **confectioners' sugar**
¼ cup *(60ml)* **fresh lemon or orange juice**

YIELD: 1 Loaf or 12-18 Muffins
CALORIES PER LOAF: 3727
CARBOHYDRATES: 585g
PROTEIN: 43g
FAT: 135g
SODIUM: High
CALORIES PER MUFFIN: 206
CARBOHYDRATES: 32.5g
PROTEIN: 2g
FAT: 7.5g
PREPARING: 15 Minutes
BAKING: 60 Minutes — Bread
   30 Minutes — Muffins
FREEZING: Yes

Plum Bread

This is an unusual, fragrant, moist loaf. Good as a dessert bread with cheese, fruit and brandy.

1 can (30 oz.) *(850g)* **purple plums, drained**
½ cup *(115g)* **butter, melted**
2 tsp. **baking soda**
1 cup *(200g)* **sugar**
2 cups *(225g)* **flour**
1 tsp. **cinnamon**
½ tsp. **cloves**
1 tsp. **salt**
½ cup *(85g)* **raisins**
½ cup *(60g)* **nuts, chopped**

Pit and mash plums; add melted butter, then baking soda (it will bubble and foam); set aside to cool. When cool, add remaining ingredients. *[FOOD PROCESSOR: Combine flour, soda, salt and unchopped nuts in work bowl; process 10 seconds or until nuts are coarsely chopped. Remove mixture and set aside. Process plums, butter and spices 10 seconds or until plums are pureed. Add sugar and process mixture 1 full minute. Add reserved flour/nut mixture and combine batter by turning machine on/off 5 or 6 times or until flour has just disappeared.]* Place batter in greased and floured 8½ × 4½ × 2½-inch *(21.5 × 11.5 × 6.25cm)* loaf pan or greased 2¼-inch *(6cm)* muffin tins.

Bake in preheated 350° oven for 60 minutes for bread, or until a wooden toothpick inserted in center comes out clean; for muffins bake 25 to 30 minutes or until browned. Cool on wire racks.

If bread is to be frozen, cool completely before wrapping.

John Lander, Collinsville, CT

Nutritional Notes: 2 cups *(240g)* whole wheat flour may be substituted for white flour. Unsalted polyunsaturated margarine may be used and salt reduced. Use ½ cup honey instead of sugar for a less sweet bread.

Microwave Conversion Instructions: Melt cut-up butter on High 1 minute. Prepare batter as for conventional recipe.

Loaf: Line bottom of 9 × 5-inch *(22.5 × 12.5cm)* loaf pan or 1½-qt. *(1½L)* mini-bundt or ring mold with waxed paper. Pour in batter. Elevate loaf pan or mold by placing on an inverted saucer. Cook on Medium (50%) 9 minutes turning ¼ turn every 2½ minutes. Continue to cook on High 4 minutes.

Muffins: Prepare microwave muffin pan with 2 paper liners per cup. Fill cups ½ with batter. Cook on High 3 minutes. Remove muffins from pan; replace paper liners and repeat process with remaining batter.

Lekakh

HONEY CAKE

"Lekakh" is Yiddish for honey cake, the traditional East European cake served on the first night of Rosh Hashanah and Simhat Torah. It is also served at the birth of a boy, at weddings, and at other happy occasions.

YIELD: 2 Loaves or 20 Slices
TOTAL CALORIES: 4220
CALORIES PER SLICE: 211
CARBOHYDRATES: 35g
PROTEIN: 2g
FAT: 7g
CHOLESTEROL: High
PREPARING: 35 Minutes
BAKING: 50-60 Minutes
FREEZING: Yes

Sift together flour, cloves, allspice, cinnamon, instant coffee, baking soda and salt; set aside.

Beat egg yolks, brown sugar, butter and honey until smooth and well-blended. Add flour mixture alternately with sour cream, beginning and ending with flour. Beat until smooth. *[FOOD PROCESSOR: Combine flour, cloves, cinnamon, allspice, instant coffee, baking soda and salt in work bowl; process 2 seconds. Remove mixture and reserve. Process eggs and brown sugar for 1 full minute, stopping machine once to scrape down sides of bowl. Add butter and process 1 full minute. Add honey and sour cream and process 10 seconds. Add reserved flour mixture and combine by turning machine on/off 4 or 5 times, or until flour just disappears. Do not overprocess.]*

In separate bowl, beat egg whites until stiff. Fold egg whites into flour mixture. Divide batter between two well-buttered 8½ × 4½ × 2½-inch *(21.5 × 11.5 × 6.25cm)* loaf pans.

Bake in preheated 350° oven 45 to 50 minutes, until browned. Cool in pan 10 minutes. Turn out on rack to cool completely. Do not serve for at least 24 hours so that the honey has a chance to develop its flavor.

Lois Reiner, West Hartford, CT

Microwave Conversion Instructions: Combine ingredients as in recipe. Line bottoms of two 8½ × 4½ × 2½-inch glass loaf pans with waxed paper. Do *not* grease and flour pan. Divide batter between pans. Shield ends of pans with 2-inch wide strips of foil, covering over 1 inch of batter and molding remainder around handles. Cook one loaf at a time. Center loaf pan on inverted saucer in oven. Cook on Medium (50%) 9 minutes, rotating ¼ turn every 3 minutes. Remove foil, increase power to High, cook 2 to 5 minutes. Check for doneness by looking through bottom. No unbaked batter should appear in center. Let stand 5 to 10 minutes before removing from pan. Loosen edges and turn out on cake rack. Removed waxed paper.

2 cups *(225g)* flour
1 tsp. ground cloves
1 tsp. allspice
1 tsp. cinnamon
1 tsp. instant coffee
1 tsp. baking soda
¼ tsp. salt
3 eggs, separated
1 cup *(200g)* brown sugar, firmly packed
½ cup *(115g)* softened butter
1 cup *(340g)* excellent quality honey
1 cup *(225g)* sour cream

YIELD: 1 Loaf
TOTAL CALORIES: 2189
CARBOHYDRATES: 439g
PROTEIN: 34g
FAT: 33g
PREPARING: 10 Minutes
BAKING: 1 Hour 10 Minutes
FREEZING: Yes

Blueberry Orange Bread

An unusual bread which is unusually good.

BATTER:

2 T. *(30g)* butter
¼ cup *(60ml)* boiling water
½ cup *(120ml)* fresh orange juice
4 tsp. grated orange rind
1 egg
1 cup *(200g)* sugar
2 cups *(225g)* flour
1 tsp. baking powder
¼ tsp. baking soda
½ tsp. salt
1 cup *(150g)* fresh blueberries

TOPPING:

2 T. *(30ml)* fresh lemon juice
2 T. *(40g)* honey
1 tsp. grated lemon rind

Put butter in small bowl, pour in boiling water, stir until melted. Add orange juice and rind.

In another small bowl, beat egg with sugar until light. In large bowl, mix dry ingredients. Alternately add orange mixture and egg mixture, beating until smooth. *[FOOD PROCESSOR: Process flour, baking powder, soda and salt to blend. Remove from bowl; set aside. Process sugar and egg 1 full minute. Add softened butter and orange rind; process 1 full minute. Quickly blend in water and juice. Blend in flour mixture by turning machine on/off 4 times or until flour just disappears. Do not overprocess. Transfer batter to a bowl.]* Fold in berries. Pour into a greased 9 × 5 × 3-inch *(22.5 × 12.5 × 7.5cm)* loaf pan.

Bake in preheated 325° oven for 1 hour and 10 minutes. Turn out onto wire rack. Mix together lemon juice, honey and lemon rind. Spoon over hot loaf. Cool completely before slicing or before wrapping and freezing.

Bunny Millan, Simsbury, CT

Variations, Advance Preparation, and Serving Suggestions: Frozen blueberries work well if you have picked them and frozen them *au naturale.*

Nutritional Notes: 2 cups minus 2 T. whole wheat flour or 2 cups whole wheat pastry flour may be substituted for white flour to add small amount trace minerals and fiber. The texture will be somewhat heavier, but delicious nevertheless.

Microwave Conversion Instructions: Prepare batter as for conventional recipe. Line bottom of glass loaf pan with waxed paper. Pour batter into pan. Cook on Medium (50%) 9 to 10 minutes, rotating dish ¼ turn after 5 minutes. Continue to cook on High 5 to 7 minutes, turning dish ¼ turn after 4 minutes. Let stand 5 minutes; remove bread from pan.

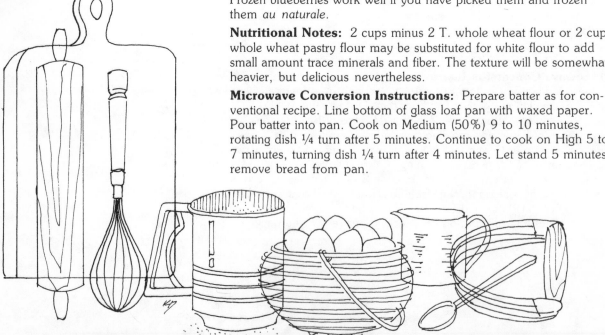

Cranberry Orange Bread

If you are trying to cut down on white flour, try this fruit bread that uses half whole wheat flour.

YIELD: 2 Loaves
CALORIES PER LOAF: 2897
CARBOHYDRATES: 453g
PROTEIN: 53g
FAT: 97g
SODIUM: High
PREPARING: 10 Minutes
BAKING: 55-60 Minutes
FREEZING: Yes

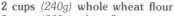

Sift dry ingredients together into a bowl. Cut in butter until mixture resembles coarse meal.

In another bowl, combine orange rind, fresh orange juice and eggs. Add to dry ingredients, mixing just to moisten. Fold in cranberries, nuts and raisins. *[FOOD PROCESSOR: Chop cranberries; remove from work bowl, but do not wash. Combine flours, baking powder, soda, salt and unchopped nuts in work bowl; process 10 seconds or until nuts are coarsely chopped. Remove mixture and set aside. Add eggs and sugars; process 1 full minute. Add softened butter, cinnamon, nutmeg and orange rind; process 1 full minute. With machine running add orange juice through feed tube. Add reserved nut/flour mixture by turning machine on/off 4 times or just until flour disappears. Do not overprocess. Transfer batter to a bowl; fold in cranberries and raisins.]* Put into 2 buttered and floured 9 x 5 x 3-inch *(22.5 x 12.5 x 7.5cm)* loaf pans.

Bake in a preheated 350° oven 55 to 60 minutes, or until a wooden toothpick inserted in the center comes out clean. Cool on wire rack. This bread slices best a day after it is baked.

To freeze: Cool completely; wrap tightly before freezing.

Greta Kemp, West Hartford, CT

Nutritional Notes: The use of fruit, nuts and whole wheat flour adds additional vitamins, trace elements and fiber. For increased food value, add ¼ to ½ cup *(30-60g)* wheat germ.

Microwave Conversion Instructions: Note: Divide prepared batter in half. Grease but do not flour 2 1½-qt. *(1.5L)* mini-bundt or ring molds. *Bake each mold separately.* Place mold on flat surface to trap heat for continued cooking on bottom. Bake on Medium (50%) 7 minutes. Then bake on High 7 to 9 minutes, just until bread begins to shrink from sides and a wooden pick inserted in center comes out almost clean. Bread will continue to set after cooking. Allow to cool slightly before unmolding.

2 cups *(240g)* whole wheat flour
2 cups *(225g)* white flour
1 T. baking powder
1 tsp. baking soda
1 tsp. salt
½ tsp. cinnamon
¼ tsp. nutmeg
1 cup *(200g)* brown sugar
1 cup *(200g)* granulated sugar
½ cup *(115g)* chilled butter
1 T. grated orange rind
1½ cups *(355ml)* fresh orange juice
2 eggs
2 cups *(225g)* fresh cranberries, coarsely chopped
1 cup *(115g)* chopped nuts
⅔ cup *(115g)* raisins

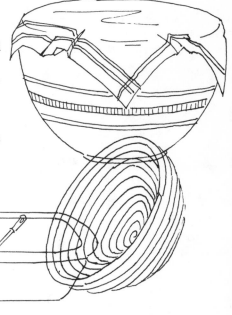

La Mouclade

YIELD: 8 Servings
TOTAL CALORIES: 2320
CALORIES PER SERVING: 290
CARBOHYDRATES: 10g
PROTEIN: 17g
FAT: 20g
CHOLESTEROL: High
PREPARING: 30 Minutes
SOAKING: 1-2 Hours
COOKING: 45 Minutes
FREEZING: No

This is a main-dish soup from the town of La Rochelle, the famous Huguenot stronghold in the southwestern coastal province of France known as Aunis. It is served at the Hotel D'Angleterre in La Rochelle. The inhabitants of this town call their mussels "moucles" instead of "moules", as most French people do, and their mussel soup "mouclade". It is not unlike "Moules Mariniere" but is more complicated with the subtle taste of curry.

MUSSELS:

6 lbs. *(2725g)* mussels (the smaller in size, the better)
3 T. *(30g)* minced shallots or white part of scallions
1½ cups *(355ml)* dry white burgundy wine

SAUCE:

4 T. *(60g)* butter
¼ cup *(30g)* flour
Mussel cooking liquid (about 6 cups) *(1400ml)*
1½ T. fresh lemon juice
3 cloves garlic, mashed
¼ scant tsp. curry powder
1 cup *(240ml)* heavy cream
Salt
Freshly ground white pepper
1 T. chopped parsley
Puff pastry croutons (optional)

MUSSELS: Discard any mussels that are open and do not close when put in water. Scrub mussels clean with a brush under cold running water. Soak mussels for 1 to 2 hours in cold water to which 3 T. flour has been added. (This should make them disgorge any sand remaining in their shells.) Remove to colander, rinse in cold water and drain. Cleaning can be done several hours ahead and mussels refrigerated until cooking time. Place minced shallots and white wine in large stock pot with lid. Turn flame to high; add mussels and cover pot. Shake pot every few seconds until mussels have opened. This should take only between 3 to 5 minutes. Any further cooking will toughen mussels. Remove mussels with slotted spoon to separate bowl; reserve cooking liquid. Shell mussels over stock pot, adding all their juices to liquid in the pot. (The best way to shell them is to use the shell from one half to scoop the mussel from the other half. This avoids tearing mussels.) Keep shelled mussels warm in top of a double boiler placed over warm water.

SAUCE: Make a roux of the butter and flour over medium flame. Cook for 1 minute, stirring with wooden spoon. Add liquid from stock pot which has been strained through cheesecloth or coffee filter paper. Add lemon juice, garlic, and curry powder; simmer for 30 minutes, whisking once in a while. (You can prepare soup ahead to this point but reheat to warm before next step.) Add cream. Heat mussels until warm; add to soup along with any liquid that has collected around them. Correct seasonings. Serve from a tureen or place in individual soup platters. Sprinkle parsley over each serving and garnish each with a few puff pastry croutons.

Lydie Marshall, New York, NY
via Melinda M. Vance, West Hartford, CT

Variations, Advance Preparation, and Serving Suggestions:
3 lbs. fresh mussels equals 1 lb. mussel meat and 1 lb. mussel meat equals 2 cups mussel meat.

Nutritional Notes: Mussels rank with other shellfish in providing quality protein for the calories.

Wine Suggestion: French Chablis, dry white; serve chilled.

Cuban Black Bean Soup

SOPA DE FRIJOL NEGRO

This soup is a meal in itself and a culinary treat for the "eco-gourmet." The dried black beans or turtle soup beans are a dietary staple throughout the Carribean and Mexico. They are an excellent and less expensive substitute for meat protein.

YIELD: 8 Servings
TOTAL CALORIES: 3616
CALORIES PER SERVING: 452
CARBOHYDRATES: 55g
PROTEIN: 22g
FAT: 16g
SODIUM: High
PREPARING: 30 Minutes
SIMMERING: 8 Hours
FREEZING: Yes

In a large pan, cover rinsed beans with beef stock and water; add ham bone and salt pork; simmer partially covered for 4 to 6 hours.

Remove bone; puree remaining contents of pan in blender or food processor in batches.

Return mixture to pan; add all remaining ingredients except sherry and lemon slices. Add more chicken stock or water if soup is too thick. Simmer slowly, partially covered, for 2 hours.

Add sherry just before serving. Float a lemon slice on top of each serving.

Gail Moore, West Hartford, CT

1 pkg. (16 oz.) *(450g)* black beans
1 qt. *(950ml)* beef stock
1 qt. *(950ml)* water
1 large meaty ham bone
¼-½ lb. *(115-225g)* salt pork
2 green peppers, chopped
2 tomatoes, peeled and chopped
1 cup *(150g)* chopped onions
½ cup *(55g)* chopped celery with leaves
1 clove garlic, minced
1 bay leaf
1 can (6 oz.) *(170g)* tomato paste
2 T. *(30ml)* Worcestershire sauce
6 green chilies, seeded and chopped (optional)
Tabasco sauce to taste
Salt and pepper
½ cup *(120ml)* dry sherry
8 thin lemon slices

Variations, Advance Preparation, and Serving Suggestions:
Add ½ cup cooked natural brown rice to each soup plate just before serving.

Nutritional Notes: Sodium, although still moderately high in this recipe due to ham and salt pork, can be decreased somewhat by using salt-free stock or broth (homemade or canned). One cup of regular canned broth contains over 800 milligrams of sodium.

Grains and beans balance one another nutritionally. If rice is added to each serving as suggested above, a complete protein balance is achieved. The few protein components lacking in many legumes are contained in grains and nuts; while those lacking in grains and nuts are usually present in legumes. Furthermore, eating beans and grains at the same meal aids in the assimilation of the essential amino acids present in these foods since the body can only absorb them when all are present simultaneously.

Microwave Conversion Instructions: Note: Reduce chilies by ½; Tabasco and black pepper should be used sparingly. Salt should be added after soup is completed and before reheating because of the use of salt pork and meaty ham bone. Thoroughly rinse beans; place in a 3-qt. *(3L)* casserole with 1 qt. *(1L)* water. Cover, cook on High 8 to 10 minutes or until just boiling; reduce power to Medium (50%), continue cooking 20 minutes. Allow 8 hours standing time, or overnight. Drain beans, reserving liquid; add enough water to liquid to make 1 qt. *(1L)*. Combine with broth in 3-qt. casserole; cover, cook on High 10 to 12 minutes or until just boiling. Stir; reduce power to Medium (50%), cook 25 to 30 minutes or until beans are tender. Allow 15 minutes standing time; puree in blender. Continue with additions as for conventional recipe. Return ingredients to 3-qt. casserole; cover, cook on High 15 minutes. Uncover, continue to cook on Medium (50%) 30 minutes, stirring twice. Allow 15 minutes standing time. Add sherry and lemon garnish.

YIELD: 6 Servings
TOTAL CALORIES: 888
CALORIES PER SERVING: 148
CARBOHYDRATES: 19g
PROTEIN: 9g
FAT: 4g
CHOLESTEROL: High
SODIUM: High
PREPARING: 10 Minutes
COOKING: 25 Minutes
FREEZING: No

6 cups *(1425ml)* chicken stock or
  vegetable stock
1 cup *(200g)* uncooked long grain rice
2 T. chopped fresh parsley
4 eggs
1 T. fresh lemon juice

Soupa Avgolemono

GREEK EGG AND LEMON SOUP

Bring stock to a boil in a 3 to 4-qt. *(3-4L)* saucepan. Add rice and parsley; simmer 15 minutes or until grains are just tender but still slightly resistant to the bite.

Beat eggs until frothy. Beat in lemon juice; stir in ¼ cup simmering chicken stock. Slowly pour egg mixture into broth, stirring constantly. Cook 3 to 5 minutes until thickened enough to coat a spoon. Serve garnished with chopped parsley.

Joyce Anne Vitelli, Manchester, CT

Variations, Advance Preparation, and Serving Suggestions:
Garnish with 2 T. finely chopped fresh mint or 1 T. dried mint.
Lemon juice can be increased to 3 T.

Microwave Conversion Instructions: Note: Reduce amount of chicken stock to 4½ cups *(1070ml)*. Bring stock to boil on High 9 minutes. Add rice and parsley. Simmer on Medium (50%) 15 minutes (a minute longer if rice is too hard). Beat eggs until frothy. Beat in lemon juice and stir in ¼ cup simmering chicken stock. Slowly pour into remaining broth, stirring constantly. Cook on Medium (50%) 2 to 3 minutes until thick enough to coat spoon.

YIELD: 4 Servings
TOTAL CALORIES: 1768
CALORIES PER SERVING: 442
CARBOHYDRATES: 19g
PROTEIN: 6g
FAT: 38g
CHOLESTEROL: High
SODIUM: High
PREPARING: 10 Minutes
SIMMERING: 30 Minutes
CHILLING: 3-4 Hours

2 large apples, cored, peeled, and sliced
2 medium onions, peeled and sliced
2 cans (10½ oz. each) *(620ml)* beef
  consomme
1 pt. *(475ml)* medium whipping cream
2 tsp. curry powder
Salt to taste

Apple Curry Soup

A delicious soup with a very subtle flavor.

Combine apples, onions, and consomme in saucepan; simmer for 30 minutes; cool and strain.

Heat cream in double boiler; slowly add strained soup, curry powder, and salt.

Chill several hours before serving. The soup may also be served hot.

Betty C. Blackburn, West Hartford, CT

Nutritional Notes: Calories, fat, and cholesterol can be significantly decreased by using evaporated skim milk instead of cream. Each serving would provide 116 *fewer* calories, 22 *fewer* grams fat, and an additional 7 grams protein. If desired, just a portion of the cream can be replaced by evaporated skim milk. Salt-free broth may be used to substantially decrease the sodium content of this recipe.

Microwave Conversion Instructions: Chop onion and peeled apples; place in 2-qt. *(2L)* casserole with consomme. Cook on High 12 to 15 minutes, or until apples are tender. Drain liquid; (or for more apple flavor, process mixture through food mill.) Put cream in empty casserole; cook on High 2½ to 3 minutes — do not boil. Stir once. Whisk in small amounts into consomme mixture along with curry, ½ tsp. at a time, checking after each addition of curry since microwaving intensifies flavors.

Florentine Cream Soup

YIELD: 6 Servings
CALORIES PER SERVING: 333
CARBOHYDRATES: 17g
PROTEIN: 10g
FAT: 25g
CHOLESTEROL: High
SODIUM: High
PREPARING: 15 Minutes
COOKING: 60 Minutes

Melt butter in saucepan; add flour and cook, stirring constantly until golden brown. Add chicken broth; cook, stirring constantly until smooth. Add onion, celery, parsley, and salt; simmer uncovered for 30 minutes, removing any scum which may accumulate on surface. Strain soup through fine colander.

Add spinach to soup; remove about 1 cup of soup to which you add egg yolks and cream; blend carefully; return to soup pot.

Cook for 3 to 5 minutes over medium heat; *do not allow to boil* or it will curdle.

Correct seasoning. Serve with croutons.

Joseph F. Spada, West Simsbury, CT

¼ cup *(60g)* butter
½ cup *(60g)* flour
8 cups *(1.9L)* chicken broth or vegetable stock
1 medium onion, chopped
1 stalk celery, chopped
¼ cup parsley, chopped
Dash of salt
1 lb. *(450g)* spinach, washed, cooked, drained, and pureed
2 egg yolks
1 cup *(240ml)* heavy cream
Croutons

Variations, Advance Preparation, and Serving Suggestions:
Cauliflower or broccoli may be substituted for the spinach.

Nutritional Notes: When not absolutely necessary, do not squeeze or drain spinach as valuable vitamins and minerals are also removed. One cup of evaporated skim milk can be used to replace the heavy cream. This saves approximately 110 calories per serving!

Microwave Conversion Instructions: Note: Reduce amount of chicken broth to 6 cups *(1.4L)*. Melt butter on High 1 minute. Stir in flour and cook on Medium (50%) 1 minute. Add chicken broth; cook on Medium (50%) 1 to 1½ minutes until smooth when stirred. Add onion, celery, parsley and salt and simmer on Medium (50%) for 15 minutes. Remove any scum which may accumulate on surface. Strain soup through fine colander. Remove about 1 cup, add egg yolks and cream; stir carefully. Add pureed spinach to remainder of soup; add soup mixed with egg and cream, cook on Medium (50%) for 2 to 3 minutes. Do not boil.

YIELD: 4 Servings
TOTAL CALORIES: 484
CALORIES PER SERVING: 121
CARBOHYDRATES: 6g
PROTEIN: 4g
FAT: 9g
SODIUM: High
PREPARING: 10 Minutes
COOKING: 20 Minutes

1 T. *(15g)* butter
¼ cup *(20g)* sliced scallions
1½ tsp. flour
¼ tsp. salt
¼ tsp. dried chervil
Freshly ground pepper
½ tsp. chopped parsley
1¼ cups *(300ml)* chicken stock
½ cup *(120ml)* light cream
1 pt. fresh *(350g)* or 1 pkg. (10 oz.)
   (285g) frozen Brussels sprouts, cooked
Chopped chervil or parsley

YIELD: 8-10 Servings
TOTAL CALORIES: 3840
CALORIES PER SERVING: 384
CARBOHYDRATES: 11g
PROTEIN: 4g
FAT: 36g
SODIUM High
PREPARING: 30 Minutes
CHILLING: Overnight

¼ cup *(30g)* ground almonds
2 shallots, peeled and chopped
1 tsp. salt
1 tsp. white pepper
2 eggs
1 cup *(240ml)* vegetable oil
½ cup *(120ml)* cider vinegar
1 can (16 oz.) *(450g)* Italian tomatoes,
   or 1 lb. fresh tomatoes
2 medium cucumbers, peeled and
   chopped
1 tsp. ground cloves
1 tsp. ground cumin
Pinch cayenne pepper
3 slices white bread, crusts removed
4 cups *(950ml)* chicken stock or
   vegetable broth
1 cup *(240ml)* heavy cream
Seedless white grapes, peeled

Belgian Herb Soup

See if your friends can correctly guess the main ingredient in this soup!

Melt butter in saucepan. Saute scallions until tender. Mix in flour, salt, chervil, pepper and parsley to form a smooth paste. Gradually stir in stock. Cook and stir until mixture boils; boil 1 minute. Remove from heat and add cream.

Combine cream mixture and sprouts. Put in a blender or food processor in batches, and process until the mixture is smooth. Return the soup to a saucepan. When ready to serve, gently heat but *do not boil.* Serve in warmed soup bowls. Garnish with chopped chervil or parsley.

Mary Benoit, Bristol, CT

Microwave Conversion Instructions: To cook fresh Brussels sprouts: Cut a shallow "x" in bottom of each stem. Combine sprouts and ¼ cup *(60ml)* water in shallow 1-qt. *(1L)* baking dish. Cover and cook on High 7 minutes per pound. Let rest, covered, 3 minutes. Place scallions in 4-cup *(1L)* measure; put butter on top. Cook on High 1 minute. Stir in flour, salt, chervil, pepper and parsley to form a smooth paste. Gradually stir in stock. Cook on High until mixture boils; continue boiling 1 minute. Place sprouts in large bowl; add cream mixture. Continue as directed above.

Gazpacho Andaluz

A refreshing, quite different example of this cold Spanish vegetable soup.

Place almonds, shallots, salt, pepper, eggs, oil, and vinegar in a blender or food processor; mix until smooth; remove and set aside.

Combine tomatoes, cucumbers, spices, bread, stock, and cream in processor; blend until smooth.

Combine both mixtures; blend. Chill thoroughly several hours or overnight.

Place 6 grapes in bottom of each soup bowl; fill with chilled soup and serve.

James Boyd II, West Hartford, CT

Wine Suggestion: Spanish Fino Sherry, dry white; serve chilled.

Basil Soup

Basil used to be known as a "royal plant", as only a sovereign could cut it and only with a golden sickle!

YIELD: 6 Servings
TOTAL CALORIES: 1992
CALORIES PER SERVING: 332
CARBOHYDRATES: 11g
PROTEIN: 18g
FAT: 24g
SODIUM: High
PREPARING: 20 Minutes
COOKING: 20 Minutes

In a blender or food processor, puree spinach, parsley, and 1 cup chicken broth; add basil, walnuts, and garlic, puree until smooth; add olive oil and blend.

Pour mixture into large pot; stir in remaining 7 cups chicken broth; heat to boiling; add orzo. Bring back to boil, reduce heat, simmer, covered, 15 minutes or until orzo is tender.

Beat egg in ½ cup water; add 1 cup cheese; gradually stir 1 cup hot soup into egg mixture. Pour egg mixture into remaining soup.

Serve with remaining cheese passed on the side.

Winnie White, North Conway, NH

Nutritional Notes: Sodium content is significantly decreased if unsalted chicken broth is used. However, Parmesan cheese provides approximately 93 milligrams per tablespoon and, therefore, adds 500 milligrams sodium to each serving if all the cheese is used. Parsley is rich in vitamins and minerals. Consumption of this nutritious vegetable rather than its common use as merely a decorative garnish is highly recommended.

2 cups *(75g)* firmly packed fresh spinach with stems removed
1 cup firmly packed parsley sprigs
8 cups *(2L)* chicken broth or vegetable stock, divided
¾ cup fresh basil leaves or ¼ cup dry basil
¼ cup *(30g)* walnut pieces
1 large clove garlic, minced
¼ cup *(60ml)* olive oil
½ cup *(80g)* orzo (rice-shaped pasta) or small noodles
1 egg
½ cup *(120ml)* water
2 cups *(260g)* freshly grated Parmesan cheese

YIELD: 6-8 Servings
TOTAL CALORIES: 2024
CALORIES PER SERVING: 253
CARBOHYDRATES: 7.5g
PROTEIN: 4g
FAT: 23g
CHOLESTEROL: High
SODIUM: High
PREPARING: 25 Minutes
SIMMERING: 20 Minutes
FREEZING: Yes

Parsnip and Curry Soup

In large saucepan heat butter; saute parsnips and onions 5 minutes. Add flour and curry powder; stir until well blended.

Add stock; simmer for 20 minutes. Remove from heat and cool slightly. Puree in blender or food processor.

Serve warm with a spoonful of whipped cream or sour cream garnished with parsley.

Lucy T. Mink, Morris, CT

Microwave Conversion Instructions: In 3-qt. *(3L)* casserole, melt butter on High 2½ minutes. Add parsnips and onions; cook 6 to 8 minutes on Medium High (70%). Add flour, curry and stock; cook on High 18 to 20 minutes, or until vegetables are tender. Cool; process in blender. Return soup to casserole; cook on High 8 to 10 minutes or until soup is hot.

½ lb. *(225g)* butter
4 large parsnips, peeled and thinly sliced
4 medium onions, peeled and thinly sliced
4 T. *(30g)* flour
4 tsp. (or more to taste) strong curry powder
8 cups *(2L)* beef stock

Whipped cream or sour cream
Chopped parsley

YIELD: 4-6 Servings
TOTAL CALORIES: 858
CALORIES PER SERVING: 143
CARBOHYDRATES: 5g
PROTEIN: 15g
FAT: 7g
SODIUM: High
PREPARING: 45 Minutes
STEAMING: 20 Minutes
FREEZING: No

Molded San Sze Soup

The artistic arrangement of textures and colors of this "molded" soup make a very dramatic presentation.

1 medium chicken breast
3 scallions, cut into pieces
3 slices fresh ginger root
1 very large dried Chinese mushroom
Hot water
2 eggs
A few drops sesame seed oil
½-¾ cup *(70-105g)* ham, cut into julienne strips ⅛ inch *(3mm)* wide and 2½ inches *(6.25cm)* long
½-¾ cup *(50-75g)* snow peas, cut into julienne strips
½-¾ cup *(70-105g)* bamboo shoots, cut into julienne strips
½ tsp. salt
3 cups *(710ml)* chicken stock

Poach chicken breast with scallions and ginger root; bone and cut into julienne strips.

Soak the mushroom in hot water for 30 minutes.

Lightly beat eggs with sesame seed oil; fry in skillet. Remove and cut into strips. Place mushroom in center bottom of a 4 to 5-cup *(1-1.25L)* rice bowl. Arrange chicken, ham, egg and snow pea strips in radiating pattern around mushroom in 1-inch *(2.5cm)* segments extending to edge of bowl in alternating colors. Fill center with bamboo shoot strips. Sprinkle with salt, add chicken stock until bowl is filled. Steam 20 minutes in steamer or large covered pot.

Place large shallow serving bowl over rice bowl. Invert and remove rice bowl. Carefully add remaining hot chicken broth. Serve, breaking up from center so that each person gets a portion of various ingredients.

Tracy Atkinson, Avon, CT

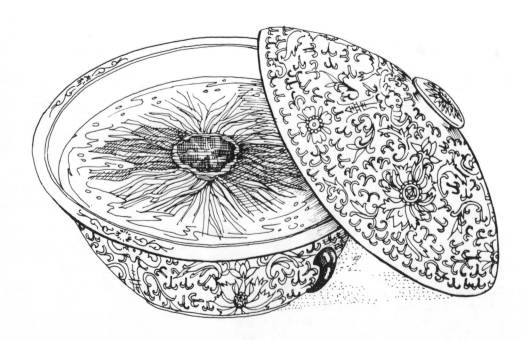

Chinese Hot and Sour Soup

Excellent as part of a Chinese meal or absolutely perfect as an entree on a cold winter day.

The tree ears used in this soup are also known as cloud ears and are a speciality of the Szechwan province. They are a tree fungus and contain calcium. Tree ears are rubbery in consistency after soaking, have very little flavor, but absorb the flavor of other ingredients used in a dish.

YIELD: 12 First Course Servings or
   6 Entree Servings
TOTAL CALORIES: 1716
CALORIES PER FIRST COURSE
   SERVING: 143
CARBOHYDRATES: 9g
PROTEIN: 11g
FAT: 7g
SODIUM: High
PREPARING: 1 Hour
COOKING: 20 Minutes
FREEZING: No

Place mushrooms, tiger lily buds, and tree ears in separate bowls. Pour hot water over each to cover; steep 30 minutes. Rinse tree ears in cold water; remove hard end of each and shred. Drain mushrooms and shred. Trim off the tough ends of the tiger lily buds and cut them in half. Combine the sherry and cornstarch; mix well. Dredge the pork shreds in cornstarch mixture. Place mushrooms, tiger lily buds, tree ears, pork shreds, bamboo shoots, bean cake, chicken broth and water in a kettle or wok. Bring contents to a boil and then simmer until pork is cooked. Add soy, sugar, salt, pepper, vinegars, and hot sauce; simmer 5 minutes. Combine cornstarch with cold water and add to soup. Simmer another minute or two, stirring. Add slightly beaten eggs with one hand while stirring with the other. Garnish with sesame oil. Serve immediately.

Lucy Goodridge, West Hartford, CT

Nutritional Notes: The nutritional values of tiger lily buds, tree ears and dried black mushrooms are not included in the above nutritional data, but they represent an insignificant number of calories and provide some vitamins and trace minerals. Bean cake is a good source of protein that is low in cholesterol/fat and sodium.

8 Chinese dried black mushrooms
1 cup *(45g)* tiger lily buds
½ cup *(25g)* tree ears
4 tsp. dry sherry
4 tsp. cornstarch
1 cup (½ lb.) *(225g)* finely shredded raw
   pork
1 cup *(140g)* bamboo shoots, shredded
1 fresh bean cake, shredded
4 cans (13¾ oz. each) *(1650ml)* chicken
   broth
4 cups *(950ml)* water
2 T. thin or light soy sauce
1 tsp. sugar
1 tsp. salt
½ tsp. freshly ground black pepper
3 T. *(45ml)* Chenkong vinegar or black
   rice vinegar
3 T. *(45ml)* red wine vinegar
½ tsp. hot sauce
6 T. *(70g)* cornstarch
½ cup *(120ml)* cold water
2 eggs, slightly beaten
2 tsp. sesame oil

YIELD: 6-8 Servings
TOTAL CALORIES: 2456
CALORIES PER SERVING: 307
CARBOHYDRATES: 19g
PROTEIN: 15g
FAT: 19g
SODIUM: High
PREPARING: 20 Minutes
COOKING: 40 Minutes

Curried Ham and Sprout Soup

4 T. *(60g)* butter
2 onions, peeled and chopped
2 carrots, peeled and chopped
1 tsp. mace
12 oz. (2 cups) *(340g)* cooked ham
2 cups *(350g)* fresh Brussels sprouts
1-2 tsp. curry powder
1 cup *(100g)* chopped tomato
½ cup *(100g)* uncooked rice
2 qts. *(2L)* chicken stock
Freshly ground pepper
Freshly chopped parsley

Melt butter in large, deep skillet; add onions, carrots, mace, ham, sprouts, and curry powder. Cook 10 minutes, stirring constantly. Add tomatoes and stir in rice, tossing to coat with the butter.

Add chicken stock and simmer, uncovered, until rice softens.

Season with pepper. Serve garnished with chopped fresh parsley.

*Ann Howard Cookery, Farmington, CT
via Sarah C. Seymour, West Hartford, CT*

Microwave Conversion Instructions: Note: Heat stock before using. Place 1 cup *(240ml)* stock and rice in casserole. Cook, covered, on High 5 minutes. Reduce power to Medium (50%) and continue cooking 5 to 6 minutes or until water is almost absorbed and rice is tender. Put onions and carrots in 3-qt. *(3L)* casserole; put butter on top of vegetables. Cook, covered, 5 minutes. Add mace, ham, sprouts and curry powder. Cook on High, covered, 5 minutes, or until sprouts are fork tender. Stir in tomatoes, cooked rice and 5 cups *(1.25L)* heated stock. Cook on High 5 minutes, or until soup simmers; continue to cook on Medium (50%) 5 minutes. Correct seasonings.

Chicken Cheese Chowder

This chowder is a superb way to use leftover chicken!

YIELD: 4-6 Servings
TOTAL CALORIES: 1644
CALORIES PER SERVING: 274
CARBOHYDRATES: 12g
PROTEIN: 16g
FAT: 18g
SODIUM: High
PREPARING: 20 Minutes
COOKING: 20 Minutes

1 cup *(120g)* shredded carrots
¼ cup *(40g)* chopped onion
¼ cup *(60g)* butter
¼ cup *(30g)* flour
2 cups *(475ml)* milk
1¾ cups *(420ml)* chicken stock
1 cup *(150g)* diced, cooked chicken or turkey
½ tsp. celery seed
½ tsp. Worcestershire sauce
1 T. dry white wine
1 cup (¼ lb.) *(115g)* grated sharp Cheddar cheese
Chopped chives

Saute carrots and onion in butter until tender but not brown. Blend in flour; cook 1 minute; add milk and stock. Over medium heat, stir until thick and bubbling. Add chicken, celery seed, Worcestershire sauce and wine. When simmering, add cheese; stir until melted.

Serve in warmed soup bowls; garnish with chopped chives.

Alice F. Evans, Simsbury, CT

Nutritional Notes: By using salt-free homemade chicken broth and unsalted margarine the sodium content is decreased by approximately 200 milligrams per serving. If skim milk replaces whole milk, 30 calories per serving are subtracted. This chowder is high in protein and calcium. Combine it with a green salad or fresh fruit salad and whole grain bread for a well balanced meal.

Wine Suggestion: Harvey's Tico Sherry, semi-dry white; serve chilled.

Microwave Conversion Instructions: To prepare chicken use 1 whole large chicken breast skinned and split, 1 tsp. chicken bouillon granules, ½ cup boiling water. Place chicken pieces in 3-qt. *(3L)* casserole with bouillon dissolved in water. Cover; cook on High 5 to 6 minutes, basting once. Drain broth; combine with wine and enough water to make 1 cup liquid. Set aside. Remove chicken, set aside to cool, then remove from bones and dice. Combine carrot, onion, celery seed, and Worcestershire sauce with melted butter, stirring well. Cover, cook on High 7 to 10 minutes, stirring once. Meanwhile, combine 4 T. plus 1 tsp. flour in ¼ cup milk; blend until smooth. Stir flour mixture into remaining milk, along with broth/wine mixture, chicken, and cheese. Pour mixture into casserole with vegetables, stirring well. Cover, cook on High 3 to 5 minutes, until cheese is melted. Stir. Uncover, cook on High 7 to 10 minutes. Soup will be hot and nicely thickened.

Spiced Lentil Soup

Another hearty soup for a Sunday night supper. Lentils, containing more protein than any other vegetable, were cultivated in pre-historic times in central Asia.

YIELD: 6-8 Servings
TOTAL CALORIES: 1984
CALORIES PER SERVING: 248
CARBOHYDRATES: 25g
PROTEIN: 10g
FAT: 12g
SODIUM: High
PREPARING: 20 Minutes
SIMMERING: 2½ Hours
FREEZING: Yes

Combine lentils, water, and salt in large pot and bring to boil. Lower heat and simmer for one hour.

Heat olive oil in skillet. Add onions, garlic, and bay leaves. Saute, stirring often, until onions begin to brown. Add cinnamon, cloves, ginger, and cumin, continuing to stir over low heat for approximately 2 minutes. Add to soup along with chilies, cilantro, and parsley. Simmer another hour, stirring occasionally.

When lentils are completely soft, puree soup in batches in blender or food processor, or force through a sieve. Return puree to pot and stir in butter. Add salt and pepper to taste.

Serve hot, sprinkled with a little paprika, or garnish each bowl with sprigs of cilantro.

Gretchen V. Swibold, North Canton, CT

Nutritional Notes: This soup is appropriate for many sodium-restricted diets if salt is eliminated. Lentils are high in B vitamins and protein. A barley or rice dish would go well with this soup, since lentils and grain products balance each other nutritionally (i.e. protein complementation in the vegetarian diet.)

Microwave Conversion Instructions: Divide recipe in half for microwave conversion. Use boiling water for the lentils. Combine lentils, water and salt in a 5-qt. *(5L)* casserole. Cook, covered, on High 30 minutes, stirring several times. Cover and continue to cook 15 minutes. Remove, keep covered. In a separate bowl, combine olive oil, onions, garlic, and bay leaves. Saute uncovered, on High 7 to 9 minutes, until onions begin to color. Add cinnamon, cloves, ginger and cumin, cook an additional 2 minutes. Add to soup, along with chilies, cilantro, and parsley. Continue cooking on High 40 to 50 minutes, until lentils are completely soft. Follow above directions for completion.

2½ cups (1 lb.) *(450g)* lentils
3½ qts. *(3½L)* water
1½ tsp. salt plus more to taste
¼ cup *(60ml)* olive oil
2 onions, peeled and chopped
4 large cloves garlic, peeled and sliced
2 large bay leaves
½ tsp. cinnamon
½ tsp. ground cloves
½ tsp. ginger
1½ tsp. ground cumin
2½ T. minced green chilies
2-3 T. chopped fresh cilantro (coriander leaves)
¼ cup chopped fresh parsley
3 T. *(45g)* butter
Freshly ground black pepper
Paprika (optional)
Sprigs of cilantro

YIELD: 4 Servings
TOTAL CALORIES: 868
CALORIES PER SERVING: 217
CARBOHYDRATES: 29g
PROTEIN: 5g
FAT: 9g
PREPARING: 15 Minutes
SIMMERING: 30 Minutes

1 cup *(170g)* peppers, seeded and
   finely chopped (a combination
   of green, red, orange, yellow,
   and hot peppers)
2 lbs. *(900g)* ripe garden tomatoes,
   scalded and peeled (use canned when
   fresh not flavorful)
1 onion, chopped
1½ cups *(355ml)* water
3 T. *(45g)* butter
3 T. *(20g)* flour
1½ tsp. freshly grated lemon rind
Salt
Freshly ground pepper
1 cup *(60g raw)* cooked brown rice
Yogurt or sour cream
Fresh dill or parsley
Cayenne pepper (optional)

YIELD: 6 Sandwiches
TOTAL CALORIES: 3220
CALORIES PER SANDWICH: 537
CARBOHYDRATES: 20g
PROTEIN: 31g
FAT: 37g
CHOLESTEROL: High
PREPARING: 15 Minutes
BROILING: 5 Minutes
FREEZING: No

⅓ cup each of minced:
Cabbage *(30g)*
Carrot *(40g)*
Green Pepper *(55g)*
Celery *(40g)*
Radishes *(40g)*
Red Onion *(65g)*

6 slices white bread
Butter
6 cups *(680g)* Cheddar cheese, grated
½ cup *(120ml)* beer
Freshly ground white pepper
Cayenne pepper

Savory Pepper Soup

Puree all vegetables in blender or food processor. Transfer mixture to large saucepan; add water; simmer for 20 minutes.

Melt butter in small saucepan; stir in flour to make a roux; cook a few minutes; add to heated soup; simmer 10 minutes more; add lemon rind, salt, and pepper; stir in rice.

Serve hot with dollop of yogurt or sour cream; garnish with dill or parsley and cayenne pepper.

Terry Oakes Bourret, Cromwell, CT

Nutritional Notes: Peppers are an excellent source of vitamin C, and, along with tomatoes and onions, represent a substantial amount of this vitamin. Vitamin C, however, is partially destroyed through the heat of cooking (and canning). If using canned tomatoes, be sure to include the juices which are also rich in vitamins and minerals. Brown rice adds fiber and trace minerals to this soup.

Microwave Conversion Instructions: Place vegetables in large glass casserole, add water, 1 cup *only*. Cook, uncovered, on High 10 minutes. Set aside. In small glass bowl, cook butter until melted; stir in flour to make a roux; cook on High 1 minute. Add to heated soup, whisking constantly to prevent lumps; cook on High, un-covered, 10 minutes. Add lemon rind, salt and pepper; stir in cooked rice.

Spirited Hot Vegetable Sandwiches

The spirit is beer in this very different luncheon offering.

In a bowl, combine minced vegetables. Lightly toast and butter bread. In a saucepan, melt cheese with beer, stirring. Season with pepper and cayenne to taste. Place ⅓ cup of the vegetable mixture on each piece of toast. Carefully place sandwiches on a baking sheet; divide the sauce among the sandwiches and broil the sandwiches ap-proximately 3 minutes or until the cheese is lightly browned and bub-bly. Serve hot.

Kristy and Dale Harris, Manchester, CT

Nutritional Notes: You can substitute whole grain bread and cheese made from skim milk.

Wine Suggestion: California Dry Sauvignon Blanc, dry white; serve chilled.

Stuffed Eggs à la Parisienne

This recipe originated in Northern Italy and is served as an antipasto or as part of a cold buffet.

YIELD: 8-10 Servings
TOTAL CALORIES: 1380
CALORIES PER SERVING: 138
CARBOHYDRATES: 2g
PROTEIN: 10g
FAT: 10g
CHOLESTEROL: High
SODIUM: High
PREPARING: 20 Minutes
COOKING: 20 Minutes

Remove yolks from eggs. Mash. Combine anchovy, green pepper, onion, and parsley with yolks and blend well. Divide mixture in half; one portion will be used for stuffing and remainder will be used for sauce.

SAUCE: Combine and thoroughly mix sauce ingredients with half of yolk mixture.

To assemble: Place enough shredded cabbage to cover an oblong serving dish or platter; sprinkle with reserved anchovy liquid. Set stuffed eggs, filled side down, atop cabbage. (Up to this point may be made in morning and refrigerated). Just before serving, pour sauce on and around eggs.

Marilyn Peracchio, Manchester, CT

Wine Suggestion: Italian Soave, dry white; serve chilled.

12 eggs, hard-boiled and halved
  lengthwise
2 cans (2 oz. each) *(115g)* flat anchovy
  filets drained, reserving liquid, finely
  chopped
1 small green pepper, finely chopped
1 onion or 3-4 scallions, minced
Parsley, minced
Shredded cabbage

SAUCE:
2-3 T. *(30-45g)* mayonnaise
¾ T. chili sauce
1-2 drops Worcestershire sauce

Fresh Vegetable Cheese Frittata

A nice idea for a brunch, buffet, or to tote along with some wine for a portable feast.

YIELD: 6-8 Servings
CALORIES PER SERVING: 514
CARBOHYDRATES: 24g
PROTEIN: 19g
FAT: 38g
CHOLESTEROL: High
SODIUM: High
PREPARING: 30 Minutes
BAKING: 55 Minutes
FREEZING: No

In large skillet, saute zucchini, mushrooms, pepper, onion, and garlic in oil 5 minutes or until vegetables are softened.

Cool. Beat eggs with cream, add cream cheese, bread, Cheddar cheese, the vegetable mixture, salt and pepper. Mix well. Pour into well-buttered 10-inch *(25cm)* springform pan. Bake in preheated 350° oven, 55 minutes or until browned. Cool 10 minutes before removing sides of pan. Cut in wedges to serve.

Kristy and Dale Harris, Manchester, CT

Wine Suggestion: California Beauclair Johannisberg Riesling, clean white; serve chilled.

Microwave Conversion Instructions: Coat prepared vegetables as evenly as possible with oil. Place vegetables in casserole; cook on High 6 minutes. Cool. Combine beaten eggs, cream cheese, bread, Cheddar cheese, vegetables, salt and pepper. Pour into lightly-buttered ring mold. Cook on High, covered, 18 minutes or until browned. Let stand 5 minutes before serving.

1½ cups *(155g)* zucchini, chopped
1½ cups *(115g)* mushrooms, sliced
¾ cup *(125g)* green pepper, chopped
¾ cup *(115g)* onion, chopped
1 clove garlic, minced
3 T. *(45ml)* oil
6 eggs
¼ cup *(60ml)* light cream
1 lb. *(450g)* cream cheese, diced
2 cups *(50g)* day old bread, crusts
  removed, cubed
1½ cups *(170g)* sharp Cheddar cheese,
  grated
Salt
Freshly ground pepper

Herbed Garden Tomato Quiche

The *quiche* or *kiche* (sometimes spelled this way) originated in Lorraine, France, although it is suggested that this kind of savory custard tart belongs to German cookery, since in Germany the *quiche* is known under the name *kuchen*, from which the word *kiche* could have come. Originally quiche was an open flan, made from bread dough, with a variety of fillings. Nowadays the dough is replaced by *pate brisee* and each quiche takes its name from the main ingredient of the filling. Quiche is one of the most popular of American culinary adaptations. While essentially a simple dish, it is infinitely accommodating. Quiches can be served as a cocktail food, a first course, a luncheon dish, a dessert, or with an entree as a substitute for both starch and vegetable dishes.

YIELD: 8 Servings
TOTAL CALORIES: 5230
CALORIES PER SERVING: 654
CARBOHYDRATES: 39g
PROTEIN: 12g
FAT: 50g
CHOLESTEROL: High
SODIUM: High
PREPARING: 20 Minutes
BAKING: 60 Minutes
CHILLING: 60 Minutes
COOKING: 25 Minutes
FREEZING: No

FRESH TOMATO PUREE:

¾ cup *(150g)* minced onion
2 T. *(30g)* butter
4 large garden tomatoes, peeled, seeded, squeezed and chopped
½ tsp. salt
¼ tsp. freshly ground pepper
¼ tsp. sugar
Bouquet garni consisting of thyme, bay leaf and fresh parsley

BASIC PIE DOUGH:

(page 198) for 1 12-inch *(30cm)* quiche pan

FILLING:

1 cup *(240ml)* heavy cream
½ cup *(120ml)* light cream
2 eggs
2 egg yolks
¼ cup *(30g)* freshly grated Swiss cheese
½ cup *(65g)* freshly grated Parmesan cheese
½ tsp. salt
¼ tsp. freshly ground white pepper
8 ½-inch *(1.5cm)* thick garden fresh tomato slices
¼ tsp. thyme or fresh basil or tarragon
2 T. *(30g)* butter

1 T. chopped fresh parsley

FRESH TOMATO PUREE: Saute onion in butter until soft and golden. Add remaining puree ingredients. Cook mixture, covered, over low heat, 10 minutes. Remove cover, increase heat and cook until liquid has evaporated and mixture is reduced to a thick, dry puree. Remove bouquet garni. Cool puree.

BASIC PIE DOUGH: Roll chilled dough out into 15-inch *(38cm)* circle. Line 12-inch *(30cm)* flan or quiche pan with removable bottom, with the pastry. Cut off excess dough. Prick bottom of shell and chill at least one hour. When ready to bake, line pastry with waxed paper and fill with raw beans, rice, or pie weights. Bake shell in lower third of preheated 400° oven for 10 to 15 minutes. Remove waxed paper and weights; bake 10 to 15 minutes more. Cool shell.

FILLING: Combine creams, eggs, tomato puree, ¼ cup each Swiss and Parmesan cheeses, salt and white pepper. Mix thoroughly.

Fill empty shell with custard mixture. Cover top with tomato slices; sprinkle with salt, pepper and thyme. Sprinkle remaining ¼ cup Parmesan cheese over top. Dot with butter. Bake on top rack of preheated 375° oven for 25 to 30 minutes. Remove quiche from pan and cool on wire rack. Before serving, sprinkle with chopped parsley.

Joyce Brown, Columbia, SC

Nutritional Notes: This recipe was tested using 1½ cups of evaporated milk instead of cream to cut calories and add protein. The reader may wish to try evaporated *skim* milk, although cholesterol content will remain high due to the egg yolks and cheese ingredients.

Microwave Conversion Instructions: Tomato Puree: Cook onion in melted butter on Medium High (70%) 2 minutes; add remaining ingredients, continue to cook on Medium High (70%) covered 5 to 7 minutes. Set aside to cool.

Prepare 12-inch pie shell in porcelain quiche pan; prick sides and bottom. Cook on High 4½ minutes, or until flaky.

Pour in filling, top with tomato slices; season and sprinkle with Parmesan. Dot with butter. Cook on Medium High (70%) 9 to 11 minutes, rotating ¼ turn twice, until slightly set in center. Additional firming will occur during standing time.

Cheese Soufflé in Tomato Cups

A tomato is really a fruit and not a vegetable. Even before the Inca civilizations of Ecuador and Peru, tomatoes were found growing wild in those areas. When these people migrated northward to Mexico and Central America they took tomatoes with them. In Mexico, they were called "tomatl". It wasn't until the 19th century, when the canning industry began, that tomatoes became widely used as food, not just as an ornamental plant.

YIELD: 6 Servings
CALORIES PER SERVING: 114
CARBOHYDRATES: 8g
PROTEIN: 7g
FAT: 6g
DRAINING: 30 Minutes
PREPARING: 45 Minutes
BAKING: 25-30 Minutes

Cut tops off tomatoes, scoop out pulp. Sprinkle insides with salt; invert on paper towels and allow to drain 30 minutes.

Make a roux by melting butter, adding flour and cooking mixture for 1 minute. Then add milk mixing with wire whisk until mixture is smooth. Add salt, pepper and nutmeg; cook until thick. Remove from heat and allow to cool several minutes; then add egg yolks, one at a time, beating well after each addition. Stir in cheese.

In another bowl, beat egg whites until stiff but not dry. Gently fold into the cheese mixture. Spoon the souffle mixture into tomato cups. Place in a shallow baking dish, about 7 × 11-inch *(18 × 28cm)*.

Bake in a preheated 350° oven, 20 to 25 minutes until puffed and golden brown. Serve immediately.

Diane Whitney, Windsor, CT

6 large flavorful garden tomatoes
Salt
1 T. *(15g)* butter
1½ T. *(10g)* flour
⅓ cup *(80ml)* milk
Freshly ground white pepper
Freshly grated nutmeg
2 eggs, separated
½ cup *(60g)* grated Swiss cheese

Microwave Conversion Instructions: Note: Use evaporated milk instead of regular milk. Melt butter in a 4-cup *(950ml)* measure for 20 seconds on High. Add flour, cover and cook 20 seconds on High. Add evaporated milk and seasonings; cover, cook on High 2 minutes, stirring every 30 seconds. Add the yolks, one at a time and ⅓ of cheese. Fold remaining cheese into stiffly beaten egg whites. Stir ⅓ of egg whites into roux; when well-blended, add remaining egg white mixture. Spoon into tomato cups, ¾ full. Place on round plate; cook on Medium Low (30%) 12 to 14 minutes, rotating plate every 3 to 4 minutes, until souffle is puffed. If desired, brown tops under broiler.

YIELD: 6 Servings
CALORIES PER SERVING: 324
CARBOHYDRATES: 8g
PROTEIN: 10g
FAT: 28g
CHOLESTEROL: High
PREPARING: 15 Minutes
COOKING: 10 Minutes
FREEZING: No

Vegetable oil

6 ½-inch (1.25cm) thick slices whole milk mozzarella cheese, about 4 inches (10cm) square (about 1150g)
1 cup (115g) flour
3 eggs, beaten
½ tsp. finely minced fresh parsley
1 tsp. freshly grated Romano cheese
Salt, freshly ground black pepper to taste
1 cup (120g) fine breadcrumbs

Fried Mozzarella Cheese

Pour oil 1½ inches deep *(4cm)* into frying pan or electric skillet; heat to 375°.

Coat cheese with flour. Mix eggs with parsley, cheese, salt, pepper. Dip cheese in egg, then coat with breadcrumbs. Dip again in egg. Fry in hot oil until golden brown on both sides. Drain cheese on paper towels. Serve immediately.

Leon's Restaurant, New Haven, CT

Variations, Advance Preparation, and Serving Suggestions:
The cheese may be breaded several hours ahead of time and refrigerated. Just before serving, do final egg dip and fry.

Serve topped with tomato sauce, or with a sauce of anchovies and capers in melted butter.

Nutritional Notes: Fat value assumes that 1 T. oil will be absorbed per serving.

Wine Suggestion: Italian Chianti, dry red; serve at room temperature.

YIELD: 10-12 Servings
TOTAL CALORIES: 4750
CALORIES PER SERVING: 396
CARBOHYDRATES: 20g
PROTEIN: 25g
FAT: 24g
CHOLESTEROL: High
SODIUM: High
PREPARING: 45 Minutes
BAKING: 60 Minutes
STANDING: 20 Minutes

3 lbs. (1350g) large zucchini, scrubbed and with ends removed
1 qt. (950ml) thick tomato sauce
1 cup (120g) breadcrumbs
2 lbs. (900g) ricotta cheese
4 eggs, lightly beaten
2 T. chopped parsley
½ tsp. oregano
½ tsp. basil
Salt
Freshly ground pepper
1 cup (225g) grated Parmesan or Romano cheese
1 lb. (450g) mozzarella cheese, coarsely grated

Zucchini "Lasagna"

This is an excellent recipe for lasagna lovers who wish to avoid white flour. Because the zucchini takes the place of the pasta, the dish is much lighter.

Bring about 1 inch *(2.5cm)* water and salt to a boil in a soup kettle; meanwhile, cut zucchini into long thin slices. When water is boiling add zucchini slices, cover and cook about 5 minutes until limp and translucent. Drain on absorbent towels.

Into a 9 x 13 x 2-inch *(22.5 x 33 x 5cm)* pan, spoon a thin layer of tomato sauce. Sprinkle with ¼ cup breadcrumbs; completely cover with a layer of zucchini, placing slices side-by-side.

Combine ricotta cheese, eggs, parsley, seasonings, ½ cup Parmesan or Romano cheese and one half of the remaining bread crumbs. Spoon half of the mixture on top of the zucchini slices, sprinkle with half the mozzarella cheese and repeat the layers of tomato sauce, zucchini slices (reserve 6 slices), and ricotta mixture. Cover with most of the remaining tomato sauce; arrange 6 zucchini slices on top and drizzle with remaining sauce and mozzarella. Combine remaining bread crumbs and Parmesan cheese. Sprinkle over top.

Bake in preheated 350° oven, 60 minutes or until top is browned. Let stand 20 minutes before cutting.

Renee Pregulman Dubin, West Hartford, CT

Nutritional Notes: Cholesterol can be moderately decreased if ricotta and mozzarella *made from skim milk* are used.

Wine Suggestion: Italian Verdicchio, dry white; serve chilled.

Microwave Conversion Instructions: *Note:* For Microwave preparation all ingredients are halved; except zucchini is reduced to 1½-2 lbs. *(675g-900g)* and tomato sauce to one cup *(240ml) plus* ⅓ cup *(85g)* tomato paste.

Prepare zucchini as for conventional recipe; place in 9 × 13 × 2-inch glass casserole. Cover with plastic wrap, cook on High 6 to 8 minutes or until limp and translucent; drain carefully.

Assemble "lasagna" as for conventional recipe being sure to add tomato paste to sauce. Cook on High 5 minutes. Reduce power to Medium (50%), continue to cook 30 to 40 minutes or until set and hot in center. Let stand 15 minutes before serving.

Tofu Lasagna

This is a good introduction to tofu, an excellent inexpensive source of protein.

YIELD: 6-8 Servings
TOTAL CALORIES: 2792
CALORIES PER SERVING: 349
CARBOHYDRATES: 32g
PROTEIN: 17g
FAT: 17g
PREPARING: 45 Minutes
BAKING: 45 Minutes

In 9-10-inch *(22.5-25cm)* skillet, melt butter; saute mushrooms with garlic, salt and pepper. Cook until mushrooms are tender, approx. 5 minutes. Stir in sauce and wheat germ; heat. In a small bowl, combine tofu and Parmesan; in another small bowl, combine mozzarella and parsley. Place ⅓ of lasagna noodles in bottom of 11¾ × 7½-inch *(30 × 20cm)* baking dish. Spread half of the tofu mixture on top of the noodles; cover with ⅓ of the sauce and top with ⅓ of the mozzarella mixture. Repeat layers once, make final layer of noodles followed by sauce and mozzarella. (Up to this point, lasagna can be prepared ahead, covered and refrigerated; let stand uncovered at room temperature 1 hour and increase baking time by 15 minutes.) Bake in preheated 350° oven 45 minutes, or until hot and bubbly. Cool 15 minutes before cutting.

Kristy and Dale Harris, Manchester, CT

¼ cup *(60g)* butter
½ lb. *(225g)* fresh mushrooms, thinly sliced
3 cloves garlic, minced
½ tsp. salt
⅛ tsp. freshly ground pepper
3 cups *(710ml)* bottled spaghetti sauce (preferably Aunt Millie's)
½ cup *(60g)* wheat germ
1 cup *(180g)* mashed tofu
¼ cup *(35g)* freshly grated Parmesan cheese
½ lb. *(225g)* shredded mozzarella cheese, about 2 cups
¼ cup parsley, chopped
1 egg worth fresh Whole Wheat Pasta (page 192) lasagna or 8 oz. *(225g)* store-bought, cooked and drained

Nutritional Notes: Tofu is a good source of protein for the vegetarian or non-vegetarian, and is low in fat, cholesterol, and sodium. In addition, it is mild-flavored and can be adapted to many recipes, since it absorbs the flavor of accompanying ingredients. Homemade spaghetti sauce may be utilized to decrease sodium content. Mozzarella cheese made from skim milk will help to decrease calories, fat, and cholesterol.

Wine Suggestion: Italian Chianti Classico, dry red; serve at room temperature.

Microwave Conversion Instructions: Note: Prepare pasta conventionally. Reduce butter to 2 T. Place butter, mushrooms, garlic and salt and pepper in 2-qt. *(2L)* casserole. Cook on High 3 minutes. Stir in sauce and wheat germ. Cook on High 7 to 8 minutes or until it reaches boiling, stirring once or twice. Assemble as directed above. Cook on Medium (50%), covered with waxed paper, 20 to 30 minutes, until heated through. If cooking appears to be uneven, turn dish after 10 minutes.

YIELD: 4 Servings
CALORIES PER SERVING: 557
CARBOHYDRATES: 55g
PROTEIN: 28g
FAT: 25g
CHOLESTEROL: High
PREPARING: 45 Minutes
BAKING: 30 Minutes
FREEZING: Yes

Lasagna Swirls

An excellent informal buffet entree for a large party. Finally, a neat and tidy way to serve lasagna!

8 uncooked lasagna noodles *(200g)*

FILLING:

1 pkg. (10 oz.) *(285g)* **frozen chopped spinach, thawed, squeezed**
¾ cup *(100g)* **freshly grated Parmesan cheese**
1⅓ cups *(345g)* **ricotta cheese**
½ tsp. salt
¼ tsp. freshly ground pepper
¼ tsp. freshly grated nutmeg

SAUCE:

2 cloves garlic, minced
1 large onion, chopped
2 T. *(30ml)* **salad oil**
1 can (15 oz.) *(425g)* **tomato sauce**
1 tsp. sugar
½ tsp. salt
¼ tsp. freshly ground pepper
½ tsp. dried basil
½ tsp. dried oregano
¼ cup *(35g)* **freshly grated Parmesan cheese**

Cook noodles as directed on package. Rinse thoroughly with cold water; drain.

FILLING: Mix together by hand or in food processor, spinach, Parmesan cheese, ricotta, salt, pepper, nutmeg. Spread about ⅓ cup mixture along entire length of each noodle. Roll up, stand on end in greased 7 or 8-inch *(17.5 or 20cm)* round casserole, at least 2½ inches *(6.5cm)* deep.

SAUCE: Saute garlic and onion in oil over medium heat until limp. Add tomato sauce, sugar, salt, pepper, basil, oregano. Simmer, uncovered, 5 minutes. Pour over noodles in casserole.

Bake casserole, covered, on middle or lowest rack of preheated 350° oven 30 minutes or until hot and bubbly. Remove from oven, sprinkle with Parmesan cheese.

Sally Johnson, West Simsbury, CT

Variations, Advance Preparation, and Serving Suggestions: The casserole may be prepared a day ahead and refrigerated or frozen. When ready to serve, bake in preheated 350° oven until hot and bubbly as above. The *swirl method* can easily be applied to various other fillings and homemade sauces.

Nutritional Notes: Whole wheat lasagna noodles may be used in this recipe. In addition, saturated fat/cholesterol can be decreased somewhat if ricotta cheese made from skim milk is used.

Wine Suggestion: Italian Chiaretto del Garda Rose, dry rose; serve chilled.

Microwave Conversion Instructions: Prepare noodles in conventional manner. *Sauce:* Combine onion and garlic with oil, cook covered 3 minutes on High. Add tomato sauce and seasonings; cook on High 4 to 5 minutes. Spread cheese-spinach mixture on cooked noodles and roll up. Place in 2½-inch-deep *(6.25cm)* round casserole; pour sauce over rolled noodles; cook on Medium High (70%) covered 15 to 16 minutes. Allow 5 to 10 minutes standing time. (If rolled noodles are refrigerated before cooking, bring to room temperature before final cooking.)

Paglia e Fieno alla Ghiotta

STRAW AND HAY PASTA WITH SAUCE

YIELD: 24 First Course Servings or
  12 Entree Servings
TOTAL CALORIES: 7200
CALORIES PER ENTREE SERVING: 600
CARBOHYDRATES: 39g
PROTEIN: 18g
FAT: 41g
CHOLESTEROL: High
SODIUM: High
PREPARING: 40 Minutes
COOKING: 20 Minutes
FREEZING: No

Slice off ends of the mushroom stems and wipe clean with damp cloth. Quarter each mushroom or dice into ¼-inch *(6mm)* cubes if mushrooms are large.

Melt half the butter in a large skillet and saute shallots over medium heat until they turn gold in color. Turn the heat to high and add mushrooms. When mushrooms have absorbed all butter, briefly turn heat to low; add 1½ tsp. salt and pepper, and shake pan, moving and tossing the mushrooms. As soon as juices come to the surface, turn heat up to high; cook for 3 minutes, stirring frequently. Turn heat down and add ham, stirring and cooking for 1 minute. Add half of the cream; cook stirring just until it thickens. Taste and correct for seasonings. Remove sauce from heat and set aside until ready to serve. If made ahead, gently reheat sauce before pouring over the pasta.

In a large flameproof casserole that later can accommodate all noodles without piling them too high, melt the rest of butter and cream. Turn off heat. Bring 6 qts. *(6L)* water to boil in a large pot; add 1 T. salt. First drop yellow noodles into pot, as they take slightly longer to cook. Then drop in spinach noodles; stir with a spoon. As soon as the water returns to a boil, taste for doneness. Cook *al dente*. Quickly drain noodles and transfer to waiting casserole. Turn heat to low and start tossing noodles, coating with butter and cream. Add half mushroom sauce, mixing well; add 1 cup Parmesan; mix well. Turn off heat and make a depression in center of noodles; add remaining sauce. Serve with bowl of remaining Parmesan cheese.

Dr. Colin Atterbury, West Haven, CT

Variations, Advance Preparation, and Serving Suggestions:
You can add or substitute fresh green peas, which are traditionally part of this dish, rather than mushrooms.

1¼ lbs. *(565g)* crisp white mushrooms
9 T. *(130g)* butter
¼ cup *(40g)* finely chopped shallots or yellow onions
Salt
Freshly ground black pepper
9 oz. *(250g)* unsmoked ham, shredded
1½ cups *(360ml)* heavy cream
2 eggs worth fresh Egg Pasta (page 192) cut into fettuccine or 1 lb. *(450g)* store-bought
2 eggs worth fresh Spinach Pasta (page 192) fettuccine or 1 lb. *(450g)* store-bought
2½ cups *(325g)* freshly grated Parmesan cheese

Scallops on a Bed of Homemade Spinach Pasta

A most delicate smooth combination of flavors that tastes as beautiful as it looks — saucy, green with touches of red.

YIELD: 6 Entree Servings
TOTAL CALORIES: 2988
CALORIES PER SERVING: 498
CARBOHYDRATES: 39g
PROTEIN: 27g
FAT: 26g
CHOLESTEROL: High
SODIUM: High
PREPARING: 1½ Hours
FREEZING: No

SCALLOP BROTH:

3 cups *(710ml)* water
1 cup *(240ml)* dry white wine or vermouth
1 carrot, sliced
1 stalk celery, sliced
1 medium onion, sliced
¾ tsp. salt
½ tsp. thyme
White pepper
1 lb. *(450g)* bay scallops (or sea scallops quartered)

SAUCE:

2½ T. *(40g)* butter
2 T. *(15g)* flour
2 cups *(475ml)* scallop broth
½ cup *(120ml)* heavy cream
⅛ tsp. freshly grated nutmeg
Salt and freshly ground white pepper to taste

PARSLEY MIXTURE:

4 cloves garlic
Big handful parsley leaves

GARNITURE:

12 cherry tomatoes
4 T. *(60g)* butter
¾ cup mixture freshly grated Parmesan *(50g)* and freshly grated Gruyere *(40g)* cheese

2 eggs worth fresh Egg or Spinach Pasta (page 192) tagliatelle or 1 lb. *(450g)* imported ¼-inch *(6mm)* store-bought noodles
4 T. *(60g)* butter for the noodles

SCALLOP BROTH: Place water, wine, carrot, celery and onion in large saucepan; add seasonings. Bring to a boil; cover ajar and simmer 20 minutes. If not reduced to 2 cups, continue to simmer until you have 2 cups. Bring this liquid to a boil; add scallops and cover tightly. Immediately turn off heat and let scallops sit 10 minutes. Drain immediately so as not to overcook. Reserve scallops and broth separately.

SAUCE: Melt butter, whisk in flour rapidly. When mixture bubbles, add the reserved 2 cups scallop broth; bring to a boil, lower heat and simmer gently for at least 20 minutes. Add heavy cream, nutmeg, and salt and pepper to taste. Simmer another 15 minutes; add scallops and set aside.

PARSLEY MIXTURE: Mince garlic cloves and parsley; set aside.

GARNITURE: Prick each cherry tomato with a fork to prevent bursting during cooking. Melt butter in saute pan; add tomatoes and 1 T. of parsley mixture. Toss over low heat 3 minutes; set aside.

Boil several quarts of water for the pasta; cook until *al dente*. The time will depend on dryness of noodles. Drain. While the noodles are cooking, reheat the scallops in their sauce 5 minutes. At the same time, reheat tomatoes. In a separate pan, large enough to accommodate all the noodles and scallops, melt 4 T. butter. Add noodles; saute 1 minute over high heat. Add scallops in their sauce, tomatoes, ½ cup of the grated cheese, and remaining parsley mixture. Serve on heated plates and pass remaining cheese separately.

Melinda M. Vance, West Hartford, CT

Variations, Advance Preparation, and Serving Suggestions:
1 lb. raw shrimp may be substituted for scallops, but be sure they are very tender, not tough or overcooked. All except cooking of pasta may be done early in day or 1 day ahead and refrigerated. Gently reheat while pasta is cooking. If serving this dish as the first course of a Northern Italian meal, follow with Italian Baby Lamb Chops in Parmesan Cheese Batter (page 291) and a green vegetable, Variegated Salad (page 175), and Italian Zuccotto (page 176) for dessert.

Wine Suggestion: Italian Orvieto or Est! Est!! Est!!!, dry white; serve chilled.

Microwave Conversion Instructions: Note: Microwave may increase strength of garlic taste. Reduce to 2 cloves, if desired. Combine 2¼ *(530ml)* cups water, ¾ *(180ml)* cup wine, vegetables and seasonings in large covered casserole; bring to boil on High for 5 minutes. Leave cover ajar and boil hard for 18 minutes or until reduced to 2 cups. Add scallops; cover and set on Warm (10%) 5 minutes until fork tender. Let sit 2 minutes, covered; drain, reserving broth. For sauce combine butter, flour, and broth; mix well and cover. Cook on High 4 minutes, stir, cook another 6 minutes until thickened. Add cream; cook on Medium (50%) 5 minutes. Melt butter on High 30 seconds; add tomatoes. Cook on High 1 minute, covered. For pasta, heat 3 qts. *(3L)* hot tap water to boiling on High 12 to 16 minutes. Add pasta; cook, covered, on Medium Low (30%) 20 to 24 minutes. Drain. Melt butter in same pasta pot for 30 seconds on High; add pasta and cook 20 seconds on High. Reheat scallops 1½ minutes on Medium High (80%). Reheat tomatoes 15 seconds on Medium High (80%). Combine and serve.

Fettucce

Gnocchi

Farfalle

Fusilli

Grandine

Ditali

Cresto di Gallo

Tagliatelle all'uovo

Fusilli

Manicotti

Lasagne

Ciocca di Capellini

Conchighe Rigate

YIELD: 16 First Course Servings
   or 8 Entree Servings
TOTAL CALORIES: 4900
CALORIES PER ENTREE SERVING: 614
CARBOHYDRATES: 33g
PROTEIN: 26g
FAT: 42g
CHOLESTEROL: Very High
SODIUM: High
PREPARING: 45 Minutes
SOAKING: 2 Hours
COOKING: 1 Hour
SIMMERING: 15 Minutes
FREEZING: No

Pasta with Sweetbreads

Sweetbread is the name of the thymus gland of cattle and lamb, situated at the top of the breast. This organ is in two parts, hence the common usage of the plural, sweetbreads. Sweetbreads are only found fully developed in young animals. They are considered to be the most delicate products of butchery.

SWEETBREADS:

1½ lbs. *(680g)* sweetbreads (They should look like nice fresh veal, should be firm, nicely rounded, and all held together, not straggly.)
1 lemon

5 medium onions
8 T. *(115g)* butter
1½ tsp. salt
⅛ tsp. freshly ground pepper
1 lb. *(450g)* baby carrots, peeled
1 cup *(200g)* shelled fresh peas
2 eggs worth fresh Egg Pasta (page 192) fettuccine or 1 lb. *(450g)* store-bought imported fettuccine
1 cup *(240ml)* heavy cream
1 cup *(130g)* freshly grated Parmesan cheese

SWEETBREADS: Soak sweetbreads in cold water 2 hours with juice of ½ a lemon. Change water every 30 minutes and each time squeeze a few drops lemon juice into new water. Discard lemon and transfer sweetbreads to saucepan. Cover with cold water; bring to a boil. Simmer for 15 minutes partly covered. Then drain and rinse sweetbreads under cold water. Remove pieces of gristly cartilage found on surface and discard. Also remove any fine membrane which comes loose. Cut or separate sweetbreads into ½-inch *(1.25cm)* cubes; reserve.

Thinly slice onions; braise in 4 T. butter for 20 minutes, covered, over low heat, stirring occasionally. Add sweetbreads, salt and pepper; braise (covered) for 30 minutes. When done, remove from heat and set aside.

Parboil carrots 8 to 10 minutes; drain and place carrots in pan with sweetbreads. Parboil fresh peas; drain and place in pan with sweetbreads.

Just 10 minutes before serving have plenty of salted boiling water ready. Cook pasta until just *al dente*. Drain well. While pasta is cooking, in a pan large enough to hold all the pasta and vegetables, melt the remaining 4 T. butter; add ½ cup of Parmesan and heavy cream and cook until slightly thickened. Gently reheat sweetbreads and vegetables in another pan. Now add the hot pasta to cream sauce mixture; toss to coat. Add about ⅓ of the sweetbread/vegetables to pasta; toss again. Season to taste with more salt, pepper and Parmesan. Place pasta on a *heated* serving platter. Make a well in the center of noodles; add remaining sweetbread/vegetable mixture. To serve, divide pasta among 8 plates, each topped with the sweetbread mixture. Pass a bowl of the grated Parmesan cheese.

Melinda M. Vance, West Hartford, CT

Variations, Advance Preparation, and Serving Suggestions:
This makes an excellent party dish as all but cooking of pasta can be ready and waiting.

Substitute for sweetbreads 1½ lbs. *(680g)* mussel meat. (You will need 4½ lbs. *(2kg)* fresh mussels in shell to get this amount mussel meat.) Use some of reduced mussel cooking liquid in the sauce.

Nutritional Notes: Sweetbreads provide protein as well as significant amounts of cholesterol. Like other organ meats, they also contain appreciable amounts of vitamin A, which is not readily found in mussel meats.

Wine Suggestion: Italian Frascati, firm dry white; serve chilled.

Pasta Primavera

PASTA GARNISHED WITH SPRINGTIME VEGETABLES

This inspired blend of pasta and crisp-tender vegetables such as zucchini, snow peas and asparagus, is a creation of Italian origin, made famous by Le Cirque, a popular French restaurant in New York City. There it is made with spaghetti, but served all year long with the fresh vegetables appropriate to each season.

YIELD: 10-12 First Course Servings
    or 6 Entree Servings
TOTAL CALORIES: 3960
CALORIES PER ENTREE SERVING: 660
CARBOHYDRATES: 54g
PROTEIN: 22g
FAT: 40g
CHOLESTEROL: High
SODIUM: High
PREPARING: 1½ Hours
COOKING: 30 Minutes
FREEZING: No

Blanch zucchini, broccoli, snow peas, baby peas, and asparagus in boiling salted water for 1 to 2 minutes each until just crisp tender. Drain and refresh under cold water which will set bright green color; set aside. (This can be done several hours ahead.)

Saute pine nuts in 1 tsp. oil until brown; set aside. Saute garlic in olive oil; add mushrooms, parsley, salt and pepper and saute 1 minute; add cherry tomatoes and set aside.

Cook pasta in lots of salted boiling water until *al dente.* Drain well.

Meanwhile, in a pan large enough to hold all the pasta and vegetables, melt the butter; add ½ cup Parmesan, the heavy cream and basil; stir to blend and melt cheese until sauce is slightly thickened. At the same time, gently reheat all the vegetables in the saute pan the garlic and cherry tomatoes were set aside in. Now add the hot pasta to the sauce mixture; toss to coat. Add about ⅓ of the vegetables to pasta; toss again. Make a well in center of pasta and add all remaining vegetables. Season to taste with more salt, pepper and Parmesan. Sprinkle dish with pine nuts.

To serve, divide pasta among 6 broad soup plates and top each with some of remaining vegetables. Pass extra bowl of grated Parmesan.

Matthew Kopcza, West Hartford, CT

Variations, Advance Preparation, and Serving Suggestions: Substitute equal quantities other seasonal fresh vegetables. Keep in mind the contrasts of color and texture in the final dish.

Nutritional Notes: This recipe was successfully tested with evaporated skim milk substituted for cream. Unsalted polyunsaturated margarine can be used, and salt can be eliminated.

Wine Suggestion: Italian Soave, dry white; serve chilled.

1 cup *(135g)* sliced zucchini (slice into finger-size sticks)
1½ cups *(90g)* broccoli flowerets
1½ cups *(150g)* slant-cut snow peas
1 cup *(200g)* fresh shelled peas
6 stalks asparagus, slant-cut into 1½-inch *(4cm)* pieces
½ cup *(80g)* pine nuts
4 cloves garlic, minced
3 T. *(45ml)* good quality olive oil
10 fresh mushrooms, quartered
¼ cup chopped parsley
Salt
Freshly ground black pepper
18 small cherry tomatoes, pricked
2 eggs worth fresh Egg Pasta (page 192) fettuccine or 1 lb. *(450g)* store-bought fettuccine
¼ cup *(60g)* butter
1 cup *(130g)* freshly grated Parmesan cheese
1 cup *(240ml)* heavy cream
⅓ cup fresh basil, coarsely chopped

Extra freshly grated Parmesan cheese to pass separately

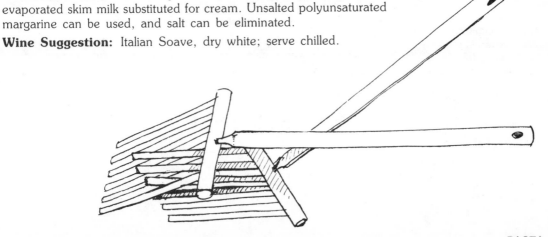

YIELD: 6 Servings
CALORIES PER SERVING: 401
CARBOHYDRATES: 50g
PROTEIN: 12g
FAT: 17g
SODIUM: High
PREPARING: 25 Minutes
COOKING: 12 Minutes
FREEZING: No

Pasta Zucchini

3 T. *(45g)* butter
3 T. *(45ml)* olive oil
½ cup *(75g)* onion, finely chopped
2 T. *(20g)* shallots, finely minced
2 lbs. *(900g)* small zucchini, sliced
   thickly in rounds, then in quarters
½ cup *(200g)* prosciutto, diced
Freshly ground pepper
Salt to taste
1 lb. *(450g)* fresh Egg Pasta (page 192)
   linguine, cooked *al dente* and drained
Freshly ground Parmesan cheese

In very large skillet, melt butter, add oil. Add onions and shallots; cook until transparent. Add zucchini, stir, cook 2 to 3 minutes. Add prosciutto, pepper and salt. Stir mixture. Toss with drained pasta in heated bowl or platter. Pass Parmesan cheese.

Mary Breen, West Hartford, CT

Nutritional Notes: The vitamin A in zucchini is found mostly in the skin.

Wine Suggestion: Italian Nebbiolo, dry red; serve at room temperature.

YIELD: 6 First Course Servings or
   4 Entree Servings
CALORIES PER ENTREE SERVING: 361
CARBOHYDRATES: 32g
PROTEIN: 11g
FAT: 21g
PREPARING: 30 Minutes
COOKING: 30 Minutes

Orecchiette with Cauliflower

Orecchiette means little ears. The shape traps whatever sauce is served on them, turning each piece into a juicy cup of flavor.

¼ cup *(60ml)* imported olive oil
4 anchovy fillets, rinsed and thoroughly
   mashed (do not omit)
1 medium onion, peeled and chopped
3 large cloves garlic, peeled, pressed or
   finely chopped
1 medium head cauliflower, with
   flowerets trimmed and cut into bite-
   size pieces; then steamed until tender
⅓ cup *(80ml)* white wine (optional)
1 lb. *(450g)* orecchiette (penne may be
   substituted)
¼ cup *(40g)* pignoli (pine) nuts
Fresh parsley, chopped
Salt and freshly ground pepper to taste
Freshly grated Parmesan cheese

In a large skillet, heat olive oil; stir in anchovies and onions; cook gently until onion is transparent. Add garlic, cauliflower, and optional wine; simmer about 10 minutes.

Meanwhile, bring 4 to 6 qts. *(4-6L)* salted water to a boil and cook pasta according to package directions.

Add pignoli nuts to vegetable mixture; cook 5 minutes.

Place drained pasta in heated serving dish; toss with cauliflower mixture; garnish with parsley and season with salt and pepper.

Serve immediately with Parmesan cheese.

Auden di Corcia, Hartford, CT

Wine Suggestion: Italian Barbera, dry red; serve at room temperature.

Microwave Conversion Instructions: Cook flowerets with 3 T. water, covered, on High 5 to 6 minutes, or until just fork tender. Allow to remain covered until needed for increased tenderness; drain before using. Place oil, anchovies, garlic and onion in casserole. Cook on High 5 minutes, stirring once, or until onion is transparent. Add drained cauliflower and nuts. Cook 1 to 2 minutes until heated, stirring once. While vegetable garnish is cooking, cook pasta conventionally. Complete recipe as directed above.

Pasta with Chilled Uncooked Tomato Sauce

You have never had a more vitamin-C-rich tomato sauce!

YIELD: 10 First Course Servings or
    4-6 Entree Servings
CALORIES PER ENTREE SERVING: 410
CARBOHYDRATES: 47g
PROTEIN: 8g
FAT: 21g
SODIUM: High
PREPARING: 30 Minutes
MARINATING: 2 Hours
COOKING: 10 Minutes
FREEZING: No

At least 2 hours before serving, remove the stems and cores from tomatoes. Cut each in half lengthwise, and remove seeds, leaving as much moisture in tomatoes as possible. Slice each tomato half into 4 long wedges; place in a glass or porcelain container. Add the olive oil; toss together very lightly. Slice the garlic cloves very thinly; add to tomatoes. Pit olives and chop coarsley; add to the tomatoes. Sprinkle on the salt and pepper, the pepper flakes, and the basil; toss all gently and refrigerate for at least 2 hours.

When ready to serve, bring a large pot of salted water to a boil. Add the pasta to the water and cook until it is *al dente*. Drain the pasta and place in a large serving bowl; add the cold sauce and toss well. Serve immediately.

Shari Kopcza, West Hartford, CT

1½ lbs. *(675g)* **fresh ripe garden
    tomatoes**
½ cup *(120ml)* **good quality olive oil**
2 **cloves garlic, peeled**
½ cup *(85g)* **black oil-cured olives (can
    substitute green olives but must
    refrigerate sauce 4 hours)**
Salt
Freshly ground black pepper
½ tsp. **dried hot pepper flakes**
3 T. **chopped fresh basil leaves**
2 **eggs worth fresh Spinach Pasta
    (page 192) fettuccine or 1 lb.** *(450g)*
    store-bought spaghetti

Nutritional Notes: Tomatoes, next to citrus fruit, are one of the greatest sources of vitamin C. Growing conditions, method and degree of ripening, handling, storage temperature, length of storage, type of storage and cooking method all effect the vitamin C content of foods. It is far better to ripen green tomatoes naturally at home than to buy the "gased" ones, and better yet use freshly harvested vine-ripened tomatoes. In this recipe most of the Vitamin C in the tomatoes is retained, since they are not exposed to heat. Olives and salt should be omitted for a low-sodium version; polyunsaturated oil (such as safflower, corn, or soybean) should be used in the restricted saturated fat/low-cholesterol regimen.

Wine Suggestion: Italian Orvieto Secco, dry white; serve chilled.

YIELD: 8 First Course Servings or
  4-6 Entree Servings
TOTAL CALORIES: 4020
CALORIES PER ENTREE SERVING: 670
CARBOHYDRATES: 63g
PROTEIN: 15g
FAT: 40g
SODIUM: High
PREPARING: 35 Minutes
BAKING: 25 Minutes
COOKING: 10 Minutes
FREEZING: Pesto-Yes

**6 large fresh sweet red peppers (select
  very red as they are sweeter)**
½ cup *(120ml)* **olive oil**

PESTO SAUCE:
Yield: 1 cup *(240ml)*

2 cups fresh basil leaves
½ cup *(120ml)* **olive oil**
2 T. *(30ml)* **water**
¼ cup *(40g)* **pine nuts**
3 cloves garlic, peeled
Salt to taste
¼ cup *(35g)* **freshly grated Romano
  cheese**
¼ cup *(35g)* **freshly grated Parmesan
  cheese**
3 T. *(45g)* **butter, softened**

**2 eggs worth Spinach pasta (page 192)
  bows or 1 lb.** *(450g)* **imported bows**
5 T. *(75g)* **butter**

1 cup *(140g)* **freshly grated Parmesan
  cheese**
2 T. chopped fresh parsley

Pronto Pesto Pimiento Pasta

Do not try to pronounce the name of this dish quickly! Just
prepare it and enjoy.

Wash and dry peppers. Seed and core them; cut into strips approximately same size as pasta bows. Put olive oil in baking dish; add
pepper strips, tossing to coat. Bake in preheated 400 ° oven about
25 minutes.

PESTO SAUCE: Put basil, olive oil, water, pine nuts, garlic cloves,
and salt into blender or food processor. When ingredients are evenly
blended, pour into a bowl and beat the two cheeses in by hand. (The
texture and flavor are better if it is not all processed together.) When
cheese has been evenly incorporated, beat in softened butter.

Cook pasta in lots of salted boiling water until *al dente*. Taste test
pasta to be sure it is crisp tender, but not soft. Drain pasta well.

While pasta is cooking, melt butter in large heatproof platter; add
Pesto and stir to blend. Add peppers which have been drained of ex-
cess oil. Add drained pasta; toss to coat. Toss pasta with half of the
Parmesan cheese. Season with salt as desired. Garnish with parsley.
Serve immediately.

Pass remaining Parmesan in separate bowl.

Melinda M. Vance, West Hartford, CT

Variations, Advance Preparation, and Serving Suggestions:
Pesto Sauce recipe can be doubled, tripled, etc. Freeze it in ½-cup
(120ml) containers or plastic ice-cube trays and use as needed. It is
also fabulous tossed with rice or small boiled potatoes, green beans,
or on broiled fish or poached skinned chicken breasts.

Microwave Conversion Instructions: Prepare peppers as for
conventional recipe. Add olive oil to glass baking dish; add pepper
strips, tossing to coat. Cook on High, covered, 15 minutes, stirring
every 5 minutes. (Note: While peppers are cooking, boil pasta on
regular range and prepare Pesto Sauce in blender or food processor.)

Melt butter on High, about 90 seconds; combine with Pesto Sauce
on heated platter and blend well. Cook on High 1 minute. Complete
recipe as directed above.

Italian Steak Ancora

YIELD: 2 Servings
CALORIES PER SERVING: 292
CARBOHYDRATES: 16g
PROTEIN: 30g
FAT: 12g
SODIUM: High
PREPARING: 15 Minutes
COOKING: 15 Minutes

In a non-stick skillet, combine onion, green pepper, tomato juice, cayenne pepper, and basil; simmer uncovered over low heat until most of liquid is evaporated and green pepper is tender-crisp. Add steak; stir over moderate heat until meat is thoroughly heated.

Sprinkle with cheese; serve immediately with optional garnish.

Roberta Lawson, Plainville, CT

Variations, Advance Preparation, and Serving Suggestions:
Serve with Bulgur Pignoli Pilaf (page 350), yellow squash, and fresh fruit salad. Herb Batter Corn Bread (page 124) is delicious with it too.

Wine Suggestion: Italian Bardolino, light red; serve at room temperature.

Microwave Conversion Instructions: Note: Reduce juice to 1½ cups. Combine vegetables, juice and seasonings in 9-inch (22.5cm) pie plate. Cover with waxed paper. Cook 10 minutes on High. Remove paper and stir. Cook 5 minutes. Add steak and spoon sauce over meat. Cook on High 1 to 3 minutes.

1 large Bermuda onion, peeled, thinly sliced, and separated into rings
1 green pepper, seeded and sliced
1 can (16 oz.) *(475ml)* tomato juice
Pinch cayenne pepper
¼ tsp. basil or oregano
7 oz. *(200g)* sliced, rare leftover broiled lean sirloin, well-trimmed
1 T. grated Romano cheese
Rings of raw onion and green pepper (optional)

Mushroom Stuffed Beef Tenderloin with Madeira Sauce

YIELD: 6-8 Servings
TOTAL CALORIES: 3328
CALORIES PER SERVING: 416
CARBOHYDRATES: 4g
PROTEIN: 37g
FAT: 28g
CHOLESTEROL: High
SODIUM: High
PREPARING: 20 Minutes
ROASTING: 1 Hour

Make a 1½-inch *(4cm)* slash on top of meat, lengthwise, to form a pocket. (Do not cut through the two ends of meat.)

Saute mushrooms and onions in butter over medium heat for 3 to 5 minutes. Sprinkle flour over mixture and add brandy; stir until slightly thickened. Simmer 5 minutes, stirring frequently. Stuff mushroom mixture into pocket in meat. Layer strips of bacon around meat.

Roast in preheated 375° oven, 60 minutes or until 130° on meat thermometer. Let stand 10 minutes before slicing.

MADEIRA SAUCE: While meat is standing, melt 3 T. butter in a saucepan. Add flour, stirring well and cook 5 minutes. Add beef stock, Bovril, Madeira and Worcestershire sauce. Cook over medium heat 3 minutes.

In another pan, saute mushrooms in 2 T. butter. Add to the sauce and serve with the tenderloin.

Katie B. Wells, West Hartford, CT

Wine Suggestion: Beaulieu Vineyard Cabernet Sauvignon, sturdy red; serve at room temperature.

1 4-lb. *(1800g)* well-trimmed tenderloin of beef
¼ lb. *(115g)* fresh mushrooms, chopped
½ small onion, finely chopped
3 T. *(45g)* butter
½ tsp. flour
2 T. *(30ml)* brandy
¼ lb. *(115g)* bacon

MADEIRA SAUCE:
5 T. *(75g)* butter
1½ T. *(10g)* flour
¾ cup *(180ml)* beef stock
1 tsp. Bovril
¼ cup *(60ml)* Madeira wine
1 tsp. Worcestershire sauce
⅓ cup *(80g)* fresh, minced mushrooms

YIELD: 6-8 Servings
CALORIES PER SERVING: 453
CARBOHYDRATES: 16g
PROTEIN: 32g
FAT: 29g
CHOLESTEROL: High
SODIUM: High
PREPARING: 2 Hours
MARINATING: 24 Hours
CHILLING: 24 Hours
BRAISING: 3 Hours
FREEZING: Yes

Daube de Boeuf à la Provençale

CASSEROLE OF BEEF WITH WINE AND VEGETABLES

An easy-to-assemble classic. A dish cooked *en daube* is braised in stock.

MARINADE:

¼ cup *(60ml)* olive oil
2 yellow onions, sliced
1 stalk celery, diced
1 carrot, diced
3 cloves garlic, minced
1 tsp. salt
½ tsp. rosemary
½ tsp. thyme
12 peppercorns
1½ cups *(355ml)* white wine

DAUBE:

3 lbs. *(1350g)* boneless beef, cut in
   1½-inch *(4cm)* cubes
¼ lb. *(115g)* salt pork
12 small white onions, peeled
½ cup *(120ml)* white wine
2 cups *(475ml)* beef stock
½ tsp. salt
¼ tsp. rosemary
¼ tsp. thyme
2 cloves garlic, crushed
12 small carrots, peeled
¾ cup *(90g)* pitted green olives, drained
¾ cup *(90g)* pitted black olives, drained
24 cherry tomatoes, peeled
Freshly ground pepper

Two days before serving: Make marinade. Heat oil in saucepan; add onions, celery, carrot, and garlic. Saute until onions are transparent, stirring several times. Add remaining ingredients and simmer 15 minutes, stirring occasionally. Transfer to bowl and let cool. Add cubed beef. Cover and refrigerate overnight, stirring once or twice.

The day before serving: Remove beef from marinade and pat each piece dry with paper towels. Strain marinade and set liquid (about 1 cup) aside. Discard vegetables. Blanch salt pork in boiling water for 10 minutes. Remove and cut into ½-inch *(1cm)* cubes or lardons. Brown lardons to render fat. Brown meat in batches, not crowding pan, in the rendered fat. Transfer beef cubes and salt pork to a large casserole. Brown onions quickly in remaining fat; set aside. Pour drained marinade into casserole, add the wine and enough beef stock (about 2 cups) to barely cover meat. Add seasonings and garlic. Cover tightly. Bring stew to a simmer on top of stove, then transfer to a preheated 350° oven and cook 1½ hours. Add onions and carrots, cover again and cook 1 hour longer or until tender. Remove from oven, let cool slightly, refrigerate covered overnight or freeze.

Remove from refrigerator 1 hour before serving. Skim fat from surface. Slowly bring to a simmer on top of the stove. Rinse and drain olives and add to stew with tomatoes. Stir in a generous grinding of black pepper. The olives and tomatoes should be warmed through.

Dr. Sybille Brewer, West Hartford, CT

Variations, Advance Preparation, and Serving Suggestions:
You can prepare this dish almost to completion two days ahead or sooner to freeze. With Marinated Bell Peppers Julienne (page 370) it could be the nucleus of a simple buffet. Serve in a chafing dish and spoon over hot noodles or boiled potatoes.

Wine Suggestion: French Beaujolais Villages, fresh red; serve slightly chilled.

Microwave Conversion Instructions: *Two days before serving:* In covered glass casserole mix oil, onions, celery, carrot and garlic; cook on High 5 minutes. Add remaining marinade ingredients, cover, cook on High 5 minutes. Add beef and continue as for conventional recipe.

Day before serving: Prepare meat and marinade as for conventional recipe. (Note: Liquid may be more than 1 cup). Blanch salt pork by putting ½-inch cubes *(1cm)* in 1½ cups water in large measuring cup; cook on High 3 minutes. Render fat by cooking cubes 3 minutes on bacon rack and draining off fat. For microwave preparation beef does not need to be browned. Place onions in covered glass casserole, cook on High 5 minutes. Assemble recipe as for conventional recipe in large glass casserole, cover, cook on High 10 minutes, stir, recover; cook on Medium (50%) 30 minutes, stirring occasionally. Add onions and carrots, cover, cook on Medium (50%) 30 minutes, stirring occasionally. Cool, refrigerate overnight.

Day of serving: Prepare casserole, olives and tomatoes as indicated. Cook covered casserole on High 10 minutes, stir, recover. Cook on Medium (50%) 5 minutes. Add pepper, olives and tomatoes. If needed, cook 5 minutes on Medium (50%) to warm through — covered. *Note:* Juices may not appear to be smooth. If this happens, drain and put in blender, pour back over meat and vegetables.

Stifado

SPICED BRAISED BEEF AND ONIONS
Serve this Greek beef stew at your next buffet.

YIELD: 8 Servings
CALORIES PER SERVING: 392
CARBOHYDRATES: 17g
PROTEIN: 36g
FAT: 20g
CHOLESTEROL: High
PREPARING: 30 Minutes
SIMMERING: 3 Hours
FREEZING: Yes

Season meat with salt and pepper. Melt butter in Dutch oven or deep casserole dish. Add meat, tossing to cover with butter over moderate heat; do not brown. Arrange onions on top of meat. Combine tomato paste, wine, vinegar, sugar, garlic; pour over meat and onions. Add bay leaf, cinnamon, cloves, cumin and currants to casserole and cover with plate or weight to hold down onions (optional). Simmer covered 3 hours, or until meat is very tender. Do not stir during cooking. As you serve, stir sauce gently to blend.

Bernice Kuzma, West Hartford, CT

Variations, Advance Preparation, and Serving Suggestions:
Can be made a day or two ahead. Refrigerate covered. Bring to room temperature before reheating on top of stove. Serve over rice with a Caesar salad or Romaine, Endive and Walnut Salad (page 160).

Wine Suggestion: California Burgundy, full red; serve at room temperature.

Microwave Conversion Instructions: Note: Reduce butter to ¼ cup *(60g)* and wine to ¼ cup *(60ml)*. Cut meat into ¾-inch *(2cm)* cubes. Melt butter in a round glass casserole. Add meat, stir to coat as evenly as possible. Combine tomato paste, red wine, vinegar, sugar, garlic to make sauce. Assemble onions and spices as for conventional recipe; cover with sauce. Cover casserole with plate or plastic wrap; cook on High 5 to 7 minutes. Continue to cook on Medium (50%) 50 to 60 minutes longer, turning casserole ¼ turn after each 15 minutes. Do not stir if pan has center tube or glass in it.

3 lbs. *(1350g)* lean beef (such as sirloin tip) cut in 1½-inch *(4cm)* cubes
Salt
Freshly ground pepper
½ cup *(115g)* butter
2½ lbs. *(1125g)* small boiling onions, peeled
1 can (6 oz.) *(170g)* tomato paste
⅓ cup *(80ml)* red table wine
2 T. *(30ml)* red wine vinegar
1 T. *(12.5g)* brown sugar
1 clove garlic, minced
1 bay leaf
1 3-inch *(7.5cm)* cinnamon stick
½ tsp. whole cloves
¼ tsp. ground cumin
2 T. *(20g)* currants or raisins

YIELD: 4 Servings
CALORIES PER SERVING: 409
CARBOHYDRATES: 13g
PROTEIN: 42g
FAT: 21g
CHOLESTEROL: High
SODIUM: High
PREPARING: 15 Minutes
COOKING: 55 Minutes
FREEZING: No

Smoor Djawa

JAVANESE BEEF

In Indonesia this dish is part of a *Rijsttafel*, but is marvelous by itself as an entree.

1½ lbs. *(680g)* London broil
6 medium-sized onions, chopped
3 T. *(45g)* butter
1 T. garlic powder
¼ tsp. freshly ground pepper
½ tsp. salt
¼ tsp. freshly grated nutmeg
1 tsp. sambal oelek (Reduce if you do not want the dish too spicy.)
¾ cup *(175ml)* ketjab benteng manis (Dutch soy sauce)
1½ cups *(355ml)* water

With a sharp knife cut beef into ¼-inch *(6mm)* cubes. In a large skillet brown onions in butter until tender. Add meat and remaining ingredients.

Allow mixture to cook about 45 minutes over low heat, uncovered. Allow sauce to reduce. Serve warm or refrigerate a day ahead and gently reheat at serving time.

Ann Feenstra, Houston, TX

Wine Suggestion: California Zinfandel, dry red; serve at room temperature.

YIELD: 10-12 Servings
TOTAL CALORIES: 9984
CALORIES PER SERVING: 832
CARBOHYDRATES: 14g
PROTEIN: 32g
FAT: 72g
CHOLESTEROL: High
SODIUM: High
PREPARING: 1 Hour
COOKING: 4 Hours
FREEZING: Yes

Smoky Barbecued Brisket

1 6-lb. *(2700g)* fresh brisket
1 bottle (3½ oz.) *(100ml)* Wright's liquid smoke

BARBECUE SAUCE:
1 bottle (14 oz.) *(400g)* ketchup
½ cup *(100g)* brown sugar
½ cup *(120ml)* water
¼ cup *(60ml)* A-1 steak sauce
1 T. *(15ml)* Worcestershire sauce
⅛ tsp. hot pepper sauce
¾ cup *(175ml)* chili sauce
½ cup *(120ml)* red wine vinegar
¼ cup *(60ml)* fresh lemon juice
½ cup *(130g)* prepared hot mustard (Gulden's spicy German or Kosciusko preferred)
3 tsp. celery seed
Salt and pepper to taste

Cover brisket with boiling water to which liquid smoke has been added; simmer 2 to 3 hours. Let meat cool in cooking liquid or refrigerate overnight.

Remove excess fat and chill meat in order to facilitate slicing.

Make barbecue sauce by combining all ingredients and simmering 30 minutes.

Place meat slices in 9 × 12 × 2-inch *(22.5 × 30 × 5cm)* dish. Cover with Barbecue Sauce; bake in preheated 350° oven 45 minutes to 1 hour.

May be kept warm for an hour before serving.

Ann Feenstra, Houston, TX

Variations, Advance Preparation, and Serving Suggestions: Serve with Great Grandmother's Green Corn Pudding (page 46).

Nutritional Notes: Calories were calculated assuming that one third of sauce is utilized. A reduction in calories is possible if all visible fat is skimmed from meat after refrigeration and if a minimal amount of sauce is utilized.

Wine Suggestion: California Pinot Noir, soft red; serve at room temperature.

Microwave Conversion Instructions: Note: Use 3 lbs. fresh brisket. Place brisket in water-soaked clay pot. Add ½ bottle liquid smoke; cover with water-soaked lid. Cook 30 minutes on Medium (50%). Turn brisket over, cover and continue to cook 60 to 65 minutes on Medium (50%). Continue as for conventional recipe. Combine ingredients for Barbecue Sauce in 3-qt. *(3L)* casserole, cover; cook on High 15 minutes, stirring occasionally. Complete as directed above.

Grilled Ginger Marinated Flank Steak

YIELD: 4 Servings
CALORIES PER SERVING: 326
CARBOHYDRATES: 5g
PROTEIN: 36g
FAT: 18g
CHOLESTEROL: High
SODIUM: High
PREPARING: 5 Minutes
MARINATING: 4 Hours or Overnight
GRILLING: 10 Minutes

Remove all fat from flank steak. Lightly score meat on both sides. Place in shallow flameproof dish.

Select Marinade I or II and pour over steak; turn to coat both sides; cover with plastic wrap. Let marinate at room temperature 2 to 4 hours, or overnight in refrigerator.

Broil steak under preheated broiler as close to heat as possible, turning it once, or over charcoal, on grill, for 3 to 5 minutes per side, depending upon the degree of doneness desired. Transfer steak to cutting board; cut it across the grain, on diagonal, into very thin slices.

MARINADE I: Place all ingredients in blender or food processor and puree.

MARINADE II: Thoroughly combine all ingredients.

Lee Grimmeisen, West Hartford, CT
Nancy Bailey, Prospect, KY

Nutritional Notes: The nutritional analysis above used all of Marinade I. Marinade II with its more acidic ingredients would be an excellent tenderizer and the dish would yield 339 calories, 6g carbohydrates and 19g fat per serving.

Wine Suggestion: Chateauneuf-du-Pape, dry French red; serve at room temperature.

1½-1¾ lbs. *(675-800g)* **flank steak**

MARINADE I:
2 T. *(30g)* **peeled, minced fresh ginger root**
¼ cup *(20g)* **minced scallion**
¼ cup *(60ml)* **imported soy sauce**
2 T. *(30ml)* **peanut oil**
1 T. **imported sesame seed oil**
1 tsp. **honey**

MARINADE II:
¾ cup *(175ml)* **Italian dressing (Wishbone preferred)**
¾ cup *(175ml)* **imported soy sauce**
2½ T. *(30g)* **brown sugar**
½ tsp. **ground ginger**

Beef Curry and Pilaf Indienne

YIELD: 12 Servings
CALORIES PER SERVING: 380
CARBOHYDRATES: 35g
PROTEIN: 33g
FAT: 12g
CHOLESTEROL: High
SODIUM: High
PREPARING: 45 Minutes
COOKING: 4 Hours

A family treasure, passed down from my husband's parents, who were missionaries in India.

2 T. *(30ml)* oil
8 large onions, sliced
5 cloves garlic, minced
4-5 lbs. *(1800-2265g)* beef, cubed round steak or stewing beef
3 tsp. imported Indian curry powder
1 tsp. coriander
1 tsp. cardamom
1 tsp. cumin
1 tsp. turmeric
1 tsp. cinnamon
1 tsp. whole cloves
1 tsp. oregano
3 T. salt
Tamarind water (a walnut-sized piece of tamarind soaked in ½ cup *(120ml)* hot water, cooled, squeezed, and strained). Juice of 2 lemons or ⅓ cup *(80ml)* vinegar may be substituted
1 can (12 oz.) *(340g)* tomato paste
1 can (8 oz.) *(225g)* tomato sauce
1 can (29 oz.) *(820g)* tomato puree or tomatoes
4 large potatoes, peeled and cubed
5 small zucchini, thinly sliced
1 lb. *(450g)* fresh mushrooms, sliced
1 recipe Rice Pilaf Indienne (page 353)

In an 8-qt. *(8L)* pot saute onions in oil until golden brown. Add garlic.

Toss beef with curry powder and add to onions. Add spices, salt and tamarind water, which acts as a souring agent. Add tomato paste, tomato sauce, and tomato puree.

Begin cooking on low heat, adding vegetables as they are prepared, ending with the mushrooms. Cover and simmer 3 to 4 hours. Serve hot or refrigerate a day ahead and gently reheat 40 minutes before serving.

Ann Janzen, Avon, CT

Variations, Advance Preparation, and Serving Suggestions:
Serve with condiments such as chutney, mango pickle, lemon pickle, Bombay duck, Indian breads (paratha, chapati, puri,) and sliced bananas.

Wine Suggestion: Portuguese Vinya Rose, semi-dry rose; serve chilled.

Microwave Conversion Instructions: Saute onion and garlic in oil in a 5-qt. *(5L)* covered casserole on High 10 minutes, stirring twice. Toss beef with curry powder and add to onions and garlic. Add spices. Cook, covered, on High 5 minutes. Add tamarind water, tomato paste, tomato sauce and tomato puree. Continue cooking, covered, on Medium High (70%), adding vegetables as they are prepared, ending with mushrooms. Cook 50 to 60 minutes, stirring twice, or until meat and vegetables are tender. Let stand 15 minutes.

Spicy Baked Corned Beef

YIELD: 8-10 Servings
CALORIES PER SERVING: 512
CARBOHYDRATES: 10g
PROTEIN: 28g
FAT: 40g
CHOLESTEROL: High
SODIUM: High
PREPARING: 40 Minutes
BAKING: 5 Hours

Four different testers gave this easy-to-prepare dish top billing! The name *corned beef* originated from Anglo-Saxon times when granular salt the size of a kernel of corn was used in the salt curing process.

4-6 lbs. *(1800-2700g)* corned beef
¼ cup *(60ml)* water
2 T. pickling spice
1 orange with rind, sliced
1 onion, peeled and sliced
1 stalk of celery with leaves, sliced
1 carrot, sliced

GLAZE:

⅓ cup *(65g)* brown sugar
1 T. prepared mustard

Soak beef in fresh water to cover 30 minutes.

In shallow pan place large sheet of aluminum foil; pat meat dry to remove any salt from the surface; place on foil and pour water over top.

Sprinkle with pickling spice and arrange orange and vegetable slices over and around meat. Bring long ends of foil up over meat and seal with a double fold; seal side ends, turning them up to contain liquid.

Bake in preheated 300° oven 4 hours; cool meat slightly, unwrap and discard vegetables. (Up to this point may be baked early in the day.)

GLAZE: Combine sugar and mustard; spread on meat; bake in preheated 375° oven 20 minutes or until glazed.

Dr. Sybille Brewer, West Hartford, CT

Variations, Advance Preparation, and Serving Suggestions:
Delicious cold for sandwiches. Serve with Pickled Oranges (page 100).

Wine Suggestion: Italian Lambrusco, semi-dry sparkling red; serve chilled.

Microwave Conversion Instructions: Place 3 lbs. corned beef in clay pot that has been soaked in water 10 to 15 minutes. Add pickling spice, orange, onions, celery and carrot. Cover with clay top, cook on Medium (50%) 30 minutes. Meanwhile, mix brown sugar and mustard. Paint beef with mixture. Continue to cook on Medium (50%) another 60 to 65 minutes, or until fork tender. Let stand, covered, 5 minutes before serving.

Dry Cooked Oriental Beef

YIELD: 4-6 Servings
CALORIES PER SERVING: 279
CARBOHYDRATES: 16g
PROTEIN: 20g
FAT: 15g
SODIUM: High
PREPARING: 25 Minutes
COOKING: 10 Minutes
FREEZING: No

Partially freeze beef and slice meat across grain into ¼-inch *(6mm)* slices. Marinate beef in mixture of soy sauce, scallions, sesame oil and garlic for at least 30 minutes or up to 12 hours.

Mix cornstarch with water and set aside.

Heat wok until very hot. Heat peanut oil 20 seconds until hot but not smoking. Add meat, reserving marinade. Stir-fry quickly until meat is browned. Reduce heat to medium temperature; add water chestnuts, peppers, and mushrooms; stir-fry until vegetables are tender but still crisp. Add spinach, remainder of soy sauce, reserved marinade and cornstarch mixture. When spinach is wilted, season with ginger and pepper.

Serve immediately over a bed of brown rice.

Monica C. Goldman, Glastonbury, CT

Nutritional Notes: Stir-frying is an excellent method of cooking that aids in maintenance of vegetable texture and nutritional value. The 1 cup soy sauce amounts to approximately 2400 milligrams sodium per serving. The estimated safe and adequate daily intake for sodium is 1100-3300 milligrams for adults according to the 1979 Recommended Dietary Allowances. You may experiment with reducing soy sauce.

Wine Suggestion: California Gamay Beaujolais, light red; serve at room temperature.

1 lb. *(450g)* **flank steak**

MARINADE:
⅓ cup *(80ml)* **soy sauce**
1 **scallion, sliced (both white and green part)**
2 T. *(30ml)* **sesame oil**
1 **clove garlic, minced**

1 T. *(10g)* **cornstarch**
¼ cup *(60ml)* **water**
2 T. *(30ml)* **peanut oil**
2 **cans (8 oz. each)** *(450g)* **water chestnuts, drained**
3 **sweet red peppers, seeded and sliced**
12 oz. *(340g)* **small fresh mushrooms**
8 oz. *(225g)* **fresh spinach**
⅔ cup *(160ml)* **soy sauce**
Ginger to taste
Freshly ground pepper to taste

YIELD: 3 Servings
TOTAL CALORIES: 1122
CALORIES PER SERVING: 374
CARBOHYDRATES: 15g
PROTEIN: 29g
FAT: 22g
CHOLESTEROL: High
SODIUM: High
PREPARING: 1 Hour
MARINATING: 30 Minutes Minimum
STIR-FRYING: 6 Minutes
FREEZING: No

Szechwan Shredded Beef

Szechuan is a province in the inland area of mainland China with a penchant for more highly seasoned food.

¾ lb. *(340g)* **flank steak**

MARINADE:
2 tsp. *(10ml)* **light soy sauce**
1 T. *(10g)* **water chestnut powder or cornstarch**
1 T. *(15ml)* **dry sherry**
½ **beaten egg white**

½ cup *(60g)* **shredded carrots**
1 cup *(100g)* **snow peas, shredded**
½ cup *(85g)* **seeded and shredded sweet red pepper**
1 fresh **hot pepper, shredded**
4 **scallions, shredded**
1 clove **garlic, minced**
2 tsp. **minced fresh ginger root**

SEASONING SAUCE:
1 T. *(15ml)* **hoisin sauce**
1 T. *(15ml)* **bean sauce**
2 tsp. *(10ml)* **plum sauce**
1 T. *(15ml)* **dry sherry**
1 T. *(15ml)* **Chinese red vinegar**
1-2 tsp. **Chinese hot sauce**
1 T. *(15ml)* **dark soy sauce**
1 tsp. **water chestnut powder**
1 tsp. **sesame seed oil**

3 T. *(45ml)* **peanut oil**

Partially freeze beef, and slice meat across grain into ¼-inch *(6mm)* slices; then shred it with the grain. Marinate beef in mixture of soy sauce, water chestnut powder, sherry and egg white for at least 30 minutes or up to 12 hours.

Place carrots and peas in a bowl. Place sweet and hot peppers and scallions in another bowl. Put garlic and ginger in small cup. In a third bowl, mix all the seasoning sauce ingredients. Refrigerate everything until ready to stir-fry.

Place wok over medium heat 30 seconds. Add 1 T. oil; heat for 20 seconds until oil is hot but not smoking. Add garlic and ginger; stir-fry 15 seconds. Add snow peas and carrots, stir-fry 60 seconds. Turn heat to high; add peppers and scallions and stir-fry 60 seconds. Empty contents of wok into heated serving dish. Do not wash wok.

Heat 2 T. oil in wok. Stir marinated beef with chopsticks and put in wok; stir-fry 2 minutes. Re-stir seasoning sauce and add along with vegetables; stir-fry 60 seconds more. Empty contents of wok into a heated serving dish and serve immediately.

Adapted from Karen Lee's *Chinese Cooking for the American Kitchen*

Variations, Advance Preparation, and Serving Suggestions: Veal, pork or poultry may be substituted for beef.

Nutritional Notes: Stir-frying helps to maintain the nutritional value and texture of vegetables. Soy sauce, hoisin sauce, bean sauce and plum sauce are all high in sodium.

Wine Suggestion: California Charbono, sturdy red; serve at room temperature.

Calves Liver with Mustard and Caper Sauce

Stop searching for a new way to appreciate this somewhat ignored meat — here is a spectacular dish. Variety meats are highly nutritious, are generally economical and contain little waste.

YIELD: 4-6 Servings
CALORIES PER SERVING: 375
CARBOHYDRATES: 10g
PROTEIN: 23g
FAT: 26g
CHOLESTEROL: High
SODIUM: High
PREPARING: 30 Minutes
COOKING: 10 Minutes
FREEZING: No

Dissolve dry mustard in 1 T. water, let stand 10 minutes. In a small bowl combine softened butter, Dijon mustard and dry mustard mixture. Blend and reserve. Season liver with salt and pepper; dredge lightly in flour. Heat 3 T. butter in skillet. When very hot, saute liver — should be browned on outside and pink inside. Remove to platter and keep warm. Remove all but 2 T. fat from skillet. Add shallots and wine, cook over high heat scraping pan, until liquid is reduced to 3 T. Add brown stock and cream, continue cooking over high heat until it is reduced by ⅓. Remove from heat and beat in mustard butter until well blended. Add capers, correct seasoning. Pour over calves liver, sprinkle with parsley.

Sandra P. Robinson, Farmington, CT

Variations, Advance Preparation, and Serving Suggestions:
Substitute chicken livers or use sauce over pork chops. Accompany with New Potatoes in Savory Sauce (page 91) and sauteed sugar snap peas.

Wine Suggestion: California Cabernet Sauvignon, dry red; serve at room temperature.

Nutritional Notes: Although liver is high in cholesterol it is exceptionally high in vitamin A, B vitamins (including B_{12}) and minerals (particularly iron). Vitamin A promotes tissue formation, increases blood platelets, and promotes growth. Overcooking results not only in tough meat, but also in losses of protein and vitamins. Even with proper cooking (medium-high heat, quickly), vitamin B_1 is reduced by 30%, B_2 by 10%, Niacin by 15%. Some of this loss can be minimized by blanching. It is best to buy liver that has never been frozen and never to re-freeze liver (uncooked or cooked).

1 tsp. dry hot mustard
4 T. *(60g)* unsalted sweet butter, softened
1 tsp. Dijon mustard
6 slices *(750g)* calves liver, ½-inch *(1.25cm)* thick
Salt
Freshly ground white pepper
Flour for dredging
3 T. *(45g)* unsalted sweet butter
2 T. *(20g)* minced shallots
½ cup *(120ml)* dry white wine
1 cup *(240ml)* concentrated brown stock
½ cup *(120ml)* heavy cream
1-2 T. capers
3 T. parsley, minced

Veal Jerusalem

Jonathan Walker, restaurant consultant and Chef/Operator of the Wadsworth Atheneum restaurant, developed this recipe while in private service in England. He presented it to the public in 1976 in New York City at the Roosevelt Hotel.

YIELD: 1 Serving
CALORIES PER SERVING: 452
CARBOHYDRATES: 35g
PROTEIN: 33g
FAT: 20g
SODIUM: High
PREPARING: 10 Minutes
COOKING: 5 Minutes

2 2-oz. *(60g each)* pieces veal scallopini
  cut across grain
Flour
½ oz. *(15g)* clarified butter
4-6 small mushrooms
⅛ tsp. dried basil
1 artichoke heart, halved
3 slices of an artichoke bottom
1 shallot, chopped
3 T. *(45ml)* Madeira wine
6 T. *(90ml)* veal or beef stock
Beurre manie (1 T. butter and 1 T. flour
  mixed to a paste)
Salt
Freshly ground pepper
Dash of Worcestershire sauce

Pound veal to flatten. Dredge with flour, gently shaking off excess.

Put clarified butter in a saute pan. Over high heat, cook and brown veal 1½ to 2 minutes. Turn and add mushrooms, basil, artichoke heart, artichoke bottom slices and shallot. Cook veal another 1½ to 2 minutes. Remove veal to plate and keep warm.

Raise heat to high, deglaze with Madeira wine and reduce wine a little. Then add stock and thicken with beurre manie. Taste for seasonings; add salt and pepper as desired and Worcestershire sauce.

Wine Suggestion: Cote de Beaune Villages Bouchard Pere & Fils, dry red; serve at room temperature.

Baked Stuffed Veal Chops

YIELD: 6 Servings
CALORIES PER SERVING: 600
CARBOHYDRATES: 7g
PROTEIN: 34g
FAT: 48.5g
CHOLESTEROL: High
SODIUM: High
PREPARING: 35 Minutes
BAKING: 1 Hour

6 shoulder veal chops (3 lbs.) *(1350g)*,
  cut 1 inch *(2.5cm)* thick
Salt
Freshly ground pepper
¾ cup *(180ml)* plus 2 T. *(30ml)* heavy
  cream
1 T. Dijon mustard
7 T. *(105g)* butter, divided
2 shallots, minced
¼ lb. *(115g)* mushrooms, minced
1 small clove garlic, minced
Freshly minced parsley
Flour for dredging
2 T. *(30ml)* oil
2 medium onions, thinly sliced
2 cloves garlic, finely minced
½ cup *(120ml)* white wine
½ cup *(120ml)* brown stock
Bouquet garni (omit bay leaf)
Beurre manie (1 T. butter and 1 T. flour
  mixed to a paste)
Fresh lemon juice

Have the butcher cut a pocket in each chop for stuffing. Season each chop. Combine ¾ cup cream and mustard, set aside. In 2 T. butter, saute shallots until soft; add mushrooms, garlic, parsley, cook until all liquid evaporates. Add 2 T. cream, cook again until all liquid evaporates. Season with salt and pepper. Stuff equal portions of mixture into each chop; sew or skewer to close. Dredge chops in flour, shaking off excess.

In large skillet with ovensafe handle over medium flame, heat 3 T. butter and oil. Brown chops being careful not to crowd pan. Discard burnt fat particles, removing chops to side dish. Add 2 T. butter to skillet, saute onions and garlic. Add wine to 2 T. scrapings and bring to boil adding brown stock. Return chops to skillet adding bouquet garni. Cover with foil, place lid on skillet. Braise in preheated 350° oven, 50 to 60 minutes. Remove chops to serving dish. Place skillet over high heat adding cream and mustard mixture. Cook until reduced by ⅓ and sauce heavily coats the back of a spoon. If needed, add beurre manie to thicken. Add dash of lemon juice. Pour sauce over chops. Serve or keep warm in 200° oven, covered, up to 30 to 40 minutes.

Bernice Kuzma, West Hartford, CT

Wine Suggestion: California Cabernet Sauvignon, dry red; serve at room temperature.

Navarin of Veal

For late breakfast, lunch or an afternoon treat, THE PANTRY in Washington Depot can provide a delightful, informal repast for a traveler to this charming corner of Connecticut. Typical of the casual, yet knowledgeably presented fare is this veal stew, a hearty melange of vegetables and cubed veal in a sauce seasoned with herbes de Provence.

YIELD: 8 Servings
CALORIES PER SERVING: 545
CARBOHYDRATES: 19g
PROTEIN: 34g
FAT: 37g
CHOLESTEROL: High
SODIUM: High
PREPARING: 45 Minutes
COOKING: 1½ Hours
FREEZING: Yes

Dredge veal in flour. In a heavy skillet, heat oil; brown meat in batches removing to a large 6-qt. *(6L)* casserole. Saute onions in skillet. Deglaze with white wine by scraping up particles; add to casserole. Add 1 qt. stock, garlic, and herbs; cover and bake in preheated 350° oven 1 hour.

Cook potatoes, carrots, turnips, and beans in 1 qt. stock until crisp tender. If frozen beans are used, add at end of cooking. Stir in artichoke hearts.

Add vegetables to casserole along with enough liquid to cover meat and vegetables. Cover and bake 30 minutes longer or until meat is tender. Garnish with fresh parsley.

Wine Suggestion: French Cotes de Beaune Villages, dry red; serve at room temperature.

Microwave Conversion Instructions: Note: Cornstarch is more effective in thickening gravy in microwave oven than flour. For microwave preparation, this recipe *must be cut in half.* Veal and vegetables should be cut into smaller pieces than for conventional preparation. Cook chopped onion in olive oil on High 2 to 3 minutes in a small glass covered casserole. Dredge veal cubes in seasoned flour. In large glass casserole, combine onions, meat, white wine, stock, garlic and herbes de Provence; cover, cook on High 5 minutes. Stir, cover and cook on Medium (50%) 20 minutes stirring occasionally. Add potato, carrots and turnip to mixture; add additional broth if necessary to just cover vegetables. Cover, cook 14 minutes on High adding frozen beans and artichokes during last 5 minutes. (Fresh beans would be added with potatoes.) Stir occasionally. If gravy needs thickening, add 1 to 2 tsp. cornstarch to 2 T. water, blend well to desired thickness. Adjust seasonings.

3 lbs. *(1350g)* boneless leg of veal, cubed
1 cup *(115g)* flour seasoned with salt and pepper
½ cup *(120ml)* olive oil
½ medium onion, chopped
½ cup *(120ml)* dry white wine
2 qts. *(1.9L)* veal or chicken stock
2-3 cloves garlic, minced
1 tsp. herbes de Provence (mixture of thyme, rosemary and savory)
2 potatoes, cubed
3 carrots, cubed
2 white turnips, cubed (or 1 wax turnip)
1 cup *(85g)* green beans, cut in thirds (frozen may be used)
½ cup *(70g)* artichoke hearts, quartered
Freshly chopped parsley

YIELD: 12 Servings
CALORIES PER SERVING
  VEAL STEW ONLY: 392
CARBOHYDRATES: 17g
PROTEIN: 27g
FAT: 24g
CALORIES PER TOAST BOX: 412
CHOLESTEROL: High
PREPARING: 30 Minutes
COOKING: 30 Minutes
SIMMERING: 1½ Hours
FREEZING: Yes-Very Well

Veal Marengo in Toast Boxes

A version of the original chicken Marengo Napoleon's chef created when the Emperor defeated the Austrians at Marengo in 1800.

VEAL STEW:

4 lbs. *(1800g)* boneless veal leg or veal shank, cubed
½ cup *(120ml)* good quality olive oil
1 lb. *(450g)* onions, chopped
4 cloves garlic, minced
⅔ cup *(80g)* flour
3-4 cups *(720-950ml)* dry white wine
1 bouquet garni (1 bay leaf, 1 tsp. thyme, 10 sprigs parsley tied in cheesecloth bag)
2 tsp. salt
1 tsp. black pepper
8 fresh ripe garden tomatoes, cored and quartered *(about 700g)*. Use canned if fresh are not flavorful
1 lb. *(450g)* fresh small button mushrooms, cleaned
¼ cup chopped fresh parsley

12 Toast Boxes (page 199)

Dry veal cubes on paper towel. Over high heat in large kettle, quickly brown one pound of veal at a time in 1 T. olive oil. Remove veal; set aside while browning remaining meat. Add remaining ¼ cup oil; lightly brown onions and garlic. Add flour and a little wine to onions and cook 3 minutes. Return browned veal to the casserole; add the remaining wine, bouquet garni, salt and pepper. Cover the casserole and gently simmer 30 minutes (45 if using shank). Stir frequently to prevent burning on bottom. Add the tomatoes and mushrooms; simmer covered another 30 minutes (45 if shank). Check to make sure veal is tender. Remove bouquet garni. Taste for salt and pepper. At this point, stew may be refrigerated for 2 to 3 days or frozen. Bring to room temperature; reheat on stove. Serve spooned into Toast Boxes; sprinkle parsley on top.

Melinda M. Vance, West Hartford, CT

Variations, Advance Preparation, and Serving Suggestions: Veal completely cooked freezes very well. Thaw and gently reheat before serving. Serve with fresh fruit salad with Honey Salad Dressing (page 137) or Variegated Salad with Sweet and Sour Honey Dressing (page 175). Serve Ginger Ginger Cheesecake for dessert (page 404).

Wine Suggestion: California Pinot Noir, dry red; serve at room temperature.

Microwave Conversion Instructions: Most ingredients are reduced by half for microwave. The exact measurements are as follows: 2 lbs. cubed veal, ¼ cup olive oil, ½ lb. chopped onion, 1 large clove garlic minced, ¼ cup flour, ¾ cup dry white wine, 1 tsp. salt, 1 bouquet garni, ½ tsp. pepper, 4 cored quartered tomatoes, ½ lb. mushrooms, chopped parsley. Prepare veal as directed above until after placing in covered casserole. Put casserole in oven; cook on Medium (50%) 8 to 10 minutes. Add tomatoes; cook on Medium (50%) 4 to 6 minutes longer. Remove bouquet garni. Add sliced mushrooms in ring around casserole. Spoon sauce over mushrooms; cover and cook on Medium (50%) for 4 minutes. Let stand 5 minutes. Taste and correct seasonings.

Veau à l'Orange en Brioche

VEAL WITH ORANGE SAUCE IN BRIOCHE OR TOAST BOXES

YIELD: 4 Servings
TOTAL CALORIES: 2164
CALORIES PER SERVING: 541
CARBOHYDRATES: 12g
PROTEIN: 31g
FAT: 41g
CHOLESTEROL: High
SODIUM: High
PREPARING: 45 Minutes
BAKING: Make Brioche 1 Day in Advance
COOKING: 2 Hours

In a skillet saute fatback in hot oil until golden brown and lightly crisp. Transfer to a 4-qt. *(4L)* casserole. Add a few cubes of veal to skillet; cook to brown in batches, transferring cubes as they brown to casserole. Lightly brown optional veal bones in remaining fat; pour off fat; deglaze skillet with wine. Pour pan juices over veal. Add bones if used, stock, onions, garlic, herb bouquet, tomato paste, salt, and pepper. Cover; simmer 1½ hours or until veal is very tender (a sharp knife should penetrate meat easily). Remove meat from casserole; cover; set aside.

Discard herb bouquet and bones; add orange and lemon juices to remaining liquid; boil down to 2 cups; add cream; reduce by boiling to 1½ cups. Adjust seasoning.

Simmer zest strips in boiling water 5 minutes. Drain; refresh under cold running water and drain again.

Add zest, fresh herbs and veal to sauce. Heat thoroughly. Fill large brioche (cut off top of brioche and hollow out center) with meat and sauce (replace top of brioche) or ladle into individual toast boxes.

Kathleen J. Schwartz, Avon, CT

Nutritional Notes: Brioche or Toast Boxes are not included in nutritional analysis.

Wine Suggestion: California Beauclair Johannesberg Riesling, soft white; serve chilled.

⅓ cup *(45g)* diced fatback or blanched salt pork
2 T. *(30ml)* vegetable oil
1½ lbs. *(680g)* boneless veal shoulder, cubed
1 or 2 veal bones (optional)
2 cups *(475ml)* dry white wine
1½ cups *(355ml)* rich veal or chicken stock
2 medium onions, thinly sliced
4 cloves garlic, halved
Herb bouquet (rib of celery, bay leaf, thyme, parsley sprig, and 1 leek)
½ T. tomato paste
Salt
Freshly ground pepper
⅔ cup *(160ml)* fresh orange juice
¼ cup *(60ml)* fresh lemon juice
⅔ cup *(160ml)* heavy cream
Zest of 1 medium orange, pith removed and cut into tiny julienne strips
1 tsp. snipped chives
1 tsp. minced fresh parsley
1 large brioche (made from 20 oz. *(570g)* Brioche Dough (page 226) or 4 Toast Boxes (page 199), hollowed out

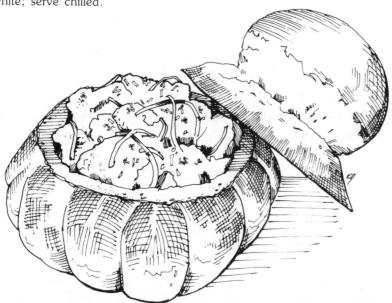

Médallions de Veau au Cresson

VEAL MEDALLIONS WITH WATERCRESS

A delectable veal preparation a la nouvelle cuisine, with a watercress beurre blanc (wine and butter sauce), from LA FINE BOUCHE Restaurant, Centerbrook, Connecticut.

YIELD: 6 Servings
CALORIES PER SERVING: 455
CARBOHYDRATES: 6g
PROTEIN: 29g
FAT: 35g
CHOLESTEROL: High
PREPARING: 20 Minutes
COOKING: 25 Minutes
FREEZING: No

WATERCRESS BUTTER:

1 bunch watercress
¼ cup chopped fresh chives
¼ lb. *(115g)* **sweet unsalted butter, cut in pieces**
Salt
Freshly ground white pepper

VEAL:

¼ cup *(30g)* **flour**
12-18 slices veal loin
Salt
Freshly ground black pepper
3 T. *(45ml)* **oil**

SAUCE:

¼ cup *(60ml)* **white wine**
1 T. minced shallots
½ cup *(120ml)* **heavy cream**

WATERCRESS BUTTER: Blanch watercress 30 seconds in rapidly boiling water. Drain immediately, refresh in ice water. Squeeze to remove as much moisture as possible. Cut off one inch of stems, discard. Chop coarsely; puree with chives in food processor 4 to 5 minutes, until very smooth. Scrape sides of processor, add butter, process until smooth, 3 to 4 minutes, scraping sides. Add salt and pepper to taste.

VEAL: Lightly flour and season veal. Heat a saute pan, add oil. Cook veal quickly over high heat in hot oil, just a few minutes on each side. Remove to hot serving dish or individual plates.

SAUCE: In small saucepan, boil white wine with shallots over high heat until liquid is reduced to about 2 T. *(30ml)*. Add cream and reduce again to about 3 T. *(45ml)*. Remove pan from heat. Quickly whisk in Watercress Butter by tablespoonfuls. Adjust seasoning if necessary. Pour sauce on sides of veal, not on top.

Variations, Advance Preparation, and Serving Suggestions:
Make the Watercress Butter a day ahead; refrigerate tightly covered. Bring to room temperature before adding to Sauce. Serve with Homemade Pasta (page 192).

Wine Suggestion: Cotes du Rhone Bouchard Pere & Fils, dry red; serve at room temperature.

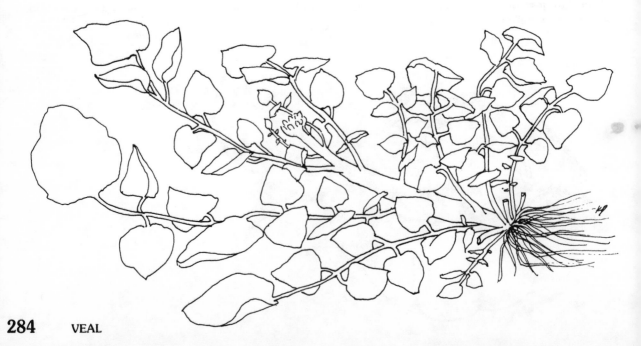

Rolled Breast of Veal

Mortadella now is a Bolognese sausage, but originally, it was any kind of forcemeat made by using a mortar and pestle.

YIELD: 6 Servings
CALORIES PER SERVING: 474
CARBOHYDRATES: 4g
PROTEIN: 29g
FAT: 38g
CHOLESTEROL: High
SODIUM: High
PREPARING: 50 Minutes
COOKING: 1½ Hours

Spread out veal, smooth side down and pound to make it as even as possible.

Finely mince celery, carrot, egg, sage, shallot and parsley; continue mincing or blend in food processor until mixture almost becomes a paste. Salt the boned side of veal; spread with vegetable paste to within 1 inch *(2.5cm)* on long sides and the wider end. Over vegetable paste, put grated mozzarella to cover, then slices of mortadella and then slices of prosciutto.

Starting at the smaller end of veal breast, roll up into a sausage shape, being careful not to squeeze out the filling, and pushing filling into place with your fingers as you roll. When rolled, skewer it together. Then tie it with string and remove skewers.

Heat olive oil in bottom of a deep 4-6-qt. *(4-6L)* Dutch oven; add veal and bones. Sprinkle with rosemary and brown meat on all sides. Add wine, cover pan, lower heat and cook approximately 1½ hours. During cooking, turn meat several times and baste with juices. There should always be 1 inch *(2.5cm)* liquid; if it gets lower, add chicken stock.

When meat is done, remove from Dutch oven and let cool 15 minutes before slicing. During that time, add ¼-½ cup chicken stock to the Dutch oven to deglaze pan; reduce liquid if desired; strain and serve with veal.

Runa Wassermann, West Hartford, CT

Variations, Advance Preparation, and Serving Suggestions:
If using a smaller veal breast, do not decrease the amounts of ingredients for the filling. Recipe easily doubles.

Wine Suggestion: Cotes du Rhone Bouchard Pere & Fils, dry red; serve at room temperature.

Microwave Conversion Instructions: Note: Omit 4 T. olive oil and substitute 3 T. melted butter with 1 tsp. paprika. Reduce dry white wine to ½ cup. Prepare veal roast as for conventional recipe. After veal has been rolled, coat it with butter/paprika mixture. Place roast on roasting rack in large covered casserole, along with bones and wine. Cover, cook 10 minutes on High; reduce to Medium (50%) and continue to cook 50 to 55 minutes (allow 18 to 19 minutes per pound). Internal temperature should be 160°. If ends of roast begin to overcook "patch" with small pieces of aluminum foil if oven manufacturer allows this procedure.

3 lbs. *(1350g)* breast of veal, boned but reserving bones
½ rib celery with leaves
1 carrot
1 jumbo egg, hard cooked
¼ tsp. dried sage or 1 leaf
¼ of a large shallot or ⅛ of a red onion
4 sprigs parsley
½ tsp. salt
¼ lb. *(115g)* whole milk mozzarella cheese, grated
3 slices *(100g)* mortadella
6 slices *(120g)* prosciutto ham
¼ cup *(60ml)* olive oil
1 tsp. rosemary
1 cup *(240ml)* dry white wine
1 cup *(240ml)* chicken stock

Red and Green Country-Style Veal Scallops

YIELD: 6 Servings
CALORIES PER SERVING: 321
CARBOHYDRATES: 7g
PROTEIN: 26g
FAT: 21g
PREPARING: 15 Minutes
COOKING: 30 Minutes
FREEZING: No

This is an elegant, colorful but simple veal entree.

2 lbs. *(900g)* veal scallops (cutlets), cut
  ¼-inch *(6mm)* thick and across the
  grain
Salt
Freshly ground pepper
¼ cup *(60ml)* olive oil
1 large onion, thinly sliced
2-3 cloves garlic, finely chopped
2 large sweet red peppers, thinly sliced
  lengthwise
¼ cup capers
¼ cup *(120ml)* Marsala wine
Fresh chopped parsley

Season veal with salt and pepper and set aside. Heat 2 T. oil in skillet large enough to accommodate all the veal at once. Saute onions and garlic 5 minutes. Add peppers and continue gentle cooking until peppers are just tender (be careful not to overcook). Remove vegetables and cooking juices from skillet. Add remaining 2 T. olive oil; saute meat, cooking very slightly on each side. Return vegetables to pan along with capers and Marsala. Cook for 10 to 12 minutes, until flavors are blended and meat is just cooked. Arrange on heated serving platter, garnish with fresh parsley. Serve immediately.

Auden di Corcia, Hartford, CT

Variations, Advance Preparation, and Serving Suggestions:
Spinach Linguini ai Quattro Fromaggi (page 173) or risotto and peas would be a complimentary pasta course. Turkey cutlets can be used as an inexpensive substitute for veal.

Wine Suggestion: Italian Valpolicella, dry red; serve at room temperature.

Microwave Conversion Instructions: Note: Use a browning dish. Place onion in 1-qt. *(1L)* casserole. Add garlic and 3 T. oil. Cook on High 4 minutes. Add peppers and cook on High 2 to 3 minutes, just until tender. Preheat browning dish to its maximum absorption. When heated, quickly add 2 T. oil and coat bottom of dish. Add veal and cook on High 1 minute. Turn veal over and cook on High 1 minute. (Rearrange veal when turning to place less cooked pieces facing outside of dish. If veal appears almost done when turning, omit the additional 1 minute on High.) Add vegetables, capers and wine. Cook on High 3 minutes, just until flavors are blended.

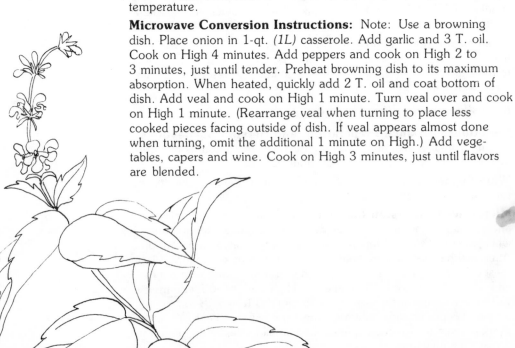

Vitello con Basilico

VEAL IN BASIL SAUCE

YIELD: 6 Servings
CALORIES PER SERVING: 368
CARBOHYDRATES: 2g
PROTEIN: 27g
FAT: 28g
PREPARING: 30 Minutes
BAKING: 25 Minutes
COOKING: 15 Minutes
FREEZING: No

SAUCE: Combine butter, basil, garlic in blender or food processor; puree until smooth. Chill.

VEAL: Butter large, shallow flameproof casserole. Combine salt, pepper and flour; dust veal with mixture. In skillet over high heat, quickly brown ¼ of the veal in butter and oil. Remove to casserole and brown remaining meat. Add shallots to same skillet; saute until tender over moderate heat; add wine, reducing liquid to 2 T. Add stock, bring to boil, scraping particles from bottom of skillet. Pour over veal. Cover with buttered foil. Bake 25 minutes in a preheated 325° oven.

GARNISH: In a skillet heat butter and oil until very hot. Add tomatoes and quickly roll to coat. Add salt and pepper; cook 3 minutes. Sprinkle with parsley; set aside.

Remove veal to serving platter and lightly sprinkle with lemon juice. Circle veal with tomatoes.

SAUCE: Place casserole over moderately high heat. Add meat glaze to liquid; stir and reduce slightly. Using a whisk, slowly add cornstarch mixture; cook until mixture coats the back of a spoon. Add chilled basil sauce mixture, using whisk until blended. Spoon sauce over veal and tomatoes.

Bernice Kuzma, West Hartford, CT

Variations, Advance Preparation, and Serving Suggestions:
Serve with rice ring filled with quickly sauteed or stir-fried sugar snap peas.

Wine Suggestion: Italian Baralo, full red; serve at room temperature.

Microwave Conversion Instructions: Follow above directions for basil sauce, and for preparing dish up to baking. Cover with waxed paper. Cook on Medium High (70%), 5 minutes. Prepare garnish on conventional cook top while veal is cooking. Remove veal to warm serving platter. Add meat glaze to liquid in dish; stir. Cook, uncovered, on High 2 minutes. Dissolve cornstarch in 3 T. beef stock; whisk into dish. Cook, uncovered, on High until thickened, whisking once or twice. Add chilled basil sauce; whisk until blended. Serve as directed above.

SAUCE:
4 T. *(60g)* unsalted sweet butter, softened
3 T. fresh basil, finely minced
2 cloves garlic, mashed
1 tsp. meat glaze (optional)
1 tsp. cornstarch mixed with 2-3 tsp. stock or water

VEAL:
2 lbs. *(900g)* veal scallops (cutlets), cut ¼-inch *(6mm)* thick and across the grain
Salt
Freshly ground white pepper
Flour
2 T. *(30g)* unsalted sweet butter
2 T. *(30ml)* oil
3 T. *(30g)* shallots, finely chopped
½ cup *(120ml)* white wine
1 cup *(240ml)* brown stock
Fresh lemon juice

GARNISH:
2 T. *(30g)* unsalted sweet butter
2 T. *(30ml)* olive oil
2 cups *(450g)* cherry tomatoes
Salt and white pepper
2 T. Italian parsley, minced

YIELD: 4-6 Servings
CALORIES PER SERVING: 565
CARBOHYDRATES: 30g
PROTEIN: 55g
FAT: 25g
CHOLESTEROL: High
PREPARING: 15 Minutes
MARINATING: 8 Hours Minimum
COOKING: 30-45 Minutes

Lamb Riblets

A very versatile dish — an unusual chafing dish hors d'oeuvre, a luncheon entree, or a picnic basket offering.

4 lbs. *(1800g)* lamb riblets, cut into sections

MARINADE:
1 medium onion, chopped
1 piece fresh ginger (about the size of a quarter), finely minced
1 cup *(240ml)* unsweetened pineapple juice
¾ cup *(175ml)* dry sherry
¼ cup *(85g)* honey
⅛ tsp. dry mustard
¼ cup *(50g)* brown sugar
Salt and pepper

1 T. *(10g)* cornstarch dissolved in 2 T. *(30ml)* cold water

Place riblets in shallow pan.

Combine marinade ingredients in saucepan and bring to a boil. Immediately pour over ribs. Cover and refrigerate 8 hours or overnight, turning occasionally.

Grill or broil riblets 8 inches *(20cm)* from heat, basting frequently, 30 minutes or until cooked to desired doneness.

Remove meat to heated platter. Reduce sauce by boiling rapidly. Thicken with cornstarch and water mixture. Pour over hot riblets to glaze.

Bobbi Hendsey Leavitt, North Canton, CT

Wine Suggestion: Hungarian Villanyi Burgundy, dry red; serve at room temperature.

Microwave Conversion Instructions: Marinate riblets as directed above. Cook on Medium High (70%), covered with waxed paper 15 to 20 minutes, turning riblets over and rearranging and basting several times. To prepare sauce, place liquid in large measuring cup. Dissolve cornstarch in 2 T. pineapple juice. Stir into liquid. Cook, uncovered, on High 2 to 3 minutes until thickened.

Lamb Tagine with Fruit and Honey

In Morocco a shallow covered ceramic pot is called a *tagine* as well as any combination of ingredients cooked in this pot. It is essentially a stew encompassing poultry, fish or meats combined with either fruits or vegetables. No matter what the month, there is a tree in Morocco bearing fruit for the tagine pot. In the spring use greening or winesap apples. In summer try fresh apricots. In fall use Seckel pears or quince, which are especially delightful. In winter use prunes or dates for a very hearty version.

YIELD: 4-6 Servings
TOTAL CALORIES: 2196
CALORIES PER SERVING: 366
CARBOHYDRATES: 22g
PROTEIN: 29g
FAT: 18g
PREPARING: 20 Minutes
SIMMERING: 1¼ Hours
FREEZING: No

2 lbs. *(900g)* lamb, cut in 2-inch *(5cm)* cubes
⅛ tsp. each ginger, saffron, salt
3 T. *(45ml)* olive oil
1 tsp. ground coriander
1½-inch *(4cm)* cinnamon stick
Freshly ground pepper
1 small onion, chopped
1 lb. *(450g)* prune plums, pears or apples
¼ cup *(85g)* honey
1 tsp. orange flower water
1 T. sesame seeds, toasted

In 3-qt. *(3L)* pan combine lamb, ginger, saffron, salt, oil, coriander, cinnamon, pepper and onion. Barely cover with water and simmer until meat is well cooked and liquid substantially reduced, about 45 minutes. Remove cinnamon stick. Prepare fruit. If using plums, pit but leave whole; core and quarter pears or apples, do not peel. Add fruit and simmer slowly, about 15 minutes. Add honey, cook additional 15 minutes. Add orange flower water and bring to a boil. Sprinkle with sesame seeds. Serve immediately.

Bernice Kuzma, West Hartford, CT

Variations, Advance Preparation, and Serving Suggestions: An attractive and tasteful accompaniment is a marinated cucumber and green pepper salad garnished with pimento.

Nutritional Notes: Nutritional analysis is based on a choice grade of lamb shoulder, well-trimmed and uses 4 oz. *(115g)* cooked lamb meat per serving. If total edible lamb (not trimmed) is used, the analysis changes to 517 calories per serving, 22g carbohydrates, 24g protein, and 37g fat.

Wine Suggestion: German Moselle Auslese, semi-sweet flowery white; serve chilled.

Microwave Conversion Instructions: Note: Cut lamb into ¾-inch *(2cm)* cubes. In 3-qt. deep casserole, combine lamb, spices, oil and onion. Add 1 cup *(240ml)* water. Cook, covered, on High 10 minutes, stirring once or twice. Remove cinnamon stick; continue to cook on Medium (50%) 15 minutes. Add fruit; cook, covered, on High 5 minutes. Remove 1 cup of hot liquid, into which is blended 3 T. flour until dissolved. Pour back into casserole. Add honey; cook 5 minutes on High. Add orange flower water; continue to cook, uncovered, on High until boiling. Garnish and serve.

Lamb Chops Florentine

"Florentine" means served with spinach and usually also with grated cheese or a Mornay sauce. Catherine de Medici popularized spinach, a specialty of her native Florence, when she went to France to marry King Henri II.

YIELD: 4 Servings
CALORIES PER SERVING: 310
CARBOHYDRATES: 9g
PROTEIN: 30g
FAT: 18g
PREPARING: 10 Minutes
BROILING: 8 Minutes
COOKING: 20 Minutes
FREEZING: No

Heat oil in small saucepan. Add onion and garlic and saute gently until soft. Add ½ cup wine, stock, tomato paste and thyme; simmer 10 minutes.

Meanwhile, clean spinach; cook in boiling salted water until wilted. Drain well.

Broil lamb chops 3 to 4 minutes per side for medium rare or to desired doneness.

When ready to serve, mix 1 T. wine and cornstarch; add to sauce and boil 1 minute to thicken.

Arrange chops on platter. Place equal amounts of spinach on each chop. Garnish with slices of fresh mushrooms, two for each chop. Top with sauce. Garnish with parsley and serve immediately. Pass extra sauce separately.

Lynn S. Gail, Hartford, CT

Wine Suggestion: Italian Chianti Classico, dry red; serve at room temperature.

Microwave Conversion Instructions: In a 4-cup *(1L)* glass measure, cook oil, onion and garlic, uncovered, on High 3 minutes. Add only ¼ cup wine, ½ cup chicken or lamb stock, 2 T. tomato paste, and thyme; cook, uncovered, 3 minutes on High. Dissolve cornstarch in 2 T. wine and stir into sauce; cook 2 minutes, or until thick. Cook spinach with 3 T. water, covered, on High 2 minutes, or just long enough to promote steaming. Leave spinach in dish, covered, 3 to 4 minutes or until wilted. To "broil" lamb chops: Preheat browning dish to maximum absorption. Grill chops on browning dish. Place "browner" side up and finish garnishing as directed above. Extra sauce can be reheated on High 1 to 2 minutes.

2 T. *(30ml)* olive oil
1 small onion, finely chopped
1 clove garlic, crushed
½ cup *(120ml)* plus 1 T. dry
  white wine
1 cup *(240ml)* chicken or lamb stock
2 T. *(30g)* tomato paste
½ tsp. dried thyme
10 oz. *(285g)* fresh spinach
4 loin lamb chops about ¾ inch *(2cm)*
  thick, very well trimmed
1 T. cornstarch
8 slices fresh mushrooms
Fresh parsley sprigs

YIELD: 8 Servings
CALORIES PER SERVING: 505
CARBOHYDRATES: 13g
PROTEIN: 48g
FAT: 29g
CHOLESTEROL: High
SODIUM: High
PREPARING: 30 Minutes
CHILLING: Overnight
COOKING: 1½ Hours

Blanquette d'Agneau

SPRING LAMB STEW WITH DILL

A *blanquette* is a white ragout, fricassee or stew of lamb, veal or chicken with a sauce made from the liquid in which the meat has been cooked, bound with egg yolks and cream.

2 onions, each stuck with 3 cloves
2 large carrots, peeled
1 celery stalk
2 leeks, thoroughly washed
1 parsnip, peeled
6 peppercorns
Salt
6 cups *(1425ml)* light chicken stock
Lamb bones (or veal bones)
4 lbs. *(1800g)* boned shoulder of lamb, cubed (or 4 lbs. boneless leg of veal or veal shank, cubed)

SAUCE:

4 T. *(60g)* butter
1 onion, finely minced
1 tsp. sugar
4 T. *(30g)* flour
2½-3 cups *(600-725ml)* reserved stock
1 cup *(240ml)* Creme Fraiche (page 200) (may use commercial sour cream but watch so it won't curdle)
3 T. *(45ml)* fresh lemon juice
Salt
Freshly ground white pepper
½ cup freshly-snipped dill, or more to taste
Whole sprigs of fresh dill

In large, heavy casserole combine vegetables, seasonings, lamb bones and stock. Bring to a simmer and add meat. (Always start stock cold for better flavor, but only add meat when hot, as cold water toughens meat.) Cook lamb for 1½ hours or until meat is tender but not falling apart. Refrigerate overnight. Degrease stock, reserving 3 cups. Reserve lamb, discarding vegetables and spices.

SAUCE: In large saucepan, melt butter; add onion and sugar. Cook over low heat until onion is soft and transparent. Add flour and cook 1 minute. Off heat add stock all at once, stirring constantly. Return to heat; cook until thickened. Add Creme Fraiche, blend well. Add lemon juice. Add reserved lamb and gently reheat. Season to taste with salt and pepper. Add dill.

Garnish with sprigs of fresh dill.

Melinda M. Vance, West Hartford, CT

Nutritional Notes: While lamb shoulder is more flavorful and less expensive than leg of lamb, the leg has about half as much fat. Using leg of lamb would result in 406 calories and 18g fat per serving. If using shoulder, calorie and fat content can be reduced considerably if all visible fat is removed before cooking and if stock is very carefully degreased.

Wine Suggestion: French Meursault, full white; serve chilled.

Microwave Conversion Instructions: In large casserole combine bones, *sliced* vegetables, seasonings and 4½ cups *(1100ml)* chicken stock. Cover; cook on Medium High (70%) 15 minutes. Add meat; continue to cook for 65 minutes on Medium (50%), stirring every 15 minutes. In large casserole, melt butter by cooking on High 45 seconds. Add onion and sugar; cover, continue cooking 3 minutes on High. Add flour; cook 30 seconds on High. Add 2 cups skimmed lamb stock with fat removed; cook 5 minutes on High, stirring halfway through. Follow above directions to complete sauce by adding Creme Fraiche, lemon juice and dill. To reheat for serving, use Medium (50%) power.

Italian Baby Lamb Chops in Parmesan Cheese Batter

The crisp and delicious cheese crust seals in all the sweetness of the lamb and keeps it very succulent.

YIELD: 6 Servings
CALORIES PER SERVING: 565
CARBOHYDRATES: 12g
PROTEIN: 28g
FAT: 45g
PREPARING: 15 Minutes
COOKING: 5-10 Minutes
FREEZING: No

With a meat pounder, flatten the eye of the chop. Turn both sides of chops in cheese, coating as heavily as possible. Immediately dip each chop into beaten eggs, letting excess flow back into dish. Then turn chops into crumbs, coating on both sides. (Prepare up to this point 1 hour ahead of time or 4 hours, if refrigerated. If refrigerated, bring to room temperature before frying.)

Heat oil in skillet over medium heat until very hot. Fry as many chops at one time as will fit loosely in skillet. As soon as they have formed a nice crust on one side, season with salt and pepper and turn them. When crust has formed on other side, add salt and pepper. Transfer to warm platter and do next batch. (If lamb is truly young and tender, and cut very thin, it will take a total of 4 to 5 minutes to cook 1 batch.) Serve immediately.

Wine Suggestion: French Camponac Rouge Bordeaux, dry red; serve at room temperature.

12 single rib young lamb chops corner bone cut off and visible fat removed
½ cup *(65g)* fresh, finely grated Parmesan cheese
2 eggs, lightly beaten in shallow dish
1 cup *(120g)* fine, dry, unflavored bread crumbs
Vegetable oil and butter, enough to come ¼ inch *(0.6cm)* up side of skillet
Salt
Freshly ground pepper

Sausage Vegetable Potpourri

Use your freshly-picked garden harvest for this delicious family supper. The title of this recipe is most appropriate as the original definition of a potpourri was a stew.

YIELD: 5 Servings
TOTAL CALORIES: 2405
CALORIES PER SERVING: 481
CARBOHYDRATES: 12g
PROTEIN: 16g
FAT: 41g
SODIUM: High
PREPARING: 10 Minutes
COOKING: 40 Minutes

In a large pan, brown sausage. Remove from pan when cooked; drain.

In another pan, fry bacon until crisp. Remove to drain. In the bacon fat, saute onion and green pepper until soft. Add tomatoes, salt, pepper, sugar and herbs. Simmer, uncovered, 20 minutes. Add squash; cover pan. Simmer 10 minutes; squash will still be firm. Stir in sausage and sprinkle with crumbled bacon.

Bunny Millan, Simsbury, CT

Wine Suggestion: California Zinfandel, fruity red; serve at room temperature.

Microwave Conversion Instructions: Place sausage pieces in a bowl. Cook, uncovered, on High 6 minutes, stirring once or twice to keep meat crumbly. Place bacon on rack with baking dish beneath. Cook, covered with paper towel, on High 3 to 4 minutes until crisp. Drain bacon fat into a separate bowl, add onion and pepper and cook 5 minutes on High. Add tomatoes, salt and pepper, sugar and herbs. Cook, covered, on High 10 minutes. Add sliced squash. Cook, covered, on High 7 minutes. Stir in sausage and sprinkle with crumbled bacon.

1 lb. *(450g)* Italian sweet sausage, cut into pieces
4 slices *(100g)* bacon
1 large onion, thinly sliced
1 large green pepper, diced
4-5 tomatoes peeled and chopped or 1 can (35 oz.) *(990g)* tomatoes
Salt
Freshly ground pepper
1 tsp. sugar
2 basil leaves, chopped, or ½ tsp. dried basil
2 T. fresh parsley, chopped
1 lb. *(450g)* yellow summer squash or zucchini, thinly sliced

Bolognese Pork Loin Braised in Milk

YIELD: 6-8 Servings
CALORIES PER SERVING: 555
CARBOHYDRATES: 7.5g
PROTEIN: 39g
FAT: 41g
CHOLESTEROL: High
PREPARING: 30 Minutes
COOKING: 2 Hours

Should the title of this recipe cause some skepticism, it will change to avid enthusiasm upon first taste and become a family favorite. Pork cooked by this method is exceptionally tender and moist. It is delicate in flavor, because the pork loses all its fat, and the milk disappears to be replaced by clusters of delicious, nut-brown sauce.

---

2 T. *(30g)* butter
2 T. *(30ml)* corn oil
4-5 lb. *(1800-2250g)* boneless pork loin with some fat on it, rolled and tied (pork will weigh 6-7 lbs. *(2700-3150g)* before trimming)
1 T. salt
½ tsp. freshly ground pepper
4-5 cups *(1-1.2L)* milk
6 T. *(90ml)* warm water

Heat butter and oil over medium/high heat in a casserole with lid in which pork loin will fit snugly. When butter foam subsides, add pork, fat side down. Brown meat thoroughly on all sides, lowering heat if butter starts to brown. Add salt and pepper and a *little* milk. After milk boils and settles down, add a little more milk; wait until it becomes caramel color, then add enough milk to immerse ⅔ of pork. Reduce heat to medium; cover casserole leaving top slightly ajar; cook slowly for approximately 2 hours or until meat is easily pierced with fork. Turn and baste meat occasionally, adding any remaining milk. When meat is cooked, remove it to a platter; keep warm. Milk in casserole should have coagulated into small nut-brown clusters. If not, raise heat to high, cook, uncovered, briskly until milk further reduces and darkens. Skim off fat and discard, being careful not to remove any coagulated milk clusters. Add warm water, turn heat to high; boil away all water while scraping and loosening all cooking residue in casserole. Taste and correct seasonings.

Remove trussing string from pork; carve into ⅜-inch *(1cm)* thick slices. Arrange slices on warm platter. Spoon sauce over pork. Serve immediately.

Patricia M. Mitchell, Avon, CT

Variations, Advance Preparation, and Serving Suggestions: A 4-lb. boned veal roast can be substituted for the pork. Rather than brown veal on top of the stove, rub it with the oil and butter and place it in a roasting pan along with a few sprigs of rosemary and some sage leaves. Put the pan in a preheated 400° oven 30 minutes. Turn frequently and baste from time to time with the meat juices. Remove veal from pan; place in casserole, add milk and proceed as directed above. Exact timing will depend on quality of meat used. Precede this entree with Pronto Pasta Pimento Pesto (page 270) or Pasta with Uncooked Tomato Sauce (page 269). Serve with fried artichoke wedges and Variegated Salad (page 175). Chocolate Amaretto Cheesecake (page 116) could serve as the grand finale.

Nutritional Notes: Of all the meats pork is richest in vitamin B complex. Over a quart of milk is utilized in this dish, adding a significant amount of calcium.

Wine Suggestion: California Rutherford Cabernet Sauvignon, dry red; serve at room temperature.

Microwave Conversion Instructions: Brown pork on conventional range as directed above. Transfer contents of casserole to covered casserole. Season meat and add enough milk to immerse about ⅔ of pork. Cover casserole, leaving top slightly ajar. Cook on 60% power for 40 minutes, turning roast and basting after 20 minutes. When roast is done (internal temperature 140° to 160°), remove to a platter and keep it warm. Complete recipe as directed above.

Roast Pork with Mustard in Puff Pastry

YIELD: 10 Servings
CALORIES PER SERVING: 582
CARBOHYDRATES: 7g
PROTEIN: 35g
FAT: 46g
CHOLESTEROL: High
SODIUM: High
PREPARING: 3 Hours
ROASTING: 2-2½ Hours
FREEZING: No

Sprinkle roast with salt and pepper; rub with mustard.

Roast in preheated 325° oven to an inner temperature of 140° to 160°, 2 to 2½ hours. Remove from oven; let rest 1 hour. When roast has cooled, wrap in puff pastry. Make a few slashes in pastry; bake in preheated 425° oven for 20 to 30 minutes or until pastry is golden brown.

MOCK PUFF PASTRY: Cut butter in strips; roll between waxed paper; refrigerate. In a bowl, mix flour, salt and pepper; sprinkle with water and blend. Gather dough into a ball; knead briefly; let rest in refrigerator for 10 minutes. Roll dough into an oblong shape; place butter on top. Fold over sides, roll lightly. Fold into thirds, roll again; repeat process twice. Return to refrigerator to rest. Repeat process 4 to 6 times. Roll thinly.

Katherine B. Wells, West Hartford, CT

1 8-lb. *(3600g)* pork roast, boned and tied
Salt
Freshly ground pepper
¼ cup *(65g)* Dijon mustard
1 recipe pastry

MOCK PUFF PASTRY:
½ cup *(115g)* butter
¾ cup *(85g)* flour
¼ tsp. salt
Freshly ground pepper
¼ cup *(60ml)* ice water

Variations, Advance Preparation, and Serving Suggestions: Pastry may be made a day ahead. The roast may be cooked day ahead and reheated in a preheated 300° oven, covered, for 1 hour; let rest. When cool wrap in pastry and proceed with the recipe. You may substitute 1 recipe Classic Puff Pastry (page 194) for above pastry.

Nutritional Notes: Pork is high in protein and vitamin B_1. Unfortunately, it is too often served tasteless and dry, overcooked in an effort to make it safe to eat. It is true that pork should be sufficiently cooked. An internal temperature of 140° is considered safe; you can be absolutely sure when a thermometer registers 160°, well before the pork loses its wonderful succulence.

Wine Suggestion: California Petite Sirah, peppery red; serve at room temperature.

Microwave Conversion Instructions: Prepare pork as directed above. Place in glass baking dish with rack. Cook on High 5 minutes. Cook on Medium (50%) 25 minutes. Turn pork over and cook on Medium (50%) 30 minutes or until internal temperature reaches 140° to 160°. Allow roast to cool and continue as directed above.

YIELD: 8 Servings
TOTAL CALORIES: 3344
CALORIES PER SERVING PORK
   ONLY: 418
CARBOHYDRATES: 2g
PROTEIN: 35g
FAT: 30g
CHOLESTEROL: High
CALORIES RHUBARB SAUCE
   PER SERVING: 105
CALORIES CRANBERRY GLAZE
   PER SERVING: 140
PREPARING: 30 Minutes
ROASTING: 2½ Hours
FREEZING: No

Roast Loin
of Pork Either/Or

ROAST PORK WITH SPRING RHUBARB SAUCE
OR FALL CRANBERRY GLAZE

1 5-lb. *(2.3kg)* boned, rolled and tied
   loin of pork
1 clove garlic, peeled, split
Salt
Freshly ground pepper to taste
2 tsp. dried rosemary leaves, crushed
2 large carrots, peeled, coarsely
   chopped
2 ribs celery, coarsely chopped
1 large onion, peeled, chopped
1 cup *(240ml)* white wine

RHUBARB SAUCE:

3 lbs. *(1360g)* rhubarb (frozen may be
   used if fresh is not available)
Juice of 1 large orange
¾ cup *(150g)* sugar

CRANBERRY GLAZE:

1 can (16 oz.) *(450g)* whole cranberry
   sauce
½ cup *(140g)* mint jelly
1 T. fresh lemon juice

Rub pork all over with garlic. Discard garlic. With your fingers, work salt, pepper and crushed rosemary into surface of meat. Combine chopped vegetables; place on bottom of roasting pan. Pour wine around vegetables. Place pork on top of vegetables in a preheated 350° oven. Roast meat 2½ hours, or to 160°, 25 to 30 minutes per lb. Baste with pan juices occasionally.

SPRING RHUBARB SAUCE: Wash rhubarb, but do not peel as the rosy color will be lost. Cut the stalks into ½-inch *(1.25cm)* pieces. Place rhubarb in a buttered baking dish with orange juice and sugar. Bake in preheated 300° oven for 30 minutes or until tender. If necessary, sweeten with more sugar.

Carve pork into ¾-inch *(2cm)* slices and arrange on a bed of baked rhubarb.

FALL CRANBERRY GLAZE: Combine cranberry sauce, mint jelly and lemon juice in a saucepan and bring to a boil. After 1½ hours, remove roast from oven and spoon half the glaze over it. Return the pork to oven for another hour, basting it twice with remaining sauce. Slice the roast to serve.

Kathleen J. Schwartz, Avon, CT
Melinda M. Vance, West Hartford, CT

Nutritional Notes: The same roast carefully trimmed would result in a decrease of fat by 16g per serving and reduce the calories by about one third.

Wine Suggestion: California Pinot Noir, soft red; serve at room temperature.

Microwave Conversion Instructions: Note: With microwave preparation, certain portions of meat may begin to overcook. If microwave manufacturer permits, small "patches" of aluminum foil may be placed on meat to insure more even cooking. Prepare pork as for conventional recipe, eliminating salt; prepare vegetables as for conventional recipe. Combine chopped vegetables and place on bottom of a glass roasting dish. Pour wine around vegetables. Place pork, fatty side down, on top of vegetables; cook on Medium (50%) 30 minutes or until internal temperature reaches 145°, basting occasionally with pan juices. If using cranberry glaze, baste roast with glaze. Cover roast with aluminum foil and let stand 10 to 15 minutes, until internal temperature reaches 160°.

Cranberry Glaze: Prepare as for conventional recipe; place in glass bowl, cook on High 5 minutes or until mixture boils.

Rhubarb Sauce: Prepare as for conventional recipe; place in buttered baking dish, cover, cook on High until tender.

Chinese Roast Pork

Hanging racks of roast pork are a familiar sight in Chinese markets. This Cantonese specialty is considered a staple ingredient in Chinese cuisine. Sliced, it is an ever-popular appetizer. Cut into various forms it is used as the main ingredient in such familiar dishes as Pork Fried Rice.

YIELD: 6-8 Appetizer Servings or
   4 Entree Servings
TOTAL CALORIES: 1504
CALORIES PER ENTREE SERVING: 376
CARBOHYDRATES: 8g
PROTEIN: 23g
FAT: 28g
CHOLESTEROL: High
SODIUM: High
MARINATING: 2-8 Hours
ROASTING: 1 Hour

Mix together marinade ingredients. Marinate pork strips for 2 to 8 hours, turning once during this period. Do not marinate longer than 8 hours, as it makes meat tough. When ready to roast, remove meat from marinade; dribble honey over each piece.

Pierce each strip with a metal hook. (Make from a coat hanger cut and bent into hooks or use drapery hooks.) Hang each hook from rungs of oven rack placed on highest position. Place water to a depth of 1 inch *(2.5cm)* in a pan below to catch drippings and to keep pork moist. Roast in preheated 350° oven for 40 minutes; raise temperature to 450°; roast 15 minutes longer. Remove pork from oven; cool on rack resting on a plate for 5 minutes. Slice and serve.

If a natural sauce is desired, skim fat from pork drippings; boil down to ¾ cup *(180ml)*. Add 2 T. marinade; boil again 1 minute. Thicken if needed with 2 tsp. water chestnut powder dissolved in 1 T. sherry. Serve sauce on side or pour over pork slices.

Patricia Mitchell, Avon, CT

Variations, Advance Preparation, and Serving Suggestions:
May be made a day or two ahead and reheated, or frozen. Serve as part of Chinese meal or use pork in other dishes such as fried rice. If preparing pork ahead, reduce the final 15 minutes of roasting to 10 minutes. When ready to serve, bring pork to room temperature; place on rack in preheated 450° oven 5 to 7 minutes.

Wine Suggestion: California Gamay Beaujolais, light red; serve at room temperature.

MARINADE:
4 large slices fresh ginger root
2 scallions, sliced
2 T. *(30ml)* dark soy sauce
4 T. *(60ml)* hoisin sauce
2 T. *(30ml)* American chili sauce
¼ tsp. pepper
1 T. *(15ml)* plum sauce
1 T. *(15ml)* bean sauce
2 cloves garlic, crushed
¼ cup *(60ml)* dry sherry

2 lbs. *(900g)* boneless pork (lean part of Boston Butt is best), cut into strips 5 × 3 × 1½-inches *(12.5 × 7.5 × 4cm)* and each strip scored on all sides at 1½-inch *(4cm)* intervals in diamond crisscross pattern

GLAZE:
¼ cup *(85g)* honey

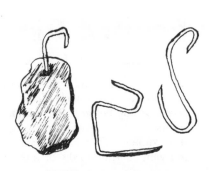

YIELD: 5-6 Servings
CALORIES PER SERVING: 600
CARBOHYDRATES: 6g
PROTEIN: 36g
FAT: 48g
CHOLESTEROL: High
SODIUM: High
PREPARING: 30 Minutes
COOKING: 30 Minutes
FREEZING: No

Pork Filet with Mustard Cream

There are few pork recipes that surpass this one!

20 pieces pork tenderloin (1 inch *(2.5cm)*
   thick each), about 2½ lbs. *(1.1kg)*
          or
10 pieces boneless pork loin, center cut,
   (1 inch thick each)
Salt
Freshly ground pepper
Flour for dredging pork
2 T. *(30g)* **butter**
1 T. oil
1½ cups *(200g)* **very finely sliced onions**
   (julienne threads)
2-3 cloves garlic, pressed
2-3 T. *(30-45ml)* **white wine vinegar**
1 bay leaf
1 cup *(240ml)* **brown stock**
1 cup *(240ml)* **heavy cream**
1 T. Dijon mustard
Beurre manie (1 T. butter and 1 T. flour,
   mixed to a paste), optional

GARNISH:

2 pints *(700g)* **braised Brussels sprouts**
Minced fresh parsley
2 T. well-drained capers

Season meat with salt and pepper. Dredge pork lightly in flour, shaking off excess.

Heat butter and oil in large skillet; brown filets on both sides without crowding them in pan; remove to side dish and reserve.

Discard all but 2 T. fat from pan; add onions and garlic; saute until nicely browned. Deglaze pan with vinegar; add bay leaf and brown stock and bring to a boil; reduce the contents of the pan by half.

Return filets to the pan; cover and cook over low heat for 20 to 30 minutes; remove meat to serving platter and keep warm.

Raise heat, add cream mixed with mustard; cook until sauce thickens. (This should be done quickly so that mustard does not become bitter.) Add beurre manie if you want sauce thicker. Taste and correct seasonings. Return meat to pan and heat through very gently.

Serve garnished with braised Brussels sprouts and/or minced parsley and capers.

Wine Suggestion: California Petite Sirah, peppery red; serve at room temperature.

Microwave Conversion Instructions: Prepare recipe conventionally until stock is reduced by half. Return filets to baking dish. Cook, covered, on Medium (50%) 8 to 9 minutes, stirring once. Remove meat from dish, but keep it covered. Add cream mixed with mustard to dish. Cook, uncovered, on Medium (50%) 5 to 7 minutes or until sauce thickens. Add beurre manie and cook 1 minute on High; stir. If sauce is not thick enough, add more beurre manie and cook an additional 1 minute on High. Correct seasonings. Return pork to dish and cook on Medium (50%) until heated through.

YIELD: 6-8 Servings
CALORIES PER SERVING: 616
CARBOHYDRATES: 20g
PROTEIN: 44g
FAT: 40g
CHOLESTEROL: High
PREPARING: 30 Minutes
ROASTING: 2 Hours

Fruited Pork Loin

1 4-5-lb. *(1800-2250g)* **boneless pork**
   loin with lengthwise pocket
1 cup *(180g)* **pitted prunes, chopped**
   coarsely
1 cup *(100g)* **apples, cut in 1-inch**
   (2.5cm) **cubes**
1 cup *(240ml)* **dry white wine**
¾ cup *(175ml)* **heavy cream**
1 T. currant jelly
¼ cup *(35g)* **currants**

Combine prunes and apples and insert into the pork pocket. Tie the loin with twine at 2-inch *(5cm)* intervals. (Up to this point, may be prepared day before). Place meat in roasting pan and brown in preheated 350° oven, turning occasionally. This should take approximately 20 minutes. Remove meat from pan. Degrease pan, add wine, stirring to dissolve brown particles that cling to bottom and sides of pan. Stir in cream, jelly, and currants. Return meat to pan and cover. Continue to roast for 1 to 1½ hours. Remove loin to heated platter and let stand 15 minutes before carving into ¾-inch

(2cm) slices. Serve sliced meat with some gravy from roasting pan.
Pass remaining sauce separately.

Donald G. Riley, Sr., Simsbury, CT

Variations, Advance Preparation, and Serving Instructions:
Serve with Wethersfield Onion Shortcake (page 38).

Wine Suggestion: Portuguese Lancers Rubio, semi-dry red; serve
slightly chilled.

Microwave Conversion Instructions: Stuff pork loin with apples
and prunes; coat with soy sauce. Place on meat rack in baking dish.
Cook 10 minutes on High; pour off fat and remove meat rack. Add
½ cup white wine, ⅓ cup cream, 1 T. currant jelly; cover tightly.
Cook on Medium (50%) 30 minutes; turn, continue to cook on
Medium (50%) 20 minutes more, or until meat registers 165° on
thermometer. Serve with pan juices.

Boudin Noir
aux Pommes

BLACK PUDDING SAUSAGE WITH APPLES

A hearty provincial French dish offered by RESTAURANT DU
VILLAGE, this savory sausage preparation is a stand-out.

YIELD: 4-6 Servings
TOTAL CALORIES: 3468
CALORIES PER SERVING: 578
CARBOHYDRATES: 8g
PROTEIN: 15g
FAT: 54g
CHOLESTEROL: High
SODIUM: High
PREPARING: 15 Minutes
COOKING: 30 Minutes
FREEZING: No

Saute blood sausage in butter and vegetable oil over medium heat
until skins begin to split. Remove sausage from pan; keep warm in
preheated 250° oven until ready to serve with sauce.

SAUCE: Remove excess fat from pan, deglaze with Calvados. Heat
for 1 minute, then add cream and sliced apples. Cook sauce over
moderately high heat until liquid is reduced by half. Season with salt,
pepper and nutmeg to taste. Just before serving, remove sauce from
heat and swirl in remaining 2 T. butter to finish sauce.

Place sausages on warm plates, cover with sauce and garnish with
watercress.

Wine Suggestion: French Valbon Rouge, dry red; serve at room
temperature.

4 blood sausages (8 oz. each) (900g),
   availabe in German and French
   butcher shops
2 T. (30g) unsalted sweet butter
2 T. (30ml) vegetable oil (not olive oil)

SAUCE:
¼ cup (2 oz.) (60ml) Calvados or cognac
¾ cup (175ml) heavy cream
2-3 hard green apples, peeled, cored and
   sliced (Granny Smith preferred)
Salt
Freshly ground pepper
Freshly grated nutmeg
2 T. (30g) unsalted sweet butter
Sprigs of fresh watercress

Sausage and Prune Stuffing for Crown Roast of Pork

An elegant dish for a gala occasion like New Year's Eve.

YIELD: 12 Servings
TOTAL CALORIES: 4788
CALORIES PER SERVING
  STUFFING: 399
CARBOHYDRATES: 19g
PROTEIN: 20g
FAT: 27g
CHOLESTEROL: High
SODIUM: High
PREPARING: 30 Minutes
COOKING: 20 Minutes

1½ lbs. *(675g)* **sausage meat**
1½ lbs. *(675g)* **ground pork** (may use trimmings from roast)
¾ cup *(75g)* **onion,** diced
¾ cup *(75g)* **celery,** diced
¾ cup *(120g)* **prunes,** cooked and snipped
1½ cups *(90g)* **soft bread crumbs**
3 T. *(40g)* **brown sugar**
¾ cup **parsley,** chopped
¾ tsp. **poultry seasoning**
¾ tsp. **cinnamon**
2 tsp. **salt**
Freshly ground pepper
2 **eggs,** beaten
⅔ cups *(120g)* **dried apricots,** snipped
Raw cranberries

Place sausage meat and pork in large skillet, breaking up with a fork, and cook until brown. Drain and remove meat from skillet, reserving 3 T. of fat.

In same skillet, saute onions and celery until golden brown.

Transfer meat, onions, and celery to a large mixing bowl. Add remaining ingredients except apricots and mix thoroughly. Check seasonings.

Fill center of crown roast with stuffing during the last hour of roasting. Remove roast to serving platter and garnish with chopped apricots and a string of cranberries winding between each rib.

Joyce Anne Vitelli, Manchester, CT

Variations, Advance Preparation, and Serving Suggestions:
For a family meal, halve or quarter stuffing to use as filling for acorn squash.

German Marinated Pork Slices

Perfect picnic fare!

YIELD: 6-8 Servings
CALORIES PER SERVING: 412
CARBOHYDRATES: 1g
PROTEIN: 30g
FAT: 32g
CHOLESTEROL: High
PREPARING: 10 Minutes
MARINATING: 4 Hours
ROASTING: 1 Hour
FREEZING: Yes

8-rib loin of pork, or any boneless pork roast
½ cup *(120ml)* **good quality olive oil**
3 T. *(45ml)* **wine vinegar**
1½ tsp. **salt**
3 T. *(40g)* **chopped sweet peppers** or pimiento
4 T. *(50g)* **fresh grated onion**
3 cloves **garlic**
½ tsp. **dried oregano**

Have loin boned and cut in half lengthwise into 2 long strips. Mix rest of ingredients together in shallow, non-metal dish large enough to fit pork. Marinate pork, covered, at least 4 hours, turning frequently.

Drain pork; reserve marinade. Place pork in shallow roasting pan. Roast, uncovered, in 425° oven 10 minutes. Pour marinade over meat, roast 50 minutes more, basting occasionally with marinade. Remove from oven. Let stand 10 minutes.

Serve pork hot or cold, sliced thinly.

Emily M-S. MacKenzie, Manchester, CT

Variations, Advance Preparation, and Serving Suggestions:
Can be made a day or even two in advance and refrigerated. Leftover pork works well in combination with fried rice or other vegetables.

Nutritional Notes: It is a common misconception that pork is high in sodium. Cured pork (such as ham, sausage or bacon) does contain a large amount of sodium. However, fresh pork, as in this recipe, contains a relatively low amount of sodium (similar to beef, lamb or poultry). Nutritional analysis uses 3½ oz. *(100g)* cooked pork loin per serving and assumes that half the marinade is consumed. Salt may be eliminated from the marinade if desired, and the result may provide gourmet variety to sodium-restricted diets.

Wine Suggestion: California Inglenook Merlot, soft red; serve at room temperature.

Pizza Rustica

ITALIAN EASTER PIE

An Easter specialty of Naples, where each family serves its own variety.

YIELD: 36 Hors d'Oeuvre Servings
or 8 Entree Servings
TOTAL CALORIES: 3736
CALORIES PER ENTREE SERVING: 467
CARBOHYDRATES: 26g
PROTEIN: 21g
FAT: 31g
CHOLESTEROL: High
SODIUM: High
PREPARING: 30 Minutes
COOKING: 50 Minutes

CRUST: With hands, blend ingredients, adding flour as needed until dough keeps together; divide into 2 pieces and roll between 2 pieces of floured waxed paper.

FILLING: In mixer bowl, blend at low speed all ingredients except prosciutto ham; when thoroughly mixed, add prosciutto.

Place one piece of rolled dough on bottom of 8 or 9-inch *(20 or 22.5cm)* pie plate; add filling; cover with top crust. Wet hand with cold water and brush crust; make 4 slashes in crust; bake in preheated 350° oven for 45 minutes or until crust is golden brown. To serve, cut in wedges for an entree or bite-size pieces for hors d'oeuvres.

Jacqueline A. Gfeller, West Hartford, CT

Variations, Advance Preparation, and Serving Suggestions: Diced ham, pepperoni, sausage, hard-boiled eggs, or a combination may be added or substituted to the filling.

Nutritional Notes: Cheeses made from skim milk may be used in this recipe to help control calories and fat/cholesterol.

Wine Suggestion: Italian Chianti, dry red; serve at room temperature.

Microwave Conversion Instructions: Crust: Use only 1½ eggs and 6 T. butter as top crust is omitted from microwave version. Let sit 15 to 30 minutes before rolling out. Put thinly rolled crust in a glass 9-inch pie plate and prick well with fork on side and bottom. (Dried beans or another glass dish can be set on crust while baking to prevent bubbles forming.) Cook on Medium High (70%) 7 minutes, turning ¼ turn halfway through and pushing down any bubbles that form. Filling: In a glass bowl combine ingredients. Cook on Medium (50%) 5 to 8 minutes or until thoroughly heated, stirring frequently. Pour into crust and cook on Medium (50%) 15 to 20 minutes or until knife inserted between center and edge comes out clean. Let stand 15 minutes before serving.

CRUST:
2 cups *(225g)* **flour**
¼ lb. *(115g)* **melted and cooled butter**
2 eggs

FILLING:
1 lb. *(450g)* **ricotta cheese**
½ cup *(65g)* **freshly grated Parmesan cheese**
3 eggs
1 tsp. salt
¼ lb. *(115g)* **diced mozzarella cheese**
Dash of pepper
¼ lb. *(115g)* **diced prosciutto ham**

YIELD: 3 Quarts Pate or
  32 ½-Inch Slices
TOTAL CALORIES: 8704
CALORIES PER SLICE: 272
CARBOHYDRATES: 3g
PROTEIN: 11g
FAT: 24g
CHOLESTEROL: High
SODIUM: High
PREPARING: 45 Minutes
BAKING: 3 Hours
CHILLING: 24 Hours
FREEZING: Not Preferred

1½ lbs. *(675g)* **fresh pork fat**
1 lb. *(450g)* **boneless veal**
1 lb. *(450g)* **boneless pork shoulder**
1 lb. *(450g)* **ham**
½ lb. *(225g)* **chicken or pork livers**
8 cloves **garlic**, peeled
¼ cup *(60ml)* **heavy cream**
3 **eggs**
½ cup *(120ml)* **cognac**
4 tsp. **salt**
2 tsp. **white pepper**
½ tsp. **allspice**
½ tsp. **cinnamon**
½ cup *(60g)* **flour**

Pâté de Campagne

Since its inception during the early Middle Ages, pate has been a wonderful and versatile creation. This rustic combination is one of the most popular versions.

Thinly slice ½ lb. of the pork fat. Finely grind half remaining pork fat with all the veal and pork shoulder. Line one 3-qt. *(3L)* mold or two 1½-qt. *(1.5L)* molds with the sliced pork fat, letting long ends hang over the edge of pan. Grind ham and remaining pork fat, using coarse blade of meat grinder, or dice meat finely with sharp knife. In blender or processor, puree livers with garlic, cream, eggs, and cognac. Gradually add to blender about ⅓ of veal-pork mixture. In mixing bowl, combine all ground and pureed meats and add remaining seasonings and flour; mix thoroughly. Fill prepared mold or molds with pate mixture. Fold overhanging strips of pork fat over top. Cover tightly with double thickness of aluminum foil. Place mold in pan of boiling water and bake in preheated 400° oven for 1½ hours (1½-qt. molds) or 3 hours (3-qt. mold). Remove foil and continue baking until top of pate is brown, about 20 minutes. After taking pate from oven, do not remove mold from larger baking pan; it will be needed to catch overflow of fat when pate is weighted. Place a brick or pan slightly smaller than pate mold right on top of baked pate. Weigh it down with heavy objects. Do not remove weights until pate is completely cool. This is necessary for easy slicing. Refrigerate, covered, until pate is served. Unmold to serving board.

Bernice Kuzma, West Hartford, CT

Variations, Advance Preparation, and Serving Suggestions:
Prepare several days ahead of serving. To keep pates at their best, seal well in fat in which they were cooked, then they will keep 2 to 3 weeks refrigerated. Freezing is not recommended as texture changes. Pate is traditionally served with French bread, pickled onions, cornichons and mustard. Veal and pork shoulder may be replaced by an equal amount of available game such as venison, hare or pheasant.

Wine Suggestion: French Macon Rouge, dry red; serve at room temperature.

Bigos

POLISH HUNTER'S STEW

Bigos is a stew of mixed meats and mushrooms, which was traditionally added to the freshly-caught game of the day. It is most characteristic of the fare served to the kings in hunting lodges of the Tatra Mountains in Poland. Large black kettles were placed over open fires to prepare Bigos. It was consumed with quantities of stout or Polish vodka. Continue the mountain tradition and serve Bigos after skiing!

YIELD: 8-10 Entree Servings
CALORIES PER SERVING: 357
CARBOHYDRATES: 7g
PROTEIN: 26g
FAT: 25g
CHOLESTEROL: High
SODIUM: High
PREPARING: 1 Hour
BAKING: 1 Hour
CHILLING: 24 Hours
SIMMERING: 1 Hour 20 Minutes

Day before serving: In Dutch oven render bacon. Add garlic and onion. Cook until wilted. Add sauerkraut, mushrooms, broth, tomato paste, salt, pepper, caraway seeds, bay leaf and wine. Bring to a boil. Simmer 15 to 20 minutes. Add meats. Cover. Simmer 45 to 60 minutes. Cover and refrigerate.

To serve: Reheat in preheated 375° oven 1 hour. Add wine before serving and simmer 15 minutes longer. Garnish with fresh dill sprigs.

Dr. Walter J. Wiechetek, Hartford, CT

Variations, Advance Preparation, and Serving Suggestions:
If a sour taste is desired, do not rinse the sauerkraut. The kielbasa, ham steak and pork meatballs can be replaced with leftover hot dogs, pork chops, or cubed beef or chicken. Typical accompaniments are Cucumber Salata (page 91), boiled potatoes and dark breads.

Wine Suggestion: Hungarian Egri Bikaver, fiery red; serve at room temperature.

Microwave Conversion Instructions: Note: Many people feel kielbasa casing toughens in microwave oven. Therefore, it is best simmered on regular range or substitute fully-cooked packaged kielbasa. To make ground pork meatballs, shape and place meat in circular pattern on paper plate. Cook on High 5 minutes. All other meat should be cubed in ½ to ¾-inch *(1.5cm)* chunks.

Cook bacon on High 1½ to 2 minutes or until crisp. In glass casserole, combine onion and garlic; cover, cook 4 minutes on High. Add sauerkraut, mushrooms, broth, tomato paste, salt, pepper, caraway seeds, bay leaf and wine; cook on High 5 minutes, stirring halfway through. Stir again, cook on Medium (50%) 10 minutes. Add meats, stir to blend, cover and cook 30 minutes on Medium (50%). Allow to cool before refrigerating, covered. Next day: Remove casserole from refrigerator approximately 1 hour before baking. Cook on Medium (50%) 30 minutes or until well-heated, covered.

2 slices *(50g)* bacon, cut into several pieces
1 tsp. minced garlic
1 cup *(200g)* minced onion
1 can (27 oz.) *(765g)* sauerkraut, rinsed and drained
1 cup *(80g)* sliced mushrooms
½ cup *(120ml)* chicken broth
3 T. *(50g)* tomato paste
Salt
Freshly ground pepper
½ tsp. caraway seeds
1 bay leaf
½ cup *(120ml)* white wine

MEATS:
1 lb. *(450g)* kielbasa (Polish sausage) simmered 30 minutes, cubed
1 lb. *(450g)* ham steak, cubed
½ lb. *(225g)* fresh ground pork, rolled into small meatballs and browned
Fresh dill

Medallions of Pork with Chestnuts

YIELD: 4 Servings
CALORIES PER SERVING: 544
CARBOHYDRATES: 23g
PROTEIN: 32g
FAT: 36g
SODIUM: High
CHOLESTEROL: High
PREPARING: 30 Minutes
COOKING: 30 Minutes
FREEZING: No

An Inn of longstanding excellence in Ridgefield, STONE-HENGE has come to be a landmark of quality in Connecticut. Its merit is attested to in this recipe for Medallions of Pork, flavorfully teamed with a sauce of bacon, onion and chestnuts.

14 oz. *(400g)* boneless loin of pork, trimmed of all fat
4 T. *(60g)* butter
Flour for dredging
Salt
Freshly ground pepper
Paprika
1½ oz. *(40g)* shallots, minced
1 T. chopped chives
1½ cups *(355ml)* dry white wine
3 cups *(710ml)* brown stock
3 oz. *(85g)* bacon (3-4 slices), cut cross-wise into ¼-inch *(0.6cm)* strips
1 small onion, finely diced
16-20 canned whole chestnuts

Slice pork about 1 inch *(2.5cm)* thick to obtain 12 pieces. Melt butter in two large skillets. Dredge meat lightly in flour combined with salt, pepper and paprika. Saute medallions quickly on each side until golden brown, being careful not to overcook and dry meat. Remove to serving platter, keep warm. Add shallots to one skillet with wine, stock and chives. Bring to a boil and reduce by ¼. Meanwhile in other skillet, saute bacon; add onion and chestnuts and cook until onion is golden. Add to reduced stock. Spoon some of sauce over meat and pass remaining sauce.

Variations, Advance Preparation, and Serving Suggestions:
Pork medallions can also be served with a bit of Bearnaise Sauce (page 191) spooned over the brown sauce.

Wine Suggestion: California Los Carneros Pinot Noir, full red; serve at room temperature.

YIELD: 8 Entree Servings or 16 Triangles
TOTAL CALORIES: 4616
CALORIES PER ENTREE SERVING: 577
CARBOHYDRATES: 11.5g
PROTEIN: 18g
FAT: 51g
CHOLESTEROL: High
SODIUM: High
PREPARING: 1½ Hours
BAKING: 25 Minutes
FREEZING: Yes

Mushroom and Sausage Triangles

2 lbs. *(900g)* Italian sausage, hot or sweet
2 T. *(30ml)* oil
2 T. *(30g)* butter
2 bunches scallions, chopped
1 lb. *(450g)* fresh mushrooms, sliced
8-10 oz. *(225-285g)* cream cheese
2 oz. *(60ml)* Sambuca liqueur
¼ cup *(30g)* freshly grated Asiago or Parmesan cheese
¼ tsp. freshly grated nutmeg
Salt
Freshly ground pepper
Butter, melted
1 pkg. (1 lb.) *(450g)* phyllo (entire amount will not be used)
Tomato wedges
Pitted ripe olives

Cook sausage in oil, drain and set aside. Saute scallions in butter; add mushrooms. Cook slightly; add sausage. Add cream cheese. Remove from heat. Stir until mixture is smooth. Add cheese, Sambuca, nutmeg, salt, pepper. Stir until completely blended. Carefully unroll phyllo leaves and cut lengthwise into 3 equal parts. Working with 3 leaves at a time, spread each layer with melted butter, stacking as you work. Place 3 or 4 T. of filling on bottom of stacked strips. Fold over and continue in flag fashion to make triangle. Place on baking sheet and brush with melted butter. Continue until filling completed. Bake in preheated 350° oven, 25 to 30 minutes or until golden brown. Garnish with tomato wedges and olives.

Donna F. Peacock, Winsted, CT

Variations, Advance Preparation, and Serving Suggestions:
To prepare hors d'oeuvre-size triangles, cut phyllo sheets into 4 strips lengthwise. Place 1 T. filling on each and fold. One-half cup *(60g)* walnut pieces can be added to filling to enhance texture.

After baking and cooling, triangles may be frozen. To serve, take directly from freezer; place on baking sheet in 350° oven until heated through.

Wine Suggestion: California Navalle Rose, semi-dry rose, serve chilled.

Microwave Conversion Instructions: In a 2-qt. *(2L)* casserole saute scallions in 1 T. butter, uncovered, on High 2 minutes. Remove with slotted spoon and set aside. Add mushrooms and 1 T. butter, cook on Medium (50%), covered, 5 minutes, until just softened, stirring once. Remove mushrooms, drain, pour off liquid. Crumble sausage into casserole. Cook on High, uncovered, 5 to 6 minutes, stirring several times and using a fork to keep sausage crumbly. When sausage is no longer pink, pour off liquid, add cream cheese, scallions, and mushrooms, stir until smooth. Add remaining ingredients and follow above directions for completion. Bake in conventional oven, since phyllo dough needs a hot, dry environment for crisping.

Shenendoah Valley Stuffed Ham

A country ham is processed by traditional, slow, old-fashioned methods. The curing, smoking and aging process cannot be artificially hastened. Brine-cured ham is cured in a salt solution and then smoked. New England-style ham has maple syrup or molasses added to brine.

YIELD: 20-35 Servings
CALORIES PER SERVING: 370
CARBOHYDRATES: 28g
PROTEIN: 24g
FAT: 18g
CHOLESTEROL: High
SODIUM: High
PREPARING: 30 Minutes
COOKING: 4-5 Hours

Blend together cornbread, nuts, fruits, and spices; moisten with honey and bourbon. Stuff boned cavity of ham; close opening with skewers and tie ham securely. Place, skin and fat side down in roasting pan. Pour in enough wine or cider to immerse about ⅓ of ham.

Cover ham with foil, making it almost airtight. Bake in preheated 350° oven, allowing 25 minutes per pound. Remove from oven; cut off heavy rind, leaving about ⅜-inch *(1cm)* fat. Score fat; rub with bread crumbs and brown sugar. Return ham to preheated 400° oven; baste occasionally with sherry until coating mixture forms a crust. Remove from oven; let rest 20 to 30 minutes before carving.

Victoria Trainer, Bloomfield, CT

Nutritional Notes: Nutritional analysis uses approximately 3¼ oz. *(90g) lean* ham per serving.

Wine Suggestion: California Beaulieu Muscat Blanc, semi-sweet white; serve chilled.

1 10-16-lb. *(4.5-7.25kg)* brine-cured or New England ham, boned but with shank bone left in
1½ cups *(140g)* cornbread crumbs
1 cup *(100g)* finely chopped pecans
1 cup *(225g)* finely chopped mixed candied fruits
1 cup *(170g)* sultana raisins
½ cup *(70g)* currants
½ tsp. mace
½ tsp. cinnamon
½ tsp. cloves
½ cup *(170g)* honey
1 cup *(240ml)* bourbon
White wine or cider
1 cup *(120g)* bread crumbs
1½ cups *(300g)* dark brown sugar
1 cup *(240ml)* sherry

Chicken alla Marsala

YIELD: 4 Servings
CALORIES PER ½ BREAST: 299
CARBOHYDRATES: 12g
PROTEIN: 29g
FAT: 15g
PREPARING: 20 Minutes
BAKING: 30 Minutes
FREEZING: Yes

2 whole large chicken breasts, boned,
   split (4 pieces), but skin not removed
Flour for coating chicken
Salt
Freshly ground pepper to taste
4 T. *(60g)* butter, divided
1 clove garlic, crushed
½ lb. *(225g)* mushrooms, sliced
½ cup *(120ml)* good quality Marsala
   wine

Marsala, created by the English brothers Woodhouse, is Sicily's famous wine. It has been a well-known name in England since the 18th century. Like sherry and port, Marsala is a fortified wine. As a dessert wine, it has the virtue that it does not deteriorate after the bottle is opened.

Coat chicken breasts with flour, salt and pepper.

Melt 3 T. butter in skillet; saute garlic until golden brown. Add chicken and brown well on both sides. Transfer to heavy, shallow baking pan.

Add 1 T. butter to skillet, add mushrooms. Cook, stirring, 2 to 3 minutes. Add Marsala, simmer 2 minutes. Pour over chicken in baking pan. Bake, covered, in preheated 350° oven 20 minutes, or until chicken is done, but still moist.

Jacqueline A. Gfeller, West Hartford, CT

Variations, Advance Preparation, and Serving Suggestions:
1 lb. *(450g)* veal scaloppine, very thinly sliced and pounded flat, may be substituted for chicken.

May be prepared up to a day ahead and refrigerated. Bring to room temperature, reheat, covered, in 325° oven, just until hot. Serve with Baked Rice with Tomatoes and Cheese (page 350) and Homemade Noodles (page 192) or Risi Bisi, an ultra thick soup of rice and peas which must be eaten with a fork.

Nutritional Notes: Adaptation to low sodium diet is possible with use of unsalted butter and elimination of salt. Recipe is well suited to low cholesterol diet especially if unsalted, polyunsaturated margarine is used. If made ahead and refrigerated, the solidified fat layer can be removed prior to reheating, to reduce calories and fat/cholesterol.

Wine Suggestion: California Chenin Blanc, full white; serve chilled.

Microwave Conversion Instructions: Preheat browning dish to maximum absorption. When heated, quickly place butter in center, coating dish. Place coated chicken breasts on hot surface. Cook on High 2 minutes, until chicken is just brown on bottom. Use spatula to turn breasts over. Cook 1 minute. Remove chicken and set aside. Add butter and garlic to browning dish. Cook on High 1 minute. Stir in mushrooms; cook on High 2 minutes. Stir in Marsala; cook 2 minutes; stir again. Replace chicken in center of dish, spooning mushroom sauce over top. Cook on High 2 to 3 minutes, until heated through. If thicker sauce is desired, dissolve 1 T. cornstarch in 3 T. Marsala. Stir into sauce before adding chicken. Cook on High 3 minutes or until cornstarch thickens sauce.

Chicken Breasts with Wild Mushrooms

YIELD: 6 Servings
CALORIES PER ½ BREAST: 390
CARBOHYDRATES: 6g
PROTEIN: 33g
FAT: 26g
SODIUM: High
PREPARING: 1½ Hours
MARINATING: Cepes 3 Hours
SIMMERING: Stock 4-5 Hours
FREEZING: No

Cepe is the French word for boletus, a kind of mushroom found in woods under oak, chestnut, and beech trees. Fresh, it is glossy and yellowish to warm brown, and the gills are honeycombed. It is native to Central and Northern Europe.

Season chicken with salt and pepper. Heat oil in 12-inch *(30cm)* skillet; quickly brown chicken on skin side. Sprinkle with shallots, lemon juice and vermouth. Add ¼ cup Poultry Stock Sauce Base. Cover and cook over low heat 20 to 25 minutes, turning chicken over once during cooking.

Meanwhile, drain cepes, reserving liquid. Rinse cepes well to rid them of sand. In smaller skillet, saute cepes and fresh mushrooms in olive oil 5 minutes, tossing. Add reserved cepe soaking liquid; quickly reduce to glaze. Toss with garlic, parsley, salt and pepper; set aside.

In same skillet, slowly soften cubes of prosciutto in its own fat, covered, 2 to 3 minutes.

Remove chicken from large skillet to heated serving platter and keep warm. Degrease skillet. Add remaining Poultry Stock Sauce Base and boil down by ⅓. Swirl in butter to thicken if necessary. Adjust seasoning with salt and pepper. Swirl in cognac.

Reheat cepes and mushrooms with pine nuts, tossing to combine. Strain sauce over chicken. Garnish chicken with prosciutto and mushroom mixture.

Maureen Moghtader, West Hartford, CT

Variations, Advance Preparation, and Serving Suggestions:
Serve with buttered Homemade Noodles (page 192) and a fresh green vegetable. Accompany with fresh fruit salad with Honey Dressing (page 137).

Wine Suggestion: French Puligny-Montrachet White Burgundy, full white; serve chilled.

Microwave Conversion Instructions: Note: Eliminate 3 T. vegetable oil as chicken will not be browned first. Place seasoned chicken in ring in large oval baking dish. Combine shallots, lemon juice, wine and ¼ cup Poultry Stock Sauce Base. Pour over chicken. Cook on High, covered with waxed paper, 18 to 22 minutes, or just until done. Turn chicken over once half way through cooking.

Drain cepes, reserving liquid. In shallow bowl, saute cepes and fresh mushrooms in olive oil 3 minutes on Medium (50%), stirring once. Add reserved cepe soaking liquid, cook uncovered on High 3 to 4 minutes, or until reduced to glaze. Toss with garlic, parsley, salt and pepper; set aside. In same bowl soften cubes of prosciutto in its own fat, covered with a paper towel, 2 to 3 minutes on High. Remove chicken from baking dish and degrease. Add remaining Poultry Stock Sauce Base and cook uncovered on High until it is boiling; continue cooking on High until it is reduced by a third. Swirl in butter to thicken if necessary. Adjust seasoning with salt and pepper. Swirl in cognac. Reheat cepes and mushrooms with pine nuts on High for 2 to 3 minutes, toss to combine. Strain sauce over chicken. Garnish chicken as directed above.

3 whole large chicken breasts, split (6 pieces)
Salt
Freshly ground pepper
3 T. *(45ml)* vegetable oil
2 T. *(20g)* chopped shallots
2 T. *(30ml)* fresh lemon juice
2 T. *(30ml)* vermouth or dry white wine
1 cup *(240ml)* Poultry Stock Sauce Base (page 198)
2 oz. *(60g)* dried cepes or porcini mushrooms soaked in warm water 2-3 hours
½ lb. *(225g)* fresh mushrooms, quartered
2 T. *(30ml)* olive oil
1 clove garlic, chopped
2 T. chopped parsley
¼ lb. *(115g)* prosciutto ham, fat and all, cubed
4 T. *(60g)* unsalted sweet butter (optional)
1 T. cognac
⅓ cup *(60g)* pine nuts, lightly toasted

Braised Chicken with Prosciutto

YIELD: 4 Servings
CALORIES PER SERVING: 547
CARBOHYDRATES: 12g
PROTEIN: 37g
FAT: 39g
SODIUM: High
PREPARING: 35 Minutes
COOKING: 1 Hour
FREEZING: No

To braise is to cook in a covered container, usually in the oven, with very little liquid. In this recipe, the method insures a moist chicken. Fennel and Pernod impart a unique favor.

CHICKEN:

1 whole chicken, 3½ lbs. *(1575g)*
4 oz. *(115g)* prosciutto ham
1 tsp. dried basil, divided
1 tsp. dried thyme, divided
1 tsp. dried rosemary, divided
3 cloves garlic, crushed, divided
Salt
Freshly ground pepper to taste
2 T. *(30ml)* olive oil
2 T. *(30g)* unsalted sweet butter
1 medium onion, coarsely chopped
1 medium fennel bulb, coarsely chopped
1 stalk celery, coarsely chopped
1 cup *(240ml)* dry white wine
1 can (16 oz.) *(450g)* Italian plum tomatoes
½ cup *(120ml)* chicken stock
1 bay leaf
2 T. *(30g)* unsalted sweet butter, softened

SAUCE:

Reserved pan juices
2 tsp. cornstarch
2 T. *(30ml)* Pernod
3 T. *(45g)* unsalted sweet butter, cut in bits

CHICKEN: Loosen chicken skin, except that on wings, by slipping fingers between the skin and flesh, being careful not to pierce the skin. Begin at neck and work down to and including legs. Slip 2 oz. prosciutto, thinly sliced, carefully under the skin; smooth the skin to expel any bubbles. Sprinkle chicken with ½ tsp. each basil, thyme and rosemary, 1 clove garlic, salt and pepper to taste.

Truss the chicken. Brown in ovenproof, stainless steel or enameled casserole in olive oil over moderately high heat. Transfer to plate. Pour off fat from casserole. Add butter, onion, fennel and celery. Cook 5 minutes over moderate heat. Add wine and boil to reduce liquid by half.

In food processor or blender, puree tomatoes and their juice; add to casserole with 2 oz. prosciutto, chopped coarsely, chicken stock, ½ tsp. each basil, thyme, rosemary, 2 cloves garlic and bay leaf. Bring liquid to boil, add chicken, breast side up; baste with liquid. Braise chicken, covered, in preheated 400° oven, basting 2 to 3 times, for 35 minutes, or until juices run clear when thigh is pricked with skewer.

Transfer chicken to ovenproof platter, reserving pan juices. Rub chicken with softened butter. Place under preheated broiler, about 8 inches from heat, rotating until lightly colored and crisp-skinned. Remove trussing string, transfer chicken to a serving platter and keep warm.

SAUCE: Strain reserved pan juices into saucepan. Boil over high heat to reduce by half. Whisk in cornstarch dissolved in Pernod. Add butter, whisking. Pour sauce over chicken.

Kathleen J. Schwartz, Avon, CT

Variations, Advance Preparation, and Serving Suggestions:
This dish can be prepared with chicken breasts and/or legs if desired. Be careful to keep the skin securely attached. The chicken can be prepared and braised several hours ahead. Complete the dish by broiling, and prepare the sauce just before serving.

Nutritional Notes: Nutritional analysis uses 4½ oz. *(125g)* cooked chicken meat per serving.

Wine Suggestion: California Grenache Rose, dry rose; serve chilled.

Microwave Conversion Instructions: Prepare chicken as directed with prosciutto placed under skin. Brush entire chicken with olive oil; sprinkle with dried basil, thyme, rosemary, 1 clove garlic, salt and pepper, adding ½ tsp. paprika sprinkled over entire chicken.

Place butter, onion, fennel and celery in center of round or oval casserole. Place chicken, breast side down, on top of vegetables. Cook, covered with waxed paper, on High 15 minutes. Remove chicken and set aside. Add wine and continue to cook, uncovered, on High 5 minutes. In food processor or blender, puree tomatoes and their juices. Add to casserole with remaining prosciutto (chopped coarsely), ¼ cup chicken stock, ½ tsp. each basil, thyme and rosemary, 2 cloves garlic and bay leaf. Bring liquid to boil on High. Add chicken, breast side up, sprinkling with additional paprika for color, if necessary, after basting with juices. Cook, covered with waxed paper on High 10 to 15 minutes, basting several times. If using temperature probe, cook to internal temperature of 175° to 180°. Transfer chicken to ovenproof platter; follow directions for broiling. *Sauce:* Strain reserved pan juices into large bowl or measuring cup. Cook on High, uncovered, 5 minutes. Dissolve 1 T. cornstarch in 2 T. Pernod. Stir into hot liquid. Continue cooking on High until sauce is thickened, 3 to 4 minutes.

Chicken Breasts Harpin

This dish adapts well to large crowds and buffets.

YIELD: 4-6 Servings
CALORIES PER ½ BREAST: 575
CARBOHYDRATES: 23g
PROTEIN: 33g
FAT: 39g
CHOLESTEROL: High
SODIUM: High
PREPARING: 45 Minutes
BAKING: 45 Minutes
CHILLING: 12-24 Hours

Day before: Simmer chicken in water to cover, covered, 30 minutes. Drain; reserve 3 cups broth. Bone chicken; arrange in 12 × 8 × 2-inch *(30 × 20 × 5cm)* baking dish; top with sliced olives. In skillet, heat ¼ cup butter; saute mushrooms 5 minutes. Remove, stir in flour, salt, pepper and mace; gradually stir in broth and cream. Cook, stirring until thickened. Saute toast triangles in ¼ cup butter. Pour sauce over chicken; top with toast triangles, sprinkle with paprika. Cover and refrigerate.

To serve following day: Bring chicken to room temperature. Bake uncovered in preheated 325° oven 45 minutes.

Carol C. Dowd, Avon, CT

Wine Suggestion: California Beaufort Pinot Chardonnay, full white; serve chilled.

Microwave Conversion Instructions: Using round or oval dish, place chicken breasts, skin side up in ring with ends touching. Pour 2 cups water over chicken. Cook, covered, on High 20 minutes, or just until chicken is tender. Allow chicken to cool slightly in broth. Drain, reserving broth. Bone chicken. Place in large baking dish and top with sliced olives. In bowl, saute mushrooms and butter 3 minutes on Medium (50%), stirring once or twice. Remove mushrooms. Stir in flour, salt, pepper and mace; gradually stir in broth and cream. Stir until flour is completely dissolved. Cook, uncovered, on High until thickened, stirring several times. Add mushrooms to sauce. Prepare toast triangles as directed. Pour sauce over chicken. Top with toast and sprinkle with paprika. Refrigerate when cool. To serve following day: Bring chicken to room temperature; cook on Medium (50%) 7 to 10 minutes, until heated to serving temperature.

3 whole large chicken breasts
1 can (4½ to 9 oz.) *(125-250g)* pitted ripe olives
½ cup *(115g)* butter
¾ lb. *(340g)* mushrooms, sliced
6 T. *(40g)* flour
1½ tsp. salt
¼ tsp. freshly ground pepper
Pinch mace
3 cups *(710ml)* reserved chicken broth
1 cup *(240ml)* heavy cream
5 thin bread slices, toasted, each cut into 4 triangles
Paprika

Summer Garden Stuffed Chicken

YIELD: 4-5 Servings
TOTAL CALORIES PER SERVING
 WITH TOMATO STUFFING: 578
CARBOHYDRATES: 25g
PROTEIN: 34g
FAT: 38g
CHOLESTEROL: High
SODIUM: High
PREPARING: 1½ Hours
BAKING: 1½ Hours
FREEZING: No

Something out of the ordinary — stuffing under the skin! This unorthodox method is given with a chicken and your choice of stuffing, but the technique can be applied to game hen and capon as well. The advantages include protecting the breast meat from drying out, elegant final presentation and ease of carving and serving.

1 3½-5-lb. *(1600-2250g)* chicken
1 tsp. mixed herbs (oregano, thyme, basil)
3 T. *(45ml)* olive oil

HERB TOMATO SAUSAGE STUFFING:

1 cup *(285g)* mild sausage meat
1 cup *(250g)* chopped raw bacon
2 cloves garlic, minced
3 small onions, chopped
Salt, pepper, paprika to taste
⅓ tsp. mace
1 tsp. sage
½ tsp. thyme
1-1½ tsp. tarragon (use whatever herb you like and want to predominate)
1-2 cups *(120-240g)* breadcrumbs (enough to make filling fit bird)
1 cup *(240ml)* bouillon
12 black pitted olives, chopped
2 large tomatoes, skinned, seeded, and sliced

SPINACH SORREL STUFFING:

8 oz. *(225g)* fresh spinach, washed and stems removed
4 T. *(60g)* butter
1 onion, minced
4 oz. *(115g)* fresh sorrel, shredded
8 oz. *(225g)* ricotta cheese
½ cup *(120ml)* heavy cream
½ cup *(65g)* freshly grated imported Parmesan cheese
2 egg yolks
Salt
Freshly ground pepper
Freshly grated nutmeg to taste

ZUCCHINI STUFFING:

1 lb. *(450g)* zucchini, washed
2 T. *(30ml)* olive oil
8 T. *(115g)* butter
1 onion, chopped
½ cup *(130g)* ricotta
½ cup *(65g)* freshly grated imported Parmesan cheese
1 egg
1 tsp. oregano

Remove back bone of chicken using kitchen or poultry shears, cutting from neck down on either side of back bone. Open out chicken, skin side up, so that it resembles a butterfly with spread wings. Press down on the breast bone (you will hear it crack) to flatten it as much as possible. Loosen skin on breast, beginning at neck. Loosen skin on legs being careful not to puncture it. Loosen membrane attached to the flesh. Loosen all skin in this manner from the neck across the breast and down to leg. Then stuff this area between skin and meat with stuffing of your choice. Truss neck and tail of chicken so that stuffing will not ooze out. Combine mixed herbs and olive oil; rub skin with this mixture. Place chicken in a shallow baking dish. Bake at 425° for 10 minutes; lower temperature to 350° for 1 to 1½ hours, depending on size of chicken (about 20 minutes per lb.). Baste chicken every 10 minutes. If breast browns too fast cover it loosely with foil.

HERB TOMATO SAUSAGE STUFFING: Saute sausage, bacon, garlic and onions until thoroughly cooked; drain off excess fat. Season with salt and pepper, and paprika. Add herbs. Saute a few minutes longer. Add olives, tomatoes, and breadcrumbs. Add bouillon; simmer a few minutes. Allow mixture to cool; stuff chicken.

SPINACH SORREL STUFFING: Blanch spinach for 2 minutes in boiling salted water. Drain spinach and squeeze dry in your hand or corner of kitchen towel; chop fine. Melt half the butter; cook onion until soft and yellow; add remaining butter and sorrel; wilt to a puree over medium flame, stirring constantly for 2 minutes or so. Add spinach and continue stirring until liquids evaporate. Cream ricotta with heavy cream; blend in spinach-sorrel mixture until smooth; add Parmesan, yolks, salt and pepper, and nutmeg. Chill to facilitate stuffing.

ZUCCHINI STUFFING: Grate zucchini with medium blade of grater or food processor. Sprinkle salt on zucchini and let stand 1 hour. Squeeze zucchini to extract all liquid. Wash under cold water to remove salt. Press zucchini again to remove all liquid. Heat olive oil and saute zucchini until dry; set aside to cool. Melt 2 T. butter and saute onion until yellow gold. Cream remaining 6 T. butter; add zucchini, onion, ricotta, Parmesan, egg and oregano to make a mixture as smooth as possible. Taste for seasonings and correct. Chill to facilitate stuffing.

Melinda M. Vance, West Hartford, CT

Variations, Advance Preparation, and Serving Suggestions:
Individual whole skinned and boned chicken breasts may be used instead of whole chicken. Stuff cavity of breast with selected filling;

secure with toothpicks and/or wrap with slice of bacon. Brown breasts in butter until golden. Remove to baking dish. Pour 1 cup (240ml) stock over chicken. Cover tightly with foil; bake at 350° 1¼ hours.

Zucchini Stuffing and Spinach Sorrel Stuffing also make excellent fillings for omelettes, crepes, ravioli, and quiches. For a quiche: Use 2 cups stuffing. Eliminate eggs and cream when making stuffing. Sprinkle filling over pre-baked crust. Beat 4 eggs with 1½ cups (355ml) heavy cream; pour over filling. Bake at 350° for 30 to 35 minutes or until set and golden.

Nutritional Notes: The nutritional information was calculated on basis of using Herb Tomato Sausage Stuffing. This stuffing is very high in sodium and cholesterol due to inclusion of sausage, bacon, olives and bouillon. The Spinach Sorrel and Zucchini Stuffings, however, are lower in sodium although still moderately high in cholesterol.

Wine Suggestion: California Gamay Rose, dry rose; serve chilled.

Southern Fried Chicken

YIELD: 4 Servings
TOTAL CALORIES: 1776
CALORIES PER SERVING: 444
CARBOHYDRATES: 16g
PROTEIN: 32g
FAT: 28g
SODIUM: High
PREPARING: 10 Minutes
SOAKING: 2 Hours Minimum
FRYING: 25-30 Minutes

Soak chicken in water mixed with salt in a large bowl for 2 hours or longer.

COATING MIX: Combine garlic salt, salt, flour, and pepper in plastic or paper bag. Remove chicken from water, partially pat dry with paper towel. Add chicken to bag, a few pieces at a time; shake to coat well. As chicken is coated, place on piece of waxed paper.

Put vegetable shortening (enough to fill skillet half full) in large deep skillet or Dutch oven electric fry pan. Heat to 365° on a deep fat thermometer. Add chicken, skin side down. (Shortening must be deep enough to cover chicken). When underside of chicken begins to brown, turn heat down and *cover* skillet. Turn chicken when completely brown on underside, after about 15 minutes. Continue cooking, *uncovered*, until second side is brown. Drain thoroughly on paper toweling before serving. Keep warm in 250° oven while making gravy.

CREAM GRAVY: Pour off all shortening, leaving brown bits; return 3 T. melted shortening to skillet. Add flour and cook, stirring and scraping brown bits from bottom, until lightly browned. Remove from heat; gradually whisk in 1 cup milk. Return to heat; cook until thickened. If too thick, add more milk. Season with salt and pepper.

Elizabeth Propp, via Joyce Brown, Columbia, SC

Nutritional Notes: Nutritional analysis assumes that 2 T. melted shortening is absorbed during frying and uses 4 oz. (115g) cooked chicken meat per serving.

Wine Suggestion: California Inglenook Vintage Burgundy, dry red; serve at room temperature.

1 3-3½-lb. (1350-1575g) broiler fryer chicken, cut up
1 qt. (950ml) cold water
1 T. salt

COATING MIX:
Garlic salt
1 cup (115g) self-rising flour
1½ tsp. salt
1½ tsp. freshly ground pepper
1 qt. (770g) vegetable shortening (Crisco preferred)

CREAM GRAVY:
3 T. melted shortening from pan
2 T. (15g) all-purpose flour
1-1½ cups (240-355ml) milk
Salt
Freshly ground pepper

YIELD: 2 Servings
CALORIES PER SERVING: 512
CARBOHYDRATES: 3g
PROTEIN: 35g
FAT: 40g
CHOLESTEROL: High
SODIUM: High
PREPARING: 10 Minutes
COOKING: 20 Minutes

2 links *(150g)* hot Italian sausage, skin
   removed and broken into pieces
1 whole large chicken breast, boned and
   sliced into several pieces
½ cup *(120ml)* chicken stock
1 green pepper, sliced
¼ cup *(60ml)* heavy cream

Chicken Armando

If hot Italian sausages are too spicy for your palate, use sweet
Italian sausages instead.

Brown sausage and chicken pieces until done. Add chicken stock
and green peppers; simmer until peppers are done, but still crisp.
Add heavy cream and heat until hot. Serve immediately with a rice
pilaf.

Donna F. Peacock, Winsted, CT

Variations, Advance Preparation, and Serving Suggestions:
This may be used as a crepe filling. This dish may be done ahead,
brought to room temperature and reheated in a 450° oven 5 to 10
minutes. It adapts well to large crowds and for buffets; the amount of
ingredients can easily be increased.

Wine Suggestion: Italian Bardolino, zesty red; serve at room
temperature.

YIELD: 8-12 Servings
CALORIES PER ½ BREAST: 264
CARBOHYDRATES: 8g
PROTEIN: 31g
FAT: 12g
SODIUM: High
PREPARING: 45 Minutes
COOKING: 50 Minutes
FREEZING: Yes

6 whole large chicken breasts, boned,
   skinned and split (12 pieces)
1 cup *(115g)* shredded Cheddar cheese,
   about 4 oz.
½ cup *(60g)* walnuts, coarsely chopped
½ cup *(30g)* fresh breadcrumbs
2 T. *(30g)* fresh onions, minced
¼ tsp. salt
⅛ tsp. freshly ground black pepper
½ cup *(60g)* flour
3 T. *(45g)* butter
1 cup *(240ml)* chicken broth
½ cup *(120ml)* white wine
2 T. fresh parsley, chopped

Parsley sprigs to garnish

Walnut Stuffed Chicken Breasts

A most pleasing combination of walnuts, cheese and chicken!

Flatten each chicken breast half to ¼-inch *(6mm)* thickness between
sheets of waxed paper with a mallet or rolling pin. In small bowl,
combine cheese, walnuts, crumbs, onions, salt and pepper. Spoon
1½ T. filling into center of each breast; spread filling, leaving ½-inch
(1.2cm) edge all around. From narrow end, roll each breast jelly-roll
fashion; fasten with a toothpick. Roll chicken in flour, let stand
10 minutes.

Melt butter in skillet. Add chicken; saute in butter until lightly
browned on all sides. Pour in broth, wine; cover. Cook over low
heat 20 minutes. (May be prepared 24 hours in advance. Refrigerate. Return to room temperature and reheat, covered.

Remove chicken to warm plate, remove toothpicks. Keep chicken
warm. Increase heat to high. Stir sauce until slightly thickened. Add
chopped parsley, pour over chicken. Garnish with parsley sprigs.

Lorraine Neff, Farmington, CT

Wine Suggestion: French Chateau La Garde Rouge, dry red;
serve at room temperature.

Microwave Conversion Instructions: Prepare and stuff chicken
as directed. Add 1 tsp. paprika to flour. Roll chicken in flour; let
stand 10 minutes. Melt butter in round or oval baking dish; add
chicken and saute on High, uncovered, 2 to 3 minutes, until lightly
browned on all sides. Pour in heated broth and wine; cook, covered
with waxed paper, on High 7 to 10 minutes, until just cooked
through.

Remove chicken to warm plate. Cook sauce, uncovered, on High
until slightly thickened, stirring once. Add chopped parsley and pour
over chicken.

Jyoti's Chicken Curry

Most people have a misconception about curry. By definition, curry is any dish with richly spiced sauce, carefully cooked to blend all spices together with flavor of meat, fish or vegetables.

YIELD: 3-4 Servings
TOTAL CALORIES: 1864
CALORIES PER SERVING: 466
CARBOHYDRATES: 13g
PROTEIN: 27g
FAT: 34g
SODIUM: High
PREPARING: 30 Minutes
COOKING: 30-40 Minutes
FREEZING: Yes

Mix together onion, garlic, ginger root, coconut and ¼ cup water. Heat oil in a large pan; add mixture. Cook over moderate heat 8 minutes, stirring often. Add 1 cup water and all other ingredients except chicken; simmer over low heat 10 minutes. Add chicken; cover and simmer, stirring occasionally, 30 minutes, or until chicken is tender. Serve with Tamarind Chutney.

Maryann Reuben, West Hartford, CT

Variations, Advance Preparation, and Serving Suggestions: Serve as part of authentic Indian menu or with rice, fresh green vegetable and a fresh fruit salad. This dish may be prepared, cooled completely and frozen. Recipe doubles or triples easily.

Nutritional Notes: Salt can be omitted from this dish because of the large amount of other spices and seasonings. Prepared in this manner, it is appropriate for moderate sodium restriction. Nutritional analysis uses 4¾ oz. *(135g)* cooked chicken meat per serving.

Wine Suggestion: California Navalle Burgundy, soft red; serve at room temperature.

Microwave Conversion Instructions: Mix together onion, garlic, ginger root, coconut, ¼ cup water and oil in 3-qt. *(3L)* casserole. Cook on High 7 to 8 minutes, stirring once. Add remaining water and all other ingredients except chicken. Cook on High 5 minutes. Add chicken. Cook, covered, on High 25 minutes or until chicken is tender, stirring occasionally.

2 medium onions, chopped
6 cloves garlic, peeled and crushed
1½ inch *(4cm)* piece fresh ginger root, peeled
3 T. *(40g)* chopped fresh coconut or packaged coconut
1¼ cups *(300ml)* water
½ cup *(120ml)* vegetable oil
2 tsp. salt
1 tsp. ground cumin
1 tsp. ground turmeric
1 tsp. ground coriander
½ tsp. ground hot red pepper, or to taste
1 16 oz. *(450g)* can tomatoes
½ tsp. ground cinnamon
½ tsp. ground cloves
2 T. *(30g)* tomato paste
1 3½-lb. *(1.5kg)* chicken, cut into parts and skin removed
Tamarind Chutney (page 374)

YIELD: 6 Servings
TOTAL CALORIES: 3648
CALORIES PER SERVING: 608
CARBOHYDRATES: 38g
PROTEIN: 42g
FAT: 32g
SODIUM: High
PREPARING: 1½ Hours
COOKING: 30 Minutes
FREEZING: No

Coq au Vin aux Pruneaux

CHICKEN IN WINE WITH PRUNES

---

18 large prunes, pitted
2 cups *(475ml)* dry red wine
18 small white onions, peeled
2 T. *(30g)* unsalted butter
1 tsp. sugar
½ lb. *(225g)* slab bacon, rind removed
   and cut into 1-inch *(2.5cm)* sticks
1 5-lb. *(2250g)* chicken, cut into 6-8
   serving pieces or 4 whole breasts, split
Flour
1 large onion, coarsely chopped
1 cup *(240ml)* chicken stock
2 cloves garlic, minced
1 tsp. thyme
1 tsp. savory
1 bay leaf
1 T. arrowroot
¼ cup *(60ml)* port wine

Combine prunes and wine in saucepan; bring to boil; simmer mixture until prunes are tender. Drain prunes, reserving liquid.

In another saucepan combine onions, butter and sugar; barely cover with water and cook over high heat until onions are tender and water almost evaporates. Cook another 2 minutes to glaze onions. Set aside.

Combine bacon and 6 cups water in saucepan; bring to boil and cook 5 minutes. Drain bacon.

In large skillet or saute pan, brown bacon pieces. Transfer to paper towels. Reserve 2 T. bacon grease in skillet. Dredge chicken pieces in flour, shaking off excess. Add chicken to skillet; saute 5 minutes per side or until golden; transfer to plate.

Saute chopped onion 3 minutes in skillet. Add reserved liquid from prunes; cook over high heat 2 to 3 minutes to reduce liquid. Add stock, garlic, thyme, savory and bay leaf; bring to boil; add chicken and cook, covered, 25 minutes or until tender.

Combine onions, prunes, bacon and chicken in flameproof casserole. Bring liquid in skillet to boil; dissolve arrowroot in port and whisk into liquid. Strain sauce over chicken and simmer covered, for 5 minutes or until heated through.

Joyce Brown, Columbia, SC

Variations, Advance Preparation, and Serving Suggestions:
1 4½-5-lb. rabbit (approximately 3¼ lbs. after cleaning) cut into 12 pieces can be substituted for chicken. Dish can be prepared a day in advance and refrigerated overnight; bring to room temperature before gently reheating. If preparing ahead, omit arrowroot and port. Add arrowroot dissolved in port just before serving.

Wine Suggestion: French Chateauneuf-du-Pape, robust red; serve at room temperature.

Microwave Conversion Instructions: Note: Reduce wine to 1¼ cups *(300ml)*. Combine prunes and wine in casserole. Cook covered on High 5 minutes or until prunes are fork tender. Stir and set aside. Combine onions, butter, sugar and ¼ cup water in small casserole. Cook, covered, on High 7 to 8 minutes per pound, or until fork tender. When onions are done, pour off remaining water and cook on High 1 minute to glaze. Set aside. Place bacon on bacon rack, with drip pan underneath. Cook on High, covered with paper towel, 3 to 5 minutes, or until bacon is crisp. Reserve 2 T. bacon grease. Add 1 tsp. paprika to flour. Dredge chicken pieces in flour. Preheat browning dish to maximum absorption. Place 2 T. butter in center of dish; allow to melt quickly and place coated chicken pieces in melted butter. Cook on High 2 minutes; turn over with spatula and cook 1 minute. Set aside. Saute onion with 2 T. butter in covered casserole on High 4 to 5 minutes, until well-cooked. Add reserved liquid from prunes; cook, uncovered, on High 3 minutes. Add heated chicken broth, garlic, thyme, savory and bay leaf; cook on High until boiling. Add chicken; cook, covered, on High 7 to 9 minutes, or until tender. Dissolve arrowroot in port. Remove chicken and all ingredients from dish, leaving liquid. Stir arrowroot mixture into liquid. Cook on High, uncovered, 3 to 4 minutes, until thickened. Strain sauce over chicken. Reheat on Medium (50%) 2 to 3 minutes, just until heated through for serving.

Chicken Neptune

The clam juice adds an unusual flavor. If the lemon juice and wine are omitted and the chicken marinated with the clam juice, the result is quite a good imitation of California abalone.

YIELD: 4-6 Servings
TOTAL CALORIES: 1356
CALORIES PER ½ BREAST: 226
CARBOHYDRATES: 6g
PROTEIN: 28g
FAT: 10g
PREPARING: 20 Minutes
MARINATING: 24 Hours
COOKING: 10 Minutes
FREEZING: No

Combine clam juice, wine, and lemon juice in a ceramic or glass bowl; add chicken breasts; store covered in refrigerator for 24 to 36 hours, turning several times.

Combine breadcrumbs, salt and pepper in a paper bag; add chicken breasts; shake until well coated.

Heat 2 T. butter in skillet over moderate heat; saute breasts approximately 2 minutes on each side; remove to a warm platter as they are cooked.

Add remaining butter and lemon juice to skillet; cook briefly and pour over breasts.

Garnish with parsley and serve immediately.

James McE. Brown, Stonington, CT

1 bottle (8 oz.) *(240ml)* clam juice or
  6 oz. *(180ml)* fresh clam juice
½ cup *(120ml)* dry white wine
¼ cup *(60ml)* fresh lemon juice
3 whole large chicken breasts, skinned,
  boned and split (6 pieces), pounded
  between sheets of waxed paper to a
  uniform thicknesss of ¼ inch *(6mm)*
Breadcrumbs
Salt and pepper to taste
4 T. *(60g)* butter
1 T. fresh lemon juice
Freshly chopped parsley

Variations, Advance Preparation, and Serving Suggestions: If using dark meat of chicken, the cooking time will be longer.

Nutritional Notes: Nutritional data based on use of ½ cup breadcrumbs and 2 T. butter. It does not include final butter to be poured over dish.

Wine Suggestion: California Pinot Chardonnay, full white; serve chilled.

Microwave Conversion Instructions: Marinate chicken as directed above. Combine very dry breadcrumbs, salt, pepper and 1 tsp. paprika in paper bag. Melt butter in shallow dish. Pat chicken breasts dry. Dip in butter; then shake in breadcrumbs. Arrange chicken in ring, with ends of chicken touching, in round shallow baking dish. Cook, covered with paper towel, on High 5 minutes. Turn chicken breasts over; cook, uncovered, an additional 1 to 2 minutes, just until cooked through. Remove to warm platter. Add butter and lemon juice to pan; cook on High 1 to 2 minutes until bubbly; then pour over chicken breasts. Garnish and serve.

YIELD: 4 Servings
TOTAL CALORIES: 1828
CALORIES PER SERVING: 421
CARBOHYDRATES: 9g
PROTEIN: 31g
FAT: 29g
SODIUM: High
PREPARING: 10 Minutes
COOKING: 50 Minutes
FREEZING: No

Poulet au Vinaigre de Framboises

SAUTEED CHICKEN WITH RASPBERRY VINEGAR SAUCE

Raspberry vinegar lends a subtle hint of the essence of the fruit to this velvety sauced chicken.

1 chicken, cut in pieces
Salt
Freshly ground pepper to taste
3 T. *(45g)* unsalted sweet butter, divided
2 T. *(30ml)* peanut oil
2 carrots, finely chopped
2 medium onions, finely chopped
1 T. minced fresh garlic
⅓ cup *(80ml)* Raspberry Vinegar (page 372)
1 tsp. tomato paste
1 bay leaf
½ cup *(120ml)* demi-glace or Poultry Stock Sauce Base (page 198)
2 cups *(240ml)* chicken broth, approximately
½ cup *(120ml)* Creme Fraiche (page 200)
Chopped parsley to garnish

Season chicken pieces with salt and pepper. In heavy skillet, brown lightly in 2 T. butter and the oil. Transfer chicken to dish. Pour off most of fat in pan. Add remaining butter and saute carrots, onions and garlic until tender and lightly colored. Stir in vinegar and tomato paste. Add bay leaf.

Return chicken pieces except breasts to pan. Add demi-glace and chicken broth to almost cover. Simmer, covered, 15 minutes. Add breasts, simmer 10 to 15 minutes more until done. Transfer chicken to a serving dish, keep warm.

Add Creme Fraiche to pan; boil sauce over high heat to reduce until thickened. Salt and pepper to taste. Pour sauce over chicken in serving dish. Sprinkle with chopped parsley.

Kathleen J. Schwartz, Avon, CT

Variations, Advance Preparation, and Serving Suggestions: Steamed, buttered rice, Homemade Pasta (page 192) or new red potatoes are nice accompaniments to this dish.

Nutritional Notes: Chicken as well as turkey are excellent sources of protein, generally providing less fat, and therefore less cholesterol than most meats if only the flesh is consumed. Fresh chicken and turkey usually have more flavor than frozen. The commercial freezing process usually involves a pre-soaking (water is absorbed and adds to the weight and also the cost). When birds are defrosted, natural flavors and some water-soluble nutrients are lost through the excess water as it drains.

Wine Suggestion: French Cotes de Beaune Villages, dry red; serve at room temperature.

Microwave Conversion Instructions: Melt 2 T. butter and 1 T. peanut oil in a 2-qt. *(2L)* casserole; add carrots, onion and 2 tsp. garlic. Cover, cook on High 2 minutes. Arrange chicken in 13 × 9-inch *(33 × 22.5cm)* glass casserole, placing thicker pieces toward outer edges. Add demi-glace and ½ to 1 cup chicken broth to raspberry vinegar, stir well, spoon mixture over chicken pieces. Cover with plastic wrap; cook on High, allowing 7 to 9 minutes per pound of chicken, turning over and rearranging once during cooking time. Chicken is done when no pink appears around bones, and joints move freely. Remove chicken from dish and degrease by blotting paper towel on surface. Add Creme Fraiche to sauce; cook, uncovered, 1½ to 2½ minutes on Medium (50%), or until heated. Pour over chicken, garnish with parsley.

Bisteeya

MOROCCAN CHICKEN PIE

This is perhaps the greatest of all Moroccan dishes, a pie of fine pastry stuffed with chicken, eggs, almonds, spices, and covered with cinnamon and sugar. Absolutely worth the extra time and effort!

YIELD: 6 Servings
TOTAL CALORIES: 3828
CALORIES PER SERVING: 638
CARBOHYDRATES: 23g
PROTEIN: 33g
FAT: 46g
CHOLESTEROL: High
SODIUM: High
PREPARING: 1 Hour
BAKING: 55 Minutes
SIMMERING: 2 Hours
FREEZING: Yes

Simmer chicken in water, butter, onion, seasonings, and parsley 2 hours or until flesh falls from bones. Drain stock and reserve. Skin and bone chicken; cut meat into small pieces.

Beat ½ cup reserved stock with eggs. Season with salt and pepper and stir over low heat until mixture starts to set, but is still creamy. Brush a round or square pie pan or oven dish approximately 13 inches *(33cm)* in diameter and 1½ to 2 inches *(4-5cm)* deep with melted butter. Fit a sheet of phyllo dough in dish so ends fold up and overlap edges. If this is not possible, overlap the sheets. Layer 6 sheets of phyllo, brushing melted butter evenly between each sheet. Sprinkle top layer with most of cinnamon and sugar mixture and all of sauteed almonds.

Spread more than half egg mixture over phyllo layers and sprinkle with a little stock. Add 4 more sheets phyllo, brushing each with melted butter.

Place boned chicken on top and cover with rest of egg mixture. Sprinkle with chicken stock and cover with remaining phyllo, brushing each layer with melted butter. Tuck in phyllo sheets. Bake in preheated 350° oven 40 minutes. Raise oven temperature to 425°; bake 15 minutes longer or until pastry is a deep golden color. Sprinkle with remaining cinnamon and sugar. Serve hot or cold, cut into wedges.

Susan Grody, West Hartford, CT

Variations, Advance Preparation, and Serving Suggestions:
This dish may be prepared the day before serving; bring to room temperature before reheating. It may also be frozen; defrost in refrigerator before reheating. Individual Bisteeya make a very elegant first course.

Nutritional Notes: Nutritional analysis uses 3½ oz. *(100g)* cooked chicken meat per serving.

Microwave Conversion Instructions: To cook chicken: Cut chicken into pieces. Place in large casserole. Cover chicken with water, using at least 3 cups *(710ml)*. Add seasonings and onion. Cook, covered, on High 1 hour, or until chicken flesh falls from bones.

Wine Suggestion: German Rhine Spaetlese, semi-sweet white; served chilled.

1 large chicken
2-3 cups *(475-710ml)* water
2½ T. *(35g)* butter
1 large onion, chopped
½ tsp. ground ginger
¼ tsp. powdered saffron
½ tsp. cinnamon
½ tsp. allspice
4 T. fresh parsley, chopped
Reserved stock from cooking chicken
8 eggs
Salt and pepper
¾ cup *(170g)* butter, melted
16 sheets phyllo dough
Cinnamon and sugar (about 2 T. each) mixed together
1 cup *(150g)* almonds, sauteed

Curry de Volaille à l'Indienne

CHICKEN CURRY CREPES

From *Donna F. Peacock,* formerly of THE DECK, a lovely restaurant overlooking a scenic spot in West Cornwall.

YIELD: 4 Servings or 8 Crepes
CALORIES PER CREPE: 412
CARBOHYDRATES: 21g
PROTEIN: 19g
FAT: 28g
PREPARING: 20 Minutes
COOKING: 20 Minutes
FREEZING: Yes

2-3 T. good curry powder
3 T. *(45ml)* cooking oil
3 T. *(45g)* butter
1 large onion, sliced
1 small head garlic, cloves crushed
1 lb. *(450g)* mushrooms, sliced
2 whole large chicken breasts, boned, skinned and cut into bite-size pieces
½ cup *(120ml)* chicken stock
½ cup *(120ml)* orange juice
1 cup *(240ml)* heavy cream
2 apples, peeled, quartered
⅓ cup *(60g)* seedless raisins
½ cup *(75g)* slivered almonds
2 T. chopped parsley
Salt
Freshly ground pepper to taste
8 thin crepes

In small saute pan, *heat* curry powder to develop full flavor.

In a large skillet, heat oil and butter; saute onion 1 minute. Add garlic, mushrooms, curry powder. Stir. Add chicken, stock, orange juice. Simmer, uncovered, until chicken is just cooked, about 10 minutes, stirring occasionally. With slotted spoon, transfer chicken to covered dish; keep warm. Add cream to skillet. Simmer sauce 10 to 15 minutes. Return chicken to skillet. Add apples, raisins, almonds, parsley; mix well. Over low heat, cook until all ingredients are heated through, 2 to 3 minutes more. Adjust sauce by adding more stock or cream if desired. Add salt and pepper.

Place 2 crepes in each of 4 individual crepe or oval gratin dishes. Spoon ⅛ of chicken mixture into center of each crepe. Fold crepes over mixture. Spoon sauce over top. Place dishes, uncovered, in preheated 350° oven until bubbly.

Variations, Advance Preparation, and Serving Suggestions: This can be made a day ahead, assembled in crepe dishes and refrigerated. Bring to room temperature before placing in oven. Serve with chutney or curry condiments. Garnish with orange wheels.

Wine Suggestion: California Johannisberg Riesling, semi-dry; served chilled.

Microwave Conversion Instructions: Put 3 T. butter in 5-qt. *(5L)* casserole. Add onion, crushed garlic, mushrooms and curry powder. Cover; cook on High 1 minute. Add chicken, stock, orange juice, apples, raisins, almonds, chopped parsley and cook on Medium High (70%) 12 to 15 minutes, stirring occasionally. Carefully stir in cream. Cook 2 to 3 minutes on Medium (50%), until heated through. More cream or stock may be added to make more sauce, stirring well after each addition. Fill prepared crepes and top with sauce.

Chicken Scallops Arlésienne

This chicken dish is as colorful as the landscapes Van Gogh painted near Arles in France.

YIELD: 4 Servings
CALORIES PER SERVING: 540
CARBOHYDRATES: 23g
PROTEIN: 40g
FAT: 32g
PREPARING: 30 Minutes
BAKING: 15 Minutes

2 large whole chicken breasts, halved, boned and skinned
Flour for dredging
4 T. *(60g)* butter

Slice chicken pieces in half parallel to cutting surface. (If chicken is partially frozen it will facilitate this procedure.) Place chicken scallops between waxed paper; gently pound to flatten. Lightly flour scallops. Quickly saute scallops in heated butter, only 15 to 20 seconds per side, being careful not to burn butter. Remove scallops and place in a single layer in 9 × 11-inch *(23 × 28cm)* baking dish.

VEGETABLE TOPPING: Gently saute onion, pepper and garlic in olive oil 5 minutes. Add tomatoes, basil, salt and pepper. Cook uncovered stirring occasionally until mixture forms a thick paste, about 20 minutes. Cool.

Coat scallops with vegetable mixture. Top with thin slices cheese. Up to this point dish can be prepared a day ahead, refrigerated and brought to room temperature before baking. Bake in preheated 350° oven 10 to 15 minutes or until heated through and cheese is melted.

Sarah C. Seymour, West Hartford, CT

VEGETABLE TOPPING:
1 medium onion, minced
1 red or green pepper or a combination of, chopped
1-2 cloves garlic, minced
4 T. *(60ml)* olive oil
8 medium tomatoes, peeled, seeded and chopped or 1 can (35 oz.) *(985g)* peeled tomatoes, drained
1 tsp. dried basil, crumbled or 3 tsp. chopped fresh
1 tsp. salt
Freshly ground pepper
5 oz. *(140g)* Gruyere or Swiss cheese, thinly sliced.

Rock Cornish Game Hens with Saffron Rice Stuffing

Excellent all-purpose poultry stuffing.

YIELD: 4 Servings
CALORIES PER SERVING: 611
CARBOHYDRATES: 42g
PROTEIN: 41g
FAT: 31g
PREPARING: 45 Minutes
ROASTING: 1 Hour 45 Minutes

Soak raisins in cognac 15 minutes. While raisins are soaking, saute onions in 2 T. butter until tender; add cognac, raisins and 6 T. butter, bring to a simmer. In a bowl, combine onion mixture, rice, walnuts and salt; toss lightly. Stuff hens with rice mixture; close with skewers.

Roast hens in preheated 450° oven 15 minutes. Reduce oven temperature to 350°; roast 1½ hours longer, basting hens occasionally with melted butter.

Kathryn Masius, West Hartford, CT

½ cup *(85g)* white raisins
½ cup *(120ml)* cognac
½ cup *(75g)* chopped onions
8 T. *(115g)* butter
1 pkg. (7 oz.) *(200g)* saffron rice, cooked and cooled
¼ cup *(30g)* chopped walnuts
½ tsp. salt

4 1-lb. *(450g)* Rock Cornish Game Hens, washed, well drained and seasoned with salt, freshly ground pepper and paprika
Additional melted butter for basting

Variations, Advance Preparation, and Serving Suggestions: Use this stuffing in same manner as described in Summer Garden Stuffed Chicken (page 308).

Nutritional Notes: For additional fiber, brown rice seasoned with saffron can be substituted. Nutritional analysis uses 5¼ oz. *(150g)* cooked meat per serving.

Wine Suggestion: Hungarian Szekszardi Voros, dry red; serve at room temperature.

Microwave Conversion Instructions: Note: Add 1 T. oil mixed with 1 T. commercial browning sauce. Saute onion in 3 T. butter on High 2 minutes. Add cognac and soaked raisins. Continue cooking on High 2 minutes, or until sauce boils. Combine sauce with walnuts, rice and salt. Toss lightly. Stuff hens with rice mixture and close with toothpicks or place heel of bread over opening. Brush hens with mixture of oil and browning sauce. Place breast side down in ring fashion on shallow round platter. Cover loosely with waxed paper. Cook on High 7 minutes per pound, turning hens over half way through cooking time. Finish cooking breast side up. Baste once or twice with drippings. If using temperature probe, cook to internal temperature of 175°. Allow to stand, covered, 5 to 10 minutes. Temperature will rise about 10 degrees.

Steak de Canard van Over

YIELD: 4-6 Servings
CALORIES PER SERVING: 553
CARBOHYDRATES: 8g
PROTEIN: 33g
FAT: 43g
CHOLESTEROL: High
SODIUM: High
PREPARING: 50-60 Minutes
MARINATING: 2 Hours
SIMMERING: Stock 3 Hours

A taste of country French living in a Connecticut River town is RESTAURANT DU VILLAGE in Chester. The following is a sampling of the entrees appearing on du Village's short sophisticated French menu . . .

4 whole ducks (only breast meat will be used)
¼ cup *(60ml)* soy sauce

DUCK STOCK:

4 carrots, peeled and chopped
3 medium onion, roughly chopped
4 cloves
2 large stalks celery, coarsely chopped
1 cup *(240ml)* dry white wine
3 tomatoes, chopped and seeded
1 bay leaf
Several black peppercorns
Bunch of parsley
Duck carcasses

6 T. *(90g)* butter
3 T. *(45ml)* Cognac
3 T. *(45ml)* Raspberry Vinegar
   (page 372)
2 T. pink peppercorns
4 peaches, sliced
Arrowroot (optional)

Make an incision along the breastbone of the duck; work knife along rib cage until entire breast is removed from bones. Carefully peel skin and fat from boned breasts; then remove legs and thighs and reserve for another recipe. Repeat instructions for each of the remaining ducks. Marinate duck breasts in soy sauce at least 2 hours.

DUCK STOCK: In a 6-qt. *(6L)* stock pot put carrots, onions, cloves, celery, white wine, tomatoes, bay leaf, black peppercorns and parsley. Put in duck carcasses; cover with cold water and place on stove. Bring to a boil, then simmer stock 3 hours. Remove bones; strain stock into saucepan and continue to cook stock until reduced to 4 cups.

In a heavy fry pan, non-stick finish preferred, saute duck breasts in 4 T. butter until browned. Lower heat; continue to cook until breasts are rare or medium rare. Immediately remove from heat. Flambe breasts with Cognac, then remove breasts from pan and place on heated plate.

Deglaze pan with raspberry vinegar; add about 2 cups *(475ml)* duck stock, pink peppercorns, fresh peach slices and cook briskly to reduce to a thick sauce. If necessary, thicken with arrowroot. Before serving, stir in 2 T. butter to sauce to enrich it.

When ready to serve, spoon sauce onto a heated dinner plate and lay duck breasts in center of plate.

Variations, Advance Preparation, and Serving Suggestions:
Serve with turned carrots and turnips. Reserved duck legs and thighs can be used to prepare Duck Rillettes (page 74).

Nutritional Notes: Nutritional analysis uses 4¾ oz. *(135g)* cooked duck meat per serving.

Wine Suggestion: French Cotes de Beaune Villages, medium red; serve at room temperature.

Roast Duck Normandy

Normandy is a French province of high gastronomic repute, known for its excellent butter and cream as well as superior apples and the spirit Calvados.

YIELD: 2-3 Servings
CALORIES PER SERVING: 655
CARBOHYDRATES: 13g
PROTEIN: 36g
FAT: 51g
CHOLESTEROL: High
PREPARING: 30 Minutes
ROASTING: 1½ Hours

Remove wing tips and second joints of duck, leaving main wingbone intact. Cut neck and wings into 1-inch *(2.5cm)* pieces.

Sprinkle duck cavity with salt and pepper. Truss duck; arrange in roasting pan breast side up, scattering quartered giblets, neck and wing pieces around duck. Coat skin with glaze.

Roast duck in preheated 400° oven for 1 hour, pouring off fat as it accumulates, occasionally scraping loose the particles from bottom of pan. Add carrots, onions, celery, and garlic; roast ½ hour longer or until duck is tender. Remove duck from pan lifting it so the juices run from cavity; set aside on warm platter.

Pour off fat from roasting pan reserving all bones and vegetables. Add Calvados; over high heat, scrape loose particles; add chicken stock; simmer 2 minutes.

Pour contents of roasting pan into saucepan; add tomatoes, apricot preserves and lemon juice; simmer 30 minutes.

Strain sauce; skim off any accumulated fat. Add cream; gently simmer 5 minutes. As sauce is simmering, melt butter in a skillet. Sprinkle apples with sugar and Calvados; saute, turning occasionally to brown lightly. Cook until just fork tender. Carve or quarter duck; arrange skin side up on serving platter; arrange apples around duck; spoon sauce over both. Extra sauce may be passed on the side.

Sarah C. Seymour, West Hartford, CT

Nutritional Notes: Nutritional analysis uses 5¼ oz. *(150g)* cooked duck meat per serving.

Wine Suggestion: California Beau Tour Cabernet Sauvignon, dry red; serve at room temperature.

Microwave Conversion Instructions: Prepare duck as directed. Place ¼ cup each carrots, onion and celery inside cavity. Put duck on rack placed in a shallow oval baking dish. Sprinkle remaining vegetables, garlic and giblets around duck. Coat duck skin with glaze. Sprinkle with paprika. Cover with waxed paper. Cook on High, skin side up, 20 minutes, pouring off fat as it accumulates. Baste again with glaze, turn duck over. Baste with glaze and sprinkle with additional paprika, if needed. Continue to cook 15 to 20 minutes until duck is just tender. (Duck is cooked at 7 minutes per pound.) Remove duck from baking dish, lifting it so juices run from cavity. Remove vegetables from cavity. Pour off fat from dish, reserving all bones and vegetables. Add Calvados, cook on High, covered, 3 to 4 minutes until hot. Add heated chicken stock; cook additional 5 minutes on High. Pour entire contents into 8-cup *(2L)* measure or large bowl. Add tomatoes, apricot preserves and lemon juice. Cook on High, covered with paper towel, 10 minutes. Strain sauce and skim off any fat; add cream and cook on Medium (50%), uncovered, 5 minutes, stirring once. If additional crisping is desired, place duck in 400° oven, or under broiler, until it is brown and crisp.

1 4-5-lb. *(1800-2250g)* duckling with neck and gizzards reserved and quartered (discard liver)
Salt
Ground pepper

2 tsp. sugar dissolved in ¼ cup *(60ml)* warm water to make glaze

¾ cup *(90g)* coarsely chopped carrots
¾ cup *(115g)* coarsely chopped onions
¾ cup *(85g)* coarsely chopped celery
1 clove garlic, minced
⅓ cup *(80ml)* Calvados
1¼ cups *(300ml)* chicken stock
1 large ripe garden tomato, peeled and diced (2-3 canned tomatoes if fresh not flavorful)
1 T. apricot preserves
1 tsp. fresh lemon juice
½ cup *(120ml)* heavy cream

APPLE GARNISH:

1½ T. *(20g)* butter
4 baking apples peeled, cored and quartered
¼ cup *(60ml)* Calvados
1½ T. *(10g)* sugar

YIELD: 6 Servings
TOTAL CALORIES: 2070
CALORIES PER SERVING: 345
CARBOHYDRATES: 11g
PROTEIN: 19g
FAT: 25g
SODIUM: High
PREPARING: 55 Minutes
STIR-FRYING: 3 Minutes

Ch'Ao Ya Syu

SHREDDED DUCK WITH VEGETABLES

2 cups *(240g)* 1/16-inch *(0.2cm)*
    carrot shreds
2 cups *(225g)* 1/16-inch *(0.2cm)*
    celery shreds
2 cups *(160g)* bean sprouts
2 T. *(10g)* minced scallions
1 T. minced garlic
2 tsp. peeled, minced ginger root
1½ tsp. crushed red pepper
3 T. *(45ml)* soy sauce
1½ T. *(22ml)* rice wine
2 tsp. sugar
½ tsp. salt
1 tsp. Chinkiang vinegar
2 tsp. dark sesame oil
2 T. *(30ml)* peanut oil
2 cups cooked, shredded duck meat
    (about 1 4-lb. *(1800g)* duck)

Blanch carrot, celery and bean sprouts in separate saucepans with boiling water, 1 minute each for carrot and celery, 30 seconds for bean sprouts. Drain vegetables separately in colander, refresh under cold running water, drain again. Mix scallion, garlic, ginger and red pepper in small dish.

Combine soy sauce, rice wine, sugar, salt, vinegar and 1 tsp. of sesame oil in a small bowl.

Arrange a tray containing blanched carrot and celery in one bowl, bean sprouts in another small bowl, scallion dish, soy sauce mixture, shredded duck and remaining sesame oil in separate bowls. Set tray aside until just before serving time.

Heat wok over high heat until it is very hot. Add peanut oil; heat until very hot. Add the scallion mixture; stir-fry 30 seconds. Add duck, carrot and celery; stir-fry 1 minute. Add soy sauce mixture and bean sprouts; stir-fry 1 minute. Add the teaspoon sesame oil; toss all together well.

Transfer to heated serving dish. Serve at once.

Kathleen J. Schwartz, Avon, CT

Nutritional Notes: Nutritional analysis uses 2¾ oz. *(75g)* cooked duck meat per serving.

Wine Suggestion: California Beaulieu Grenache Rose, dry rose; serve chilled.

Roast Pheasant with Red Cabbage and Glazed Apples

YIELD: 4-6 Servings
CALORIES PER SERVING
  PHEASANT ONLY: 498
  CARBOHYDRATES: 23g
  PROTEIN: 34g
  FAT: 30g
CALORIES PER SERVING
  RED CABBAGE GARNISH: 153
  CARBOHYDRATES: 16g
  PROTEIN: 2g
  FAT: 9g
PREPARING: 30 Minutes
COOKING: 30 Minutes
ROASTING: 1¼ Hours

Not only does this combination of pheasant, apples, onions and cabbage present a delectable contrast of flavors, but the finished entree is a feast for the eyes.

Place bacon and butter in low, heavy oven-proof casserole. Melt butter; add onion and carrot and cook gently 3 to 4 minutes. Remove bacon and reserve. Raise heat and brown pheasants on all sides. Remove birds to heated platter. Add spices, salt, brandy and wine to casserole; simmer 3 minutes.

Meanwhile, secure strips of bacon across breasts of pheasants with toothpicks. Return birds, breast side up, to casserole; surround them with whole apples and onions. Roast in preheated 300° oven 1¼ hours, basting birds, apples and onions frequently. Remove birds and arrange attractively on top of Red Cabbage Garnish along with apples and onions. Pour pan juices over birds.

RED CABBAGE GARNISH: Melt butter and gently saute onion for 3 to 4 minutes. Stir in apple slices; then all remaining ingredients. Season to taste; if necessary, add a few tablespoons water. Cover tightly and simmer 20 to 25 minutes. Check before serving to see if more salt should be added.

Alice F. Evans, Simsbury, CT

Variations, Advance Preparation, and Serving Suggestions:
2 large (2 lbs. each) *(900g each)* Cornish Game Hens can be used when pheasant is not available.

Nutritional Notes: Nutritional analysis uses 4½ oz. *(125g)* cooked pheasant meat per serving. Wild birds are always lower in fat than domestic birds. Pheasants are also always leaner than waterfowl (ducks and geese) and therefore do not need to be cooked as long.

Wine Suggestion: German Liebfraumilch, semi-dry white; serve chilled.

Microwave Conversion Instructions: Cook bacon 4 minutes on High so it is partially cooked and some fat is rendered; drain fat. Combine butter, onion and carrot in covered glass casserole. Add spices, salt, brandy and wine to vegetable mixture. Cover and cook 2 minutes on High; add onions. Secure bacon on pheasant breasts; place birds breast side down on top of mixture, basting with liquids. Cook on High 8 minutes, rotate birds to their sides, cook on High 8 more minutes. Baste and rotate birds to opposite side. Add apples and baste. Cook on High 8 minutes; place birds breast side up, baste; cook on High 8 minutes or until legs move easily and juices run clear. *Red Cabbage Garnish:* Add butter and onion to casserole. Cook 5 minutes on High. Add apples and stir. Add remaining ingredients, cover and cook 6 minutes or until cabbage is softened.

6 slices *(150g)* bacon
4 T. *(60g)* butter
1 small onion, finely chopped
¼ cup *(30g)* finely chopped carrot
2 pheasants
¼ tsp. ground mace
¼ tsp. cayenne pepper
Salt
¼ cup *(60ml)* brandy
½ cup *(120ml)* port, sherry or red wine
4 medium apples (Golden Delicious) peeled and left whole
8-12 small onions, peeled

RED CABBAGE GARNISH:
6 T. *(85g)* butter
1 large onion, finely sliced
1 large green apple, peeled, cored and sliced
1 T. *(15ml)* fresh lemon juice
Water as needed
Salt
Freshly ground pepper
½ tsp. thyme
2 T. chopped parsley
½ red cabbage, shredded

Pheasant Bar-le-Duc

Bar-le-Duc is a town in France famed for its red currant preserves. The preserve itself was famous for being made from whole white currants. Bar-le-Duc preserves are now made from both white and red currants.

YIELD: 4 Servings
CALORIES PER SERVING: 520
CARBOHYDRATES: 9g
PROTEIN: 33g
FAT: 40g
PREPARING: 15 Minutes
ROASTING: 45 Minutes

PHEASANT:

2 pheasants, cleaned
Salt
Freshly ground pepper
2 apples, peeled and quartered
1 cup *(240ml)* dry vermouth mixed with
   1 cup water

SAUCE:

2 T. *(30g)* butter
2 T. *(15g)* flour
½ cup *(140g)* Bar-le-Duc preserves or
   currant jelly
1 tsp. garlic powder
⅛ tsp. curry powder
1 cup *(240ml)* heavy cream
½ cup *(120ml)* dry vermouth
¾ cup *(180ml)* pan drippings

PHEASANT: Sprinkle birds with salt and pepper and stuff cavities with apples. Roast on a rack in 450° oven 45 minutes. Baste every 10 minutes with watered vermouth and pan drippings to prevent birds from drying out.

SAUCE: Melt butter; stir in flour and cook 1 minute. Add preserves, garlic powder, curry, cream and vermouth. Cook and stir until thickened. Stir in drippings. Correct seasonings with salt and pepper.

Cut pheasants into serving pieces. Pass sauce separately.

Nutritional Notes: Nutritional analysis uses 4½ oz. *(125g)* cooked pheasant meat per serving.

YIELD: 8 Quail
CALORIES PER QUAIL: 368
CARBOHYDRATES: 14g
PROTEIN: 33g
FAT: 20g
PREPARING: 45 Minutes
BAKING: 1 Hour

Quail with Grapes

Quail has true distinction not only as a game bird, but as a mouth watering morsel. This particular recipe keeps the meat very moist while retaining the delicate flavor.

8 wild or domestic quail, (if frozen, thaw
   completely before preparing)
½ fresh lemon, quartered
1 medium red onion, finely chopped
10-12 fresh mushrooms, finely chopped
3 T. *(45g)* butter
½ cup plus 2 T. *(150ml)* whipping cream
1½ lbs. *(680g)* green seedless grapes
Salt and pepper
Dash of nutmeg
⅓ cup *(80ml)* dry white vermouth

Gently dry quail with paper towels; rub inside and out with lemon.

Over medium heat, saute onions and mushrooms in 1 T. butter; add 2 T. cream to moisten; remove from heat; let cool slightly. Loosely fill quail cavities with mixture taking care not to tear skin; add 2 to 3 halved grapes to each bird; press legs down to close cavity; tie with string.

In heavy skillet, brown birds in 2 T. butter until golden. Place quail *breast down* in baking dish; sprinkle with salt, pepper, and nutmeg. Combine vermouth and ½ cup cream; coat birds with mixture. Cover tightly. Bake in preheated 325° oven 45 minutes, basting occasionally. Add remaining grapes to pan; bake uncovered 15 minutes.

Alice F. Evans, Simsbury, CT

Variations, Advance Preparation, and Serving Suggestions: Serve with Wild Rice Casserole (page 77) or Grits Souffle (page 352) and fresh spinach salad.

Nutritional Notes: Nutritional analysis uses 4½ oz. *(125g)* cooked quail meat with skin per serving.

Wine Suggestion: California Inglenook Cabernet Sauvignon, dry red; serve at room temperature.

Francie Bergquist

Pheasant Cumberland

An adaptation of a traditional English sauce served with cold meats and game.

YIELD: 4 Servings
CALORIES PER SERVING
  PHEASANT ONLY: 250
  CARBOHYDRATES: Trace
  PROTEIN: 31g
  FAT: 14g
CALORIES PER ⅓ CUP
  SAUCE: 85
  CARBOHYDRATES: 18g
  PROTEIN: 1g
  FAT: 1g
PREPARING: 30 Minutes
COOKING: 35 Minutes
ROASTING: 45 Minutes
FREEZING: No

PHEASANT: Rub birds generously with butter. Stuff birds with orange and apple slices. Place in roasting pan. Cover with foil. Roast in preheated 375° oven 30 minutes. Remove foil; baste with pan juices. Roast 15 minutes more uncovered. Remove from oven; set pheasant aside until cool enough to handle. Reserve and degrease pan juices.

SAUCE: Combine all ingredients in medium saucepan. Bring to a boil, stirring. Boil 1 minute, skimming off froth as it forms. Reduce heat to low; simmer 30 minutes, stirring occasionally. Add salt and pepper.

Remove meat from cooled birds. Remove tendons from legs. Slice meat from breasts, thighs, legs into neat thin slices. (Reserve remaining meat for other use.) Place slices in baking dish; cover with sauce. Heat in preheated 300° oven to desired serving temperature. Pheasant and sauce may also be heated in skillet on stovetop.

James McE. Brown, Stonington, CT

Variations, Advance Preparation, and Serving Suggestions:
This dish is at its best when pheasant and sauce have been combined at least 2 hours before serving. They may be prepared up to one day ahead and refrigerated.

Serve with Wild Rice Casserole (page 77) and braised endive.

Nutritional Notes: Nutritional analysis uses 4½ oz. *(125g)* cooked pheasant meat per serving.

Wine Suggestion: French Chateau Olivier Rouge, full red; serve at room temperature.

PHEASANT:

2 pheasants, cleaned
¼ cup *(60g)* butter, softened
1 large orange, sliced
1 large apple, cored, sliced

SAUCE: (about 3 cups)

1 cup *(240ml)* beef stock or canned bouillon
1 cup *(240ml)* red wine
1 cup *(240ml)* fresh orange juice
¼ cup *(60ml)* fresh lemon juice
½ cup *(140g)* tart currant jelly
1 tsp. dry mustard
½ cup *(120ml)* port wine
¼ cup *(60ml)* good orange liqueur, preferably Cointreau
¼ cup freshly grated orange rind
1 tsp. freshly grated lemon rind
½ cup *(120ml)* degreased pan juices
Salt
Freshly ground pepper to taste

Flounder Florentine

YIELD: 4 Servings
CALORIES PER SERVING: 418
CARBOHYDRATES: 10g
PROTEIN: 36g
FAT: 26g
PREPARING: 15 Minutes
COOKING: 10 Minutes
FREEZING: No

Olive oil
6 slices flounder fillets
1 cup *(115g)* **flour**
2 eggs, beaten
1 tsp. freshly grated Romano cheese
Salt
Freshly ground black pepper to taste
4 T. *(60g)* **butter**
1 clove garlic, minced
2 T. *(30ml)* **dry sherry**
Juice of ½ fresh lemon
2 cups *(375g)* **steamed spinach**
½ lemon, thinly sliced

LEON'S RESTAURANT has become an Italian family tradition in New Haven, Connecticut. The Varipappa brothers, owners of the establishment, are on hand to oversee the presentation of some of Connecticut's best Italian food from Leon's extensive menu. Given here is a sauteed fish, served "a la Firenze" with steamed spinach.

Pour olive oil ¼-inch *(0.5cm)* deep in frying pan or electric skillet. Heat oil to 375°. Coat flounder with flour; shake off excess. Mix eggs with cheese, salt and pepper. Dip fillets in mixture. Saute in oil until golden brown.

Meanwhile, place butter, garlic, sherry and lemon juice in a small pan. Bring to boil over high heat. Boil 30 seconds and set aside.

Season warm spinach with salt and pepper. Arrange on serving platter. Place fillets on top of spinach and pour butter mixture over. Garnish with lemon slices. Serve hot.

Variations, Advance Preparation, and Serving Suggestions: This dish should be prepared just before serving, using flounder purchased the same day.

Wine Suggestion: Italian Trebbiano Toscano, dry white; serve chilled.

Filets de Sole Duglère

FILLETS OF SOLE WITH TOMATOES

An easy fish dish that looks pretty and tastes delicious. This method for cooking and serving white fish such as halibut, turbot, sole, etc. was devised by the French chef Duglere at "Aux Trois Freres Provencaux" restaurant in 1786.

YIELD: 4 Servings
CALORIES PER SERVING: 279
CARBOHYDRATES: 6g
PROTEIN: 39g
FAT: 11g
SODIUM: High
PREPARING: 20 Minutes
COOKING: 5-10 Minutes

2 lbs. *(900g)* **fresh sole or flounder fillets**
1 tsp. salt
¼ tsp. freshly ground pepper
2 T. *(30g)* **butter**
1 medium onion, chopped
1 minced shallot
1 clove garlic, minced
1 large ripe tomato, peeled, seeded and chopped or ¾ cup *(160g)* **canned tomatoes, well drained**
2 T. chopped parsley
¼ cup *(60ml)* **dry white wine**
¼ cup *(60ml)* **light cream**
1 tsp. flour

Cut out circle of waxed paper to fit 10-inch *(25cm)* skillet; punch a hole in center and set aside.

Sprinkle fish with salt and pepper.

Melt 1 T. butter in skillet; add onion, shallot, and garlic. Arrange fillets on top; spoon tomatoes on fish, sprinkle with 1 T. parsley; pour wine around fish, cover with waxed paper.

Bring to boil, cover and cook over high heat 5 to 10 minutes. Remove paper.

Pour cream around fish; mix 1 T. butter with flour; stir into cream. Move skillet in circular motion to combine and thicken sauce. Spoon sauce over fish and sprinkle with remaining parsley.

Betty Roberts, Hartford, CT

Wine Suggestion: Alsatian Riesling, dry white; serve chilled.

Microwave Conversion Instructions: Note: Increase flour to 1½ T. Saute onion and garlic in butter in a 10-inch quiche dish on High 4 minutes, stirring once. Sprinkle fish with salt and pepper. Arrange fish on top of onions. Spoon tomatoes on fish. Sprinkle with parsley. Pour wine around fish. Cook, covered with waxed paper on High 7 to 9 minutes, just until fish turns opaque. Remove fish and set aside. Stir in cream, butter and flour. Cook on High 1 to 2 minutes, until sauce thickens. Add fish. Spoon sauce over fish and sprinkle with parsley.

Filet de Sole aux Raisins Blanc

FILLET OF SOLE WITH WHITE RAISIN SAUCE

YIELD: 2-3 Servings
CALORIES PER SERVING: 506
CARBOHYDRATES: 29g
PROTEIN: 30g
FAT: 30g
CHOLESTEROL: High
PREPARING: 15 Minutes
MARINATING: 30 Minutes
COOKING: 15 Minutes

In a small saucepan, bring raisins to boil in white wine. Remove from heat. Let remain at room temperature 30 minutes.

Dredge fillets in flour, shaking off excess. Dip fillets in eggs. Pour the clarified butter into a hot saute pan. Over moderately high heat, brown the fillets quickly on both sides. Remove to a heated serving platter.

Drain fat from pan. Add unclarified butter to pan. When melted, add wine drained from raisins. Boil quickly until liquid is reduced by half. Add raisins and Beurre Manie as needed to thicken, starting with a small piece the size of a hazelnut, stirring or whisking constantly. Whisk in lemon juice, salt and pepper. Stir in chopped parsley. Pour sauce over fish on platter.

Marcel Godbout, Hartford, CT

Variations, Advance Preparation, and Serving Suggestions:
Raisins and Beurre Manie may be made several hours ahead and set aside at room temperature, but prepare fish and sauce just before serving.

A simple and light entree as this provides good opportunity to serve more complicated accompaniments. Try it with a pasta with red pepper, Spinach Timbales (page 159), a salade composee.

Wine Suggestion: French Camponac Blanc Bordeaux, dry white, serve chilled.

½ cup *(85g)* California white raisins
½ cup *(120ml)* white wine
4 fillets (3½-4 oz. each) *(100-115g)* sole
1 cup *(115g)* flour
3 eggs, lightly beaten
3 T. *(45g)* clarified butter
2 T. *(30g)* unclarified butter
Beurre Manie, as needed
Juice of ½ fresh lemon
Salt
Freshly ground black pepper
1 T. finely chopped fresh parsley

BEURRE MANIE:
2 oz. *(60g)* butter, at room temperature and 1½ oz. *(45g)* flour, sifted, blended to smooth paste

YIELD: 6 Servings
CALORIES PER SERVING: 348
CARBOHYDRATES: 1g
PROTEIN: 41g
FAT: 20g
SODIUM: High
PREPARING: 5 Minutes
MARINATING: 3-48 Hours
BROILING: 15 Minutes
FREEZING: No

Lemon Soy Grilled Fish Steaks

Even people who dislike fish like swordfish, because its firm, oily texture so resembles meat. Avocado butter is a delectable accompaniment.

---

3 lbs. *(1350g)* salmon or swordfish steaks, cut 1 inch *(2.5cm)* thick

MARINADE:
⅓ cup *(80ml)* soy sauce
¼ cup *(60ml)* fresh lemon juice
½ cup *(120ml)* salad oil
1 large clove garlic, crushed
1 tsp. grated lemon rind
2 tsp. Dijon mustard
Handful fresh parsley, chopped
Lemon wedges

With a fork, pierce fish on both sides so more of marinade can be absorbed. Blend marinade ingredients. Place fish in shallow container; pour marinade over. Cover and marinate 3 to 48 hours, turning and piercing fish occasionally.

Heat outdoor grill or broiler to very hot. (If using outdoor barbecue or open fire, generously oil a double-hinged two-sided wire grill with long handle. Place fish between grills; close and lock to secure fish.) Grill or broil fish on the first side, 6 to 8 minutes, keeping cover on most of time and brushing with marinade. Turn fish and repeat on second side. Adjust barbecue rack according to the heat of coals. Continue grilling or broiling until fish is browned. If fish flakes easily it is overcooked!

Remove to serving board and garnish with lemon wedges.

Bernice Kuzma, West Hartford, CT

Wine Suggestion: Chateau Olivier Blanc, dry white; serve chilled.
Nutritional Notes: Nutritional analysis assumes that no more than half the marinade is consumed and uses 5¼ oz. *(150g)* cooked fish per serving. Salmon and swordfish are oilier or fatter than other ocean fish such as flounder or haddock. Salmon and swordfish have 120 calories and 4g fat per 3½ oz. *(100g)* while flounder and haddock average 74 calories and .3g fat.
Microwave Conversion Instructions: Note: Use browning dish. Heat browning dish to maximum absorption. Place marinated steaks on heating dish. Cook on High 2 minutes or just until tiny drops of juice begin to appear to top. Turn fish and cook 1 minute on High.

YIELD: 6 Servings
CALORIES PER SERVING: 160
CARBOHYDRATES: 5g
PROTEIN: 26g
FAT: 4g
SODIUM: High
PREPARING: 15 Minutes
COOKING: 8 Minutes

Creole Flounder or Haddock

2 lbs. *(900g)* flounder or haddock fillets
2 cups *(200g)* tomatoes, drained and chopped
1 cup *(170g)* green or red pepper, chopped
⅓ cup *(80ml)* fresh lemon juice
1 T. *(15ml)* oil
1 tsp. salt
2 tsp. minced fresh onion
1 tsp. basil, crumbled
2 tsp. fresh parsley, chopped
¼ tsp. thyme, crumbled
¼ tsp. freshly ground pepper

1 lemon, thinly sliced
Parsley sprigs

Place fillets in a greased 13½ × 9 × 2-inch *(34 × 22.5 × 5cm)* baking dish.

Combine remaining ingredients except sliced lemon and parsley sprigs. Spoon over fish. Bake in preheated 500° oven 5 to 8 minutes.

Place fish on platter. Garnish with lemon slices and parsley sprigs.

Linda Woronick Desmond, Hartford, CT

Wine Suggestion: French Valbon Blanc, dry white; serve chilled.
Microwave Conversion Instructions: Place fish in shallow oval baking dish. Combine remaining ingredients except garnish. Cook, covered with waxed paper, on High 9 to 11 minutes, just until fish turns opaque. Garnish and serve.

Baked Stuffed Red Snapper

One of America's finest fish from the Gulf Coast, so handsome on the platter when served whole with its glistening silver and pinkish-red skin.

YIELD: 6 Servings
CALORIES PER SERVING: 268
CARBOHYDRATES: 15g
PROTEIN: 34g
FAT: 8g
SODIUM: High
PREPARING: 20 Minutes
BAKING: 1 Hour

Saute celery and onion in butter until tender; add stuffing, sour cream, lemon, lemon rind, paprika, salt, and pepper. The mixture should be moist *not* soggy. Cool.

Fill cavity of fish with stuffing and skewer or sew up the opening. Wrap in buttered foil. (Can be stuffed and refrigerated day before serving.) Bake in preheated 350° oven 40 to 60 minutes.

Kinny Hull, West Hartford, CT

Wine Suggestion: California Inglenook Grey Riesling, clean white; serve chilled.

Microwave Conversion Instructions: Note: Add 1 lemon very thinly sliced and chopped fresh parsley. Saute celery, onion and butter on High 2 to 3 minutes, or until tender. Mix in seasoned stuffing, spices and just enough sour cream to hold stuffing together. Stuff fish. Place fish in oval *au gratin* dish. Place lemon slices overlapping on top of fish. Sprinkle with chopped parsley. Cover dish with plastic wrap. Cook on High 5 to 6 minutes per lb. Let stand 5 minutes before serving.

½ cup *(55g)* chopped celery
¼ cup *(35g)* chopped onion
2 T. *(30g)* butter
4 oz. *(115g)* packaged seasoned stuffing
¼-½ cup *(60-115g)* sour cream
½ cup peeled, seeded and diced lemon
1 T. grated lemon rind
½ tsp. imported paprika
½ tsp. salt
Dash cayenne pepper

1 4-lb. *(1800g)* whole red snapper

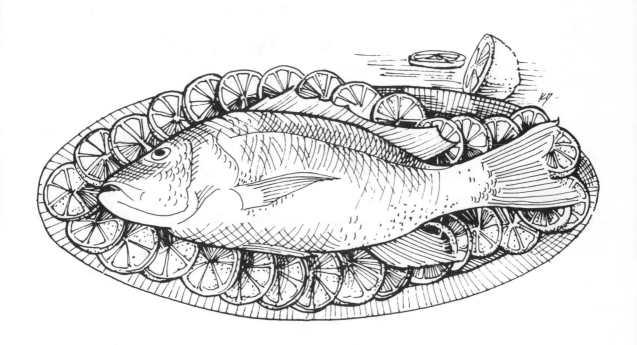

Crab Mousseline

There are three types of crab on the market: blue crabs from the Atlantic and Gulf coasts, Dungeness crabs from the Pacific, and king crab from North Pacific waters. Crab is sold live, frozen, or cleaned and packed in refrigerated tins. Canned crab is good, but lacks the delicate flavor of fresh.

YIELD: 4 Servings
CALORIES PER SERVING: 563
CARBOHYDRATES: 7g
PROTEIN: 28g
FAT: 47g
CHOLESTEROL: High
SODIUM: High
PREPARING: 20 Minutes
BROILING: 30 Seconds

3 T. *(45g)* butter
½ lb. *(225g)* fresh mushrooms, sliced
1 T. fresh lemon juice
¼ tsp. garlic salt
1 lb. *(450g)* fresh crabmeat (or a combination shrimp, crabmeat and lobster)
1 pkg. *(255g)* frozen artichoke hearts, cooked and sliced
2 T. *(30ml)* cognac
1 cup *(240ml)* Hollandaise Sauce (page 191)
½ cup *(120ml)* cream, whipped

Melt butter in skillet; saute mushrooms with lemon juice and garlic salt 2 minutes. Add crab meat; heat, stirring lightly until well coated with butter; add artichoke hearts, sprinkle with cognac and cook a few minutes longer. Place in buttered pie plate or divide into buttered scallop shells.

Fold whipped cream into hollandaise sauce; spread over crab mixture; brown under preheated broiler, watching carefully.

Robin Worcester, Weston, MA

Wine Suggestion: French Puligny-Montrachet, elegant white; serve chilled.

Baked Fillet of Sole Mustard

YIELD: 4 Servings
CALORIES PER SERVING: 375
CARBOHYDRATES: 6g
PROTEIN: 29g
FAT: 26g
PREPARING: 15 Minutes
BAKING: 20 Minutes
FREEZING: No

SAUCE:
8 T. *(115g)* butter
1 T. vinegar
1 T. fresh lemon juice
1 T. Worcestershire sauce
½ T. Dijon mustard

FISH:
1½-2 lbs. *(675-900g)* fillet of sole
Breadcrumbs
Freshly chopped parsley

SAUCE: In small saucepan melt butter; add vinegar, lemon juice, Worcestershire sauce, and mustard; stir to combine.

FISH: Roll fillets in bread crumbs and place in shallow baking dish just large enough to hold them without overlapping. Pour sauce mixture over fish.

Bake in preheated 400° oven 20 minutes. Garnish with chopped parsley and serve immediately.

Clare Edwards, West Hartford, CT

Variations, Advance Preparation, and Serving Suggestions: Any other firm white fish such as flounder or haddock may be substituted for the sole.

Wine Suggestion: Meursault Blanc Burgundy, rich white; serve chilled.

Microwave Conversion Instructions: Melt butter in 2-cup measure on High 1 minute. Add remaining sauce ingredients. Roll fillets in breadcrumbs and place in baking dish, with thicker portions at outer edges. Pour butter mixture over fish. Cover with plastic wrap; cook on High 8 minutes.

Calamari Ripieni

STUFFED SQUID

Squid, also called inkfish or cuttlefish, is a cousin of the octopus. Small squid are usually served whole; larger squid are cut into rings and pieces. The larger pieces are commonly used in Cioppino or Zuppa di Pesce.

YIELD: 4-6 Servings
CALORIES PER SERVING: 515
CARBOHYDRATES: 46g
PROTEIN: 49g
FAT: 15g
SODIUM: High
PREPARING: 3 Hours
BAKING: 45 Minutes
COOKING: 1 Hour

Refrigerate cleaned squid covered with cold water. Chop tentacles and saute in butter. Add onion, lemon juice, parsley and stuffing. Add either mushrooms, salami, or ham. Remove from heat and add egg, mixing with fork until well-blended and combined. Use a teaspoon to stuff each squid with 2 to 3 teaspoons mixture. Do not overstuff or the sac will crack. Secure opening of each squid sac with wooden pick or sew up with cotton thread.

SAUCE: In saucepan, saute onion in oil 5 minutes. Add remaining ingredients. Bring to boil. Reduce heat and simmer 1 hour.

Place squid in a 7 x 11-inch *(17.5 x 28cm)* casserole. Cover with sauce. Bake in preheated 350° oven 45 minutes. Serve hot or cold. Garnish with lemon.

Joseph Mehan, New Britain, CT

Wine Suggestion: Italian Frascati or Soave, dry white; serve chilled.

Microwave Conversion Instructions: Note: Decrease oil to 3 T. Prepare ingredients as directed above. Saute chopped onions in butter, uncovered, on High 3 minutes. Add chopped tentacles and cook on High 6 to 7 minutes, until fairly tender. Add remaining stuffing ingredients. Stuff squid. Do not overstuff. Secure opening of each squid. *Sauce:* In oval or round casserole saute onion in 3 T. oil on High 3 to 4 minutes. Add remaining ingredients. Continue to cook on High until boiling. Place squid in casserole. Spoon sauce over squid and cook on Medium (50%) 15 to 20 minutes.

3 lbs. *(1360g)* **squid, cleaned**

STUFFING:
2 T. *(30g)* butter
1 onion, chopped
1 cup *(75g)* prepared bread stuffing
2 T. *(30ml)* fresh lemon juice
¼ cup chopped parsley
Add one of the following:
   ¼ lb. *(115g)* mushrooms, chopped or
   2 oz. *(60g)* Genoa salami, chopped or
   2 oz. *(60g)* ham, chopped
1 egg, slightly beaten

SAUCE:
⅓ cup *(80ml)* oil
1 small onion, chopped
1 can (2 lb. 3 oz.) *(990g)* chopped
   tomatoes
1 can (6 oz.) *(170g)* tomato paste
1½ cups *(355ml)* water
2 T. parsley, chopped
1 T. salt
1 T. sugar
1 tsp. oregano, crumbled
1 tsp. basil, crumbled
1 tsp. freshly ground pepper
Lemon slices for garnish

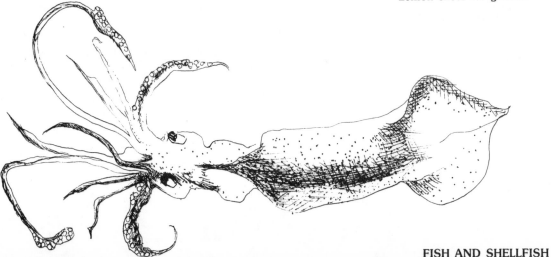

Jambalaya

YIELD: 12 Servings
TOTAL CALORIES: 7044
CALORIES PER SERVING: 587
CARBOHYDRATES: 67g
PROTEIN: 28g
FAT: 23g
CHOLESTEROL: High
SODIUM: High
PREPARING: 1-1½ Hours
COOKING: 1 Hour

This is certainly the most famous of all Acadian dishes. And like its Spanish ancestor paella, jambalaya is simply rice with whatever kind of meat or poultry or seafood you happen to have available, in whatever combination your taste buds tell you is right.

2 tsp. oregano
4 peppercorns
2 cloves garlic, peeled
3 tsp. salt
¾ cup (175ml) olive oil
2 tsp. vinegar
12 pieces chicken, boned (breasts and thighs)
4-8 oz. (115-225g) ham, cut into thin strips
2 chorizo sausages, sliced
2 oz. (60g) salt pork (optional)
2 green peppers, seeded and chopped
2 cups (300g) onion, peeled and chopped
1 tsp. ground coriander
2 tsp. capers
4½ cups (900g) rice, washed and drained
8 cups (2L) boiling water or chicken broth
2 tsp. saffron
12-24 medium shrimp, shelled and deveined
1 large pkg. (20 oz.) (570g) frozen peas
½ tsp. thyme, crumbled
A few drops Tabasco
1 can (4 oz.) (115g) pimiento or fresh tomato, chopped
Chopped parsley

With the back of a spoon, or in a mortar pulverize oregano, peppercorns, garlic, salt, 4 T. olive oil, and vinegar. Rub chicken with the mixture.

Heat remaining olive oil in a deep, heavy skillet; brown chicken lightly over moderate heat; add ham, sausage, salt pork, onion, green pepper, coriander, and capers; cook 10 minutes over low heat; add rice and cook 5 minutes stirring constantly.

Add boiling liquid, saffron, shrimp, peas, thyme and Tabasco; mix well and cook, covered, until liquid is absorbed. Gently combine rice from top to bottom.

Garnish with pimiento or tomato and parsley.

Gloria J. Holtsinger, West Hartford, CT

Variations, Advance Preparation, and Serving Suggestions:
May be made a day ahead, omitting shrimp and pea. Bring to room temperature, reheat, add shrimp and peas; cook until shrimp is just done.

Wine Suggestion: Alsatian Gewurztraminer, spicy white; serve chilled.

Microwave Conversion Instructions: Note: Cut recipe in half and add 1 tsp. browning sauce. Saute onion with 2 T. olive oil on High 4 minutes. Rub chicken with seasoning mixture as directed above. Put chicken in oval or round baking dish with thicker pieces of chicken at outer edges. Cover with waxed paper. Cook on High 10 minutes. Rearrange chicken in dish with less cooked pieces at edges. Cook on High 10 minutes. (Total time for chicken should be based on 5 minutes per lb.) Remove chicken. Add ham, sausage, salt pork, onion, green pepper, coriander and capers. Cook 5 minutes on High. Add rice, boiling liquid, saffron and peas. Mix well. Cook, covered, until liquid is absorbed. Add shrimp. Cover and cook on High 3 to 5 minutes. Do not allow shrimp to overcook. Add chicken; let stand 5 minutes. Garnish and serve.

Mariscos à la Costa Brava

SHELLFISH IN SPICED TOMATO SAUCE

This dish originated in Mallorca. As prepared in Spain, it is quite spicy and may be made with a mixture of shellfish.

YIELD: 6 Entree Servings
TOTAL CALORIES: 2430
CALORIES PER SERVING: 405
CARBOHYDRATES: 14g
PROTEIN: 31g
FAT: 25g
CHOLESTEROL: High-Shrimp
SODIUM: High
PREPARING: 30 Minutes
COOKING: 25 Minutes
FREEZING: No

In a bowl, combine parsley, vinegar, garlic, and anchovies; set aside.

In a large skillet, heat olive oil; add chili peppers and onion; cook until onion is soft. Add wine and bring to boil; reduce liquid by half; add tomatoes, salt, and pepper. Cook until most of tomato juice has evaporated. Add shrimp and cook for 5 minutes, do not overcook. Add capers, olives, and the parsley, vinegar, garlic, anchovy mixture; heat through.

Correct seasonings; sprinkle garnish on top. Serve on bed of saffron rice.

Sandra P. Robinson, Farmington, CT

Nutritional Notes: Shellfish is considered a good source of protein in comparison to its fat and carbohydrate content.

Per 100 grams raw meat	Calories	Protein	Fat	Carbohydrates
Oysters, Eastern	66	9g	2g	3g
Oysters, Western and Pacific	86	11g	2g	6g
Clams	77	11g	1g	6g
Scallops	74	15g	.2g	3g
Shrimp	89	18g	1g	2g

Wine Suggestion: California Sauvignon Blanc, herbaceous white; serve chilled.

Microwave Conversion Instructions: Note: Reduce olive oil to ¼ cup and wine to ¼ cup. Place chili peppers, onion and oil in 3-qt. *(3L)* bowl. Cook on High 3 to 4 minutes until onion is soft, stirring once. Add wine and cook on High until liquid comes to boil. Continue to cook 2 to 3 minutes until liquid is reduced by half. Add tomatoes, salt and pepper. Cook 4 to 5 minutes on High, until most of tomato juice has evaporated. Place half of shrimp on round 9-inch *(23cm)* plate, with thickest part facing outside of dish, and thin section facing inside, in a single layer. Cook on High 1½ to 2 minutes, just until shrimp turns pink. As soon as shrimp turns color, remove it from plate. Repeat this process with remaining shrimp. Add capers, olives, parsley, vinegar, garlic and anchovy mixture; heat through on High 2 minutes. Stir in cooked shrimp. If additional heating is necessary, watch closely to avoid overcooking shrimp. Correct seasonings; sprinkle garnish on top.

4 T. freshly minced parsley
3 T. *(45ml)* wine vinegar
2 large cloves garlic, minced
6 anchovy fillets, minced
½ cup *(120ml)* good quality olive oil
2 small hot chili peppers, or use dried peppers depending on desired spiciness
1 onion, finely minced
½ cup *(120ml)* dry white wine
8 ripe tomatoes, seeded, peeled, and chopped
Salt
Freshly ground pepper
2 lbs. *(900g)* fresh raw shrimp, peeled, or scallops
1 T. (heaping) capers, well drained
1 cup *(170g)* Greek black olives, pitted

GARNISH:

1 tsp. grated lemon rind
2 T. finely minced parsley
2 cloves garlic, minced

YIELD: 6 Servings
CALORIES PER SERVING: 367
CARBOHYDRATES: 14g
PROTEIN: 26g
FAT: 23g
SODIUM: High
PREPARING: 20 Minutes
BAKING: 10 Minutes
COOKING: 15 Minutes

Scallops à la Russe

2 lbs. *(900g)* bay scallops, rinsed
Milk
Salt
Flour for dredging
Oil or butter
1¼ cups *(285g)* mayonnaise
¼ cup *(60ml)* ketchup
Dash Worcestershire sauce
1 tsp. fresh lemon juice
½ pkg. dry chicken broth with
   seasonings (George Washington
   preferred)
⅛-¼ tsp. celery seed
¼ tsp. tarragon, crumbled
¼ tsp. chervil, crumbled
Dash Lawrey's seasoned salt
Dash freshly ground pepper
1 tsp. Dijon mustard
Freshly grated Parmesan cheese

Soak scallops in milk to cover 15 minutes; drain. Dredge in salt and flour and saute in oil or butter just until scallops turn white — 2 to 3 minutes. Drain when cooked.

Make sauce by combining remaining ingredients except cheese; gently mix with scallops.

Place in individual shells, ramekins, or a shallow baking dish. Sprinkle liberally with cheese and bake in preheated 300° oven until thoroughly heated. Place under broiler to brown.

Sandy Milliken, West Hartford, CT

Variations, Advance Preparation, and Serving Suggestions:
Dish may be prepared ahead, covered and refrigerated before heating and broiling. Serve with a rice pilaf.

Wine Suggestion: California Chenin Blanc, soft white; serve chilled.

YIELD: 4 Servings
TOTAL CALORIES: 1345
CALORIES PER SERVING: 337
CARBOHYDRATES: 10g
PROTEIN: 27g
FAT: 21g
SODIUM: High
PREPARING: 30 Minutes
COOKING: 10 Minutes
FREEZING: No

Sautéed Scallops Provençale

1½ lbs. *(680g)* bay or sea scallops
   rinsed, drained, dried
6 T. *(90ml)* olive oil
2 cloves garlic, finely chopped
1 shallot, finely chopped
1 tsp. fresh lemon juice
1 large ripe tomato, peeled, seeded,
   chopped
Salt
Freshly ground pepper
¼ cup finely chopped fresh parsley

If using sea scallops and they are quite large, quarter them.

In large heavy skillet or wok, heat oil. Saute garlic and shallot until tender but not browned. Increase heat to high; add scallops. Do not crowd pan or they will poach. Saute until scallops are lightly browned and opaque but not overcooked, 5 minutes. Add remaining ingredients; cook just to heat through and combine flavors.

Muriel Fleischmann, West Hartford, CT

Variations, Advance Preparation, and Serving Suggestions:
On serving platter, lightly mound cooked rice with parsley garnish in center, sauteed scallops on two sides, green peas around perimeter interspersed with tomato wedges. For a first course: divide prepared scallops among individual scallop shells, serve with hot, crusty baguettes.

Wine Suggestion: French Macon Villages Blanc, dry white; serve chilled.

Microwave Conversion Instructions: Note: For microwave preparation reduce olive oil to 4 T. Combine olive oil, shallots and garlic in 2-qt. *(2L)* casserole and cook on High 2 minutes. Add towel-dried scallops and remaining ingredients, cover with plastic wrap, cook on Medium (50%) 5 to 6 minutes, stirring once. Check for doneness — do not overcook.

Kung Pao Scallops

Ding Kung-Pao was a government official in China. Kung-Pao was his title and Ding was his family name. It is said that he liked to be served this peppery dish when in Szechuan. If your palate does not match his, the hot pepper can be reduced!

YIELD: 4 Entree Servings
CALORIES PER SERVING: 331
CARBOHYDRATES: 16g
PROTEIN: 24g
FAT: 19g
CHOLESTEROL: High-Shrimp
SODIUM: High
PREPARING: 50 Minutes
COOKING: 5 Minutes
FREEZING: No

Mix seafood in marinade for 30 minutes or up to 12 hours before cooking. Mix together ingredients for seasoning sauce. Mix together binder ingredients. Up to this point, everything may be prepared and refrigerated early in the day. When ready to cook, remove ingredients from refrigerator.

Place 2 cups oil in wok; heat to 325°. Re-stir seafood in marinade; add to wok all at once, stirring with a pair of chopsticks, one in each hand. Cook seafood about 1 minute. With large wire strainer, remove seafood from oil and let drain in colander set over bowl.

Pour oil from the wok into a bowl. Place wok over high flame; heat 30 seconds. Add ginger, garlic, dried peppers, and scallions; stir-fry 30 seconds. Add water chestnuts, pea pods, and peanuts; mix briefly. Re-add seafood along with seasoning sauce; mix briefly. Re-stir binder and add with one hand while stir-frying with the other for 1 minute.

Remove contents of wok to heated platter and serve immediately.

Susan Flynn, Avon, CT

Variations, Advance Preparation, and Serving Suggestions: 2 whole chicken breasts, 12-14 oz. each *(340-400g each)*, cut into ¾-inch *(2cm)* pieces can be substituted for shellfish.

Wine Suggestion: California Chablis, clean white; serve chilled.

1 lb. *(450g)* scallops or shrimp, shelled, deveined, butterflied, washed, and dried

MARINADE:

1 egg white
1 T. water chestnut powder
1 T. dry sherry

SEASONING SAUCE:

2 T. *(30ml)* dark soy sauce
1½ tsp. hot sauce
1½ tsp. sugar
1½ tsp. white vinegar
1 tsp. dry sherry

BINDER:

3 T. *(45ml)* chicken stock
1 tsp. water chestnut powder

2 cups *(475ml)* peanut or corn oil
2 tsp. ginger root, minced
1 clove garlic, minced
4 whole dried hot peppers, seeds removed (optional)
4 scallions, thinly sliced crosswise
10-12 fresh water chestnuts, peeled, washed, and cut in half
½ cup *(50g)* slant-cut pea pods (optional)
½ cup *(70g)* raw peanuts, roasted in preheated 325° oven 10 minutes

Lobster Pot

A cooking schedule for an indoor clam bake!

YIELD: 6 Minimum
PREPARING: 15 Minutes
COOKING: 1¼ Hours
FREEZING: No

Chicken pieces
Whole kielbasa sausage
Small potatoes, scrubbed
Fresh ears of corn, in husks
Eggs
Steamer clams, scrubbed
Whole live lobsters

Place ¾ inch *(2cm)* water in bottom of large steamer pot.

Countdown to serving time, add to pot:
    1¼ hours — Chicken pieces
    55 minutes — Kielbasa and potatoes
    30 minutes — Corn and eggs
    10-15 minutes — Clams and lobsters

Karen Roberts, Wrightsville Beach, NC

Wine Suggestion: California Inglenook Gamay Rose, dry rose; serve chilled.

Shellfish Mold

This recipe received the top rating from no less than 6 different testers!

YIELD: Hors d'Oeuvre Spread or
    12 Appetizer Servings or
    6 Entree Servings
TOTAL CALORIES: 1938
CALORIES PER
    ENTREE SERVING: 323
CARBOHYDRATES: 10g
PROTEIN: 10g
FAT: 27g
CHOLESTEROL: High
SODIUM: High
PREPARING: 30 Minutes
CHILLING: 4 Hours Minimum
COOKING: 15 Minutes
FREEZING: No

¼ cup *(60ml)* cold milk
1 envelope *(7g)* plain gelatin
2 T. *(30g)* butter
1 tsp. curry powder
1 small apple, pared, cored, and diced
1 small onion, diced
½ cup *(120ml)* chicken broth
½ tsp. Worcestershire sauce
2 T. *(30ml)* fresh lemon juice
¼ tsp. Tabasco sauce
½ cup *(115g)* mayonnaise
1 cup *(225g)* sour cream
2 T. chutney
2 cups *(½ lb.) (225g)* fresh lump crabmeat or cooked lobster, diced, or a combination
Watercress to garnish

Place cold milk and gelatin in a blender or food processor. Cover and blend at slow speed to soften gelatin.

Melt butter in skillet; add curry, apple, and onion. Cook until tender, but do not brown. Add chicken broth and bring to a boil. Add contents of skillet to milk mixture in blender. Turn speed to high and add all remaining ingredients except seafood. Blend until smooth.

Combine mixture from blender or food processor with seafood; mix thoroughly. Place mixture in lightly oiled 5-cup *(1.2L)* mold. Chill at least 4 hours or overnight. Unmold before serving and fill center with watercress.

Marshall Beirne, Wethersfield, CT

Variations, Advance Preparation, and Serving Suggestions: Serve with fresh asparagus and Croissants (page 220) or Blueberry Orange Bread (page 244) for a lovely luncheon.

Wine Suggestion: California Johannisberg Riesling, fruity white; serve chilled.

Nancie Bergquist

Szechuan Red Cooked Shrimp

Red Cooked refers to the fact that the shrimp are cooked in soy sauce. The Chinese call it red cooked even though it looks brown because the color red simply has more pleasing associations for them!

YIELD: 4 Servings
CALORIES PER SERVING: 246
CARBOHYDRATES: 10g
PROTEIN: 21g
FAT: 13.5g
CHOLESTEROL: High
SODIUM: High
PREPARING: 20 Minutes
STIR-FRYING: 5 Minutes

Sprinkle 1 tsp. of ginger and salt evenly over shrimp. Set aside to marinate at least 15 minutes.

Combine cornstarch and 2 T. water in small bowl; set aside.

Heat wok over moderately high heat 15 seconds; add 2 T. oil. It will be hot enough to cook when tiny bubbles form and a few wisps of smoke appear.

Add shrimp; stir-fry 45 seconds. Pour in wine, cover wok, cook over fairly high heat another 45 seconds. Remove from wok, set aside. Wipe out wok with paper towels, reheat over moderate heat; pour in remaining 3 T. oil. When hot enough, toss in chopped garlic and remaining ginger; stir-fry vigorously 30 seconds; reduce heat slightly; stir in hot pepper paste, soy sauce, ½ cup water, sugar and vinegar. May be prepared ahead of time up to this point.

Return shrimp to pan along with scallions. Cook over moderately high heat 2 minutes. Stir in cornstarch and water mixture; stir-fry until thick and clear, about 15 seconds; serve immediately.

Muriel Fleischmann, West Hartford, CT

Variations, Advance Preparation, and Serving Suggestions:
This dish is very hot, so reduce hot pepper paste to ¾ tsp. first time. If doubling recipe, stir-fry shrimp in two batches, then combine with seasoning sauce adding all shrimp to wok during final stir-frying. Serve with rice accompanied by pea pods and cherry tomatoes quickly stir-fried in sesame oil.

Wine Suggestion: California Ingelnook Gewurztraminer, spicy white; serve chilled.

1 lb. *(450g)* medium, raw shrimp (about 25), shells removed except tail piece, rinsed under cold running water
1-inch *(2.5cm)* piece fresh ginger, minced
1 tsp. salt
1 T. cornstarch
2 T. *(30ml)* plus ½ cup *(120ml)* water
5 T. *(75ml)* peanut oil, divided
2 T. *(30ml)* rice wine or dry sherry
9 cloves garlic, peeled and chopped to size of raw rice grains
2 tsp. Chinese hot pepper paste (can use garlic/chili paste)
2 T. *(30ml)* soy sauce
1¼ tsp. sugar
1¼ tsp. rice wine vinegar
4 scallions white and green sliced ⅛-inch *(0.3cm)* thick

YIELD: 8 First Course Servings
or 4 Entree Servings
CALORIES PER
ENTREE SERVING: 319
CARBOHYDRATES: 10g
PROTEIN: 27g
FAT: 19g
CHOLESTEROL: High
SODIUM: High
PREPARING: 15 Minutes
MARINATING: 30 Minutes
BROILING: 6-10 Minutes

½ cup *(70g)* **peanuts**
2-3 cloves garlic, minced
½ tsp. chili powder
2 T. *(30ml)* fresh lemon juice
2 T. *(30ml)* sherry
2 T. *(25g)* brown sugar
5 T. *(75ml)* soy sauce
½ cup *(120ml)* chicken stock
2 T. *(30g)* butter
24 medium-large shrimp, shelled and
deveined
1 large green pepper, cubed
8-12 cherry tomatoes
¼ cup *(60g)* butter, melted

Shrimp Saté

Sate, a national food in Indonesia, comes in endless variety. It means meat or fish cut in small pieces and grilled over charcoal on bamboo-skewers. Each town has a different recipe for sate sauce, and most are hot, hot! This is a mild version.

Combine peanuts, garlic, chili powder, lemon juice, sherry, brown sugar, soy sauce, chicken stock and butter in blender or food processor. Process until smooth. Heat the sauce to simmering; cool. Pour over shrimp. Marinate 30 minutes or longer.

Thread shrimp on skewers, alternating with pepper cubes and tomatoes. Brush vegetables with melted butter; grill or broil 3 to 5 minutes on each side until shrimp are just cooked. Serve with rice.

Katherine B. Wells, West Hartford, CT

Nutritional Notes: Nutritional analysis assumes that no more than half the marinade is absorbed by shrimp.

Wine Suggestion: California Fume Blanc, dry white; serve chilled.

YIELD: 12 Quiches
CALORIES PER QUICHE: 255
CARBOHYDRATES: 12g
PROTEIN: 9g
FAT: 19g
CHOLESTEROL: High
SODIUM: High
PREPARING: 30 Minutes
BAKING: 20 Minutes

CRUSTS:
Pastry for 2-crust pie (page 198)

FILLING:
¾ cup *(170-200g)* chopped, cooked
shrimp, about 6-7 oz.
¼ cup *(25g)* sliced scallions, green and
white parts
4 oz. *(115g)* imported Swiss cheese,
shredded, about 1 cup
½ cup *(115g)* mayonnaise (Hellmann's
preferred)
2 eggs
⅓ cup *(80ml)* milk
¼ tsp. salt
¼ tsp. dried dill weed

Individual Shrimp Quiches

CRUSTS: On floured surface, roll half of pastry into a 12-inch *(30cm)* circle. From it, cut 6 4-inch *(10cm)* circles. Repeat with remaining pastry. Fit into 12 2½-inch *(6.25cm)* muffin pan cups.

FILLING: Divide shrimp, scallions, cheese evenly among cups. Beat remaining ingredients. Pour into cups. Place on middle rack of preheated 400° oven; bake 15 to 20 minutes or until browned. Remove from oven; let cool on rack 5 to 10 minutes before serving.

Greta Kemp, West Hartford, CT

Variations, Advance Preparation, and Serving Suggestions: Pastry and filling can be prepared up to 24 hours ahead. Place shrimp mixture in pastry cups, wrap muffin tins well, refrigerate. Prepare liquid for filling and refrigerate separately. Pour into cups just before baking. This recipe can easily be doubled or tripled for party brunches or buffets.

Wine Suggestion: French Macon Villages Blanc, dry white; serve chilled.

Oyster Loaf

Oysters have a long history on this continent; ancient Indian settlements have been located because their inhabitants left heaps of empty oyster shells. Oysters are two-shelled mollusks, having one half of their shell flatter than the other. They vary in size from tiny western Olympias to the huge Japanese variety. On the East Coast, Maryland's Chincoteagues are famous.

YIELD: 8 Servings
CALORIES PER SERVING: 464
CARBOHYDRATES: 37g
PROTEIN: 16g
FAT: 28g
CHOLESTEROL: High
PREPARING: 30 Minutes
BAKING: 45 Minutes
FREEZING: No

Cut the bread crosswise to create top hat or lid. Scoop out most of center leaving a ½-inch *(1.25cm)* shell; reserve crumbs. Remove and reserve any soft bread remaining from lid. Rub interior of loaf with split garlic clove. Butter loaf and lid, inside and outside. Combine eggs with spinach, mayonnaise, nutmeg, salt and pepper. Place a layer of oysters in bottom of loaf (slice oysters in half if large), top with a layer of spinach mixture. Continue layering with tomato slices, reserved breadcrumbs and cheese. Repeat sequence until loaf is filled, ending with crumbs and cheese. Replace lid. Set loaf on buttered baking sheet. Bake in preheated 350° oven, 45 minutes or until mixture is set. Cover with foil, if crust is browning too rapidly. Cool 5 to 10 minutes before cutting in pie-shaped slices. Pass lemon wedges.

Bernice Kuzma, West Hartford, CT

Variations, Advance Preparation, and Serving Suggestions:
If sourdough bread is not available, substitute a French or Italian bread of same size obtained at specialty bakery.

1 large round, 12-inch *(30cm)* diameter sourdough French bread
1 large clove garlic split
Butter softened
3 eggs, slightly beaten
1 pkg. (10oz.) *(285g)* frozen, chopped spinach, thawed, drained
¾ cup *(170g)* mayonnaise
⅛ tsp. freshly grated nutmeg
Salt
Freshly ground pepper
1 pt. *(475ml)* fresh oysters, minimum 15 count
2 medium fresh tomatoes, sliced thinly
½ cup *(65g)* freshly grated Parmesan cheese
Lemon wedges

Grilled Shrimp

A must for a summer barbecue and wonderful all year round.

YIELD: 4 Servings
CALORIES PER SERVING: 283
CARBOHYDRATES: 3g
PROTEIN: 34g
FAT: 15g
CHOLESTEROL: High
PREPARING: 20 Minutes
MARINATING: 6 Hours Minimum
GRILLING: 6-10 Minutes

Leaving shells on, cut shrimps up back with scissors and remove black vein.

In a large bowl, combine garlic, parsley, dill, olive oil, wine, salt and pepper. Add shrimp; toss lightly. Cover and refrigerate 6 to 12 hours, tossing two to three times.

Grill shrimp over medium coals about 3 minutes on each side. Shells will be slightly charred and shrimp pink.

Timothy W. Goodrich II, Farmington, CT

Variations, Advance Preparation, and Serving Suggestions:
Serve with hot French Bread (page 229) and Couscous Salad (page 367). Follow with Fresh Fruit Terrine (page 70) for dessert.

Nutritional Notes: Nutritional analysis assumes that no more than half the marinade is absorbed by shrimp.

Wine Suggestion: Pouilly-Fuisse Bouchard Pere & Fils, rich white; serve chilled.

2 lbs. *(900g)* fresh, raw jumbo or medium shrimp in their shells
3 cloves garlic, finely chopped
3 T. freshly chopped parsley
1 T. chopped fresh dill
½ cup *(120ml)* olive oil
¼ cup *(60ml)* white wine
1 tsp. salt
2 tsp. freshly ground pepper

YIELD: 4 Servings
CALORIES PER SERVING: 222
CARBOHYDRATES: 19g
PROTEIN: 5g
FAT: 14g
PREPARING: 30 Minutes
COOKING: 30 Minutes
FREEZING: No

Tangy Braised Green Beans

Here is a lovely way to enjoy your own crop. Green beans and tomatoes team up with herbs for this creative preparation.

1 lb. *(450g)* small fresh green beans, washed
¼ cup *(60ml)* olive oil
1 dried hot chili pepper, cut in half, soaked in warm water 10 minutes, seeds removed
2 cloves garlic, finely minced
¼ cup fresh parsley, finely minced
5-6 large ripe tomatoes, peeled, seeded and chopped
1 large sprig fresh oregano, or 1 tsp. dried, crumbled
1 large sprig fresh thyme, or 1 tsp. dried, crumbled
3 large basil leaves, cut into thin julienne strips
Salt
Freshly ground pepper
Sugar
Finely minced fresh parsley for garnish

Steam beans until tender but still crisp. Drain. Rinse under cold water to stop cooking and to retain green color. Set aside.

In large skillet, heat oil; add chili pepper. When chili pepper has darkened, discard it. Add garlic, parsley, tomatoes, herbs; season with salt, pepper, and sugar. Bring to boil; reduce heat, partially cover and simmer 20 minutes or until liquid has evaporated and sauce is thickened. (Up to this point, can be made earlier in day. Combine green beans with sauce just before serving to finish cooking.) Add green beans to skillet and stir thoroughly into sauce. Cover and simmer 5 to 10 minutes to heat through. Taste and correct seasoning. Garnish with parsley.

Bernice Kuzma, West Hartford, CT

Variations, Advance Preparation, and Serving Suggestions: Leftover steamed beans may be resurrected with this recipe and taste like "the first time around". Delicious side dish for a cheese omelet with hot bread, as well as any meat or fish. Also good served chilled.

Nutritional Notes: If a non-stick pan is utilized with *1 T. oil*, the caloric content becomes approximately 100 per serving, making this a low-calorie vegetable.

Microwave Conversion Instructions: Place beans in 1½-qt. *(1½L)* casserole with ¼ cup water; cover, cook on High 5 minutes. Drain; let stand. Heat 2 T. oil and chili on High 1 to 2 minutes in deep narrow bowl, uncovered, or until oil darkens. Remove chili. Add garlic, parsley, tomatoes, herbs, salt, pepper, and sugar to oil. Cook uncovered 8 to 10 minutes on High. Pour oil mixture over green beans. Hold 2 to 3 minutes. Serve.

YIELD: 10 Servings
CALORIES PER SERVING: 280
CARBOHYDRATES: 18g
PROTEIN: 7g
FAT: 20g
PREPARING: 15 Minutes
BAKING: 30 Minutes

Pod Potpourri

This dish has an unusual texture.

1 pkg. (9 oz.) *(255g)* frozen French-style green beans
1 pkg. (10 oz.) *(285g)* frozen lima beans
1 pkg. (10 oz.) *(285g)* frozen peas
1 can (5.33 oz.) *(160ml)* evaporated milk
1 cup *(225g)* mayonnaise
1½ T. Worcestershire sauce
1 medium onion, finely chopped
1 can (8 oz.) *(225g)* water chestnuts, drained and sliced
Buttered breadcrumbs

Cook beans and peas according to package directions. Drain. Add remaining ingredients except breadcrumbs and mix together. Place in buttered 2-qt. *(2L)* casserole. Top with crumbs. Bake in preheated 350° oven 30 minutes.

Evelyn H. Beach, West Hartford, CT

Variations, Advance Preparation, and Serving Suggestions: Substitute water chestnuts with ½ cup sliced celery and 2 oz. *(55g)* chopped pimiento. Can also add chopped pecans or slivered almonds for crunch. Can use herb stuffing mix for topping.

Nutritional Notes: The caloric content of each serving may be decreased by 80 calories if imitation low-fat mayonnaise and evaporated skim milk are substituted.

Wine Suggestion: California French Colombard, semi-dry white; serve chilled.

Microwave Conversion Instructions: Note: Add ¼ tsp. paprika to buttered breadcrumbs. Place the 3 frozen packages beans in a ring formation standing on the side of the package rather than flat on the floor of the microwave oven. Cook on High 10 to 12 minutes, until steaming hot. Leave in unopened package until slightly cooled; drain. Place 1 cup *(120g)* breadcrumbs in a 2-cup *(½L)* glass measure. Add paprika and place 2 T. butter on top. Cook on High 2 minutes, stirring after 1 minute. Mix together all ingredients except breadcrumbs. Place in 10-cup *(2½L)* ring mold. Sprinkle crumbs over top. Cook, covered with waxed paper, on Medium (50%) 10 to 15 minutes.

Autumn Apple Butternut

A supermarket staple all fall and winter — its versatility makes it a delicious spicy or sweet accompaniment to poultry or roast pork.

YIELD: 8 Servings
TOTAL CALORIES: 2928
CALORIES PER SERVING: 366
CARBOHYDRATES: 57g
PROTEIN: 3g
FAT: 14g
PREPARING: 15 Minutes
BAKING: 15 Minutes
COOKING: 40 Minutes
FREEZING: Yes

Cut squash in half lengthwise; clean out seeds and membranes. Steam 30 minutes or until tender. Scrape out pulp and mash with electric mixer until smooth. Stir in 4 T. butter, salt, brown sugar and pepper; set aside. In skillet, melt 1½ T. butter; add apples and sugar. Cover and simmer over low heat until barely tender. Spread apple mixture in 9-inch *(22.5cm)* round buttered casserole. Spoon squash evenly over apples.

TOPPING: Combine cornflakes, nuts, sugar and melted butter, mixing well. Spread over squash. Bake in preheated 350° oven, 12 to 15 minutes, uncovered, until lightly browned.

Louise D'Aquila, Newington, CT

Nutritional Notes: A crushed whole grain cereal can be substituted for cornflakes.

Microwave Conversion Instructions: Wash squash; break off stem, pierce surface several times. Cook on High 20 minutes, turning squash halfway through cooking time. Prepare squash mixture as for conventional recipe; set aside. In large glass casserole, melt butter; add apples and sugar, cover with waxed paper, cook 5 minutes on High. Continue with casserole preparation as directed above. *Topping:* Melt butter in a glass bowl; add remaining ingredients, continue as for conventional recipe. Cook casserole 5 minutes on High, rotate dish ¼ turn, continue to cook on High 5 minutes. Allow 5 minutes standing time.

1 large butternut squash, 2½ to 3 lbs. *(1100-1350g)*
5½ T. *(80g)* butter, divided
¼ tsp. salt
1 T. brown sugar
Pinch white pepper
1½ qts. sliced apples, about 2 lbs. *(900g)*
¼ cup *(50g)* sugar

TOPPING:
3 cups *(85g)* cornflakes, coarsely crushed
½ cup *(60g)* chopped pecans
½ cup *(100g)* brown sugar
2 T. *(30g)* butter, melted

San Mateo Brussels Sprouts

Many people who have once eaten soggy Brussels sprouts forever more avoid them. It is a shame because, properly cooked, they are a pleasure to eat.

YIELD: 6-8 Servings
CALORIES PER SERVING: 152
CARBOHYDRATES: 13g
PROTEIN: 7g
FAT: 8g
CHOLESTEROL: High
SODIUM: High
PREPARING: 15 Minutes
COOKING: 12 Minutes
FREEZING: No

2 cartons (12 oz. each) (680g) fresh Brussels sprouts
2 T. (30g) butter
¼ cup (60ml) lemon juice
1 cup (225g) sour cream or Creme Fraiche (240ml) (page 200)
¼ cup chopped fresh parsley
½ tsp. salt
⅛ tsp. pepper
Pimiento stuffed olives, sliced or chopped

Remove loose leaves from sprouts. Cut an X ¼-inch (0.6cm) deep in the root ends. Cover sprouts with cold, salted water. Let sit 5 minutes. Drain. In skillet, melt butter over medium heat. Add sprouts. Cover and cook 10 to 20 minutes or until fork tender. Shake skillet occasionally to prevent burning. Add lemon juice, cover again and steam additional 2 minutes. Add mixture of sour cream, parsley, salt and pepper, stir gently; heat but do not let come to a boil. Garnish with olives.

Emily M.S. MacKenzie, Manchester, CT

Nutritional Notes: If olives are omitted as final garnish, sodium content is no longer high.

Brussels Sprouts Soufflé

Unlike most, this souffle can be prepared the day before serving. Blue cheese provides added intrigue.

YIELD: 6 Servings
CALORIES PER SERVING: 297
CARBOHYDRATES: 10g
PROTEIN: 12.5g
FAT: 23g
CHOLESTEROL: High
PREPARING: 20 Minutes
BAKING: 50 Minutes
FREEZING: No

4 T. (60g) butter
¼ cup (30g) flour
½ tsp. salt
1 cup (240ml) half-and-half
2 oz. (60g) grated sharp Cheddar cheese
2 oz. (60g) crumbled blue cheese
4 eggs, separated
1 pkg. (10 oz.) (285g) frozen Brussels sprouts, steamed, drained and chopped or use 1 carton (12 oz.) (340g) fresh Brussels sprouts

Melt butter in 3-qt. (3L) saucepan; add flour and salt. Cook several minutes, stirring constantly to blend. Add half-and-half at once and stir until mixture is thickened and slightly bubbly. Stir in cheeses until melted. Remove from heat. Beat egg yolks in large bowl until thick and lemon-colored. Slowly stir cheese mixture into yolks. Add Brussels sprouts. Blend well. Cool slightly. Beat egg whites until stiff but not dry. Thoroughly fold ⅓ of the egg whites into the egg yolk mixture. Take remaining ⅔ and fold in carefully. Gently pour mixture into ungreased 1½-qt. (1½L) souffle dish. (Up to this point, may be prepared in morning or day ahead, refrigerated, and removed one hour before baking). Bake in preheated 350° oven 45 to 50 minutes.

Janice Niehaus, West Hartford, CT

Microwave Conversion Instructions: Cook Brussels sprouts 9 minutes on High. Melt butter in 1-qt. (1L) casserole; blend in flour and half-and-half, stirring well. Cook on High 3½ to 4 minutes stirring after 2 minutes, again after 1 more minute. Add cheese and sprouts. Cool. Beat egg whites and fold in cheese mixture. Cook on Medium Low (30%) 25 minutes turning ¼ turn twice during this time.

Cabbage with Caraway or Fennel

Choose your seasoning — either way this cabbage recipe is outstanding, and tribute to the GOLDEN LAMB BUTTERY, Brooklyn, Connecticut, for demonstrating the versatility and deliciousness of freshly prepared vegetables.

YIELD: 6 Servings
CALORIES PER SERVING
  WITH CARAWAY: 347
CARBOHYDRATES: 11g
PROTEIN: 15g
FAT: 27g
CHOLESTEROL: High
CALORIES PER SERVING
  WITH FENNEL: 383
CARBOHYDRATES: 9g
PROTEIN: 8g
FAT: 35g
PREPARING: 45 Minutes
COOKING: 3½ Hours
FREEZING: No

DUCK OR PORK STOCK: Place all stock ingredients in stockpot or large kettle. Bring to boil, reduce to simmer. Cook slowly 2 to 3 hours, partially covered. Cool; strain, remove meat (discard bones). Chop meat coarsely.

CABBAGE: Meanwhile, soak shredded cabbage in large bowl cold water and lemon juice to cover 30 minutes. Drain well.

Melt 2 T. butter in large saucepan. Place ⅓ of cabbage in pan. Layer with ⅓ duck or pork meat, sprinkle with 1 T. caraway or fennel. Repeat, making three layers. Add just enough duck or pork stock to cover. Cook, uncovered over medium heat, to *al dente*, about 15 to 20 minutes. Drain off juices. Salt to taste. Transfer cabbage mixture to serving dish. Melt remaining butter in saucepan. Saute garlic briefly. Pour over cabbage.

For Cabbage with Caraway, sprinkle with paprika and parsley.

Variations, Advance Preparation, and Serving Suggestions: May be prepared a day ahead. Reheat in oven, serve hot.

Nutritional Notes: *Cabbage with Caraway:* This recipe is low in sodium and can also be reduced in calories by decreasing amount of butter used in the final step. Since the hearts and livers are significant sources of cholesterol, you may substitute other duck meat. *Cabbage with Fennel:* In order to decrease fat and calories, stock may be degreased by cooling and removing fat layer prior to using in recipe. Also, the amount of butter poured over cabbage in the final step can be decreased to taste.

Raw cabbage is an excellent source of vitamin C. An average serving of raw cabbage can supply 50 milligrams vitamin C (adult RDA is 60 milligrams). This delicate vitamin is especially susceptible to heat. Vitamin C is also water soluble and the soaking process will leach out some. Stir-frying in oil is a good alternative for maximizing vitamin and mineral retention in cabbage.

WITH CARAWAY:

Duck Stock:

4-6 duck necks, hearts and livers
2 medium onions, quartered
2 cloves garlic
Tops of 6 celery stalks, about ¾ cup
Dash freshly ground black pepper
8 cups *(2L)* water

Seasoning:

3 T. caraway seeds
1 clove garlic, minced
Salt to taste
Imported hot or sweet paprika, to taste
Fresh parsley, minced

WITH FENNEL:

Pork Stock::

3-4 lbs. *(1350-1800g)* pork rib bones
3 medium onions, quartered
3 stalks celery, in pieces
3 cloves garlic
½ lemon
Dash freshly ground black pepper
8 cups *(2L)* water

Seasoning:

3 T. fennel seeds or chopped fuzzy part
  of fresh fennel
1 clove garlic, minced
Salt to taste

CABBAGE:

1 medium head green cabbage,
  shredded
Dash fresh lemon juice
10 T. *(140g)* unsalted sweet butter,
  divided

Palsternackor och Morotter Suffle

PARSNIP AND CARROT SOUFFLE

If you have not explored the delight of parsnips, this light mixture is a wonderful introduction to the mildly sweet and flavorful vegetable. In Scandinavia, where this dish originated, root vegetables are widely grown and served because they retain their high quality during the long winters.

YIELD: 8 Servings
CALORIES PER SERVING: 150
CARBOHYDRATES: 13g
PROTEIN: 2g
FAT: 10g
CHOLESTEROL: High
PREPARING: 30 Minutes
MARINATING: 50-55 Minutes

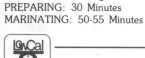

1 cup *(120g)* **finely shredded carrots**
4½-5 cups *(450-500g)* **peeled, sliced parsnips**
¼ cup *(60g)* **butter**
1 tsp. **sugar**
1 tsp. **salt**
1 cup *(240ml)* **milk**
4 **eggs, separated**
½ tsp. **freshly grated nutmeg**

Cook carrots, covered, 5 minutes; drain. Cook parsnips, covered, 15 to 20 minutes until tender; drain. Mash parsnips with butter, sugar and salt. Blend in milk and carrots. Beat egg yolks and nutmeg about 5 minutes until thick. Blend 1 cup parsnip mixture into yolks and return all to parsnip mixture. Beat egg whites until stiff; fold into parsnip mixture. Turn into buttered 2½-qt. *(2.5L)* souffle dish with prepared collar. (Souffle can be prepared 2 hours before baking.) Bake in preheated 350° oven 50 to 55 minutes.

Arlene J. Parmelee, West Hartford, CT

Sunshine Carrots

YIELD: 4 Servings
CALORIES PER SERVING: 160
CARBOHYDRATES: 25g
PROTEIN: 1.5g
FAT: 6g
PREPARING: 15 Minutes
COOKING: 30 Minutes

1 lb. *(450g)* **carrots, pared, bias cut**
    1 inch *(2.5cm)*

SAUCE:
¼ cup *(50g)* **sugar**
1 tsp. **cornstarch**
¼ tsp. **salt**
¼ tsp. **ground ginger**
¼ cup *(60ml)* **fresh orange juice**
2 T. *(30g)* **butter**

Cook carrots in salted boiling water about 25 minutes. Drain and set aside.

SAUCE: In saucepan, combine sugar, cornstarch, salt and ginger. Add orange juice, stir. Cook, stirring constantly until mixture thickens and bubbles slightly. Boil 1 minute. Stir in butter. Pour over carrots, tossing to coat evenly.

Rosalie M. Borst, South Windsor, CT

Nutritional Notes: Carrots are very rich in Vitamin A! This particular vitamin is not destroyed by heat and is not water soluble. Therefore, the preferred method of cooking fresh vegetables by steaming to preserve more vitamins is not as essential when cooking carrots. Steaming, however, will preserve some calcium, minerals and other vitamins as well as preserving more flavor.

Microwave Conversion Instructions: Note: For very tart orange flavor, ¼ cup orange juice concentrate may be substituted for the fresh orange juice. Place ¼-inch *(0.6cm)* sliced carrots in a 2-qt. *(2L)* covered casserole with ¼ cup water; cook 12 minutes on High, or until fork tender. Drain. *Sauce:* In a 4-cup *(1L)* glass measure combine sugar, cornstarch, salt and ginger; add orange juice; stir. Cook 1 minute on High; stir, cook 1 minute on High. Stir in butter, pour over carrots, tossing to coat evenly.

Soused Gourmet Onions

YIELD: 6 Servings
CALORIES PER SERVING: 143
CARBOHYDRATES: 9g
PROTEIN: 2g
FAT: 11g
SODIUM: High
PREPARING: 5 Minutes
COOKING: 15 Minutes
FREEZING: No

Sprinkle onions with sugar, salt and pepper. In skillet saute onions in melted butter 5 to 8 minutes, separating into rings. Add sherry; cover and cook 2 to 3 minutes or until tender. Sprinkle with cheese. Serve immediately.

Anne T. Shafer, Hartford, CT

Microwave Conversion Instructions: Note: Reduce butter to ¼ cup *(60g)* and sherry to ¼ cup *(60ml)*. Melt butter in uncovered casserole. Add seasoned sliced onions. Cook 10 to 12 minutes on High, covered, turning once. Add sherry. Cover and cook 3 minutes on High, stirring once. Sprinkle with cheese.

5 medium onions, thinly sliced
½ tsp. sugar
½ tsp. salt
½ tsp. freshly ground pepper
⅓ cup *(75g)* butter, melted
½ cup *(120ml)* sherry
2 T. *(20g)* freshly grated Parmesan cheese

Baked Stuffed Mushrooms in Cream

This easy-to-prepare vegetable is especially elegant served in a chafing dish on a buffet table.

YIELD: 6-8 Servings
CALORIES PER SERVING: 143
CARBOHYDRATES: 7g
PROTEIN: 4g
FAT: 11g
SODIUM: High
PREPARING: 20 Minutes
BAKING: 20 Minutes
FREEZING: No

Clean mushrooms and remove stems from caps. Set caps aside. Finely chop stems. Heat butter in skillet; add onions and mushroom stems and slowly saute until onions are slightly glazed, 3 to 4 minutes. Add mixture of breadcrumbs, salt, pepper, paprika, sherry and gently toss. Lightly pile mixture into mushroom caps and place in greased casserole or chafing dish liner. Sprinkle top with chopped bacon pieces and pour mixture of cream and Worcestershire sauce over all. Bake in preheated oven at 400°, 15 to 20 minutes, until bacon is cooked and casserole is bubbly.

Anne Healey, West Hartford, CT

Variations, Advance Preparation, and Serving Suggestions: Mushrooms may be prepared a day ahead, placed in refrigerator, and brought to room temperature before placing in oven. Serve as a first course in puff pastry cases.

Microwave Conversion Instructions: Cook bacon 2 to 3 minutes on High, between pieces of paper towel on a paper plate, until crisp. Chop and set aside. Place butter and onion in a bowl; cook on High 1 minute. Add mushroom stems and continue to cook 2 minutes. Add mixture of breadcrumbs, salt, pepper, paprika and 1 T. sherry and toss gently. Lightly pile mixture into mushroom caps; arrange in ungreased round pie plate or quiche dish just large enough to hold mushrooms close together. Cook, uncovered, on High 2 minutes. Sprinkle with bacon. Combine cream and Worcestershire sauce. Pour over mushrooms and cook until bubbly.

1 lb. *(450g)* mushrooms, 1- to 2-inch *(2.5-5cm)* caps
¼ cup *(60g)* butter
1 T. minced onion
⅓ cup *(40g)* fine, dry unseasoned breadcrumbs
½ tsp. salt
⅛ tsp. freshly ground pepper
¼ tsp. paprika
2 T. *(30ml)* sherry
3 slices bacon, finely chopped
1 cup *(240ml)* half-and-half
½ tsp. Worcestershire sauce

Vegetable Charlotte with Tomato Sauce

YIELD: 8 Servings
TOTAL CALORIES: 2560
CALORIES PER SERVING: 320
CARBOHYDRATES: 32.5g
PROTEIN: 7g
FAT: 18g
SODIUM: High
PREPARING: 1 Hour
BAKING: 25 Minutes

The interesting combination of tastes and beautiful presentation is worth the effort.

12 slices day-old bread, crusts removed, cut in half
10 T. *(140g)* butter, melted
2 cups steamed pureed carrots (about 4 large)
2 cups steamed pureed turnips (about 1 large)
2 cups steamed pureed Brussels sprouts (about 1 12-oz. *(340g)* carton)
Salt
Freshly ground pepper

TOMATO SAUCE:

2 lbs. *(900g)* flavorful tomatoes, peeled and sliced
Salt
Freshly ground pepper
6 shallots, finely chopped
1 T. brown sugar
1 bay leaf
2 T. *(30g)* butter
2 T. *(15g)* flour
1 cup *(240ml)* beef stock or vegetable stock

Line 2-qt. *(2L)* charlotte mold, including the bottom with pieces of bread that have been dipped in butter. Reserve a few pieces for the top.

Combine pureed vegetables; add salt and pepper to taste. Spoon puree into mold; cover with reserved bread.

Bake in preheated 425° oven 20 minutes. Unmold onto an oven-proof dish; place in oven again until bread is lightly browned.

Pour tomato sauce over charlotte. Slice in wedges.

TOMATO SAUCE: Place tomatoes, salt, pepper, shallots, sugar, and bay leaf in saucepan; bring to boil; reduce heat and simmer until tomatoes are well cooked; remove bay leaf; place sauce in blender or food processor and puree. Melt butter in a saucepan; stir in flour; cook stirring until lightly browned; add stock and continue cooking until thickened. Combine with tomato mixture.

Janice Niehaus, West Hartford, CT

Garden Fresh Tomato Pie

YIELD: 6 Servings
CALORIES PER SERVING: 338
CARBOHYDRATES: 17g
PROTEIN: 18g
FAT: 22g
CHOLESTEROL: High
SODIUM: High
PREPARING: 20 Minutes
BAKING: 30-35 Minutes
FREEZING: No

This recipe originally came from Maryland and has been served in the Sener family for many years. Excellent for brunches or buffets or as a sidedish with roasts or grilled meats.

2 cups *(120g)* fresh soft breadcrumbs
4 large garden fresh tomatoes, thinly sliced
2 large onions, sliced
2 cups *(225g)* grated sharp Cheddar cheese
½ cup *(400g raw)* crumbled bacon
2 large or 3 small eggs
½ tsp. salt
⅛ tsp. freshly ground pepper
3 strips bacon
Parsley

Cover bottom of buttered 9-inch *(22.5cm)* pie pan with half the soft breadcrumbs; reserve remaining breadcrumbs. Add layers of tomatoes, onions, cheese and finally bacon. Alternate these four layers until all ingredients are used.

Beat eggs well; add salt and pepper; pour over pie. Top with remaining breadcrumbs and strips of bacon. Bake in preheated 350° oven 30 to 35 minutes.

Garnish with parsley and serve hot.

Marcie Sener, West Hartford, CT

Creamed Parsley

The tedious stemming of the parsley is rewarded with this new and unusual vegetable side dish. Fill sauteed mushroom caps with cooked parsley mixture and serve as an hors d'oeuvre.

YIELD: 4 Cups or 8 Servings
TOTAL CALORIES: 2944
CALORIES PER ½-CUP SERVING: 368
CARBOHYDRATES: 14g
PROTEIN: 6g
FAT: 32g
CHOLESTEROL: High
PREPARING: 1½ Hours
COOKING: 45 Minutes

Bring 3 qts. *(3L)* water and salt to a boil in a very large pot. Add parsley leaves, return to a boil, simmer 2 minutes, stirring. Drain and refresh under cold running water. Wrap parsley in a towel and extract as much moisture as possible. Chop parsley or process 5 seconds in food processor. Do not completely puree parsley.

Melt butter in 2-qt. *(2L)* saucepan. Add shallots and cook about 10 minutes or until softened. Add parsley and mix thoroughly. Cook 10 minutes, stirring occasionally. Add cream and simmer very gently until cream has almost evaporated. Only traces of white cream should remain visible. Adjust seasonings. Serve immediately or reheat at serving time.

Dr. Colin Atterbury, West Haven, CT

Nutritional Notes: Parsley is high in vitamin A as well as other valuable vitamins and minerals. It is a nutritious vegetable and should be eaten more often — not just pushed aside as a garnish.

- 2 tsp. salt
- 2½ lbs. *(1.1kg)* fresh parsley, all stems removed
- 12 medium shallots (4 oz.) *(115g)* peeled and minced
- 6 T. *(85g)* unsalted sweet butter
- 2 cups *(475ml)* heavy cream
- Freshly ground black pepper
- A few grinds freshly grated nutmeg

Layered Vegetable Cheese Bake

An elegant side dish or an easy one-dish meal of everyone's favorite ingredients.

YIELD: 8 Vegetable Servings or
    4 Entree Servings
TOTAL CALORIES: 2264
CALORIES PER
   VEGETABLE SERVING: 283
CARBOHYDRATES: 18g
PROTEIN: 10g
FAT: 19g
CHOLESTEROL: High
SODIUM: High
PREPARING: 1 Hour
BAKING: 1 Hour

Butter an earthenware 1½-qt. *(1.5L)* casserole or baking dish. Layer with ⅓ of zucchini and potato slices. Sprinkle with ⅓ of cheeses, breadcrumbs, parsley, garlic, salt and pepper. Drizzle with 1 T. oil. Repeat each layer twice, drizzling each with 1 T. oil. Dot top with butter. Pour water over top. Cover and bake in preheated 350° oven 1 hour.

Olga Ippedico, West Hartford, CT

Wine Suggestion: California Chenin Blanc, soft white; serve chilled.

Microwave Conversion Instructions: Assemble ingredients in glass dish as for conventional recipe. Cover and cook 10 minutes on High. Rotate dish ¼ turn, continue to cook on Medium (50%) 15 minutes rotating ¼ turn every 5 minutes. Vegetables should be fork tender. Let stand 5 minutes covered. Place under preheated broiler 2 to 3 minutes to crisp topping if desired.

- 1 lb. *(450g)* zucchini, thinly sliced
- 3 potatoes, peeled, thinly sliced
- 1 cup *(115g)* sharp Cheddar cheese, grated
- 1 cup *(115g)* Monterey Jack cheese, grated
- 1 cup *(120g)* flavored breadcrumbs
- ½ cup chopped parsley
- 2 large cloves garlic, minced
- Salt
- Freshly ground pepper to taste
- 3 T. *(45ml)* olive oil
- 3 T. *(45g)* butter
- ¼ cup *(60ml)* water

Baked Apples with Spiced Sweet Potatoes

YIELD: 6 Servings
CALORIES PER SERVING: 335
CARBOHYDRATES: 48g
PROTEIN: 2g
FAT: 15g
PREPARING: 15 Minutes
COOKING: 45 Minutes
BROILING: 1-2 Minutes

Apples were known by primitive man. In Switzerland, carbonized remains of apples were found in prehistoric Iron Age lake dwellings and in the recorded history of Babylonia, China and Egypt, apples were mentioned. But in the New World there were no apple trees, so when the pilgrims arrived in New England, they lost no time in starting trees from seed.

**6 firm apples, Golden Delicious
   suggested**

PER APPLE:

½ tsp. sugar
⅛ tsp. grated lemon rind
1½ tsp. butter

**2 medium sweet potatoes, cooked,
   peeled and mashed**
3 T. *(45g)* butter
Salt to taste
⅛ tsp. freshly grated nutmeg
1 tsp. cinnamon
2 T. *(30ml)* cream
2 T. *(25g)* brown sugar
¼ cup *(30g)* chopped pecans
¼ cup *(40g)* raisins
6 marshmallows

Wash and core apples without cutting all the way through. Cut a piece off bottom of each apple, if necessary, so it will sit firmly. Pare one third down sides. Make foil cups to cover bottom one third of apple and shape to fit. Place in 11 × 7-inch *(28 × 17.5cm)* shallow pan. Fill centers of apples with sugar, lemon rind and butter. Put 6 T. water in bottom of baking pan. Bake, uncovered, in preheated 400° oven until tender, basting often. After 35 minutes, poke apples with straw to see if they are done. Do not overcook.

In mixing bowl, beat mashed potatoes until fluffy. Add butter, salt, nutmeg, cinnamon, cream and brown sugar; beat until well-mixed. Fold in pecans and raisins.

Fill each apple with sweet potato mixture, top with a marshmallow. In preheated 350° oven, warm apples several minutes, then put under broiler to toast marshmallow. Serve warm.

Joyce Anne Vitelli, Manchester, CT

Nutritional Notes: Sweet potatoes are extremely rich in vitamin A. The amount varies with the color of the flesh. The deep-orange varieties contain up to 10,000 *I.U.* per 100 grams whereas the light yellow variety can be as low as 600 *I.U.* per 100 grams. Sweet potatoes also provide a good amount of fiber to the diet. This particular dish could also be served as a dessert for family meals.

Microwave Conversion Instructions: Note: Delete water, foil cups and marshmallows. Place apples in glass baking dish with sugar, lemon rind and butter. Do not cover. Cook on High 8 minutes. Two long thin sweet potatoes can be baked with apples at same time. Remove all from oven. Mash potatoes; add seasonings. Fill each apple with sweet potato mixture. When ready to serve, reheat, uncovered, on Medium (50%) 2 minutes, more or less depending whether apples were cold. Be careful not to let them get mushy. Can be quickly put under broiler if browning is desired. If using broiler, marshmallows can be used.

Hawaiian Sweet Potatoes

Sweet potatoes were first found in Central America. According to Sir Francis Drake, "these potatoes be the most delicate roots that may be eaten."

YIELD: 6 Servings
TOTAL CALORIES: 2064
CALORIES PER SERVING: 344
CARBOHYDRATES: 55g
PROTEIN: 4g
FAT: 12g
PREPARING: 15 Minutes
BAKING: 45 Minutes
COOKING: 20 Minutes

Boil sweet potatoes just until tender; peel. In medium bowl, mash potatoes. Stir in pineapple to taste, 2 T. butter, salt and pepper. Spoon into 1-qt. *(1L)* ungreased casserole. Combine remaining butter with breadcrumbs, brown sugar and allspice. Sprinkle over potato mixture. (Up to this point, can be prepared as much as 8 hours before baking). Bake in preheated 350° oven, 45 minutes.

Geraldine C. Snelgrove, Windsor, CT

Microwave Conversion Instructions: Note: Reduce liquid — use only half of pineapple juice drained from 9-oz. can. Pierce potato skins. Cook 4 potatoes 8 to 9 minutes on High or 5 potatoes 9 to 10 minutes. Peel and mash potatoes in large bowl. To potato pulp, add 4 T. melted butter, salt and pepper, pineapple juice and pineapple. Turn into casserole. Place breadcrumbs, 2 T. butter, brown sugar and allspice in 1 cup measure. Cook, uncovered, on High 1 to 2 minutes or until crumbs are lightly toasted. Sprinkle crumbs over casserole. Cook on High 7 to 8 minutes or until heated through.

4-5 large sweet potatoes
9-16 oz. *(255-450g)* **crushed pineapple, undrained**
6 T. *(85g)* **butter, melted**
¾ tsp. salt
Freshly ground pepper
½ cup *(60g)* **dry breadcrumbs**
2 T. *(25g)* **brown sugar**
Dash allspice

Pommes de Terre à la Savoyarde

BAKED SLICED POTATOES WITH CHEESE

More than 5000 years ago the Indians who preceded the Incas in the valleys of the Andes Mountains of South America were cultivating potatoes. When the Spanish conquistador Pizarro introduced the potato (called *patata,* after the Haitian *batata*) in Europe, few were willing to eat them. King Louis XVI of France failed in his effort to convince his subjects to eat these "apples of the earth." The English also rejected potatoes at first, but the Irish adopted them.

YIELD: 6-8 Servings
CALORIES PER SERVING: 224
CARBOHYDRATES: 23g
PROTEIN: 6g
FAT: 12g
CHOLESTEROL: High
PREPARING: 30 Minutes
BAKING: 15-20 Minutes
COOKING: 25 Minutes
FREEZING: No

Melt butter in heavy skillet; add onions and potatoes; season well with salt and pepper. Cover with waxed paper, then place lid on skillet. Cook over gentle heat until vegetables are tender 25 to 30 minutes. Remove to buttered shallow casserole or au gratin dish. Add enough stock to partially cover vegetables. Cover with cheese. Sprinkle with paprika. (Up to this point, can be prepared ahead and refrigerated; bring to room temperature 1 hour before baking). Bake in preheated 400° oven 15 to 20 minutes, uncovered.

Sara Conrad, Hartford, CT

Microwave Conversion Instructions: Note: Use only 2 lbs. potatoes. Melt butter in casserole large enough to hold potatoes, on High 1 minute. Add potatoes, onions and seasonings. Cover and cook on High 15 minutes, stirring halfway through. Pour stock over potatoes and place cheese on top. Dust with paprika. Cover and cook on High 6 minutes.

6 T. *(85g)* **butter**
3 medium onions, thinly sliced
2-3 lbs. *(900-1350g)* **old potatoes, peeled and finely diced**
Salt
Freshly ground pepper
Chicken stock or vegetable stock
4 oz. *(115g)* **Gruyere cheese, thinly sliced or grated**
Imported sweet paprika

YIELD: 8-10 Servings
CALORIES PER SERVING: 428
CARBOHYDRATES: 26g
PROTEIN: 9g
FAT: 32g
SODIUM: High
PREPARING: 60 Minutes
BAKING: 30 Minutes
COOKING: 30 Minutes
FREEZING: Yes

Eggplant Provençale

This casserole is an excellent accompaniment to beef, pork and lamb roasts and plain grilled meats.

3 medium eggplants, peeled
Salt
2 T. *(30g)* butter, melted
1 T. flour
¾ cup *(175ml)* beef stock or
   vegetable stock
1½ lbs. *(680g)* garden ripe tomatoes,
   peeled, seeded and quartered or
   1 can (28 oz.) *(790g)* Italian plum
   tomatoes, drained
3 onions, finely chopped
1 tsp. sugar
Bouquet garni (bay leaf, thyme, parsley,
   in cheesecloth bag)
Freshly ground pepper
Flour for dredging
Olive oil for frying, about 1 cup *(240ml)*
Breadcrumbs
1¼ cups *(145g)* grated Gruyere cheese
2 T. *(30g)* butter

Cut eggplant into ½-inch *(1.2cm)* slices.

Make a roux of butter and flour; add stock gradually. Add tomatoes, onions, sugar, bouquet garni, salt and pepper to taste. Cook, covered over low heat 30 minutes. Remove bouquet garni; puree sauce in blender or food processor. Check seasonings. Coat eggplant with flour; saute in oil until browned on both sides. Drain on paper towel.

Layer slices in buttered baking dish, pouring sauce and sprinkling cheese over each layer. Sprinkle top with breadcrumbs and cheese; dot with butter.

Bake in preheated 350° oven 25 to 30 minutes, or until bubbly. Place under broiler until top is brown.

Mary Buschek, Chicago, IL

Variations, Advance Preparation, and Serving Suggestions:
This casserole freezes very well completely baked. To serve, thaw casserole, bring to room temperature, reheat in 350° oven 20 minutes and run under broiler.

Wine Suggestion: Italian Azura, soft white; serve chilled.

YIELD: 8 Servings
CALORIES PER SERVING: 296
CARBOHYDRATES: 12g
PROTEIN: 8g
FAT: 24g
CHOLESTEROL: High
SODIUM: High
PREPARING: 20 Minutes
BAKING: 25 Minutes

Peppers Roquefort

An unusual and pretty pepper dish that is equally delicious served cold.

4 red or green peppers
1 cup *(120g)* breadcrumbs
1 cup *(225g)* Roquefort cheese
⅔ cup *(150g)* mayonnaise
½ cup *(120ml)* milk
Fresh parsley sprigs for garnish

Cut peppers in half lengthwise. Remove seeds. Place in saucepan with water to cover. Bring to boil over high heat, boil 1 minute. Remove peppers from heat, drain well.

Mix remaining ingredients. Fill pepper halves with mixture. Place in shallow baking dish with a small amount of water in the bottom. Bake uncovered in preheated 350° oven 25 minutes.

Garnish each pepper with parsley.

Gloria J. Holtsinger, West Hartford, CT

Microwave Conversion Instructions: Note: Reduce milk to ¼ cup. After seeds have been removed from pepper halves, rinse in water and allow some water to cling to peppers. Place cut side down in shallow 2½-qt. *(2½L)* glass baking dish. Cook, covered, on High 2½ minutes. Mix remaining ingredients except 3 T. crumbs. Fill pepper halves and sprinkle remaining crumbs evenly over each. Cover and cook on Medium (50%) 6 to 8 minutes. Allow 2 minutes standing time before serving.

Francis Bergquist

Stir-Fried Zucchini and Yellow Summer Squash

YIELD: 4 Servings
CALORIES PER SERVING: 108
CARBOHYDRATES: 14g
PROTEIN: 4g
FAT: 4g
SODIUM: High
PREPARING: 15 Minutes
COOKING: 5 Minutes

Place wok over high flame 30 seconds.

Add oil and heat 20 seconds until it is hot but not smoking. Add scallions; let sizzle 15 seconds. Add zucchini and summer squash; stir-fry 2 minutes. Add sugar and salt; mix well. Add dill and stir-fry 1 minute.

Mix together water chestnut powder, sherry and soy sauce. Add mixture to wok while stir-frying squash 1 more minute.

Pour mixture onto heated serving dish and *serve immediately.*

Carol Kohn, West Hartford, CT

Nutritional Notes: Stir-frying is an excellent means of maintaining the nutritional value and texture of vegetables.

1½ T. *(22.5ml)* peanut oil
4 scallions, white and green parts, chopped
4 cups *(480g) small* zucchini, very thinly slant-cut
4 cups *(450g) small* yellow squash, very thinly slant-cut
1 tsp. sugar
1 tsp. salt
2 T. minced fresh dill
1 tsp. water chestnut powder or cornstarch
1 T. dry sherry
1 T. dark soy sauce (or bean sauce, spicy bean sauce, hoisin sauce, or oyster sauce; if used, omit fresh dill)

Zucchini Rounds

YIELD: 12 Rounds
TOTAL CALORIES: 684
CALORIES PER ROUND: 57
CARBOHYDRATES: 3g
PROTEIN: 2g
FAT: 4g
PREPARING: 5 Minutes
COOKING: 12 Minutes
FREEZING: Yes

An unusual way to use those prolific summer vegetables.

Combine biscuit mix, cheese, pepper. Stir in eggs just until mixture is moistened. Fold in zucchini. *[FOOD PROCESSOR: Put cheese in work bowl and process until finely grated. Add biscuit mix and pepper; process 2 seconds to combine. Remove and set aside. Insert shredding disc; put zucchini in feed tube vertically and shred using medium pressure, leave in work bowl. Insert metal blade. Add eggs and combine by turning machine on/off about 4 times. Add reserved cheese mixture and combine by turning machine on/off 3 or 4 times or just until flour disappears.]* If time permits, refrigerate several hours. This will stiffen mixture, making rounds easier to form. In 10-inch *(25cm)* skillet, melt butter over medium heat. Use 2 T. mixture for each round. Cook 4 at a time, 2 to 3 minutes on each side or until browned. Keep warm while cooking remaining batter. Spread with a little butter to serve.

Roberta Lawson, New Britain, CT

Variations, Advance Preparation, and Serving Suggestions:
After rounds have browned and cooled, wrap well and freeze. Remove directly from freezer onto baking sheet and heat in 350° oven 10 minutes.

⅓ cup *(40g)* packaged biscuit mix
¼ cup *(35g)* freshly grated Parmesan cheese
⅛ tsp. freshly ground pepper
2 eggs, lightly beaten
2 cups *(210g)* shredded zucchini or yellow squash
2 T. *(30g)* butter

YIELD: 4-6 Servings
TOTAL CALORIES: 1250
CALORIES PER SERVING: 208
CARBOHYDRATES: 28g
PROTEIN: 6g
FAT: 8g
SODIUM: High
PREPARING: 10 Minutes
BAKING: 17 Minutes
FREEZING: No

3 T. *(45g)* butter, divided
⅓ cup *(50g)* finely chopped onion
1 clove garlic, finely minced
⅓ cup *(70g)* diced fresh ripe tomatoes
  (use canned if fresh are not flavorful)
1 cup *(200g)* rice
2 sprigs fresh thyme or ½ tsp. dried,
  crumbled
½ bay leaf
1¼ cups *(300ml)* chicken broth
2 T. *(15g)* freshly grated Parmesan
  cheese
3 T. *(20g)* grated imported Gruyere or
  Swiss cheese
1 T. finely chopped parsley

Baked Rice with Tomatoes and Cheese

This method for cooking rice ensures a perfect batch every time
— the cheese and tomatoes are an added bonus.

Melt 1 T. butter in heavy ovenproof saucepan. Add onion and garlic;
cook, stirring, until onion is translucent. Add tomatoes, rice, thyme,
bay leaf; mix well. Stir in broth. Bring to a boil. Cover and place
saucepan in preheated 400° oven *exactly 17 minutes*. Remove from
oven, discard thyme and bay leaf. With fork, stir in remaining 2 T.
butter, cheese and parsley. Serve at once.

Dr. Sybille Brewer, West Hartford, CT

Variations, Advance Preparation, and Serving Suggestions:
Basic rice formula to use when not adding cheese and tomatoes, is
one cup of rice for each 1½ cups liquid.

Microwave Conversion Instructions: Melt butter in 2-qt. *(2L)*
casserole on High 20 seconds. Add onion and garlic. Cover, cook
2 minutes on High. Add rice, seasonings and tomato. Stir well and
add stock. Cover, cook on High 5 minutes. Continue to cook on
Medium (50%) 13 minutes. Allow 10 minutes standing time.

YIELD: 12 Servings
CALORIES PER SERVING: 395
CARBOHYDRATES: 47g
PROTEIN: 9g
FAT: 19g
SODIUM: High
PREPARING: 20 Minutes
BAKING: 40 Minutes
FREEZING: Yes

¾ cup *(170g)* butter
3 cups *(500g)* coarse bulgur (cracked
  wheat)
2 onions, finely chopped
6 cups *(1400ml)* chicken or beef broth or
  vegetable stock
2 tsp. salt
1 tsp. freshly ground pepper
1 tsp. curry powder
1 cup *(160g)* pine nuts (pignoli)
Freshly chopped parsley

Bulgur Pignoli Pilaf

Bulgur is the Turkish word for cracked wheat and is used in the
Mideast in place of rice for a pilaf. This bulgur casserole is a
delicious and more unusual alternative to rice. It accompanies
most lamb, beef, pork and chicken stews or ragouts beautifully.

Melt ½ cup butter in skillet; add bulgur and saute well.

In separate pan, saute onion in remaining butter until yellow gold.

In large, deep casserole, combine all ingredients except for parsley;
stir well. Bake uncovered in preheated 375° oven 30 minutes.
Check seasonings; bake 10 minutes longer. (Up to this point, make a
day or two ahead or freeze. Bring to room temperature and reheat in
325° oven 20 to 30 minutes.)

Serve garnished with fresh parsley.

Variations, Advance Preparation, and Serving Suggestions:
For a delicious meatless protein dish, substitute up to 1½ cups
(255g) soybean granules for bulgur. Also, 4 oz. *(115g)* grated
Cheddar cheese can be mixed into casserole before baking. Leftovers
can be reheated easily or can be combined with Sauce Gribiche
(page 367) and cooked vegetables as described in Couscous Salad
(page 367).

Nutritional Notes: Bulgur, a parboiled, dried and cracked whole-
grain wheat with the bran and germ intact is an excellent source of
vegetable protein that also contains valuable minerals and vitamins.
Eaten along with a bean, pea or lentil dish, these vegetable proteins
will form complete proteins.

Pineapple Bread Pudding

Excellent for brunch and especially good with ham or pork.

YIELD: 6-8 Servings
TOTAL CALORIES: 2704
CALORIES PER SERVING: 338
CARBOHYDRATES: 44g
PROTEIN: 4.5g
FAT: 16g
CHOLESTEROL: High
PREPARING: 15 Minutes
BAKING: 1 Hour

Cream butter and sugar. Add eggs and beat until mixture is thick and pale lemon colored. Add crushed pineapple and bread; mix well. Place in buttered 2-qt. *(2L)* casserole. Bake in preheated 325° oven 1 hour.

Linda Cadigan, TX   .

Nutritional Notes: Pineapple canned in its own juice contains approximately 15 fewer calories per serving than that canned in heavy syrup. Experiment with substituting whole wheat bread for white bread.

Microwave Conversion Instructions: Drain liquid from pineapple. Prepare as directed above. Cook on Medium (50%) 15 minutes.

¼ lb. *(115g)* butter
1 cup *(200g)* sugar
4 eggs
1 can (20 oz.) *(565g)* crushed pineapple (do not drain)
6 slices good quality white bread, crusts removed, cubed

Traditional Noodle Pudding

Some like to serve the pudding as a meat accompaniment or as a meatless main dish. Some like it as a dessert, warm or cold. Everyone enjoys it.

YIELD: 12 Servings
CALORIES PER SERVING: 234
CARBOHYDRATES: 39g
PROTEIN: 6g
FAT: 6g
CHOLESTEROL: High
PREPARING: 20 Minutes
BAKING: 2 Hours
FREEZING: Yes

Cook noodles according to package directions. Drain and set aside. Heat buttered 9 x 13-inch *(22.5 x 33cm)* baking dish in a preheated 400° oven. With electric mixer, beat together eggs, sugar, salt, oil, lemon juice and cinnamon. By hand, stir in raisins and apples. Combine with cooked noodles with folding motion. Quickly pour into heated baking dish. Bake at 400° (Reduce heat 25° if using glass container.) 15 minutes, reduce to 350°, bake 45 minutes or until golden brown. Let stand 5 minutes before cutting into 3 x 3-inch *(7.5 x 7.5cm)* portions. Garnish with chopped parsley.

Renee Pregulman Dubin, West Hartford, CT

Variations, Advance Preparation, and Serving Suggestions: May be frozen and reheated. To serve, thaw overnight at room temperature. Place in preheated 350° oven until heated through. Noodle Pudding is versatile and can easily be altered to taste. If serving as a dessert, sugar should be increased. Whole wheat noodles may be used, for example, and other fruits, cottage cheese, sour cream, yogurt, etc. may add variety.

Nutritional Notes: Fewer eggs may be utilized to decrease cholesterol content.

1 pkg. (12 oz.) *(340g)* egg noodles, medium width
4-6 eggs, well beaten
½ cup *(100g)* sugar
Salt
2 T. *(30ml)* oil
Juice of ½ lemon (optional)
1 tsp. cinnamon
½ cup *(85g)* raisins
4 apples, peeled, thinly sliced
Parsley

YIELD: 10-12 Servings
CALORIES PER SERVING: 357
CARBOHYDRATES: 24g
PROTEIN: 9g
FAT: 25g
CHOLESTEROL: High
SODIUM: High
PREPARING: 30 Minutes
BAKING: 1 Hour
FREEZING: No

4 cups *(950ml)* **water**
2 tsp. **salt**
2 cups *(300g) quick* **grits (not regular or instant)**
2 cups *(475ml)* **whole milk**
2 cups *(225g)* **grated extra sharp Cheddar**
4 **egg yolks**
Cayenne pepper to taste (about 1 tsp.)
½ **lb.** *(225g)* **butter**
Grated cheese (optional)
Paprika (optional)

Cheese Grits

Grits is a dish commonly found in the southern region of the United States. The casserole is flavored with butter and cheese and makes a good substitute for rice when serving veal, chicken, ham or lamb dishes.

Bring water and salt to boil in large saucepan. Over low heat, add grits; cook stirring constantly 5 minutes. Add milk; stir. Let cook, covered, over low heat 10 minutes. Add grated cheese and then egg yolks; stir. Add cayenne to taste. Add butter and stir until well-blended. Place in buttered 3-qt. *(3L)* casserole. (Up to this point may be done a day ahead and refrigerated; bring to room temperature before heating.) Add additional grated cheese and a dusting of paprika on top if desired. Bake in a preheated 350° oven 1 hour.

Betty Lynn Wright, West Hartford, CT

Nutritional Notes: Hominy grits or corn grits are ground grains of corn with the hull and germ removed. White hominy is somewhat lower in vitamin A than yellow hominy. White hominy usually has vitamins and minerals added by the manufacturer.

Microwave Conversion Instructions: Note: Reduce butter to ¼ lb. and add 1 additional cup grated cheese for topping. Place grits and salt in 3-qt. casserole. Add 4 cups boiling water. Cook on High 3 to 4 minutes, stirring once. Stir in milk; cook on Medium (50%) 7 minutes. Stir in grated cheese. Take some of hot mixture and whisk with egg yolks; add to casserole along with cayenne and butter and stir until blended. Cook on Medium (50%) 25 minutes, stirring once after 15 minutes. Sprinkle with additional 1 cup cheese and paprika. Cook on High 3 to 4 minutes, until bubbling hot and cheese is completely melted.

YIELD: 6-8 Servings
CALORIES PER SERVING: 228
CARBOHYDRATES: 22g
PROTEIN: 8g
FAT: 12g
PREPARING: 20 Minutes
BAKING: 30 Minutes

1 cup *(150g)* **grits**
4 cups *(950ml)* **milk**
4 T. *(60g)* **butter**
1 tsp. **sugar**
1 tsp. **salt**
2 **eggs, separated**

Grits Soufflé

Even non-grit eaters rate this dish highly. It is a perfect accompaniment for ham or game. It is also a hit at breakfast.

In top of double boiler combine grits, milk, butter, and sugar. Cook, stirring often, until slightly thickened. Add salt. Remove from heat and beat in egg yolks one at a time. Beat egg whites until stiff peaks form. Fold into souffle base. Pour mixture into buttered 2-qt. *(2L)* souffle dish or casserole. Bake in preheated 350° oven 30 minutes or until set. Recipe easily doubles.

Alice Evans, Simsbury, CT

Microwave Conversion Instructions: In glass bowl combine grits, milk, butter and sugar; cook 3 minutes on High, stirring occasionally with wire whip. Remove from oven and beat in egg yolks one at a time. Beat egg whites until stiff peaks form; fold into souffle base. Pour mixture into buttered, 2-qt. round shallow baking dish. Cook on Medium Low (30%) 20 to 25 minutes or until top is dry, rotating dish ¼ turn at least 4 times. Note: If there is uneven rising, rotate dish more frequently, placing high of souffle in area of oven where lowest side was located.

Rice Pilaf Indienne

A pilaf or pilau is rice cooked in the eastern manner — or more accurately, in one of the many ways used from the Balkans to Burma.

YIELD: 12 Servings
TOTAL CALORIES: 3480
CALORIES PER SERVING: 290
CARBOHYDRATES: 51g
PROTEIN: 5g
FAT: 7g
SODIUM: High
PREPARING: 1 Hour
MARINATING: 1½ Hours
COOKING: 1½ Hours

COCONUT MILK: Scrape meat from fresh coconut; chop finely in food processor or blender. Add 2 cups *(474ml)* hot water to each cup coconut meat. Let stand 1½ hours. Then squeeze mixture through cheesecloth to extract milk. The coconut milk or coconut cream makes up part of the 8 cups water used in cooking rice.

PILAF: In large enamel pot, melt 8 T. butter. Lightly saute raisins until they puff; remove to side dish with slotted spoon. Saute almonds until golden brown. (It may be necessary to add more butter). Remove to side dish with slotted spoon.

Melt remaining 2 to 4 T. butter in pot and add rice. Saute 5 to 10 minutes until lightly browned. Add garlic, water (coconut milk included) and spices. Cover and simmer slowly until all water is absorbed, approximately 1 hour. Serve on large platter garnished with slivered almonds, raisins, and egg slices.

Ann Janzen, Avon, CT

2 oz. *(60ml)* coconut cream or coconut milk obtained from 1 fresh coconut
12 T. *(170g)* butter, divided
2 cups *(340g)* raisins
¼ lb. *(115g)* slivered almonds
4 cups *(800g)* white rice
1 clove garlic, minced
8 cups *(2L)* water (coconut milk included)
1 tsp. ginger
1 tsp. turmeric
1 tsp. cardamom
½ tsp. whole cloves
2 sticks whole cinnamon
4 tsp. salt
6 hard-cooked eggs, sliced

Spicy Rice Ortega

A Mexican twist turns this rice dish into a delicious and unusual meat accompaniment.

YIELD: 10-12 Servings
CALORIES PER SERVING: 248
CARBOHYDRATES: 16g
PROTEIN: 10g
FAT: 16g
CHOLESTEROL: High
SODIUM: High
PREPARING: 30 Minutes
BAKING: 35 Minutes

½ cup *(75g)* chopped onion
3 T. *(45g)* butter
4 cups cooked rice *(265g raw)*
1 small red or green pepper, minced
2 cups *(450g)* sour cream
1 cup *(225g)* cottage cheese
2½ cups *(280g)* grated Longhorn or Monterey Jack cheese
½ bay leaf, crumbled
1 can (4 oz.) *(115g)* green chilies, chopped
Salt
Freshly ground black pepper

Saute onion in butter until lightly browned; combine well with remaining ingredients, reserving ½ cup cheese. Place mixture in buttered 2-qt. *(2L)* casserole. Cover, bake in preheated 375° oven 25 minutes. Remove casserole from oven, sprinkle with reserved cheese. Bake uncovered 10 minutes longer. Can be prepared in advance and reheated before serving. Serve hot.

Carle Mowell, Birmingham, MI

Variations, Advance Preparation, and Serving Suggestions: Hot onion cheese, chopped spinach and pine nuts can be used instead of chilies and green pepper.

Nutritional Notes: Brown rice can be used as a high fiber variation, although cooking time will be longer.

Microwave Conversion Instructions: Note: Reduce butter to 2 T. and add 2 T. chopped fresh parsley for garnish. Place onion and 2 T. butter in 2-qt. casserole. Cook 3 minutes on High. Stir in rice to blend well. Add all remaining ingredients, reserving ½ cup grated cheese. Cook, covered, on Medium (50%) 15 to 17 minutes, stirring once. Timing depends on starting temperature of ingredients. When heated through, sprinkle with reserved cheese. Cook on High 2 to 3 minutes, just until cheese is melted. Sprinkle with parsley.

YIELD: 6 Entree Servings
CALORIES PER SERVING: 148
CARBOHYDRATES: 2g
PROTEIN: 17g
FAT: 8g
SODIUM: High
PREPARING: 20 Minutes
CHILLING: Overnight

Dilled Tuna Salad

This raises the lowly tuna salad to a more exalted taste level.

1 can (13 oz.) *(370g)* water-packed solid
   white tuna, well-drained
MARINADE:
½ cup *(120ml)* white wine vinegar
1 medium onion, chopped
½ tsp. dill seed
1 bay leaf
⅛ tsp. allspice
½ tsp. dry mustard

½ cup *(53g)* sliced celery
¼ cup *(60g)* mayonnaise (page 190)

GARNISH: Lettuce

Choose 2 or more from the following,
   keeping color contrast in mind:
   Tomatoes, ripe olives, dill pickles
   (sliced), tiny whole beets, or
   asparagus spears

Place tuna in workbowl and gently break into pieces with fork. In small saucepan combine vinegar, onion, dill seed, bay leaf, allspice and mustard; bring to boil. Pour marinade over tuna; refrigerate several hours or overnight. Just before serving, drain tuna thoroughly; combine with celery and mayonnaise. Serve on lettuce bed with choice of garnishes.

Beaubette Kagey, Simsbury, CT

Nutritional Notes: Imitation mayonnaise may be used to further decrease calories. Low-sodium tuna may also be used for sodium-restricted diets.

YIELD: 6-8 Entree Servings
CALORIES PER SERVING: 450
CARBOHYDRATES: 19g
PROTEIN: 15g
FAT: 35g
SODIUM: High
CHOLESTEROL: High
PREPARING: 1 Hour
CHILLING: 24 Hours

Curried Shrimp Salad

1 pkg. (6 oz.) *(170g)* curried rice mix,
   cooked according to package
   directions, cooled
2 cups *(300g)* cooked small shrimp
1 cup *(110g)* chopped celery
½ cup *(85g)* chopped green pepper
8 slices *(200g)* bacon, cooked and
   crumbled
½ cup *(120ml)* heavy cream, whipped
½ cup *(115g)* mayonnaise (page 190)
4 tsp. curry powder
3-4 ripe avocados, halved
Leafy lettuce
GARNISH:

Mango chutney
Salted cashews
Shredded coconut

Combine shrimp, celery, pepper, bacon, with cooked, cooled rice. Blend curry powder and mayonnaise with whipped cream; stir into rice mixture. Cover and chill overnight.

Serve on avocado half placed on lettuce-lined, chilled plate. Place chutney, cashews, and coconut in individual small bowls to be served as accompaniments.

Ann Houston Feenstra, Houston, TX

Nutritional Notes: This salad becomes low-calorie only if avocado halves are omitted. One half avocado contributes about 170 calories to each serving, and about half the fat content. On the positive side, avocados are loaded with essential vitamins and minerals. They are high in vitamins A and E. In addition, they are an excellent source of iron and potassium. And they contain no cholesterol!

Wine Suggestion: California Grey Riesling, clean white; serve chilled.

Chilled Scallop Salad

The fresh green beans and new potatoes make this salad heartier than it appears.

YIELD: 8 Entree Servings
CALORIES PER SERVING: 309
CARBOHYDRATES: 17g
PROTEIN: 13g
FAT: 21g
SODIUM: High
PREPARING: 15 Minutes
CHILLING: 4 Hours Minimum
COOKING: 35 Minutes

Steam unpeeled potatoes until tender, about 25 minutes. Let cool to room temperature. Steam green beans *al dente,* about 10 minutes, depending on size.

Meanwhile, bring water, wine, lemon juice, salt and bay leaf to boil in medium saucepan. Add scallops; return to boil. Reduce heat and simmer 1 minute. Drain.

Peel and slice potatoes; combine with scallops and green beans. Add Italian dressing and mix gently. Chill at least 4 hours or overnight. Drain. At serving time or not more than several hours before, add celery, scallions, mayonnaise, sour cream and dill. Mix gently. Pile salad in shallow bowl. Garnish with romaine leaves and twisted lemon slices.

Kathleen J. Schwartz, Avon, CT

Variations, Advance Preparation, and Serving Suggestions: Radish roses or pimientos cut in fancy shapes could also garnish this pretty salad which should be presented in a crystal bowl. For a complete luncheon entree, just add flaky Croissants (page 220) and butter curls.

Nutritional Notes: Plain lowfat yogurt can be substituted for a portion of mayonnaise and/or sour cream in order to decrease calories. The flavor will be somewhat more tart and the consistency slightly thinner.

6 small new potatoes
1 lb. *(450g)* small fresh green string beans
1¾ cups *(415ml)* water
½ cup *(120ml)* white wine
3 T. *(45ml)* fresh lemon juice
½ tsp. salt
1 bay leaf
1 lb. *(450g)* bay scallops or 1¼ lbs. *(570g)* sea scallops, cut in bite-size pieces
½ cup *(120ml)* Italian dressing
1 cup *(100g)* sliced celery
3 T. *(15g)* chopped scallions, white and green parts
½ cup *(115g)* mayonnaise, Homemade (page 190) or Hellmann's preferred
¼ cup *(60g)* sour cream or Creme Fraiche (page 200)
½ tsp. dried dill weed
Romaine leaves
Fresh lemon slices

YIELD: 6 Entree Servings
TOTAL CALORIES: 2022
CALORIES PER SERVING: 337
CARBOHYDRATES: 5g
PROTEIN: 14g
FAT: 29g
CHOLESTEROL: High
PREPARING: 30 Minutes
CHILLING: 2 Hours

Crab and Cucumber Salad

Remove any cartilage from crabmeat. Slice cucumbers crosswise into ½-inch *(1.2cm)* thick pieces. Place in saucepan with wine to cover. Simmer gently about 3 minutes, until translucent around edges but not limp. Drain on paper towels; cool thoroughly.

Whisk egg and mustard together in small bowl. Whisking constantly, add oil in small stream. Whisk in lemon juice, salt and pepper. Stir in sour cream or creme fraiche to desired consistency. Correct seasonings to taste. Gently fold in crabmeat, cucumbers. Chill several hours before serving.

Kathleen J. Schwartz, Avon, CT

1 lb. *(450g)* fresh lump crabmeat (if not available, use frozen langostinos, thawed and drained)
2½ medium cucumbers, peeled, halved lengthwise, seeded
About ⅓ bottle *(250ml)* dry white wine
CREME FRAICHE DIJON DRESSING:
1 egg yolk
1 tsp. Dijon mustard
⅓ cup *(80ml)* peanut oil
⅓ cup *(80ml)* olive oil
Juice of ½ lemon
Salt
Freshly ground pepper to taste
About ¾ cup *(170g)* sour cream or Creme Fraiche (page 200)

Szechuan Peppercorn Chicken Salad

This is not just another chicken salad, but a marvelous variation on an old theme! Szechuan is a province in the inland area of China with a penchant for more highly seasoned food. It is their Szechuan pepper that has given this region's dishes a fiery reputation. This piquant spice differs from the pepper we know; these tiny reddish-brown peppercorns have a strong, pungent smell that distinguishes them from black peppercorns, which are actually hotter. They cause a peculiar delayed reaction, for at first they seem to have no taste at all. Then suddenly there it is, strong and hot. In fact, if enough is taken, it makes the mouth numb for a little while. Used in cooking, this reaction is not so noticeable.

YIELD: 6 First Course Servings
  or 3-4 Entree Salads
TOTAL CALORIES: 1136
CALORIES PER ENTREE
  SERVING: 284
CARBOHYDRATES: 16g
PROTEIN: 37g
FAT: 8g
SODIUM: High
PREPARING: 15 Minutes
CHILLING: 4 Hours Minimum
COOKING: 1 Hour

2 whole chicken breasts (12-14 oz. each)
  (340-400g each)
2 cups (170g) sliced leek tops
2 slices fresh ginger root
4 cups (300g) shredded Chinese or
  Shantung cabbage

SZECHUAN PEPPERCORN DRESSING:
2 T. (30ml) peanut oil
½ cup (40g) chopped scallion
1 tsp. minced fresh ginger root
½ tsp. ground Szechuan peppercorns
1 fresh hot chili, chopped
2 T. (30ml) dark soy sauce
1 T. hoisin sauce
2 T. (40g) honey
2 cloves garlic, minced
1-2 tsp. hot red pepper sauce

CHICKEN: Rinse chicken breasts in water. Place leeks and ginger in 2 qts. (2L) boiling water. Return water to boil; add chicken, cover, and cook over high flame 15 minutes. Turn off heat; allow chicken to cool in water 45 minutes, leaving cover askew. Remove chicken from pan and refrigerate, covered, until cold; then remove skin and bone and coarsely shred chicken meat. Refrigerate until ready to use.

Shred cabbage; refrigerate until ready to serve.

DRESSING: Combine the oil, scallions, minced ginger, ground peppercorns, and chopped chili in a saucepan; heat until it bubbles, then simmer 1 minute; combine with remaining dressing ingredients. Pour dressing over chicken and cabbage; toss well. Serve immediately.

Karen Lee, New York, NY
adapted from her book Chinese Cooking for the American Kitchen

Variations, Advance Preparation, and Serving Suggestions:
Serve as part of a Chinese banquet, a luncheon entree with Croissants (page 220) or Gougere (page 145), or as part of a salad buffet with Shellfish Mold (page 334) and Shrimp Filled Tomato Aspic with Dressing (page 90).

Pon Pon Chicken

An adaptation of a Szechuan chicken and vegetable salad, to be served as hot and spicy as you please.

YIELD: 4 Entree Servings or
   6 as Part of Chinese Meal
TOTAL CALORIES: 2190
CALORIES PER ENTREE
   SERVING: 336
CARBOHYDRATES: 9g
PROTEIN: 30g
FAT: 20g
PREPARING: 20 Minutes
CHILLING: 2-3 Hours
COOKING: 35 Minutes

CHICKEN: Bring enough water and/or chicken broth to boil in a pot (liquid need not completely cover). Add chicken and remaining ingredients. Bring to a boil, covered. Reduce heat, simmer gently 15 minutes. Turn chicken over, simmer additional 15 minutes. Remove from heat, let cool to room temperature. Drain, skin and bone chicken. Tear into shreds, refrigerate, covered.

VEGETABLE BED: Coarsely shred vegetables into 1½-inch *(4cm)* long strips. Place all except bean sprouts in a large bowl; pour boiling water over vegetables and let remain 2 minutes. Quickly cool in ice water, drain. Repeat process for bean sprouts, blanching 30 seconds only.

Heat wok, add oil, salt. Quickly stir-fry vegetables, about 1 minute. Remove with slotted spoon, drain. Chill.

SAUCE: Place all ingredients in bowl; blend well. To serve, arrange vegetables in a dish, mound chicken on top and pour sauce over chicken.

Sonya Wetstone, Hartford, CT

Variations, Advance Preparation, and Serving Suggestions:
Prepare chicken, vegetables and sauce a day ahead. Assemble just before serving. The amount of hot oil may be varied to taste, or substituted with chopped fresh green chili peppers or hot red pepper sauce.

Nutritional Notes: Nutritional analysis allows 3½ oz. *(100g)* chicken per serving.

Wine Suggestion: California Inglenook Petite Sirah, peppery red; serve at room temperature.

Microwave Conversion Instructions: *Chicken:* Place chicken and water (¾ way up chicken) in pot; cook, covered, 15 minutes on High or until boiling. Then simmer 10 minutes on Medium (50%). Cool chicken in broth until room temperature. Drain and shred. *Vegetable Bed:* Put all shredded vegetables on round platter in following manner: carrot, celery and bok choy stems on outside of plate; bean sprouts in mid-section; green pepper and bok choy leaves in center of plate. Cover with plastic wrap and cook 2½ to 3 minutes on High or just until crisp tender. Immediately cool in cold water. Proceed with sauce and assembly.

CHICKEN:
Water or chicken broth
3½-4-lb. *(1575-1800g)* chicken
2 scallions, white and green parts, cut in 2-inch *(5cm)* pieces
2 slices ginger root
2-3 stalks celery, cut in 2-inch *(5cm)* pieces
1½ tsp. salt

VEGETABLE BED: **3 cups** *(710ml)* combination of any or all:
Bok Choy
Celery
Green peppers
Carrots (very thin)
Bean sprouts
2 T. *(30ml)* peanut oil
½ tsp. salt

SAUCE:
3 T. *(45ml)* peanut oil
2 scallions, white and green parts, finely chopped
1 T. ginger root, finely chopped
1½ T. soy sauce
3 T. *(50g)* chunky peanut butter
2 T. *(30ml)* white vinegar
2½ tsp. sugar
¾ tsp. salt
1 tsp. sesame oil
½ tsp. hot oil

Chez Bach Salad

NOM TRAI BUOI

From Madame Bach Ngo, a remarkably talented chef and owner of CHEZ BACH restaurant, Branford. Bach Ngo's culinary knowledge includes both classic French as well as Vietnamese cuisine. Her restaurant gives evidence of her commitment to the use of only the freshest and best of ingredients. The following is a deliciously piquant sample of the Vietnamese dishes to be found at Chez Bach.

YIELD: 6 Entree Servings or
   8 as Part of Vietnamese Meal
TOTAL CALORIES SALAD: 704
CALORIES PER SERVING: 88
CARBOHYDRATES: 2g
PROTEIN: 7g
FAT: 4g
CALORIES PER TABLESPOON
   NOUC CHAM: 8
CARBOHYDRATES: 6g
SODIUM: High
PREPARING: 1 Hour
COOKING: 25 Minutes

1 medium onion
1 cup *(240ml)* white vinegar
2 cups *(160g)* fresh bean sprouts
4 oz. *(115g)* pork butt or loin
1 large carrot
Skin of 1 large cucumber
2 oz. *(60g)* raw shrimp in shell
1 small dried squid (optional)
2 T. sesame seeds, toasted
2-3 large grapefruits
2-3 fresh hot red chili peppers, or
   several dried

NUOC CHAM:
½ fresh hot red chili pepper, or 2 dried,
   seeds and membrane removed
1 clove garlic, peeled
1 T. sugar
⅛ fresh lime
2 T. *(30ml)* bottled fish sauce (nuoc am)
3 T. *(45ml)* water, or to taste

FRIED SHRIMP CHIPS:
Dried shrimp chips
1-2 cups *(240-475ml)* vegetable, peanut
   or safflower oil

Slice onion in half lengthwise; cut across in paper-thin horizontal slices. Place in bowl with vinegar 20 minutes; drain vinegar and discard. Squeeze onion slices dry with your hands.

Plunge bean sprouts in boiling water; drain immediately.

Simmer pork in covered saucepan in water to cover 20 minutes; drain. Cut into thin slices, then long narrow strips. Cut carrot and cucumber skin into strips the same size as pork. Simmer shrimp in water to cover 3 minutes; drain, shell and devein. Cut into small thin strips.

Toast dried squid in broiler until slightly brown. Remove from heat; pound with back of knife or cleaver to tenderize. With your hands shred squid.

Combine onions, bean sprouts, pork, carrot, cucumber skin, shrimp and squid in large bowl. Sprinkle with sesame seeds. Add Nuoc Cham, toss well. Slice top off grapefruits. Scoop out pulp. Cut 2 to 3 sections into bite-size pieces. Add to Nuoc Cham mixture. (Reserve remaining pulp for other use.) Fill grapefruit shells with mixture.

Garnish grapefruit tops with chili pepper "flowers": Slice each chili vertically into 8 strips without cutting through to stem. Spread "petals" apart in grapefruit.

NUOC CHAM: Chop chili pepper. Pound in mortar to paste with garlic and sugar. Squeeze lime juice into mortar, add lime pulp. Mash well; mix in fish sauce and water.

FRIED SHRIMP CHIPS: Heat oil to 375° in small pan; oil should be about 1 inch *(2.5cm)* deep. Drop in 3 to 4 chips at a time, pressing down with a spoon or chopsticks so that chips expand into large crackers.

Remove from oil with slotted spoon. Drain on paper towels. Serve with salad.

Variations, Advance Preparation, and Serving Suggestions:
The salad, Nuoc Cham and Shrimp Chips may be prepared early in the day. Garnish with chili peppers just before serving. Arrange grapefruits on spinach or red lettuce leaves on rattan tray or straw mat in center of table.

Nutritional Notes: 1 oz. *(30g)* Shrimp Chips contain 180 calories and are high in sodium.

Shortest Salad

Kudos to the recipe with the least amount of ingredients and a delicious taste.

YIELD: 2 Servings
TOTAL CALORIES: 420
CALORIES PER SERVING: 210
CARBOHYDRATES: 50g
PROTEIN: 2.5g
PREPARING: 15 Minutes

Combine ingredients. Place on lettuce and chicory. Serve with dressing of your choice.

Ruth E. Shepherd, Bolton, CT

Nutritional Notes: The nutritional analysis does not include the dressing which adds an average of 60 calories per 1 T. and 15 calories per 1 T. for low-calorie dressing.

1 grapefruit, sectioned
1 small green pepper, cut in small chunks
10 dates, pitted, cut in half
Favorite dressing (Italian is a good choice)
Iceberg lettuce
Chicory

Purslane Salad

Purslane is a prolific weed with a crisp texture and vinegary flavor that can be used in salads. It has mucilaginous stems; therefore, it is also used to thicken soups and stews. It is a nutritious vegetable.

YIELD: 8 Servings
CALORIES PER SERVING
    NOT INCLUDING DRESSING: 110
CARBOHYDRATES: 5.5g
PROTEIN: 2g
FAT: 9g
PREPARING: 10 Minutes
STANDING: 30 Minutes

PURSLANE: Steam purslane in boiling water in a covered pan 5 minutes, drain and let cool.

Add onion, tomatoes, dillweed, vinegar and oil. Put in large bowl and toss thoroughly. Serve as is, if desired.

SUMMER SALAD: Mix together scallions, watercress, wild lettuce, sorrel, mint and dillweed. Toss with dressing or add to Purslane Salad.

DRESSING: Blend together vinegar, oil, dillweed, thyme and mustard. Add to summer salad, toss and let stand 30 minutes to develop flavor. Toss again and serve with your favorite garnishes.

Barrie Kavasch, Bridgewater, CT, from her book Native Harvests

Variations, Advance Preparation, and Serving Suggestions: Wood sorrel should be eaten in moderation because of its high oxalic acid content.

Nutritional Notes: Purslane is a relatively low calorie vegetable which raw or cooked yields a good amount of vitamin A and calcium.

PURSLANE SALAD:
2 qts. purslane, washed twice
1 cup *(240ml)* boiling water
1 medium onion, thinly sliced
2 ripe tomatoes, cubed
¼ cup chopped fresh dillweed
½ cup *(120ml)* cider vinegar
⅓ cup *(80ml)* nut oil

SUMMER SALAD:
2 scallions, sliced including tops
1 qt. watercress sprigs
1 qt. wild lettuce leaves
1 cup sorrel leaves and blossoms
1 cup fresh mint leaves
½ cup chopped fresh dillweed

WILD HERB SUNFLOWER DRESSING:
1 cup *(240ml)* apple cider vinegar
1 cup *(240ml)* sunflower seed oil
½ cup dillweed, chopped
½ cup creeping wild thyme leaves
½ cup *(120g)* prepared mustard

YIELD: 16 ½-Cup Servings
TOTAL CALORIES: 2640
CALORIES PER SERVING: 165
CARBOHYDRATES: 23g
PROTEIN: 2g
FAT: 7g
SODIUM: High
MARINATING: 24 Hours

Copper Penny Carrots

Wonderful relish or summer salad or vegetable dish.

2 lbs. *(900g)* carrots, peeled, sliced
   crosswise
1 medium red onion, thinly sliced
1 pkg. (10 oz.) *(285g)* frozen peas
1 small green pepper, sliced in strips
1 can (10¾ oz.) *(300g)* condensed
   tomato soup, undiluted
½ cup *(120ml)* vegetable oil
1 cup *(200g)* sugar
¾ cup *(175ml)* cider vinegar
1 tsp. prepared mustard
1 tsp. Worcestershire sauce
½ tsp. salt
¼ tsp. freshly ground pepper

Cook carrots until just crisp-tender, about 5 minutes. Do not over-cook. Rinse under cold water to stop cooking; drain and cool. Separate onion slices into rings. In serving bowl, alternate layers of carrots, peas, onion rings, and green pepper. Combine all remaining ingredients to make marinade; mix until smooth. Pour over vegetables. Cover and refrigerate overnight. Keeps well up to 2 weeks refrigerated.

The Happy Cookers, Bloomfield, CT, Anita MacDonald and Mary Cagenello

Variations, Advance Preparation, and Serving Suggestions:
Serve in a crystal bowl or in individual lettuce cups. Fresh blanched green pepper halves or hollowed tomato halves also make attractive holders.

Topopo

YIELD: 6-8 Entree Servings
CALORIES PER SERVING: 593
CARBOHYDRATES: 37g
PROTEIN: 28g
FAT: 37g
SODIUM: High
PREPARING: 35 Minutes
COOKING: 10 Minutes
CHILLING: 30 Minutes

Mexican cooking is an ancient but very much alive cuisine. The food is bursting with color, flavor and excitement. This recipe is festive and different for entertaining or family suppers. It is a delicious alternative to chef's salad. The Topopo traditionally consists of a crisp tortilla laden with shredded lettuce, a mixed vegetable salad, meat or seafood and cheese. The ingredients offer contrasts of soft and crisp, hot and cold, savory or sharp and mild.

1 lb. *(450g)* ground chuck
1 head iceberg lettuce
½ lb. *(225g)* Cheddar cheese, grated
1 can (16 oz.) *(450g)* red kidney beans,
   drained
1 pkg. (9 oz.) *(255g)* Dorito chips,
   coarsely chopped
2-3 tomatoes, chopped
1 large onion, chopped
1 large avocado cut in bite-size pieces

PICANTE CHILI DRESSING:

8 oz. *(225g)* sour cream
3 T. chili powder
1 jar (5.3 oz.) *(150g)* picante sauce (use
   ½ jar of sauce)

In large skillet, brown ground chuck, separating meat while cooking. Drain and cool. Place lettuce in large salad bowl. Add meat, cheese, kidney beans, Doritos, tomatoes, onion and avocado. Mix gently.
DRESSING: Combine sour cream with chili powder and picante sauce. Add dressing to salad. Toss again. Chill 30 minutes before serving.

Dee Gordon, Avon, CT

Variations, Advance Preparation, and Serving Suggestions:
Although this Topopo does not contain a chili pepper, you might carefully add one of the 61 varieties available for extra zip. For luncheon, serve with corn muffins. For dinner, serve with enchiladas or chile rellenos. If making salad 24 hours ahead, do not add avocado until serving time. Substitute for salad dressing can be your favorite bottled Catalina or Russian dressing.

Curried Spinach Salad

YIELD: 6 Servings
CALORIES PER SERVING: 399
CARBOHYDRATES: 5g
PROTEIN: 9.5g
FAT: 38g
SODIUM: High
PREPARING: 30 Minutes
CHILLING: 2 Hours

DRESSING: Combine oil, vinegar, wine, soy sauce, sugar, curry powder, salt, garlic salt and pepper. Chill at least 2 hours.

SALAD: Cook bacon until crisp, drain and crumble. Remove tough stems from spinach, wash and drain well. Toss spinach with dressing; sprinkle with bacon, toss lightly. Garnish with egg.

Bonnie W. Chapman, West Hartford, CT

Nutritional Notes: A very significant amount of sodium is present, contributed by bacon, salt, garlic salt, and soy sauce. Eliminate salt and use garlic powder instead of garlic salt to decrease sodium.

CURRY DRESSING:

⅔ **cup** *(160ml)* **salad oil**
¼ **cup** *(60ml)* **white wine vinegar**
2 **T.** *(30ml)* **white wine**
2 **tsp. soy sauce**
1 **tsp. sugar**
1 **tsp. curry powder**
½ **tsp. salt**
½ **tsp. garlic salt**
1 **tsp. freshly ground pepper**

SALAD:

1 **lb.** *(450g)* **bacon**
2 **pkgs. (10 oz. each)** *(570g)* **fresh spinach**
2 **hard-cooked eggs, chopped**

Molded Spinach Salad

A novel way to make spinach more delicious and decorative.

YIELD: 6 ½-Cup Servings
CALORIES PER SERVING: 232
CARBOHYDRATES: 16g
PROTEIN: 6g
FAT: 16g
PREPARING: 15 Minutes
CHILLING: 4 Hours Minimum

Dissolve gelatin in ¾ cup *(175ml)* boiling water. Add 1 cup *(240ml)* cold water. Stir in vinegar, mayonnaise and salt. Put in freezer tray and chill until very firm 1 inch *(2.5cm)* around sides of tray; check after 30 minutes. Turn into mixing bowl and beat with electric beater until fluffy. Fold in celery, spinach, cottage cheese and onion. Pour into 1-qt. *(1L)* mold and chill in refrigerator until firm, at least 4 hours. Flavor is enhanced if made day before. Unmold and garnish with cherry tomatoes.

Joyce Anne Vitelli, Manchester, CT

1 **pkg. (3 oz.)** *(85g)* **lemon gelatin**
1½ **T. white vinegar**
½ **cup** *(115g)* **mayonnaise (page 190)**
¼ **tsp. salt**
¼ **cup** *(30g)* **chopped celery**
1 **pkg. (10 oz.)** *(285g)* **frozen spinach, thawed, chopped, drained**
¾ **cup** *(170g)* **cottage cheese**
1 **T. onion, minced**
Cherry tomatoes

Variations, Advance Preparation, and Serving Suggestions:
To successfully triple this recipe add 1 envelope unflavored gelatin to ingredients. 1 pkg. (10 oz.) frozen chopped broccoli, cooked and well-drained may be substituted for spinach. Use ring mold for salad and fill center with curried chicken salad, Dilled Tuna Salad (page 354), Curried Shrimp Salad (page 354) or marinated mushrooms.

Nutritional Notes: Calories can be decreased to approximately 110 per serving by using low-fat cottage cheese and imitation mayonnaise.

Cauliflower Slaw

YIELD: 6 Servings
CALORIES PER SERVING: 108
CARBOHYDRATES: 7g
PROTEIN: 2g
FAT: 8g
SODIUM: High
PREPARING: 20 Minutes
CHILLING: 3 Hours Minimum

Here is a different salad — a change from the popular cole-slaw, using cauliflower in place of cabbage.

4 cups *(450g)* **fresh uncooked cauliflower**
½ cup *(115g)* **mayonnaise (page 190)**
¼ cup *(60ml)* **milk**
1 T. fresh lemon juice
1 tsp. finely chopped fresh dill
¼ tsp. salt
Dash of freshly ground white pepper

GARNISH:

Fresh dill
Cherry tomatoes
Carrot curls
Radicchio

To prepare cauliflower: Remove stalks from major stem, then remove buds from small stalks. Using knife or shredding blade of food processor, shred stalks; using knife or slicing disc of food processor, shred buds.

Blend together mayonnaise, milk, lemon juice, dill, salt and pepper. Mix well; toss with cauliflower. Chill at least 3 hours. Garnish with more fresh dill, cherry tomatoes, radicchio, or carrot curls.

Diane Burgess, Hartford, CT

Nutritional Notes: Sodium is high primarily due to mayonnaise. Low sodium mayonnaise can be used. To lower calories and cholesterol, use imitation mayonnaise and lowfat/skim milk.

Molded Beet Salad

YIELD: 8 Servings
CALORIES PER SERVING: 318
CARBOHYDRATES: 19g
PROTEIN: 2g
FAT: 26g
CHOLESTEROL: High in Dressing
SODIUM: High
CALORIES PER TABLESPOON
  DRESSING: 45
PREPARING: 45 Minutes
CHILLING: 4 Hours Minimum

MOLD:

½ env. *(3.5g)* **plain gelatin**
¼ cup *(60ml)* **cold water**
1 pkg. (3 oz.) *(85g)* **lemon gelatin**
1 cup *(240ml)* **boiling water**
¾ cup *(175ml)* **canned pickled beet juice**
3 T. *(45ml)* **red wine vinegar**
½ tsp. salt
4 tsp. *(15g)* **minced fresh onion**
½ cup *(55g)* **peeled, seeded and finely chopped cucumbers**
½ cup *(55g)* **finely chopped celery**
1 cup *(190g)* **finely diced pickled beets**
2 T. prepared horseradish
SOUR CREAM HORSERADISH
  DRESSING:

1 cup *(225g)* **mayonnaise (page 190)**
1 cup *(225g)* **sour cream or Creme Fraiche (page 200)**
Horseradish to taste
½ cup *(40g)* **chopped green onion**

MOLD: Sprinkle gelatin in cold water; let stand 5 minutes. Add lemon gelatin and boiling water; stir until dissolved. Add pickled beet juice; chill mixture until consistency of egg whites. Stir in remaining ingredients. Pour into a greased 5-6 cup *(1¼-1½L)* ring mold. Chill until firm.

DRESSING: Combine all ingredients; blend very thoroughly. Chill until ready to serve.

When ready to serve, unmold salad and place a small bowl of the dressing in center. Garnish with watercress.

Mary Buschek, Chicago, IL

Variations, Advance Preparation, and Serving Suggestions: Mold easily doubles or triples and may be made several days ahead of serving. This mold is especially good with baked ham or Shenendoah Valley Stuffed Ham (page 303) accompanied by Cheese Grits (page 352).

Nutritional Notes: The nutritional analysis includes all of the dressing which amounts to 244 calories per serving and all of the fat in the recipe. The salad alone is only 74 calories per serving and contains no fat.

Autumn Vegetable Mosaic

Chervil is a relative of parsley, widely used in Europe but not well-known in this country. It is one of the herbs in "fines herbes".

YIELD: 6-8 Servings
TOTAL CALORIES: 2000
CALORIES PER SERVING: 250
CARBOHYDRATES: 8g
PROTEIN: 3g
FAT: 23g
PREPARING: 15 Minutes
CHILLING: 1 Hour Minimum

LEMON HERB DRESSING: Mix together wine vinegar, lemon juice, parsley, salt, basil, tarragon and chervil. Add salad oil slowly, beating with wire whisk until mixture is thick and oil is incorporated in mixture.

SALAD: Combine mushrooms, avocado and tomatoes in 13 × 9 × 2-inch *(33 × 23 × 5cm)* pan. Pour dressing over the mixture. Chill at least 60 minutes.

When ready to serve, tear spinach leaves into bite-size pieces and arrange on serving plate. Drain marinated vegetables, reserving dressing. Spoon vegetables over spinach. Serve reserved dressing separately.

Winnie White, North Conway, NH

LEMON HERB DRESSING:
2 T. *(30ml)* wine vinegar
⅓ cup *(80ml)* fresh lemon juice
2 tsp. chopped fresh parsley
1 tsp. salt
½ tsp. basil
¼ tsp. tarragon
¼ tsp. chervil
⅔ cup *(160ml)* salad oil

SALAD:
½ lb. *(225g)* fresh mushrooms, if large cut in half
1 large avocado, peeled and thinly sliced
3 medium tomatoes, cut into wedges
½ lb. *(225g)* fresh spinach leaves

Poireaux Vinaigrette

LEEKS VINAIGRETTE

Leeks are a native European vegetable, and the most delicately flavored member of the onion family. They star here in this recipe from the elegant and handsomely-appointed COPPER BEECH INN restaurant in Ivoryton.

YIELD: 2 Servings
CALORIES OF LEEKS
   PER SERVING: 30
CARBOHYDRATES: 6g
PROTEIN: 1g
CALORIES PER TABLESPOON
   VINAIGRETTE: 64
FAT: 7g
PREPARING: 15 Minutes
COOKING: 15 Minutes

LEEKS: Cut leeks where green leaves meet end of white. Cut whites in half (reserve greens for another use.) Rinse leeks thoroughly, retaining shape. Place leeks in boiling salted water. Poach 15 minutes or until tender. Plunge leeks immediately in cold water. Drain well.

VINAIGRETTE: Place mustard in medium mixing bowl. Whip half of olive oil into mustard slowly. Add half of vinegar and all lemon juice, whipping. Add remaining oil, whip thoroughly. Whip in remaining vinegar, salt and pepper.

To serve, arrange warm leeks on individual plates. Spoon vinaigrette over leeks. Garnish with sprinkling of crumbled Roquefort.

Variations, Advance Preparation, and Serving Suggestions: The vinaigrette may be prepared a day ahead and refrigerated. Bring to room temperature to serve. Leeks and vinaigrette may also be served cold.

Nutritional Notes: Leeks, slightly milder and sweeter than onions, are only slightly more caloric. They have a little more vegetable protein and carbohydrates than raw onions of an equal weight.

LEEKS:
4 medium firm leeks
1 qt. *(950ml)* water
1 tsp. salt

VINAIGRETTE:
2 tsp. Dijon mustard
1 cup *(240ml)* olive oil
½ cup *(120ml)* red wine vinegar
Juice of 2 lemons
Salt
Freshly ground pepper to taste
Crumbled Roquefort cheese, optional

YIELD: 8 Servings
CALORIES PER SERVING: 300
CARBOHYDRATES: 16g
PROTEIN: 1g
FAT: 26g
CHOLESTEROL: High
SODIUM: High
PREPARING: 20 Minutes
CHILLING: 30 Minutes Minimum

Heavenly Pineapple Coleslaw

1 medium cabbage, shredded
1 medium onion, diced
1 can (15½ oz.) *(440g)* crushed
   pineapple, drained, reserving the juice
1 cup *(225g)* mayonnaise (page 190)
1 cup *(225g)* sour cream
1 tsp. salt
1 T. sugar or honey

Combine cabbage and onion; add pineapple and mix well.

In separate bowl, combine mayonnaise, sour cream, reserved pineapple juice, salt, and sugar or honey; mix well.

Toss cabbage mixture with dressing until well blended. Refrigerate at least 30 minutes before serving. Serve on a bed of lettuce garnished with green pepper rings and carrot curls and sprinkled lavishly with paprika.

Irene and Vicki Roschefsky, West Hartford, CT

YIELD: 6-8 Servings
CALORIES PER SERVING: 177
CARBOHYDRATES: 18g
PROTEIN: 6g
FAT: 9g
PREPARING: 15 Minutes
SOAKING: 1 Hour
CHILLING: 4 Hours Minimum
COOKING: 1 Hour

White Bean Salad with Fresh Herbs

Navy beans were so named because they were the beans once served for breakfast to the men in the Navy. They are also called Yankee beans.

SALAD:

4 cups *(950ml)* water
1 cup *(225g)* dried Navy or pea beans
2 tsp. salt
2 T. finely cut fresh basil
2 T. finely cut fresh chives
2 T. finely chopped fresh parsley
1 tsp. finely cut fresh dill
3 small mint leaves, finely cut
½ tsp. finely chopped garlic
2 medium firm ripe tomatoes, peeled,
   seeded and coarsely chopped

DRESSING:

1 T. tarragon vinegar
2 tsp. prepared mustard
2 drops Tabasco
¼ tsp. freshly ground pepper
⅓ cup *(80ml)* olive oil

SALAD: In a heavy 2 to 3 qt. *(2-3L)* saucepan, bring water to a boil. Drop in beans; boil uncovered 2 minutes. Turn off heat and let beans soak uncovered 1 hour. Add ½ tsp. salt; bring to boil again. Reduce heat to low, partially cover pan; simmer 1 hour until beans are tender but intact. Drain and set aside to cool to room temperature.

DRESSING: Combine vinegar, mustard, Tabasco, 1½ tsp. salt and pepper in small bowl; whisk to a smooth paste. Whisking constantly, add oil in small stream; beat until dressing is thick and creamy.

TO ASSEMBLE: Place basil, chives, parsley, dill, mint and garlic in large serving bowl; mix well. Add cooled beans and tomatoes; stir gently together. Pour in mustard dressing; stir gently until ingredients are coated with dressing. Cover tightly with plastic wrap or foil. Chill in refrigerator 4 hours or longer. Before serving, taste for seasonings and mix together gently.

Nancy Webster Woodworth, West Hartford, CT

Nutritional Notes: Eliminate salt for a low-sodium recipe as this salad contains 20 milligrams sodium per serving. In vegetarian diet, a complimentary protein is obtained when beans and grain products are eaten together. A brown rice casserole or other whole grain dish or bread would enhance the quality of protein in this salad.

Sesame Rice Stick Salad

With its origin in Oriental cuisine, this salad makes a great accompaniment to shellfish, especially scallops. The dressing itself is excellent on all tossed salads.

In deep, heavy skillet, heat oil to 375°. Add rice sticks a few at a time. As soon as they are puffed, remove with wire strainer; drain on paper towel. Set aside until needed.

When ready to serve, mix rice sticks with shredded cabbage in large bowl; toss with dressing.

SESAME SEED DRESSING: Place all ingredients in covered jar; shake well.

Diane Burgess, Hartford, CT

YIELD: 6 Servings
CALORIES PER SERVING: 85
CARBOHYDRATES: 9g
PROTEIN: 1g
FAT: 5g
SODIUM: High
CALORIES PER TABLESPOON
  DRESSING: 30
PREPARING: 15 Minutes
COOKING: 20 Minutes

1 cup *(240ml)* fresh oil
2 oz. *(55g)* Misua (Chinese vermicelli) or rice sticks
4 cups *(300g)* thinly shredded Chinese cabbage or iceberg lettuce

SESAME SEED DRESSING:

6 T. *(90ml)* vinegar
2 T. *(30ml)* soy sauce
2 tsp. salt
2 T. *(25g)* sugar
2 T. *(30ml)* sesame oil
2 T. *(30ml)* dry sherry
2 tsp. finely chopped fresh ginger
2 tsp. toasted sesame seeds
2 drops Tabasco sauce

Dilled Chicken with Sorrel Chiffonnade

In cooking, all plants, herbal or otherwise, which are cut into fine strips or ribbons are denoted by the term *chiffonnade*. It is more specifically used to denote a mixture of sorrel and lettuce cut into julienne strips and cooked in butter. Most chiffonnades are used as a garnish for clear or thick soups.

This original adaptation was inspired by a chicken vinaigrette served at George Blanc's Chez La Mere Blanc in Vonnas, France.

VINAIGRETTE: Using a large mixing bowl and wire whisk, combine vinegar, oil and lemon juice. Add remaining ingredients. Toss chicken with vinaigrette to coat evenly. Chill 30 minutes.

When ready to serve, either arrange sorrel on a platter with dressed chicken on top or place chicken in a shallow crystal bowl and sprinkle sorrel on top; toss at the table.

Glenn Recchia, New York, NY

Microwave Conversion Instructions: How to poach chicken breasts: Place chicken in casserole and add ½ cup *(120ml)* chicken stock. Cook, covered, on High 4 to 5 minutes per pound, just until chicken is tender. Turn chicken pieces over and allow them to cool, covered, in liquid.

YIELD: 6 Entree Servings
CALORIES PER SERVING: 302
CARBOHYDRATES: 5.5g
PROTEIN: 26g
FAT: 19.5g
PREPARING: 1 Hour
CHILLING: 30 Minutes
COOKING: 35 Minutes

3 whole chicken breasts, lightly poached, skinned, boned, julienned
MINT VINAIGRETTE:

2 T. *(30ml)* mint, raspberry, or sherry vinegar
¼ cup *(60ml)* olive oil
Juice of ½ fresh lemon
Salt
Freshly ground pepper
2 T. minced fresh dill or to taste
2 T. minced Italian parsley
1 bunch scallions (white parts only), minced
½ tsp. coriander seeds, crushed in mortar
1 small to medium clove garlic, pounded to paste in mortar
2 cups *(65g)* sorrel leaves, chiffonnade (shredded)

Milkweed Pods Vinaigrette

YIELD: 10-12 Servings
PREPARING: 15 Minutes
COOKING: 25 Minutes
MARINATING: Overnight
FREEZING: Yes-Partially

A most fragrant, wild native vegetable, sometimes referred to as Indian Broccoli. This superlative relish captivates everyone who tastes it!

MILKWEED:

1 qt. *(1L)* young whole milkweed pods, less than ½ inch *(1.2cm)* long
1 cup milkweed buds and blossoms (optional)
2 cups *(250g)* small white onions, peeled
1 qt. *(1L)* water
½ cup *(120ml)* real maple syrup

PIMIENTO DILL VINAIGRETTE:

2 cups *(400g)* chopped pimientos
1 cup fresh dillweed, chopped
1 qt. *(1L)* cider vinegar
2 cups *(475ml)* corn oil

MILKWEED: Combine all ingredients in enamel pot and bring to boil. Cover and simmer 25 minutes. Stir occasionally. Drain, rinse with cold water. Place ingredients in stoneware crock or glass bowl.

VINAIGRETTE: Blend all ingredients. Pour over milkweed, stir gently. Cover, refrigerate overnight to enhance flavors before serving. The relish will keep, refrigerated, about 1 month.

Barrie Kavasch, Bridgewater, CT, from her book Native Harvests

Variations, Advance Preparation, and Serving Suggestions:
Milkweed pods abound in meadows and along roadside borders in July and August in all regions of the United States. Gather blossoms and buds when they first appear; blanch twice and freeze a week or so before the pods are ready to be harvested; then use all together in this delightful salad. Blossoms, buds, and pods may also be "put by" in brine to preserve your harvest all winter long.

Nutritional Notes: Very little nutritional information is available at this time for the wild edibles that are gaining increasing public interest.

YIELD: 3½ Cups
CALORIES PER TABLESPOON: 44
CARBOHYDRATES: 2g
FAT: 4g
SODIUM: High
PREPARING: 5 Minutes
CHILLING: 4 Hours Minimum
FREEZING: Not Necessary

Rosy Dressing

A dressing that goes well with lettuce and tomato salad, or cottage cheese.

1 can (10½ oz.) *(300g)* tomato soup, undiluted
1 cup *(240ml)* good quality olive oil
¾ cup *(175ml)* red wine vinegar
½ cup *(100g)* sugar
Scant 1 tsp. salt
Paprika
1 onion, quartered
Basil or any favorite herb (dill is a good choice)

Combine all ingredients in 1-qt. *(1L)* jar with lid. Shake to mix thoroughly. Refrigerate at least 4 hours so onion flavor is absorbed. Remove onion and shake well before using.

Carol H. Maynard, West Hartford, CT

Nutritional Notes: One can of tomato soup contains approximately 2400 milligrams sodium. A low sodium tomato soup, available in the dietetic section of most supermarkets, can be substituted. This dressing is 25% lower in calories and fat than most commercial French-type salad dressings.

Francis Bergquist

Couscous Salad

Couscous is both the name of the national dish of many North African countries, as well as the principal grain ingredient in that dish. It is a granular wheat product also known as semolina. In Russia, a similar product made from buckwheat is called *kasha*.

YIELD: 16 Salad Servings or
8-10 Entree Servings
TOTAL CALORIES: 4840
CALORIES PER ENTREE
  SERVING: 480
CARBOHYDRATES: 57g
PROTEIN: 10g
FAT: 24g
CALORIES PER SALAD
  SERVING: 300
STANDING: 3 Hours, Then Overnight
PREPARING: 30 Minutes
COOKING: 20 Minutes
STEAMING: 40 Minutes

Place couscous in large mixing bowl; sprinkle ½ cup water over it. Rub couscous in your hands about 5 minutes or until all grains are damp. Cover bowl with wet towel and let stand 3 hours. After 3 hours, repeat rubbing procedure and let couscous stand overnight with damp cloth covering it. Then sprinkle couscous with 1 T. water and rub again 5 minutes. Boil several quarts water in couscousier or stock pot, to which has been added cumin and coriander. Wrap couscous in cheesecloth; put in top section of couscousier or in sieve secured to the stock pot. Cover and steam couscous 40 minutes. (The above steps can be eliminated if pre-cooked couscous is being used. Follow directions on package. The texture of pre-cooked is not as nice.)

While couscous is cooking, prepare vegetables and fruit: cook corn about 8 minutes in boiling water; drain, cool and cut off kernels and reserve. Boil peas 5 minutes or until tender; drain and reserve with corn. Season with salt and pepper. Peel and section grapefruit, being sure to remove all the skin. Cut each section into halves; set aside. Cut each tomato into 6 to 8 wedges. Coarsely chop peppers. Cook carrots until tender.

SAUCE GRIBICHE: Peel eggs; remove yolks. Put yolks in a small bowl and mash with fork. Add mustard and garlic; mix in vinegar. Add oil, the herbs and capers; mix. Mince egg whites and add to sauce. Season to taste with salt and pepper.

Remove couscous from cheesecloth. Put into large salad bowl and fluff.

Add butter and olive oil; mix well with couscous. Season to taste with salt and pepper. Finally add fruits and vegetables. Pour Sauce Gribiche over all and mix well. Correct seasonings and serve.

Melinda M. Vance, West Hartford, CT

Variations, Advance Preparation, and Serving Suggestions:
Salad may be made several days in advance but it must be brought to room temperature before serving. It keeps refrigerated for 1 week.

Nutritional Notes: Couscous, used in many Middle Eastern recipes, is a partially refined wheat product. Often utilized in vegetarian diets, couscous forms a complete protein when combined with dried beans or dried peas. If desired, part of couscous can be replaced by cooked soybean granules to achieve a more complete protein.

1 lb. *(450g)* medium-grain couscous
½ cup *(120ml)* plus 1 T. water
½ tsp. cumin
1½ tsp. ground coriander or several fresh sprigs
4 ears fresh corn (or enough to equal 1 cup)
1 cup *(200g)* shelled fresh green peas
Salt
Freshly ground pepper
3 medium grapefruit
4 fresh tomatoes or 20 cherry tomatoes, halved
4 large canned Italian peppers
1 lb. *(450g)* carrots, peeled and shaped into nuggets

SAUCE GRIBICHE DRESSING:

2 hard-cooked eggs
2 tsp. hot mustard
2 cloves garlic, mashed
¼ cup *(60ml)* red wine vinegar
¾ cup *(175ml)* good quality green olive oil
¼ cup minced parsley, dill and/or tarragon
¼ cup capers
Salt
Freshly ground pepper
2 T. *(30g)* unsalted sweet butter
2 T. *(30ml)* olive oil

Cranberry Pear Butter

Fruit butter is an old fashioned name for preserves made with fruit puree and sugar as opposed to a jelly which is made of fruit juice only, a jam which is both juice and pieces of fruit, and a marmalade which must be made with citrus fruits. This particular butter is a beautiful rosy-pink, especially appropriate for holiday gift-giving.

YIELD: 3½ Pints
CALORIES PER TABLESPOON: 40
CARBOHYDRATES: 10g
PREPARING: 30 Minutes
COOKING: 1½ Hours

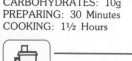

4 lbs. *(1800g)* **firm Bosc pears, cored and chopped**
3 firm tart apples, cored
¾ cup *(85g)* **raw cranberries**
Juice of 1 lemon
½ cup *(120ml)* **water**
4 cups *(800g)* **sugar**
½ tsp. cinnamon

Combine chopped pears, apples, cranberries, lemon juice and water in heavy enamel or stainless kettle. Bring to boil; reduce heat and simmer until tender. Remove from heat and puree fruit in blender or food processor. Return puree to kettle, adding sugar and cinnamon. Cook over low heat until sugar is dissolved. Increase heat, stirring frequently. Cook until butter is thick and glossy. It is done when it sheets from spoon. Ladle into hot sterilized jars and seal.

Melinda M. Vance, West Hartford, CT

Microwave Conversion Instructions: Note: Reduce sugar to 3½ cups *(700g)* and water to ⅓ cup *(80ml)*. Combine pears, apples, cranberries, lemon juice and water in 5-qt. *(5L)* casserole. Cook on High, covered, 5 minutes, or until tender. Puree fruit mixture and return to casserole. Add sugar and cinnamon. Cook on High 12 minutes, stirring occasionally, or until thick and glossy.

Rhubarb Orange Marmalade

The original marmalade was made with quince, in Portuguese called *marmelo*. It has come to refer to any thick jam made of citrus fruit; most commonly, orange. Here is another excellent version.

YIELD: 2 Pints
TOTAL CALORIES: 2600
CALORIES PER TABLESPOON: 36
CARBOHYDRATES: 9g
PREPARING: 20 Minutes
COOKING: 20 Minutes
FREEZING: Yes

2 lbs. *(900g)* fresh rhubarb, washed, not dried
3 oranges, quartered, thinly sliced
1 lemon, thinly sliced
3 cups *(600g)* sugar
½ cup *(120ml)* fresh lemon juice

Cut rhubarb in ½-inch *(1.5cm)* pieces. Place all ingredients in heavy 10-qt. *(10L)* preserving pan. Heat stirring frequently until sugar is dissolved; bring mixture to a boil and boil rapidly 10 to 15 minutes until jelling point is reached. Seal.

Nancy Bailey, Prospect, KY

Variations, Advance Preparation, and Serving Suggestions:
1 cup *(120g)* chopped walnuts or pecans can be added to marmalade just before pouring into jars. Serve as a condiment with meats, especially ham. For dessert, layer marmalade between crepes, alternating with applesauce. Cut in wedges. Pass Creme Fraiche (page 200).

Microwave Conversion Instructions: Note: Reduce sugar to 1 cup *(200g)*. Place prepared rhubarb and fruit in 3-qt. *(3L)* casserole. Cover; cook on High 5 minutes. Add sugar. Cook uncovered on High, stirring often, 30 minutes or until jelly point is reached. Cool. Pour into plastic freezer containers. Freeze when thoroughly cooled.

Marmalade Gold

YIELD: 8 Cups
TOTAL CALORIES: 5213
CALORIES PER TABLESPOON: 42
CARBOHYDRATES: 10g
PREPARING: 40 Minutes
COOKING: 15 Minutes

1 orange
1 lemon
1 cup *(240ml)* water
2 T. *(30ml)* fresh lemon juice
1 lb. *(450g)* fully ripe apricots, peeled, pitted and finely chopped
1 lb. *(450g)* fully ripe nectarines, peeled, pitted and finely chopped
7 cups *(1360g)* sugar
3 oz. *(90ml)* liquid fruit pectin

Cut orange and lemon in half; remove seeds. Do not peel, but chop finely. Simmer chopped citrus fruits with water and lemon juice in covered pan for 20 minutes.

Add enough of mixture of nectarines and apricots to simmered citrus fruits to make a total of 4½ cups *(1L)*. Put into 5-qt. *(5L)* kettle; add sugar and stir to mix thoroughly. Over high heat, bring to full rolling boil. Boil hard, stirring constantly, 1 minute. Remove from heat. Stir in pectin all at once with large metal spoon; skim off foam. Stir and skim 5 minutes to cool slightly and prevent floating fruit.

Ladle quickly into hot sterilized jars. If using jars, adjust caps and bands according to manufacturer's directions; if using jelly glasses, cover at once with ⅛ inch *(0.3cm)* hot melted paraffin.

Lorraine Neff, Farmington, CT

Microwave Conversion Instructions: Note: Reduce ingredients by half. Prepare orange and lemon as for conventional recipe, place in 3-qt. *(3L)* casserole with ¼ cup *(60ml)* water (fruit will produce additional liquid). Cover and cook 5 to 7 minutes on High power. Meanwhile prepare remaining fruit as for conventional recipe; add to orange-lemon mixture along with sugar. Cook on High 7 to 10 minutes. Stir and continue to cook 10 to 12 minutes more. Stir in pectin and complete recipe as for conventional recipe.

Mother's Sweet Pepper Relish

YIELD: 6 Pints
CALORIES PER TABLESPOON: 16
CARBOHYDRATES: 4g
SODIUM: High
PREPARING: 30 Minutes
COOKING: 30 Minutes

This really is Mother's relish recipe. Try it with pork chops and baked beans, or hot dogs and hamburgers.

12 medium sweet red peppers, *coarsely* chopped
12 medium sweet green peppers *coarsely* chopped
12 medium onions, *coarsely* chopped
1 pt. *(475ml)* vinegar
3 cups *(600g)* sugar
2 T. pickling (coarse or Kosher) salt

Place peppers and onions in saucepan. Cover with boiling water; let stand 5 minutes. Drain. Cover again with boiling water; let stand 10 minutes more. Drain well. Add vinegar, sugar and salt. Bring to boil; cook 15 to 20 minutes at low boiling point. Ladle into hot, sterilized jars; seal. Process in boiling water bath 5 minutes.

Debbie Fuller, Essex, CT

Marinated Bell Peppers Julienne

YIELD: 40 ¼-Cup Servings
TOTAL CALORIES: 2160
CALORIES PER SERVING: 54
CARBOHYDRATES: 1g
FAT: 5.5g
SODIUM: High
PREPARING: 15 Minutes
COOKING: 8 Minutes
CHILLING: 7 Days Minimum

When your garden runs rampant with sweet red and green peppers and your neighbor refuses to take anymore, you'll be thankful you kept them for this delightful treat.

6 large bell peppers, red and green for nice color
3 large cloves garlic, thinly sliced
1 cup *(240ml)* oil
1 cup *(240ml)* vinegar
1 cup *(240ml)* water
2 tsp. sugar
4 tsp. seasoned salt
½ tsp. pepper
2 medium onions, thinly sliced and separated

Julienne each pepper in ½ to ¾-inch *(1.2 to 2cm)* strips. In 5-qt. *(5L)* pot, combine garlic, oil, vinegar, water, sugar, salt and pepper. Bring to boil; add peppers. Boil gently 3 minutes, stirring with wooden spoon. Add onions and stir. Spoon into 4-qt. *(4L)* glass container. Allow to cool at room temperature. Cover tightly. Refrigerate 1 week before serving. Stir occasionally. The vegetables keep 3 to 4 months if refrigerated in tightly-closed container.

Jean Speck, Hartford, CT

Nutritional Notes: Bell peppers are an excellent source of vitamin C. One ripe bell pepper can contain 150 to 300 milligrams vitamin C (3 to 6 times the RDA). Red peppers contain more vitamin C than green peppers, and the redder the pepper, the more vitamin C. Vitamin C is water-soluble as well as light- and heat-sensitive; therefore, soaking and heating will destroy some of this vitamin. Sufficient quantities will remain, however, to make this a very nutritious vegetable dish.

Microwave Conversion Instructions: Combine garlic, oil, vinegar, water, sugar and salt and pepper in a large casserole. Cook on High until boiling, about 7 to 9 minutes. Add julienned peppers. Cook on High 3 minutes. Stir in onions and follow above directions to complete.

Zucchini Relish

This is a recipe for non-canners.

YIELD: 10 Cups
CALORIES PER CUP: 132
CARBOHYDRATES: 31g
PROTEIN: 2g
PREPARING: 20 Minutes
CHILLING: 24 Hours
SIMMERING: 1 Hour
FREEZING: Yes

In large bowl, combine zucchini, onions and salt; cover with water. Cover and refrigerate overnight. Drain vegetables; rinse and drain again. In 5-qt. *(5L)* pot combine vegetables with pepper, vinegar, sugar and seasonings. Simmer uncovered for 1 hour or until thickened and total volume is reduced to 2½ qts. *(2.3L)*. Ladle relish into 5 1-pt. *(½L)* refrigerator containers. Cover. Refrigerate as long as one month or freeze.

Millie Linehan, West Hartford, CT

Microwave Conversion Instructions: In 5-qt. pot, combine vegetables with peppers, vinegar, sugar and seasonings. Cook on High 15 minutes. Then cook on Medium (50%) 10 minutes. Stir several times during cooking.

3-3½ lbs. *(1350-1595g)* zucchini, chopped to equal 10 cups
4 medium onions, chopped
5 T. *(55g)* coarse salt
1 cup *(170g)* chopped red or green bell pepper
2¼ cups *(535ml)* white vinegar
1¼ cups *(250g)* sugar
2 tsp. celery seed
2 tsp. mustard seed
1 tsp. cinnamon
1 tsp. freshly grated nutmeg
½ tsp. freshly ground pepper

Connecticut Garden Uncooked Tomato Relish

The explosive abundance of even the smallest planting of tomatoes calls for ingenuity — soups, sauces, pies, aspics, salads and especially preserves.

YIELD: 5 Pints
TOTAL CALORIES: 1443
CALORIES PER TABLESPOON: 9
CARBOHYDRATES: 2g
SODIUM: High
PREPARING: 30 Minutes
CHILLING: 1 Week

Combine tomatoes, celery, sugar, onions, salt, mustard seed, cinnamon and cloves. Stir in cider vinegar and blend well. Spoon into hot sterilized jars; seal. Refrigerate at least one week before serving. Will keep several months in refrigerator.

Peggy Stanwood, Bloomfield, CT

Variations, Advance Preparation, and Serving Suggestions: Serve this relish anytime you would like a change from ketchup. It is great at cookouts with hamburgers and potato salad or beside a cheese omelet for breakfast or with just plain scrambled eggs and toast.

Nutritional Notes: Because this relish is not cooked and is exposed to a minimal amount of heat, most of the vitamin C found in the tomatoes, onions and celery is preserved. Keeping the relish in a sealed jar in the refrigerator also retards loss of vitamin C which deteriorates when exposed to heat, light and air.

14 to 15 ripe tomatoes, (or enough to yield 1½ qts.), peeled and chopped
1 cup *(110g)* chopped celery
1 cup *(200g)* dark brown sugar
¾ cup *(125g)* finely chopped onions
¼ cup *(75g)* salt
¼ cup *(40g)* mustard seed
1 tsp. cinnamon
⅓ tsp. ground cloves
1½ cups *(355ml)* cider vinegar

YIELD: 1½ Cups
TOTAL CALORIES: 90
CALORIES PER TABLESPOON: 4
CARBOHYDRATES: 1g
PREPARING: 10 Minutes
STANDING: 12 Hours Minimum

Raspberry Vinegar

1 bottle (12.7 oz.) *(375ml)* **white wine vinegar**
½ pt. *(140g)* **fresh raspberries**

Pour white wine vinegar into saucepan and bring to a boil but do not let it boil.

While vinegar is heating, scald a large canning jar. Place raspberries in jar; pour heated vinegar over. Cover and set aside 12 hours or overnight, gently shaking jar several times during this period.

Strain vinegar through cheesecloth-lined sieve; discard raspberries. Pour vinegar into canning jar and seal.

Maryann Reuben, West Hartford, CT

Jezebel Sauce

A recipe from the deep South — hot stuff! Serve as an accompaniment to plain meats, especially ham.

1 jar (12 oz.) *(340g)* **apple jelly**
1 jar (12 oz.) *(340g)* **pineapple preserves**
1 bottle (5 oz.) *(140g)* **horseradish**
1 small can (1½ oz.) *(40g)* **dry mustard**

Blend all ingredients thoroughly and refrigerate.

Gail Moore, West Hartford, CT

Hot Red Pepper Jelly

Make this jelly as hot as you like with crushed red pepper. Serve with cream cheese on crackers, or as a meat accompaniment.

1 large fresh red pepper, finely chopped
1¾ cup *(415ml)* **white vinegar, divided**
1 T. **crushed red pepper** (available whole in bags at oriental shops)
4 cups *(800g)* **sugar**
6 oz. *(180ml)* **liquid pectin**
Paraffin for sealing

Puree fresh pepper in blender or food processor. Add ½ cup vinegar and blend. Add crushed red pepper.

Over low heat, bring sugar and remaining vinegar slowly to boil. Cook until sugar is dissolved, about 15 minutes, stirring constantly. Add pepper mixture and cook 7 minutes more, stirring. Remove from heat; stir in pectin and mix well. Return to heat and bring to rolling boil. Boil 1 minute without stirring.

Pour into sterilized jars; seal with paraffin. If desired, omit paraffin and store in refrigerator several months.

Helen Paluch, West Hartford, CT

Microwave Conversion Instructions: Puree fresh peppers with ½ cup vinegar as directed above; set aside. Place crushed red pepper, remaining vinegar and sugar in 3-qt. *(3L)* bowl. Cook, uncovered, on High 10 to 12 minutes or until sugar is dissolved, stirring once or twice. Add fresh pepper puree. Cook on High 7 minutes, stirring once. Stir in liquid pectin. Cook on High until it boils for 1 full minute. Complete as directed above.

Mustard Dip

Served in small dishes, it is particularly good with Oriental deep-fried foods and is usually served with the following recipe for Plum Dip.

YIELD: 1 Cup
CALORIES PER SERVING: Negligible

Add boiling water to dry mustard until it is consistency of thick batter. Add vermouth a tablespoon at a time until mustard reaches desired consistency. The thicker it is, the hotter it will be. Refrigerate, covered, and use as needed.

½ cup *(50g)* **dry mustard**
Boiling water
1-4 T. dry vermouth

Plum Dip

Plum Dip is not to be confused with *plum sauce* which is purchased in a can and is a separate ingredient in this recipe. Plum Dip is similar to *Duck Sauce* available commercially. Neither is authentically Chinese, but rather a concession to American palates.

YIELD: 1 Quart
TOTAL CALORIES: 3072
CALORIES PER TABLESPOON: 48
CARBOHYDRATES: 12g
PREPARING: 10 Minutes
FREEZING: Not Necessary

Mix all ingredients together. (Dip will be smoother if done in blender or food processor.) Sauce keeps 4 to 6 months refrigerated in tightly-closed glass jar.

Variations, Advance Preparation, and Serving Suggestions:
Serve along with Mustard Dip with deep-fried foods, especially Oriental dishes such as Shrimp Toast (page 213), Shanghai Spring Rolls (page 212), Pearl Balls (page 182) or Chinese Rumaki (page 205).

10 oz. *(285g)* **canned Chinese plum sauce**
10 oz. *(285g)* **peach preserves**
10 oz. *(285g)* **apricot preserves**
10 oz. *(285g)* **applesauce**
4 T. *(60ml)* **hoisin sauce**
2 cloves **garlic, minced**
1 T. **dry mustard**

Hot Mustard Sauce

The Chinese cultivated mustard seeds over 3000 years ago. Hippocrates praised mustard for its medicinal value and Thomas Jefferson introduced it to America. Today, mustard is the most popular condiment.

YIELD: 6 Cups
TOTAL CALORIES: 2976
CALORIES PER TABLESPOON: 31
CARBOHYDRATES: 6g
PROTEIN: .5g
FAT: .5g
SOAKING: Overnight
COOKING: 20-30 Minutes

Combine dry mustard and vinegar; soak overnight.

Add eggs and sugar, put in saucepan and cook over low heat 20 to 30 minutes, beating with electric beater to avoid lumps. Refrigerated, sauce keeps 1 year. Sauce should be heated before serving.

Phyllis B. Abrahms, West Hartford, CT

Variations, Advance Preparation, and Serving Suggestions:
Use as topping for meat loaf, for buffet tables, tailgate picnics, lunch boxes and middle-of-the-night refrigerator raids. A flavored vinegar such as Champagne or tarragon can be used.

3 cups *(300g)* **ground dry mustard (Coleman's preferred)**
3 cups *(710ml)* **cider or malt vinegar**
9 **eggs**
3 cups *(600g)* **sugar**

Tamarind Chutney

Tamarind is an evergreen tree of the tropics. It bears a cinnamon-colored flat pod filled with seeds and pulp that tastes like a combination of dates and apricots. In Arabic, *tamarind* means "Indian date," indicating that it entered medieval trade from India, although it is generally considered native to eastern tropical Africa. In India and Arabia, the pulp of the seed pods is pressed into cakes and sold as a delicacy or used in Oriental curries, chutneys and syrup.

YIELD: 6-8 Servings
TOTAL CALORIES: 510
CALORIES PER SERVING: 64
CARBOHYDRATES: 16g
PREPARING: 5 Minutes
SOAKING: 3 Hours
CHILLING: 3 Hours
FREEZING: Yes

1 cup *(240ml)* boiling water
4½ oz. *(130g)* dried tamarind cake
  (available in Indian markets)
½ cup *(100g)* sugar
1 tsp. salt
1 tsp. ground coriander
1 tsp. ground cumin

Soak tamarind in boiling water 3 hours. As tamarind begins to soften, break it up with a fork.

Puree tamarind and soaking liquid through a food mill; discard seeds left in the food mill.

Add sugar, salt, coriander and cumin to puree. Chill several hours. Chutney keeps well in freezer.

Maryann Reuben, West Hartford, CT

Watermelon Rind Chutney

Don't throw away the rind when your summer fruit salad calls for watermelon balls — make this unique and spicy chutney.

YIELD: 6-8 Cups
TOTAL CALORIES: 2430
CALORIES PER TABLESPOON: 19
CARBOHYDRATES: 4.5g
SODIUM: High
PREPARING: 25 Minutes
STANDING: 3 Hours
COOKING: 35 Minutes
CHILLING: Overnight

1 piece watermelon, 3½-6 lbs.
  (1.6-2.7kg)
2½ T. salt, divided
2 cups *(300g)* tart apples, peeled, cored
  and diced
2 cups *(475ml)* white vinegar
1 cup *(150g)* chopped onion
1½ cups *(300g)* firmly packed light
  brown sugar
½ cup *(100g)* sugar
¾ cup *(100g)* dried currants
¾ cup *(125g)* golden raisins
¾ cup *(170g)* minced preserved ginger
1 lemon, seeded, thinly sliced
3 cloves garlic, minced
1 T. mustard seed
1 tsp. celery seed
1 tsp. cinnamon
1 tsp. ground clove
1 tsp. ground allspice
1 tsp. cayenne pepper
1 T. cornstarch, dissolved in 1 T. cold
  water
Salt
Freshly ground black pepper to taste

Peel and discard green skin from watermelon. Cut flesh away from rind, leaving small amount of pink flesh on rind. Cut rind into 1-inch *(2.5cm)* cubes. There should be 6 to 7 cups. Reserve flesh for another use. Put rind in large saucepan with water to cover and 1 T. salt. Bring water to boil over high heat; boil rind 3 minutes until just tender. Drain and let cool.

In a 3½-qt. *(3.3L)* ceramic or glass bowl, combine apples, vinegar, onion, rind and 1½ T. salt. Cover and let stand at room temperature 3 hours.

In large stainless steel or enameled saucepan, combine sugars, currants, raisins, ginger, lemon, garlic and spices. Strain liquid from rind mixture into saucepan; bring to a boil over high heat. Cook, stirring, until sugar dissolves. Add rind mixture and cook 30 minutes, stirring frequently. Stir in cornstarch mixture. Remove from heat; cool. Chill, covered, overnight.

Bring mixture to boil, add salt and pepper to taste and transfer to sterilized jars, filling to ½ inch *(1.2cm)* of top. Seal jars. If desired, process jars in boiling water bath 10 minutes. Let cool completely; store in cool, dark, dry place. Processing is not necessary if jars are stored in refrigerator.

Kathleen J. Schwartz, Avon, CT

Variations, Advance Preparation, and Serving Suggestions:
This chutney makes a good hors d'oeuvre or snack with plain crackers and cream cheese. It also performs well as a lively condiment with crisp broiled chicken, roasted pork or ham.

Aunt Lilly's Mincemeat

Aunt Lilly, age 101, brought this recipe to Hartford from her native England many years ago.

YIELD: 5 Pints
TOTAL CALORIES: 11,200
CALORIES PER TABLESPOON: 70
CARBOHYDRATES: 10g
FAT: 2.5g
PREPARING: 20 Minutes
STANDING: 1 Week Minimum

Mix all ingredients together. Pack in sterilized pint jars; seal. Mincemeat does not need to be processed. Let stand at least 1 week, preferably 1 month, before using, to fully develop flavor.

Dorothy W. Mather, Windsor, CT

Nutritional Notes: Suet contains approximately the same amount of fat by volume as most vegetable oils and lard and more than butter. The raisins and currants make this preserve rich in iron. It also contains magnesium and potassium and, therefore, is not an "empty"-caloried condiment or sweet.

1 pkg. (15 oz.) *(425g)* seeded muscat raisins, chopped
1 pkg. (10 oz.) *(285g)* currants
1 pkg. (15 oz.) *(425g)* seedless golden raisins, chopped
2 lbs. *(900g)* apples, peeled, chopped
1 lb. *(450g)* sugar
1 lb. *(450g)* suet, finely chopped
Juice of 2 fresh lemons
Juice of 2 fresh oranges
Grated rind of 1 fresh lemon
2 oz. *(60g)* each candied citron, lemon peel, and orange peel
½ tsp. each salt, cloves, cinnamon, ginger
2 cups *(475ml)* brandy

Pickled Watermelon Rind

YIELD: 6 Pints
TOTAL CALORIES: 6000
CALORIES PER ¼ CUP: 120
CALORIES PER CHUNK: 32
CARBOHYDRATES: 8g
PREPARING: 1½ Hours
STANDING: 3 Days

With large, sharp knife, cut watermelon in half crosswise; then cut each half lengthwise into quarters.

Remove all watermelon pulp first with knife, then scrape any excess with large spoon; refrigerate pulp for another use. With sharp knife or vegetable peeler, cut off and discard green skin leaving only white inner rind. Cut rind into 1-inch *(2.5cm)* chunks. Cover chunks with hot water; boil until they can be pierced with a fork. Drain well and place in large bowl.

Combine syrup ingredients in large kettle; bring to boiling point. Remove from heat; pour over rind. Let stand overnight. In morning, drain, heat syrup to boiling again. Pour over rind and let stand overnight. Repeat process 1 more time. The third morning, reheat both syrup and rind together. Seal in sterilized jars. Let stand in cool dark place at least 2 weeks before serving.

Edith Bruce, Evanston, IL

1 large oval watermelon *(2kg)* with as thick a rind as possible. (Yield should be 3½ lbs. *(1.6kg)* rind)
Syrup for every 3½ lbs. prepared rind:
7 cups *(1.4kg)* sugar
2 cups *(475ml)* vinegar
⅛ tsp. cinnamon oil
⅛ tsp. oil of cloves

YIELD: 75 Bars
TOTAL CALORIES: 7500
CALORIES PER BAR: 100
CARBOHYDRATES: 15g
PROTEIN: 1g
FAT: 4g
PREPARING: 20 Minutes
BAKING: 35-40 Minutes

½ cup *(115g)* butter
½ cup *(100g)* brown sugar
1 egg yolk
1 tsp. pure vanilla extract
2 cups *(225g)* flour
½ tsp. baking soda
¼ tsp. salt
¼ cup *(60ml)* milk
1 cup *(285g)* red raspberry jelly
ALMOND PASTE FILLING:

8 oz. *(225g)* almond paste, cut into
    small pieces
1 egg white
½ cup *(100g)* sugar
1 tsp. pure vanilla extract
3 T. *(45g)* butter
3 eggs
Green food coloring (optional for holidays)
CHOCOLATE ICING:

2 oz. *(60g)* unsweetened chocolate,
    melted
1 T. butter
1 tsp. pure vanilla extract
2 cups *(260g)* confectioners' sugar, sifted
¼ cup *(60ml)* hot milk

Marzipan Bars

A very rich cookie that will add color to an assortment of Christmas cookies, but which can also be served any time of year.

Cream butter and sugar. Beat in egg yolk and vanilla. Sift together flour, baking soda and salt. Add to egg yolk mixture together with milk. Spread onto bottom of greased 10 × 15 × 1-inch *(25 × 37.5 × 2.5cm)* pan; cover with jelly.

ALMOND PASTE FILLING: Blend together or process almond paste, egg white, sugar, vanilla and butter until smooth. Add eggs one at a time, beating well after each addition. Tint mixture a delicate green; pour over jelly layer.

Bake in preheated 350° oven 35 to 40 minutes. Cool completely before icing the bars.

CHOCOLATE ICING: Combine all ingredients in a small bowl; beat until smooth. Spread over almond paste layer; cut into 1 × 2-inch *(2.5 × 5cm)* bars.

Ann Howard, Farmington, CT

YIELD: 120 Small Confections
TOTAL CALORIES: 3840
CALORIES PER CONFECTION: 32
CARBOHYDRATES: 5g
PROTEIN: .5g
FAT: 1g
PREPARING: 30 Minutes
CHILLING: 45 Minutes
BAKING: 15 Minutes Per Sheet

4 small egg whites
1 lb. *(450g)* confectioners' sugar
½ lb. *(225g)* ground pecans
½ lb. *(225g)* ground walnuts
1 tsp. dark rum (Myers's preferred)

ICING:

Confectioners' sugar
Rum to moisten

Von Trapp Rum Stangerln

Stangerl is Austrian dialect for a small stick.

Beat egg whites until stiff; fold in sugar and ground nuts; flavor with vanilla or rum. (If grinding nuts in a food processor rather than by hand, add 1 cup confectioners' sugar to each batch of nuts before processing to prevent them from becoming wet.)

Form into rolls ¾ inch *(2cm)* in diameter; chill 45 minutes. Cut into ⅓-inch *(0.8cm)* thick slices.

Bake on greased baking sheet in preheated 350° oven approximately 15 minutes. While still warm, ice with confectioners' sugar moistened with enough rum to spread.

Emilie de Brigard, Haddam, CT

Chocolate Pecan Jumbles

YIELD: 39 Cookies
TOTAL CALORIES: 3393
CALORIES PER COOKIE: 87
CARBOHYDRATES: 9g
PROTEIN: 1.5g
FAT: 5g
PREPARING: 15 Minutes
BAKING: 5 Minutes Per Sheet

In 1770 in Norwich, Connecticut, the first chocolate mill in America was founded by Christopher Leffingwell.

In saucepan combine sugar, butter, maple syrup and chocolate bits. Heat slowly until melted. Remove from heat and cool.

Meanwhile, sift together flour, baking soda and salt. When chocolate mixture is cool, blend in egg, vanilla, and dry ingredients. Beat well; stir in chopped nuts.

Drop by heaping teaspoonfuls onto greased baking sheets. Bake in preheated 350° oven until set, about 5 minutes.

Bobbi Evans, Duxbury, MA

½ cup *(100g)* **sugar**
½ cup *(115g)* **butter**
¼ cup *(60ml)* **real maple syrup**
1 cup (6 oz.) *(170g)* **chocolate bits**
1 cup *(115g)* **sifted flour**
½ tsp. **baking soda**
½ tsp. **salt**
1 **egg,** unbeaten
1½ tsp. **pure vanilla extract**
1 cup *(120g)* **chopped pecans**

Colonial Pumpkin Bars

YIELD: 48 Bars
TOTAL CALORIES: 7200
CALORIES PER BAR: 150
CARBOHYDRATES: 20g
PROTEIN: 2g
FAT: 7g
PREPARING: 20 Minutes
BAKING: 35 Minutes
FREEZING: Yes

Pumpkins or "pompions," as the Pilgrims called them, were used in various ways on colonial tables. Edward Johnson said in 1651, "Let no man make a jest of pumpkin, for with this fruit the Lord was pleased to feed his people till corn and cattle were increased."

Cream butter and sugar together until light and fluffy. Blend in pumpkin and eggs. Add remaining ingredients and blend thoroughly. Turn into well-greased and floured 15½ × 10½-inch *(40 × 26.5cm)* jelly roll pan. Bake in preheated 350° oven 35 minutes or until wooden pick inserted in center comes out clean. Cool on wire rack. (At this point, cake may be frozen).

ICING: In small mixing bowl, combine cream cheese with butter until fluffy. Gradually add sugar beating well after each addition. Add vanilla and beat until smooth. Ice cake and cut into serving pieces.

Rosalie Borst, South Windsor, CT

Variations, Advance Preparation, and Serving Suggestions:
For 18 muffins: Increase flour by ½ cup *(60g)*, change spices to 1 tsp. each cloves, cinnamon; ½ tsp. each ginger, nutmeg and 1½ tsp. allspice. Omit nuts and add 1 cup *(170g)* plumped raisins or chopped dates. Pour batter into greased muffin tins. Bake in preheated 350° oven 40 minutes. *Variation for bars:* A 9 × 13-inch *(22.5 × 33cm)* pan may be used to obtain a thicker, cake-like bar or square.

Nutritional Notes: If frosting is omitted, calories are decreased by approximately 50 per bar. Whole wheat flour may be substituted for the white flour in this recipe.

¾ cup *(175g)* **butter**
2 cups *(400g)* **sugar**
1 can (16 oz.) *(450g)* **pumpkin**
4 **eggs**
2 cups *(225g)* **flour**
2 tsp. **baking powder**
1 tsp. **cinnamon**
½ tsp. **baking soda**
½ tsp. **salt**
¼ tsp. **nutmeg**
1 cup *(120g)* **chopped walnuts**

ICING:

1 pkg. (3 oz.) *(85g)* **cream cheese,** softened
⅓ cup *(75g)* **butter,** softened
3 cups *(390g)* **confectioners' sugar**
1 tsp. **pure vanilla extract**

Frosted Coconut Squares

Very easy recipe for a very sweet delicacy.

YIELD: 64 Squares
TOTAL CALORIES: 4864
CALORIES PER SQUARE: 76
CARBOHYDRATES: 9g
PROTEIN: 1g
FAT: 4g
PREPARING: 30 Minutes
BAKING: 45 Minutes

CRUST:

½ cup (115g) butter, softened
1 cup (115g) flour
2 T. (15g) confectioners' sugar

FILLING:

2 eggs
1¼ cups (250g) packed brown sugar
1 tsp. pure vanilla extract
2 T. (15g) flour
¾ tsp. salt
½ tsp. baking powder
1 cup (115g) chopped nuts
1 cup (75g) moist flaked coconut

FROSTING:

1½ cups (200g) confectioners' sugar
2 T. (30g) melted butter
2 T. (30ml) fresh orange juice
1 T. (15ml) fresh lemon juice

CRUST: Line 8-inch (20cm) square pan with greased waxed paper. Blend butter, sugar and flour together until thoroughly mixed. Press evenly into pan; bake in preheated 350° oven 15 minutes.

FILLING: Meanwhile, beat eggs, brown sugar, and vanilla together. Sift flour, salt, and baking powder; add to egg-sugar mixture; mix well; add nuts and coconut. Spread mixture over baked crust; return to oven for 30 minutes.

FROSTING: Beat sugar, butter, and juices together. When squares are cooled, frost. After frosting has settled (about ½ hour) cut into 1-inch (2.5cm) squares.

Patricia L. Rougvie, Hartford, CT

Variations, Advance Preparation, and Serving Suggestions: May be served as candy in petit four wrappers.

Microwave Conversion Instructions: Melt butter in 8-inch square glass dish 45 seconds on High. Stir in flour and sugar. Mix well. Spread evenly to form crust. Cook on Medium (50%) 5 to 6 minutes. Spread filling over crust and cook 5 to 7 minutes on High. *Frosting:* Melt butter 30 seconds on High. Add confectioners' sugar, orange juice and lemon juice.

Best Lemon Bars Ever

In 1856, while living in Torrington, Connecticut, Gail Borden conducted numerous experiments and successfully produced the first commercially available condensed milk. This was the first product sold by the Borden Company. The product begins as fresh whole milk. Then sugar is added and water is removed. Its special flavor and smooth consistency make it ideal for use in desserts, sauces, and cookies such as Best Lemon Bars Ever.

YIELD: 24-32 Bars
TOTAL CALORIES: 4640
CALORIES PER BAR: 145
CARBOHYDRATES: 23g
PROTEIN: 2g
FAT: 5g
PREPARING: 20 Minutes
BAKING: 35 Minutes

1½ cups (170g) flour
1 tsp. baking powder
½ tsp. salt
1 can (14 oz.) (415ml) sweetened
   condensed milk
Finely grated rind from 1 large lemon
½ cup (120ml) fresh lemon juice
⅔ cup (150g) butter
1 cup (200g) packed dark brown sugar
1 cup (85g) old fashioned oats

Sift together flour, baking powder and salt; set aside.

Pour condensed milk into medium-sized mixing bowl; add grated lemon rind, then gradually add lemon juice, stirring with a small whisk to keep mixture smooth set aside.

In large bowl cream butter; add sugar and beat well. On lowest speed, gradually add sifted dry ingredients, beat until thoroughly blended; mix in oats. Mixture will be crunchy.

Sprinkle a bit more than half the oat mixture (2 generous cups) evenly over bottom of buttered 9 × 13-inch (22.5 × 33cm) pan; pat crumbs firmly to make smooth firm layer; drizzle or spoon lemon mixture evenly over crumb layer and spread to make a thin, smooth layer. Sprinkle remaining oat mixture evenly over lemon layer; pat crumbs gently with palms to smooth them.

Bake on rack ⅓ up from bottom of preheated 350° oven 30 to 35 minutes until lightly colored. Cool completely in pan; then refrigerate 1 hour. With small sharp knife cut around sides of pan and then cut into squares; remove and refrigerate.

Lee Grimmeisen, West Hartford, CT

Nutritional Notes: Sweetened condensed milk is actually evaporated milk with a sweetener (sucrose, dextrose or corn syrup) added. The sweetener added accounts for approximately 50% of the volume of sweetened condensed milk.

Rocky Ripple Fudge Bars

YIELD: 36 Bars
TOTAL CALORIES: 10580
CALORIES PER BAR: 294
CARBOHYDRATES: 48g
PROTEIN: 3g
FAT: 10g
CHOLESTEROL: High
PREPARING: 45 Minutes
BAKING: 25-35 Minutes
FREEZING: Yes-Very Well

CRUST: In 3-qt. *(3L)* saucepan, melt butter and chocolate over moderately low heat. Stir constantly until melted. Remove from heat. Add vanilla and sugar; stir to mix well. Add eggs, one at a time, stirring until thoroughly incorporated after each addition. Stir in flour and baking powder. Then stir in nuts and/or coconut. Spread mixture in well-buttered and floured 9 × 13-inch *(22.5 × 33cm)* glass baking dish.

FILLING: In small bowl, combine cream cheese, sugar, flour, butter, egg and vanilla. Beat until smooth and fluffy. Stir in nuts and/or coconut. Sprinkle with chocolate bits. Spread filling over crust. Bake on center rack in preheated 350° oven 25 to 35 minutes or until toothpick inserted in center of crust barely comes out dry. Do not overbake. Remove pan from oven. Quickly sprinkle with marshmallows. Return to oven for 2 minutes or until marshmallows just begin to puff.

FROSTING: While bars are baking, prepare frosting. Melt chocolate and butter in top of small double boiler over hot water on moderate heat. Add remaining ingredients and stir until smooth. As soon as marshmallows have puffed, remove pan from oven. Immediately pour warm frosting over marshmallows. Quickly swirl marshmallows and frosting.

Let stand uncovered overnight or 5 to 6 hours to facilitate cutting. Cut around sides with small sharp knife. Then cut into bars, dipping knife in cold water after each cut to prevent sticking. Cutting into bars will be a bit messy and frustrating, but well worth the effort.

Leland W. Morgan, East Haddam, CT

CRUST:
½ cup *(115g)* butter
1 oz. *(30g)* unsweetened chocolate
1 tsp. pure vanilla extract
1 cup *(200g)* sugar
2 eggs
1 cup *(115g)* flour
1 tsp. baking powder
½-1 cup chopped nuts *(60-120g)* or coconut *(40-75g)* or combination of both

FILLING:
6 oz. *(170g)* cream cheese, softened
½ cup *(100g)* sugar
2 T. *(15g)* flour
¼ cup *(60g)* butter, softened
1 egg
½ tsp. pure vanilla extract
¼ cup chopped nuts *(30g)* or coconut *(20g)*, or combination of both
1 pkg. (6 oz.) *(170g)* semi-sweet chocolate bits (mini-bits preferred)
2 cups *(55g)* miniature marshmallows

FROSTING:
¼ cup *(60g)* butter
1 oz. *(30g)* unsweetened chocolate
2 oz. *(55g)* cream cheese, softened
¼ cup *(60ml)* milk
1 lb. *(450g)* confectioners' sugar
1 tsp. pure vanilla extract

YIELD: 48-60 Cookies
TOTAL CALORIES: 6600
CALORIES PER COOKIE: 110
CARBOHYDRATES: 13g
PROTEIN: 1.5g
FAT: 6g
PREPARING: 20 Minutes
BAKING: 12-15 Minutes Per Sheet

Chocolate Oatmeal Fruit Drops

1 cup *(225g)* butter, softened
1 cup *(200g)* brown sugar
½ cup *(100g)* granulated sugar
1 egg (a second egg may be used if batter seems too dry)
¼ cup *(60ml)* water
1 tsp. pure vanilla extract
3 cups *(255g)* regular oats
1 cup *(115g)* flour (half may be whole wheat)
1 tsp. salt
½ tsp. baking soda
¾ cup *(90g)* chopped nuts
¾ cup *(130g)* mini chocolate chips
¾ cup *(130g)* raisins
⅔ cup *(75g)* wheat germ
¾ cup *(135g)* dried apricots, snipped into small slices

Cream butter with sugars; add eggs, water, and vanilla; blend well. Add oats, flour, salt, and baking soda, mixing well. Add remaining ingredients, continuing to mix.

Drop by rounded teaspoonfuls onto greased baking sheet. Bake in preheated 350° oven 12 to 15 minutes.

Denise Walker, West Hartford, CT

Nutritional Notes: These cookies are relatively high in calories, but they are "valuable" calories due to use of such ingredients as whole wheat flour, wheat germ, oats, raisins and apricots. Approximately 10 to 13 calories per cookie can be eliminated if chocolate chips are eliminated.

YIELD: 54 Cookies
TOTAL CALORIES: 4752
CALORIES PER COOKIE: 88
CARBOHYDRATES: 11g
PROTEIN: 2g
FAT: 4g
PREPARING: 15 Minutes
BAKING: 10-11 Minutes Per Sheet

Granola Apricot Nut Drops

¾ cup *(90g)* whole wheat flour
¼ cup *(30g)* wheat germ
¼ cup *(20g)* nonfat dry milk powder
¾ tsp. salt
¼ tsp. baking powder
¼ tsp. baking soda
½ cup *(115g)* butter
½ cup *(130g)* peanut butter
¾ cup *(250g)* honey
1 egg
1 tsp. pure vanilla extract
1 cup *(170g)* raisins
1 cup *(180g)* dried apricots, snipped in small pieces
¾ cup *(60g)* quick-cooking oats
½ cup *(60g)* chopped walnuts
⅓ cup *(25g)* shredded coconut

Stir together flour, wheat germ, milk powder, salt, baking powder and soda.

In a large mixer, beat butter, peanut butter, and honey; add egg and vanilla; beat well. Add flour mixture to butter mixture. Stir together remaining ingredients; add to the above mixture.

Drop dough by heaping teaspoonfuls onto *ungreased* baking sheet. Bake in preheated 350° oven 10 to 11 minutes. Cool 1 minute on baking sheet; then remove to wire racks to finish cooling.

Maryann Reuben, West Hartford, CT

Nutritional Notes: These cookies provide a vitamin, mineral, and fiber rich alternative to the normal empty-calorie variety. They are especially appropriate for children's lunch boxes and for after-school snacks.

Chewy Molasses Spice Cookies

YIELD: 24-30 Cookies
TOTAL CALORIES: 3420
CALORIES PER COOKIE: 114
CARBOHYDRATES: 14g
PROTEIN: 1g
FAT: 6g
PREPARING: 15 Minutes
BAKING: 5-6 Minutes Per Sheet

Cream butter. Add sugar and beat until fluffy; blend in egg, molasses, dry ingredients, and spices.

Drop by teaspoonfuls onto greased baking sheet, no more than eight cookies to a sheet. Flatten each cookie with bottom of a glass which has first been coated with a little batter and then dipped into granulated sugar.

Bake in preheated 375° oven until just set, about 5 to 6 minutes.

Bobbi M. Evans, Duxbury, MA

1 cup *(225g)* butter, softened
1 cup *(200g)* packed brown sugar
1 egg
4 T. *(60ml)* light molasses
1½ cups *(170g)* sifted flour (no more)
½ tsp. salt
1 tsp. baking soda
½ tsp. ground cloves
1 tsp. cinnamon
1 tsp. ginger

Toffee Bars

Toffee is a generic name for many kinds of hard sweetmeats made from sugar and butter. The addition of egg and flour produces a cross between a cookie and candy.

YIELD: 30-48 Bars
TOTAL CALORIES: 4944
CALORIES PER BAR: 103
CARBOHYDRATES: 9g
PROTEIN: 1g
FAT: 7g
PREPARING: 15 Minutes
BAKING: 15 Minutes
DECORATING: 30-60 Minutes
FREEZING: Yes

BARS: Cream butter, add sugar gradually, beating by hand or with electric mixer until light and fluffy. Add yolk, beat well. Stir in flour. Spread evenly in lightly buttered 11 × 15-inch *(27.5 × 37.5cm)* baking pan. Place on middle rack of preheated 350° oven. Bake 15 minutes. Remove from oven.

TOPPING: While bars are baking, melt chocolate. Pour chocolate over bars while they are still warm. Spread quickly with spatula. Sprinkle with chopped nuts. Let cool to room temperature. Cut into bars.

ALTERNATE HOLIDAY TOPPING: Melt white chocolate and spread as above. Cool until chocolate is firm to touch. Cut into bars. Beat confectioners' sugar with egg white and cream of tartar. Tint green. Pipe "holly" leaves onto each bar. Decorate centers with cinnamon candy "berries".

Kathleen J. Schwartz, Avon, CT

Microwave Conversion Instructions: *Bars:* Follow above directions to prepare bars. Spread mixture evenly in lightly buttered 10 or 12-inch *(25cm or 30.5cm)* round shallow plate. Cook on High about 9 to 10 minutes, turning if cooking unevenly, just until it appears barely cooked. Toffee will firm as it cools. *Topping:* Place chocolate in glass measure. Cook on High 2 minutes, just until softened (chocolate will not dissolve until stirred). Complete as directed above.

BARS:

1 cup *(225g)* butter, room temperature
1 cup *(200g)* dark brown sugar
1 egg yolk
1 cup *(115g)* flour

TOPPING:

7 oz. *(200g)* milk chocolate, Lindt preferred
1 cup *(115g)* chopped walnuts

ALTERNATE HOLIDAY TOPPING:

14 oz. *(400g)* white chocolate, Lindt preferred
3 cups *(385g)* confectioners' sugar
1 egg white
⅛ tsp. cream of tartar
Green food coloring
Red cinnamon candies

Fortune Cookies

YIELD: 48 Cookies
TOTAL CALORIES: 4080
CALORIES PER COOKIE: 85
CARBOHYDRATES: 9g
PROTEIN: 1g
FAT: 5g
PREPARING: 15 Minutes
BAKING: 10 Minutes Per Sheet

Write fortunes on thin paper strips, 3 x ¾ inches. Personalize remarks for guests and occasions. These will make a party!

¾ cup *(175ml)* unbeaten egg whites
   (5-6 eggs)
1⅔ cups *(335g)* sugar
¼ tsp. salt
1 cup *(225g)* melted butter
1 cup *(115g)* flour
¾ cup *(85g)* very finely chopped,
   blanched almonds
½ tsp. pure vanilla extract

Combine egg whites, sugar and salt and mix until sugar is dissolved. Stir remaining ingredients in separately and beat until well blended.

Drop dough by level teaspoonfuls, well apart, onto an ungreased baking sheet, (6 cookies to a sheet). Bake in preheated 350° oven 10 minutes or until edges are golden brown.

One at a time, remove cookies from baking sheet. Place a fortune in center of each cookie, fold over in half and pinch sides together. They should resemble nurses' caps. Work very quickly since cookies cool and harden rapidly.

Carol M. Locandro, Simsbury, CT

Almond Lace Wafers

YIELD: 30 Wafers
TOTAL CALORIES: 1860
CALORIES PER WAFER: 62
CARBOHYDRATES: 6g
PROTEIN: .4g
FAT: 4g
PREPARING: 15 Minutes
BAKING: 8-10 Minutes Per Sheet
FREEZING: Yes

A crisp, extremely delicate and fragile wafer, delicious all by itself or wonderful for shaping into small cups to be filled with ice cream or a mousse.

4 oz. *(115g)* blanched almonds, finely
   ground
½ cup *(100g)* sugar
¼ lb. *(115g)* butter
1 T. (exactly level) sifted flour
2 T. *(30ml)* milk

Place all ingredients in large heavy skillet. Stir over low heat until butter melts and ingredients are thoroughly mixed; remove from heat.

Drop dough by slightly rounded teaspoonfuls about 4 inches *(10cm)* apart on buttered and lightly floured non-stick coated baking sheets. Place only 4 or 5 cookies on each sheet. Bake 1 sheet at a time in preheated 350° oven on rack ⅓ down from top of oven. Bake cookies 8 to 10 minutes, reversing position of sheet if cookies are not browning evenly, or until golden brown with no light spots in centers.

Remove from oven; let stand *a few seconds* until they can be removed with a wide spatula. Working *very quickly*, remove a cookie and place it over a rolling pin to shape. If cookies cool too quickly, reheat in oven long enough to soften. Once cookies are set, remove from rolling pin to make room for others.

As soon as cookies are cool, store in airtight containers to prevent them from becoming limp. May be frozen.

Susan Flynn, Avon, CT

Vanilj Bullar

SWEDISH VANILLA COOKIES

The dry ammonia makes these cookies extremely light and delicate.

YIELD: 60 Cookies
CALORIES PER COOKIE: 55
CARBOHYDRATES: 7g
PROTEIN: Trace
FAT: 3g
PREPARING: 45 Minutes
BAKING: 15 Minutes Per Sheet

Cream butter and then add sugar. Add egg yolk and vanilla. Sift together flour and ammonium powder; add a little at a time to butter mixture. Roll dough into small ¾-inch (2cm) balls. Place balls 2 inches (5cm) apart on greased baking sheet. Bake in preheated 325° oven 15 minutes or until very lightly golden. When cookies have cooled, sprinkle with confectioners' sugar.

Arlene Johanson Parmelee, West Hartford, CT

1 cup (225g) butter, softened
1 cup (200g) sugar
1 egg yolk
1 tsp. pure vanilla extract
1½ cups (170g) flour
1 tsp. powdered ammonium carbonate (Hjortronsalt) (available at Scandinavian food stores).
Confectioners' sugar

Orange Butter Wafers

A crispy, buttery cookie, delicious all by itself or wonderful for shaping into fluted cups to serve with scoops of sorbet, ice cream or mousse.

YIELD: 24 Wafers
TOTAL CALORIES: 1080
CALORIES PER WAFER: 45
CARBOHYDRATES: 6g
PROTEIN: 1g
FAT: 2g
PREPARING: 15 Minutes
BAKING: 10 Minutes Per Sheet
FREEZING: No

In bowl, beat butter and sugar until light and fluffy; add orange and lemon rind.

In another bowl, beat whites with salt until stiff. Fold half of the whites into butter mixture; add remaining whites alternately with flour. Drop batter by teaspoonfuls onto buttered and floured baking sheets, only 4 or 5 per sheet, 3½ inches (9cm) apart. Flatten each mound into 3-inch (7.5cm) circle with narrow spatula or spoon dipped in water. Bake cookies on center rack of preheated 325° oven, 1 sheet at a time, for 10 minutes, or until edges are lightly browned. Watch carefully to prevent overbaking. Remove cookies from sheet, 1 at a time; roll around a sharpening steel or other narrow, cylindrical object. Slip each roll onto rack; let cool. If cookies become too hard to roll, return to oven for several seconds.

As soon as cookies are completely cool, carefully store in airtight container for several days to a week.

Maria M. Rossi, Brewster, MA

¼ cup (60g) unsalted sweet butter, softened
½ cup (100g) sugar
1½ tsp. freshly grated orange rind
¼ tsp. freshly grated lemon rind
2 egg whites, room temperature
Pinch salt
½ cup (55g) sifted flour

Almond Star Cookie Tree

An impressive, elegant and delicious must for any holiday table.

YIELD: 1 Cookie Tree
TOTAL CALORIES: 7700
CARBOHYDRATES: 935g
PROTEIN: 195g
FAT: 354g
PREPARING: 48 Hours
BAKING: 20-30 Minutes Per Sheet

DOUGH:

1½ cups *(340g)* butter, softened
1¾ cups *(350g)* sugar
3 eggs
1½ tsp. cinnamon
¼ tsp. ground cloves
3 cups *(340g)* finely ground unblanched almonds
5½ cups *(625g)* sifted flour
1¾-inch round cookie cutter

GLAZE:

1 T. milk mixed with 1 beaten egg
½ cup *(75g)* blanched whole almonds, split in half lengthwise

SPECIAL EQUIPMENT:

Cardboard, cut into 11 8-pointed stars in the following graduated sizes measured from point to point across center:
10-inch *(25cm)*, 9½-inch *(23.75cm)*, 9-inch *(22.5cm)*, 8½-inch *(21.25cm)*, 8-inch *(20cm)*, 7-inch *(17.5cm)*, 6-inch *(15cm)*, 5-inch *(12.5cm)*, 4-inch *(10cm)*, 3-inch *(7.5cm)*, and 2-inch *(5cm)*
9-inch high *(22.5cm)* wooden hat stand with dowel ¾-inch *(2cm)* thick and a 1-inch *(2.5cm)* deep hole made in top with ice pick or nail
1 tsp. confectioners' sugar mixed with a little water
1 toothpick

DOUGH: In large mixer bowl, cream butter. Gradually add sugar beating until mixture is light; add eggs, continue to beat until well blended. Add spices and almonds, blend; stir in flour; mix thoroughly. Wrap dough in waxed paper or foil; refrigerate overnight.

Cutting off pieces of dough as you use them and refrigerating the rest, roll dough with well-floured rolling pin on well-floured board to ¼-inch *(0.6cm)* thickness. Use cardboard stars to cut out 12 stars (2 2-inch stars). Cut out approximately 18 small rounds with 1¾-inch *(4.5cm)* cookie cutter. With narrow end of (large #9) pastry tube, cut a hole in center of all rounds and stars except the 2-inch ones.

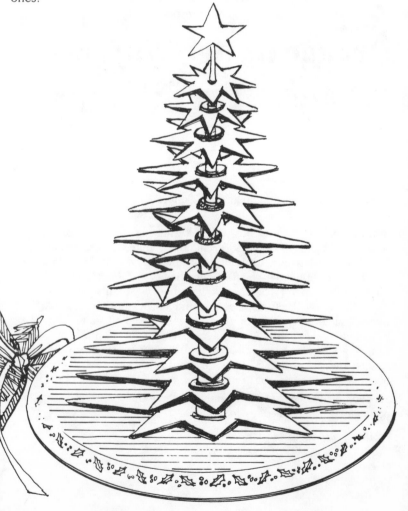

With two broad, floured spatulas, lift cookies to ungreased baking sheets. Brush stars and rounds with milk-egg mixture. Place 1 almond half on each point of all but 2-inch stars. Decorate 2-inch stars by cutting 4 almonds each into 4 lengthwise pieces.

Bake in preheated 350° oven, the cookies 20 minutes and the stars 30 minutes. Cool on wire racks. Cookies may be stored in a cool place until ready to assemble tree.

Assemble tree by first slipping 2 round cookies onto dowel. Start with 10-inch star; alternate with cookie rounds until only the 2 2-inch stars are left and the dowel is covered. Put 2-inch stars together with confectioners' sugar and water; let dry. Insert one end of toothpick into hole on top of dowel and other end between pinned stars, holding them in an upright position. Trim toothpick as needed.

Completed tree may be wrapped in plastic wrap.

Renee Pregulman Dubin, West Hartford, CT

Zimtsterne

CINNAMON CHRISTMAS STARS

A flourless cookie. In Switzerland, a land of sweet confections, Cinnamon Stars are a holiday tradition.

YIELD: 30 Cookies
TOTAL CALORIES: 2640
CALORIES PER COOKIE: 88
CARBOHYDRATES: 11g
PROTEIN: 2g
FAT: 4g
PREPARING: 1 Hour
CHILLING: Overnight
STANDING: 2 Hours
BAKING: 25 Minutes Per Sheet
FREEZING: Yes-Very Well

DOUGH: Beat egg whites with electric mixer at medium speed until soft peaks form. Add granulated sugar, 2 T. at a time, beating after each addition; continue to beat until mixture is very glossy, about 10 minutes. Combine almonds with cinnamon. Stir in egg white mixture; stir to combine well. Refrigerate dough, covered, overnight.

Lightly sprinkle wooden board or pastry cloth with 2 T. flour mixed with 2 T. granulated sugar. Roll out dough, one half at a time until ¼-inch (0.3cm) thick. Using 3-inch (7.5cm) star-shaped cookie cutter, cut out cookies and place 1 inch (2.5cm) apart on lightly greased baking sheets. Let cookies stand, uncovered, at room temperature 2 hours.

GLAZE: Combine confectioners' sugar with water; mix until smooth. Bake cookies in preheated 300° oven 20 minutes. Brush tops with glaze; bake 5 minutes longer. Remove to wire rack and let cool.

Ruth S. Hennessy, Morristown, NJ

DOUGH:
⅓ cup (80ml) egg whites (2 egg whites) at room temperature
1¼ cups (250g) granulated sugar
1½ cups (175g) unblanched almonds, ground
1½ T. cinnamon

2 T. (15g) flour
2 T. (25g) sugar

GLAZE:
1 cup (130g) sifted confectioners' sugar
2 T. (30ml) water

Variations, Advance Preparation, and Serving Suggestions: Add 1 tsp. grated lemon rind if desired. Recipe easily doubles. To store or freeze, place in tightly covered tin with waxed paper between layers.

Nutritional Notes: These cookies are low in sodium and cholesterol since only the egg white is used and no butter or margarine is added. The fat component is contributed by the almonds.

YIELD: 40 Cookies
TOTAL CALORIES: 5120
CALORIES PER COOKIE: 128
CARBOHYDRATES: 15g
PROTEIN: 1g
FAT: 7g
PREPARING: 30 Minutes
BAKING: 13-15 Minutes Per Sheet

Florentines

ECHTE FLORENTINER

An Austrian cookie despite its Italian-sounding name.

DOUGH:

¼ cup *(60g)* **unsalted sweet butter**
⅓ cup *(80g)* **firmly packed brown sugar**
1 T. **heavy cream**
2 T. *(40g)* **honey**
2 T. *(30ml)* **light corn syrup**
¾ cup *(85g)* **sifted cake flour**
¼ tsp. **salt**
4 oz. *(115g)* **blanched slivered almonds**
3 oz. *(85g)* **candied cherries, quartered**
3 oz. *(85g)* **candied orange peel, finely chopped**

ICING:

6 T. *(85g)* **unsalted sweet butter**
3 oz. *(85g)* **semisweet chocolate (Lindt preferred)**
3 oz. *(85g)* **sweet chocolate**
1 tsp. **pure vanilla extract**

DOUGH: Cream butter and brown sugar until light. Add cream, honey and corn syrup; beat until smooth and well blended.

Sift flour and salt over mixture; beat well. Mix in almonds, cherries and orange peel. Drop about 1 tsp. dough (slightly rounded) onto greased baking sheet leaving 2 inches *(5cm)* between cookies. Bake in preheated 300° oven 13 to 15 minutes. Dough should be bubbly and almost carmelized, no longer cakey or doughy looking. Cool *only* 1 minute on baking sheet; remove to wire rack with broad spatula.

ICING: Combine icing ingredients; melt over hot water or in microwave 2 minutes. When cookie is completely cool, ice flat side. Refrigerate iced cookies until chocolate is almost set. Draw wavy lines through the glaze. Store in airtight container between layers of waxed paper. If room is warm, store in refrigerator, bringing cookies back to room temperature before serving.

Margaret McClure, Highland Park, IL

YIELD: 15 Cookies
TOTAL CALORIES: 3450
CALORIES PER COOKIE: 230
CARBOHYDRATES: 14g
PROTEIN: 3g
FAT: 18g
PREPARING: 10 Minutes
BAKING: 8-10 Minutes Per Sheet

Nötkakor

SWEDISH CHOCOLATE HAZELNUT COOKIES

---

1 **egg, very lightly beaten**
½ scant cup *(100g)* **sugar**
2 cups *(275g)* **ground hazelnuts**
15 **whole perfect hazelnuts**
4 oz. *(115g)* **German sweet chocolate**
1 T. **shortening or corn oil**

Gently but thoroughly mix egg, sugar and ground hazelnuts. Mixture will be airy and sticky.

Place rounded tablespoons of dough on greased baking sheet and put whole hazelnut in center of each cookie. Bake in preheated 400° oven 8 to 10 minutes, watching carefully so bottoms of cookies do not burn. Cool on a wire rack.

While cookies cool, melt chocolate and shortening in double boiler. When cookies are cool, dip bottom half into chocolate and place on waxed paper-lined baking sheet. Refrigerate just long enough to set chocolate.

Eva Pollock, West Hartford, CT

Variations, Advance Preparation, and Serving Suggestions:
Cookies can be made smaller in size if desired.

Deep Dish Fruit Pie

This is one of those recipes that every cook as well as every non-cook needs in their repertoire — fast, easy, delicious, versatile, and enjoyed by all.

YIELD: 6-8 Servings
TOTAL CALORIES: 2864
CALORIES PER SERVING: 358
CARBOHYDRATES: 55g
PROTEIN: 3g
FAT: 14g
SODIUM: High
PREPARING: 10 Minutes
BAKING: 50 Minutes

CRUST: Melt butter in deep 3-qt. *(3L)* casserole in preheated 350° oven. Watch so that butter does not burn; when butter is melted, remove casserole from oven.

Sift together flour, baking powder, salt, and ¾ cup sugar. Stir milk into dry ingredients until just wet but not thoroughly blended. Pour mixture into melted butter; *do not stir.*

FRUIT: Toss fruit with sugar, lemon juice and cinnamon. Place fruit on top of milk mixture; *do not stir.*

Bake in preheated 350° oven 50 to 60 minutes.

Serve with vanilla ice cream or sweetened whipped cream.

Mary Fish, Cashiers, NC

Microwave Conversion Instructions: Note: Reduce milk to ¾ cup. Use cinnamon on top of crust for color. Melt butter in deep 3-qt. casserole on High 1 minute. Pour prepared mixture into melted butter and then add fruit. Sprinkle with cinnamon. Cook on High 12 to 15 minutes, rotating ¼ turn every 3 minutes.

CRUST:
¼ lb. *(115g)* butter
¾ cup *(85g)* flour
2 tsp. baking powder
¼ tsp. salt
¾ cup *(150g)* sugar
1 cup *(240ml)* milk

FRUIT:
4 cups sliced fresh fruit of your choice:
   Blueberries *(600g)*
   Peaches *(800g whole fruit)*
   Nectarines *(850g whole fruit)*
   Strawberries *(600g)*
   Rhubarb *(550g)*
   Strawberry-Rhubarb
   Plums *(900g) (use half dark brown sugar, 1 tsp. grated orange rind)*
¾ cup *(150g)* sugar
Juice of 1 lemon
¼ tsp. cinnamon for whichever above fruit you feel is enhanced by cinnamon

Macadamia Nut Chiffon Pie

Macadamia nuts are native to Australia, but grown commercially in Hawaii. One full-grown Macadamia nut tree yields between 100 to 150 pounds of nuts a year.

YIELD: 8 Servings
TOTAL CALORIES: 4130
CALORIES PER SERVING: 517
CARBOHYDRATES: 48g
PROTEIN: 7g
FAT: 33g
CHOLESTEROL: High
PREPARING: 1 Hour
CHILLING: 1 Hour Minimum

Roll out dough ⅛-inch *(0.3cm)* thick. Put in 9-inch *(22.5cm)* pie dish. Prick bottom; chill 60 minutes. Line dough with waxed paper and fill with beans. Bake in preheated 400° oven 12 minutes. Remove paper and beans and bake an additional 12 minutes. Cool.

FILLING: Soften gelatin in cold water. Set aside. In saucepan, combine yolks, ½ cup sugar, salt and milk. Cook over moderate heat, stirring until thickened and mixture coats spoon. Do not boil. Remove from heat; stir in gelatin and cool.

Beat egg whites with pinch salt until foamy; gradually beat in ½ cup sugar until stiff peaks form. Fold whites into cooled yolk mixture. Add half of Macadamia nuts and almond extract. Spoon into pie shell and chill.

Mix whipped cream and sugar. Spread on top of pie. Sprinkle with remaining Macadamia nuts and serve.

Lee M. Grimmeisen, West Hartford, CT

Dough for 1 9-inch *(22.5cm)* Pie Crust (page 198)

FILLING:
1 env. *(¼ oz.) (7g)* unflavored gelatin
¼ cup *(60ml)* cold water
4 eggs, separated
1 cup *(200g)* sugar, divided
¼ tsp. salt
1 cup *(240ml)* milk
⅛ tsp. salt
½ cup *(80g)* Macadamia nuts, chopped
¼ tsp. almond extract
1 cup *(240ml)* heavy cream, whipped and sugar to taste

YIELD: 6 Servings
TOTAL CALORIES: 2250
CALORIES PER SERVING WITH
   APPLE FILLING: 375
CARBOHYDRATES: 59g
PROTEIN: 1g
FAT: 15g
PREPARING: 30 Minutes
BAKING: 35 Minutes
MARINATING: Prunes 6 Weeks
COOKING: 30 Minutes
FREEZING: No

Flower Petal Apple Croustade

Crispy butter-glazed phyllo "petals" create a spectacular floral bouquet enclosing a fresh fruit filling.

STRUDEL PASTRY:

½ lb. *(225g)* phyllo or strudel leaves (Krino's brand preferred), approximately 10 leaves
½ cup *(115g)* unsalted sweet clarified butter, melted
Confectioners' sugar
Orange flower water
1 T. Armagnac

APPLE OR PEAR FILLING:

3 lbs. *(1.4kg)* Granny Smith or Greening apples or Bartlett pears (or mixture of both) pared, cored and thickly sliced
½ cup *(100g)* sugar
2 pieces lemon peel
1 vanilla bean split or 1 tsp. pure vanilla extract
1 T. orange flower water
3 T. *(45ml)* Armagnac

PRUNE FILLING:

1 box (1 lb.) *(450g)* unsweetened pitted prunes
Steeped tea, cooled
½ cup *(100g)* sugar
¼ cup *(60ml)* water
2 cups *(475ml)* Armagnac
1 cup *(240ml)* white wine

Lightly brush flat baking sheet with non-stick finish or large pizza pan with some of melted butter.

Unroll strudel pastry. Place pile of leaves in front of you and cover with damp towel to prevent drying out. Working quickly, lightly brush with butter lengthwise half a sheet phyllo. Fold unbuttered half over onto buttered half. You now have a rectangular strip of buttered phyllo. Place the narrow end of this strip in the center of pan, allowing the excess to extend over edge of pan. Butter and fold all remaining phyllo strips in the same manner, placing them side-by-side, like the spokes of a wheel, until the entire pan is covered with a circular arrangement of phyllo leaves. Place the fruit filling of your choice (you can also combine the apple filling with 1 or 2 prunes per serving placed on top of apple filling) in 10-inch *(25cm)* circle in center of leaves. Sprinkle with additional orange flower water, if desired.

To complete croustade, starting with last leaf placed on pan, bring one leaf at a time toward center of filling as if to cover. Twist leaf once in counterclockwise direction. Pinch twisted portion and lightly set it into fruit filling. Form end of strip into an open petal resembling a tulip. Continue with remaining phyllo strips in same twisting fashion, placing petals close together so they cover fruit filling. Sprinkle top very lightly with additional orange flower water, 1 T. Armagnac and confectioners' sugar. Bake on lower shelf in preheated 400° oven 15 minutes. Lower oven to 350° and bake 20 minutes. Cool slightly on rack before dusting with additional confectioners' sugar. Using 2 large spatulas, transfer croustade to serving platter. Cut into wedges with kitchen shears.

APPLE OR PEAR FILLING: Cook apples with sugar, lemon peel, vanilla, and orange flower water in large covered skillet over low heat until mixture is chunky applesauce. Flavor with Armagnac. Cool. Refrigerate overnight. Remove lemon peel.

PRUNE FILLING: Soak prunes in tea overnight; drain. In small saucepan, combine sugar and water and cook without stirring 10 minutes or until 220° is reached on candy thermometer. Place prunes in large glass jar; pour hot syrup over them. Add Armagnac and wine to cover. Let soak 6 weeks in cool place. If using only prunes for filling, partially mash them before placing on phyllo leaves.

Bernice Kuzma, West Hartford, CT

Variations, Advance Preparation, and Serving Suggestions:
For drama at serving time, flame Armagnac over petal edges. Create your own combinations of fruit filling, using apples and apricots, etc.

Wine Suggestion: French Comte Zafond Sancerre, semi-sweet; serve chilled.

Francis Bergquist

Apple Puff Pastry Tart with Ground Pecan Filling

A tart that everyone raves about!

YIELD: 2 Tarts or 12 Servings
TOTAL CALORIES: 5800
CALORIES PER SERVING: 484
CARBOHYDRATES: 53g
PROTEIN: 5g
FAT: 28g
CHOLESTEROL: High
PREPARING: 1½ Hours
BAKING: 40 Minutes

PASTRY: Cut puff pastry in half crosswise, roll out each piece into rectangle 16 x 20-inches *(40 x 50cm)*. Trim edges so they are perfectly straight. Place each rectangle on separate baking sheet, cover with waxed paper, refrigerate and let rest 15 minutes to facilitate cutting strips.

Then cut ½-inch *(1.5cm)* strips from all 4 sides of each rectangle. Moisten edges of strips with water, gently place on edges of rectangles, and then miter corners of each rectangle. *Firmly* press strips in place so they will rise straight up rather than fan out. Prick interior of pastry all over with fork. Cover tart with waxed paper and refrigerate overnight or freeze.

Remove pastry from refrigerator or freezer. Prick interior of pastry again with fork. Line interior of tart with aluminum foil, then weigh it down with rice or dried beans. Rub edges of pastry with milk to glaze.

Bake tarts in preheated 425° oven 15 minutes. Remove from oven, carefully remove beans and foil, reduce heat to 400° and continue baking empty tart shells, 5 minutes more to dry out bottom.

Peel, core and *very thinly* slice apples. Toss slices with lemon juice. Cover and set aside.

NUT FILLING: Combine all ingredients in mixer bowl or food processor and beat together or process until well-mixed.

APRICOT GLAZE: Put all ingredients in a small pan, bring just to the boil, then strain. It must be warm when brushed on.

One hour before serving, spread half nut filling mixture over bottom of each tart shell. Then overlap apple slices almost standing upright over filling. Brush apple slices with warm apricot glaze.

Bake tart in preheated 400° oven 20 minutes. Cool briefly. Serve tart warm and decorated with sweetened whipped cream.

Lydie Marshall, New York, NY
via Melinda M. Vance, West Hartford, CT

Wine Suggestion: French Comte Lafond Sancerre, semi-sweet white; serve chilled.

PASTRY:
1 recipe Puff Pastry (page 194), chilled and ready to roll out
Milk
5 apples (Cortland, Granny Smith, or Northern Spies)
Lemon juice

NUT FILLING:
1 cup ground, pecans *(90g)* or almonds *(120g)*
4 T. *(60g)* butter
1 egg
1 tsp. pure vanilla extract
2 T. *(30ml)* dark rum (Myers's preferred)
½ cup *(100g)* sugar

APRICOT GLAZE:
1 cup *(285g)* apricot jam
¼ cup *(50g)* sugar
1 T. freshly squeezed lemon juice
1 T. dark rum or Calvados
Sweetened whipped cream

Fruit Tarts or Tartlets

A tart is not a pie. It is a delicate pastry shell filled with raw or cooked fruit and sometimes a custard. A tart is never covered by a top crust. Listed below are just a few of the possible combinations. The fruits or mixture of fruits, flavored custards, or various nut crusts are only limited by your imagination.

Rich Tart Pastry (page 196)
Almond Short Pastry (page 197)
Walnut Tart Pastry (page 197)

CINNAMON SUGAR:
　CALORIES PER TABLESPOON: 46
2 cups *(400g)* **granulated sugar mixed with 2 T. cinnamon**

APRICOT GLAZE:
　TOTAL CALORIES: 1180
　CARBOHYDRATES: 288g
1 cup *(285g)* **apricot jam**
¼ cup *(50g)* **sugar**
2-4 T. *(30-60ml)* **liqueur (dark rum or your choice)**
1 T. fresh lemon juice

CURRANT GLAZE:
　TOTAL CALORIES: 1100
　CARBOHYDRATES: 269g
1 cup *(285g)* **currant jelly**
2-4 T. *(30-60ml)* **liqueur (dark rum or your choice)**
¼ cup *(50g)* **sugar**
1 T. fresh lemon juice

PASTRY CREAM (Creme Patissiere):
　YIELD: 1½ Cups
　TOTAL CALORIES: 1050
　CARBOHYDRATES: 174g
　PROTEIN: 21g
　FAT: 30g
2 T. *(15g)* **flour**
1 cup *(240ml)* **milk**
⅛ tsp. salt
⅜ cup *(75g)* **sugar**
4 egg yolks, slightly beaten
1 T. vanilla or dark rum

STRAWBERRY TART:
1 cup *(240ml)* **cold Pastry Cream**
1 9-inch *(22.5cm)* **baked Rich Tart Pastry (page 196) or Almond Short Pastry (page 197) shell**
2 cups *(300g)* **perfect medium-size stawberries, hulled (slice vertically if they are too big)**
½ cup Currant Glaze

APRICOT GLAZE: Heat jam and sugar in saucepan until boiling. Strain and immediately add flavoring. Brush glaze on while it is still warm. Extra glaze keeps indefinitely refrigerated. Gently reheat each time before using. Use on light-colored fruit or cakes.

CURRANT GLAZE: Heat jelly to boiling. Immediately add remaining ingredients. Brush glaze on while it is still warm. Extra glaze keeps indefinitely refrigerated. Gently reheat each time before using. Use on red or dark-colored fruit.

PASTRY CREAM: Combine flour with ¼ cup milk; stir until smooth. Gradually add remaining ¾ cup milk. Place in heavy saucepan. Stir in salt and sugar. Cook over medium heat, stirring until mixture becomes as thick as medium white sauce. Stir a little of hot sauce into egg yolks. Then pour egg yolks into saucepan, stirring briskly. Return pan to low heat for few minutes to thicken a little more, continuing to stir. Be careful not to let sauce boil. Remove from heat. Add flavoring. Cool in refrigerator until ready to use, covered with plastic wrap.

STRAWBERRY TART: Spread pastry cream in bottom of baked tart shell, making thin layer. Arrange strawberries on top, close together, using largest ones in center. Strawberries should cover pastry cream. Spoon or lightly brush currant glaze over berries. Refrigerate until serving time.

RHUBARB TART: Line 9-inch flan ring with pastry. Save trimmings for top of tart. Chill pastry-lined flan in freezer at least 1 hour. Roll pastry trimmings out into strips 10 inches (22.5cm) long and ¼ inch (0.6cm) thick. Brush with beaten egg mixture and sprinkle with cinnamon sugar. Cut into strips ½ inch (1.2cm) wide to be used for lattice top.

Press ground nuts into bottom of pastry shell. Mix together flour, sugar and rhubarb. Fill pastry shell. Make lattice on top. Place tart in lowest rack in oven. Bake in preheated 350° oven 1 hour 15 minutes. While tart is still hot, brush currant glaze over rhubarb filling showing through lattice.

GRAPE TART: Brush bottom of tart shell with some apricot glaze. Spread 1½ cups pastry cream over bottom. Arrange grape halves on top of pastry cream in attractive pattern. Brush entire top of tart with warm apricot glaze.

GLAZED FRUIT TART: Line 9-inch flan ring and chill in freezer 1 hour. Add cinnamon to nuts. Sprinkle nuts over bottom of unbaked pastry shell, pressing them in gently but firmly. Sprinkle sugar over prepared fruit. Toss lightly together. Place fruit neatly in unbaked shell, arranging top slices to form a design. Place on lowest rack in 350° oven. Bake 1 hour 10 minutes, or until fruit bubbles slightly in center. While tart is hot, brush light-colored fruit with apricot glaze and dark-colored fruit with currant glaze.

BLUEBERRY TART: In heavy saucepan, combine 1½ cups blueberries, sugar, lemon rind and juice, and cinnamon. Cook over low heat, stirring until sugar is dissolved. Raise heat and boil rapidly about 8 minutes, or until blueberries thicken and acquire consistency of jam. Cool. Combine raw blueberries with cooled jam, mixing gently. Spoon into baked tart shell.

APPLE CUSTARD TART: Line 9-inch flan ring with pastry. Chill, preferably in freezer, at least 1 hour. Combine grated apple, lemon juice, lemon rind and sugar in saucepan. Cook over medium heat, uncovered, until almost boiling. Stir in flour which has been mixed with water. Stir until apple mixture is thickened. Stir 3 T. hot filling into yolks. Pour yolk mixture into pan with filling and stir briskly. Stir in vanilla and butter. Pour into unbaked tart shell. Bake on lowest rack in preheated 350° oven 35 to 45 minutes or until custard is set. Dust with sugar just before serving.

SOUR CREAM CHERRY TART: Line 9-inch flan ring with pastry. Chill, preferably in freezer, at least 1 hour. Beat eggs with sugar, sour cream and vanilla. Arrange pitted cherries in unbaked tart shell. Pour egg mixture over them. Bake in preheated 350° oven about 45 minutes on lowest rack of oven, or until custard is firm and crust brown. Serve chilled.

Melinda M. Vance, West Hartford, CT

RHUBARB TART:
1 recipe Rich Tart Pastry (page 196)
1 beaten egg mixed with 1 T. milk
2 T. cinnamon sugar
1 cup (170g) ground walnuts, pecans or filberts
3 T. (20g) flour
1¼ cups (250g) sugar
4 cups (560g) rhubarb, cut in 1-inch (2.5cm) pieces
½ cup Currant Glaze

FRESH GRAPE TART:
1 9-inch (22.5cm) baked Rich Tart Pastry shell (page 196)
Apricot Glaze
1 recipe Pastry Cream
3 cups (570g) fresh grapes, assorted colors, halved and seeded

GLAZED FRUIT TART:
1 recipe Rich Tart Pastry (page 196)
⅛ tsp. cinnamon
¾ cup (130g) ground pecans, walnuts or almonds
4 cups raw pitted fruit of your choice
Sugar
½ cup Apricot or Currant Glaze

BLUEBERRY TART:
4 cups (600g) blueberries
⅜ cup (75g) sugar
Grated rind and juice of ½ lemon
½ tsp. cinnamon
1 9-inch (22.5cm) baked Rich Tart Pastry (page 196) or Almond Short Pastry (page 197) shell
1 cup Pastry Cream (optional)

APPLE CUSTARD TART:
    TOTAL CALORIES FILLING ONLY: 1400
1 recipe Rich Tart Pastry (page 196)
3 large apples, peeled, cored and grated
Grated rind and juice of 1 lemon
¾ cup (150g) sugar
1 T. flour
3 T. (45ml) water
2 egg yolks
1 tsp. pure vanilla extract
2 T. (30g) butter
Confectioners' sugar

SOUR CREAM CHERRY TART:
    TOTAL CALORIES FILLING ONLY: 1050
1 recipe Rich Tart Pastry (page 196)
3 eggs
⅓ cup (65g) sugar
¾ cup (170g) sour cream
1 tsp. pure vanilla extract
2 cups (300g) pitted sweet cherries

YIELD: 8 Servings
TOTAL CALORIES: 2975
CALORIES PER SERVING: 372
CARBOHYDRATES: 81g
PROTEIN: 3g
FAT: 4g
SODIUM: High
PREPARING: 10 Minutes
BAKING: 50 Minutes

6 medium cooking apples, peeled, cored
   and sliced
1½ cups *(300g)* sugar
⅓ cup *(40g)* flour
½ tsp. nutmeg
2 cups *(475ml)* cranberry juice cocktail
2 cups *(225g)* biscuit mix
⅔ cups *(160ml)* milk
1 tsp. grated lemon rind

Yankee Cobbler

Webster's defines a cobbler as "a deep-dish fruit pie with no
bottom crust and a thick top crust of biscuit dough."

Place apple slices in *shallow* 8-cup *(2L)* baking dish. In small bowl,
combine 1¼ cups sugar, flour and nutmeg; stir in cranberry juice until smooth. Pour mixture over the apples. Cover with foil. Bake in
preheated 400° oven 30 minutes or until apples are tender.

Combine biscuit mix, 2 T. sugar and milk in bowl; stir until moistened. Drop from a tablespoon onto the hot apples to form
8 mounds. Mix 2 T. sugar and lemon rind; sprinkle over dough.
Bake uncovered at 400° 20 minutes or until biscuits are golden.
Serve warm.

Bernice Kuzma, West Hartford, CT

Microwave Conversion Instructions: Note: Reduce sugar to
1¼ cups and cranberry juice to 1½ cups. Slice apples into 2½-qt.
(2½L) souffle dish. Combine sugar, flour, nutmeg, and cranberry
juice. Pour over apples, cover and cook on High 10 minutes. Stir,
and continue to cook on High 5 minutes. Combine biscuit mix and
milk. Drop mixture in mounds around edge of dish. Cook, uncovered, on Medium (50%) 4 minutes. Rotate ¼ turn, and continue
to cook on Medium (50%) 3 to 5 minutes, or until top is dry.
Sprinkle with sugar and lemon rind. Brown under preheated broiler.

YIELD: 10-12 Servings
TOTAL CALORIES: 2400
CALORIES PER SERVING: 200
CARBOHYDRATES: 12g
PROTEIN: 4g
FAT: 15g
CHOLESTEROL: High
PREPARING: 1½ Hours
BAKING: 1 Hour
FREEZING: No

1 cup *(200g)* freshly grated coconut, *no
   substitute,* toasted
2 cups *(250g)* confectioners' sugar
2 tsp. vanilla
3 T. *(30g)* cornstarch
1 cup plus 1 T. *(250g)* Creme Fraiche
   (page 200)
6 egg yolks, lightly beaten
6 egg whites, stiffly beaten

Gâteau à la Noix de Coco

PREPARING COCONUT: With screwdriver and hammer, puncture
"eyes" of coconut; drain juice into jar, (reserve and drink as is, or
use in other recipes: salads, added to hot sauces, curries, or as a
substitute for dairy products.) Open shell by cracking very hard with
a hammer at widest part; hit firmly all around middle. An alternative
method is to place coconut in preheated 400° oven for 20 minutes
before tapping. Pry out white meat in pieces with strong, small knife.
Pare off dark skin. Shred meat with coarse grater. To toast shredded
coconut: Spread in shallow pan. Bake in 350° oven 20 to
30 minutes until delicately brown, stirring occasionally. A medium-
sized coconut yields 3 to 4 cups grated. Shredded coconut will keep
in refrigerator 1 to 2 days.

GATEAU: In large mixing bowl, combine coconut, confectioners'
sugar, vanilla, cornstarch and creme fraiche. Add egg yolks; gently
fold in egg whites. Turn mixture into well-buttered 9½-inch *(24cm)*
springform pan. Bake in preheated 425° oven 25 to 30 minutes.
Cool on rack 10 minutes. With knife, loosen edges gently; unmold
onto flat serving platter. Dust with additional confectioners' sugar.
Serve warm or cold.

Glenn Recchia, New York, NY

Gâteau Moka

MULTILAYERED MOCHA CAKE

Madame Bach Ngo of CHEZ BACH restaurant, Branford, gives us a very special French mocha layer cake to decorate with candied violets or fresh flowers.

YIELD: 12 Servings or
1 8-Inch Layer Cake
TOTAL CALORIES: 5544
CALORIES PER SERVING: 462
CARBOHYDRATES: 53g
PROTEIN: 4g
FAT: 26g
CHOLESTEROL: High
PREPARING: 2 Hours
BAKING: 25 Minutes
FREEZING: Yes

GENOISE: Butter and flour 2 8 × 1½-inch *(20 × 4cm)* round cake pans.

Thoroughly combine eggs, sugar and vanilla in large mixer bowl. Place bowl over (not in) simmering water on stove until mixture is barely lukewarm. Remove from stove; beat on medium, then high speed for 10 minutes until mixture is pale yellow, tripled in volume and forms a thick ribbon when beaters are lifted. Sift flour into batter, folding with large rubber spatula. Add butter, folding in with spatula.

Fill cake pans about ¾ full. Place pans on baking sheet on lowest rack of preheated 350° oven. Bake 22 to 25 minutes. Remove pans from oven; place on rack, let cool 5 minutes. Invert cakes onto rack to cool thoroughly.

MOCHA BUTTER CREAM: Combine sugar and coffee in saucepan. Boil 2½ to 3 minutes. Place yolks in mixer bowl; beat at medium speed, adding sugar slowly. Then beat on high until mixture is like mayonnaise in consistency, 5 to 6 minutes. At medium speed, add butter in pieces until mixture is smooth.

ASSEMBLY: Using a long serrated knife, cut each genoise into three even horizontal slices. Place one layer, crust side down, on cake plate or 8¼-inch round cardboard. Moisten with about 3 T. Rum Syrup, spread with about 3 T. Apricot Glaze. Cover with a second cake layer. Moisten with 3 T. Rum Syrup, spread thin layer Mocha Butter Cream. Cover with a third cake layer. Moisten with Rum Syrup, spread with Apricot Glaze. Continue using cake layers, moistening with Rum Syrup, alternating Apricot Glaze and Mocha Butter Cream fillings.

Spread Mocha Butter Cream smoothly over top and sides of cakes. Decorate cake to your fancy.

Variations, Advance Preparation, and Serving Suggestions:
Cooled genoise may be kept 1 to 2 days well wrapped in airtight container. Or freeze, well wrapped. Mocha Butter Cream, Rum Syrup and Apricot Glaze may be prepared several days before assembly. Assembled cake will remain moist at least one day, refrigerated.

Wine Suggestion: California Beaulieu Muscat Blanc, semi-sweet; serve chilled.

GENOISE:

6 eggs, room temperature
¾ cup *(150g)* sugar
½ tsp. pure vanilla extract
1 cup *(115g)* flour (may use ⅔ all-purpose plus ⅓ cake flour)
6 T. *(85g)* unsalted sweet butter, melted

MOCHA BUTTER CREAM:

½ cup *(100g)* sugar
½ cup *(120ml)* very strong espresso coffee
3 egg yolks
½ lb. *(225g)* unsalted sweet butter, softened

RUM SYRUP:

1 cup *(240ml)* strong, lukewarm coffee, mixed with 3 T. *(37.5g)* sugar and 2 T. *(30ml)* dark rum (Myers's preferred)

APRICOT GLAZE:

1 jar (10 oz.) *(285g)* good quality apricot jam, melted and strained

YIELD: 12 Servings
TOTAL CALORIES: 5460
CALORIES PER SERVING: 455
CARBOHYDRATES: 67g
PROTEIN: 4g
FAT: 19g
CHOLESTEROL: High
SODIUM: High
PREPARING: 40 Minutes
BAKING: 1 Hour 20 Minutes

CAKE:

2 oz. *(60g)* unsweetened chocolate
¾ cup *(175ml)* hot black coffee
½ cup *(115g)* butter
2 cups *(400g)* sugar
2 eggs
2 cups *(225g)* flour
1 tsp. baking soda
¾ cup *(170g)* sour cream
1 tsp. pure vanilla extract

FROSTING:

1 cup *(200g)* sugar
½ cup *(120ml)* milk
2 oz. *(60g)* unsweetened chocolate,
   grated
2 T. *(30g)* butter
1 tsp. pure vanilla extract

Chocolate Sour Cream Cake

Chocoholics take note! This is a moist chocolate cake with sinfully delicious real fudge frosting!

CAKE: Dissolve chocolate in hot coffee. Cream together butter and sugar; when light and fluffy, add eggs and mix thoroughly. Add chocolate and coffee; add flour, baking soda, sour cream and vanilla. Mix thoroughly. *[FOOD PROCESSOR: Process eggs, vanilla and sugar 1 full minute or until light colored. Add butter and process 1 full minute, stopping machine once to scrape down sides of bowl. With machine running, add chocolate mixture through feed tube. Add sour cream and process 20 seconds. Add flour and baking soda and combine batter by turning machine on/off 5 or 6 times, or until flour just disappears.]* Pour into well-buttered and floured 10-inch *(25cm)* tube pan.

Bake in preheated 300° oven 1 hour 20 minutes. Cool on wire rack.

FROSTING: Mix together sugar, milk and grated chocolate in heavy pan; bring to a boil. Cover and boil 3 minutes. Uncover, wash sugar crystals off side of pan with wet pastry brush; cook mixture to 240° on candy thermometer. Remove from heat; add butter and vanilla; mix. Cool slightly, but spread on cake while quite warm, before frosting thickens.

Elizabeth Daggerhart, Granby, CT

YIELD: 16-20 Servings
TOTAL CALORIES: 8700
CALORIES PER SERVING: 435
CARBOHYDRATES: 44g
PROTEIN: 4g
FAT: 27g
CHOLESTEROL: High
PREPARING: 35 Minutes
DRYING OUT: Macaroons 4-6 Hours
CHILLING: Overnight
FREEZING: Yes-Very Well

Almond Macaroon Torte

¾ lb. *(340g)* almond macaroons
   (purchased from bakery, not pre-
   packaged variety)
½ lb. *(225g)* butter, softened
2 cups *(250g)* confectioners' sugar
6 eggs, separated
1 tsp. almond extract
5-6 dozen ladyfingers, split

FROSTING:

2 cups *(475ml)* heavy cream, whipped
1 can (3½ oz.) *(100g)* flaked coconut

Place macaroons in preheated 200° oven 4 to 6 hours to dry them out; finely crush in blender or food processor.

Cream butter and sugar until light; add one egg yolk at a time, beating well after each addition. Add almond extract. Fold macaroon crumbs into yolk mixture.

Beat egg whites until stiff; fold into yolk mixture.

Line bottom and sides of greased 10-inch *(25cm)* tube pan with split ladyfingers. Cover bottom layer of ladyfingers with approximately 1/5 of almond macaroon filling. Add another layer of ladyfingers; spread with another 1/5 almond macaroon filling. Repeat process until all filling has been used, ending with layer of ladyfingers.

Place torte, covered, in refrigerator overnight or a minimum of 3 hours. When torte is solid, remove from pan; cover with whipped cream and sprinkle with coconut.

Whipped cream may be piped onto top and sides of torte, but then torte must be briefly placed in freezer to set whipped cream.

Nancy Ball, West Hartford, CT

Variations, Advance Preparation, and Serving Suggestions:
Unfrosted torte may be frozen, well wrapped.

Carolina Prune Cake

This is an extremely moist cake. It will last an hour after the first slice only if you padlock the pantry or refrigerator!

Prunes, dried sweet prune plums, were brought to the United States from France by a French fruit grower, Louis Pellier in 1856. Today, 90% of the prunes from California are French prune plums (prune d'agen).

YIELD: 12 Servings
TOTAL CALORIES: 6660
CALORIES PER SERVING: 555
CARBOHYDRATES: 62g
PROTEIN: 7g
FAT: 31g
PREPARING: 20 Minutes
BAKING: 45-60 Minutes
FREEZING: Yes

CAKE: Mix together sugar and oil; add eggs and stir. Sift together dry ingredients; add to sugar mixture alternately with buttermilk, stirring to avoid lumps. Add vanilla, nuts and prunes; stir.
[FOOD PROCESSOR: Put flour, soda, salt and spices in work bowl; process 2 seconds. Leave 2 T. in work bowl; remove rest of flour and set aside. Put prunes in work bowl and process about 10 seconds to chop them. Add nuts and process 5 seconds. Transfer mixture to large bowl. Add eggs and sugar to work bowl and process 1 full minute or until mixture is light colored. Add oil and process 1 full minute or until mixture is fluffy, stopping once to scrape down sides of bowl. With machine running add buttermilk and vanilla through feed tube. Add dry ingredients and combine by turning machine on/off 5 or 6 times, or only until flour just disappears. Do not overprocess. Combine batter with prune/nut mixture in large bowl.] Pour into a buttered 13 × 9 × 2-inch (33 × 22.5 × 5cm) pan. Bake at 350° 45 to 60 minutes or until cake is brown and pulls away from sides of pan.

ICING: Make icing while cake is baking. Put all ingredients in heavy pan. Bring to boil and boil until the temperature reaches 236° on a candy thermometer (5 to 7 minutes). Be careful that it does not boil over. Pour over cake while icing and cake are both still hot. It soaks into the cake somewhat but does not become soggy.

William Gephart, Hartford, CT

Variations, Advance Preparation, and Serving Suggestions:
Prunes can be cooked according to directions for Prune Filling (page 388). Cake can be baked in greased and floured bundt pan in preheated 350° oven 55 minutes.

Nutritional Notes: Calories can be decreased by approximately 125 per serving if icing is omitted.

Wine Suggestion: California Angelica, sweet amber; serve slightly chilled.

CAKE:
1½ cups (300g) sugar
1 cup (240ml) vegetable oil
3 eggs
2 cups (225g) flour
1 tsp. baking soda
½ tsp. salt
1 tsp. cinnamon
1 tsp. nutmeg
1 tsp. allspice
1 cup (240ml) buttermilk
1 cup (225g before cooking) cooked prunes, cut up
1 cup (120g) chopped nuts (black walnuts or pecans preferred)
1 tsp. pure vanilla extract

ICING:
1 cup (200g) sugar
½ tsp. baking soda
¼ cup (60g) butter
½ cup (120ml) buttermilk
1 T. light corn syrup
1 tsp. pure vanilla extract

YIELD: 10-12 Servings
TOTAL CALORIES: 3768
CALORIES PER SERVING: 314
CARBOHYDRATES: 35g
PROTEIN: 3g
FAT: 18g
CHOLESTEROL: High
PREPARING: 20 Minutes
CHILLING: 3 Hours
COOKING: 15 Minutes
FREEZING: Yes

Dutch Apricot Log

1 box (11 oz.) *(310g)* dried apricots
¼-½ cup *(50-100g)* sugar (to taste)
2 pkgs. (3 oz. each) *(170g)* ladyfingers
2 cups *(475ml)* heavy cream
2 T. *(25g)* sugar

Day before or several hours before serving: Cook apricots according to package directions. Add sugar last 5 minutes. Puree in blender or food processor. Cool 25 minutes. On oblong serving dish with waxed paper placed around edges, make layer of unsplit ladyfingers using half of 1 package. Spread ⅓ of apricot filling on ladyfingers. Repeat twice, ending with a layer of ladyfingers. Reserve a small amount of apricot for final decoration. Chill. Just before serving, whip cream with sugar until spreading consistency. Frost sides and top of log. Place small spoonfuls of remaining apricot mixture down center of log. Remove waxed paper. Serve in thin slices.

Ingrid Boelhouwer, Wethersfield, CT

Variations, Advance Preparation, and Serving Suggestions:
Two small logs can be made by equally dividing the ladyfingers, filling and icing. For variety, brush ladyfingers with favorite liqueur.

Nutritional Notes: Dried apricots are especially high in vitamin A as well as rich in iron, potassium and copper.

YIELD: 8 Servings
TOTAL CALORIES: 4344
CALORIES PER SERVING: 543
CARBOHYDRATES: 85g
PROTEIN: 8g
FAT: 19g
SODIUM: High
PREPARING: 20 Minutes
BAKING: 45 Minutes
FREEZING: Yes

Rhubarb Cake

An ideal take-along for a summer picnic.

2 cups *(400g)* sugar
2 cups *(285g)* finely chopped rhubarb
½ cup *(115g)* butter, softened
1 egg
1 tsp. pure vanilla extract
2 cups plus 2 T. *(240g)* flour
1 tsp. cinnamon
1 tsp. baking powder
1 tsp. baking soda
½ tsp. salt
1 cup *(240ml)* buttermilk or sour milk
½ cup *(40g)* shredded coconut
½ cup *(60g)* chopped walnuts or pecans
½ cup *(85g)* golden raisins
¼ tsp. grated lemon or orange rind

Mix ½ cup sugar with rhubarb and set aside.

Blend together butter, remaining 1½ cups sugar, egg and vanilla.

In separate bowl mix flour, cinnamon, baking powder, baking soda, and salt. Add this mixture alternately with buttermilk to the sugar and egg mixture. Add rhubarb, coconut, nuts, raisins, and grated rind.
[FOOD PROCESSOR: Put unsifted flour, cinnamon, baking powder and soda, and salt in work bowl. Process 2 seconds; set aside. Add nuts to work bowl and process 5 seconds; set aside. Process eggs and vanilla and 1½ cups sugar 1 full minute, stopping machine once to scrape down sides of bowl. Add butter and process 1 full minute. With machine running pour buttermilk through feed tube and process 20 seconds. Add reserved flour and combine by turning machine on/off 5 or 6 times, or until flour just disappears. Do not overprocess. In large bowl combine batter with remaining ingredients.] Mix well.

Pour into a greased 7 × 12-inch *(17.5 × 30cm)* pan. Bake in preheated 350° oven 45 minutes.

Roselyn Sedlezky, West Hartford, CT

Variations, Advance Preparation, and Serving Suggestions:
Make this in June when rhubarb is plentiful, and freeze for later. Good served warm with hard sauce.

Norwegian Apple Cake

YIELD: 4-6 Servings
TOTAL CALORIES: 1440
CALORIES PER SERVING: 248
CARBOHYDRATES: 39g
PROTEIN: 5g
FAT: 8g
PREPARING: 10 Minutes
BAKING: 25-30 Minutes

Mix together sugar, flour, salt and baking powder. Break an egg into middle of mixture and stir it together to mix well. Add apples and nuts; mix all together. Pour batter into a greased 8-inch *(20cm)* pie pan.

Bake in preheated 350° oven 25 to 30 minutes. Serve warm or cold, topped with whipped cream or vanilla ice cream. It is even more delicious the next day.

Martha Hornbacher, Springfield, MA

Wine Suggestion: French Sauternes, sweet white; serve chilled.

Microwave Conversion Instructions: Combine all ingredients as for conventional recipe. Pour into 8-inch pie plate and cook on High 7 minutes. Sprinkle lightly with sugar and brown under preheated broiler.

¾ cup *(150g)* **sugar**
½ cup *(60g)* **flour**
½ tsp. **salt**
1 tsp. **baking powder**
1 **egg**
1 rounded cup *(160g)* **diced apples**
½ cup *(60g)* **chopped nuts**

Blueberry Sour Cream Cake

YIELD: 12 Servings or
  1 9- or 10-Inch Cake
TOTAL CALORIES: 3480
CALORIES PER SERVING: 290
CARBOHYDRATES: 36g
PROTEIN: 3g
FAT: 15g
CHOLESTEROL: High
PREPARING: 15 Minutes
BAKING: 1 Hour

Although blueberries grow wild in many parts of the world, the United States and Canada supply almost 95% of all blueberries used by the food industry.

In large bowl combine flour, sugar, butter, baking powder, egg, vanilla and nutmeg; mix thoroughly. Press into buttered 9- or 10-inch *(22.5 or 25cm)* springform pan. Sprinkle blueberries evenly over top.

In another bowl combine sour cream, egg yolks, sugar and vanilla; blend well with a wire whisk. Pour over berries.

Bake on rack in center of preheated 350° oven 60 minutes or until edges of custard are lightly browned. Cool on wire rack until cake is set. Then unmold onto serving platter and serve with Creme Fraiche. This cake can be made a day or two ahead and refrigerated.

Lois F. Sykes, Bronxville, NY

Microwave Conversion Instructions: Line bottom of 10-inch round dish with waxed paper; do not grease. Place a small custard cup right side up in center. Prepare batter as for conventional recipe; press into prepared dish. Prepare sour cream-egg yolk mixture; pour over blueberries. Place an inverted saucer under baking dish; cook on Medium (50%) 8 minutes. Turn dish and continue to cook on High 3 to 4 minutes, just until it begins to pull away from sides of dish. For additional browning, place under conventional broiler. Allow to set before unmolding.

BATTER:

1½ cups *(170g)* **flour**
½ cup *(100g)* **sugar**
½ cup *(115g)* **butter, at room temperature**
½ tsp. **baking powder**
1 **egg**
1 tsp. **pure vanilla extract**
½ tsp. **nutmeg**
1 qt. *(600g)* **fresh blueberries, or unthawed frozen blueberries**

TOPPING:

2 cups *(450g)* **sour cream**
2 **egg yolks**
½ cup *(100g)* **sugar**
1 tsp. **pure vanilla extract**
Creme Fraiche (page 200)

YIELD: 6-9 Servings
TOTAL CALORIES: 2200
CALORIES PER SERVING: 244
CARBOHYDRATES: 48g
PROTEIN: 4g
FAT: 4g
PREPARING: 15 Minutes
BAKING: 30 Minutes
SIMMERING: 3-4 Minutes

Sherried Fruit Delight

A lovely easy-to-make dessert that gives the impression of having spent a great deal of time in the kitchen.

1 cup *(115g)* flour
1 tsp. baking powder
½ tsp. salt
2 eggs
1½ cups *(300g)* sugar
2 T. *(30g)* butter
2 T. *(30ml)* milk
½ cup *(120ml) cream* sherry
3 cups *(340g)* fresh fruit, sliced (apricots, plums, peaches and apples recommended)

Sift together flour, baking powder and salt; set aside.

Beat together eggs, 1 cup sugar, butter and milk. Add flour mixture; mix well. Pour into buttered 9-inch *(23cm)* square pan.

Simmer sherry and ½ cup sugar for 3 to 4 minutes; add fruit. Pour hot fruit mixture over batter.

Bake in preheated 375° oven 30 minutes. Serve warm, cut into squares, with whipped cream, vanilla ice cream or granulated sugar sprinkled over the top.

Millie Linehan, West Hartford, CT

YIELD: 10 Servings
TOTAL CALORIES: 4070
CALORIES PER SERVING: 407
CARBOHYDRATES: 62g
PROTEIN: 6g
FAT: 15g
PREPARING: 45 Minutes
BAKING: 1 Hour 10 Minutes

Fresh Plum Cake

A delicious moist cake to be made during that short time when fresh Italian plums are available.

TOPPING:
⅓ cup *(40g)* flour
½ cup *(60g)* chopped nuts
1 tsp. cinnamon
½ cup *(100g)* sugar
2 T. *(30g)* butter, softened
CAKE:
¼ cup *(30g)* crisp cookie crumbs (vanilla or lemon wafers, graham crackers, macaroons) or dry cereal
6 T. *(85g)* butter, softened
¾ cup *(150g)* sugar
1 egg
1 T. freshly grated lemon rind
1 tsp. pure vanilla extract
2 cups *(225g)* flour
2 tsp. baking powder
½ cup *(120ml)* milk
⅓ cup *(75g)* sour cream
3 cups Italian purple plums, pitted and quartered or 1½ lbs. *(675g)*, tossed with lemon juice and sugar (add cinnamon, allspice or freshly grated nutmeg if desired)

TOPPING: Combine Topping ingredients, blending in butter with fork or fingertips or in food processor. Set aside.

CAKE: Dust well-buttered 9-inch *(22.5cm)* springform pan with cookie crumbs. Set aside. In mixing bowl, cream butter and sugar. Beat in egg, lemon peel and vanilla. Add flour and baking powder alternately with milk. Fold in sour cream and plums. *[FOOD PROCESSOR: Process egg, lemon rind, vanilla and sugar 1 full minute. Add butter and process 1 full minute. Add milk and sour cream and process 20 seconds. Add flour and baking powder and combine batter by turning machine on/off 5 or 6 times, or until flour just disappears. Do not overprocess. In large bowl combine batter and plums.]* Spread in prepared pan and cover evenly with Topping. Bake in preheated 375° oven 60 to 70 minutes. Cool 10 minutes before removing outer ring. Serve warm or cool with whipped cream or ice cream.

Marion Kuzma, West Hartford, CT

Wine Suggestion: Japanese Plum Wine, sweet amber; serve chilled.

Lemon Poppy Seed Pound Cake

A taste of American heritage is captured in this contemporary version of a teatime favorite. It is guaranteed to become an often repeated recipe!

YIELD: 16-20 Slices or
1 10-Inch Bundt Cake
TOTAL CALORIES: 5000
CALORIES PER SLICE: 250
CARBOHYDRATES: 17.5g
PROTEIN: 4g
FAT: 18.5g
CHOLESTEROL: High
PREPARING: 45 Minutes
SOAKING: 4 Hours Minimum
BAKING: 1 Hour
FREEZING: Yes

CAKE: Soak poppy seeds in milk 4 hours or overnight in refrigerator. Rinse seeds with cold running water; drain well.

Cream butter in large mixer bowl. Gradually beat in 1¼ cups sugar (reserve remaining ¼ cup). Beat in lemon and orange rinds, then poppy seeds. Add egg yolks, one at a time, beating well after each addition. Beat until mixture is very light, about 5 minutes.

Beat egg whites in clean large mixer bowl until soft peaks form. Gradually beat in ¼ cup sugar; continue beating until stiff but not dry.

Sift flour and salt, a third at a time, over egg yolk mixture, gently folding in after each addition. Fold in ¼ of egg white; gently fold in remaining egg whites. Pour batter into greased 10-inch (25cm) bundt pan; bake in center of preheated 350° oven until wooden pick inserted in center is clean, about 50 to 60 minutes. Cool in pan on wire rack 5 minutes. Unmold cake onto rack over large baking sheet.

GLAZE: Combine lemon and orange juices with sugar until sugar is dissolved. Slowly dribble mixture over warm cake until outside is evenly moistened. Cool cake completely before serving.

Sarah C. Seymour, West Hartford, CT

Variations, Advance Preparation, and Serving Suggestions:
If a sauce is desired to make this more of a dessert rather than a tea cake, use Grand Marnier Sauce (page 188) or Creme Anglaise (page 200).

Wine Suggestion: French or New York Sauternes, sweet white; serve chilled.

Microwave Conversion Instructions: Prepare batter as directed above. Then grease 10-inch ceramic or plastic bundt pan and sprinkle evenly with granulated sugar. Bake on shelf or inverted glass bowl 12 to 14 minutes on Medium (50%); then 6 minutes on High (longer if center starts to sink as cake is removed from oven.) Cool as directed and coat with juices and sugar.

CAKE:
½ cup *(70g)* poppy seeds
½ cup *(120ml)* milk
1½ cups *(340g)* unsalted sweet butter, softened
1½ cups *(300g)* sugar
2 T. grated lemon rind
1 T. grated orange rind
8 eggs, separated, at room temperature
2 cups *(225g)* sifted cake flour
¾ tsp. salt

GLAZE:
½ cup *(120ml)* fresh lemon juice
¼ cup *(60ml)* fresh orange juice
⅓ cup *(65g)* superfine sugar

YIELD: 2 Loaf Cakes
CALORIES PER LOAF: 5327
CARBOHYDRATES: 753g
PROTEIN: 86g
FAT: 219g
PREPARING: 2 Hours
BAKING: 65 Minutes
FREEZING: Yes

Gift-Wrapped Fruitcake

This cake makes a wonderful gift for a very special friend.

CAKE:

17 T. *(250g)* unsalted sweet butter,
   softened
1¼ cups *(250g)* sugar
7 eggs
3¾ cups *(425g)* bread flour
1 lb. *(450g)* candied mixed fruit,
   chopped
½ vanilla bean
4 T. *(60ml)* dark rum (Myers's preferred)
¼ tsp. ground cinnamon
¼ tsp. ground ginger
Grated peel of 1 small lemon
2 T. *(30ml)* fresh lemon juice
⅔ cup *(80g)* coarsely chopped walnuts

SYRUP:

½ cup *(120ml)* water
¼ cup *(50g)* sugar

MARZIPAN WRAPPING:

2 cups *(450g)* almond paste, softened
1⅓ cups *(175g)* confectioners' sugar
2 egg whites

OPTIONAL TRIMMING:

3 oz. *(85g)* semisweet chocolate (Lindt
   Extra-Bittersweet preferred)
Chocolate Holly Leaves (see following
   page)
Red cinnamon candies

CAKE: Butter and flour 2 8½ × 4½ × 2½-inch
(21.5 × 11.5 × 6.5cm) loaf pans.

Cream butter in large mixing bowl with electric mixer. Gradually add sugar, beating until light and fluffy. Add 3 eggs, one at a time, beating well after each. Add 2 cups flour, beating. Add 4 remaining eggs, one at a time, again beating well after each.

Place baking sheet on next-to-lowest rack in oven. Set oven to 400°. In small bowl, toss ⅓ cup flour with chopped fruits. Stir remaining flour into cake batter. Split vanilla bean lengthwise; scrape seeds into batter. Lightly fold in rum, spices, lemon peel and juice, fruits, nuts; blend until just mixed. Divide batter between pans. Batter will be heavy. Tap against counter to settle mixture; smooth top of batter with spatula, indenting center slightly as cake will rise slightly in center during baking.

Set pans on baking sheet in preheated oven. Bake 65 minutes, watching closely at end of baking time to prevent burning. Remove pans from oven; set on racks. Let cool completely.

SYRUP: Combine water and sugar in small saucepan. Bring to boil over medium low heat, stirring just until sugar is dissolved. Wash down any sugar clinging to sides of pan with brush dipped in cold water. Let syrup simmer 5 minutes. Cool to room temperature.

MARZIPAN WRAPPING: Mix almond paste, sugar and egg whites in bowl with electric mixer until well blended. Divide marzipan in half, roll each half into ¼-inch *(0.3cm)* thick rectangle on work surface which has been sprinkled with confectioners' sugar to prevent sticking. Trim each to 8 × 14-inch *(20 × 35cm)* rectangle. Brush with syrup.

Remove cakes from pans. Trim to even tops and sides. Set each on a marzipan rectangle and roll to wrap completely. Trim overlapping marzipan to make a neat "present." Sprinkle granulated sugar on a sheet of waxed paper. Brush tops and sides of cakes with syrup. Dip in sugar to coat. Using thin, sharp knife, make cross-hatch design on top. Decorate with melted chocolate, cooled just enough to spoon into small pastry bag fitted with plain tip. Pipe one line of chocolate across width of each cake, one line lengthwise to form a chocolate "ribbon" tied around each present. Place Chocolate Holly Leaves and red cinnamon candies at intersection of lines.

Kathleen J. Schwartz, Avon, CT

Variations, Advance Preparation, and Serving Suggestions:
At Christmas, present cake on platter decorated with fresh holly. Cakes will remain fresh up to one week in airtight container. Marzipan Wrapping and Syrup can be made several days ahead of assembling cakes. Gift-Wrapped Fruitcake, without chocolate decorations and leaves, will freeze for a short period of time; wrap in foil or freezer wrap after freezing; thaw still wrapped.

Wine Suggestion: Harveys Bristol Cream Sherry, sweet golden; serve at room temperature.

Chocolate Leaves

Leaves which work best are those having waxy or thick surfaces with prominent veins. Melt chocolate and oil or shortening in top of double boiler. Using a spoon, generously coat the underside of the leaf with chocolate, holding the leaf by its stem end and being careful not to let the chocolate run onto the top of the leaf. With your fingertip, wipe the edges of the leaf to remove any chocolate. Place leaf on small plate and chill or freeze until firm. Separate chocolate from leaf by peeling leaf away, starting with stem end.

Variations, Advance Preparation, and Serving Suggestions:
Use to decorate Gift-Wrapped Fruitcake.

Also pretty to overlap white and chocolate leaves alternately in a circle on top of a round cake or torte. Leaves can be stored for several weeks in refrigerator or freezer in an airtight container.

8 oz. *(227g)* semisweet, bittersweet, sweet or white chocolate
1 T. vegetable oil or shortening (omit if using white chocolate)
Fresh camellia, rose, ivy, holly or other leaves

YIELD: 10-12 Servings
TOTAL CALORIES: 8880
CALORIES PER SERVING: 740
CARBOHYDRATES: 90g
PROTEIN: 6g
FAT: 40g
PREPARING: 30 Minutes
BAKING: 45-60 Minutes
FREEZING: Yes-Unfrosted

Carrot Layer Cake

The results of years of experimenting with carrot cake recipes and cream cheese frostings! This is without a doubt the ultimate carrot cake.

CAKE:

4 extra large eggs
2 cups *(400g)* **sugar**
1 cup *(240ml)* **salad oil**
2 cups *(225g)* **sifted flour**
2 tsp. baking soda
1 tsp. salt
1 tsp. cinnamon
3 cups *(360g)* **grated carrots**

FROSTING:

1 pkg. (8 oz.) *(225g)* **cream cheese**
¼ lb. *(115g)* **butter, softened**
1 lb. *(450g)* **confectioners' sugar**
1 T. pure vanilla extract
1 cup *(120g)* **chopped pecans**

CAKE: In large mixer bowl, beat eggs and sugar together until light and fluffy; add oil; beat.

Sift together dry ingredients; beat into egg-sugar mixture; stir in carrots. *[FOOD PROCESSOR: Put unsifted flour, baking soda, salt and cinnamon in work bowl with metal blade and process 2 seconds; set aside. If using nuts process 5 seconds and set aside. Shred carrots with shredding disc, using firm pressure; set aside. Return metal blade to work bowl. Add eggs and sugar and process 1 full minute, or until mixture is light colored. Add oil and process 1 full minute, or until mixture is fluffy, stopping once to scrape down sides of bowl. Add dry ingredients and combine by turning machine on/off 5 or 6 times, or until flour just disappears. Do not overprocess. In large bowl combine batter and shredded carrots.]* Using 2 8-inch *(20cm)* well greased and waxed paper-lined square pans or 2 9-inch *(22.5cm)* round pans, bake in preheated 325° oven 45 to 60 minutes. Test for doneness with toothpick. Cool completely before frosting.

FROSTING: Cream butter and cream cheese together; gradually add sugar and vanilla; beat well. Add pecans. *[FOOD PROCESSOR: Coarsely chop nuts and set aside. Process all remaining ingredients until frosting is creamy. Add chopped nuts and process until nuts are finely chopped.]* Spread frosting between layers and then frost top and sides of cake.

Rhoda Chase, West Hartford, CT

Variations, Advance Preparation, and Serving Suggestions:
For 3 9-inch round layers, use the following variation: 1½ cups *(355ml)* oil, 2 cups *(400g)* sugar, 4 eggs, 2 cups *(225g)* sifted flour, 2 tsp. baking powder, 2 tsp. soda, 2 tsp. cinnamon, ½ tsp. salt, ¼ tsp. nutmeg, 1 cup *(120g)* chopped pecans, 3 cups *(360g)* grated carrots, 1 cup *(170g)* golden raisins, 1 T. pure vanilla. Bake in preheated 350° oven 25 minutes. (If baking in single layer in bundt pan, bake 1 hour 10 minutes.) Use above frosting. Frost and assemble cake 24 hours before serving. Unfrosted layers freeze well. Wrap airtight.

Wine Suggestion: California Chateau Beaulieu Sauvignon Blanc, sweet white; serve chilled.

Microwave Conversion Instructions: Note: Conversion is for the 3-layer carrot cake given in the variation section above. Line bottom of 3 glass 8 × 8-inch dishes with waxed paper. Do not grease and flour. Prepare cake batter as directed above. Bake each layer separately 9 minutes on Medium (50%) and then 2 minutes on High. If making cake in a tube or bundt pan, reduce all ingredients by half. Line bottom of pan with circle of waxed paper. Cook 9 to 12 minutes on Medium (50%) and then 2½ to 3 minutes on High. Turn ¼ turn twice during cooking time.

Orange Date Nut Layer Cake

YIELD: 12-14 Servings
TOTAL CALORIES: 10,600
CALORIES PER SERVING: 758
CARBOHYDRATES: 107g
PROTEIN: 6g
FAT: 34g
PREPARING: 45 Minutes
BAKING: 35 Minutes
FREEZING: Yes-Unfrosted

CAKE: Cream butter and sugar together. Add eggs and beat well. Sprinkle a little flour over nuts and dates; reserve. Add rind to butter. Sift dry ingredients together; add to butter mixture alternately with buttermilk and vinegar. Mix well; add nuts and dates. *[FOOD PROCESSOR: Put flour, baking powder and soda, and salt into work bowl; process 2 seconds. Leave 2 T. in work bowl; remove rest of flour and set aside. Put dates in work bowl and process about 10 seconds to chop them. Add nuts and process 5 seconds. Transfer mixture to large bowl. Put eggs and sugar in work bowl and process 1 full minute, or until thick and light colored. Add butter and orange rind and process 1 full minute, stopping machine once to scrape down sides of bowl. With machine running, pour buttermilk and vinegar through feed tube and process 20 seconds. Add reserved flour mixture and combine batter by turning machine on/off 5 or 6 times, or until flour just disappears. Do not overprocess. Combine batter and date/nut mixture.]* Turn into 2 greased and waxed paper-lined 9-inch *(22.5cm)* round cake pans. Bake in preheated 350° oven about 25 to 35 minutes. Remove cake from oven; leave in pans.

TOPPING: Combine orange juice and sugar; pour over cake while still warm. Leave in pans until cool.

FROSTING: Beat butter until fluffy; add orange rind and salt; add confectioners' sugar gradually. Thin with enough orange juice until frosting is of spreading consistency. Let cake sit at least 24 hours before serving.

Eloise Martin, Kenilworth, IL

Microwave Conversion Instructions: Combine ingredients as directed above. Place circle of waxed paper on bottom of 2 9-inch ungreased round glass cake pans. Cook 1 layer at a time on Medium (50%) 6 minutes. Cook on High 2 to 5 minutes or until inserted knife comes out clean. Let stand on counter top 5 to 10 minutes. Pour juice topping over cake while still warm. Leave in pans to cool. Frost in conventional manner.

CAKE:

1 cup *(225g)* butter, softened
1 cup *(200g)* sugar
2 eggs, beaten
2½ cups *(285g)* sifted flour
1 cup *(115g)* chopped pecans or walnuts
1 cup *(160g)* dates, cut up
Grated rind of 2 oranges
1 tsp. baking powder
½ tsp. baking soda
½ tsp. salt
1 cup *(240ml)* buttermilk
1 tsp. white vinegar

JUICE TOPPING:

1 cup *(200g)* sugar
Juice of 2 oranges

ORANGE BUTTER FROSTING:

1 cup *(225g)* butter, softened
Grated rind of 1 orange
Pinch salt
4 cups *(520g)* confectioners' sugar
Juice of 2 oranges

YIELD: 12-14 Servings
TOTAL CALORIES: 7448
CALORIES PER SERVING: 532
CARBOHYDRATES: 44g
PROTEIN: 8g
FAT: 36g
CHOLESTEROL: High
PREPARING: 10 Minutes
BAKING: 2¾ Hours
COOLING: 2 Hours
CHILLING: 5-6 Hours
FREEZING: Yes

Ginger Ginger Cheesecake

Ginger, brought to Mexico by a Spanish envoy in 1535, was the first Oriental spice to come to North America. The ginger root is the rhizome of an orchid-like plant found in many tropical countries.

½ cup *(60g)* crushed ginger snaps
½ cup *(60g)* crushed chocolate wafers
⅓ cup *(75g)* butter, melted
2 lbs. *(900g)* cream cheese softened
1½ cups *(300g)* sugar
4 eggs
½ cup *(120ml)* heavy cream
1 tsp. pure vanilla extract
2 T. *(30g)* freshly grated ginger root
1 cup *(200g)* candied ginger, finely chopped (about 7 oz.)

Mix crushed cookies with melted butter; press onto bottom and halfway up sides of buttered 8-inch *(20cm)* or 9-inch *(22.5cm)* by 3¼-inch *(8.2cm)* cheesecake pan, not springform pan.

In large bowl of electric mixer or in food processor beat cream cheese until smooth. Add sugar, eggs, heavy cream, vanilla and grated ginger root; beat until smooth. Add candied ginger. Pour into prepared pan and shake gently to level. Put pan into larger pan filled with 2 inches *(5cm)* boiling water.

Bake in preheated 300° oven 1 hour 40 minutes. Turn off oven and let sit 1 hour. Remove from oven; cool on rack at least 2 hours before unmolding. Refrigerate 5 to 6 hours or overnight.

Lora Apter Brody via Rena Koopman, Newton, MA

Variations, Advance Preparation, and Serving Suggestions: Can be frozen, wrapped airtight when completely cooled.

Microwave Conversion Instructions: Note: Construct a microwave-safe springform pan as follows. Bottom: Cut an 8-inch circle from heavy cardboard; place on the bottom of an 8-inch microwave-safe cake plate. Side: Cut a strip of cardboard 2½ inches wide and long enough to ring an 8-inch circle. Tape edges with masking tape, so that sides can be cut away after cheesecake has been allowed to set. Note: Filling ingredients must be cut in half, but crust ingredients remain the same. Melt butter in medium-sized glass bowl. Blend with cookie crumbs; press well onto bottom and halfway up sides of buttered pan. Soften each 8 oz. *(225g)* block cream cheese by removing from foil wrap and placing on paper plate; cook on Low (10%) 2 to 4 minutes. Prepare filling as for conventional recipe, in a glass bowl; cook on High 4 minutes, stirring with wire whisk after each minute. Pour warmed filling into prepared crust; cook on Medium (50%) 10 minutes or until filling is set, rotating dish ¼ turn every 2 to 3 minutes. Sprinkle additional cookie crumbs on top of cake immediately after taking from oven, if desired. Cool on wire rack and refrigerate overnight before removing from cardboard pan and serving.

Creamy Deluxe Cheesecake

YIELD: 12-16 Servings
TOTAL CALORIES: 7680
CALORIES PER SERVING: 480
CARBOHYDRATES: 32g
PROTEIN: 8g
FAT: 36g
CHOLESTEROL: High
SODIUM: High
PREPARING: 20 Minutes
BAKING: 1 Hours 35 Minutes
COOLING: 5 Hours
CHILLING: 24 Hours
FREEZING: Yes

CRUST: Mix together melted butter, graham cracker crumbs, sugar and cinnamon. Reserve a little of mixture; with remaining mixture, line bottom and ⅔ up sides of a 10-inch *(25cm)* springform pan or 9-inch *(22.5cm)* cheesecake pan. Refrigerate, unbaked, until ready to fill.

FILLING: In large bowl of electric mixer or in food processor beat sugar and cream cheese until smooth. Add eggs, one at a time, beating well after each addition. Add vanilla and mix. Fold in sour cream. Place mixture in prepared pan and sprinkle with remaining crumbs.

Bake in preheated 350° oven 35 minutes. Turn off oven but *do not open oven door.* Let sit in oven 60 minutes. Remove from oven and cool at room temperature 5 hours. Refrigerate at least 24 hours before serving.

Shelia Holincheck, West Hartford, CT

CRUST:

½ cup *(115g)* butter, melted
2 cups *(180g)* graham cracker crumbs
3 T. *(35g)* sugar
1 tsp. cinnamon (optional)

FILLING:

1½ cups *(300g)* sugar
4 pkgs. (8 oz. each) *(900g)* cream cheese, at room temperature
6 eggs, at room temperature
2 tsp. pure vanilla extract
1 qt. *(900g)* sour cream, at room temperature

Blueberries in Lemon Mousse

YIELD: 6 Servings
CALORIES PER SERVING: 338
CARBOHYDRATES: 47g
PROTEIN: 6g
FAT: 14g
CHOLESTEROL: High
PREPARING: 15 Minutes
COOKING: 10 Minutes
CHILLING: 2 Hours Minimum

Place berries in glass serving bowl; sprinkle with ¼ cup sugar.

In top of *stainless* or *enamel* double boiler, beat egg yolks with remaining sugar until mixture is light lemon color; add lemon juice, continuing to cook over simmering water, whisking constantly until mixture coats spoon. Do not boil; remove from heat and let cool.

Beat egg whites until stiff, but not dry; gently fold into lemon mixture. Fold in whipped cream and lemon rind. Incorporate well so that mousse is very smooth.

Chill. Just before serving pour over berries.

Sandra P. Robinson, Farmington, CT

1 qt. *(600g)* blueberries, washed
1 cup *(200g)* sugar
5 eggs, separated
Juice of 2 large lemons
1 cup *(240ml)* cream, whipped
2 tsp. grated lemon rind

Variations, Advance Preparation, and Serving Suggestions:
Any other berry can be used. For a firmer version that can be prepared in parfait glasses, use the following proportions: 6 egg yolks, ¾ cup sugar *(150g)*; ½ cup *(120ml)* fresh lemon juice, 1 T. grated lemon rind, 3 egg whites, ¾ cup *(175ml)* heavy cream. Finally fold in 1½ cups *(225g)* fresh blueberries.

Old-Fashioned Rice Pudding with Fruit

YIELD: 6 Servings
TOTAL CALORIES: 2660
CALORIES PER SERVING: 443
CARBOHYDRATES: 60g
PROTEIN: 8g
FAT: 19g
CHOLESTEROL: High
BAKING: 35 Minutes
COOKING: 40 Minutes

Long before the English set up their colonies on the eastern seaboard, the Spanish were establishing a foothold in Florida and in the vast territory north of the Rio Grande. They brought with them their favorite foods — rice being one of them. Rice Pudding was a favorite dessert spiced with cinnamon, enriched with cream, or sweetened with raisins — or all three.

⅔ cup *(115g)* **golden raisins plumped in**
    ¼ cup *(60ml)* **Grand Marnier**
1 cup *(200g)* **long-grain rice**
1 tsp. **salt**
2 cups *(475ml)* **water**
½ cup *(100g)* **sugar**
3 cups *(710ml)* **milk**
3 **egg yolks**
¾ cup *(180ml)* **heavy cream**
1 T. **pure vanilla extract**

Combine rice, salt and water in medium saucepan; simmer 3 minutes. Drain off water. Add sugar and milk; bring to simmer over low heat, stirring occasionally. Cook uncovered, until milk is absorbed and rice is creamy, about 30 minutes. Let cool.

Whisk yolks with cream and vanilla. Combine with cooled rice, mixing well. Stir in raisins. Put into well-buttered 2-qt. *(2L)* round or oval *shallow* baking dish.

Bake in preheated 300° oven, uncovered, about 25 minutes or until set on edges but creamy in center. Serve warm, not hot.

David W. Parmelee, West Hartford, CT

Variations, Advance Preparation, and Serving Suggestions:
The pudding can be topped with meringue and baked or broiled until brown. It can also be served with a favorite fruit sauce. You can add 2 T. *(30g)* chopped candied orange peel or 1 T. *(15g)* chopped citron or crystallized ginger for taste variations.

Wine Suggestion: Hungarian Tokaji Assu, breadlike sweet white; serve chilled.

Microwave Conversion Instructions: Combine rice, salt and water in 4-qt. *(4L)* covered casserole. Cook on High 10 minutes. Drain. Add sugar and cold milk and cook, uncovered, on Medium High (70%) until milk is absorbed and rice is creamy, about 20 to 22 minutes. Let cool. Combine cooled rice with prepared egg yolk mixture. Stir in raisins. Place mixture in buttered 9-inch *(23cm)* round 2-qt. baking dish. Cook on Medium (50%) 15 to 20 minutes, or until set on edges but creamy in center.

Pear Ice Cream

YIELD: 6-8 Servings
CALORIES PER SERVING: 236
CARBOHYDRATES: 35g
PROTEIN: 1.5g
FAT: 10g
CHOLESTEROL: High
PREPARING: 15 Minutes
FREEZING: Overnight Minimum

Place pears and pineapple juice in blender or food processor; puree until smooth; add sugar, salt, cream cheese, cream and lemon juice gradually; process until well blended and completely smooth. Pour into container; freeze overnight.

Several hours before serving, cut ice cream into chunks; place in food processor; blend until smooth. Freeze again before serving.

Sarah C. Seymour, West Hartford, CT

3 large ripe Bartlett pears, peeled, cored and cut into quarters
½ cup (120ml) pineapple juice
1 cup (200g) sugar
½ tsp. salt
1 pkg. (3 oz.) (85g) cream cheese, cut in chunks
½ cup (120ml) heavy cream
2 T. (30ml) fresh lemon juice

Pear Sherbet

YIELD: 8 Servings
CALORIES PER SERVING: 240
CARBOHYDRATES: 56g
PROTEIN: 2g
FAT: 1g
PREPARING: 30 Minutes
FREEZING: Overnight

Using pan large enough to hold pears, make syrup by boiling sugar and water together 10 minutes.

Remove pears from cold water; drop into bubbling syrup; cover; simmer slowly basting often. When soft and easily pierced by knife (about 15 minutes), turn off heat and let fruit cool in syrup.

Drain pears reserving syrup; in batches puree pears in blender or food processor with small amount of syrup. There should be about 1 qt. (1L) of puree. Add vodka, egg white, and lemon juice, mix well; add extra syrup as needed for desired sweetness.

Place puree in container and freeze; after 12 hours remove and return to food processor. Process until fluffy; refreeze in serving container. Remove to refrigerator 1 hour before serving.

Auden di Corcia, Hartford, CT

3 lbs. (1.35kg) ripe eating pears, peeled, cored, quartered, and submerged in cold water with juice of ½ lemon to prevent discoloring
1¼ cups (250g) sugar
1¼ cups (300ml) water
3 T. (45ml) vodka
1 egg white, lightly beaten
3 T. (45ml) fresh lemon juice

Variations, Advance Preparation, and Serving Suggestions: Serve with a chocolate cookie, since the combination of pears and chocolate is sublime, or Notkakor (page 386).

Wine Suggestion: California Lejon Champagne, semi-sweet sparkling white; serve chilled.

Fresh Apple Mousse with Apricot Sauce

YIELD: 12-14 Servings
CALORIES PER SERVING: 286
CARBOHYDRATES: 37g
PROTEIN: 3g
FAT: 14g
CHOLESTEROL: High
CALORIES PER TABLESPOON
  SAUCE: 38
PREPARING: 1½ Hours
CHILLING: 8 Hours Minimum

This is a very simple, light and refreshing dessert. Much of its appeal lies in its subtle delicate flavor. You may find that the apricot sauce takes away from the apple flavor. Try it both ways and decide for yourself.

APPLE MOUSSE:

8 medium apples (McIntosh or other firm cooking apple) peeled, cored and quartered
¾ tsp. cinnamon
⅓ cup (95g) apricot preserves
⅛ tsp. freshly grated nutmeg
¼ tsp. freshly grated lemon rind
6 egg yolks
1½ tsp. cornstarch
1¼ cups (250g) sugar
2¼ cups (530ml) warm milk
2 T. (14g) unflavored gelatin
¾ cup (180ml) fresh orange juice
2 tsp. pure vanilla extract
1½ cups (355ml) heavy cream, whipped

APRICOT SAUCE:

1¼ cups (355g) apricot preserves
2 T. (30ml) fresh lemon juice
1 tsp. grated lemon rind
½ cup (120ml) apricot or peach brandy
3 T. (25g) confectioners' sugar
½ cup (120ml) water

APPLE MOUSSE: In heavy-bottomed saucepan, combine apples, cinnamon, apricot preserves, nutmeg and lemon rind. Cook over low heat until apples are very soft and mixture can easily be mashed with fork. Be careful that apples on bottom of pan do not burn. When done, pass them through a sieve and reserve apple puree.

In top of double boiler, combine egg yolks, cornstarch and sugar; beat until pale yellow and fluffy. Add warm milk and place over simmering water. Stir constantly until custard coats spoon; do not let it boil or it will curdle. Remove from heat and reserve.

Heat gelatin softened in orange juice in small saucepan. Whisk melted gelatin into still hot custard. Pour custard into large, clean bowl; chill 2 hours, stirring occasionally or cool over ice, beating every few minutes, until it starts to set. Remove from refrigerator and whisk in vanilla, apple puree and whipped cream. Pour mousse into individual dessert cups or large glass bowl. Chill at least 6 hours or up to 48 hours before serving. Serve with Apricot Sauce passed separately.

APRICOT SAUCE: Combine apricot preserves, lemon juice, lemon rind, apricot or peach brandy and confectioners' sugar and water in small saucepan. Heat until preserves are thoroughly dissolved. Pass sauce through fine sieve. Taste and add more sugar if necessary. Chill.

Dr. Colin Atterbury, West Haven, CT

Variations, Advance Preparation, and Serving Suggestions: The apricot sauce is delicious with a variety of fruits, such as poached pears, bananas, apple compote, ice cream or crepes or Riz a l'Imperatrice (page 78).

Wine Suggestion: French Sauternes, sweet white; serve cold.

Microwave Conversion Instructions: *Apple Mousse:* Combine apples, cinnamon, apricot preserves, nutmeg and lemon rind in 2-qt. *(2L)* bowl. Cook on High 13 to 15 minutes, stirring twice, until mixture can easily be mashed with fork. Pass through a sieve; reserve apple puree. Heat milk on High in 4-cup *(1L)* glass measure 3½ to 4 minutes, until heated through. Slowly add beaten egg yolks that have been combined with cornstarch and sugar. Heat on Medium High (70%) 5 minutes, stirring every minute. Do not let custard boil. It if begins to boil, reduce to Medium (50%). Cook until custard coats a spoon. Heat gelatin, softened in orange juice in glass measure 45 seconds. Whisk into hot custard. Follow above directions to complete. *Apricot Sauce:* Combine all ingredients in 4-cup measure. Cook on High 7 to 9 minutes, until preserves are thoroughly dissolved, stirring once. Follow above directions to complete.

Apple Fritters

When Caesar's Roman Legion invaded Britain, they brought apples with them, and apples have grown in the British Isles ever since that time. STONEHENGE restaurant of Ridgefield, Connecticut, gives us this dessert recipe putting our Connecticut apples to good use in a versatile beer batter coating.

YIELD: 16 Fritters
TOTAL CALORIES: 3360
CALORIES PER FRITTER: 210
CARBOHYDRATES: 19g
PROTEIN: 2g
FAT: 14g
PREPARING: 40 Minutes
DEEP FRYING: 15 Minutes

BEER BATTER: Sift flour into bowl. Add paprika, salt and pepper. Pour in beer; whisk briskly to thoroughly mix.

FRITTERS: Cut apples into ½-inch (1.2cm) thick slices; flour on all sides and completely cover with beer batter. Remove from batter and place in hot oil heated to 350°. When cooked, in 4 to 5 minutes, batter will become crisp and golden brown. Remove from oil; drain on paper towels.

Mix together cinnamon and sugar. Place hot fritters in sugar mixture and spoon mixture over all sides.

To serve, spoon a small amount Bavarian Cream Sauce onto warm plate. Arrange fritter rings on sauce and serve immediately.

Variations, Advance Preparation, and Serving Suggestions: This batter may be made several days ahead and refrigerated. Eggplant or summer squash coated with the batter and deep fried are delicious variations.

Wine Suggestion: California late-picked Johannisberg Riesling, semi-sweet white; serve chilled.

BEER BATTER:
1½ cups (170g) flour
1 tsp. paprika
⅛ tsp. salt
⅛ tsp. freshly ground white pepper
12 oz. (355ml) beer, at room temperature

FRITTERS:
4 large unbruised apples, peeled and cored
Flour
Beer batter
½ cup (100g) superfine sugar
½ tsp. cinnamon
6 cups (1.5L) oil for deep frying
Bavarian Cream Sauce (see following recipe)

Bavarian Cream Sauce

A Bavarian Cream is an egg custard to which gelatin is added for body. Then whipped cream is folded in for rich flavor. STONEHENGE restaurant, Ridgefield, Connecticut, has developed this recipe, adding further flavor with Kirschwasser.

YIELD: 3½ Cups
TOTAL CALORIES: 1400
CALORIES PER TABLESPOON: 25
CARBOHYDRATES: 1g
PROTEIN: .5g
FAT: 2g
PREPARING: 20 Minutes
COOKING: 10 Minutes

In bowl mix together eggs, vanilla, cornstarch and ½ cup milk.

In saucepan mix 1½ cups milk and sugar; bring to boil. Then add egg mixture and bring to rolling boil. Remove from heat, cool and refrigerate.

Whip cream until stiff peaks form. Fold into cold egg mixture. Add Kirschwasser; stir with fork to incorporate.

Variations, Advance Preparation, and Serving Suggestions: The cream sauce can be cooked a day ahead, then add whipped cream and Kirschwasser just before serving.

2 eggs
2 drops pure vanilla extract
1 T. (10g) cornstarch
2 cups (475ml) milk
3 T. (40g) sugar
½ cup (120ml) heavy cream
½ cup (120ml) Kirschwasser

YIELD: 10-12 Servings
CALORIES PER SERVING: 70
CARBOHYDRATES: 17g
PREPARING: 15 Minutes
CHILLING: 3 Hours Minimum
COOKING: 20 Minutes
FREEZING: No

This "soup" is traditionally served as a dessert, but it is equally delightful and refreshing as a cold summer soup.

6 cups fresh rhubarb or 1 pkg. (20 oz.) (570g) frozen rhubarb, cut in pieces
4 cups (950ml) water
¾ cup (150g) sugar
¼ tsp. salt
½ cup (120ml) cold water
¼ cup (40g) potato starch
1 lb. (450g) fresh strawberries, sliced or 1 pkg. (16 oz.) frozen sliced strawberries
Creme Fraiche (page 200) or sour cream to garnish

Combine rhubarb and water in large saucepan; bring to boil; lower heat and cook until fruit is soft, stirring from time to time.

Strain fruit through medium sieve or puree in blender or food processor; return to pan; reheat to hot temperature; add sugar and salt. Test for sweetness; add more sugar if desired.

Combine water and potato starch; gradually add to fruit liquid, stirring constantly. Cook until fully thickened, about 5 to 7 minutes.

Pour into large bowl; cool to room temperature; add strawberries; stir gently. Chill thoroughly; serve very cold with garnish of your choice.

Betty Ahlin, Windsor, CT

Variations, Advance Preparation, and Serving Suggestions: If using as dessert, serve with a rich Swedish coffee bread or a plain cake or assorted cookies. Substitute any tart fruit (red plums, blueberries, raspberries) for rhubarb and cook in same manner.

Nutritional Notes: Caloric analysis based on the use of *unsweetened* fruit. This refreshing fruit soup may provide calorie-controlled variety to many restricted diets.

Microwave Conversion Instructions: Note: Finely dice rhubarb and use only ½ cup water. Place rhubarb and water in casserole. Cook, covered, on High until fruit is soft. Timing will depend on tenderness of fruit. Strain or puree rhubarb. Return to casserole and reheat on Medium (50%) until hot, stirring once. Add sugar and salt. Add more sugar if desired. Combine ½ cup cold water with potato starch; stir to dissolve. Gradually add to fruit puree. Cook on Medium (50%) until fully thickened, about 7 minutes. Complete as directed above.

Lollipops

The first use of a confectionary machine to manufacture lollipops was in New Haven, Connecticut, in 1908. The first lollipop ever manufactured was made by Bradley & Smith of New Haven. They named their confection for a popular race-horse of the day.

YIELD: 15 Lollipops
TOTAL CALORIES: 1080
CALORIES PER LOLLIPOP: 72
CARBOHYDRATES: 18g
PREPARING: 20 Minutes
COOKING: 25 Minutes

Prepare baking sheets, lollipop molds or a marble slab by brushing with butter. Arrange lollipop sticks on selected surface, leaving enough space between sticks, so that when lollipops are formed they will not run together.

In large heavy pan, bring water to boil. Remove from heat. Add sugar, corn syrup and butter and stir until dissolved. Return to heat; when boiling, cover mixture 2 to 3 minutes so that any sugar crystals on side of pan will be washed down into mixture. Then uncover and cook over high heat, stirring until candy thermometer reaches 280°. Turn heat down to low and add few drops food coloring, if desired. Then add flavoring and mix well.

Allow syrup to cool slightly. *Working quickly*, pour syrup onto upper end of each lollipop stick. It will shape itself into a circle. Allow to cool, then remove from baking sheets. When completely cool, wrap each lollipop in cellophane.

Kim McDonagh, West Hartford, CT

Variations, Advance Preparation, and Serving Suggestions:
To make fresh fruit lollipops, replace the water and flavoring with ½ cup fruit juice. Juicy fruits such as raspberries, blackberries, blueberries, grapes or chopped pineapple are all suitable. *Gently* heat fruit in saucepan until juice begins to flow. Strain juice through a jelly bag. Do not allow temperature of syrup to rise above 280° or it may discolor.

Microwave Conversion Instructions: Heat water in 3-qt. *(3L)* bowl until it comes to rolling boil, 30 to 45 seconds. Stir in remaining ingredients, except flavoring; cook on High 7 to 9 minutes, stirring once, or until candy thermometer registers 280°. If using a microwave candy thermometer it may be left in the oven. If using a regular candy thermometer, test mixture out of the oven.

½ cup *(120ml)* **water**
1 cup *(200g)* **sugar**
⅓ cup plus 1 T. *(95ml)* **light corn syrup**
1½ tsp. *(7g)* **butter**
Food coloring (optional)
2-3 tsp. flavoring (butterscotch, root beer, or flavoring of your choice)

SPECIAL EQUIPMENT:

Lollipop sticks or popsicle sticks

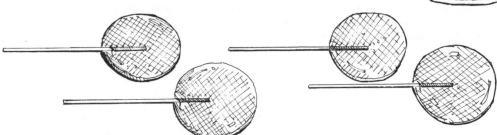

Cover Design and Color Plates

The cover and color illustrations of *Connecticut à la Carte* are developed by Francie Bergquist through the art of theorem painting. Theorem art came to America from England at the beginning of the 19th century where it had been adapted from forms used in the Orient called Poonah, Oriental tinting and Chinese painting.

In New England theorem painting was considered a "ladies art" and was used in the first finishing schools as a teaching tool. Initially it was taught in conjunction with embroidery, but later became an art form on its own merit. With the advent of the theorem, this quicker and more pleasant way of displaying one's artistic talents began to supersede embroidered pictures. Theorem painting flourished from about 1800 to 1835, and marked the decline of embroidery as a young ladies accomplishment. But by the mid-1800s its popularity declined.

The word *theorem* means a formula, a theory or logic deduced or to be deduced from other formulas. Thus theorem refers to the way the artist must analyze the subject matter he wants to paint and divide it into numerical parts in order to cut stencils (theorems). Separate stencils are combined to create pleasing compositions. Each element of design is first traced on oiled paper and then cut out to form a stencil. The stencils are held carefully in place on white velvet fabric or paper background, while watercolors mixed with gum arabic or oil paints are rubbed or brushed through the stencil openings to color in the major portions of the design. Details are added with a fine brush or pen.

Due to the efforts of a number of enthusiastic preservationists, early examples of theorem painting have survived and can be seen today in many museums. One of the most extensive collections is in the Abby Aldrich Rockefeller Folk Art Center in Williamsburg, Virginia where Mrs. Bergquist first researched this technique and developed the form for use in *Connecticut à la Carte*. In New England early theorem paintings can be seen in Old Sturbridge Village in Sturbridge, Massachusetts, the Concord Antiquarian Society in Concord, Massachusetts, the Shelburne Museum in Shelburne, Vermont, and the New York State Historical Association in Cooperstown, New York.

The early technique of theorem painting has been carefully handed down and is growing in popularity in Connecticut today. Although the mediums have improved considerably, the use of stencils to create basic forms on fabric remains true to the antique technique. The cover of *Connecticut à la Carte* is a faithful reflection of that antique style and composition. It depicts now as then, the popular subject of still-life arrangements of fruits. One of the favorite motifs for 19th century theorem paintings was the watermelon, cut open to expose its pink flesh punctuated by dark seeds.

The eight color plates, however, represent contemporary subjects executed in theorem tradition. The artist used theorem stencils for the basic layout and then finished each print with a dry brush technique. Mrs. Bergquist incorporates the honeybee in each illustration as her personal signature. This style was developed especially for this publication as a blending of flavors of 19th century Connecticut theorem design to 20th century taste. The art work evolves as each recipe comes from our heritage to be shared and enjoyed as a reflection of New England today.

Recipe Index

C

E

F

G

M

Q

R

T

U

V

W

Y

Z

Please send me _____ copies of *Connecticut à la Carte* at $21.95 each $ _____
plus postage/handling $ 2.00 each $ _____
add sales tax for delivery in Connecticut $ 1.65 each $ _____
please gift wrap $ 1.50 each $ _____
please furnish gift enclosure card $ .50 each $ _____
CHECK OR CREDIT CARD TOTAL $ _____

Connecticut à la Carte

☐ Charge to my   ☐ Mastercard   ☐ Visa

Account # ☐☐☐☐☐☐☐☐☐☐☐☐☐☐☐☐

Expiration date ☐☐☐☐   Interbank # ☐☐☐☐

Signature _____
(required if using charge card)

NAME _____

STREET _____

CITY _____ STATE _____ ZIP _____

P.O. Box 17-158 West Hartford, CT 06117

All copies will be sent to same address unless otherwise specified. If you wish one or any number of books sent as gifts, furnish a list of names and addresses of recipients. If you wish to enclose your own gift card with each book, please write name of recipient on outside of envelope, enclose with order, and we will include it with your gift.

- -

Please send me _____ copies of *Connecticut à la Carte* at $21.95 each $ _____
plus postage/handling $ 2.00 each $ _____
add sales tax for delivery in Connecticut $ 1.65 each $ _____
please gift wrap $ 1.50 each $ _____
please furnish gift enclosure card $ .50 each $ _____
CHECK OR CREDIT CARD TOTAL $ _____

Connecticut à la Carte

☐ Charge to my   ☐ Mastercard   ☐ Visa

Account # ☐☐☐☐☐☐☐☐☐☐☐☐☐☐☐☐

Expiration date ☐☐☐☐   Interbank # ☐☐☐☐

Signature _____
(required if using charge card)

NAME _____

STREET _____

CITY _____ STATE _____ ZIP _____

P.O. Box 17-158 West Hartford, CT 06117

All copies will be sent to same address unless otherwise specified. If you wish one or any number of books sent as gifts, furnish a list of names and addresses of recipients. If you wish to enclose your own gift card with each book, please write name of recipient on outside of envelope, enclose with order, and we will include it with your gift.

Distinctive features of **Connecticut à la Carte**

- 495 unusual and scrupulously tested recipes plus tested variations or adaptations of individual recipes
- 6 symbols identifying recipes in these catagories:

 First Course Dishes

 Food Processor

 Luncheon Dishes

 Quick Gourmet

 Vegetarian Dishes

 Low Calorie Dishes

- Connecticut and food folklore and culinary definitions
- 440 pages (8 × 10) locked spiral bound between hardboard covers

- Microwave Conversion Instructions for 188 of the recipes *printed immediately following* conventional preparation method
- 8 full-color illustrations and individual pen and ink drawings for specific recipes
- Specific wine selection for recipes
- 20 menus with recipes giving a pictorial and historical overview of Connecticut
- Computerized nutritional analysis of every recipe giving calories per serving as well as grams of carbohydrates, protein, fat, cholesterol and sodium per serving
- Nutritional adaptations of many recipes
- Food Processor directions for 120 recipes incorporating special techniques required to prepare the recipe in the food processor
- Metric Equivalents of every ingredient given in italics immediately following conventional measurement
- Comprehensive cross-referenced Index

Distinctive features of **Connecticut à la Carte**

- 495 unusual and scrupulously tested recipes plus tested variations or adaptations of individual recipes
- 6 symbols identifying recipes in these catagories:

 First Course Dishes

 Food Processor

 Luncheon Dishes

 Quick Gourmet

 Vegetarian Dishes

 Low Calorie Dishes

- Connecticut and food folklore and culinary definitions
- 440 pages (8 × 10) locked spiral bound between hardboard covers

- Microwave Conversion Instructions for 188 of the recipes *printed immediately following* conventional preparation method
- 8 full-color illustrations and individual pen and ink drawings for specific recipes
- Specific wine selection for recipes
- 20 menus with recipes giving a pictorial and historical overview of Connecticut
- Computerized nutritional analysis of every recipe giving calories per serving as well as grams of carbohydrates, protein, fat, cholesterol and sodium per serving
- Nutritional adaptations of many recipes
- Food Processor directions for 120 recipes incorporating special techniques required to prepare the recipe in the food processor
- Metric Equivalents of every ingredient given in italics immediately following conventional measurement
- Comprehensive cross-referenced Index